GRASPING GOD'S WORD

GRASPING GOD'S WORD

A Hands-On Approach to Reading, Interpreting, and Applying the Bible

FOURTH EDITION

J. SCOTT DUVALL

J. DANIEL HAYS

FOREWORDS BY MARK L. STRAUSS AND KEVIN J. VANHOOZER

ZONDERVAN ACADEMIC

ZONDERVAN ACADEMIC

Grasping God's Word

Published in Grand Rapids, Michigan, by Zondervan. Zondervan is a registered trademark of The Zondervan Corporation, L.L.C., a wholly owned subsidiary of HarperCollins Christian Publishing, Inc.

Requests for information should be addressed to customercare@harpercollins.com.

Zondervan titles may be purchased in bulk for educational, business, fundraising, or sales promotional use. For information, please email SpecialMarkets@Zondervan.com.

ISBN 978-0-310-10917-4 (hardcover)
ISBN 978-0-310-10918-1 (ebook)

Cover design: Chris Tobias | Tobiasdesign.com
Cover photo: © PlusONE | Shutterstock
Interior design: Kait Lamphere

Printed in the United States of America

26 27 28 29 30 31 32 33 34 35 36 37 38 /TRM/ 24 23 22 21 20 19 18 17 16 15 14 13 12 11

To our wives, Judy Duvall and Donna Hays—
Our discussion of Song of Songs (chapter 22) summarizes our love for you.

CONTENTS

PART 5: THE INTERPRETIVE JOURNEY—OLD TESTAMENT

FOREWORDS

Through the four editions of *Grasping God's Word*, we have asked fellow scholars to provide for our readers supportive statements that place our book in its proper context and to offer their recommendations for using the book. We think you will find the forewords by Kevin J. Vanhoozer and Mark L. Strauss insightful for delineating what we're trying to accomplish in our book.

This is a wonderful user-friendly book for serious readers who desire to journey into the world of the Bible to understand it better and to live faithfully in today's world. J. Scott Duvall and J. Daniel Hays have chosen an apt title: *Grasping God's Word*. The metaphor of grasping is a useful one for thinking through what is involved in biblical interpretation. As you embark on that lifelong journey, as well as the shorter one of studying the present work, keeping four senses of the term *grasping* in mind will be useful.

To begin with, grasping is an act of violence: "to seize greedily." This is not what the present authors intended! It is, however, what many so-called postmodern readers think about the process of interpretation. In our disenchanted, disbelieving age, many no longer believe that there is a "meaning" in texts. Interpretation is more like a power struggle in which the reader imposes or forces his or her will on the text: *This is what it means to me*. In the opinion of many contemporary readers, we can never see beyond ourselves so as to attain an "objective" meaning. For these postmodern readers, there is no such thing as "correct" interpretation.

Grasping God's Word lays great emphasis on the importance of observing the small details and the overall design of biblical texts. Yet Duvall and Hays are not unaware of the current skeptical trend. They well know that the observer-reader is not an impersonal recording device but rather a person with a specific identity, history, and cultural background—all of which affect what one sees. Readers are not godlike, hovering in disembodied fashion over literary creations; no, readers, like authors, are rooted in particular historical situations—in what our authors call "towns."

Not wreaking violence on texts is hard work, for it is all too easy to read our own ideas and prejudices into the text. Accordingly, the authors call readers both to undertake serious observation and to be honest about their background and their location. Readers must be prepared to have their values and beliefs called into question by the text. If they are not, they will grasp the Bible in the wrong way, twisting its words and conforming them to what they want the text to say. This book is about avoiding such violent grasping.

Second, *Grasping God's Word* is really about another kind of grasping: understanding. We grasp an idea or a story or a poem when we can make good sense of the words in their context. For only when an interpretation makes sense of the parts and the whole can one say, "I've got it." To grasp, or understand, or "get it" is to recognize what an author is saying and doing in his or her text. The present book equips serious readers to "get it."

What is especially valuable is the authors' attention to both the "parts" and the "whole" of the Bible. They are as concerned with the Bible's words and sentences as they are with its paragraphs and books. Why? Because they rightly see that one can understand the whole only in light of the parts, and the parts only in light of the whole. We are not to grasp at the interpretative straws of word studies and proof texts. No, as the Israelites in ancient Egypt knew, straw can be used to make bricks. The "bricks" in this case are sentences and paragraphs that, when put together, are in turn used to make a variety of larger structures. One therefore finds chapters on word studies (the parts), as well as chapters on how to read the different kinds of "wholes" (e.g., the different types of literature) that make up the Bible. Indeed, the authors rightly devote almost half of the book to the practical challenges of interpreting and applying different kinds of biblical discourse.

Third, this book is about grasping in the literal sense of hands-on and practical know-how. For this is a book for interpreters who are willing to get their hands dirty with concrete examples and practical assignments. Readers will receive the equipment, tools, and training to "correctly handle the word of truth" (2 Tim. 2:15). Everything the contemporary tourist needs to know and to take on the journey into the world of the Bible is provided herein, along with instructions on how to get back again—application!

In the fourth place, this book is about "grasping" God's Word in the sense of holding on firmly. It is not enough merely to grasp God's Word intellectually to make sense of it. No, we need to grasp God's Word practically to make use of it. To what use should the Scriptures be put? One important answer lies within the text itself:

"for teaching, rebuking, correcting and training in righteousness" (2 Tim. 3:16). We need not only to understand but to hold on to and obey God's Word. For the Scriptures contain the words of eternal life—the words, when grasped, that enable the reader to lay hold of Jesus Christ, God's living Word, in faith. Of course, grasping the Scriptures, or holding on to Jesus Christ in faith, is only a figure of speech. The truth of the matter is that when we grasp the message of God's love for us, it—or rather, God—grasps us. This is the true end of biblical interpretation: to know as we are known.

In the final analysis, grasping God's Word is a matter of life and death. Needy sinners, we need to let go of the cultural baggage that weighs us down and to hold firmly on to the words of Scripture for dear life. For it is only in Scripture that we come to know, and be known, by him who is the way, the truth, and the life.

Kevin J. Vanhoozer

The Bible is the most revered, respected, and celebrated book of all time. Since the first published book rolled off Gutenberg's press over five hundred years ago (a Bible, of course!), it has been a perpetual bestseller, far surpassing sales of any other volume in human history. For Christians, the Bible is not just a bestseller; it is "God's Word"—a divine message to us in human language. It holds the answers to life's toughest questions: "Where did we come from?" "Why are we here?" "Is there a God?" and "How is this all going to end?"

Yet the Bible is also a book of bizarre events and strange mysteries. Read through the Bible and you'll find angels and demons, giants and dragons, seven-headed beasts rising from the sea, human-faced locusts coming out of the abyss, sea monsters with names like Leviathan and Rahab inhabiting the ocean depths, and "sons of God" cohabitating with the "daughters of men." The whole earth is covered by a flood, killing everyone but one family who escape on a barge. Fire and brimstone rains down on cities, obliterating them, and a woman turns into a pillar of salt. The mighty river Nile turns blood red. A powerful wind rolls back the sea and an entire nation walks through on dry land. An iron ax-head floats and dead people come back to life. This is strange stuff indeed!

Also strange to our ears are the many commands given in the Bible. People are told to cut the throats of animals and offer them as sacrifices to the Lord. They are commanded not to eat certain foods, like pork and shellfish, and not to plant two different crops in the same field. They must not wear clothing made of more than one material (cotton and polyester blend?) or tattoo their bodies. They absolutely must not work on Saturday (the Sabbath) but face execution if they do! Even in the New Testament, where most Christians feel a little more "at home," people are commanded to greet one another with a kiss, to wash one another's feet, and to sell everything they have and give the money to the poor. Women are told not to wear pearls or gold jewelry, to cover their heads with a veil, and to keep quiet in church. Christians today obviously do not obey all of these commands—but why not? Some say they're just part of the culture of the ancient world and don't apply today. But then what about other commands in the Bible, like those forbidding homosexual behavior? Are these "just cultural" as well?

Obviously, to navigate these challenging and potentially treacherous waters, we're going to need steady and experienced guides—those who know both the world of the text and the ways of God in human history. I can think of no better guides for this journey than Drs. Scott Duvall and Danny Hays. This volume, *Grasping God's Word*, is a clear, accurate, engaging, and balanced introduction to interpreting and applying God's Word. It leads students through the basic questions of how language works and where meaning resides in a written text. Using the metaphor of a journey across a river, the authors discuss how to cross the bridge from our modern world to the ancient world of the Bible and then back again to determine the text's abiding value for today. They discuss the various literary forms, or genres, of the Bible, from the primeval history of Genesis to the odd lists of laws given to Israel, to the everyday letters of the apostle Paul, to the bizarre apocalyptic imagery of the book of Revelation. Each genre has its own rules for reading, which determine both the meaning of the text in its original context and its significance for believers today.

Most importantly, as followers of Jesus Christ, the authors affirm that the Bible is not just a history of religious people doing religious things. It is the self-revelation of God, inspired by his Spirit and teaching us his ways in the past so we can live for him in the present. The journey of discovery introduced in *Grasping God's Word* is an invitation into a relationship with God and his purpose in the world. I hope you will enjoy the journey; but most of all, I pray that you will accept the invitation to find your place in the Bible's great story.

Mark L. Strauss

PREFACE

If you are interested in studying and applying God's Word, *Grasping God's Word* may be just the book for you. We applaud your commitment to the Bible and thank you for taking a few minutes to find out about our book. Our goal is to provide you with a resource that combines reliable hermeneutical theory with clear, practical explanations and interpretive examples from the Bible.

WHERE DID THE IDEA COME FROM?

As evangelical Christians, we believe that the Bible is important. But despite such claims, biblical illiteracy seems to be commonplace within our circles. At Ouachita Baptist University (pronounced WASH-u-taw), where both of us teach, we once required the courses Old Testament Survey and New Testament Survey for all students. Throughout the years, these traditional courses supplied students with a healthy dose of historical background and theological content along with a nice touch of the devotional. It's what we sensed our students were *not* getting that began to concern us. Were these courses helping them to see the overarching story of the Bible clearly enough to be able to live for Christ in a culture of competing stories? We also wondered whether we were teaching our students how to read the biblical story for themselves. How would they handle the Bible after leaving the class?

We now require all students to take Survey of the Bible and Interpreting the Bible in place of the Old and New Testament survey courses. In Survey of the Bible, we retell the biblical story from Genesis to Revelation in hopes of helping students see the big picture and understand how the grand story of Scripture answers the basic questions of life. In Interpreting the Bible, we teach students how to read, interpret, and apply the Bible for themselves. As the old adage says, we are trying to teach students how to fish rather than merely giving them fish to eat. The idea for *Grasping God's Word* grew out of this classroom strategy for equipping students for life and ministry, and this book serves as the textbook for the Interpreting the Bible course.

WHY IS THE BOOK CALLED *GRASPING GOD'S WORD*?

We write as evangelicals. The full title bears this out: *Grasping God's Word: A Hands-On Approach to Reading, Interpreting, and Applying the Bible.* Our fundamental assumption is that the Bible is the inspired and authoritative *Word of God* (see 2 Tim. 3:16–17).

This book emphasizes *grasping* the Bible. This is not to suggest that the Bible is nothing more than an object to be analyzed or scrutinized. The Bible is more than a deposit of static truth that must be manipulated. It is God's great story that is to be understood and lived out. Our approach underscores careful reading and wise interpretation, culminating in commitment to apply what we know (John 14:21). A person who truly grasps God's Word will find that Word grasping them.

Our approach is also *hands-on*. Through the abundant use of biblical examples and hands-on assignments, we hope to involve students in the nitty-gritty of biblical interpretation while guiding them through the process. Students should plan on getting their hands dirty as they learn how to dig deeper into God's Word.

WHAT KIND OF BOOK IS *GRASPING GOD'S WORD*?

Most books on interpreting the Bible fall into one of two categories. There are plenty of popular guides to understanding the Bible. At the other extreme, you will find a number of excellent graduate-level hermeneutics texts (e.g., Jeannine K. Brown, *Scripture as Communication*; William Klein, Craig Blomberg, and Robert Hubbard Jr., *Introduction to Biblical Interpretation*; Grant Osborne, *The Hermeneutical Spiral*; Walter Kaiser Jr. and Moisés Silva, *Introduction to Biblical Hermeneutics*). But there is not much in between to choose from. We hope that our book will help bridge that gap.

Grasping God's Word is intended to help serious believers (especially college and beginning seminary students) learn how to read, interpret, and apply the Bible. We are writing for our students rather than interacting with our colleagues in the professional guild. Although our book was never intended to be a comprehensive manual on biblical hermeneutics, it goes well beyond the introductory guides. We have tried to give students plain-language explanations informed by the best of evangelical biblical scholarship.

This book has three basic components:

1. We give serious attention to reading the Bible carefully. Much of the *hands-on* flavor comes through in the opening chapters as we lay a foundation of thoughtful reading. This section may look a lot like the inductive Bible study approach promoted by Robert Traina and Howard Hendricks.

2. We address general hermeneutical issues that confront every interpreter (e.g., preunderstanding, the role of the Holy Spirit).
3. We offer guidelines for interpreting and applying every major literary genre in both the Old and New Testaments.

HOW IS THE BOOK ORGANIZED?

Grasping God's Word is organized pedagogically rather than logically. A logical organization would begin with theory before moving to practice. But that is boring to students, and they lose interest before they ever get to the "good stuff." We have organized the book in a manner that motivates students to learn. Therefore, generally speaking, we begin with practice, move to theory, and then go back to practice. We have discovered in our teaching that after students have spent some time digging into the process of reading the Scriptures closely, they begin to ask more theoretical questions. We are extremely encouraged by the positive reception our students have given to the pedagogical arrangement. The book unfolds in five parts:

More practical	Part 1: How to Read the Book—Basic Tools
More theoretical	Part 2: Contexts—Now and Then Part 3: Meaning and Application
Theoretical and practical	Part 4: The Interpretive Journey—New Testament Part 5: The Interpretive Journey—Old Testament

Each chapter begins with an attention-getting introduction before moving into a serious but nontechnical presentation of the topic. After each chapter's conclusion, we provide several assignments to help students do what we have been discussing. Here, for example, is a sampling of the contents for the chapters on "Contexts: Now and Then—Word Studies" and "The Interpretive Journey: Old Testament—Prophets":

Contexts: Now and Then—Word Studies	**The Interpretive Journey: Old Testament—Prophets**
Introduction	Introduction
Common Word-Study Fallacies	The Nature of Old Testament Prophetic Literature
Choose Your Words Carefully	The Historical-Cultural and Theological Context

(cont.)

Contexts: Now and Then—Word Studies	**The Interpretive Journey: Old Testament—Prophets**
Determine What the Word Could Mean	The Basic Prophetic Message
Decide What the Word Does Mean in Context	Interpretation and Application
A Word Study: "Present" in Romans 12:1	Special Problems—the Predictive Passages
Conclusion	Conclusion
Assignments	Assignments

In three appendixes we provide a discussion on inspiration and canonicity, guidelines for writing exegetical papers, and suggestions for building a personal library (including a bibliography of recommended tools).

WORKBOOK

A student workbook accompanies this textbook. The workbook is designed primarily to facilitate the completion of assignments by the students and the collection of those assignments by the professor (i.e., it has tear-out sheets). This textbook can be used without the workbook, but then the student (or the professor) must photocopy the assignments in order to turn them in. The directions in this textbook for the assignments sometimes indicate this need for photocopying. Using the workbook eliminates the photocopying step because the workbook sheets themselves can be turned in. If you are using the workbook, follow the assignment directions there and ignore the ones in this textbook. We think both teachers and students will find the workbook convenient, and we recommend its use.

WEBSITE RESOURCES FOR TEACHERS

We are also offering resources for professors who adopt the textbook for use in their class on the Zondervan website.[1] You need to be logged into the site to be able to use them.

These resources include the following:

- quizzes
- exams

1. These resources may be found at www.TextbookPlus.Zondervan.com/content/Grasping-Gods-Word. Our thanks to Zondervan for making these resources available to teachers on their website.

- lesson plans (instructions about day-to-day class sessions)
- sample syllabi (including a course schedule)
- presentation slides
- online quizzes for students
- "A Short Guide to Writing Exegetical Papers"
- a sample exegetical paper

We pray the Lord continues to use this resource (and the accompanying workbook) to help his people understand and live out the Scriptures so that their relationship with the Lord grows deep and strong. As much as at any time in history, the contemporary church needs to listen carefully and faithfully to God's Word for the purpose of living in loving obedience to our triune God. To him be the glory!

J. Scott Duvall
J. Daniel Hays
Ouachita Baptist University
Arkadelphia, Arkansas

ACKNOWLEDGMENTS

We are particularly indebted to a group of teachers who have traveled the road of biblical interpretation before us and influenced our thinking in a number of ways: Howard Hendricks, Elliot Johnson, Roy Zuck, Gordon Fee, Grant Osborne, D. A. Carson, Bruce Corley, Craig Blomberg, Kevin Vanhoozer, Mark Strauss, and Jack Kuhatschek. We acknowledge that we do not address some of the scholarly, theoretical discussions that are foundational to our hermeneutical method. We would direct the reader to Kevin Vanhoozer's *Is There a Meaning in This Text?* for the theoretical foundation on which our application-oriented book is based.

We wish to thank our friends and fellow teachers for field-testing the book. We are especially grateful to Preben Vang, Randy Richards, and Dennis Tucker for reading a number of the chapters and offering valuable suggestions. In addition, we wish to thank especially David Croteau and Ernest Gray for their helpful suggestions at a recent Evangelical Theological Society meeting.

We are also grateful to our editors and publishing friends. Jack Kuhatschek has been a genuine inspiration from the beginning of the project. His passion for encouraging people to encounter God's Word is contagious. We are most appreciative of Verlyn Verbrugge's expertise in biblical interpretation and keen eye for detail. Thanks also to Jack Kragt for his friendship and encouragement during the course of the project and to other members of the academic marketing team at Zondervan. To Katya Covrett, we say thanks for your support and encouragement and strong vision to see people connect with God's Word in a meaningful way.

To the many students, friends, and relatives who have given us suggestions and assisted us in proofreading, we say thanks. We are especially grateful to Daryl White, Sam Myrick, Brad Johnson, Ellis Leagans, Jim Hays, Tracey Knight, Jason Hentschel, and Julie Bradley. We are especially grateful to the following students for reviewing and providing feedback on several chapters in the 4th edition: Sara Patterson, Kayla Whittington, Jael Winterholter, and Sam Youmans.

Finally, we want to express deep appreciation to our wives, Judy Duvall and Donna Hays, and to our kids, Ashley, Amy, and Meagan Duvall, and Hannah and J. D. Hays, for persevering to the end of the project with us.

PART 1

HOW TO READ THE BOOK—*Basic Tools*

Chapter 1 of *Grasping God's Word* delves into the whole issue of Bible translation. How did we get our English Bible? What are the various ways the Bible has been translated into English? What are the two main approaches to making a translation? And which translation is best?

In chapter 2 we introduce you to the process of reading, interpreting, and applying the Bible, a process we refer to as the "Interpretive Journey." This journey starts with a call to careful reading, because this is where we determine what the biblical text meant in its original context (*their town*). Before we are ready to apply that meaning to our lives (*our town*), however, we need to measure the width of the river that separates us from the world of the text. Once we have crossed the river, we will be able to apply the meaning of the Bible in relevant and reliable ways.

In chapter 3 we will start learning how to read with more insight and understanding. Superficial reading needs to be replaced by serious reading. We will show you how to observe smaller sections of text, looking for things like repeated words, contrasts, comparisons, lists, figures of speech, influential verbs, nouns, and conjunctions. Here we will learn how to read carefully at the sentence level. In chapters 4 and 5 we will move beyond the sentence level to the longer and more complex units of text—paragraphs and discourses. We will learn to detect things like dialogue, questions and answers, tone, connections between episodes, and story shifts. This is important to know if you really want to hear what God is saying through his Word.

In these first five chapters of *Grasping God's Word*, you will get your hands dirty as you learn about Bible translations and dig deeply into the process of biblical interpretation. The theory can wait for a few chapters as we learn how to read carefully and thoughtfully. This becomes the foundation for understanding what the Bible means and how we can live it out.

CHAPTER 1

BIBLE TRANSLATIONS

INTRODUCTION

For your birthday you get some extra cash and decide to buy a new Bible. You go online thinking you can find what you want pretty quickly. Immediately you notice more choices than you had imagined. You see the *NIV Study Bible*, *ESV Systematic Theology Study Bible*, *CSB Study Bible*, *Life Application Study Bible*, *Christian Basics Bible NLT*, *CSB Apologetics Study Bible*, *NIV Cultural Backgrounds Study Bible*, *NKJV Apply the Word Study Bible*, and about fifty other options. You didn't know buying a new Bible could be so complicated. What should you do?

> There is a big difference between the Bible version or translation and the format used by publishers to market the Bible.

The first thing to know about selecting a Bible is that there is a big difference between the Bible version or translation and the format used by publishers to market the Bible. Packaging features such as study notes, introductory articles, and devotional insights are often helpful, but they are not part of the translation of the original text. When choosing a Bible, you will want to look past the marketing format to make sure you know which translation the Bible uses. In this chapter we will be talking about Bible translations rather than marketing features.

We have a chapter on Bible translations because translation itself is unavoidable. God has revealed himself and has asked his people to make that communication known to others. Unless everyone wants to learn Hebrew and Greek (the Bible's original languages), we will need a translation. Translation is nothing more than transferring the message of one language into another language. We should not think of translation as a bad thing, since through translations we are able to hear what God has said. In other words, translations are necessary for people who speak a language other than Greek or Hebrew to understand what God is saying through his Word.

Translations are necessary for people who speak a language other than Greek or Hebrew to understand what God is saying through his Word.

We will begin our discussion of Bible translations by looking at how we got our English Bible in the first place. Then we will look back at the various ways the Bible has been translated into English from the fourteenth century to the present. Next we will turn our attention to evaluating the two main approaches to making a translation of God's Word. Since students of the Bible often ask, "Which translation is best?" we will wrap up the chapter with a few guidelines for choosing a translation.

HOW DID WE GET OUR ENGLISH BIBLE?

Kids ask the toughest theological questions. At supper one evening, right after hearing a Bible story on the Tower of Babel, Meagan Duvall (age five at the time) asked, "Who wrote the Bible anyway?" What a great question! Meagan's question is actually part of a larger question: "How did we get our English Bible?" or "Where did the English Bible come from?"[1] Since the Bible was not originally written in English, understanding the process God used to get the English Bible into our hands is important. Below is a chart illustrating the process of inspiration, transmission, translation, and interpretation.

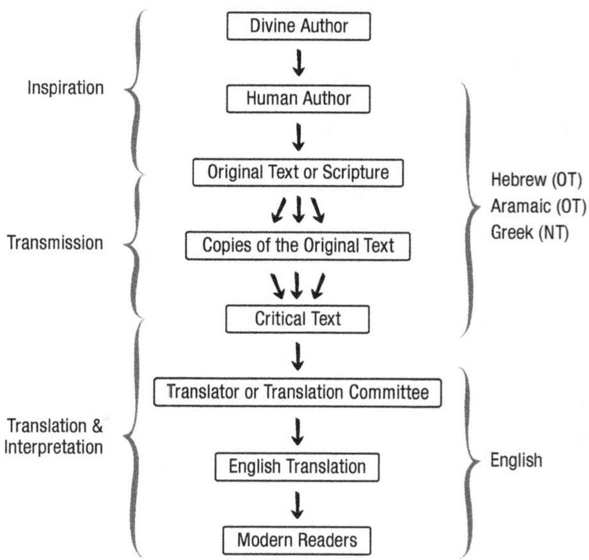

We left you hanging regarding Scott's answer to his daughter Meagan. Using the language of a five-year-old, he tried to explain that God wrote the Bible and that he used many different people to do so. The Bible is entirely the Word of God (divine

1. For a clear and engaging introduction to how the Bible came to be, see Clinton E. Arnold, *How We Got the Bible: A Visual Journey* (Grand Rapids: Zondervan, 2008). See also Timothy Paul Jones, *How We Got the Bible* (Torrance, CA: Rose, 2015); Neil R. Lightfoot, *How We Got the Bible*, 3rd ed. (Grand Rapids: Baker, 2010).

authorship), but it is at the same time the writings of human authors. John Stott clearly describes the divine-human authorship of the Bible:

> Out of whose mouth did Scripture come, then? God's or man's? [Sounds a lot like Meagan's question.] The only biblical answer is "both." Indeed, God spoke through the human authors in such a way that his words were simultaneously their words, and their words were simultaneously his. This is the double authorship of the Bible. Scripture is equally the Word of God and the words of human beings. Better, it is the Word of God through the words of human beings.[2]

God worked through the various human authors, including their backgrounds, personalities, cultural contexts, writing styles, faith commitments, research, and so on, so that what they wrote was the inspired Word of God. As Paul said to Timothy, "All Scripture is God-breathed and is useful for teaching, rebuking, correcting and training in righteousness" (2 Tim. 3:16). God's work through human authors resulted in an inspired original text.

As you might expect, in time people wanted to make copies of the original documents of Scripture (we refer to the originals as the ***autographs***). Then copies were made of those first copies and so on. As a result, although the autographs no longer exist, we do possess numerous copies of the books of the Bible. For example, there are almost six thousand manuscripts (handwritten copies) of all or parts of the New Testament in existence today. Regarding the Old Testament, in 1947 Hebrew manuscripts of Old Testament books were discovered in the caves of Qumran near the Dead Sea. The Dead Sea Scrolls, as they are called, contain a portion of almost every book of the Old Testament. Prior to the discovery of the Dead Sea Scrolls, the oldest Old Testament manuscript dated to the ninth century AD. In other words, some of the copies found in 1947 were a thousand years older than anything previously known.

Before the invention of the printing press in the 1400s, all copies of the Bible were, of course, done by hand. As you know if you have ever tried to copy a lengthy piece of writing by hand, you make mistakes. The scribes who copied the copies of Scripture occasionally did the same. They might have omitted a letter or even a line of text, misspelled a word, or reversed two letters. At times scribes might have changed a text deliberately to make it more understandable or even more theologically "correct."

Consequently, the copies we have do not look exactly alike. Make no mistake, scribes were generally very careful, and you can rest assured that there is no textual

2. John Stott, *The Contemporary Christian* (Downers Grove, IL: InterVarsity Press, 1992), 168–69.

dispute about the vast majority of the Bible.[3] Nevertheless, there are differences in the copies, and we need some way of trying to determine which copy is more likely to reflect the original text. That responsibility falls to the discipline known as *textual criticism.*

Textual criticism (or analysis) is a technical discipline that compares the various copies of a biblical text in an effort to determine what was most likely the original text. The work of textual critics is foundational to the work of Bible translation, since the first concern of any translator should be whether they are translating the most plausible rendition of a biblical text. The work of the best textual critics is set forth in modern critical editions of the Bible. For the Old Testament the standard critical text is the *Biblia Hebraica Stuttgartensia* (*BHS*). For the New Testament the work of the best textual critics is reflected in the latest edition of the United Bible Societies' *Greek New Testament* (*GNT*) or Nestle-Aland's *Novum Testamentum Graece*. These critical editions represent the best scholarly consensus regarding the autographs, and they form the basis for almost all modern English translations.

At this point in the process, a translator (or usually a translation committee) will translate the Bible from the source languages (Hebrew, Aramaic, or Greek) into the receptor language (in our case, modern English). Here you enter the picture. As a reader you pick up your English Bible and begin to read and interpret.

Think for a moment about all that has happened before you ever lay eyes on the English text. God spoke through human authors who composed an original text. The originals were copied and recopied. Textual analysts did their best to determine which copies most likely resemble the originals and produced a modern critical edition of the Old and New Testament texts. The translators then went to work moving the meaning of the ancient biblical text into our own language so that we can hear the Lord speak to us through his Word.

A BRIEF SURVEY OF ENGLISH TRANSLATIONS[4]

English Translations Prior to 1611

The early Christian leader Jerome translated the Bible into Latin around AD 400 (dubbed the *Vulgate*, from a Latin word meaning "common"), and for a thousand

3. William W. Klein, Craig L. Blomberg, and Robert L. Hubbard Jr., *Introduction to Biblical Interpretation*, 4th ed. (Grand Rapids: Zondervan, 2017), 187, conclude, "Estimates suggest that more than 99 percent of the original NT can be reconstructed from the existing manuscripts with a high degree of probability. The percentage for the OT is lower, but even a very cautious figure would be well above 90 percent."

4. For a far more complete treatment of Bible translations into English, see F. F. Bruce, *History of the Bible in English: From the Earliest Versions*, 3rd ed. (New York: Oxford University Press, 1978); David Ewert, *A General Introduction to the Bible: From Ancient Tablets to Modern Translations* (Grand Rapids: Zondervan, 1983); Paul D.

years churches in the British Isles had to use this Bible. We have John Wycliffe to thank for the first complete translation of the Bible into English. The *Wycliffe Bible* (New Testament in 1380) was actually a word-for-word translation from Latin into English rather than from the original Hebrew and Greek. Wycliffe was accused of being a heretic and suffered persecution for his willingness to translate the Bible into the language of ordinary people. People were threatened with severe penalties for even reading this forbidden Bible. Shortly after Wycliffe's death in 1384, John Purvey produced a second (and much improved) edition. Purvey's revision of the Wycliffe Bible (1388) dominated the English-speaking scene for some two hundred years—until the time of William Tyndale.

John Wycliffe was accused of being a heretic and suffered persecution for his willingness to translate the Bible into the language of ordinary people.

With the invention of the printing press in the mid-1400s, the renewed interest in the classical languages associated with the Renaissance, and the changes brought on by the Protestant Reformation (early 1500s), English Bible translation shifted into high gear. William Tyndale produced an English New Testament (1526) based on the Greek text rather than the Latin, but he did not live to complete his translation of the Old Testament. In 1536 Tyndale was executed and his body burned for his resolute commitment to Bible translation and his desire to "make the boy that drives the plough in England know more of Scripture" than many a scholar.[5]

Shortly before Tyndale's death, Miles Coverdale produced a translation of the entire Bible into English (*Coverdale Bible*, 1535). Two years later John Rogers, an associate of Tyndale, completed the *Matthew Bible*, using the pen name Thomas Matthew. The Matthew Bible was in large part a completion of Tyndale's work. Like Tyndale, John Rogers suffered martyrdom in connection with his commitment to Bible translation. In 1539 Coverdale revised the Matthew Bible, a revision that became known as the *Great Bible* because of its larger than normal size (approximately 16½ x 11-inch pages). The Great Bible was the first English translation authorized to be read in the Church of England and became popular with the people.

William Tyndale was executed and his body burned for his resolute commitment to Bible translation and his desire to "make the boy that drives the plough in England know more of Scripture" than many a scholar.

During the infamous reign of Mary I ("Bloody Mary"), many Protestants fled from England to Protestant havens

Wegner, *The Journey from Texts to Translations: The Origin and Development of the Bible* (Grand Rapids: Baker, 1999); Bruce M. Metzger, *The Bible in Translation: Ancient and English Versions* (Grand Rapids: Baker, 2001); and David Daniell, *The Bible in English* (New Haven, CT: Yale University Press, 2003).

5. F. F. Bruce, *The Books and the Parchments*, 3rd ed. (Old Tappan, NJ: Revell, 1963), 223.

of refuge, such as Geneva, Switzerland, the home of John Calvin. While in Geneva, the Oxford scholar William Whittingham (with some help from others) made a complete revision of the English Bible. The popular *Geneva Bible* (1560) was "the Bible of Shakespeare, the Bible of the Puritans, and the Bible of the Pilgrim Fathers."[6] Yet because of the Calvinistic marginal notes in the Geneva Bible, the bishops of England were unwilling to use it in English churches. Yet since the Geneva Bible was superior to the Great Bible in translation quality, the bishops knew they needed a new translation. Matthew Parker, the archbishop of Canterbury, was asked to oversee the revision of the Great Bible. The *Bishops' Bible* was completed in 1568. The Roman Catholic Church also needed an English translation with marginal notes in support of its doctrine. Although not of the same quality as the Protestant English translations (because of its close adherence to the Latin Vulgate), the *Douai-Rheims Bible* (1593) served this purpose.

The Authorized Version of 1611

Since none of the previous translations was able to satisfy all the different factions within the English church, in 1604 King James I authorized a new translation of the whole Bible for use in the churches of England. The leading university scholars in England produced the *Authorized Version* of 1611, commonly known as the *King James Version*. To generate the thousands of copies needed, two different printers were used. This resulted in two editions, named after their different translations of Ruth 3:15. The "He" edition reads, "He [Boaz] went into the city," while the "She" edition reads, "She [Ruth] went into the city." There are more than two hundred variations between these two editions as well as some mistakes.[7] For example, the "He" edition says "then cometh Judas" in Matthew 26:36 instead of "then cometh Jesus." The "She" edition repeats twenty words in Exodus 14:10. Even from the start it was difficult to determine the real KJV. The King James Version of 1611 also included the Apocrypha, a group of Jewish books recognized as canonical by Catholics but not by Protestants.

The leading university scholars in England produced the *Authorized Version* of 1611, commonly known as the *King James Version*.

The goal of the KJV translators was to translate the original Greek and Hebrew texts into the language of ordinary people, with enough dignity to be used in church. From the original preface to the 1611 version, we learn that these scholars were keenly aware that their new translation would bring opposition from those who refused to break with tradition. They wrote:

6. Ewert, *General Introduction to the Bible*, 195.

7. See Erroll F. Rhodes and Liana Lupas, eds., *The Translators to the Reader: The Original Preface to the King James Version of 1611 Revisited* (New York: American Bible Society, 1997), 5.

> For was anything ever undertaken with a touch of newness or improvement about it that didn't run into storms of argument or opposition? . . . [The king] was well aware that whoever attempts anything for the public, especially if it has to do with religion or with making the word of God accessible and understandable, sets himself up to be frowned upon by every evil eye, and casts himself headlong on a row of pikes, to be stabbed by every sharp tongue. For meddling in any way with a people's religion is meddling with their customs, with their inalienable rights. And although they may be dissatisfied with what they have, they cannot bear to have it altered.[8]

In spite of the dangers associated with Bible translation, the translators were committed to the ongoing ministry of making the Scriptures available in the language of ordinary people.

> So the Church should always be ready with translations in order to avoid the same kind of emergencies [i.e., the inability to understand because of a language barrier]. Translation is what opens the window, to let the light in. It breaks the shell, so that we may eat the kernel. It pulls the curtain aside, so that we may look into the most holy place. It removes the cover from the well, so that we may get to the water. . . . In fact, without a translation in the common language, most people are like the children at Jacob's well (which was deep) without a bucket or something to draw the water with; or like the person mentioned by Isaiah who was given a sealed book and told, "Please read this," and had to answer, "I can not, because it is sealed" (Isaiah 29.11).[9]

Early on, the KJV faced severe attacks from certain quarters. Dr. Hugh Broughton, an eminent biblical scholar of that day, was famous for his caustic remarks: "Tell His Majesty that I had rather be rent in pieces with wild horses, than any such translation by my consent should be urged upon poor churches. The new edition crosseth me. I require it to be burnt."[10] In spite of such criticism, the KJV eventually became one of the most widely used translations in the English-speaking world.

The goal of the KJV translators was to translate the original Greek and Hebrew texts into the language of ordinary people, with enough dignity to be used in church.

Because languages (including English) change over time, the KJV itself eventually needed to be revised.

8. Rhodes and Lupas, 68–69.
9. Rhodes and Lupas, 71–72.
10. Bruce, *History of the Bible in English*, 107.

There have been many major revisions (1629, 1638, 1729, 1762), but the 1769 revision by Benjamin Blayney (known as the Oxford Standard Edition) is the edition still in use today. Many people are unaware that the 1769 edition of the KJV differs in thousands of places from the original 1611 edition. Language can change a lot in the span of 150 years.

Contemporary readers face two major obstacles with the KJV.[11] First, the translators of the KJV worked from an inferior Greek text constructed from only a few late New Testament manuscripts. Since the KJV first appeared, many older manuscripts have been discovered, and scholars contend that these older manuscripts are much more likely to reflect the original text. In contrast to the Greek text on which the KJV is based, scholars today are able to translate from a Greek text that draws on almost six thousand New Testament manuscripts, some dating back to the second century. Often differences between the KJV and contemporary translations such as the New International Version are due to differences in the underlying Greek text. Here are several examples.

	King James Version	**New International Version**
Acts 8:36–38	36And as they went on *their* way, they came unto a certain water: and the eunuch said, See, *here is* water; what doth hinder me to be baptized?	36As they traveled along the road, they came to some water and the eunuch said, "Look, here is water. What can stand in the way of my being baptized?"
	37And Philip said, If thou believest with all thine heart, thou mayest. And he answered and said, I believe that Jesus Christ is the Son of God.	[No verse 37]
	38And he commanded the chariot to stand still: and they went down both into the water, both Philip and the eunuch; and he baptized him.	38And he gave orders to stop the chariot. Then both Philip and the eunuch went down into the water and Philip baptized him.
1 John 5:7–8	7For there are three that bear record in heaven, the Father, the Word, and the Holy Ghost: and these three are one.	7For there are three that testify:
	8And there are three that bear witness in earth, the Spirit, and the water, and the blood: and these three agree in one.	8the Spirit, the water and the blood; and the three are in agreement.

11. Those who insist that the KJV is the only legitimate English-language translation should consult James R. White, *The King James Only Controversy*, 2nd ed. (Minneapolis: Bethany, 2009).

	King James Version	New International Version
Rev. 22:19	[19]And if any man shall take away from the words of the book of this prophecy, God shall take away his part out of the book of life, and out of the holy city, and *from* the things which are written in this book.	[19]And if anyone takes words away from this scroll of prophecy, God will take away from that person any share in the tree of life and in the Holy City, which are described in this scroll.

A second obstacle is the KJV's use of archaic English words and phrases. In addition to the use of obsolete terms such as "aforetime," "must needs," "howbeit," "holden," "peradventure," and "whereto," the KJV is filled with out-of-date expressions that either fail to communicate with contemporary readers or mislead them entirely. Consider the following:

- Genesis 43:25: "And they made ready the present **against** Joseph came at noon."
- Exodus 19:18: "And mount Sinai was altogether **on a smoke.**"
- 1 Samuel 5:12: "And the men that died not were smitten with the **emerods.**" [What are "emerods"?]
- Psalm 5:6: "Thou shalt destroy them that **speak leasing.**"
- Luke 17:9: "Doth he thank that servant because he did the things that were commanded him? **I trow not.**"
- Acts 7:44–45: "Our fathers had the tabernacle of witness in the wilderness, as he had appointed, speaking unto Moses, that he should make it according to the fashion that he had seen. Which also our fathers that came after brought in with **Jesus** [Joshua] into the possession of the Gentiles, whom God drave out before the face of our fathers, unto the days of David."
- 2 Corinthians 8:1: "Moreover, brethren, **we do you to wit of** the grace of God bestowed on the churches of Macedonia."
- James 2:3: "And ye have respect to him that weareth **the gay clothing.**"
- James 5:11: "The Lord is **very pitiful.**"

The KJV was a good translation for the early 1600s because it was written in the English of the early 1600s. Today, however, most of us would have trouble even reading a page of the original 1611 version, since it was printed in archaic English. See for yourself.

To argue that we should still use the 1769 KJV edition (the one that is popular today) is to admit the necessity of revising a translation. This is the case because there were thousands of changes from 1611 to 1769; they are literally two different Bibles. Why not continue the process of revision by drawing on the latest in biblical scholarship and using language that today's readers can understand? Anything less seems to violate the intent of those who translated the original KJV. Let's turn our attention now to what happened in Bible translation after 1611.

English Translations since 1611

A number of more recent English translations have some connection (direct or indirect) to updating the KJV. The *English Revised Version* (1881–85) was the first such revision and the first English translation to make use of modern principles of textual criticism. As a result, the Greek text underlying the ERV was different from that of the KJV. In 1901 American scholars produced their own revision of the ERV—the *American Standard Version*. Toward the middle of the twentieth century (1946–52), the *Revised Standard Version* appeared. The goal of the RSV translators was to capture the best of modern scholarship regarding the meaning of Scriptures and to express that meaning in English designed for public and private worship—the same qualities that had given the KJV such high standing in English literature. The *English Standard Version* (2001) is a word-for-word translation that uses the RSV as its starting point. Its goal is to be as literal as possible while maintaining beauty, dignity of expression, and literary excellence.

Genesis 22 from the 1611 KJV

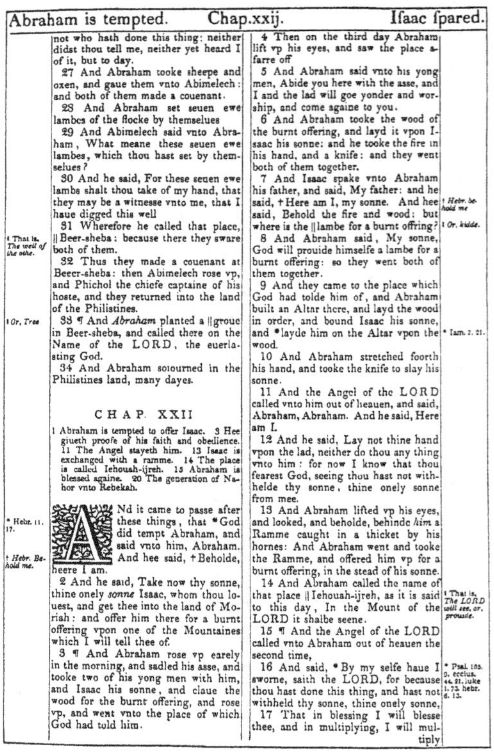

Abraham is tempted. Chap.xxij. Isaac spared.

not who hath done this thing: neither didst thou tell me, neither yet heard I of it, but to day.

27 And Abraham tooke sheepe and oxen, and gaue them vnto Abimelech: and both of them made a couenant.

28 And Abraham set seuen ewe lambes of the flocke by themselues

29 And Abimelech said vnto Abraham, What meane these seuen ewe lambes, which thou hast set by themselues?

30 And he said, For these seuen ewe lambs shalt thou take of my hand, that they may be a witnesse vnto me, that I haue digged this well

31 Wherefore he called that place, ||Beer-sheba: because there they sware both of them. (|| That is, The well of the othe.)

32 Thus they made a couenant at Beeer-sheba: then Abimelech rose vp, and Phichol the chiefe captaine of his hoste, and they returned into the land of the Philistines.

33 ¶ And *Abraham* planted a ||groue in Beer-sheba, and called there on the Name of the LORD, the euerlasting God. (|| Or, Tree)

34 And Abraham soiourned in the Philistines land, many dayes.

CHAP. XXII

1 Abraham is tempted to offer Isaac. 3 Hee giueth proofe of his faith and obedience. 11 The Angel stayeth him. 13 Isaac is exchanged with a ramme. 14 The place is called Iehouah-ijreh. 15 Abraham is blessed againe. 20 The generation of Nahor vnto Rebekah.

AND it came to passe after these things, that *God did tempt Abraham, and said vnto him, Abraham. And hee said, †Beholde, heere I am. (* Hebr. 11. 17. † Hebr. Behold me.)

2 And he said, Take now thy sonne, thine onely *sonne* Isaac, whom thou louest, and get thee into the land of Moriah: and offer him there for a burnt offering vpon one of the Mountaines which I will tell thee of.

3 ¶ And Abraham rose vp earely in the morning, and sadled his asse, and tooke two of his yong men with him, and Isaac his sonne, and claue the wood for the burnt offering, and rose vp, and went vnto the place of which God had told him.

4 Then on the third day Abraham lift vp his eyes, and saw the place afarre off

5 And Abraham said vnto his yong men, Abide you here with the asse, and I and the lad will goe yonder and worship, and come againe to you.

6 And Abraham tooke the wood of the burnt offering, and layd it vpon Isaac his sonne: and he tooke the fire in his hand, and a knife: and they went both of them together.

7 And Isaac spake vnto Abraham his father, and said, My father: and he said, †Here am I, my sonne. And hee said, Behold the fire and wood: but where is the ||lambe for a burnt offring? († Hebr. behold me || Or, kidde.)

8 And Abraham said, My sonne, God will prouide himselfe a lambe for a burnt offering: so they went both of them together.

9 And they came to the place which God had tolde him of, and Abraham built an Altar there, and layd the wood in order, and bound Isaac his sonne, and *layde him on the Altar vpon the wood. (* Iam. 2. 21.)

10 And Abraham stretched foorth his hand, and tooke the knife to slay his sonne.

11 And the Angel of the LORD called vnto him out of heauen, and said, Abraham, Abraham. And he said, Here am I.

12 And he said, Lay not thine hand vpon the lad, neither do thou any thing vnto him: for now I know that thou fearest God, seeing thou hast not withhelde thy sonne, thine onely sonne from mee.

13 And Abraham lifted vp his eyes, and looked, and beholde, behinde *him* a Ramme caught in a thicket by his hornes: And Abraham went and tooke the Ramme, and offered him vp for a burnt offering, in the stead of his sonne.

14 And Abraham called the name of that place ||Iehouah-ijreh, as it is said to this day, In the Mount of the LORD it shalbe seene. (|| That is, The LORD will see, or, prouide.)

15 ¶ And the Angel of the LORD called vnto Abraham out of heauen the second time,

16 And said, *By my selfe haue I sworne, saith the LORD, for because thou hast done this thing, and hast not withheld thy sonne, thine onely sonne, (* Psal. 105. 9. ecclus. 44. 21. luke 1. 73. hebr. 6. 13.)

17 That in blessing I will blesse thee, and in multiplying, I will multiply

The *New American Standard Bible* (1971, rev. ed. 1995) claimed to be a revision of the ASV but probably should be viewed as a new translation. The NASB (or NAS) is one of the more popular translations that adheres closely to the form of the original languages. The *New King James Version* (1979–82) attempts to update the language of the KJV while retaining the same underlying Greek text that the translators of the KJV used (commonly called the *Textus Receptus* or TR).[12] This preference for the TR distinguishes the NKJV from the other revisions, which make use

12. The *Textus Receptus* (Latin for "received text") was the Greek text published in the mid-1500s and used by the translators of the KJV. It was "received" in the sense that it was considered the standard Greek text of that time.

of a better Greek text (commonly called an *eclectic* Greek text), based on older and more reliable readings of the Greek. The *New Revised Standard Version*, a thorough revision of the RSV, was completed in 1989 with the goal of being as literal as possible and as free as necessary. The accompanying chart illustrates the relationship between translations that are related in some way to revising the KJV.

In addition to the KJV revisions noted above, committees of scholars have produced many other new translations in recent years. Catholic scholars have completed two major translations: the *New American Bible* (1941–70) and the *Jerusalem Bible* (1966). What makes these significant is that not until 1943 did the Roman Catholic Church permit scholars to translate from the original Greek and Hebrew. Until that time, their translation had to be based on the Latin Vulgate. The *New Jerusalem Bible*, a revision of the Jerusalem Bible, appeared in 1985 and the *New American Bible, Revised Edition* in 2011. Both the *New English Bible* (1961–70) and its revision, the *Revised English Bible* (1989), are translations into contemporary British idiom. The American Bible Society completed the *Good News Translation* in 1976 (also called *Good News Bible* or *Today's English Version*). The translators of this version sought to express the meaning of the original text in conversational English (even for those with English as a second language). In the *New International Version* (1973, 1978, 1984), a large committee of evangelical scholars sought to produce a translation in international English offering a middle ground between a word-for-word approach and a thought-for-thought approach.

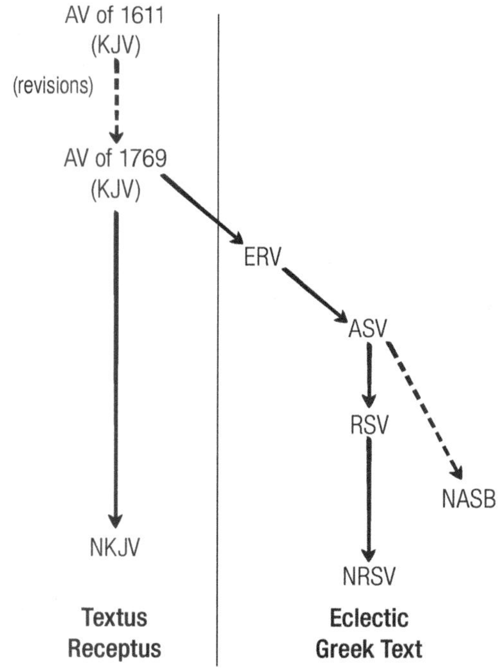

The *New Century Version* (1987) and the *Contemporary English Version* (1991–95) are recent translations that utilize a simplified, thought-for-thought approach to translation. A similar translation from the translators of the NIV is the *New International Reader's Version* (1995–96). The *New Living Translation* (1996) is a fresh, thought-for-thought translation based on the popular paraphrase *The Living Bible* (1967–71). A recent attempt by an individual (rather than a committee) to render the message of Scripture in the language of today's generation is *The Message* by Eugene Peterson (1993–2002). *The Message* claims to be a translation but reads more like a paraphrase aimed at grabbing the reader's attention. *God's Word Translation* (1995) uses the "closest natural equivalence" approach to translation in an attempt to translate the meaning of the original texts into clear, everyday language. The *New English Translation*, commonly referred to as the NET Bible (1998), offers an electronic version of a modern translation for distribution over the internet. Anyone anywhere in the world with an internet connection (including translators and missionaries) can have access to this new version, which is under continual revision. The *Lexham English Bible* (2010–11) is an online Bible released by Logos Bible Software that is closely connected to the original languages. The *Common English Bible* (2011) is a fresh translation in the liberal Protestant tradition.

Today's New International Version (2005) is an attempt to revise the NIV, using the best of contemporary biblical scholarship and changes in the English language. Most recently the Committee on Bible Translation has revised the most popular of all modern English translations of the Bible, the New International Version. The NIV 2011 incorporates many of the improvements of the NIV (1984) made by the TNIV but with more precision in the area of gender-inclusive language.

The *Holman Christian Standard Bible* (1999–2004) is a new Bible translation that promotes a word-for-word approach unless clarity and readability demand a more idiomatic translation, in which case the literal form is often put in a footnote. The *Christian Standard Bible* (2017) is a major revision of the Holman Christian Standard Bible that draws from both formal and functional translation philosophies.

Our survey of the history of English Bible translations running from the Middle English of John Wycliffe's 1380 translation to the NIV 2011 has been a brief one. We have only hit the high points in a long and rich history. We move now to explore the different approaches to Bible translation.

APPROACHES TO TRANSLATING GOD'S WORD

The process of translating is more complicated than it appears.[13] Some people think that all you have to do when making a translation is to define each word and string together all the individual word meanings. This assumes that the source language (in this case, Greek or Hebrew) and the receptor language (such as English) are exactly alike. If only the process could be so easy! In fact, no two languages are exactly alike. For example, look at a verse chosen at random—from the story of Jesus healing a demon-possessed boy (Matt. 17:18). The word-for-word English rendition is written below a transliteration of the Greek:

13. See Glen G. Scorgie, Mark L. Strauss, and Steven M. Voth, eds., *The Challenge of Bible Translation* (Grand Rapids: Zondervan, 2003).

Kai epetimēsen autō ho Iēsous kai exēlthen ap' autou to daimonion
And rebuked it the Jesus and came out from him the demon

kai etherapeuthē ho pais apo tēs hōras ekeinēs
and was healed the boy from the hour that

Should we conclude that the English line is the most accurate translation of Matthew 17:18 because it attempts a literal rendering of the verse, keeping also the word order? Is a translation better if it tries to match each word in the source language with a corresponding word in a receptor language? Could you even read an entire Bible "translated" in this way?

The fact that no two languages are exactly alike makes translation a complicated endeavor. D. A. Carson identifies a number of things that separate one language from another:[14]

- No two words are exactly alike. As we will learn in our chapter on word studies, words mean different things in different languages. Even words that are similar in meaning differ in some way. For example, the Greek verb *phileō*, often translated "to love," must be translated "to kiss" when Judas kisses Jesus in an act of betrayal (Matt. 26:48 KJV and NIV).
- The vocabulary of any two languages will vary in size. This means that it is impossible to assign a word in a source language directly to a word in a receptor language. This kind of one-to-one correspondence would be nice, but it is simply not possible.
- Languages put words together differently to form phrases, clauses, and sentences (syntax). This means that there are preset structural differences between any two languages. For example, English has an indefinite article (*a*, *an*) while Greek does not. In English, adjectives come before the noun they modify, and they use the same definite article (e.g., "the big city"). In Hebrew, however, adjectives come after the noun they modify, and they have their own definite article (e.g., "the city, the big").
- Languages have different stylistic preferences. Sophisticated Greek emphasizes passive voice verbs, while refined English stresses the active voice. Hebrew poetry sometimes uses an acrostic (ABC) pattern, which is impossible to transfer into English.

14. The following is a summary of only a few differences discussed by Carson in *The Inclusive-Language Debate* (Grand Rapids: Baker, 1998), 48–51.

Since languages differ in many ways, making a translation is not a simple, cut-and-dried, mechanical process. When it comes to translation, it is wrong to assume that *literal* automatically equals *accurate*. A more literal translation is not necessarily a more accurate translation; it could actually be a less accurate translation. Is the translation "and was healed the boy from the hour that" better than "and the boy was healed instantly" (ESV) or "and from that moment the boy was healed" (CSB)? Translation is more than just finding matching words and adding them up.

"[Translation entails] reproducing the meaning of a text that is in one language (the *source language*), as fully as possible, in another language (the *receptor language*)."
—*Mark Strauss*

Translation entails "reproducing the meaning of a text that is in one language (the *source language*), as fully as possible, in another language (the *receptor language*)."[15] The form of the original language is important, and translators should stay with it when possible, but form should not have priority over meaning. What is most important is that the contemporary reader understands the meaning of the original text. When a translator can reproduce meaning while preserving form, all the better. Translating is complicated work, and translators often must make difficult choices between two equally good but different ways of saying something. This explains why there are different approaches to translation. Individuals and committees have differences of opinion about the best way to make the tough choices involved in translation, including the relationship between form and meaning.

There are two main approaches to translation: the *formal* approach (sometimes labeled "literal" or "word-for-word") and the *functional* approach (often called "idiomatic" or "thought-for-thought"). In reality, no translation is entirely formal or entirely functional. Since source and receptor languages differ, all translations will have at least some formal features and some functional features. The situation is more like a scale, ranging from translations that are more formal to translations that are more functional (see below).

There are two main approaches to translation: the *formal* approach (sometimes labeled "literal" or "word-for-word") and the *functional* approach (often called "idiomatic" or "thought-for-thought").

The *more formal* approach tries to stay as close as possible to the structure and words of the source language. Translators using this approach feel a keen responsibility to reproduce the forms of the original Greek and Hebrew whenever possible. The NASB and ESV use this approach. On the downside, the formal approach is less sensitive to the receptor language of the contemporary reader and, as a result, may appear stilted

15. Mark L. Strauss, *Distorting Scripture?* (Downers Grove, IL: InterVarsity Press, 1998), 77.

or awkward. Formal translations run the risk of sacrificing meaning for the sake of maintaining form.

The *more functional* approach tries to express the meaning of the original text in today's language. Here the translator feels a responsibility to reproduce the meaning of the original text in English so that the effect on today's reader is equivalent to the effect on the ancient reader.

Many contemporary translations utilize this approach, including the NLT and GNB. The functional approach is not always as sensitive as it should be to the wording and structure of the source language. When it moves too far away from the form of the source language, the functional approach runs the risk of distorting the true meaning of the text. The spectrum of translations might look something like this, moving from the more formal to the more functional.

More Formal → **More Functional**

KJV	NASB	RSV	NRSV	NAB	NIV	NJB	NCV	GNB	*The Message*
ASV	NKJV	HCSB	NET		TNIV	REB	NLT	CEV	
	ESV								

In addition to the two main approaches to translation discussed above, you will encounter what is known as a *paraphrase*. Technically, a paraphrase is not a translation from the original languages at all, but merely a restatement or explanation of a particular English translation using different English words. *The Living Bible* (1967–71), perhaps the most famous paraphrase, is Kenneth Taylor's restatement of the ASV (1901) for the benefit of his children.

A paraphrase is not a translation from the original languages at all, but merely a restatement or explanation of a particular English translation using different English words.

Another well-known paraphrase, the *Amplified Bible, Classic Edition* (1954–87), tries to give the reader an understanding of the many meanings contained in a particular verse through the "creative use of amplification." For instance, John 11:25 reads, "Jesus said to her, I am [Myself] the Resurrection and the Life. Whoever believes in (adheres to, trusts in, and relies on) Me, although he may die, yet he shall live." This looks very much like the overload fallacy, which assumes that a word will bring its full range of meaning into every context.[16] The *Amplified Bible* leaves the misleading impression that the reader is free to choose from among the options presented.

16. See explanation of this fallacy in chapter 9 on word studies.

Again, paraphrases are not translations from the original language. We do not recommend using paraphrases for serious study, because they tend to explain rather than translate. We believe that the author's meaning is encoded in the details of the text. In a paraphrase the "translator" makes far too many of the interpretive decisions for you. The result is that paraphrases add many things that are simply not in the Bible. Rather than translating the Word of God, paraphrases present a commentary on the Word of God. You should treat paraphrases like commentaries and use them as such. Our advice for those who enjoy *The Living Bible* and other paraphrases is to switch to the New Living Translation.

Below are sample translations from across the spectrum, using 1 Corinthians 10:13. As you read the different translations, you will notice the subtle shift from an emphasis on form to an emphasis on function.

With all these contemporary translations to choose from, the natural question is "Which translation is best?" The next section is intended to help you choose a translation.

CHOOSING A TRANSLATION

We suggest the following guidelines for choosing a translation.[17]

1. Choose a translation that uses modern English. The whole point of making a translation is to move the message of the original text to a language you can understand. History teaches us that languages change over time, and English is no exception. The English of John Wycliffe's day or of 1611 or even of the late 1700s is simply not the same as the English of the twenty-first century. There is little to be gained by translating a Greek or Hebrew text into a kind of English that you no longer use and can no longer understand. For that reason, we recommend that you choose among the many good translations that have appeared within the last fifty years.
2. Choose a translation that is based on the standard Hebrew and Greek text. As we mentioned earlier in this chapter, the standard text for the Old Testament is the *Biblia Hebraica Stuttgartensia* (*BHS*). For the New Testament the standard text is reflected in the latest edition of the United Bible Societies' *Greek New Testament* (*GNT*) or Nestle-Aland's *Novum Testamentum Graece*. Along with the majority of scholars, we much prefer an eclectic original text rather than the *Textus Receptus* used by the KJV and the NKJV.

17. For more on choosing a translation, see Gordon D. Fee and Mark L. Strauss, *How to Choose a Translation for All Its Worth* (Grand Rapids: Zondervan, 2007).

3. Give preference to a translation by a committee over a translation by an individual. Translating requires an enormous amount of knowledge and skill. A group of qualified translators will certainly possess more expertise than any one translator possibly could. In addition, a group of scholars will usually guard against the tendency of individual scholars to read their own personal biases into their translation.
4. Choose a translation that is appropriate for your own particular purpose at the time. When you want to read devotionally or read to children, consider a simplified, functional translation such as the New Living Translation or the New Century Version. If you are reading to nontraditional or unchurched people, consider the Contemporary English Version or *The Message*. If you are reading to people with English as a second language, consider the Good News Translation. If you are reading to a "King James only" church, consider the New King James. But for serious Bible study, we suggest the New American Standard Bible, the New Revised Standard Version, the English Standard Version, the Christian Standard Bible, the NET Bible, and the New International Version (2011), depending on the audience and situation.

King James Version (KJV)
There hath no temptation taken you but such as is common to man: but God is faithful, who will not suffer you to be tempted above that ye are able; but will with the temptation also make a way to escape, that ye may be able to bear it.

New King James Version (NKJV)
No temptation has overtaken you except such as is common to man; but God is faithful, who will not allow you to be tempted beyond what you are able, but with the temptation will also make the way of escape, that you may be able to bear it.

New American Standard Bible (NASB)
No temptation has overtaken you but such as is common to man; and God is faithful, who will not allow you to be tempted beyond what you are able, but with the temptation will provide the way of escape also, so that you will be able to endure it.

English Standard Version (ESV)
No temptation has overtaken you that is not common to man. God is faithful, and he will not let you be tempted beyond your ability, but with the temptation he will also provide the way of escape, that you may be able to endure it.

Holman Christian Standard Bible (HCSB)
No temptation has overtaken you except what is common to humanity. God is faithful and He will not allow you to be tempted beyond what you are able, but with the temptation He will also provide a way of escape so that you are able to bear it.

New Revised Standard Version (NRSV)
No testing has overtaken you that is not common to everyone. God is faithful, and he will not let you be tested beyond your strength, but with the testing he will also provide the way out so that you may be able to endure it.

New English Translation (NET Bible)
No trial has overtaken you that is not faced by others. And God is faithful: He will not let you be tried beyond what you are able to bear, but with the trial will also provide a way out so that you may be able to endure it.

Christian Standard Bible (CSB)
No temptation has come upon you except what is common to humanity. But God is faithful; he will not allow you to be tempted beyond what you are able, but with the temptation he will also provide a way out so that you may be able to bear it.

New International Version (NIV [2011])
No temptation has overtaken you except what is common to mankind. And God is faithful; he will not let you be tempted beyond what you can bear. But when you are tempted, he will also provide a way out so that you can endure it.

Today's New International Version (TNIV)
No temptation has overtaken you except what is common to us all. And God is faithful; he will not let you be tempted beyond what you can bear. But when you are tempted, he will also provide a way out so that you can endure it.

God's Word Translation (GWT)
There isn't any temptation that you have experienced which is unusual for humans. God, who faithfully keeps his promises, will not allow you to be tempted beyond your power to resist. But when you are tempted, he will also give you the ability to endure the temptation as your way of escape.

New Living Translation (NLT)
The temptations in your life are no different from what others experience. And God is faithful. He will not allow the temptation to be more than you can stand. When you are tempted, he will show you a way out so that you can endure.

Good News Translation (GNT)
Every test that you have experienced is the kind that normally comes to people. But God keeps his promise, and he will not allow you to be tested beyond your power to remain firm; at the time you are put to the test, he will give you the strength to endure it, and so provide you with a way out.

Contemporary English Version (CEV)
You are tempted in the same way that everyone else is tempted. But God can be trusted not to let you be tempted too much, and he will show you how to escape from your temptations.

***The Message* (MSG)**
No test or temptation that comes your way is beyond the course of what others have had to face. All you need to remember is that God will never let you down; he'll never let you be pushed past your limit; he'll always be there to help you come through it.

Amplified Bible, Classic Edition (AMPC; paraphrase)
For no temptation (no trial regarded as enticing to sin), [no matter how it comes or where it leads] has overtaken you and laid hold on you that is not common to man [that is, no temptation or trial has come to you that is beyond human resistance and that is not adjusted and adapted and belonging to human experience, and such as man can bear]. But God is faithful [to His Word and to His compassionate nature], and He [can be trusted] not to let you be tempted and tried and assayed beyond your ability and strength of resistance and power to endure, but with the temptation He will [always] also provide the way out (the means of escape to a landing place), that you may be capable and strong and powerful to bear up under it patiently.

CONCLUSION

When it comes to studying Scripture, few things are as important as how the Bible has been translated. We can be thankful that God has used translators to get the message of the original text into our hands. Can you imagine the Christian life without your own copy of God's Word? In the past, many Christians have lived under those circumstances, but it would be difficult for us today. In spite of the many good Bible translations available to us, there is no such thing as a perfect translation. Furthermore, languages change over time. For these reasons, committed scholars and linguists must continue to work hard to get the message of the original text into a language that people can understand. Who knows, God may call you to serve as a Bible translator.

ASSIGNMENTS

Assignment 1–1

Select five translations that we talked about in this chapter. Select a passage from the Bible (it must be at least two verses long) and write out how the translations render this passage. Next, mark or highlight the differences among the five translations. Write a paragraph summarizing what you have observed by comparing the translations.

Assignment 1–2

Answer the following questions:

1. Do you agree that the Bible is a divine-human book? Why or why not?
2. What is textual criticism? How is it possible to have a high view of the authority of Scripture and a positive view of textual criticism at the same time?
3. What is a Bible translation? Why is translation not a simple exercise? Describe the two main approaches to translation discussed in this chapter. Which approach do you feel most comfortable with? Why?

CHAPTER 2

THE INTERPRETIVE JOURNEY

INTRODUCTION

A wrinkled old man in the mountains of Ethiopia sips coffee and peers through weathered, ancient bifocals at his worn Amharic Bible to read once again the story of David and Goliath. A middle-aged woman is bouncing along on a bus in Buenos Aires, reading and reflecting on Psalm 1. A young Korean executive, on his way home to Seoul from a business trip in Singapore, flies above the clouds at thirty-five thousand feet, reading and pondering the words of the apostle Paul in Romans 5. And in a dorm room in San Diego, California, a young college student enjoys a sip of her latte and then looks back down at her laptop computer to finish reading Mark's account of how Jesus miraculously calmed a raging storm on the Sea of Galilee.

People all over the world love reading the Bible—and they have loved it for thousands of years. Why? People read the Bible because it is a fascinating book, filled with gripping stories and challenging exhortations. People read it because it is an important book, dealing with the big issues of life—God, eternal life, death, love, sin, and morals. People read it because they believe that in the Bible, God speaks to them through written words. The Bible encourages us, lifts our spirits, comforts us, guides us, chides us, builds us up, gives us hope, and brings us close to the living God.

Some parts of the Bible are easy to understand, but much of it is not. Most

Christians, however, desire to understand all of God's Word, not just the easy portions. Many of us want to be able to dig deeper into that Word. We want to see more and understand more of the biblical text. We also want to know that we understand the Bible correctly. That is, we want to be confident that we can pull the actual truth out of a text and not just develop an arbitrary, fanciful, or incorrect interpretation. Our book is designed for such people.

The process of interpreting and grasping the Bible is similar to embarking on a *journey*. Reading the text thoroughly and carefully lies at the beginning of the journey. From this careful reading, we become able to determine what the passage meant in the biblical context—that is, what it meant to the biblical audience.

Often, however, when we try to apply this meaning directly to ourselves, we run into problems. We are separated from the biblical audience by culture and customs, language, situation, and a vast expanse of time. These differences form a barrier—a *river* that separates us from the text and that often prohibits us from grasping the meaning of the text for ourselves.

We are separated from the biblical audience by culture and customs, language, situation, and a vast expanse of time.

If that were not enough, the Old Testament widens the river by adding another major interpretive barrier that separates us from the audience. Between the Old Testament biblical audience and Christian readers today lies a change in *covenant*. We as New Testament believers are under the new covenant, and we approach God through the sacrifice of Christ. The Old Testament people, however, were under the old covenant, and for them the law was central. In other words, the theological situation for the two groups is different. There is a covenant barrier between the Old Testament audience and us because we are under different covenants.

Thus, the river between the Old Testament text and us consists not only of culture, language, situation, and time, but also of covenant. We have much more in common with the New Testament audience; yet even in the New Testament, the different culture, language, and specific situations can present a formidable barrier to our desire to grasp the meaning of the text. The river is often too deep and too wide simply to wade across.

As a result, today's Christian is often uncertain about how to interpret much of the Bible. How should we understand Leviticus 19:19, which prohibits wearing a garment made of two types of material? Does this mean that obedient Christians should wear only 100-percent cotton clothes? In Judges 6:37 Gideon puts out a fleece to confirm what God has told him. Does this mean that *we* should put out fleeces when we seek God's leading?

Passages in the New Testament are not always much clearer. For example, Peter walks on the water in Matthew 14:29. Does this mean that *we* should attempt to walk on water in our obedience to Christ? If not, what does the passage mean, and how can we apply it to our lives today? Even if we cannot walk on water, how do we cross the river that separates us from the text?

Any attempt to interpret and to apply the Bible involves trying to cross the river. While often unconscious of their interpretive method, many Christians today nonetheless frequently employ an *intuitive* or *feels-right approach* to interpretation. If the text looks as if it could be applied directly, then they attempt to apply it directly. If not, then they take a *spiritualizing approach* to the meaning—an approach that borders on allegorizing the biblical text (which shows little or no sensitivity to the biblical context). Or else they simply shrug their shoulders and move on to another passage, ignoring the meaning of the text altogether.

Such approaches will never land us safely on the other side of the river. Those using the intuitive approach blindly wade out into the river, hoping that the water is not more than knee deep. Sometimes they are fortunate and stumble onto a sandbar, but often they step out into deep water, and they end up washed ashore somewhere downstream. Those who spiritualize, by contrast, try to jump the river in one grand leap, but they also end up washed ashore downstream with their intuitive buddies. Shrugging, or ignoring a passage, is to remain on the far side of the river and simply to gaze across without even attempting to cross.

Many Christians are admittedly uncomfortable with such approaches, recognizing the somewhat willy-nilly methodology and the extreme subjectivity involved, but they continue to use them because they are the only methods they know. How do we move from the world of the biblical audience to the world of today?

This book addresses how to cross over that river into the world of today. We need a valid, legitimate approach to the Bible, one that is not based strictly on intuition and feeling. We need an approach that derives meaning from within the text, but one that also crosses over to the situation for today's Christian.

How do we move from the world of the biblical audience to the world of today?

We also need a consistent approach, one that can be used on any passage. Such an approach should eliminate the habit of skipping over texts and surfing along through the Bible looking for passages that might apply. A consistent approach should allow us to dig into any passage with a method to determine the meaning of that text for us today. We need an approach that does not leave us stranded on the banks of the interpretive river and one that does not dump us into the river to be washed ashore downstream. We need a way to study the Bible to cross over the river with validity and accuracy. Our goal in this book is to take you on the journey across the river, to transport you from the text and the world of the biblical audience to a valid understanding and application of the text for Christians today.

BASICS OF THE JOURNEY

Keep in mind that our goal is to grasp the meaning of the text that God has intended. We do not create meaning out of a text; rather, we seek to find the meaning that is already there. However, we recognize that we cannot apply the meaning for the ancient audience directly to us today because of the river that separates us (culture, time, situation, covenant, etc.). Following the steps of the Interpretive Journey provides us with a reliable way to move from the meaning for the ancient audience across the river of differences to a legitimate application of that same meaning for us today.

This journey works on the premise that the Bible is a record of God's communication of himself and his will to us. We revere the Bible and treat it as holy because it is the Word of God and because God reveals himself to us through this Word. Many texts in the Bible are specific, concrete, revelatory expressions of broader, universal realities or theological principles.[1] While the specifics of a particular passage may apply only to the particular situation of the biblical audience, the theological principles revealed in that text are applicable to all of God's people at all times. The theological principle, therefore, has meaning and application both to the ancient biblical audience and to Christians today.

Constructing the principlizing bridge will be one of the critical steps in our Interpretive Journey.

Because the theological principle has meaning and application to both audiences, it functions as a bridge spanning the river of differences. Rather than blindly wading out into the river, foolishly attempting to jump across the river in one short hop, or wishfully gazing at the other shore without ever crossing, we can safely cross over the river on the bridge that the theological principle provides. Constructing this *principlizing bridge* will be one of the critical steps in our Interpretive Journey.

Thus, our journey starts with a careful reading of the text. Our final destination is to grasp the meaning of the text so that it changes our lives. It is an exciting trip, but one that requires hard work. There are no easy shortcuts.

The Interpretive Journey involves five steps:

---

1. The terminology and concept that the text reflects a "concrete expression of a universal principle" is from John Goldingay, *Models for Interpretation of Scripture* (Grand Rapids: Eerdmans, 1995), 92.

Step 1: Grasping the Text in Their Town

Question: What did the text mean to the biblical audience?

The first part of step 1 is to read the text carefully and observe it. In step 1 try to see as much as possible in the text. Look, look, and look again, observing all you can. Scrutinize the grammar and analyze all significant words. Likewise, study the historical and literary contexts. How does your passage relate to those passages that precede it and those that follow it?

After completing all this study, synthesize the meaning of the passage for the biblical audience into one or two sentences. That is, write out what the passage meant for the biblical audience. Use past-tense verbs and refer to the biblical audience. For example:

> God commanded the Israelites in Joshua 1 to . . .
> Paul exhorted the Ephesians to . . .
> Jesus encouraged his disciples by . . .

Be specific. Do not generalize or try to develop theological principles yet.

Step 2: Measuring the Width of the River to Cross

Question: What are the differences between the biblical audience and us?

As mentioned above, the Christian today is separated from the biblical audience by differences in culture, language, situation, time, and often covenant. These differences form a river that hinders us from moving straight from meaning in their context to meaning in ours. The width of the river, however, varies from passage to passage. Sometimes it is extremely wide, requiring a long, substantial bridge for crossing. Other times, however, it is a narrow creek that we can easily hop over. It is obviously important to know just how wide the river is before we start trying to construct a principlizing bridge across it.

In step 2 you will take a good, hard look at the river and determine just how wide it is for the passage you are studying. In this step you look for significant *differences* between our situation today and the situation of the biblical audience. If you are studying an Old Testament passage, also be sure to identify those significant theological differences that came as a result of the life and work of Jesus Christ.

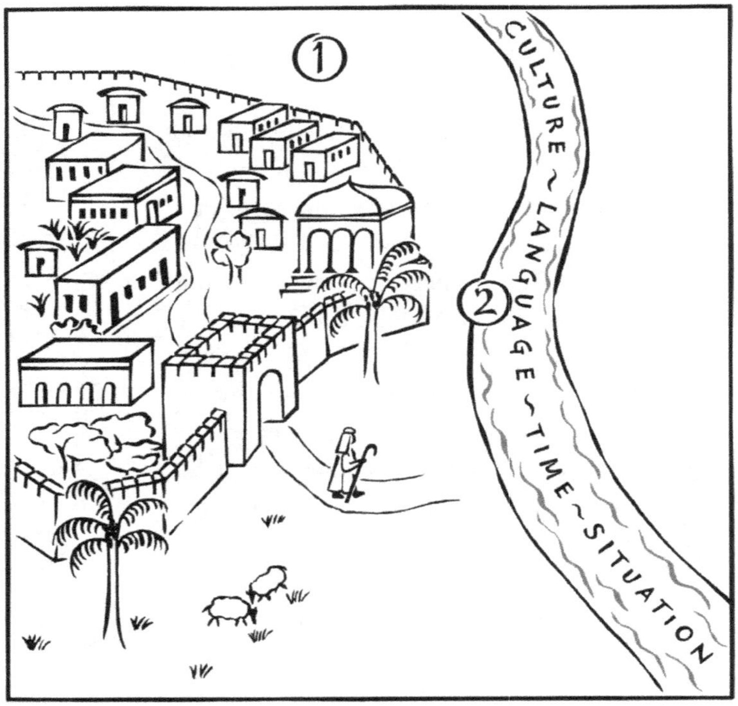

In addition, whether in the Old Testament or in the New Testament, try to identify any unique aspects of the *situation* of your passage. For example, in Joshua 1:1–9, the people of Israel are preparing to enter the promised land. Moses has just died and Joshua has been appointed to take his place. In this passage God speaks to Joshua to encourage him to be strong and faithful in the upcoming conquest of the land. What are the differences? We are not entering or conquering the promised land. We are not the new leaders of the nation of Israel. We are not under the old covenant.

Step 3: Crossing the Principlizing Bridge

Question: What is the theological principle in this text?

This is perhaps the most challenging step. In it you are looking for the theological principle or principles that are reflected in the meaning of the text you identified in step 1. Remember that this theological principle is part of the *meaning*. Your task is not to create the meaning but to discover the meaning intended by the author. As God gives specific expressions to specific biblical audiences, he is also giving universal theological teachings for all his people through these same texts.

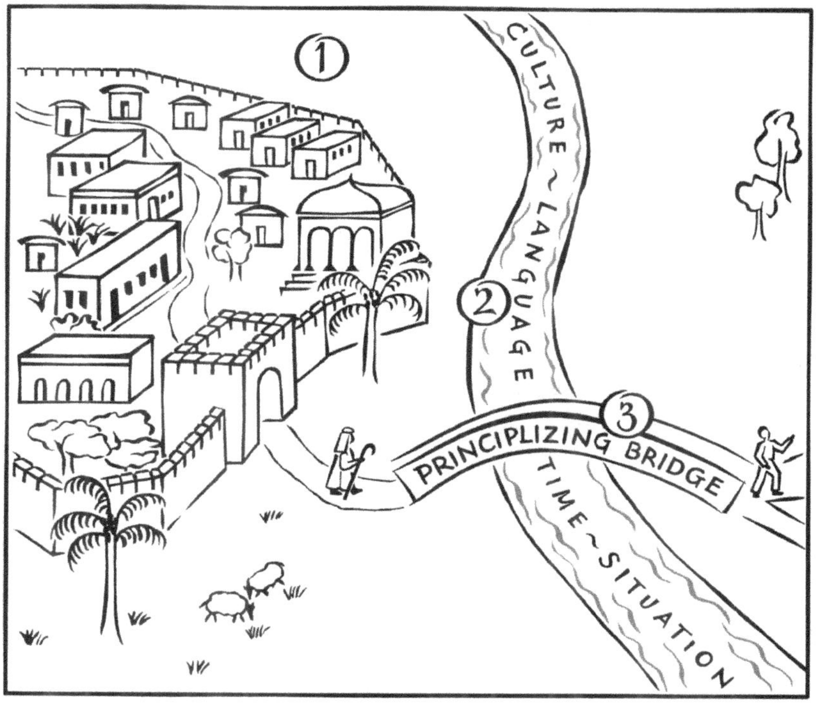

To determine the theological principle, first recall the differences you identified in step 2. Next, try to identify any *similarities* between the situation of the biblical audience and our situation. For example, consider Joshua 1:1–9 again. Recall, of course, the differences that we identified in step 2. But then note the similarities between the biblical situation and our own. We are also the people of God, in covenant relationship (new covenant); while we are not the leaders of Israel, nonetheless, many of us are in leadership positions in the church; we are not invading the promised land, but we are seeking to obey the will of God and to accomplish what he has commanded us to do.

After reviewing the differences and identifying the similarities, return to the meaning for the biblical audience that you described in step 1 and try to identify a broader theological principle reflected in the text, but also one that relates to the similarities between us and the biblical audience. In essence, the theological principle is the same as the "theological message" or the "main theological point" of the passage. (We will discuss in more detail how to develop theological principles in chapter 10.) We will use this theological principle as the *principlizing bridge* by which we can cross over the river of differences.

We can summarize the criteria for formulating the theological principle with the following:

The principle should be reflected in the text.
The principle should be timeless and not tied to a specific situation.
The principle should not be culturally bound.
The principle should correspond to the teaching of the rest of Scripture.
The principle should be relevant to both the biblical and the contemporary audience.

Write out the theological principle (or principles) in one or two sentences. Use present- or future-tense verbs.

Step 4: Consulting the Biblical Map

Question: How does our theological principle fit with the rest of the Bible?

During this step you must enter the parts-whole spiral. That is, you reflect back and forth between the text and the teachings of the rest of Scripture. Is your principle consistent with the rest of Scripture? Do other portions of Scripture add insight or qualification to the principle? If your principle is valid, it ought to "fit" or "correlate" with the rest of the Bible.

If you are studying an Old Testament passage, consulting the biblical map (step 4) is especially important, for here you will run your theological principle through the grid of the New Testament, looking for what the New Testament adds to that principle or how the New Testament modifies it. Keep in mind that we read and interpret the Old Testament as Christians. That is, although we believe that the Old Testament is part of God's inspired Word to us, we do not want to ignore the cross and thus interpret and apply this literature as if we were Old Testament Hebrews. We affirm that we are New Testament Christians, and we will interpret the Old Testament from that vantage point.

Thus, at the end of this step, sometimes you will need to reword your theological principle slightly to ensure that it fits with the rest of Scripture. Don't ignore the elements you initially drew on in step 3, but now fine-tune your principle if it needs it.

Step 5: Grasping the Text in Our Town

Question: How should individual Christians today live out the theological principles?

In step 5 we apply the theological principle to the specific situation of individual Christians in the church today. We cannot leave the meaning of the text stranded in an abstract theological principle. We must now grapple with how we should respond to that principle in our town. How does it apply in real-life situations today?

While for each passage there will usually be only a few (and often only one) theological principles relevant for all Christians today, there will be numerous applicational possibilities. This is because Christians today find themselves in many different specific situations. Each of us will grasp and apply the same theological principle in slightly different ways, depending on our current life situation and where we are in our relationship with God. In our illustration, we have tried to show the different applications possible by showing different individuals traveling on different streets. (The application step will be discussed in much more detail in chapter 13.)

So, the Interpretive Journey as a whole looks like this:

Step 1: Grasp the text in their town. What did the text mean to the original audience?

Step 2: Measure the width of the river to cross. What are the differences between the biblical audience and us?

Step 3: Cross the principlizing bridge. What is the theological principle in this text?

Step 4: Consult the biblical map. How does our theological principle fit with the rest of the Bible?

Step 5: Grasp the text in our town. How should individual Christians today live out the theological principle?

AN EXAMPLE—JOSHUA 1:1–9

We have mentioned Joshua 1:1–9 several times already. Let's make the formal trip from this Old Testament passage to life today to illustrate how the Interpretive Journey works.

The passage is as follows:

> [1]After the death of Moses the servant of the LORD, the LORD said to Joshua son
> of Nun, Moses' aide: [2]"Moses my servant is dead. Now then, you and all these
> people, get ready to cross the Jordan River into the land I am about to give to
> them—to the Israelites. [3]I will give you every place where you set your foot,
> as I promised Moses. [4]Your territory will extend from the desert to Lebanon,
> and from the great river, the Euphrates—all the Hittite country—to the
> Mediterranean Sea in the west. [5]No one will be able to stand against you all the
> days of your life. As I was with Moses, so I will be with you; I will never leave you
> nor forsake you. [6]Be strong and courageous, because you will lead these people
> to inherit the land I swore to their ancestors to give them.

> [7]"Be strong and very courageous. Be careful to obey all the law my servant Moses gave you; do not turn from it to the right or to the left, that you may be successful wherever you go. Keep this Book of the Law always on your lips; meditate on it day and night, so that you may be careful to do everything written in it. Then you will be prosperous and successful. [9]Have I not commanded you? Be strong and courageous. Do not be afraid; do not be discouraged, for the LORD your God will be with you wherever you go."

Step 1: What did the text mean to the biblical audience?

The Lord commanded Joshua, the new leader of Israel, to draw strength and courage from God's empowering presence, to be obedient to the law of Moses, and to meditate on the law so that he would be successful in the conquest of the promised land.

Step 2: What are the differences between the biblical audience and us?

We are not leaders of the nation Israel (although some of us may be leaders in the church). We are not embarking on the conquest of Canaan, the promised land. We are not under the old covenant of law.

Step 3: What is the theological principle in this text?

To be effective in serving God and successful in the task to which he has called us, we must draw strength and courage from his presence. We must also be obedient to God's Word, meditating on it constantly.

Step 4: How does our theological principle fit with the rest of the Bible?

The rest of the Bible consistently affirms that God's people can draw strength and courage from his presence. In the New Testament, believers experience God's presence through the indwelling of the Holy Spirit rather than through his presence in the tabernacle. Likewise, throughout both the Old Testament and the New Testament, God's people are exhorted to pay close, obedient attention to his Word.

Step 5: How should individual Christians today live out the theological principles?

There are numerous possible applications. Here are a few suggested ones:

- Spend more time meditating on God's Word by reading the Bible consistently, listening to trustworthy podcasts, or listening to worship music.
- If God calls you to a new, scary ministry, such as teaching fourth-grade Sunday school, then be strengthened and encouraged by his empowering presence. Be obedient, keeping a focus on the Scriptures.

- If you are in a church leadership position, realize that successful Christian leadership requires strength and courage that flows from the presence of God.

THE JOURNEY AND *GRASPING GOD'S WORD*

The Interpretive Journey is actually a blueprint for this book. In part 1 we have looked first at an overview of Bible translation and how we got the English Bible (chapter 1). In the next three chapters, we will focus on how to observe and read the biblical text carefully. We start with smaller, simpler units of text (chapter 3) and then move on to more complex and longer units of text (chapters 4 and 5).

In part 2 we spend time discussing contexts, both theirs (the ancient audience) and ours (the modern readers). We first explore historical and cultural contexts (chapter 6). Next we probe into the issue of preunderstanding (i.e., our context) in chapter 7. Then in chapter 8 we examine literary context. We wrap up this unit by learning how to do word studies within these contexts (chapter 9). All of these chapters in part 1 and part 2 give us skills necessary to get our feet firmly planted into step 1.

Part 3 focuses on the theory needed to identify and construct the principlizing bridge, to cross over the river of differences, and to grasp the meaning of the text in a way that changes our lives in the world today. Chapter 10 deals with what meaning is and who controls it (author or reader?). Chapter 11 delves into some issues related to the theological principle and the concept of meaning. Are there deeper levels of meaning? Is there one meaning or numerous meanings for a passage? Chapter 12 then explores the role of the Holy Spirit in this whole interpretive process. Step 5 (application) is the focus of chapter 13, helping us to move on from head knowledge to actual life-changing behavior. In other words, while in chapter 2 we have introduced the journey to you, the rest of part 1 as well as part 2 and part 3 expand on the Interpretive Journey, describing in more detail the interpretive issues you will face along the way.

In part 4 we focus on how to take the Interpretive Journey within the New Testament. In this unit we leave the theoretical discussions of part 3 and move into the actual practice of interpreting and applying the New Testament. We teach you how to take the journey with passages from different types or genres of New Testament literature. Chapters 14–17 cover, respectively, New Testament Letters, the Gospels, Acts, and Revelation. These chapters pull together everything you learned in parts 1–3, teaching you how to apply your new skills to the New Testament.

Finally, part 5 addresses some of the specific challenges and opportunities of interpreting and applying the Old Testament. First, in the introduction, we refine the steps of the journey to fit the Old Testament situation more closely. Then, as in part 4, we teach you how to take the Interpretive Journey with passages from the different types of Old Testament genres. Chapters 18–22 sharpen your tools for grasping passages from the entire range of Old Testament literature: narrative, law, poetry, prophetic literature, and wisdom literature.

Are you ready to move forward into the exciting realm of interpretation and application? There are lots of interesting biblical passages ahead of you. Work hard! The rewards are great.

ASSIGNMENTS

Assignment 2–1

Describe the five steps of the Interpretive Journey.

Assignment 2–2

What are the guidelines for developing theological principles?

Assignment 2–3

What are the differences that determine the width of the river to cross?

CHAPTER 3

HOW TO READ THE BOOK—SENTENCES

INTRODUCTION

If someone invited you over for dinner, what would your expectations be regarding the meal? What kind of meal would you be anticipating? We, personally, are easily satisfied. Give us a nice steak and potato with all the trimmings. Add hot rolls and a good vegetable. Top it off with apple pie or blackberry cobbler. But we are not picky. We also love hamburgers, pizza, spaghetti, lasagna, ribs, and a host of various casseroles.

What about you? What would you expect at a meal? How would you react if your expectations were not met at all? For example, what if you showed up at some friends' house and they served you nice, soft, mushy baby food? There are some really great flavors of baby food—strained peas, stewed prunes—good stuff, if you are six months old. However, since you are not six months old, you expect something more substantial—something you can sink your teeth into. Baby food would be a disappointment (and perhaps put a strain on your friendship!).

Bible study is much the same. Plunging into the Word of God is similar to sitting down at a meal. We expect to eat something nourishing, something substantial, and something appropriate to our maturity level. We want to dig into the real meat. But often we are able only to come up with baby food—soft mush for infants. This is not a reflection on the Word of God, which is loaded with meat, but rather a reflection on us and our inability to extract the meat and enjoy it. Indeed, some Christians have become so accustomed to baby food that they no longer desire the stronger food. What about you? Do you long to dig deeper into God's Word? Do you long for a more substantial diet? Our goal in this book is to help you to "eat well."

So, let's begin.

If you move straight from your initial reading of a passage to the application of that passage, you will remain tied to your previous understanding of that text. You will rarely see anything new and exciting in the text, and the Bible will become boring for you. Likewise, it is unlikely that you will hear anything new from God, and your relationship with him is likely to be stagnant. God wants to have deeper and more mature conversations with you, but if you are tied to superficial and surface readings of the Bible or if you always assume that you have already seen and understood all there is, then your relationship with God will tend to stay at the same level. Likewise, any teaching or preaching you do will tend to be flat and boring or a reflection of something other than Scripture. The Bible, however, is the Word of God, and it is not boring. We simply need to learn how to read it with more insight and understanding.

If you move straight from your initial reading of a passage to the application of that passage, you will remain tied to your previous understanding of that text.

If you want to hear and understand some of the deep and wonderful truths that God has placed in Scripture for you—if you desire to pull out of God's Word some of the serious "meat" he has placed there for us to sink our teeth into—you will have to exert considerable effort. It takes work—hard work! And you, the reader, have to decide whether you are content with shallow "baby food" that comes from casual reading or you want to work for the "mature food" that comes from serious reading.

SERIOUS READING AND LOVE LETTERS

What is serious reading? Consider the following episode about a "serious" reader.

How to Read a Love Letter (or Email)

In April Kaitlyn and Zach moved beyond being "just friends" and went out on their first real date. By mid-May Zach was thinking that "this could be love." In June, however, before the young couple had said anything specific to each other about the relationship, Kaitlyn traveled to Ghana with other members of their church on a two-month mission trip to an isolated rural area that did not have any email or phone service. Two weeks went by and anxious Zach didn't hear anything from Kaitlyn. Finally, the team in Ghana visited a city that had Wi-Fi/ internet service, and the anxious Zach received the precious email he had been longing for from Kaitlyn.

He read it over three or four times, but he was just beginning. To read it as accurately as he desired would have required several dictionaries and a good deal of close work with a few experts of etymology and philology.

However, he would do all right without them.

He would ponder over the exact shade of meaning of every word, every comma. The text started off with "Hiya!" What, he asked himself, was the exact significance of that greeting? Did she refrain from saying something more personal because she was bashful, or because they were just friends?

Maybe she would have said "Hiya" to anybody! A worried frown now appeared on his face. But it disappeared as soon as he really got to thinking about the first sentence. She certainly wouldn't have written that to just anybody!

And so he worked his way through the email, one moment perched blissfully on a cloud, the next moment huddled miserably behind an eight ball. The message had started a hundred questions in his mind. He could quote it by heart. In fact, he would—to himself—for weeks to come.[1]

This lovesick young man is a good reader because he scrutinizes the text for all the details, even the most minute. One of the most critical skills needed in reading the Bible is the ability to *see* the details. Most of us read the Bible too quickly, and we skip over the details of the text. However, the meaning of the Bible is intertwined with the details of every sentence. Our first step in grasping a biblical text is to observe as many details as possible. We want to *see* as much as possible. At this early stage of analysis, try to refrain from *interpreting* or *applying* the text. These steps are important, but they come later, after the *observing* step. Our first step is to read *carefully*, to note as many details as possible, to observe our text as closely as a CSI team reads a crime scene, and to probe into these details as energetically and seriously as Zach did in reading his email from Kaitlyn.

So, how do we develop the skill of *observing* the Bible? We read the text over and over, noting the details of the text. There are several basic features to look for that will help us get started with this *observation* stage. These features include repetition of words, contrasts, comparisons, lists, causes and effects, figures of speech, conjunctions,

1. This story has been adapted and updated from a famous anecdote that first appeared in 1940 in the *New York Times* as part of an advertisement for Mortimer J. Adler's work *How to Read a Book* (New York: Simon and Schuster, 1940). It is cited by Robert Traina, *Methodical Bible Study: A New Approach to Hermeneutics* (Wilmore, KY: Asbury Theological Seminary, 1952), 97–98.

verbs, and pronouns. This list, however, represents only some of what you might search for. Observation includes looking carefully at all the details of the text.

Keep in mind that we are not yet asking, "What does the text *mean*?" We are simply asking, "What does the text *say*?" We have not yet begun to explore the implications of our observations. Also, do not limit your observations to so-called deep insights or highly important features. At the observation step, we want to see everything, all the details. Later in the book, we will tackle the problem of sorting through the details to determine meaning.

Another thing to keep in mind as we begin is that reading and interpreting is a combination of analyzing small pieces of text and big pieces of text. We have to understand the small parts of the text (words, phrases, sentences) to understand the larger chunks (paragraphs, chapters, stories). However, the larger units of text also provide a critical context for understanding the small units. So the process requires a bit of both—reading the whole to get a general overview and then analyzing the parts to reveal the nitty-gritty details.

In chapter 2, "The Interpretive Journey," we dealt with the big picture (the whole). In the next few chapters, we will focus on reading and observing the small parts. The present chapter stresses the serious reading of small units of text, focusing generally at the sentence level. Chapter 4 will move us up to the paragraph level, and chapter 5 will help us read multiparagraph units (discourses).

Work hard! Dig deep! The feast awaits you!

THINGS TO LOOK FOR IN SENTENCES

1. Repetition of Words

Look for words that repeat. First, be sure to note any words that repeat within the sentence you are studying. Then survey the sentences around the text you are reading and look for repetition in the larger passage.

Look, for example, at 1 John 2:15–17:

> [15]Do not love the world or anything in the world. If anyone loves the world, love for the Father is not in them. [16]For everything in the world—the lust of the flesh, the lust of the eyes, and the pride of life—comes not from the Father but from the world. [17]The world and its desires pass away, but whoever does the will of God lives forever.

Which word repeats in the first sentence? Does this word ("world") appear in the next sentence as well? How many times in this passage does "world" occur? Is it in every sentence? Does it always have the definite article *the* ("the world")? Did you also notice the repetition of "love"? How many times does "love" occur? Simply by observing the repetition of words, we have an early indication of what the passage may be about. It has something to do with the world—in particular, about loving the world.

Let's try another passage. Read carefully through 2 Corinthians 1:3–7 below.

> [3]Praise be to the God and Father of our Lord Jesus Christ, the Father of compassion and the God of all comfort, [4]who comforts us in all our troubles, so that we can comfort those in any trouble with the comfort we ourselves receive from God. [5]For just as we share abundantly in the sufferings of Christ, so also our comfort abounds through Christ. [6]If we are distressed, it is for your comfort and salvation; if we are comforted, it is for your comfort, which produces in you patient endurance of the same sufferings we suffer. [7]And our hope for you is firm, because we know that just as you share in our sufferings, so also you share in our comfort.

Reread the first sentence. How many times does "comfort" occur? Four times! In one sentence! Alarms should go off in your head. You've seen the obvious: this passage has something to do with comfort. Is there more? Look back through the rest of that passage. How many times does "comfort" reappear? Is it in every sentence? Is "comfort" used in the same way each time? Where is "comfort" used as a verb, and where is it used as a noun? Which modifiers are used with "comfort," and how do they vary ("*all* comfort," "*the* comfort," "*our* comfort," "*your* comfort")? Who is being comforted? Who comforts? Also, what about "suffering"? Which verses mention "suffering"? How many times does "suffering" occur? Who is suffering? Is there a connection between suffering and comfort?

> How many times does "comfort" occur in 2 Corinthians 1:3–7?

Look at word repetition in a few other passages. Note, for example, the number of times the words listed are repeated in the following sections:

John 15:1–10 (look for "remain")
Matthew 6:1–18 (look for "Father")
1 Corinthians 15:50–54 (look for "perishable" and "imperishable")

2. Contrasts

Look for items, ideas, or individuals that are contrasted with each other. For an example of contrast, take a look at Proverbs 14:31:

> Whoever oppresses the poor shows contempt for their Maker,
> but whoever is kind to the needy honors God.

Two different types of people are contrasted in this passage, both in the way they treat the poor and in the way this behavior toward the poor reflects their attitude toward God. One type oppresses the poor, an action that reflects contempt for God, their Creator. The other type of person is kind to the poor. Their action toward the poor honors God.

What is being contrasted in Proverbs 15:1?

> A gentle answer turns away wrath,
> but a harsh word stirs up anger.

The New Testament writers frequently use contrasts as well. Read Romans 6:23 and identify the two contrasts:

> For the wages of sin is death, but the gift of God is eternal life in Christ Jesus our Lord.

What is the contrast in Ephesians 5:8?

> For you were once darkness, but now you are light in the Lord.

John likewise uses the light/darkness contrast, developing it over several verses in 1 John 1:5–7:

> 5This is the message we have heard from him and declare to you: God is light; in
> him there is no darkness at all. 6If we claim to have fellowship with him and yet
> walk in the darkness, we lie and do not live out the truth. 7But if we walk in the
> light, as he is in the light, we have fellowship with one another, and the blood of
> Jesus, his Son, purifies us from all sin.

What is the major contrast in this passage? "Light" and "darkness." Can we be more specific about the nature of the contrast? Yes. Note that the contrast breaks down into two parts: (1) the nature of God (light and no darkness), and (2) our manner of walking (in light versus in darkness).

3. Comparisons

Contrast focuses on differences. Comparison focuses on similarities. Look for items, ideas, or individuals that are compared with each other.

Proverbs 25:26 provides a good Old Testament example:

Like a muddied spring or a polluted well
are the righteous who give way to the wicked.

How are the righteous who give way to the wicked like a muddied spring? Because the spring, like the righteous person, was once clean, pure, and useful but now is contaminated and useless for service.

In James 3:3–6 the tongue is compared to three different things. What are they?

> [3]When we put *bits* into the mouths of horses to make them obey us, we can turn the whole animal. [4]Or take ships as an example. Although they are so large and are driven by strong winds, they are steered by a very small *rudder* wherever the pilot wants to go. [5]Likewise, the tongue is a small part of the body, but it makes great boasts. Consider what a great forest is set on fire by a small spark. [6]The tongue also is a *fire*, a world of evil among the parts of the body.[2]

Finally, a wonderful comparison is made in Isaiah 40:31, where the renewal of strength received from placing one's hope in the Lord is compared to the soaring of eagles:

But those who hope in the Lord
will renew their strength.
They will soar on wings like eagles;
they will run and not grow weary,
they will walk and not be faint.

Good Bible study can make you soar like an eagle too. So read on.

4. Lists

Anytime you encounter more than two itemized things, you can identify them as a list. Write the list down and explore its significance. Is there any order? Are the items grouped in any way? For example, what three things are listed in 1 John 2:16?

> For everything in the world—the lust of the flesh, the lust of the eyes, and the pride of life—comes not from the Father but from the world.

Is there any order? Are the items grouped in any way?

2. Note that in all Scripture verses cited in this book, the original has no italics. All italics (and later also bold type) have been added to point out a particular feature of the biblical text.

What is listed in Galatians 5:22–23?

> But the fruit of the Spirit is love, joy, peace, forbearance, kindness, goodness, faithfulness, gentleness and self-control.

And what is listed in Galatians 5:19–21?

> The acts of the flesh are obvious: sexual immorality, impurity and debauchery; idolatry and witchcraft; hatred, discord, jealousy, fits of rage, selfish ambition, dissensions, factions and envy; drunkenness, orgies, and the like.

5. Cause and Effect

Often the biblical writers will state a *cause* and then state the *effect* of that cause. Earlier we looked at Proverbs 15:1 and found that this verse contained a contrast. It also has two cause-and-effect relationships. Take a look at it again:

> A gentle answer turns away wrath,
> but a harsh word stirs up anger.

The first cause is "a gentle answer." What is the effect of this cause? It "turns away wrath." The second cause is "a harsh word." What does that result in? As we all well know, it "stirs up anger."

Let's also look at Romans 6:23 again:

> For the wages of sin is death, but the gift of God is eternal life in Christ Jesus our Lord.

In this passage "sin" is the cause and "death" the effect. Likewise, read Romans 12:2:

> Do not conform to the pattern of this world, but be transformed by the renewing of your mind. Then you will be able to test and approve what God's will is—his good, pleasing and perfect will.

What is the cause? Our transformation through the renewing of our minds. What is the associated effect? The ability to discern God's will.

What is the cause and effect in John 3:16? Is there more than one set of cause-and-effect relationships?

> For God so loved the world that he gave his one and only Son, that whoever believes in him shall not perish but have eternal life.

Determine the cause and the effect in each of the following passages:

> I will sing the LORD's praise,
> for he has been good to me. (Ps. 13:6)

> Since, then, you have been raised with Christ, set your hearts on things above, where Christ is, seated at the right hand of God. (Col. 3:1)

As you can see, cause-and-effect relationships play an extremely important role in the Bible. Always be on the lookout for them.

6. Figures of Speech

Figures of speech are images in which words are used in a sense other than the normal, literal sense. For example, think about the lamp image in Psalm 119:105:

> Your word is a lamp for my feet,
> a light on my path.

God's Word is not a literal lamp to light up a dark trail for us. Rather, it is a figurative lamp that allows us to see our way through life (feet/path) clearly. Note that both "lamp" and "feet/path" are figures of speech.

As you observe biblical texts, always identify any figures of speech that occur. Try to visualize the figure of speech. Ask yourself, "What image is the author trying to convey with the figure of speech?" For example, consider Isaiah 40:31 again:

> But those who hope in the LORD
> will renew their strength.
> They will soar on wings like eagles;
> they will run and not grow weary,
> they will walk and not be faint.

Soaring on wings like eagles is a figure of speech. Can you visualize the image—soaring up high . . . coasting on a warm air current . . . gliding along without even flapping your wings?

Figures of speech are powerful literary forms because they paint images to which we can relate emotionally. These can be images of blessing, like that of the eagle in Isaiah 40, but they can also be images of judgment or disgust. For example, visualize the image in Matthew 23:27 and describe your emotional reaction to this image:

> "Woe to you, teachers of the law and Pharisees, you hypocrites! You are like whitewashed tombs, which look beautiful on the outside but on the inside are full of the bones of the dead and everything unclean."

The Bible is full of figures of speech. They show up in both the Old and New Testaments. Read the following passages. After reading each one, identify what the figure of speech is. Then stop to ponder the image for a moment. Try to visualize the image; what do you see?

Figures of speech are powerful literary forms because they paint images to which we can relate emotionally.

> The Lord is my *rock*, my fortress and my deliverer. (Ps. 18:2)

> I planted the seed, Apollos watered it, but God has been making it grow. (1 Cor. 3:6)

> "Jerusalem, Jerusalem, you who kill the prophets and stone those sent to you, how often I have longed to gather your children together, as a hen gathers her chicks under her wings, and you were not willing." (Luke 13:34)

> We all, like sheep, have gone astray,
> each of us has turned to our own way;
> and the Lord has laid on him
> the iniquity of us all. (Isa. 53:6)

7. Conjunctions

If we imagine the biblical text to be like a brick house, then conjunctions are the mortar that holds the bricks (phrases and sentences) together. One critical aspect of careful reading is to note all the conjunctions (*and*, *for*, *but*, *therefore*, *since*, *because*, etc.). Our tendency is to skip over them—but don't do it! Without the mortar the bricks fall into a jumbled mess. So always take note of the conjunctions and identify their purpose or function. That is, try to determine what the conjunction connects.

Conjunctions are the mortar that holds the bricks (phrases and sentences) together.

For example, if you encounter the conjunction ***but***, you might suspect some sort of contrast. Look in the text for the things being contrasted by this conjunction. Recall Romans 6:23:

> For the wages of sin is death, ***but*** the gift of God is eternal life in Christ Jesus our Lord.

Here "but" indicates a contrast between the wages of sin (death) and the gift of God (eternal life).

Therefore or *so* usually presents some type of conclusion based on earlier arguments or reasons. When you encounter a *therefore*, look back in the text and determine what the earlier reason was. Sometimes the reason is easy to find, lying out in the open in the previous verse. At other times, however, the earlier reason is more difficult to find. It may refer to the larger argument of several previous chapters.

Romans 12:1 is a good illustration of the hard-to-find type:

> *Therefore*, I urge you, brothers and sisters, in view of God's mercy, to offer your bodies as a living sacrifice, holy and pleasing to God—this is your true and proper worship.

The word "Therefore," which opens Romans 12, connects this verse to the preceding *eleven chapters*. For eleven chapters Paul has been discussing theology—the wonderful fact of our salvation by grace through faith. In Romans 12 he switches the subject to behavior. How should we act? How should we behave? "Therefore" in 12:1 connects who we are with what we should do. Our behavior described in Romans 12 (and following) should be a direct consequence of God's grace in our lives (discussed in chapters 1–11).

An easier "therefore" is in Hebrews 12:1:

> *Therefore*, since we are surrounded by such a great cloud of witnesses, let us throw off everything that hinders and the sin that so easily entangles. And let us run with perseverance the race marked out for us.

The reason for this "therefore" can easily be found in the previous chapter, Hebrews 11. It is easy to find because 12:1 identifies it for us by saying "since we are surrounded by such a great cloud of witnesses." The people in chapter 11 are the only cloud of witnesses available in the context.

The "therefore" in Colossians 3:12 is not quite so obvious:

> *Therefore*, as God's chosen people, holy and dearly loved, clothe yourselves with compassion, kindness, humility, gentleness and patience.

What does the "therefore" refer back to? Read the previous eleven verses and look for the underlying reason behind verse 12. In the preceding verses, Paul tells the Colossians to put on the new self (see especially v. 10). Since they have put on "the new self," they "therefore" should also put on new virtues—compassion, kindness, and so on.

Other conjunctions are important too. Look, for example, at 2 Timothy 1:7–8:

> [7]*For* the Spirit God gave us does not make us timid, *but* gives us power, love *and* self-discipline. [8]*So* do not be ashamed of the testimony about our Lord *or* of me his prisoner. *Rather,* join with me in suffering for the gospel, by the power of God.

Note the conjunctions in verse 7 ("for," "but," "and") and in verse 8 ("so," "or," "rather"). Which two things are contrasted by the conjunction "but" in verse 7? How does the "so" in the next sentence relate verse 8 to verse 7? Likewise, what is it that the conjunction "rather" in verse 8 is contrasting?

How significant is the conjunction "but" in Genesis 6:8? Note the contrast presented in the previous two verses:

> [6]The Lord regretted that he had made human beings on the earth, and his heart was deeply troubled. [7]So the Lord said, "I will wipe from the face of the earth the human race I have created—and with them the animals, the birds and the creatures that move along the ground—for I regret that I have made them." [8]*But* Noah found favor in the eyes of the Lord. (Gen. 6:6–8)

8. Verbs—Where All the Action Is

Verbs are important because they communicate the action of the sentence. As you observe the text, be sure to note the verbal action. Try to identify what kind of verb is used. Is the verb a past, present, or future tense verb ("I went," "I go," "I will go")? Does it present a progressive idea; that is, does it have continued action ("I was going," "I am going," "I will be going")? Is it an imperative verb ("Go!")?

Be especially sure to note all imperative verbs! These are often God's commands to us. Note, for example, the list of imperative verbs in Ephesians 4:2–3:

> Be completely humble and gentle; be patient, bearing with one another in love. Make every effort to keep the unity of the Spirit through the bond of peace.

Another important distinction to look for in verbs is whether they are active or passive. Active verbs are those in which the subject is doing the action ("Bill *hit* the ball"). Passive verbs are those verbs where the subject is acted upon ("Bill *was hit* by the ball"). This distinction is particularly important in Paul's letters, because it often delineates between what we do and what God has done for us. Passive verbs often underscore the things God has done for us.

Passive verbs often underscore the things God has done for us.

Note the following active and passive verbs:

> Since, then, you *have been raised* [passive] with Christ, *set* [active!] your hearts on things above, where Christ is, seated at the right hand of God. (Col. 3:1)

> In him we *were* also *chosen* [passive], *having been predestined* [passive] according to the plan of him who *works out* [active] everything in conformity with the purpose of his will. (Eph. 1:11)

Passive verbs are also significant in the Old Testament. Note Genesis 12:3:

> "and all peoples on earth
> *will be blessed* [passive and future] through you."

9. Pronouns

Note all pronouns and be sure to identify the antecedent (to whom or to what the pronoun refers). Who, for example, are the "our" and "us" in Ephesians 1:3?

> Praise be to the God and Father of *our* Lord Jesus Christ, who has blessed *us* in the heavenly realms with every spiritual blessing in Christ.

Identify all of the pronouns in the following text (Phil. 1:27–30):

> [27]Whatever happens, conduct yourselves in a manner worthy of the gospel of Christ. Then, whether I come and see you or only hear about you in my absence, I will know that you stand firm in the one Spirit, striving together as one for the faith of the gospel [28]without being frightened in any way by those who oppose you. This is a sign to them that they will be destroyed, but that you will be saved—and that by God. [29]For it has been granted to you on behalf of Christ not only to believe in him, but also to suffer for him, [30]since you are going through the same struggle you saw I had, and now hear that I still have.

EXAMPLE: ROMANS 12:1–2

Up to this point we have been observing some important individual features that we encounter in the biblical text. Now let's try to pull all this together and apply it to one passage. Below is Romans 12:1–2. We have made numerous observations in this passage, but we have been far from exhaustive. Read over our observations. Identify other observations that we could have made.

Here is the example of observation in a passage:

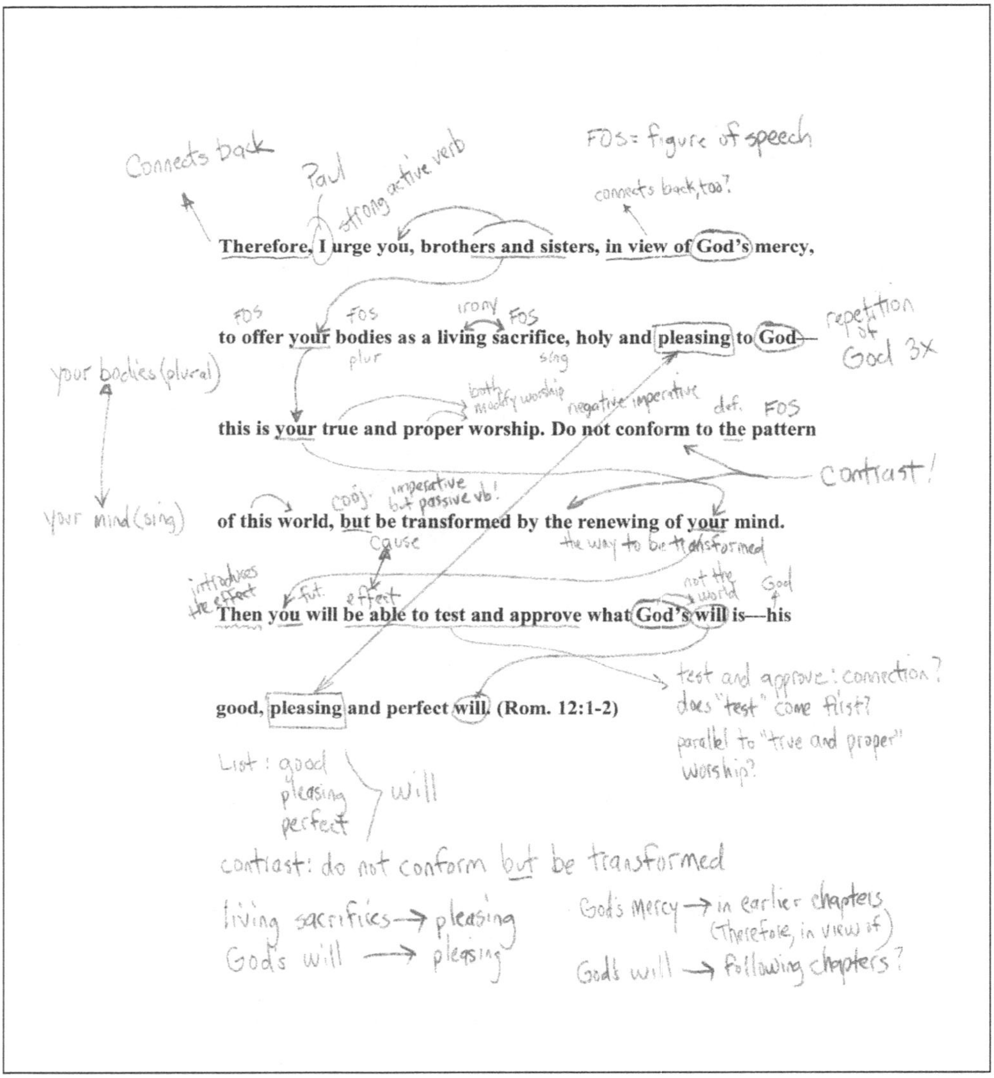

REVIEW

Let's review quickly what we have covered in this chapter.

- **Repetition of words**—Look for words and phrases that repeat.
- **Contrasts**—Look for ideas, individuals, and/or items that are contrasted with each other. Look for differences.
- **Comparisons**—Look for ideas, individuals, and/or items that are compared with each other. Look also for similarities.
- **Lists**—Note where the text mentions more than two items.
- **Cause and effect**—There may be more than one effect from a single cause mentioned in the text.
- **Figures of speech**—Look for expressions that convey an image, using words in a sense other than the literal sense.
- **Conjunctions**—Notice terms that join units, like *and*, *but*, *for*. Note what they are connecting.
- **Verbs**—Note whether a verb is past, present, or future; active or passive; also look for imperatives.
- **Pronouns**—Identify the antecedent for each pronoun.

CONCLUSION

The first step in tackling a biblical text is to make as many detailed observations as possible. We want to dig deep and to see as much as possible. The above list is far from exhaustive and is presented to help you get started. As you get into a text, observe as many details as possible. Spend time in the passage. Each sentence in the Bible has dozens and dozens of details just waiting for you to observe. Look carefully at the text. Read it over and over! Observe. Write down your observations. Read it again. Look some more. Write some more. Which observations have you missed? There is more yet to find. Don't quit! Keep digging!

ASSIGNMENTS

Assignment 3–1

Find a *minimum* of thirty observations in Acts 1:8. List them on a sheet of paper. Avoid making interpretations or applications at this stage. That is, stay with observations. For example, an observation would be to note that the passage starts off with the conjunction "but." This conjunction connects the sentence to the one above it in a contrasting way. If, however, you were to note that the Holy Spirit empowers us for evangelism, that observation falls into the category of interpretation or application. Do not enter the interpretation or application phase yet. Limit all thirty of your observations to the details and not to the interpretation of the details. Work hard! Dig deep! Read and reread the passage. Do not quit until you have found at least thirty observations. Try to find more than thirty. Happy hunting!

But you will receive power when the Holy Spirit comes on you;

and you will be my witnesses in Jerusalem,

and in all Judea and Samaria,

and to the ends of the earth.

Assignment 3–2

Photocopy this page from 1 John 1:5–7 and make as many observations as you can on this passage. Follow the format presented in the example of Romans 12:1–2. Dig deep. Think hard. Spend time on this. Mark dozens and dozens of observations. Read and reread. Look again. Observe! Observe! Observe!

5 This is the message we have heard from him

and declare to you: God is light;

in him there is no darkness at all.

6 If we claim to have fellowship with him

and yet walk in the darkness, we lie and do not live out the truth.

7 But if we walk in the light, as he is in the light,

we have fellowship with one another,

and the blood of Jesus, his Son, purifies us from all sin.

Assignment 3–3

Photocopy this page from Deuteronomy 6:4–6 and make as many observations as you can on this passage. Follow the format presented in the example of Romans 12:1–2.

4Hear, O Israel: The LORD our God, the LORD is one.

5Love the LORD your God with all your heart

and with all your soul and with all your strength.

6These commandments that I give you today

are to be on your hearts.

Assignment 3–4

Photocopy this page from 1 Timothy 6:17–19 and make as many observations as you can on this passage. Follow the format presented in the example of Romans 12:1–2.

17Command those who are rich in this present world

not to be arrogant nor to put their hope in wealth,

which is so uncertain, but to put their hope in God,

who richly provides us with everything for our enjoyment.

18Command them to do good, to be rich in good deeds,

and to be generous and willing to share.

19In this way they will lay up treasure for themselves

as a firm foundation for the coming age,

so that they may take hold of the life that is truly life.

Assignment 3–5

Photocopy this page from Matthew 28:18–20 and make as many observations as you can on this passage. Follow the format presented in the example of Romans 12:1–2.

18Then Jesus came to them and said,

"All authority in heaven and on earth

has been given to me.

19Therefore go and make disciples of all nations,

baptizing them in the name of the Father

and of the Son and of the Holy Spirit,

20and teaching them to obey

everything I have commanded you.

And surely I am with you always,

to the very end of the age."

CHAPTER 4

HOW TO READ THE BOOK—PARAGRAPHS

INTRODUCTION

In chapter 3 you learned how to make observations at the sentence level. In this chapter you will continue to develop your skill in making observations, but we will shift the focus of your observation from the sentence level to the paragraph level. Keep looking! Keep observing! Keep listening carefully to what God is saying through the Scriptures!

But first, a story . . .

THE ART OF OBSERVATION—LEARNING TO SEE

Learning to see details is a skill that does not come naturally, but it can be developed through practice. The following story is a classic tale about one student's education in the art of observation.

The Student, the Fish, and Agassiz[1]

By the Student

It was more than fifteen years ago that I entered the laboratory of Professor Agassiz, and told him I had enrolled my name in the scientific school as a student of natural history. He asked me a few questions about my object in coming, the mode in which I afterwards proposed to use the knowledge I might acquire and finally, whether I wished to study any special branch. To the latter I replied that while I wished to be well grounded in all departments of zoology, I purposed to devote myself specially to insects.

"When do you wish to begin?" he asked.

"Now," I replied.

This seemed to please him, and with an energetic "very well," he reached from a shelf a huge jar of specimens in yellow alcohol.

"Take this fish," said he, "and look at it; we call it a Haemulon; by and by I will ask what you have seen."

With that he left me. In ten minutes I had seen all that could be seen in that fish, and started in search of the professor, who had, however, left the museum; and when I returned, after lingering over some of the odd animals stored in the upper apartment, my specimen was dried all over. I dashed the fluid over the fish as if to resuscitate it from a fainting-fit, and looked with anxiety for a return of a normal, sloppy appearance. This little excitement over, nothing was to be done but return to a steadfast gaze at my mute companion. Half an hour passed, an hour, another hour; the fish began to look loathsome. I turned it over and around; looked it in the face—ghastly; from behind, beneath, above, sideways, at a three-quarters view—just as ghastly. I was in despair; at an early hour I concluded that lunch was necessary; so with infinite relief, the fish was carefully replaced in the jar, and for an hour I was free.

On my return, I learned that Professor Agassiz had been at the museum, but had gone and would not return for several hours. Slowly I drew forth that hideous fish, and with a feeling of desperation again looked at it. I might not use a magnifying glass; instruments of all kinds were interdicted. My two hands, my two eyes, and the fish; it seemed a most limited field. I pushed my fingers down its throat to see how sharp its teeth were. I began to count the scales in the different rows until I was convinced that was nonsense. At last a happy thought struck me—I would draw the fish; and now with surprise I began to discover new features in the creature. Just then the professor returned.

1. Jean Louis Rodolphe Agassiz (1807–73) was a famous scientist of the nineteenth century who taught for many years at Harvard.

"That is right," said he, "a pencil is one of the best eyes. I am glad to notice, too, that you keep your specimen wet and your bottle corked."

With these encouraging words he added, "Well, what is it like?"

He listened attentively to my brief rehearsal of the structure of parts whose names were still unknown to me: fringed gill-arches, fleshly lips, lidless eyes; the lateral line, the spinous fin, and the forked tail. When I had finished, he waited as if expecting more, and then, with an air of disappointment:

"You have not looked very carefully. Why," he continued, more earnestly, "you haven't seen one of the most conspicuous features of the animal, which is as plainly before your eyes as the fish itself. Look again; look again!" and he left me to my misery.

I was mortified. Still more of that wretched fish? But now I set myself to the task with a will, and discovered one new thing after another, until I saw how just the professor's criticism had been. The afternoon passed quickly, and when towards its close, the professor inquired, "Do you see it yet?"

"No," I replied. "I am certain I do not, but see how little I saw before."

"That is next best," said he earnestly, "but I won't hear you now; put away your fish and go home; perhaps you will be ready with a better answer in the morning. I will examine you before you look at the fish."

This was disconcerting; not only must I think of the fish all night, studying without the object before me, what this unknown but most visible feature might be, but also, without reviewing my new discoveries, I must give an exact account of them the next day.

The cordial greeting from the professor the next morning was reassuring; here was a man who seemed to be quite as anxious as I that I should see for myself what he saw.

"Do you perhaps mean," I asked, "that the fish has symmetrical sides with paired organs?"

His thoroughly pleased, "Of course, of course!" repaid the wakeful hours of the previous night. After he had discoursed most happily and enthusiastically—as he always did upon the importance of this point—I ventured to ask what I should do next.

"Oh, look at your fish!" he said, and left me again to my own devices. In a little more than an hour he returned and heard my new catalogue.

"That is good, that is good!" he repeated, "but that is not all; go on." And for three long days, he placed that fish before my eyes, forbidding me to look at anything else, or to use any artificial aid. "Look, look, look," was his repeated injunction.

This was the best entomological lesson I ever had—a lesson whose influence has extended to the details of every subsequent study; a legacy the professor has left to me, as he left it to many others, of inestimable value, which we could not buy, with which we cannot part.[2]

2. "Appendix," in *American Poems* (Boston: Houghton, Osgood & Co., 1880). Howard Hendricks has used this wonderful illustration of observation in class at Dallas Theological Seminary for many years.

Do you see similarities between studying God's Word and studying fish? Read the Bible carefully. Look for the items we discussed in chapter 3. Look for other details as well. Observe! Look some more. Observe some more. Look again. Ask questions of the text. Look again. See more. Dig! Make notes. Mark the observations you see. Reread the passage. Look for other details. There is more! Keep digging! You get the idea. God is speaking here and you want to hear him correctly.

Let's push on and learn more about what to look for in paragraphs.

THINGS TO LOOK FOR IN PARAGRAPHS

1. General and Specific

Sometimes an author will introduce an idea with a general statement—that is, an overview or summary of the main idea. The author will then follow this general statement with the specifics of the idea. Often these specifics provide the supporting details that make the general idea true or explain it more completely. For example, I can make a *general* statement: "I like dessert." I can then explain this more fully with *specific* details: "I like homemade apple pie, strawberry shortcake, rocky road ice cream, and caramel pecan turtle cheesecake." This is a movement from *general* to *specific.*

General—dessert; specific—apple pie, strawberry shortcake, rocky road ice cream, and caramel pecan turtle cheesecake.

Although the biblical writers do not write of rocky road ice cream, they do often use the *general-to-specific* literary feature to communicate to us. For example, Paul makes a *general* statement in Galatians 5:16:

> So I say, walk by the Spirit, and you will not gratify the desires of the flesh.

"Walk by the Spirit" and "gratify the desires of the flesh" are general statements. They are broad generalizations. We as readers want to know more details or *specifics* about each of these. Paul obliges us and presents the specifics of gratifying the desires of the flesh in 5:19–21a:

> [19]The acts of the flesh are obvious: sexual immorality, impurity and debauchery; [20]idolatry and witchcraft; hatred, discord, jealousy, fits of rage, selfish ambition, dissensions, factions [21]and envy; drunkenness, orgies, and the like.

He next moves on to the specifics of how to "walk by the Spirit" in 5:22–23:

> But the fruit of the Spirit is love, joy, peace, forbearance, kindness, goodness, faithfulness, gentleness and self-control.

Romans 12 is also a *general-to-specific* passage. Paul makes his *general* statement in verse 1:

> Therefore, I urge you, brothers and sisters, in view of God's mercy, to offer your bodies as a living sacrifice, holy and pleasing to God—this is your true and proper worship.

The *specifics* start a few verses later in 12:9 and continue on into chapter 15. Romans 12:9–13 is cited below as one set of examples. Note the specific nature of the exhortations:

> [9]Love must be sincere. Hate what is evil; cling to what is good. [10]Be devoted to one another in love. Honor one another above yourselves. [11]Never be lacking in zeal, but keep your spiritual fervor, serving the Lord. [12]Be joyful in hope, patient in affliction, faithful in prayer. [13]Share with the Lord's people who are in need. Practice hospitality.

Also keep in mind that the authors will frequently reverse the order and go from *specific* to *general*. The writer will first list the *specifics* ("I like homemade apple pie, strawberry shortcake, rocky road ice cream, and caramel pecan turtle cheesecake") and then recap the idea with a *general* statement summarizing the main point ("I like dessert"). A good example of this is the famous chapter on love in 1 Corinthians 13. Verses 1–12 present the *specifics*:

> If I speak in the tongues of men or of angels, but do not have love, I am only a resounding gong or a clanging cymbal. . . .
>
> Love is patient, love is kind. It does not envy, it does not boast, it is not proud. It does not dishonor others, it is not self-seeking, it is not easily angered. . . .

Verse 13 then recaps the chapter with a *general* statement that summarizes the main point:

> And now these three remain: faith, hope and love. But the greatest of these is love.

2. Questions and Answers

Occasionally an author will raise a rhetorical question and then answer that question. Paul does this several times in Romans. For instance, in Romans 6:1 he asks:

> What shall we say, then? Shall we go on sinning so that grace may increase?

Paul then answers his own question in verse 2:

> By no means! We are those who have died to sin; how can we live in it any longer?

In the verses that follow, the apostle continues to discuss the answer to his opening question in 6:1. He uses this type of *question-and-answer* format in numerous other places in Romans as well (3:1–2, 5–6, 9, 27–31; 4:1–2, 9; 6:15; 7:1, 7, 13; 8:31–35; 11:1, 7, 11).

This technique is not limited to Paul's letters. Mark uses the *question-and-answer* format in several places as the backdrop for the story of Jesus. For example, in Mark 2:1–3:6 five episodes revolve around a question and an answer. The five questions are these:

1. "Who can forgive sins but God alone?" (2:7)
2. "Why does he eat with tax collectors and sinners?" (2:16)
3. "How is it that John's disciples and the disciples of the Pharisees are fasting, but yours are not?" (2:18)
4. "Why are they doing what is unlawful on the Sabbath?" (2:24)
5. "Which is lawful on the Sabbath: to do good or to do evil, to save life or to kill?" (3:4)

The first four questions are raised by opponents of Jesus. The Pharisees and others are challenging the religious behavior of Jesus and his disciples. In the verses that follow each question, Jesus answers the inquiry with a clear justification of his actions.

1. "But I want you to know that the Son of Man has authority on earth to forgive sins." So he said to the man, "I tell you, get up, take your mat and go home." (2:10–11)
2. "I have not come to call the righteous, but sinners." (2:17b)
3. "How can the guests of the bridegroom fast while he is with them?" (2:19)
4. "Have you never read what David did . . . ? The Son of Man is Lord even of the Sabbath." (2:25, 28)

The fifth question, however, is asked by Jesus and is directed at the Pharisees. The answer to his question is obvious, for the lawful thing is to "do good," as Jesus does by healing the man's shriveled hand, and not to "do evil" and "to kill" (3:4) as the Pharisees are plotting to do to Jesus (3:6). However, even though Jesus has answered their questions, they fail to answer his.

Note that Mark balances this five-question episode that occurs early in his book with another five-question episode at the end of his book (11:27–12:40). The opponents are the same in each episode. Also, in each episode the opponents ask the first four questions and Jesus asks the last question.

3. Dialogue

Dialogue, of course, overlaps with the question-and-answer feature discussed above. The four questions in Mark 2:15–3:6 are part of an ongoing dialogue between Jesus and the Pharisees. Dialogue may seem at first glance to be too obvious to worry about. Clearly, in narrative material dialogue is employed frequently and is easy to spot. But do not simply read past the point of the dialogue. Note the fact that a dialogue is taking place. Then ask questions of the dialogue. Who are the participants? Who is speaking to whom? What is the setting? Are other people around? Are they listening? Are they participating in the dialogue? Is the dialogue an argument? A discussion? A lecture? Friendly chitchat? What is the point of the dialogue? You may find it helpful to color-code the dialogue. Assign one specific color to each participant, and then color the conversation accordingly.

The stories of the Bible contain a multitude of wonderful dialogues. Recall Jesus' conversation with the Samaritan woman at the well in John 4. Another famous dialogue occurs between Peter and Jesus in John 13:6–10, where they discuss whether Jesus will wash Peter's feet. Clearly one of the most unusual discussions in the Bible is the conversation between Balaam and his donkey in Numbers 22.

You may find it helpful to color-code the dialogue. Assign one specific color to each participant, and then color the conversation accordingly.

Some dialogues, however, are not as easy to spot. These "less-than-obvious" dialogues, however, are often important to the meaning of the passage. The book of Habakkuk, for example, consists primarily of a dialogue between God and the prophet. In 1:1–4 Habakkuk asks God why he allows injustice to continue in Judah without doing anything to stop it. God answers in 1:5–11 by promising to send the Babylonians to invade Judah and to destroy the nation. Habakkuk objects in 1:12–2:1 because an invasion is not quite what Habakkuk had in mind. Nonetheless, God answers the objection in 2:2–20 by stating that the invasion is inevitable. Once you recognize the dialogue format of Habakkuk, the message of the book becomes clear.

4. Purpose/Result Statements

Always identify *purpose/result statements*. These are phrases or sentences that describe the reason, the result, or the consequence of some action. They are frequently introduced by result-oriented conjunctions such as *that*, *in order that*, and *so that*, but they can also be introduced with the simple infinitive. The following examples illustrate the use of purpose/result statements.

> For we are God's handiwork, created in Christ Jesus *to do good works*. (Eph. 2:10)

> For God so loved the world *that he gave his one and only Son*. (John 3:16)

> "You did not choose me, but I chose you and appointed you *so that you might go and bear fruit—fruit that will last*." (John 15:16)

> Hear, Israel, and be careful to obey *so that* it may go well with you and *that* you may increase greatly in a land flowing with milk and honey. (Deut. 6:3)

Purpose/result statements are phrases or sentences that describe the reason, the result, or the consequence of some action.

> I have hidden your word in my heart *that I might not sin against you*. (Ps. 119:11)

5. Means (By Which Something Is Accomplished)

When an action, a result, or a purpose is stated, look for the *means* that brings about that action, result, or purpose. How is the action or result brought into reality? How is the purpose accomplished? For example, read the second half of Romans 8:13:

> . . . but if *by the Spirit* you put to death the misdeeds of the body, you will live.

The *means* by which the misdeeds of the body are put to death is *the Spirit*.

Likewise, ponder a moment Psalm 119:9:

> How can a young person stay on the path of purity?
> By living according to your word.

The purpose or action desired is for a young person to stay on the path of purity. What is the *means*? Living according to God's Word.

6. Conditional Clauses

Identify all conditional clauses. These are clauses that present the conditions whereby some action, consequence, reality, or result will happen. The conditional aspect will usually be introduced by the conditional conjunction *if*. The resultant action or consequence will occasionally be introduced by *then*, but often the resultant action or consequence has no specific introductory words. Whenever you encounter a conditional clause, always determine exactly what the required conditional action is (the *if* part) and what the result or consequence is (the *then* part).

Identify the conditional clause and the result or consequence in each of the following:

> If we claim to have fellowship with him and yet walk in the darkness, we lie and do not live out the truth. (1 John 1:6)

Condition: if we claim to have fellowship with him and yet walk in the darkness
Result or consequence: we lie and do not live out the truth

Whenever you encounter a conditional clause, always determine exactly what the required conditional action is (the *if* part) and what the result or consequence is (the *then* part).

> Therefore, if anyone is in Christ, the new creation has come: The old has gone, the new is here! (2 Cor. 5:17)

Condition: if anyone is in Christ
Result or consequence: the new creation has come; the old has gone, the new is here

> If you fully obey the LORD your God and carefully follow all his commands I give you today, the LORD your God will set you high above all the nations on earth. (Deut. 28:1)

Condition: if you fully obey the LORD your God and carefully follow all his commands I give you today
Result or consequence: the LORD your God will set you high above all the nations on earth

7. The Actions/Roles of People and the Actions/Roles of God

Biblical passages often refer to actions of people as well as those of God. Identify these and mark them as separate. Ask the questions: What does God (further identify as the Father, the Son, or the Holy Spirit) do in this passage? What do people do in this passage? Then ask whether there is any kind of connection between what God does and what people do.

For example, read Ephesians 5:1–2:

> [1]Follow God's example, therefore, as dearly loved children [2]and walk in the way of love, just as Christ loved us and gave himself up for us as a fragrant offering and sacrifice to God.

What are the actions or roles of people in this passage? We are told to be imitators of God in the same way children are imitators. We are also told to live a life of love as Christ did. What is Christ's or God's role in this passage? Christ's role was to offer himself up to God for us; God's role is to be the one who is imitated.

What does God do in this passage? What do people do in this passage?

In addition, be sure to observe when references to God are made in relational terms (father, husband, king). For example, in Matthew 5:43–6:34 there are *fourteen* references to God as "Father" (5:45, 48; 6:1, 4, 6, 8, 9, 14, 15, 18, 26, 32). By his repeated use of "Father" in this passage (from the Sermon on the Mount), Jesus is clearly trying to convey an idea of relationship to God as a Father (both his and ours).

8. Emotional Terms

The Bible is not a book of abstract, technical information. It is a book about relationships, primarily relationships between God and people. Emotions play a big role in relationships. This is frequently overlooked in biblical interpretation. As part of your careful reading, when you observe the text, be sure to underscore words and phrases that have emotional overtones—that is, words that convey feeling and emotion. Also be sure to note words such as "father," "mother," "child," "daughter," "son," and the like. These usually have underlying emotional connotations as well.

Read Galatians 4:12–16 and note the emotional connotations of the italicized phrases and words:

> [12]I *plead* with you, *brothers and sisters*, become like me, for I became like you. *You did me no wrong.* [13]As you know, it was because of an *illness* that I first preached the gospel to you, [14]and even though *my illness was a trial to you*, you did not *treat me with contempt or scorn*. Instead, *you welcomed me* as if I were an angel of God, as if I were Christ Jesus himself. [15]*Where, then, is your blessing of me now?* I can testify that, if you could have done so, *you would have torn out your eyes and given them to me.* [16]*Have I now become your enemy* by telling you the truth?

"Plead" is much more emotional than "ask," isn't it? Paul seems to have intentionally chosen strong emotional terms to express himself in this passage (and throughout Galatians). What feelings does Paul express here? Why does he bring up their past relationship, recalling how they once welcomed him? How strong is the phrase "torn out your eyes"? Likewise, what kind of connotations does the word "enemy" carry?

The Old Testament uses emotional terminology even more frequently than the New Testament. God himself will open up and pour out his broken heart on account of his spiteful, rebellious people, as Jeremiah 3:19–20 testifies:

> 19 I myself said,
>
> " 'How gladly would I treat you like my children
> and give you a pleasant land,
> the most beautiful inheritance of any nation.'
> I thought you would call me 'Father'
> and not turn away from following me.
> 20 But like a woman unfaithful to her husband,
> so you, Israel, have been unfaithful to me,"
> declares the LORD.

The Bible is not a book of abstract, technical information. It is a book about relationships, primarily relationships between God and people.

Observe the two emotional analogies God uses. Israel is like a son who has spurned and rejected the relationship with his father, and she is also like a wife who has cheated on her husband and had affairs with other men. These two relationships (parent/child and husband/wife) are without doubt among the most emotionally charged relationships that people experience. These relationships can bring extreme joy as well as devastating heartbreak. In Jeremiah 3, God wants his people to know that they have hurt him emotionally by their rejection of him.

9. Tone

Try to identify the tone of the passage. This will often be closely related to the identification of emotional terms (see above). However, once you have noted any emotional terms, continue on to determine the overall *tone* of the passage. Is it one of anger? A scolding tone? A sorrowful tone? Or a tone of unimpassioned explanation?

For example, contrast the tone of Colossians 3:1–4 with that of Galatians 3:1–4:

> 1Since, then, you have been raised with Christ, set your hearts on things above, where Christ is, seated at the right hand of God. 2Set your minds on things above, not on earthly things. 3For you died, and your life is now hidden with Christ in God. 4When Christ, who is your life, appears, then you also will appear with him in glory. (Col. 3:1–4)

> [1]You foolish Galatians! Who has bewitched you? Before your very eyes Jesus Christ was clearly portrayed as crucified. [2]I would like to learn just one thing from you: Did you receive the Spirit by the works of the law, or by believing what you heard? [3]Are you so foolish? After beginning by means of the Spirit, are you now trying to finish by means of the flesh? [4]Have you experienced so much in vain—if it really was in vain? (Gal. 3:1–4)

In Colossians 3:1–4 Paul is using a calm, explanatory tone. He does not use strong emotional terms. In Galatians 3:1–4, however, Paul's tone is quite different. He is chiding or scolding the Galatians. He even sounds as if he may be a little angry or at least disappointed with his readers, or both. His tone is part of his message, however, and it is important to note the tone of each passage you study.

What is Jesus' tone in Matthew 23:33–35? Is he calm, gentle, and loving in his tone?

> [33]"You snakes! You brood of vipers! How will you escape being condemned to hell? [34]Therefore I am sending you prophets and sages and teachers. Some of them you will kill and crucify; others you will flog in your synagogues and pursue from town to town. [35]And so upon you will come all the righteous blood that has been shed on earth, from the blood of righteous Abel to the blood of Zechariah son of Berekiah, whom you murdered between the temple and the altar."

Note, too, the tone of despair and gloom in Lamentations 3:1–6:

> [1]I am the man who has seen affliction
> by the rod of the LORD's wrath.
> [2]He has driven me away and made me walk
> in darkness rather than light;
> [3]indeed, he has turned his hand against me
> again and again, all day long.
>
> [4]He has made my skin and my flesh grow old
> and has broken my bones.
> [5]He has besieged me and surrounded me
> with bitterness and hardship.
> [6]He has made me dwell in darkness
> like those long dead.

EXAMPLES

The following example is from Colossians 1:3–8:

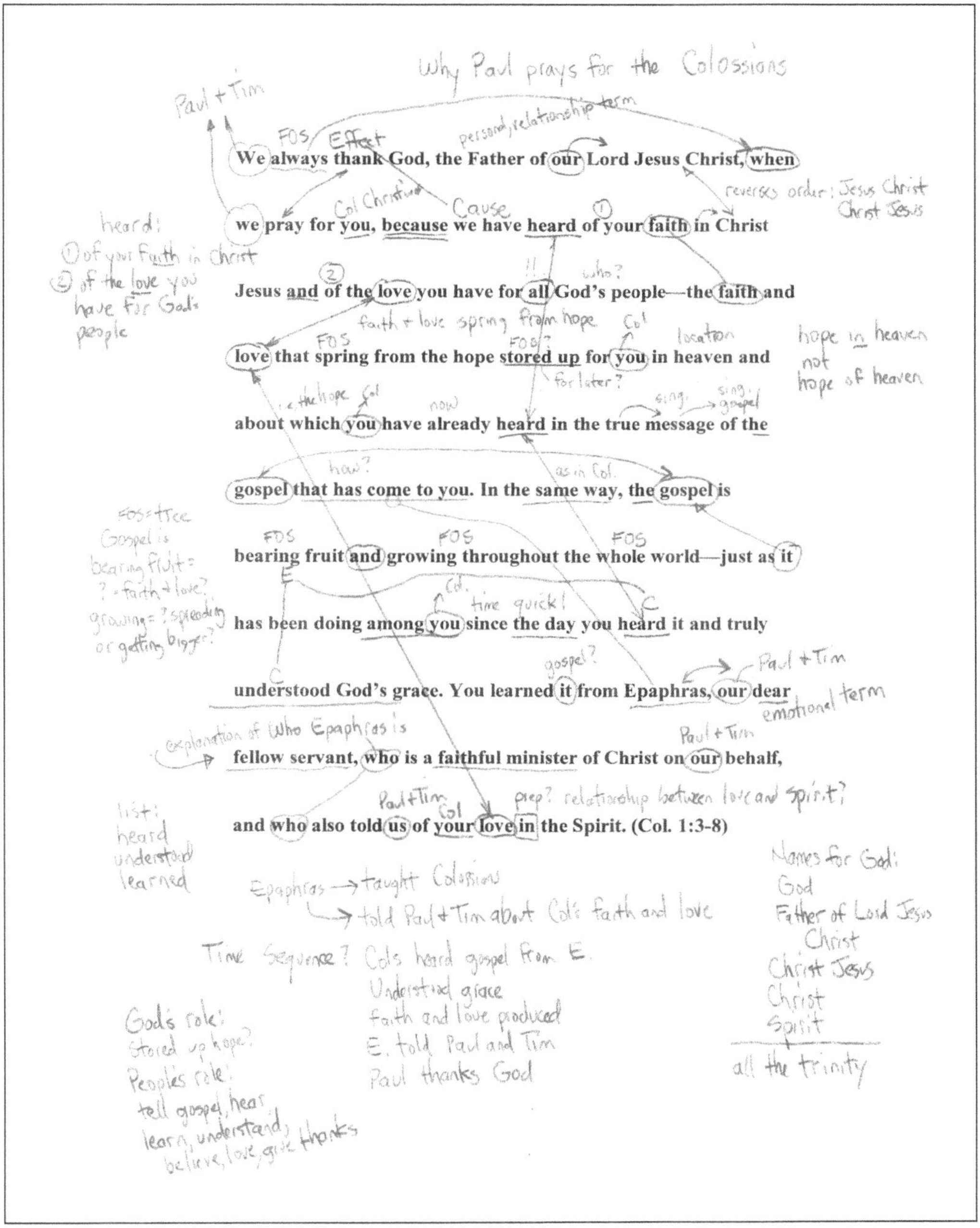

We always thank God, the Father of our Lord Jesus Christ, when we pray for you, because we have heard of your faith in Christ Jesus and of the love you have for all God's people—the faith and love that spring from the hope stored up for you in heaven and about which you have already heard in the true message of the gospel that has come to you. In the same way, the gospel is bearing fruit and growing throughout the whole world—just as it has been doing among you since the day you heard it and truly understood God's grace. You learned it from Epaphras, our dear fellow servant, who is a faithful minister of Christ on our behalf, and who also told us of your love in the Spirit. (Col. 1:3-8)

This next example is from Deuteronomy 6:1–3:

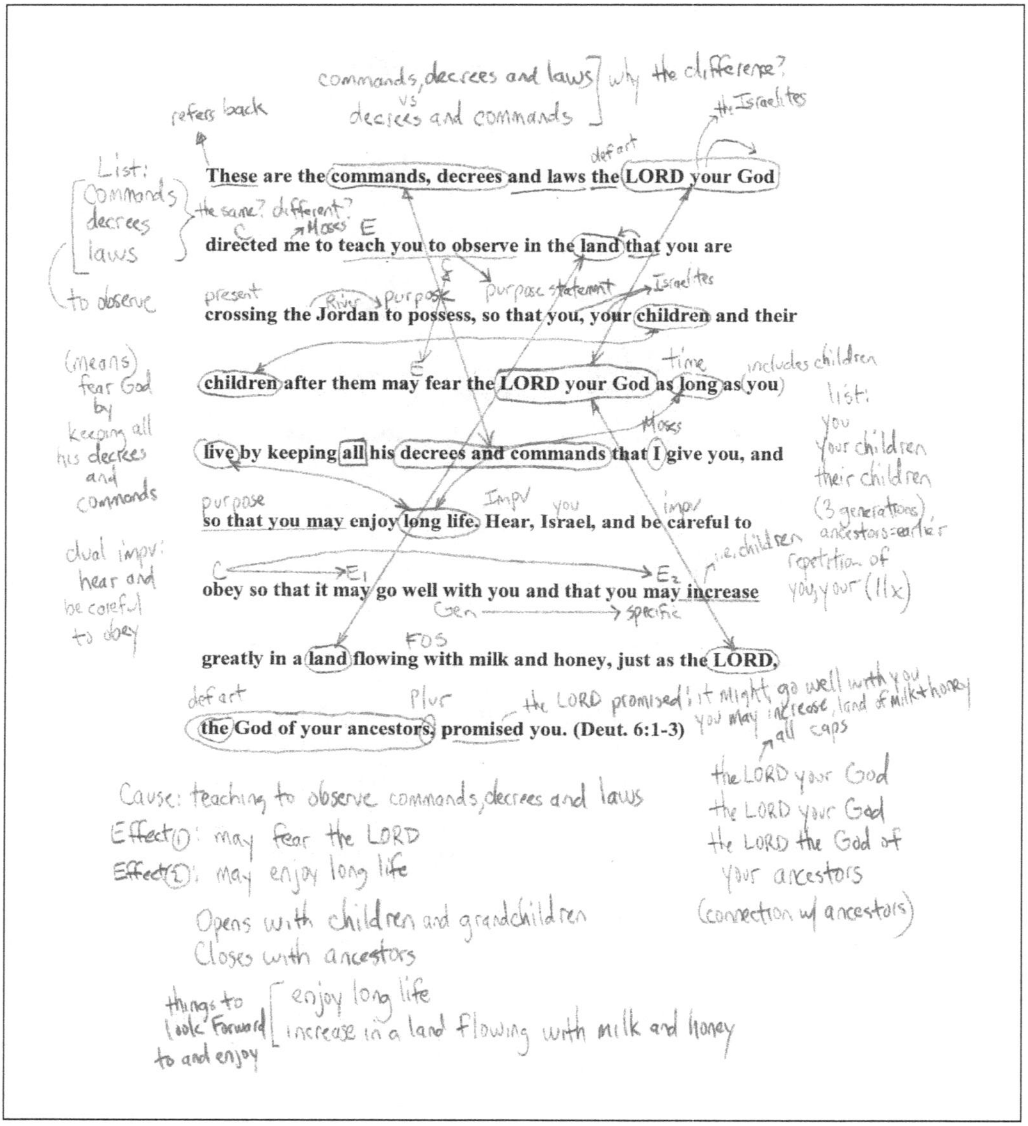

REVIEW

Here is a quick review of the items to look for during observation that we have presented in chapters 3 and 4:

- **Repetition of words**—Look for words and phrases that repeat.
- **Contrasts**—Look for ideas, individuals, and/or items that are contrasted with each other. Look for differences.
- **Comparisons**—Look for ideas, individuals, and/or items that are compared with each other. Look also for similarities.
- **Lists**—Anytime the text mentions more than two items, identify them as a list.
- **Cause and effect**—Look for cause-and-effect relationships.
- **Figures of speech**—Identify expressions that convey an image, using words in a sense other than the normal literal sense.
- **Conjunctions**—Notice terms that join units, like *and*, *but*, *for*. Note what they are connecting.
- **Verbs**—Note whether a verb is past, present, or future; active or passive; and the like.
- **Pronouns**—Identify the antecedent for each pronoun.
- **General to specific and specific to general**—Find the general statements that are followed by specific examples or applications of the general. Also find specific statements that are summarized by a general one.
- **Questions and answers**—Note if the text is built on a question-and-answer format.
- **Dialogue**—Note if the text includes dialogue. Identify who is speaking and to whom.
- **Purpose/result statements**—These are a more specific type of "means," often telling why. Purpose and result are similar and sometimes indistinguishable. In a purpose statement, you usually can insert the phrase "in order that." In a result clause, you usually can insert the phrase "so that."
- **Means**—Note if a sentence indicates that something was done *by means of* someone/something (answers "How?"). Usually you can insert the phrase "by means of" into the sentence.
- **Conditional clauses**—A clause can present the condition by which some action or consequence will result. Often such statements use an "if . . . then" framework (although in English the "then" is often left out).

- **Actions/roles of people**—Identify actions or roles that the text ascribes to people or encourages people to do/be.
- **Actions/roles of God**—Identify actions or roles that the text ascribes to God.
- **Emotional terms**—Does the passage use terms that have emotional energy, like kinship words ("father," "son") or words like "pleading"?
- **Tone**—What is the overall tone of the passage: happy, sad, encouraging, and so on?

CONCLUSION

In chapters 3 and 4 we have suggested numerous things to look for while reading the Bible. We have also encouraged you to read the Bible as closely and with as much interest as a lovesick teenager would read a love letter. We suggested that you go over and over and over the text, looking for details and connections, in the same fashion as Agassiz's student observed his *Haemulon*. The ultimate goal, remember, is to hear correctly and to grasp firmly what God is saying to us through his Word.

"A pen is a mental crowbar."
—*Howard Hendricks*

According to Howard Hendricks, "A pen is a mental crowbar." It is important that you mark these observations or write them down. Develop your own style of making observations that is legible and understandable. For example, you can mark "cause" with a big *C* and draw a connecting line to the "effect," which you could mark with (you guessed it!) a big *E*. Consider using similar notations for other features that you observe. Try photocopying and enlarging the text you are studying. Work on the photocopy sheet so that you do not completely destroy your Bible. Then fill the photocopy sheet, both the text and the margins, with all the observations that you can find. Some examples are listed above, but feel free to develop your own style.

Keep in mind that we are not trying to interpret the text yet. The interpretation phase comes later. This first phase—and a critical one—is that of observing or seeing. We are merely asking, "What does the text *say*?" So, for now, stay in this phase. Try to *see* all you can. Later in the book we will move on to interpretation (What does the text *mean*?) and application (What do I *do* about the text?).

ASSIGNMENTS

Assignment 4–1

Try making observations on Philippians 2:1–4. Write down as many observations as you can. Write in the text and in the margins.

1Therefore if you have any encouragement from being united with Christ,

if any comfort from his love,

if any common sharing in the Spirit,

if any tenderness and compassion,

2then make my joy complete by being like-minded,

having the same love, being one in spirit and of one mind.

3Do nothing out of selfish ambition or vain conceit.

Rather, in humility value others above yourselves,

4not looking to your own interests

but each of you to the interests of the others.

Assignment 4–2

Photocopy 1 Corinthians 1:18–25 and make as many observations as you can. Dig deep! Think hard. This is not an easy passage. Spend time on this. Mark dozens and dozens of observations. Read and reread! Look again! Observe! Observe! Observe!

18 For the message of the cross is foolishness to those who are

perishing, but to us who are being saved it is the power of God.

19 For it is written:

"I will destroy the wisdom of the wise;

the intelligence of the intelligent I will frustrate."

20 Where is the wise person? Where is the teacher of the law?

Where is the philosopher of this age?

Has not God made foolish the wisdom of the world?

21 For since in the wisdom of God the world

through its wisdom did not know him,

God was pleased through the foolishness of what was preached

to save those who believe.

22Jews demand signs and Greeks look for wisdom,

23but we preach Christ crucified:

a stumbling block to Jews and foolishness to Gentiles,

24but to those whom God has called, both Jews and Greeks,

Christ the power of God and the wisdom of God.

25For the foolishness of God is wiser than human wisdom,

and the weakness of God is stronger than human strength.

Assignment 4–3

Photocopy Colossians 3:1–4 and make as many observations as you. Dig deep! Think hard. Spend time on this. Mark dozens and dozens of observations. Read and reread! Look again! Observe! Observe! Observe!

[1]Since, then, you have been raised with Christ,

set your hearts on things above,

where Christ is, seated at the right hand of God.

[2]Set your minds on things above,

not on earthly things.

[3]For you died, and your life is now hidden with Christ in God.

[4]When Christ, who is your life, appears,

then you also will appear with him in glory.

Assignment 4–4

Photocopy Psalm 1:1–3 and make as many observations as you can. Dig deep! Think hard. Spend time on this. Mark dozens and dozens of observations. Read and reread! Look again! Observe! Observe! Observe!

1Blessed is the one

who does not walk in step with the wicked

or stand in the way that sinners take

or sit in the company of mockers,

2but whose delight is in the law of the Lord,

and who meditates on his law day and night.

3That person is like a tree planted by streams of water,

which yields its fruit in season

and whose leaf does not wither—

whatever they do prospers.

Assignment 4–5

Photocopy Matthew 6:25–34 and make as many observations as you can. Dig deep! Think hard. Spend time on this. Mark dozens and dozens of observations. Read and reread! Look again! Observe! Observe! Observe!

25"Therefore I tell you, do not worry about your life, what you

will eat or drink; or about your body, what you will wear.

Is not life more important than food, and the body more than clothes?

26Look at the birds of the air; they do not sow or reap or

store away in barns, and yet your heavenly Father feeds them.

Are you not much more valuable than they?

27Can any one of you by worrying add a single hour to your life?

28 And why do you worry about clothes?

See how the flowers of the field grow. They do not labor or spin.

29 Yet I tell you that not even Solomon in all his splendor was

dressed like one of these.

30 If that is how God clothes the grass of the field,

which is here today and tomorrow is thrown into the fire,

will he not much more clothe you—you of little faith?

31 So do not worry, saying, 'What shall we eat?' or

'What shall we drink?' or 'What shall we wear?'

32 For the pagans run after all these things,

and your heavenly Father knows that you need them.

33 But seek first his kingdom and his righteousness,

and all these things will be given to you as well.

34 Therefore do not worry about tomorrow,

for tomorrow will worry about itself.

Each day has enough trouble of its own."

CHAPTER 5

HOW TO READ THE BOOK—DISCOURSES

INTRODUCTION

By now, of course, you are well on your way to becoming an expert at reading and observing the Bible! We have discussed how to read sentences and how to read paragraphs. We have suggested things to look for while reading. We have encouraged you to look, look, and look some more. By now we trust you have done some serious reading and serious scrutinizing of God's Word. Keep working hard! Push on! The best is yet to come.

This chapter focuses on discourses. We are using the term *discourse* to refer to units of connected text that are longer than paragraphs.[1] There are other terms we could have used (*story*, *pericope*, *episode*, *unit of thought*, *chapter*), but we like the fluidity of the term *discourse*. A discourse can be a smaller episode within a story (David and Goliath), or it can be the longer story itself (the David narratives). A discourse can be two related paragraphs in one of Paul's letters. We are not hung up on the terminology or the definition. Our goal in this chapter is to help you to tackle longer units of biblical text.

1. The term *discourse* is used in a similar manner within the field of linguistics. For example, see Robert E. Longacre, *The Grammar of Discourse* (New York and London: Plenum, 1983). Longacre identifies four major types of discourse: narrative, hortatory, expositional, and procedural. In parts 4 and 5, where we discuss the different "discourse" types in the Bible, we will use the literary term *genre*.

The Bible is not a collection of short, disconnected sentences or unrelated paragraphs. The Bible is a story. Themes are intertwined throughout the text from paragraph to paragraph. Numerous markers and connections tie these paragraphs together. While it is critical to start with the small details at the sentence level, it is also imperative that we move on to the paragraph level and then on to the discourse level. God's message is not restricted to small units of text. Much of the message of the Bible is embedded in larger units of text. Discovering this message requires us to make observations at the discourse level. How do we *see* or *observe* large chunks of text?

The answer is not complicated. Everything you have learned in chapters 3 and 4 about sentences and paragraphs also applies to discourses. Word repetition, cause and effect, general to specific, conjunctions, and so forth—all these are applicable to the study of discourses. The basic discipline you developed in chapters 3 and 4 involving focused, intensive observation is exactly the skill you need to sink your teeth into longer units of text. However, in this chapter we will add a few more items to your list of things to look for—items that are more specific to reading at the discourse level. We will also illustrate these features for you with some intriguing passages.

But first a lesson on observation from the master of observation, Sherlock Holmes.

LESSONS FROM SHERLOCK HOLMES

> One night—it was on the twentieth of March 1888—I was returning from a journey to a patient (for I had now returned to civil practice), when my way led me through Baker Street. As I passed the well-remembered door, which must always be associated in my mind with my wooing, and with the dark incidents of the *Study in Scarlet*, I was seized with a keen desire to see Holmes again, and to know how he was employing his extraordinary powers. His rooms were brilliantly lit, and, even as I looked up, I saw his tall, spare figure pass twice in a dark silhouette against the blind. He was pacing the room swiftly, eagerly, with his head sunk upon his chest and his hands clasped behind him. To me, who knew his every mood and habit, his attitude and manner told their story. He was at work again. He had risen out of the drug-created dreams and was hot upon the scent of some new problem. I rang the bell and was shown up to the chamber, which had formerly been in part my own.
>
> His manner was not effusive. It seldom was; but he was glad, I think, to see me. With hardly a word spoken, but with a kindly eye, he waved me to an armchair, threw across his case of cigars, and indicated a spirit case and a gasogene in the corner. Then he stood before the fire and looked me over in his singular introspective fashion.

"Wedlock suits you," he remarked. "I think, Watson, that you have put on seven and a half pounds since I saw you."

"Seven!" I answered.

"Indeed, I should have thought a little more. Just a trifle more, I fancy, Watson. And in practice again, I observe. You did not tell me that you intended to go into the harness."

"Then how did you know?"

"I see it, I deduce it. How do I know that you have been getting yourself very wet lately, and that you have a most clumsy and careless servant girl?"

"My dear Holmes," said I, "this is too much. You would certainly have been burned, had you lived a few centuries ago. It is true that I had a country walk on Thursday and came home in a dreadful mess, but as I have changed my clothes I can't imagine how you deduce it. As to Mary Jane, she is incorrigible, and my wife has given her notice; but there, again, I fail to see how you work it out."

He chuckled to himself and rubbed his long, nervous hands together. "It is simplicity itself," said he. "My eyes tell me that on the inside of your left shoe, just where the firelight strikes it, the leather is scored by six parallel cuts. Obviously they have been caused by someone who has very carelessly scraped round the edges of the sole in order to remove crusted mud from it. Hence, you see, my double deduction that you had been out in vile weather, and that you had a particularly malignant bootslitting specimen of the London slavery. As to your practice, if a gentleman walks into my rooms smelling of iodoform, with a black mark of nitrate of silver upon his right forefinger, and a bulge on the right side of his top-hat to show where he has secreted his stethoscope, I must be dull, indeed, if I do not pronounce him to be an active member of the medical profession."

I could not help laughing at the ease with which he explained his process of deduction. "When I hear you give your reasons," I remarked, "the thing always appears to me to be so ridiculously simple that I could easily do it myself, though at each successive instance of your reasoning I am baffled until you explain your process. And yet I believe that my eyes are as good as yours."

"Quite so," he answered, lighting a cigarette, and throwing himself down into an armchair. "You see, but you do not observe."[2]

Sherlock Holmes continues to fascinate generation after generation through reprinted books, TV series, and updated movies. Likewise, the numerous crime scene

2. Sir Arthur Conan Doyle, "A Scandal in Bohemia," in *The Original Illustrated Sherlock Holmes* (Secaucus, NJ: Castle, n.d.), 11–12.

investigation shows on TV continue in the Sherlock Holmes tradition. The parallel between Sherlock Holmes's method and the serious kind of close observation needed in Bible study is close indeed. But keep in mind that this is just an analogy. We are not just "observing" a set of facts and data and trying to solve a problem. We are entering a dialogue with the all-powerful and loving God. We want to hear correctly what he is saying to us so that we can grow closer to him and mature in our Christian lives.

"You see [Watson], but you do not observe."

THINGS TO LOOK FOR IN DISCOURSES

1. Connections between Paragraphs and Episodes

After reading carefully and observing thoroughly at the sentence level and at the paragraph level, it is important to ask how your paragraph (in the letters) or your episode (in the narratives) relates to and connects with the other paragraphs/episodes that come before and after the one you are studying.

So far we have focused on the relationships between phrases, clauses, and sentences. We have looked at cause-and-effect relationships, general-to-specific relationships, conditional clauses with resultant or consequential effects, and other relational features within sentences and between sentences. These same features will also often connect paragraphs and episodes.

Look for connections. Look for repeated words or repeated themes. Look for logical connections like cause and effect. Be sure to note the conjunctions between the paragraphs. In narrative episodes pay attention to the time sequence of each episode. And remember—keep looking and keep digging and keep reading and keep looking and, whatever you do, don't stop after one short glance at the text. Immerse yourself in the passage. Search for these connections. They are critical to the meaning.

Example: Mark 8:22–26

Let's look at the episode in Mark 8:22–26 and see if we can determine any connections between it and the episodes that precede (8:14–21) and follow (8:27–30).

First, read Mark 8:22–26:

> 22They came to Bethsaida, and some people brought a blind man and begged
> Jesus to touch him. 23He took the blind man by the hand and led him outside
> the village. When he had spit on the man's eyes and put his hands on him, Jesus
> asked, "Do you see anything?"
>
> 24He looked up and said, "I see people; they look like trees walking around."

> [25]Once more Jesus put his hands on the man's eyes. Then his eyes were opened, his sight was restored, and he saw everything clearly. [26]Jesus sent him home, saying, "Don't even go into the village."

Taken by itself, this is a strange passage. Why does Jesus only heal the man partially at first? Is he unable to heal the blind person completely all at once? Why does Jesus ask the man if he can see anything? Doesn't he know? Is he uncertain about his healing ability? At first the man can see nothing; then he can see partially but not clearly. Finally, Jesus enables him to see clearly. Is there a point to this? Let's look at the surrounding episodes and look for some connections. Perhaps the connections will help us understand this puzzling passage.

Look for connections between episodes.

The previous episode is Mark 8:14–21:

> [14]The disciples had forgotten to bring bread, except for one loaf they had with them in the boat. [15]"Be careful," Jesus warned them. "Watch out for the yeast of the Pharisees and that of Herod."
>
> [16]They discussed this with one another and said, "It is because we have no bread."
>
> [17]Aware of their discussion, Jesus asked them: "Why are you talking about having no bread? Do you still not see or understand? Are your hearts hardened? [18]Do you have eyes but fail to see, and ears but fail to hear? And don't you remember? [19]When I broke the five loaves for the five thousand, how many basketfuls of pieces did you pick up?"
>
> "Twelve," they replied.
>
> [20]"And when I broke the seven loaves for the four thousand, how many basketfuls of pieces did you pick up?"
>
> They answered, "Seven."
>
> [21]He said to them, "Do you still not understand?"

The following episode is Mark 8:27–30:

> [27]Jesus and his disciples went on to the villages around Caesarea Philippi. On the way he asked them, "Who do people say I am?"
>
> [28]They replied, "Some say John the Baptist; others say Elijah; and still others, one of the prophets."
>
> [29]"But what about you?" he asked. "Who do you say I am?"
>
> Peter answered, "You are the Messiah."
>
> [30]Jesus warned them not to tell anyone about him.

Now let's search for connections between these three episodes. Note the following observations:

1. All three episodes are basically dialogues.
2. In all three episodes Jesus asks a question.
3. In the first episode (8:14–21) Jesus' dialogue is with his disciples. In the third episode (8:27–30) Jesus' dialogue is also with his disciples. The middle episode (8:22–26) is different: Jesus' dialogue is with a blind man. In other words, the dialogue with the blind man is bracketed on both sides by a dialogue with the disciples. Is there a suggested comparison or contrast?
4. The middle episode (8:22–26) mentions "the village" twice (8:23, 26). The third episode mentions "villages" (8:27).
5. Jesus ends the blind man episode (8:22–26) by forbidding him to go back into the village. Jesus ends the third episode (8:27–30) by forbidding the disciples to tell anyone about him.
6. The middle episode (8:22–26) revolves around terms related to seeing. Observe the following repetition:
    - a *blind* man (v. 22)
    - the *blind* man (v. 23)
    - he had spit on the *blind* man's *eyes* (v. 23)
    - "Do you *see* anything?" (v. 23)
    - he *looked* up (v. 24)
    - "I *see* people" (v. 24)
    - "they *look* like trees" (v. 24)
    - Jesus put his hands on the man's *eyes* (v. 25)
    - his *eyes* were opened (v. 25)
    - his *sight* was restored (v. 25)
    - he *saw* everything clearly (v. 25)
7. In light of the preponderance of terms related to *seeing* in the *blind man* episode, it is interesting to note similar terms used in reference to the *disciples* in the first or preceding episode (8:14–21):
    - "Do you still not *see*?" (v. 17)
    - "Do you have *eyes* but fail to *see*?" (v. 18)

    This repetition of *seeing* in the first two episodes is undoubtedly an important connection between the two.
8. Note that *seeing* in the *blind man* episode is being used literally, referring to literal vision. In the first episode, however, *seeing* is used figuratively, referring to *understanding*. Jesus makes this particularly clear when he states, "Do you

still not see *or understand*?" (8:17). Jesus repeats this nuance as he ends the episode with the repeated question, "Do you still not *understand*?" (8:21).

9. Peter's statement in 8:29, "You are the Messiah," indicates that Peter now understands who Jesus is, even though others may not. In essence he now *sees clearly*.

Conclusion about the connection. In the first episode Jesus asks his disciples some questions and realizes that they do not really understand who he is. They see only partially. By the third episode, however, they see clearly, acknowledging him as the Messiah.[3] The middle story, the *blind man* episode, is an illustration of the process that the disciples are experiencing. It is not so much a story about Jesus' healing as it is about a man's seeing. He only sees partially at first, as do the disciples. Then he sees clearly, as do the disciples. So the *blind man* episode is really an interruption in the flow of a section about the disciples' understanding of Jesus. It provides a colorful, real-life illustration of what was occurring in the lives of the disciples.

Example: Colossians 1:3–8 and 1:9–14

In chapter 4 we studied Colossians 1:3–8, making numerous observations within the paragraph. Now let's make observations in the following paragraph (1:9–14) and see if we can find any connections between the two. Here we repeat Colossians 1:3–8:

> [3]We always thank God, the Father of our Lord Jesus Christ, when we pray for you, [4]because we have heard of your faith in Christ Jesus and of the love you have for all God's people—[5]the faith and love that spring from the hope stored up for you in heaven and about which you have already heard in the true message of the gospel [6]that has come to you. In the same way, the gospel is bearing fruit and growing throughout the whole world—just as it has been doing among you since the day you heard it and truly understood God's grace. [7]You learned it from Epaphras, our dear fellow servant, who is a faithful minister of Christ on our behalf, [8]and who also told us of your love in the Spirit.

The next section, Colossians 1:9–14, reads as follows:

3. Some scholars argue that the disciples don't really see clearly until after the resurrection. However, such a view may be stretching the concept of "seeing" beyond the literary use in this passage. Peter's confession that Jesus is the Messiah is a gigantic step forward for the disciples, and his confession is central to the structure of the entire book. Obviously, Peter sees even better after the resurrection, but that does not detract from the crystal clarity of the statement, "You are the Messiah."

> [9]For this reason, since the day we heard about you, we have not stopped praying for you. We continually ask God to fill you with the knowledge of his will through all the wisdom and understanding that the Spirit gives, [10]so that you may live a life worthy of the Lord and please him in every way: bearing fruit in every good work, growing in the knowledge of God, [11]being strengthened with all power according to his glorious might so that you may have great endurance and patience, [12]and giving joyful thanks to the Father, who has qualified you to share in the inheritance of his holy people in the kingdom of light. [13]For he has rescued us from the dominion of darkness and brought us into the kingdom of the Son he loves, [14]in whom we have redemption, the forgiveness of sins.

Let's summarize the connections that seem obvious:

1. In both paragraphs Paul refers to having heard about the Colossians' conversion (1:4; 1:9).
2. In both paragraphs Paul and Timothy are praying for the Colossians (1:3; 1:9).
3. In the first paragraph Paul and Timothy are thanking God in their prayer because they have heard of the Colossians' faith and love (1:4). In the second paragraph Paul and Timothy are petitioning God in their prayer to fill the Colossian Christians with the knowledge of his will (1:9). Thus, the first paragraph is the *cause* for prayer, while the second paragraph is the *content* of the prayer.
4. In the first paragraph Paul and Timothy are thanking God (1:3), but in the second paragraph they want the Colossians to thank God (1:12).
5. In the first paragraph the gospel is producing fruit and growing (1:6). This is a figure of speech, referring to the spread of the gospel. The fruit is the new church in Colossae. Paul uses the same figure of speech (*fruit* and *growing*) in the second paragraph (1:10), but with different referents. Here the Colossians are the ones producing fruit, and they are the ones who are growing. Their fruit is "every good work" and their growth is in "the knowledge of God."

Conclusion about the connection. In the first paragraph, Paul and Timothy have heard of the Colossians' initial saving faith and love, and Paul and Timothy are thanking God for this. However, they do not stop at simply thanking God for new believers. They continue in the second paragraph to pray that these new believers will move on to maturity, being filled with the knowledge of God's will, doing good works, and continuing to grow in the knowledge of God.

2. Story Shifts: Major Breaks and Pivots

As you read larger units of text, look for critical places where the story seems to take a new turn. In the letters this takes the form of a *major break*. The writer will shift topics, frequently changing from doctrinal discussion to practical discussion. These shifts are important to note. Such shifts occur in narrative also, but they usually take the form of *pivot episodes*. Usually a shift in the direction of the story will be signaled by an unusually significant episode. Let's look at an example of each.

A pivot episode is an unusually significant episode that shifts the direction of the story.

In the first three chapters of Paul's letter to the Ephesians, he presents a doctrinal explanation about the Ephesians' new life in Christ and the implications of that new life, especially regarding the unity of Jews and gentiles in that new life. Ephesians 4:1, however, signals a *major break*, for Paul now begins to give practical exhortations about how the Ephesians ought to put the doctrine of chapters 1–3 into practice. So while chapters 1–3 deal primarily with doctrine, chapters 4–6 focus on practical living.

One way to spot this kind of break is by closely observing the change in verbs. In Ephesians 1–3 Paul uses a large number of "explanatory" or "descriptive" types of verbs. There are almost no imperative verbs in chapters 1–3; for example:

- who *has blessed* us (1:3)
- he *made known* to us the mystery of his will (1:9)
- you *were* dead in your transgressions and sins (2:1)
- God *made* us alive (2:5)
- it *is* by grace you *have been saved* (2:5)
- God *raised* us up (2:6)
- he himself *is* our peace (2:14)
- this mystery *is* that through the gospel the gentiles *are* heirs together with Israel (3:6)

Starting in Ephesians 4:1, however, the imperative verbs dominate:

- *be* completely humble (4:2)
- *make* every effort to keep the unity of the Spirit (4:3)
- you *must no longer live* as the gentiles do (4:17)
- *put off* falsehood (4:25)
- *do not give* the devil a foothold (4:27)
- *be* kind and compassionate to one another (4:32)

- *follow* God's example (5:1)
- *be filled* with the Spirit (5:18)
- husbands, *love* your wives (5:25)
- *put on* the full armor of God (6:11)

This verb change signals the major shift in the book. Overall, the two halves connect as a cause-and-effect relationship. The cause is explained in chapters 1–3 (what Christ has done for us and its implications), while the effect is stated in chapters 4–6 (live in a manner worthy of Christ and all he has done for us). A similar major break occurs between Romans 1–11 (doctrine) and Romans 12–16 (practical application).

The verb change that starts in Ephesians 4:1 signals the major shift in the book.

In narrative passages these shifts are usually episodes. They function as *pivots* because the story will pivot on that episode and take a new turn. A good example occurs in 2 Samuel. In the first half of 2 Samuel, the story is about David's rise to power. Everything is going great for David. He wins the civil war and succeeds Saul as king (chs. 1–5). He conquers Jerusalem, brings the ark to his new capital, and receives a covenant from God (chs. 5–7). He wins all his battles, defeating the Philistines, Moabites, Arameans, Edomites, and Ammonites (chs. 8–10). Life is good for David and his nation.

The second half of the book, however, is incredibly different. Events in that half are almost all negative for the king. David's oldest son, Amnon, rapes Tamar, Amnon's half sister, prompting Absalom, Tamar's brother, to kill Amnon (ch. 13). Next, Absalom, a son whom David loves, conspires against him, creating a bloody civil war. David is forced to flee Jerusalem. Eventually Absalom is defeated and killed, but David remains heartbroken (chs. 14–19). Next another rebellion arises (ch. 20). David then ends his career by fighting the Philistines again (ch. 21). In contrast to his earlier defeat of the Philistines (and his single-handed defeat of Goliath), David becomes exhausted and must be rescued by his troops; other heroes kill the giants this time (2 Sam. 21:15–22).

The difference between the first half and the second half of 2 Samuel is striking. The strong, victorious, confident David in the first half of the book is contrasted sharply with the insecure, weak, indecisive David in the second half. What happens in the middle that leads to this change? Where does the pivot occur, and what happens to bring it about?

The pivot event is in 2 Samuel 11–12. David sins by sleeping with Bathsheba and having her husband Uriah killed. Prior to this episode, David cruises through life as the beloved, respected, national hero; afterward, David's magnificent reputation begins to unravel. It is crucial for understanding 2 Samuel to see this pivot and to note the central role it plays in changing the direction of the story.

3. Interchange

Interchange is a literary device, used primarily in narrative, that involves contrasting or comparing two stories at the same time as part of the overall story development. Usually the narrative will move back and forth from one story to the other, often to show contrast.

The early chapters of 1 Samuel exhibit this feature. In the first few chapters, the story develops two contrasting families. Eli, the lazy priest, and his two decadent, disobedient sons, Hophni and Phinehas, are contrasted with devout Hannah and her pious, obedient son, Samuel. The two stories unfold at the same time, with the narrative moving back and forth from one to the other. As you read narrative, look for interchange between two different stories. Next, look for some purpose in the interchange. Why does the author employ this literary device in the telling of his story? In 1 Samuel the interchange is used to underscore the strong contrast between Samuel and the corrupt priesthood he replaces.

Interchange is a literary device, used primarily in narrative, that involves contrasting or comparing two stories at the same time as part of the overall story development.

Luke also uses interchange in the middle chapters of Acts to present the transition in central characters from Peter to Paul. Peter is the central character in the first seven chapters. Paul (as Saul) is introduced in Acts 7:58; 8:1–3. Peter returns to center stage in 8:14–25. Paul (as Saul) is the focus in 9:1–30 (his conversion), but Peter has the important encounter with Cornelius in 10:1–11:18. Paul returns briefly in 11:19–30, followed by Peter's miraculous escape from prison and his departure from Jerusalem in 12:1–19. In chapter 13 Paul moves onto center stage, and he remains the central character in the story for the next fifteen chapters.

What is the purpose of the interchange in Acts? What is Luke trying to say by switching back and forth? Clearly he is not contrasting a positive character with a negative character, as was the case in 1 Samuel. Both Peter and Paul are exemplary characters in Acts. In fact, Luke seems to be stressing the similarities of the two. Paul will do the same miracles that Peter does and preach as powerfully as Peter does. Luke uses interchange to demonstrate that Paul is as powerful (and authoritative) an apostle as Peter is and to show that the message of Christ that began with the Jews is spreading successfully to the gentiles.

4. Chiasm

Chiasm is a fascinating literary feature that is seldom used in English but is employed frequently by the biblical authors, especially in the Old Testament. In a chiasm a list of items, ideas, or events is structured in such a manner that the first item parallels the last item, the second item parallels the next to the last item, and so forth. For an illustration of chiasm, consider the following silly example:

I got up this morning, got dressed, and drove into town. I worked hard all day, returned home, put on my PJs, and went to bed.

To analyze the chiasm we list the events and look for parallels. We will list the first item as *a* and the corresponding parallel item as *a´*. The parallels of the story line up as follows:

a I got up this morning
    b got dressed
        c and drove into town
            d I worked hard all day
        c´ returned home
    b´ put on my PJs
a´ and went to bed

I got up this morning is noted as *a*, and it parallels the last event, *and went to bed*, noted as *a´*. Likewise, *got dressed* parallels *put on my PJs* and so forth. Note that the middle event (*I worked hard all day*) does not have any parallel. Frequently in chiastic structures, if the middle event does not have a parallel, it functions as the main point or the focal point of the chiasm. The stress of this ridiculous example is on the narrator's working hard all day. Often, however, there is no middle event in chiasm.

Chiasm can be simple and short. For example, consider Psalm 76:1:

God is renowned in Judah;
    in Israel his name is great.

Can you spot the chiasm in this verse? The parallels look like this:

a God is renowned
    b in Judah
    b´ in Israel
a´ his name is great.

Sometimes chiasms are lengthy and complex.[4] They can be subtle and difficult to notice. Scholars often disagree over whether the author intended the chiasm or whether perhaps the chiastic structure is merely the imagination of the reader. Read

4. For an extended discussion of chiasm and other literary structures in the Old Testament, see David A. Dorsey, *The Literary Structure of the Old Testament: A Commentary on Genesis–Malachi* (Grand Rapids: Baker, 1999).

the following story from Genesis 11:1–9 and see if you are convinced of the suggested chiastic structure.

> [1]Now the whole world had one language and a common speech. [2]As people moved eastward, they found a plain in Shinar and settled there.
>
> [3]They said to each other, "Come, let's make bricks and bake them thoroughly." They used brick instead of stone, and tar for mortar. [4]Then they said, "Come, let us build ourselves a city, with a tower that reaches to the heavens, so that we may make a name for ourselves; otherwise we will be scattered over the face of the whole earth."
>
> [5]But the LORD came down to see the city and the tower the people were building. [6]The LORD said, "If as one people speaking the same language they have begun to do this, then nothing they plan to do will be impossible for them. [7]Come, let us go down and confuse their language so they will not understand each other."
>
> [8]So the LORD scattered them from there over all the earth, and they stopped building the city. [9]That is why it was called Babel—because there the LORD confused the language of the whole world. From there the LORD scattered them over the face of the whole earth.

Read through the text and search for repeated words. Also look for similar ideas and contrasted ideas. Look to see if the end of the episode parallels the beginning. Next, line up the paralleling items and see if they fall together in order. Look to see if there is a center and an associated central idea that may be stressed. One suggested chiastic structure scholars have observed in this passage is as follows:

a *the whole world* (11:1)
  b *had one language* (11:1)
    c *Shinar* and settled *there* (11:2)
      d *"Come, let's make bricks"* (11:3)
        e "Come, let us *build*" (11:4)
          f "*a city, with a tower*" (11:4)
            g *But the* LORD *came down* (11:5)
          f′ to see *the city and the tower* (11:5)
        e′ the people were *building* (11:5)
      d′ *"Come, let us go down* and *confuse* their language" (11:7)
    c′ *Babel*—because *there* (11:9)
  b′ the LORD *confused the language* (11:9)
a′ *the whole world* (11:9)

The evidence is rather convincing that Genesis 11:1–9 has been written in a chiastic literary form.[5] Six specific words or concepts in the first half are paralleled in the second half. Note that the chiasm centers on the phrase in verse 5, "But the LORD came down." This is the central event in the story and focal point of the chiasm.

5. *Inclusio*

Inclusio is closely related to chiasm but is not as complicated. Inclusio is a literary technique in which a passage (a story or a poem, etc.) has the same or a similar word, statement, event, or theme at the beginning and at the end. This is also called "bracketing" or "framing." Psalm 8, for example, opens with, "LORD, our Lord, how majestic is your name in all the earth!" (v. 1). At the very end of the psalm we find the exact same statement, "LORD, our Lord, how majestic is your name in all the earth!" These two identical statements "frame" or "bracket" the rest of Psalm 8.

The inclusio is easy to spot if the beginning and end elements are completely identical, as in Psalm 8 (see also Eccl. 4:4–16). However, often inclusio involves similar events or themes. Sometimes the beginning and ending brackets can be separated by several chapters of narrative. For example, Joshua 3–6 is about how Israel prepares for and then captures the city of Jericho. This story is "framed" or "bracketed" by two stories about individual people. The story of Rahab (who believes and is saved) comes in Joshua 2 and the story of Achan (who disobeys God and is destroyed) comes in Joshua 7. This inclusio indicates that the opening event (Rahab) and the closing event (Achan) provide critical context for understanding the bracketed material (Josh. 3–6, the capture of Jericho). We will explore this fascinating unit (Josh. 2–7) in more depth in chapter 18.

CONCLUSION

To interpret and understand the Bible, we must first read it carefully, observing all the details. We must observe it at the sentence level, at the paragraph level, and at the discourse level. In chapters 3 and 4 we listed some features to look for—repetition, cause and effect, general to specific, and so forth. In chapter 5 we added five additional features to look for when reading at the discourse level: connections between paragraphs and episodes, story shifts (major breaks and pivots), interchange, chiasm, and inclusio. This expanded list is far from exhaustive. The purpose of the features we have listed is to get you started in careful reading. We have presented some of the major literary

5. This particular chiastic structure is presented and discussed in Allen P. Ross, *Creation and Blessing: A Guide to the Study and Exposition of Genesis* (Grand Rapids: Baker, 1988), 235–37; and in J. P. Fokkelman, *Narrative Art in Genesis* (Assen: Van Gorcum, 1975), 13–22.

features to look for. But as you are finding out, reading carefully—really observing closely—involves looking at all the details and asking numerous questions of the text.

Keep in mind that we are still only at the first step of grasping God's Word. Later in the book we will move on to *discovering* the meaning and *applying* the meaning. These early chapters, however, are critical, because if you bypass the careful reading step and move straight to application after only a superficial reading, you will almost certainly miss the meaning of the passage. In addition, the Bible will become boring for you because you will never see anything in it that you haven't already seen. If you read carefully, however, and observe, observe, observe, you will be much more likely to arrive at the true meaning, and the Bible will become interesting to you because you will be seeing new things.

Because it is God's Word, the Bible is a unique piece of literature. It is like a mine that never wears out. One can dig in it for a lifetime and not exhaust it. Likewise, when we study the Bible, we are engaging in a conversation with the infinite God. He is able, of course, to communicate with us in simple, surface terms. But God wants us to go beyond that initial conversation. He himself is neither simple nor easily grasped by just skimming surface information. He has provided us with his written Word, which is rich and deep and sometimes complex.

Both of us (Duvall and Hays) have been studying the Bible seriously for more than thirty years, yet we continue to see new things—new insights that we never noticed, new connections we never made, new truths and new understandings of God and the life he has called us to that we never saw before. This keeps the Bible fresh and exciting for us, for it keeps our relationship with God fresh and exciting. Our hope and prayer for you is that you will continue to read God's Word carefully and study the text with discipline. Make this a lifelong pursuit. The rewards are rich.

REVIEW

Below is a summary of chapters 3, 4, and 5. It serves as a review and as a reminder sheet for you to use as you observe biblical passages. It provides you with a brief summary of each item we have suggested that you look for during observation.

Things to Observe

- **Repetition of words**—Look for words and phrases that repeat.
- **Contrasts**—Look for ideas, individuals, and/or items that are contrasted with each other. Look for differences.
- **Comparisons**—Look for ideas, individuals, and/or items that are compared with each other. Look also for similarities.

- **Lists**—Anytime the text mentions more than two items, identify them as a list.
- **Cause and effect**—Look for cause-and-effect relationships.
- **Figures of speech**—Identify expressions that convey an image, using words in a sense other than the normal literal sense.
- **Conjunctions**—Notice terms that join units, like *and, but, for.* Note what they are connecting.
- **Verbs**—Note whether a verb is past, present, or future; active or passive; and the like.
- **Pronouns**—Identify the antecedent for each pronoun.
- **General to specific and specific to general**—Find the general statements that are followed by specific examples or applications of the general. Also find specific statements that are summarized by a general one.
- **Questions and answers**—Note if the text is built on a question-and-answer format.
- **Dialogue**—Note if the text includes dialogue. Identify who is speaking and to whom.
- **Purpose/result statements**—These are a more specific type of "means," often telling why. Purpose and result are similar and sometimes indistinguishable. In a purpose statement, you usually can insert the phrase "in order that." In a result clause, you usually can insert the phrase "so that."
- **Means**—Note if a sentence indicates that something was done *by means of* someone/something (answers "How?"). Usually you can insert the phrase "by means of" into the sentence.
- **Conditional clauses**—A clause can present the condition by which some action or consequence will result. Often such statements use an "if . . . then" framework (although in English the "then" is often left out).
- **Actions/roles of people**—Identify actions or roles that the text ascribes to people or encourages people to do/be.
- **Actions/roles of God**—Identify actions or roles that the text ascribes to God.
- **Emotional terms**—Does the passage use terms that have emotional energy, like kinship words ("father," "son") or words like "pleading"?
- **Tone**—What is the overall tone of the passage: happy, sad, encouraging, and so on?
- **Connections between paragraphs and episodes**—How does the passage connect to the one that precedes it and the one that follows it?

- **Story shifts and pivots**—Is the passage being used as a key to understanding a dramatic shift in the story?
- **Interchange**—Does the passage shift back and forth between two scenes or characters?
- **Chiasm**—Does the passage have any chiastic arrangements, such as a-b-c-d-c′-b′-a′?
- **Inclusio**—Does the passage open and close with similar statements or events?

ASSIGNMENTS

Assignment 5–1

Photocopy this passage (Neh. 1:1–11) and make as many observations as you can:

1The words of Nehemiah son of Hakaliah: In the month of Kislev

in the twentieth year, while I was in the citadel of Susa,

2Hanani, one of my brothers, came from Judah with some other men,

and I questioned them about the Jewish remnant

that had survived the exile, and also about Jerusalem.

3They said to me, "Those who survived the exile and are back

in the province are in great trouble and disgrace. The wall of

Jerusalem is broken down, and its gates have been burned with fire."

4When I heard these things, I sat down and wept. For some days

I mourned and fasted and prayed before the God of heaven.

5Then I said: "Lord, the God of heaven, the great and awesome God,

who keeps his covenant of love with those who love him and keep

his commandments,

6let your ear be attentive and your eyes open to hear the prayer

your servant is praying before you day and night for your servants,

the people of Israel. I confess the sins we Israelites, including

myself and my father's family, have committed against you.

[7]We have acted very wickedly toward you. We have not obeyed the

commands, decrees and laws you gave your servant Moses.

[8]Remember the instruction you gave your servant Moses, saying,

'If you are unfaithful, I will scatter you among the nations,

[9]but if you return to me and obey my commands,

then even if your exiled people are at the farthest horizon,

I will gather them from there and bring them to the place

I have chosen as a dwelling for my Name.'

[10]They are your servants and your people,

whom you redeemed by your great strength and your mighty hand.

11Lord, let your ear be attentive to the prayer of this your servant

and to the prayer of your servants who delight in revering your

name. Give your servant success today by granting him favor in the

presence of this man." I was cupbearer to the king.

Assignment 5–2

Read Mark 5:21–43, which contains two stories. The first story is about Jairus and his daughter, the second about a bleeding woman. Note that the second story interrupts the first; that is, the bleeding-woman story is presented right in the middle of the Jairus episode. This is suggestive to us. Look at the two stories and list as many direct comparisons and contrasts between the two as you can find. Read carefully! Look hard! There are many to find.

[21]When Jesus had again crossed over by boat to the other side of the lake, a large crowd gathered around him while he was by the lake. [22]Then one of the synagogue leaders, named Jairus, came, and when he saw Jesus, he fell at his feet. [23]He pleaded earnestly with him, "My little daughter is dying. Please come and put your hands on her so that she will be healed and live." [24]So Jesus went with him.

A large crowd followed and pressed around him. [25]And a woman was there who had been subject to bleeding for twelve years. [26]She had suffered a great deal under the care of many doctors and had spent all she had, yet instead of getting better she grew worse. [27]When she heard about Jesus, she came up behind him in the crowd and touched his cloak, [28]because she thought, "If I just touch his clothes, I will be healed." [29]Immediately her bleeding stopped and she felt in her body that she was freed from her suffering.

[30]At once Jesus realized that power had gone out from him. He turned around in the crowd and asked, "Who touched my clothes?"

[31]"You see the people crowding against you," his disciples answered, "and yet you can ask, 'Who touched me?' "

[32]But Jesus kept looking around to see who had done it. [33]Then the woman, knowing what had happened to her, came and fell at his feet and, trembling with fear, told him the whole truth. [34]He said to her, "Daughter, your faith has healed you. Go in peace and be freed from your suffering."

[35]While Jesus was still speaking, some people came from the house of Jairus, the synagogue leader. "Your daughter is dead," they said. "Why bother the teacher anymore?"

[36]Overhearing what they said, Jesus told him, "Don't be afraid; just believe."

[37]He did not let anyone follow him except Peter, James and John the brother of James. [38]When they came to the home of the synagogue leader, Jesus saw a commotion, with people crying and wailing loudly. [39]He went in and said to them, "Why all this commotion and wailing? The child is not dead but asleep." [40]But they laughed at him.

After he put them all out, he took the child's father and mother and the disciples who were with him, and went in where the child was. [41]He took her by the hand and said to her, "*Talitha koum!*" (which means "Little girl, I say to you, get up!"). [42]Immediately the girl stood up and began to walk around (she was twelve years old). At this they were completely astonished. [43]He gave strict orders not to let anyone know about this, and told them to give her something to eat.

Just to get you started:

Jairus	Bleeding woman
1. a man	1. a woman
2. goes to Jesus for help publicly	2. goes to Jesus for help privately

Assignment 5–3

Read the story below from Mark 11. Photocopy this page and make as many observations as you can on the text. Notice that the text has two encounters with a fig tree (vv. 12–14, 19–21) sandwiched around an event in the temple (vv. 15–18). In addition to making observations, explain how the fig tree relates to the episode in the temple.

12 The next day as they were leaving Bethany, Jesus was hungry.

13 Seeing in the distance a fig tree in leaf, he went to find out if it

had any fruit. When he reached it, he found nothing but leaves,

because it was not the season for figs.

14 Then he said to the tree, "May no one ever eat fruit from you

again." And his disciples heard him say it.

15 On reaching Jerusalem, Jesus entered the temple courts

and began driving out those who were buying and selling there.

He overturned the tables of the money changers and

the benches of those selling doves,

16and would not allow anyone to carry merchandise

through the temple courts.

17And as he taught them, he said, "Is it not written:

'My house will be called a house of prayer for all nations'?

But you have made it 'a den of robbers.' "

18The chief priests and the teachers of the law heard this

and began looking for a way to kill him, for they feared him,

because the whole crowd was amazed at his teaching.

19When evening came, Jesus and his disciples went out of the city.

20In the morning, as they went along, they saw

the fig tree withered from the roots.

21Peter remembered and said to Jesus, "Rabbi, look!

The fig tree you cursed has withered!"

PART 2

CONTENTS—*Now and Then*

In part 2 we take a closer look at context, the key to determining the meaning of the Bible. We start with the context of the Bible itself. In chapter 6 we explore the historical-cultural context, or the background, of the Bible. We look closely at the world of the Bible to see how God spoke to ancient people living in particular cultures and facing specific situations. Once we understand what God was saying to them, we can understand more clearly what he is saying to us.

We spend time in chapter 7 dealing with a context that is often overlooked—our own context as contemporary readers. What do we bring with us to the text? Here we look at the issue of preunderstanding—all of the ideas and experiences we bring to the task of interpretation. How do we handle our preunderstanding in a way that does not allow it to blind us to what God is trying to say?

In chapter 8 we learn how to discern the literary context—the texts that surround the passage we are studying.

We close this unit by discussing a topic that is closely related to both literary and historical-cultural context. In chapter 9 you will learn how to do word studies properly (i.e., in context). By the end of part 2, you should have a good feel for the importance of context, both ours and that of the biblical writers.

CHAPTER 6

THE HISTORICAL-CULTURAL CONTEXT

INTRODUCTION

If you had to choose your favorite character in the Bible, some of you might choose the apostle Paul. His passion for serving Jesus Christ continues to challenge us. In our New Testament we have thirteen letters traditionally attributed to Paul. In the last chapter of the last letter he wrote (2 Timothy), Paul verbalizes his feelings about coming to the end of his life:

> [6]For I am already being poured out like a drink offering, and the time for my departure is near. [7]I have fought the good fight, I have finished the race, I have kept the faith. [8]Now there is in store for me the crown of righteousness, which the Lord, the righteous Judge, will award to me on that day—and not only to me, but also to all who have longed for his appearing. (2 Tim. 4:6–8)

As Paul concludes the letter, he repeats a simple message to Timothy, his friend and coworker. "Do your best to come to me quickly," he writes in 4:9. Then in 4:21 he adds, "Do your best to get here before winter." We can tell that Paul wants Timothy to come visit him, but only an understanding of the historical-cultural context lying behind these words can reveal the depth and emotion of Paul's plea.

Most evangelical scholars believe Timothy is ministering in Ephesus while Paul is imprisoned in Rome. They are hundreds of miles apart. Travel by ship was considered dangerous from mid-September through the end of May and was completely closed down from early November to around early March. Both Paul and Timothy know this, of course. If Paul sent the letter of 2 Timothy by Tychicus in the summer, Timothy probably has little time to make the long journey to Rome. The historical background of this passage helps us see what Paul is really saying to his young friend: "Put things in order in Ephesus and get on a ship as soon as you can. If you don't leave now before winter sets in, the shipping lanes will shut down and you won't arrive in time. Timothy, do your best to get here before they put me to death. Come quickly, my friend, before it's too late." Knowing the historical-cultural context of this passage makes it come alive with emotion and intensity. Paul is not merely asking Timothy to come visit. He is more like a father pleading for his son to come to him before he dies.

Context takes two major forms: literary context and historical-cultural context (commonly referred to as "background").

To grasp God's Word, we must understand the meaning of the text in context and apply that meaning to our lives. Context takes two major forms: literary context and historical-cultural context (commonly referred to as "background"). In this chapter you will learn about historical-cultural context as we ask and answer some important questions. Why do we need to bother with studying the historical-cultural background of a passage? Is it really all that important? What exactly is involved in studying historical-cultural context? Are there any pitfalls along the way? What tools are available to help us get the job done? Our goal in this chapter is to show you how to study the historical-cultural context of a passage and to persuade you that knowing the background of a text can help clarify its meaning and reveal its relevance to your life.

WHY BOTHER WITH HISTORICAL-CULTURAL CONTEXT?

In his commentary on the background of the Bible, Craig Keener reminds us that God did not dictate most of the Bible in the first person. He did not say, "Because I'm God I will speak directly to everybody in all times and cultures."[1] Instead, God (the

1. Craig S. Keener, *The IVP Bible Background Commentary: New Testament* (Downers Grove, IL: InterVarsity Press, 1993), 24.

ultimate source) spoke through the human writers of Scripture (the immediate source) to address the real-life needs of people at a particular time in a particular culture. This is how God chose to speak.[2]

Please don't misunderstand what we are saying here. God has given us eternal principles in his Word that apply to every person of every age in every culture. Our goal in *Grasping God's Word* is to teach you how to discover and live out those theological truths. We are not questioning ***whether*** God has given us eternally relevant principles; we are simply noting ***how*** he has done so. We believe that the way we approach the Bible (i.e., the way we listen to God) should match how God gave us the Bible (i.e., the way God chose to speak). Otherwise, we will likely misunderstand what God is trying to say to us.

The way we approach the Bible (i.e., the way we listen to God) should match how God gave us the Bible (i.e., the way God chose to speak).

Since God spoke his message in specific, historical situations (i.e., to people living in particular places, speaking particular languages, adopting a particular way of life), we should take the ancient historical-cultural situation seriously. The bottom line is that we cannot simply ignore "those people living back then" and jump directly to what God wants to say to us. Why not? Again, because the way we listen to God (our interpretive approach) must honor the way God chose to communicate. We should not be so arrogant and prideful as to think that God cared nothing about the original audience but was merely using them to get a message to us.

The truth of the matter is that each passage of Scripture was "God's Word to other people before it became God's Word to us."[3] God cared deeply about the original hearers and spoke to them within their own historical-cultural situation. God also cares deeply about us and wants to speak to us. The time-bound message of Scripture contains eternally relevant principles that we can discover and live out.

Think again about how the Interpretive Journey moves from the meaning of the text for the biblical audience across the river of differences (e.g., time, place, culture, situation) by means of the principlizing bridge to the application of those theological principles in our lives.

---

2. We are indebted to Grant R. Osborne, *The Hermeneutical Spiral: A Comprehensive Introduction to Biblical Interpretation*, 2nd ed. (Downers Grove, IL: InterVarsity Press, 2006), 166, for the terms "ultimate source" and "immediate source" to describe the divine-human authorship of Scripture.

3. William W. Klein, Craig L. Blomberg, and Robert L. Hubbard Jr., *Introduction to Biblical Interpretation*, 4th ed. (Grand Rapids: Zondervan, 2017), 312.

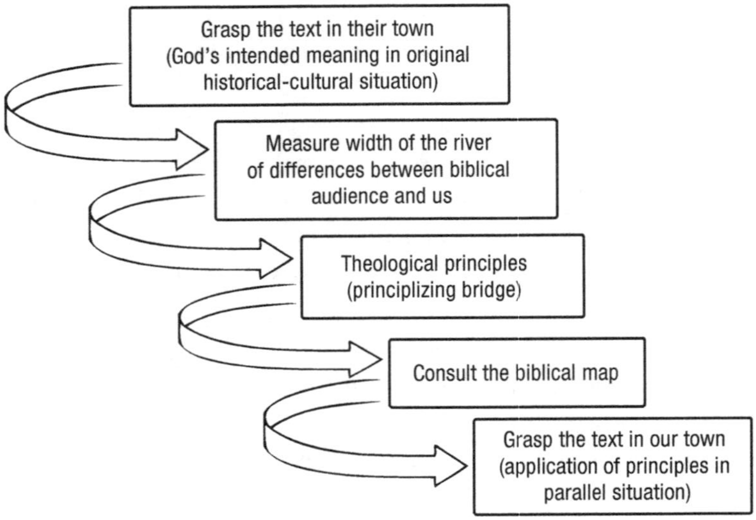

Back to our question: Why bother to become familiar with the original historical-cultural context? We do so because it offers us a window into what God was saying to the biblical audience. Since we live in a very different context, we must recapture God's original intended meaning as reflected in the text and framed by the ancient historical-cultural context. Once we understand the meaning of the text in its original context, we can apply it to our lives in ways that will be just as relevant. God's Word is eternally relevant. Our task as students of his Word is to discover that relevance by doing our contextual homework.

For the interpretation of any biblical text to be valid, it must be consistent with the historical-cultural context of that passage.

This leads us to a crucial interpretive principle: *For our interpretation of any biblical text to be valid, it must be consistent with the historical-cultural context of that text.*[4] If our interpretation would not have made sense back then, we are probably on the wrong track. Fee and Stuart rightly emphasize that "the true meaning of the biblical text for us is what God originally intended it to mean when it was first spoken."[5] We must first determine what a text meant "in their town" before we can determine what it means and how we should apply that meaning to "our town" (i.e., our own time and culture). Our *goal*, then, is to understand the historical-cultural context of the biblical passage as clearly as possible in order to grasp the meaning of the passage.

4. Cf. Klein, Blomberg, and Hubbard, 312.

5. Gordon D. Fee and Douglas K. Stuart, *How to Read the Bible for All Its Worth*, 4th ed. (Grand Rapids: Zondervan, 2014), 35.

WHAT IS HISTORICAL-CULTURAL CONTEXT?

What exactly do we mean by *historical-cultural context*? Generally speaking, this kind of context involves the biblical writer, the biblical audience, and any historical-cultural elements touched on by the passage itself. Historical-cultural context relates to just about anything outside the text that will help you understand the text itself (e.g., what life was like for the Israelites as they wandered in the wilderness, what the Pharisees believed about the Sabbath, where Paul was when he wrote Philippians). Literary context, as we will see in chapter 8, relates to the context within the book (e.g., the form a passage takes, the flow of argument within the book, and the meaning of the words and sentences that surround the passage you are studying). In this chapter we will cite resources you can use to identify the historical-cultural context, but first we want to illustrate our definition above with a few examples. Again, we need to know more about the biblical writer, the biblical audience, and background elements within the passage. We begin with the biblical writer.

The Biblical Writer

Because God chose to work through human authors as the immediate source of his inspired Word, the more we know about the human author the better. Try to find out as much as you can about the writer's background. When studying one of Paul's letters, for example, it is helpful to know that before the Lord radically changed his life, he used to get authorization from the Jewish high priest allowing him to imprison Christians. He persecuted the church out of a misdirected zeal to serve God. This explains why the early Christians feared Paul for a time even after his conversion: "All those who heard him [preach] were astonished and asked, 'Isn't he the man who raised havoc in Jerusalem among those who call on this name? And hasn't he come here to take them as prisoners to the chief priests?'" (Acts 9:21). This also helps us understand why Paul describes himself as "the worst of sinners" in 1 Timothy 1:16. We don't often think of Paul, a man whom God used to change the world, as struggling with horrible memories of the things he did before he met Christ. Paul's life is certainly a portrait of God's grace.

Still thinking about the biblical author's background, consider Amos, a prophet who preached around 760 BC. Although Amos was from Tekoa in Judah (the southern kingdom), God called him to preach in Israel, the northern kingdom. Amos says about himself, "I was neither a prophet nor the son of a prophet, but I was a shepherd, and I also took care of sycamore-fig trees" (Amos 7:14). Amos was not being paid to be a prophet, nor was he following in his dad's footsteps. The prophetic task was completely new to him. This astute farmer answered God's call to proclaim his message to a spiritually sick people facing God's judgment.

Along with knowing something about the author's background, you may also ask, "When did he write and what kind of ministry did he have?" While we are talking about eighth-century BC prophets, do you remember Hosea's infamous wife, Gomer? Have you thought about how Hosea's marriage was linked to his ministry? His heartbreaking marriage to Gomer became a vehicle for understanding and expressing the spiritual adultery of Israel against God. Just as Gomer had rejected Hosea, so Israel had rejected her true God, Yahweh, to pursue pagan gods.

Along with knowing about the writer's background and ministry, you will also want to understand more about the specific relationship between the writer and the people he was addressing. You can tell from the tone and the content of Galatians, for instance, that Paul is not happy with the churches of Galatia and their movement toward a different gospel. He even omits his customary thanksgiving at the beginning of his letter and moves directly into a rebuke. In contrast, Paul praises the Thessalonians for their faith and perseverance in spite of his premature separation from them as a result of persecution. He reminds them of his motherly (1 Thess. 2:7) and fatherly (2:11) love for them and reassures them of his longing to see them again.

What kind of relationship did Jonah have with his primary audience, the Ninevites? About the same time that Amos and Hosea were warning Israel of God's judgment soon to occur at the hands of the ominous Assyrians, Jonah was sent to warn Nineveh. What difference does it make to know that Nineveh is the capital city of Assyria? It helps to see that at the heart of the story lies Jonah's contempt for the Ninevites (Assyrians) and his fear that God might act with compassion toward his enemies. God doesn't disappoint him.

Perhaps the most important thing to know about the biblical writers is why they are writing. Why does the author of 1 and 2 Chronicles, for example, repeat much of Samuel and Kings? The answer lies in the writer's purpose. The chronicler (perhaps Ezra) is writing for Israel *after* the exile (i.e., for the restored community). He is trying to show that God is still very much interested in his people even after judging them by the exile. For example, the chronicler seems to idealize David and Solomon by omitting anything that might tarnish their image (e.g., David's sin with Bathsheba). In this way the writer reassures his audience that although God has judged his people, he still loves them and wants to use them to accomplish his purposes.

Acts offers another example of the need to know the writer's purposes. If you are studying Acts 28, you may wonder why Luke ends the book so abruptly after spending almost two whole chapters describing Paul's voyage to Rome. Why does he fail to mention anything about the outcome of Paul's trial? The most likely reason goes back to Luke's purpose in writing. He wants to show the triumphant movement of the gospel from Jerusalem, the birthplace of the church, to Rome, the center of the empire. Once he accomplishes his purpose, he wraps up the project quickly. What matters most to Luke is the success of the gospel message, not the personal history of one of its messengers.

Let's review. When we think about historical-cultural context, we first need to consider the biblical writer. What is the writer's background? Where does he come from? When does he write? What kind of ministry does he have? What is his relationship with the people he addresses? Finally, why is he writing? Answers to these kinds of questions will give you insight into the circumstances of the biblical writer and clarify the meaning of what he has written.

The Biblical Audience

Discovering the historical-cultural context also involves knowing something about the biblical audience and their circumstances. Take Mark's gospel as an example. Mark makes a point of emphasizing the cross of Christ and the demands of discipleship throughout his gospel. Many scholars believe that Mark's original audience was the church in the vicinity of Rome and that Mark was preparing them for the persecution they would soon face at the hands of Emperor Nero during the mid-60s AD. To encourage these believers to remain faithful in the midst of suffering, Mark stresses how Jesus remained faithful during his time of suffering.

When you read the Old Testament prophets, you need to know something of the general circumstances of the biblical audience to make sense of the prophetic message. When studying Jeremiah, for example, it helps to know that his prophetic ministry began about 627 BC and ended a short time after 586 BC. This means that Jeremiah witnessed the revival under King Josiah, the fall of Assyria, the rise of Babylon, the first siege of Jerusalem (598/597 BC), and the destruction of his nation in 587/586 BC. Jeremiah preached against the sins of Judah and predicted the destruction of Jerusalem and the Babylonian exile.

New Testament letters are situational or occasional, meaning that they were written to address specific situations faced by the churches.

Yet Jeremiah also spoke powerful words of encouragement and hope during the dark days of the final siege of Jerusalem. Note Jeremiah 29:11: "'For I know the plans I have for you,' declares the Lord, 'plans to prosper you and not to harm you, plans to give you hope and a future.'" These words form part of a letter that Jeremiah wrote to people already experiencing God's discipline—the exiles of 597 BC. The historical context of this verse will surely influence how we understand its meaning. In spite of the devastating consequences of Judah's disobedience, God's final word is not judgment but hope. Nevertheless, even though God's deliverance is certain, it will not be immediate (see 29:10).

Most, if not all, New Testament letters are situational or occasional, meaning that they were written to address specific situations faced by the churches. Colossians, for example, is written to a group of believers battling a false teaching that gave Christ a place, but not the supreme place that is rightfully his (Col. 2:4–5, 8, 16–23). Paul writes to refute this false teaching by emphasizing the absolute supremacy of Christ (1:15–20; 2:9–15).

In a similar fashion, John wrote his first letter to Christians wrestling with what many scholars believe was an early form of Gnosticism. Central to this heresy was the belief that spirit is entirely good and matter is entirely evil. You can probably guess some of the implications of this line of thinking: Christ wasn't a real human being; a person could either treat their material body harshly or indulge it; salvation meant escape from the body and was accomplished by means of a special knowledge (*gnōsis* is the Greek word translated "knowledge"). In the case of 1 John, knowing the historical-cultural context will clarify the main themes of the letter: the genuine incarnation of Christ (i.e., God really did become a human being), the need to walk in the light rather than in immorality, and the need for love (versus the arrogance of those who claimed to possess the special knowledge).

Other Historical-Cultural Elements

As noted earlier, historical-cultural context involves the biblical writer and the biblical audience, plus any historical-cultural elements touched on by your passage. Sometimes it is difficult to know much about the biblical author and the audience or their specific circumstances. Often you will focus more on the historical, social, geographical, religious, political, and economic elements that shape your passage. Here are a few examples of how understanding these elements can shed light on the meaning of your passage.

> Economic and political issues are important elements of the historical-cultural context.

Sometimes knowing more about the geography or topography assumed by the text can help you grasp its meaning. Jesus starts his parable of the good Samaritan with the statement: "A man was going down from Jerusalem to Jericho" (Luke 10:30). You would certainly go down from Jerusalem to Jericho, descending from about 2,500 feet above sea level to over 700 feet below sea level. In addition, the trip would not be a walk in the park. The distance is about fifteen miles and would take you through some rugged desert country that offered plenty of hiding places for thieves. Knowing the geography helps us understand how easy it would have been to pass by the dying man and how troublesome it would have been to be a loving neighbor.

One of the most productive areas of background study relates to social customs. If you are studying Ephesians 5:21–6:9, for example, you need to know something about Greco-Roman household codes to make sense of your passage. These rules were developed primarily to instruct the head of the household about how to deal with members of his family. The apostle Paul uses the household code concept, but he transforms it in powerful ways. For instance, Greco-Roman codes told husbands to make their wives submit, but they never listed love as a duty of the husband. In Ephesians 5:25 Paul breaks the mold when he instructs husbands to "love your wives, just as Christ loved the church and gave himself up for her." Paul's exhortation for all members of the household to "submit to one another out of reverence for Christ" (5:21) would have been even more radical.

Often in the Scriptures social customs are loaded with religious significance. Note again the parable of the good Samaritan. Jesus' original audience would have been shocked and insulted by the fact that Jesus has the two Jewish religious leaders doing nothing to help the wounded traveler, while the Samaritan proves to be the man's neighbor (and the story's hero). We know this because in that culture Jews despised Samaritans, who were considered half-breeds.

In the parable of the prodigal son, we think nothing of the father running to greet his returning son. But when we learn that elderly Jewish men were considered much too dignified to run, we begin to see that Jesus is telling us how God feels about and responds to sinners when they come home. If you have ever been in the far country spiritually, you'll be glad to know that when you decide to return home, God stands ready to "ditch his dignity" and run to meet you.

The book of Ruth provides another example of how social and religious elements interconnect. To understand this book, you need to know something about the role of the kinsman-redeemer. After Naomi and her daughter-in-law Ruth both lose their husbands, they meet Boaz, who turns out to be their kinsman-redeemer. As strange as this may sound to us, Boaz could legally preserve the family name and provide an heir for Naomi's two dead sons by marrying Ruth, which he does. It is interesting that Ruth gives birth to Obed, who in turn becomes the father of Jesse. Jesse then becomes the father of David—King David. At the end of this genealogy, you will find Jesus Christ, the "son of David" (cf. Matt. 1:1, 6, 16).

Sometimes your passage will touch on economic issues. On his second missionary tour (Acts 15:39–18:22), Paul plants a church at Philippi. There Paul and Silas meet a slave girl who has a spirit by which she predicts the future. She continues to bother the missionary team until Paul finally commands the spirit to come out of her. Her enraged owners then drag Paul and Silas into the marketplace, where the magistrates order them to be stripped, beaten, and later imprisoned for causing trouble. All this happens because the demon-possessed slave girl has been earning a lot of money for her owners. When the evil spirit left the girl, the money left the owners' pockets, and thus they take their revenge on Paul and Silas.

You also need to pay attention to political issues that may surface in your passage. In the Acts 16 episode just mentioned, notice what happens next to Paul and Silas. After spending time in prison (where God does some exciting things), the magistrates send word that the missionaries may leave the city. Here is the rest of the story (Acts 16:36–40):

> [36]The jailer told Paul, "The magistrates have ordered that you and Silas be released. Now you can leave. Go in peace."
>
> [37]But Paul said to the officers: "They beat us publicly without a trial, even though we are Roman citizens, and threw us into prison. And now do they want to get rid of us quietly? No! Let them come themselves and escort us out."
>
> [38]The officers reported this to the magistrates, and when they heard that Paul and Silas were Roman citizens, they were alarmed. [39]They came to appease them and escorted them from the prison, requesting them to leave the city.
> [40]After Paul and Silas came out of the prison, they went to Lydia's house, where they met with the brothers and sisters and encouraged them. Then they left.

Since it was illegal to beat publicly and imprison a Roman citizen, especially without a trial, the Roman officials act quickly to apologize for their actions. Paul and Silas probably demand an escort out of town in order to make a public statement about their innocence for the benefit of the church in Philippi.

Knowing the historical-cultural background of the Bible makes it come alive with power and relevance.

Historical-cultural context includes information about the author and the audience—their background, circumstances, and relationship—as well as geographical, social, religious, economic, and political elements connected to the passage. Some people are convinced that background studies are tedious ways of making the Bible less relevant. We have found the opposite to be true. When we take time to understand the context, the message comes alive and explodes with relevance (sometimes more than we can take). We are able to see that God was speaking to real people struggling with real life, and that he continues to speak to us.

Before citing various resources one can use to study the historical-cultural context, we want to mention a few of the dangers associated with studying this type of material.

DANGERS ASSOCIATED WITH STUDYING BACKGROUND

While the greatest danger is ignoring the historical-cultural context, there are also dangers associated with studying it. To begin with, you need to *watch out for inaccurate background information*. Take Matthew 19:23–24 as an example:

> [23]Then Jesus said to his disciples, "Truly I tell you, it is hard for someone who is rich to enter the kingdom of heaven. [24]Again I tell you, it is easier for a camel to go through the eye of a needle than for someone who is rich to enter the kingdom of God."

You may have heard it explained that the "camel's gate" was a small gate in the wall of Jerusalem through which a camel could squeeze if its load was removed and the animal got down on its knees. The problem with this explanation is that there is no evidence for this kind of gate. The "eye of a needle" meant essentially what it means today (i.e., the eye of a sewing needle). Jesus is using the largest animal in Palestine and one of the smallest openings to make a forceful statement about how hard it is for the rich and powerful to enter God's kingdom.

This is just one example of how inaccurate information can get passed down through generations of preachers and teachers. Just because background material makes a great sermon illustration does not mean it is true. Your information will only be as good as your resources, and not all resources are created equal.

A second danger associated with studying historical-cultural context is that of *elevating the background of the text above the meaning of the text*. When studying the parable of the Pharisee and the tax collector in Luke 18:9–14, for instance, you may be tempted to spend all your time learning about Pharisees and tax collectors. You certainly need to know something about these two groups and their role and reputation in Jesus' day. Yet you don't want to let your fascination with background information cause you to miss the point—God judges the proud and exalts the humble.

> **Just because background material makes a great sermon illustration does not mean it is true.**

Or take the example of King Agrippa and Bernice in Acts 25:13–26:32. It is interesting to know the family history of King Agrippa, but you cannot afford to let that interest cause you to lose sight of Luke's message. Luke portrays Paul as fulfilling the Lord's statement recorded in Acts 9:15 that he would bear witness before gentiles and their kings. Colorful characters like Agrippa and Bernice are not meant to overshadow the triumphant gospel of Jesus Christ. Keep in mind as you study historical-cultural context that there is a difference between the context of the passage and the meaning of the passage. We study background not to lose ourselves in a maze of historical trivia but to grasp the meaning of the passage more clearly.

Finally, we caution you *not to let yourself slowly evolve into nothing more than a walking database of ancient facts.* Don't lose your interpretive heart in your quest for information to deepen your understanding of the text. Keep your study of the background of the Bible in proper perspective. We study the historical-cultural context not as an end in itself, but as a tool to help us grasp and apply the meaning of the biblical text.

We must guard against equating the historical-cultural background with the meaning of the text.

In spite of these three dangers, however, the greatest danger by far is assuming that we do not need to know any background information to understand the Bible. You cannot begin the Interpretive Journey apart from step 1—grasping the text in its own town. And you cannot grasp that text in its town without knowing the historical-cultural context. We turn our attention now to the resources that can help you identify the historical-cultural context of a passage.

TOOLS FOR IDENTIFYING HISTORICAL-CULTURAL CONTEXT

To identify the historical-cultural context, you need to (1) grasp the historical-cultural context of *the book* that contains your passage and (2) recognize the specific historical-cultural context of *the passage* itself.

Historical-Cultural Context of the Entire Book

As we have explained above, grasping the historical-cultural context of the entire book means finding out about the biblical author and audience as well as the general setting for the book. The following questions will help you get started:

- Who was the author?
- What was his background?
- When did he write?
- What was the nature of his ministry?
- What kind of relationship did he have with the audience?
- Why was he writing?
- Who was the biblical audience?
- What were their circumstances?

- How was their relationship to God?
- What kind of relationship did they have with each other?
- What was happening at the time the book was written?
- Are there any other historical-cultural factors that might shed light on the book?

To find answers to these questions, you need to become familiar with some basic tools. Since we cannot possibly list all the available resources, we will mention only a few of the most reliable ones for students at this level. To understand the historical-cultural context of the entire book, we suggest you consult Bible handbooks, introductions and surveys of the Old and New Testaments, and especially good commentaries.

Bible Handbooks

Bible handbooks usually begin with general articles about the Bible and the world of the Bible (e.g., the nature of Scripture, life in Bible times). They normally include a brief introduction to each book of the Bible and an equally brief running commentary on the entire biblical text. Articles on subjects of interest are interspersed throughout. You will probably want to go beyond what is provided by a Bible handbook, but they offer a good place to begin getting acquainted with the historical-cultural context of your book.

For example, if you are studying the book of James and decide to consult a Bible handbook, what can you expect to find? The introduction to James may include a concise discussion of the authorship of the book, the date of writing, the recipients, and the main themes. As you can tell from the example below, the commentary on the text is usually brief:

> **1:5–8** *Wisdom*
>
> If we need wisdom (perhaps to handle various trials), we should ask God, trusting in his kind and generous character, and he will give us wisdom (1:5). If we doubt, however, we can be compared to a storm-tossed wave of the sea (1:6). Such an unstable, "double-minded" (lit. "double-souled") person shouldn't expect to receive anything from the Lord (1:7–8). The key to godly wisdom has always been a healthy fear of or trust in the Lord.[6]

6. J. Daniel Hays and J. Scott Duvall, eds., *The Baker Illustrated Bible Handbook* (Grand Rapids: Baker, 2011), 928.

We recommend the following Bible handbooks:

Alexander, Pat, and David Alexander, eds. *Zondervan Handbook to the Bible*. 5th ed. Grand Rapids: Zondervan, 2017.

B&H Editorial Staff, eds. *Holman Illustrated Bible Handbook*. Nashville: B&H, 2012.

Hays, J. Daniel, and J. Scott Duvall, eds. *The Baker Illustrated Bible Handbook*. Grand Rapids: Baker, 2011.

Old Testament and New Testament Introductions and Surveys

These resources supply detailed background information on each book of the Bible as well as an overview of the book's contents. Usually they discuss authorship, date, recipients, situation, purpose, and more. Generally speaking, introductions offer more technical discussions of the background issues and spend less time on the actual content of the books, while surveys touch on background issues and focus more on content.

If you consult a survey of the New Testament to look for background information on the book of Revelation, for example, here is what you are likely to find:

- definition of the term *revelation*
- discussion of authorship
- discussion of the two main options for the date of writing
- discussion of the recipients and their situation
- statement of the main theme or purpose of the book
- description of the apocalyptic style of Revelation
- explanation of the four main approaches to Revelation
- summary of specific issues (e.g., rapture, millennium)
- detailed outline of the book
- overview of the contents of the book
- bibliography for further reading

You will also notice as you look at the following list that introductions and surveys deal with either the Old Testament or the New Testament, not both. These types of books normally go into greater detail than Bible handbooks, so there is simply too much information to fit into a single volume.

Achtemeier, Paul, Joel Green, and Marianne Meye Thompson. *Introducing the New Testament*. Grand Rapids: Eerdmans, 2001.

Arnold, Bill, and Bryan Beyer. *Encountering the Old Testament: A Christian Survey*. 3rd ed. Grand Rapids: Baker, 2015.

Berding, Kenneth, and Matt Williams, eds. *What the New Testament Authors Really Cared About*. Grand Rapids: Kregel, 2008.

Burge, Gary M., and Gene L. Green. *The New Testament in Antiquity*. 2nd ed. Grand Rapids: Zondervan Academic, 2020.

Carson, D. A., and Douglas J. Moo. *An Introduction to the New Testament*. 2nd ed. Grand Rapids: Zondervan, 2005.

Dearman, J. Andrew, and Robert L. Hubbard Jr. *Introducing the Old Testament*. Grand Rapids: Eerdmans, 2018.

deSilva, David. *An Introduction to the New Testament: Contexts, Methods & Ministry Formation*. 2nd ed. Downers Grove, IL: InterVarsity Press, 2018.

Elwell, Walter, and Robert Yarbrough. *Encountering the New Testament*. 2nd ed. Grand Rapids: Baker, 2005.

Goldingay, John. *An Introduction to the Old Testament: Exploring Text, Approaches & Issues*. Downers Grove, IL: InterVarsity Press, 2015.

Gundry, Robert H. *A Survey of the New Testament*. 5th ed. Grand Rapids: Zondervan, 2012.

Guthrie, Donald. *New Testament Introduction*. 4th ed. Downers Grove, IL: InterVarsity Press, 1990.

Hagner, Donald A. *The New Testament: A Historical and Theological Introduction*. Grand Rapids: Baker Academic, 2012.

Harrison, R. K. *Introduction to the Old Testament*. Peabody, MA: Hendrickson, 2004.

Hess, Richard S. *The Old Testament: A Historical, Theological, and Critical Introduction*. Grand Rapids: Baker Academic, 2016.

Hill, Andrew E., and John H. Walton. *A Survey of the Old Testament*. 3rd ed. Grand Rapids: Zondervan, 2009.

House, Paul R., and Eric Mitchell. *Old Testament Survey*. 2nd ed. Nashville: B&H, 2007.

Köstenberger, Andreas J., L. Scott Kellum, and Charles L. Quarles. *The Cradle, the Cross, and the Crown: An Introduction to the New Testament*. 2nd ed. Nashville: B&H, 2016.

Lea, Thomas D., and David Alan Black. *The New Testament: Its Background and Message*. 2nd ed. Nashville: B&H, 2003.

Longman, Tremper, III, and Raymond B. Dillard. *An Introduction to the Old Testament*. 2nd ed. Grand Rapids: Zondervan, 2006.

Powell, Mark Allan. *Introducing the New Testament: A Historical, Literary, and Theological Survey*. 2nd ed. Grand Rapids: Baker, 2018.

Van Pelt, Miles V., ed. *A Biblical-Theological Introduction to the Old Testament: The Gospel Promised*. Wheaton, IL: Crossway, 2016.

Walton, John H., and Andrew E. Hill. *Old Testament Today*. 2nd ed. Grand Rapids: Zondervan, 2014.

Wright, N. T., and Michael F. Bird. *The New Testament in Its World: An Introduction to the History, Literature, and Theology of the First Christians*. Grand Rapids: Zondervan Academic, 2019.

Commentaries

In most cases a good commentary will be your best bet for up-to-date, detailed information about the historical-cultural context of the book that contains your passage. For example, in Gordon Fee's 462-page commentary on Philippians in the New International Commentary on the New Testament series, he devotes more than fifty pages to introductory matters. He discusses ancient letter writing, the city of Philippi and its people, the situation of the church, the situation of Paul, the argument or thought flow of the letter, and theological themes. He also provides a detailed outline of the book. By the time you finish the entire discussion, you will have a great sense of the historical-cultural context of Paul's letter to the Philippians.

Because commentaries are always written from a particular point of view and since they differ in quality and scope, it is always a good idea to consult more than one commentary. We recommend that you consult a commentary in one of the following series as you begin your study. There are certainly other fine commentaries (and some are not attached to a series), but this is a solid place to start.

Apollos Old Testament Commentary. Leicester: Apollos.
Baker Exegetical Commentary. Grand Rapids: Baker.
Bible Speaks Today. Downers Grove, IL: InterVarsity Press.
Expositor's Bible Commentary. Grand Rapids: Zondervan.
IVP New Testament Commentary. Downers Grove, IL: InterVarsity Press.
New American Commentary. Nashville: B&H.
New International Commentary on the New Testament. Grand Rapids: Eerdmans.
New International Commentary on the Old Testament. Grand Rapids: Eerdmans.
New Interpreter's Bible Commentary. Nashville: Abingdon.
NIV Application Commentary. Grand Rapids: Zondervan.
Pillar New Testament Commentary. Grand Rapids: Eerdmans.
Story of God Bible Commentary. Grand Rapids: Zondervan Academic.
Tyndale New Testament Commentaries. Downers Grove, IL: InterVarsity Press.
Tyndale Old Testament Commentaries. Downers Grove, IL: InterVarsity Press.
Word Biblical Commentary. Grand Rapids: Zondervan Academic.
Zondervan Exegetical Commentary on the New Testament. Grand Rapids: Zondervan Academic.

Historical-Cultural Context of the Passage Itself

After you have a good sense of the background of the book that contains your passage, you need to identify the historical-cultural context of the passage itself. This involves examining any elements of history and culture that are connected to or mentioned in the passage (e.g., geography, politics, religion, economics, family life, social customs). To accomplish this, we recommend using Bible atlases, Bible dictionaries or encyclopedias, commentaries, background commentaries, Old and New Testament histories, and special studies on ancient life and culture.

Bible Atlases

If you want to learn more about the people, places, and events mentioned in your passage, take a look at a Bible atlas. You will find colorful maps of the land, pictures of many of the important sites, helpful charts of political and religious leaders, discussions of the various periods of biblical history, and more.

Let's say that you want to study the last week of Jesus' earthly ministry, a week commonly known as Passion Week. You will need a map of Jerusalem during the New Testament period so that you can see where many of the significant events took place. A good Bible atlas will include such a map.

Do you see the Mount of Olives, the place from which Jesus entered Jerusalem on Palm Sunday? Can you locate the traditional site of the upper room, where Jesus shared the Passover meal with his disciples on Thursday night? Where is the garden of Gethsemane, where Jesus prayed and was later arrested? If you want to know where the Jewish and Roman rulers tried Jesus, you can see many of the traditional locations on the map (e.g., the house of the high priest). You can also find the traditional site outside the city walls where Jesus was crucified (i.e., Golgotha).

Here is a list of some reliable Bible atlases:

Aharoni, Yohanan, et al. *The Carta Bible Atlas*. 5th ed. Jerusalem: Carta, 2011.

Beck, John A. *Discovery House Bible Atlas*. Grand Rapids: Discovery House, 2015.

Beitzel, Barry J. *The New Moody Atlas of the Bible*. Chicago: Moody, 2009.

Brisco, Thomas V. *Holman Bible Atlas: A Complete Guide to the Expansive Geography of Biblical History*. Nashville: B&H, 2014.

Currid, John D., and David P. Barrett. *Crossway ESV Bible Atlas*. Wheaton, IL: Crossway, 2010.

Curtis, Adrian. *Oxford Bible Atlas*. 4th ed. Oxford: Oxford University Press, 2007.

Rasmussen, Carl G. *Zondervan Atlas of the Bible*. Rev. ed. Grand Rapids: Zondervan, 2009.

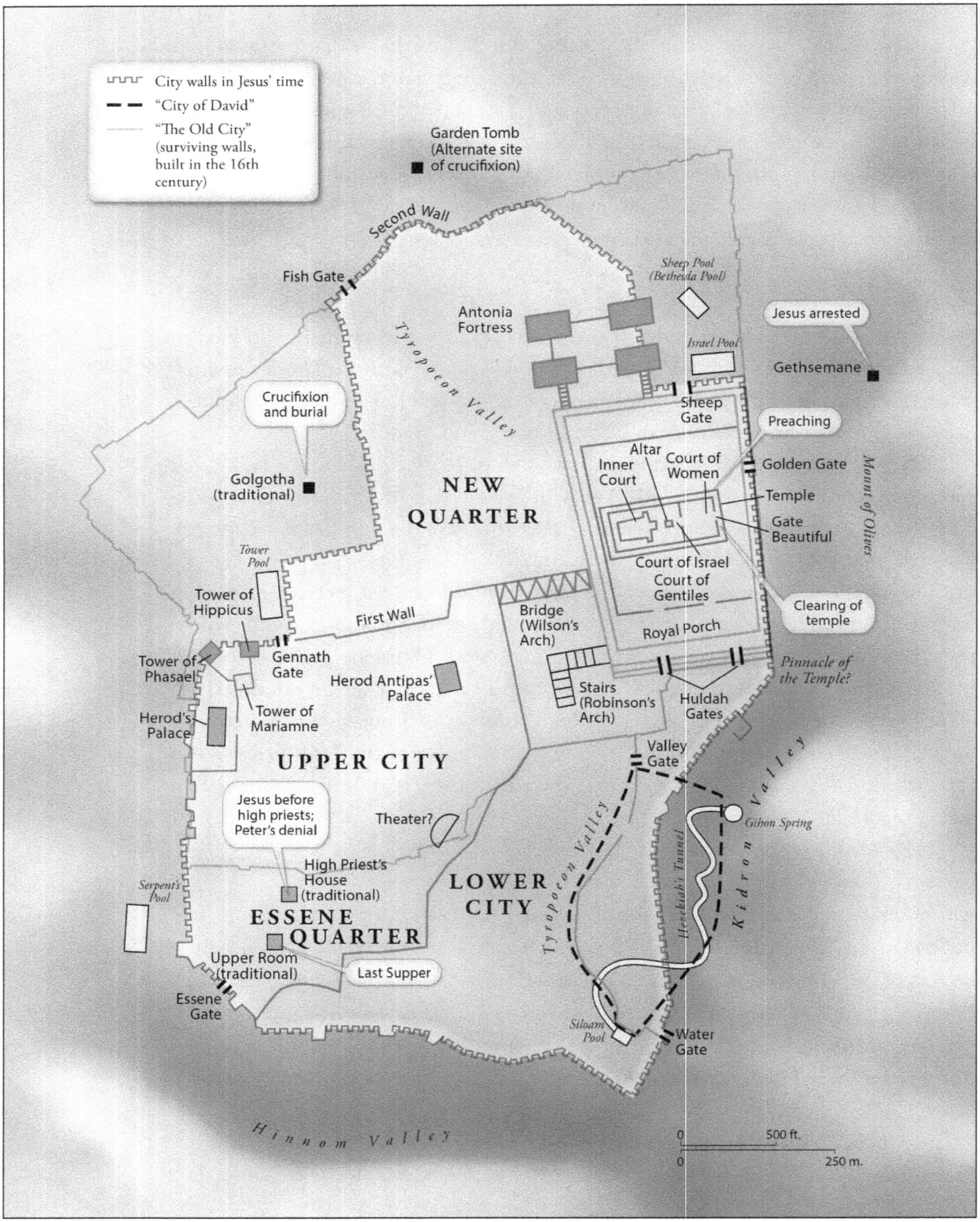
City walls in Jesus' time
"City of David"
"The Old City" (surviving walls, built in the 16th century)
Garden Tomb (Alternate site of crucifixion)
Second Wall
Fish Gate
Sheep Pool (Bethesda Pool)
Antonia Fortress
Tyropoeon Valley
Jesus arrested
Israel Pool
Gethsemane
Crucifixion and burial
Sheep Gate
Preaching
Altar
Inner Court
Court of Women
Golden Gate
Golgotha (traditional)
NEW QUARTER
Temple
Gate Beautiful
Mount of Olives
Court of Israel
Court of Gentiles
Tower Pool
Tower of Hippicus
First Wall
Bridge (Wilson's Arch)
Clearing of temple
Royal Porch
Tower of Phasael
Gennath Gate
Herod Antipas' Palace
Pinnacle of the Temple?
Stairs (Robinson's Arch)
Huldah Gates
Herod's Palace
Tower of Mariamne
Valley Gate
UPPER CITY
Kidron Valley
Jesus before high priests; Peter's denial
Theater?
Gihon Spring
Tyropoeon Valley
Hezekiah's Tunnel
High Priest's House (traditional)
Serpent's Pool
LOWER CITY
ESSENE QUARTER
Upper Room (traditional)
Last Supper
Essene Gate
Siloam Pool
Water Gate
Hinnom Valley
0 500 ft.
0 250 m.

Bible Dictionaries and Encyclopedias

This is the place to go when you need information about a particular topic mentioned in your passage. For instance, if you want to know more about the garden of Gethsemane, consult a Bible dictionary or encyclopedia. These resources cover a full range of biblical topics and arrange the topics alphabetically. All you have to do is turn to "Gethsemane" and read. Here is a sample of the kind of information you will find:

> **Gethsemane** (PLACE) [GK *Gethsemani*]. Garden located E of the Kidron Valley from Jerusalem (John 18:1), on the slopes of the Mount of Olives (Matt 26:30; Luke 22:39). Jesus often went to Gethsemane in order to rest, pray, and find fellowship with his disciples (Luke 21:37; 22:39; John 18:2). After celebrating the Passover with his disciples for the last time, Jesus went to pray in Gethsemane, where he was later betrayed by Judas Iscariot (Matt 26:36–56; Mark 14:32–52; Luke 22:39–53; John 18:1–12).
>
> The name Gethsemane derives from Hebrew and Aramaic words for "oil press." Presumably Gethsemane consisted of an olive orchard and an oil press to squeeze oil from the olives, both of which were common on the Mount of Olives. . . . It may have been a walled garden since John describes Jesus and the disciples as having entered it. From John's account we derive the traditional name of the "garden of Gethsemane." The garden must have been fairly large because Jesus led Peter, James, and John away from the rest of the disciples . . . and later Jesus withdrew further in order to pray alone. . . .
>
> In Gethsemane, Jesus warned his disciples several times to watch and pray against entering into temptation (Matt 26:41; Mark 14:38; Luke 22:40, 46). Jesus understood his own agonizing time of prayer as a time of temptation from completing the sacrificial will of God. . . . He prayed three times for deliverance (Mark 14:32–42). . . . Jesus won the spiritual battle and faithfully met his betrayer in the garden (John 18:1–11). . . . Reminiscent of Gethsemane, Heb 5:7–8 reflects upon the prayers and supplications Jesus made with loud cries and tears. As a result of his godly fear and obedience, Jesus was made perfect and became the source of eternal salvation to all who obey him. . . .
>
> Early Christians conceived of Gethsemane as analogous to the garden of Eden in the divine plan for human redemption. The sinful actions of the first Adam are contrasted with the prayerful obedience of the second Adam—Jesus Christ.[7]

7. Donald A. D. Thorsen, "Gethsemane," in *The Anchor Bible Dictionary*, ed. David Noel Freedman (New York: Doubleday, 1992), 2:997–98.

Included among the most reliable Bible dictionaries and encyclopedias are the following:

Alexander, T. Desmond, and David W. Baker, eds. *Dictionary of the Old Testament: Pentateuch*. Downers Grove, IL: InterVarsity Press, 2003.

Arnold, Bill T., and H. G. M. Williamson, eds. *Dictionary of the Old Testament: Historical Books*. Downers Grove, IL: InterVarsity Press, 2005.

Boda, Mark J., and J. Gordon McConville, eds. *Dictionary of the Old Testament Prophets*. Downers Grove, IL: InterVarsity Press, 2012.

Brand, Chad, Charles W. Draper, and Archie England, eds. *Holman Illustrated Bible Dictionary*. Rev. and exp. ed. Nashville: B&H, 2015.

Douglas, J. D., Merrill C. Tenney, and Moisés Silva, eds. *Zondervan Illustrated Bible Dictionary*. Grand Rapids: Zondervan, 2011.

Elwell, Walter, ed. *Baker Encyclopedia of the Bible*. 2 vols. Grand Rapids: Baker, 1988.

Elwell, Walter, and Philip Comfort, eds. *Tyndale Bible Dictionary*. Wheaton, IL: Tyndale, 2001.

Evans, Craig A., and Stanley E. Porter, eds. *Dictionary of New Testament Background*. Downers Grove, IL: InterVarsity Press, 2000.

Freedman, David Noel, ed. *The Anchor Bible Dictionary*. 6 vols. Garden City, NY: Doubleday, 1992.

Green, Joel B., Scot McKnight, and I. Howard Marshall, eds. *Dictionary of Jesus and the Gospels*. Downers Grove, IL: InterVarsity Press, 1992.

Green, Joel B., Jeannine K. Brown, and Nicholas Perrin, eds. *Dictionary of Jesus and the Gospels*. 2nd ed. Downers Grove, IL: InterVarsity Press, 2013.

Hawthorne, Gerald, Ralph Martin, and Daniel Reid, eds. *Dictionary of Paul and His Letters*. Downers Grove, IL: InterVarsity Press, 1993.

Longman, Tremper, III, ed. *The Baker Illustrated Bible Dictionary*. Grand Rapids: Baker, 2013.

Longman, Tremper, III, and Peter Enns, eds. *Dictionary of the Old Testament: Wisdom, Poetry and Writings*. Downers Grove, IL: InterVarsity Press, 2008.

Marshall, I. Howard, A. R. Millard, J. I. Packer, and D. J. Wiseman, eds. *New Bible Dictionary*. 3rd ed. Downers Grove, IL: InterVarsity Press, 1996.

Martin, Ralph, and Peter Davids, eds. *Dictionary of the Later New Testament and Its Developments*. Downers Grove, IL: InterVarsity Press, 1997.

Powell, Mark Allan, gen. ed. *HarperCollins Bible Dictionary*. Rev. and updated. San Francisco: HarperSanFrancisco, 2011.

Reid, Daniel G., ed. *The IVP Dictionary of the New Testament*. Downers Grove, IL: InterVarsity Press, 2004.

Ryken, Leland, James C. Wilhoit, and Tremper Longman III, eds. *Dictionary of Biblical Imagery*. Downers Grove, IL: InterVarsity Press, 1998.

Sakenfeld, Katharine D., ed. *The New Interpreter's Dictionary of the Bible*. 5 vols. Nashville: Abingdon, 2006–9.

Tenney, Merrill C., and Moisés Silva, eds. *The Zondervan Encyclopedia of the Bible*. Rev. ed. 5 vols. Grand Rapids: Zondervan, 2009.

Commentaries

We mention commentaries again because the good ones are also extremely helpful in shedding light on background matters within your passage. Do you recall Paul's harsh words for the Corinthian Christians regarding their practice of celebrating the Lord's Supper? Here is what Paul says in 1 Corinthians 11:17–22:

> [17]In the following directives I have no praise for you, for your meetings do more harm than good. [18]In the first place, I hear that when you come together as a church, there are divisions among you, and to some extent I believe it. [19]No doubt there have to be differences among you to show which of you have God's approval. [20]So then, when you come together, it is not the Lord's Supper you eat, [21]for when you are eating, some of you go ahead with your own private suppers. As a result, one person remains hungry and another gets drunk. [22]Don't you have homes to eat and drink in? Or do you despise the church of God by humiliating those who have nothing? What shall I say to you? Shall I praise you? Certainly not in this matter!

A good commentary will do what Craig Blomberg does in his commentary on 1 Corinthians—it will clarify the meaning of the passage by summarizing the historical-cultural context.

> The minority of well-to-do believers (1:26), including the major financial supporters and owners of the homes in which the believers met, would have had the leisure-time and resources to arrive earlier and bring larger quantities and finer food than the rest of the congregation. Following the practice of hosting festive gatherings in ancient Corinth, they would have quickly filled the small private dining room. Latecomers (the majority, who probably had to finish work before coming on Saturday or Sunday evening—there was as of yet no legalized day off in the Roman empire) would be seated separately in the adjacent atrium or courtyard. Those that could not afford to bring a full meal, or a very good one, did not have the opportunity to share with the rest in the way that Christian

> unity demanded. . . . The result of the lack of consideration by the wealthy for the less well-to-do implies that they are not celebrating the *Lord's* Supper at all, merely "their *own* supper."[8]

Background Commentaries

This relatively new type of commentary focuses not on the meaning of each passage, but on historical-cultural background essential to grasping the meaning. Background commentaries are helpful because they provide a wealth of information conveniently arranged in a verse-by-verse format. As you study Jesus' teaching on nonresistance in Matthew 5, you will come across the statement: "And if anyone wants to sue you and take your shirt, hand over your coat as well" (v. 40). Keener's background commentary offers the following insight into the context of the passage:

> The poorest people of the Empire (e.g., most peasants in Egypt) had only an inner and outer garment, and the theft of a cloak would lead to legal recourse. Although conditions in first-century Palestine were not quite that bad, this verse could indicate divestiture of all one's possessions, even (*hyperbolically) one's clothes, to avoid a legal dispute affecting only oneself. Jesus gives this advice in spite of the fact that, under Jewish law, a legal case to regain one's cloak would have been foolproof: a creditor could not take a poor person's outer cloak, which might serve as one's only blanket at night as well as a coat (Ex 22:26–27).[9]

It's hard to overestimate the value of the following background commentaries:

Arnold, Clint, gen. ed. *Zondervan Illustrated Bible Backgrounds Commentary: New Testament*. 4 vols. Grand Rapids: Zondervan, 2002.

Beitzel, Barry J., ed. *Lexham Geographic Commentary on the Gospels*. Bellingham, WA: Lexham, 2017.

———. *Lexham Geographic Commentary on Acts through Revelation*. Bellingham, WA: Lexham, 2019.

Hays, J. Daniel, and J. Scott Duvall, eds. *The Baker Illustrated Bible Background Commentary*. Grand Rapids: Baker, 2020.

Keener, Craig S. *The IVP Bible Background Commentary: New Testament*. 2nd ed. Downers Grove, IL: InterVarsity Press, 2014.

---

8. Craig L. Blomberg, *1 Corinthians*, NIV Application Commentary (Grand Rapids: Zondervan, 1994), 228–29.
9. Keener, *IVP Bible Background Commentary: New Testament*, 60.

Walton, John H., gen. ed. *Zondervan Illustrated Bible Backgrounds Commentary: Old Testament*. 5 vols. Grand Rapids: Zondervan, 2009.

Walton, John H., Victor H. Matthews, and Mark W. Chavalas. *The IVP Bible Background Commentary: Old Testament*. Downers Grove, IL: InterVarsity Press, 2000.

Old Testament and New Testament Histories

Histories are most useful when you want detailed background information on particular topics within your passage. You can usually locate the discussion by looking up a key word in the index. If you are examining 1 Peter 4:9 ("Offer hospitality to one another without grumbling"), you might consult a New Testament history to learn more about hospitality in the first-century world. Here is what one such history tells us about the motels of the first-century world and the resulting need for hospitality among Christians:

> The traveler was not so fortunate in the accommodations for the night as he was in the quality of the roads on which he traveled by day. Not that inns were lacking, but their reputation (in quality and morals) was notorious. The wine was often adulterated (or after the patron was drunk on good wine, bad was substituted), sleeping quarters were filthy and insect and rodent infested, innkeepers were extortionate, thieves were in wait, government spies were listening, and many were nothing more than brothels. . . . There were some excellent inns in Italy, but they seem to have been the exception. The upper classes avoided the public accommodations and stayed with friends when they traveled. The moral dangers at the inns made hospitality an important virtue in early Christianity. Hospitality occupies a prominent place in Christian literature (Rom. 16:23; 1 Pet. 4:9; 2 John 10; 3 John 5–8; Heb. 13:2; *1 Clement* 10–12; *Didache* 11–13) because of the needs of missionaries and messengers of the churches and other Christians who happened to be traveling. The churches provided an extended family, giving lodging and assistance for the journey.[10]

The most reliable Old and New Testament histories include the following:

Arnold, Bill T., and Richard S. Hess, eds. *Ancient Israel's History: An Introduction to Issues and Sources*. Grand Rapids: Baker Academic, 2014.

Barnett, Paul. *The Birth of Christianity: The First Twenty Years*. Grand Rapids: Eerdmans, 2005.

10. Everett Ferguson, *Backgrounds of Early Christianity*, 3rd ed. (Grand Rapids: Eerdmans, 2003), 81–82.

———. *Jesus and the Rise of Early Christianity: A History of New Testament Times*. Downers Grove, IL: InterVarsity Press, 1999.

Bruce, F. F. *New Testament History*. Garden City, NY: Doubleday, 1972.

Bruce, F. F., and David Payne. *Israel and the Nations*. 2nd ed. Downers Grove, IL: InterVarsity Press, 1999.

Carter, Warren. *Seven Events That Shaped the New Testament World*. Grand Rapids: Baker Academic, 2013.

Ferguson, Everett. *Backgrounds of Early Christianity*. 3rd ed. Grand Rapids: Eerdmans, 2003.

Jeffers, James S. *The Greco-Roman World of the New Testament Era*. Downers Grove, IL: InterVarsity Press, 1999.

Kaiser, Walter, Jr., and Paul D. Wegner. *A History of Israel: From the Bronze Age through the Jewish Wars*. Rev. ed. Nashville: B&H Academic, 2017.

Long, V. Philips, David Baker, and Gordon Wenham, eds. *Windows into Old Testament History*. Grand Rapids: Eerdmans, 2002.

Merrill, Eugene H. *Kingdom of Priests: A History of Old Testament Israel*. 2nd ed. Grand Rapids: Baker, 2008.

Provan, Iain, V. Philips Long, and Tremper Longman III. *A Biblical History of Israel*. Louisville: Westminster John Knox, 2003.

Witherington, Ben, III. *New Testament History: A Narrative Account*. Grand Rapids: Baker, 2001.

Special Studies in Ancient Life and Culture

These resources provide detailed discussions on selected topics. They can be helpful when you really want to dig deep on a particular topic. You can find articles on biblical cities, social life, legal matters, religious practices, warfare, economic life, and a host of other topics. These special studies are similar to Bible dictionaries but are more narrowly focused. As with many of these resources, go first to the index to locate their treatment of the topic.

Here are a few options in this category:

Arnold, Bill T., and Brent A. Strawn, eds. *The World around the Old Testament: The People and Places of the Ancient Near East*. Grand Rapids: Baker Academic, 2016.

Bailey, Kenneth E. *Jesus through Middle Eastern Eyes: Cultural Studies in the Gospels*. Downers Grove, IL: IVP Academic, 2008.

Barton, John, ed. *The Biblical World*. New York: Routledge, 2002.

Bauckham, Richard. *The Christian World around the New Testament*. Grand Rapids: Baker Academic, 2017.

———. *The Jewish World around the New Testament*. Grand Rapids: Baker Academic, 2010.

Clements, Ronald. *The World of Ancient Israel*. Cambridge: Cambridge University Press, 1989.

deSilva, David A. *Honor, Patronage, Kinship and Purity: Unlocking New Testament Culture*. Downers Grove, IL: InterVarsity Press, 2000.

DeVries, LaMoine F. *Cities of the Biblical World*. Peabody, MA: Hendrickson, 1997.

Evans, Craig A. *Ancient Texts for New Testament Studies: A Guide to the Background Literature*. Peabody, MA: Hendrickson, 2005.

Green, Joel B., and Lee Martin McDonald, eds. *The World of the New Testament: Cultural, Social, and Historical Contexts*. Grand Rapids: Baker Academic, 2013.

Greer, Jonathan S., John W. Hilber, and John H. Walton. *Behind the Scenes of the Old Testament: Cultural, Social, and Historical Contexts*. Grand Rapids: Baker Academic, 2018.

Helyer, Larry R. *Exploring Jewish Literature of the Second Temple Period*. Downers Grove, IL: InterVarsity Press, 2002.

Hoerth, Alfred, Gerald Mattingly, and Edwin Yamauchi, eds. *Peoples of the Old Testament World*. Grand Rapids: Baker, 1994.

Jeremias, Joachim. *Jerusalem in the Time of Jesus*. Philadelphia: Fortress, 1969.

King, Philip, and Lawrence Stager. *Life in Biblical Israel*. Louisville: Westminster John Knox, 2001.

Malina, Bruce. *The New Testament World*. 3rd ed. Louisville: Westminster John Knox, 2001.

Malina, Bruce, and John J. Pilch, eds. *Handbook of Biblical Social Values*. 3rd ed. Eugene, OR: Cascade, 2006.

Matthews, Victor H. *Manners and Customs in the Bible*. 3rd ed. Peabody, MA: Hendrickson, 2006.

Scott, J. Julius. *Customs and Controversies*. Grand Rapids: Baker, 1995.

Shanks, Hershel, ed. *Ancient Israel*. Rev. and exp. ed. Washington, DC: Biblical Archaeology Society, 1999.

Skarsaune, Oskar. *In the Shadow of the Temple: Jewish Influences on Early Christianity*. Downers Grove, IL: InterVarsity Press, 2002.

Vos, Howard. *Nelson's New Illustrated Bible Manners and Customs*. Nashville: Thomas Nelson, 1999.

Walton, John H. *Ancient Near Eastern Thought and the Old Testament*. 2nd ed. Grand Rapids: Baker Academic, 2018.

Computer Software and the Internet

Some of the resources mentioned above are available in electronic format. We encourage you to take full advantage of computer software packages that include the best resources. Often the convenience and price are hard to beat. But remember that you are after the best tools, not simply the least expensive deal. You can use the bibliography of resources throughout this chapter to evaluate the various electronic resources.

Be cautious when using internet resources. This is a rapidly changing environment that has not traditionally represented the best in biblical scholarship. While the internet is certainly convenient, you don't always know whether you are getting reliable information. We recommend that you stick with resources by well-known and respected authors.

CONCLUSION

We study the historical-cultural background of the Bible because God chose to speak first to ancient peoples living in cultures that are radically different from our own. As we recapture the original context of God's Word, we will be able to grasp its meaning and apply that meaning to our lives. Remember, a valid interpretation of any text must be consistent with the historical-cultural context of that text.

In this chapter we have talked about the tools you will need to identify the historical-cultural context of a book and a specific passage. Bible handbooks, Old and New Testament introductions or surveys, and commentaries are particularly useful for grasping the historical-cultural context of the book as a whole. We recommend using atlases, dictionaries or encyclopedias, commentaries, background commentaries, Old and New Testament histories, and special studies to discover the historical-cultural context of a particular passage. We strongly encourage you to add some of these tools to your personal library.

While some may label background studies "boring" and "irrelevant," we argue the opposite—that knowing the background of a passage can clarify its meaning and heighten our understanding of its relevance. Does knowing all that Paul means by "come before winter" make his words less relevant or more relevant? Does understanding the significance of God "running" in the parable of the prodigal son make the story less practical or more practical? We believe that studying the historical-cultural context of a passage is among the most practical things you can do when it comes to Bible study.

ASSIGNMENTS

Assignment 6–1

In the New Testament letter of Philemon, the apostle Paul writes on behalf of a slave named Onesimus. Part of identifying the historical-cultural context of Philemon includes knowing something about the institution of slavery in the Greco-Roman world. Consult several New Testament histories or Bible dictionaries or encyclopedias and read their articles on slavery. Then write a two-page summary of the practice of slavery in New Testament times.

Assignment 6–2

Look up Haggai in an Old Testament survey or introduction and read what the author(s) has to say by way of introduction (e.g., author, date, audience, situation, purpose). Use what you have learned to write a one- to two-page description of the historical setting of this prophetic book.

Assignment 6–3

Read Revelation 2–3 and list the seven churches that receive a letter. Next, copy a map of Asia Minor from a Bible atlas and locate the seven churches. On your copy trace the route among the seven churches that a messenger probably followed to deliver the letters. Finally, look up Revelation 3:14–22 in a commentary or background commentary and make a list of every historical-cultural fact about Laodicea that you can find.

Assignment 6–4

Read the conversation between Jesus and the Samaritan woman recorded in John 4:1–39. Then read an article on "Samaria" or "Samaritan" in a Bible dictionary or encyclopedia and make a list of all the ways the article helps you understand the conversation between Jesus and the woman.

Assignment 6–5

Use a Bible dictionary or encyclopedia to answer the following questions about the book of Nehemiah:

1. How much time passes between the month of Kislev (or Chislev) in Nehemiah 1:1 and the month of Nisan in Nehemiah 2:1?
2. Where is Susa (Neh. 1:1)?
3. For which empire did Susa serve as one of three royal cities?
4. What other biblical character lived in Susa?
5. Did this character live before Nehemiah or after?
6. Which empire did King Artaxerxes rule over, and when (Neh. 2:1)?
7. What was a cupbearer's (Neh. 1:11) status in the royal court?

CHAPTER 7

WHAT DO *WE* BRING TO THE TEXT?

INTRODUCTION

One context that is often overlooked is the context of the reader—the world from which the reader approaches the text. We as readers of the Bible are not by nature neutral and objective. We bring a lot of preconceived notions and influences with us to the text when we read. Thus, we need to discuss and evaluate these "pre-text" influences, lest they mislead us in our search for the meaning of the text.

Let's begin with a story. Danny and his family spent several years working as missionaries in Ethiopia. Right after moving "down-country," Danny was privileged to watch a Christmas pageant presented by an Ethiopian evangelical church in Dilla, Ethiopia. Was that ever a different experience! There were no Christmas trees with lights, nor was there any snow. The weather was balmy, and there were banana trees growing right outside the church. More than four hundred people crowded into the church building, which had seating for maybe one hundred fifty. Of course, we use the term "seating" loosely—the pews consisted of uncomfortable benches constructed out of rough, uneven, hand-cut lumber. The church had dirt floors (where fleas flourished), mud walls plastered white with lime plaster, rafters made of eucalyptus poles of various sizes, and a corrugated steel roof.

Whenever the sun would go behind a cloud, the change in temperature on the corrugated steel roof would cause it to contract, creating a creaking, groaning sound for several seconds. Then the sun would emerge again, causing the roof to get hot again, and the corrugated steel would repeat the ritual moans until the metal had expanded back to its original size. Thus, a certain background rhythm of "roof groaning" developed. The inside of the church was lit by only two forty-watt lightbulbs. Most of the needed light was usually provided by the numerous windows on each side, but on this particular day much of the light was blocked by the dozens of eager spectators jammed around each window outside the church, standing on their tiptoes and craning their necks, trying to see. They had arrived too late to get a seat inside.

Christmas pageants in the United States are fairly stereotypical. Danny assumed that this one would be similar. How else can you tell the story? Was he in for a shock! The pageant started out normal enough. At the beginning a "town crier" of sorts was walking back and forth shouting through a megaphone, proclaiming the new Roman census requirements (similar to Linus's proclamation of Luke 2:1 ["And it came to pass in those days, that there went out a decree from Caesar Augustus that all the world should be taxed"] at the beginning of all *Peanuts* pageants). After some preparation by Joseph's family, Joseph and Mary finally departed for Bethlehem.

Whose culture is closer to that of the Bible?

Here the pageant began to differ, for Joseph and Mary did not travel alone. Mary, quite big in her last month of pregnancy, was accompanied by over a dozen aunts and female cousins. Joseph walked alone in front, followed by all of these women, who were chatting and giggling merrily about babies and "motherly" things. *Whoa*, Danny thought, *whatever happened to the typical travel scene with Mary, Joseph, and the donkey? Where did all these women come from? They're not in the story!*

A few minutes later, the noisy entourage arrived in Bethlehem and were directed to the "sheep pen," crowded with sheep. Soon Mary started labor. Joseph paced nervously back and forth in front of the stable, while the women, several of them midwives, crowded around Mary to help deliver the baby. A short labor ensued, and soon the women all gave a shrill, vibrating cry—the typical Ethiopian joy cry that announces the birth of every child in Ethiopia. The spectators cheered, and the women in the crowd joined in the joy cry with the actors. Hearing the cry, Joseph ran into the sheep pen to see the newborn baby. Later, of course, the familiar shepherds came, followed by the wise men. All in all, the pageant took two hours!

What struck Danny was the way in which the Ethiopians had interpreted the story through their culture. They were not consciously contextualizing the story to make it Ethiopian. They were trying to portray it in the way they thought it actually happened. Yet notice what they did. As we do in our pageants, they filled in all the gaps in the story with explanations that made sense in their culture. For example, to the Ethiopians it is unthinkable that Mary's family would have allowed her to make this trip by herself. She was a young woman expecting her first baby, and the Ethiopians could not imagine her making the trip with only Joseph to help her. Who, after all, would deliver the baby? Only an irresponsible person would travel in this condition without her aunts there as midwives!

But to us in North America who live in a world of doctors and hospitals, traveling without a midwife seems like no big deal, so we don't put midwives in the story. Actually, we Americans generally skip over the question of who delivered the baby. We just check the young couple into the stable, and then—presto!—baby Jesus appears in Mary's arms. But think about it. Did Joseph deliver the baby? The Ethiopians would laugh at us for suggesting such a preposterous thing. Could a young, newlywed man with no other children deliver a baby? Such a thing would not happen in Ethiopia.

Notice what has happened. As we in America portray the story, we fill in the silent gaps in the text with an *Americanized* point of view. In our world we deal primarily with nuclear family units (mom, dad, children), and so we have no problem with Joseph and Mary traveling by themselves. It never occurs to us to consider midwives because we rarely use them. We are familiar in our culture with the scene of a young man and his pregnant wife rushing off alone to the hospital by themselves as she starts into labor. The man checks the wife in at the hospital, and after some time behind closed doors—presto!—the baby comes. Thus, we are comfortable with presenting Mary and Joseph in a similar fashion.

Rural Ethiopians, by contrast, have a different cultural experience with childbirth. The young expectant mother is surrounded by her female relatives and pampered during the final weeks of the pregnancy. She is never left alone. The birth of a baby does not normally occur in a hospital but in a home. It is an extended family affair. Either relatives or neighborhood midwives (friends of the family) deliver the baby. To send the young mother on a trip without her female relatives is unthinkable, as is the thought of the young, inexperienced Joseph somehow doubling as an obstetrician. Since Americans have seen the same basic pageant presented every Christmas, they have generally accepted that presentation as the complete truth. Yet both the Americans and the Ethiopians take some liberty with the story to fill in the gaps with things that concur with their respective cultures. Whose culture, do you suppose, is closer to that of the Bible?

PREUNDERSTANDING

One major influence that can skew our interpretive process and lead us away from the real meaning in the text is what we call *preunderstanding*. Preunderstanding refers to all of our preconceived notions and understandings that we bring to the text, which have been formulated, both consciously and subconsciously, *before* we actually study the text in detail. The preunderstanding problem is the broader issue that links with the cultural problems introduced above and discussed in more detail below. Preunderstanding includes specific experiences and previous encounters with the text that tend to make us assume that we already understand it.

Preunderstanding is formed by both good and bad influences, some accurate and some inaccurate. It includes all that you have heard in Sunday school, at church, in Bible studies, and in your private reading of the Bible. However, preunderstandings of biblical texts are also formed by hymns and other Christian music, pop songs, jokes, art, and nonbiblical literature, both Christian and secular. Likewise, culture constantly creeps in.

> The student sitting next to Albert Einstein turned to him and asked, "What do you do?" Einstein replied, "I am a student of physics. What do you do?" "Oh," the student answered, "I finished studying physics last year."[1]

Note that your preunderstanding of any given passage may indeed be correct. The problem, however, is that often it is not, and until you study the text seriously, you simply do not know whether it is accurate. The danger here is for those who assume that their preunderstanding is always correct. Vanhoozer labels this attitude *pride*. This kind of pride, he writes, "encourages us to think that we have got the correct meaning before we have made the appropriate effort to recover it. Pride does not listen. It knows."[2]

Another dangerous aspect of preunderstanding surfaces when we come to the text with a theological agenda already formulated. That is, we start into a text with a specific slant that we are looking for, and we use the text merely to search for details that fit with our agenda. Anything that does not fit in with the meaning we are looking for we simply skip or ignore. Vanhoozer humorously labels this as "overstanding" and not "understanding."[3] That is, *we* as readers stand *over* the Word of God and determine what it means, rather than placing ourselves *under* that Word, seeking diligently to determine what *God* means in the text.

A related danger is that of familiarity. If we are thoroughly familiar with a passage, we tend to think that we know all there is to know about it and are prone to skip over it without studying it carefully. Hopefully you realized in part 1 that most

---

1. 1. Taken from Penrose St. Amant, "Communicating the Gospel in the Eighties," *The Quarterly Review* 41.3 (April–June 1981): 72. Cited by Dan Kent in class notes at Southwestern Baptist Theological Seminary.

2. Kevin J. Vanhoozer, *Is There a Meaning in This Text? The Bible, the Reader, and the Morality of Literary Knowledge* (Grand Rapids: Zondervan, 1998), 462.

3. Vanhoozer, 402–3.

passages have a lot of depth to them, and we are unlikely to exhaust them or to grasp all there is to grasp in a few short visits to that text. Familiarity with a passage creates preunderstanding. As we revisit these familiar texts, we must resist the temptation of letting our familiarity dictate our conclusions before we even get started studying a text. We need to study it afresh, lest our preunderstanding turn into the pride mentioned above. Furthermore, as we mentioned in part 1, if we skip over serious fresh study of a text because we think we know it already, all we will see in the Bible is what we saw last time. Our study becomes boring and stagnant, and our growth and understanding become stunted.

Another dangerous aspect of preunderstanding surfaces when we come to the text with a theological agenda already formulated.

One of the most powerful yet subtle aspects of preunderstanding is that of culture. Our theology tells us to ask, *What would Jesus do?* Our culture, however, may subconsciously be telling us to ask, *What would Iron Man do?* Or perhaps, *What would Captain Marvel do?* Undoubtedly, our culture has a tremendous influence on how we read and interpret the Bible. For example, even though we believe that Jesus is our Lord and Savior, when he tells us to turn the other cheek, a voice in the back of our head objects. After all, turning the other cheek is not really the American way. It is not what Tony Stark would do. Perhaps he might turn his cheek once and let his adversary strike him a second time just to demonstrate his patience and control, but undoubtedly after that second strike he would thrash the bad guy soundly (and we would all cheer). None of our action heroes turns the other cheek!

What would Iron Man do?

Thus, when we read of such a command from Jesus, we immediately try to interpret it in such a way that it does not conflict with cultural norms, especially those set by the culture's heroes, be they Captain Marvel or Iron Man. This culture-driven predisposition we call *cultural baggage*. Imagine that you are about to embark on a long hike in the mountains on a hot day. You wear good hiking boots and a hat. You bring sunglasses and a canteen. Should you bring three or four suitcases along? How ridiculous! Can you imagine hiking through the mountains with a suitcase under each arm? If we are not careful, our culture will likewise weigh us down on the Interpretive Journey and hinder us from discovering and grasping God's Word to us. Our culture tends to make us skew the text as we read it, twisting it to fit with our cultural world. Or, as illustrated in the Christmas pageant story cited in the introduction, our culture works in us subconsciously to fill in all the gaps and missing details of the passage we are reading.

A good illustration of culture's subconscious influence on our understanding occurs when we read the book of Jonah and then try to visualize Jonah inside the great fish. Try to imagine this scene yourself. What do you see? Do you see Jonah scrunched up inside of the tight stomach of a whale, with no space between him and the stomach walls? Most people do not see that image. Many people, including ourselves, see Jonah inside a circular-shaped stomach, about six to eight feet in diameter, with a little bit of water at the bottom. Obviously this is not really what the inside of a whale (or fish) looks like.

So why do we see this? Where might this image come from? We suggest it comes from the movie (or book) *Pinocchio*. In this Walt Disney movie, a whale swallows the main character, Pinocchio. The movie then presents us with a scene that portrays Pinocchio sitting inside the whale (a barrel-shaped room on its side, six to eight feet in diameter, etc.). This movie thus leaves us with a subconscious image of a person sitting inside a whale. When we read of Jonah's digestive misfortune, our minds begin an image search back through our memory banks, looking for a picture from which to visualize the event. As our mind searches through the files in its memory, it hits a match in the Pinocchio file, and a picture comes to mind without our conscious reckoning of where we obtained the image. Subconsciously we begin to fill in the descriptive gaps in the Jonah story with information that comes from a Hollywood movie! Thus, we find ourselves influenced in our reading of the Bible without even realizing what has happened.

What exactly do we mean by *culture*? Our culture is a combination of family and national heritage. You learn it from your mom at breakfast, from the kids on the playground at school, and from YouTube. It is a mix of language, customs, stories, movies, jokes, literature, and national habits. For Americans it consists of SONIC Drive-Ins, American Girl dolls, Stephen Curry, and Carrie Underwood all mixed in with George Washington, Babe Ruth, the Mississippi River, Walmart, and Facebook. It can vary somewhat, however, even within the same city. If you grew up in an inner-city, blue-collar, Catholic home with both parents, your culture differs in many respects from that of someone who grew up in a suburban, white-collar, single-parent, Protestant home, but you will still share many of the same cultural influences. However, even though they share some common cultural features, black, white, Asian, and Hispanic cultures differ significantly, even within North America. Once you move out of North America, you will encounter drastic differences in culture.

For Americans culture consists of SONIC Drive-Ins, American Girl dolls, Stephen Curry, and Carrie Underwood all mixed in with George Washington, Babe Ruth, the Mississippi River, Walmart, and Facebook.

Your family background is also a central element in your cultural world. You have inherited many, many values, ideas, and images (for good and for bad) from your family. For example, what are your views about money, work, the poor, or the unemployed? Your views have undoubtedly been shaped by your family's socioeconomic setting and its outlook. If you are from an upper-middle-class family, you will probably approach biblical texts about the poor from a different frame of reference than someone born and raised in the poverty of New Delhi. We are not suggesting that the cultural reading from New Delhi is automatically right while the one from Dallas is wrong. Christians in both settings need to be aware that their family background and socioeconomic setting affect how they read the Bible.

Your family also provides you with your strongest frame of reference regarding relationships. If you were fortunate enough to grow up in a loving, caring family, it will be easy for you to transpose the imagery of this experience to the imagery of God's care for you. If you had a loving father, for example, the biblical image of God as a loving Father will be easy for you to grasp. In this case, the cultural influence of your family background helps you grasp the biblical truth about God.

All of us tend to be influenced by our culture subconsciously.

Unfortunately, however, not everyone has had a loving father. Those who have grown up with negligent or even abusive fathers carry a lot of baggage into the biblical texts that describe God as a Father. This doesn't mean that these people cannot grasp this aspect of biblical truth, but it does mean that they will have to work harder to overcome some of the negative images from their childhood. Other images of God and his care may be more relatable for them. As we all seek to understand God's Word, acknowledging and identifying the cultural influences at work in our heads and hearts is important.

We recognize full well that Christians do not culturally misread the Bible intentionally. As noted, all of us tend to be influenced by our culture subconsciously. This automatic transportation of the biblical text into our cultural world is called "interpretational reflex."[4] It is a natural thing to do, and we do it without thinking about it.

Interpretational reflex affects our interpretation in two ways. (1) As mentioned in the Christmas pageant story, we tend to fill in all of the gaps and ambiguities in the biblical texts with explanations and background from our culture.

(2) More damaging to our interpretation is the fact that our cultural background preforms a parameter of limiting possibilities for a text even before we grapple with the intended meaning. In this situation, based on our culture we subconsciously create a world of interpretive possibilities and a world of interpretive impossibilities. In other words, our cultural setting has driven us to decide possible and impossible meanings for the text even before we study them.

---

4. Charles H. Kraft, "Interpreting in Cultural Context," in *Rightly Divided: Readings in Biblical Hermeneutics*, ed. Roy B. Zuck (Grand Rapids: Kregel, 1996), 250.

Let's examine again Jesus' command to turn the other cheek. Our subconscious agenda seeks to legitimize our cultural worldview, that is, the way things are in our culture. Thus, before we even start to explore what Jesus meant when he said this, we place parameters of possibility around the text and eliminate culturally conflicting possible meanings. It cannot possibly mean that if someone bad hits you, you are to let them hit you again. However, by doing this we are placing our culture above the Bible and reading the Bible through culture-colored lenses. In this way we miss one of the main points of the Bible, namely, that the biblical message is from God and is above culture. The challenge is to critique our culture with the Bible and not vice versa.

The challenge is to critique our culture with the Bible and not vice versa.

For an evocative example, let's take a "cultural" look at Romans 13:1–7. (This section is targeted primarily at American readers. If you are not an American, please be patient with us in this section. Try to determine a similar situation in *your* culture.) Read this passage carefully:

> [1]Let everyone be subject to the governing authorities, for there is no authority except that which God has established. The authorities that exist have been established by God. [2]Consequently, whoever rebels against the authority is rebelling against what God has instituted, and those who do so will bring judgment on themselves. [3]For rulers hold no terror for those who do right, but for those who do wrong. Do you want to be free from fear of the one in authority? Then do what is right and you will be commended. [4]For the one in authority is God's servant for your good. But if you do wrong, be afraid, for rulers do not bear the sword for no reason. They are God's servants, agents of wrath to bring punishment on the wrongdoer. [5]Therefore, it is necessary to submit to the authorities, not only because of possible punishment but also as a matter of conscience.
>
> [6]This is also why you pay taxes, for the authorities are God's servants, who give their full time to governing. [7]Give to everyone what you owe them: If you owe taxes, pay taxes; if revenue, then revenue; if respect, then respect; if honor, then honor.

With this passage in mind, would it have been wrong for you to participate in the Boston Tea Party of 1773? In protest of a new tax on tea, American "patriots" dumped tons of someone else's tea into the Boston Harbor. Was that a Christian thing to do? Or suppose you were one of the Minutemen along the route between Concord and Boston on April 19, 1775. Should a Christian aim, fire, and kill the soldiers that represent the government? Does this not conflict with Romans 13?

Or perhaps the larger question should be asked: Was the American Revolution undertaken in disobedience to Romans 13:1–7? Keep in mind that the Revolution was more about economics than about religious freedom. Remember, too, that when Paul wrote Romans, the government in Rome was much more oppressive and tyrannical than the British government under King George III ever was. What do you think?

Perhaps we have angered some of you. Perhaps you are steamed up about our challenge to the legitimacy of the glorious American Revolution. Please forgive us. We are not really concerned with what you think about the Revolution. What we hope you saw was some inner emotional reaction within yourself to a fairly literal and normal reading of a biblical text. If you reacted strongly to our suggested understanding of Romans 13, you should ask yourself, *Why did I react so strongly?* We would suggest that we struck a sensitive cultural nerve.

You see, the morality of the American rebellion against Britain is *never* questioned as we grow up. It is always presented as wonderful and glorious—the epitome of patriotism (which *must* be good). It is tightly intertwined in our hearts with the flag, baseball, Mom, and apple pie. Thus, it has become sacred. We place the "rightness" of it over any critique or challenge to it that may come from the Bible. Any interpretation of Romans 13 that can possibly be legitimate must comply with respect for the Revolution. Thus, we place our culture over the Bible, and we become closed-minded to any understanding of the Bible that conflicts with the status quo of our culture.

We often become closed-minded to any understanding of the Bible that conflicts with the status quo of our culture.

Of course the Revolution is more complicated than we have admitted. Our purpose is not so much to criticize it as to use it as an illustration. However, we do want you (American readers) to see that there are *American* things that exert a powerful subconscious influence on the way we read and interpret the Bible. We need to be aware of these influences and conscious of their effect on our study. It is important that we at least be open to the *possibility* that Romans 13 may be critical of the Revolution. We are looking for what God is saying and not what our culture is saying. We must look to the details of the text and its historical setting to determine the answer, not to our own culture-driven preunderstanding.

If we start our interpretive analysis of Romans 13:1–7 with the preconceived, forgone conclusion that it *cannot* be critical of the Revolution, we are then placing our culture above the Bible. Jesus, however, calls us to a higher calling! We are citizens of *his* kingdom, pledged to follow *him* and *his* teachings. We should never place our loyalty to our country and culture above our loyalty to God. Regardless of what you think about the Revolution, we hope you grasp the idea that we must be able to put *all* of our American culture on the table under the scrutiny of Scripture. *Never* should we allow our culture to dictate the meaning of the Word of God.

This is radical stuff and may be difficult for you to digest all at once. We know that. Mull that over for a while. Talk to Christians from different cultures and get their perspective.

Preunderstanding, including culture, is not inherently bad, but it can often skew our understanding of the Bible and lead us down the trail of misinterpretation. We do not want to abandon our preunderstanding, throwing all of our previous encounters with the text into the trash. What we do want to do is to submit our preunderstanding *to* the text, placing it under the text rather than over the text. We must be able to identify our preunderstanding and then be open to changing it in accordance with a true serious study of the text. That is, after we have studied the text thoroughly, we must then evaluate our preunderstanding and modify it appropriately in light of our current study.

FOUNDATIONAL BELIEFS

Our approach to preunderstanding, however, does not suggest that we read and interpret the Bible in a completely neutral manner, apart from any foundational beliefs, such as faith. Total objectivity is impossible for any reader of any text. Neither is it our goal. Striving for objectivity in biblical interpretation does not mean abandoning faith or trying to adopt the methods of unbelievers. Trying to read the Bible apart from faith does not produce objectivity.

Striving for objectivity in biblical interpretation does not mean abandoning faith or trying to adopt the methods of unbelievers.

We define preunderstanding and foundational beliefs as two distinct entities that we deal with in two quite different ways. We must let our preunderstanding change each time we study a passage. We submit it to the text and then interact with it, evaluate it in light of our study, and, one would hope, improve it each time. Foundational beliefs, by contrast, do not change with each reading. They are not related to particular passages but to our overall view of the Bible.

As Christians we serve the living Lord and have the Holy Spirit living within us. The relationship we have with God is a critical aspect of the communication that we have with him through reading his Word. This relationship impacts us greatly as we interpret, and it is not something we want to renegotiate as we read each text, such as we do with preunderstanding aspects. Rather, it is something we want to use. We will explore the interaction between the Holy Spirit and our understanding in more detail in chapter 12, "The Role of the Holy Spirit." But for now it is important to note that we as Christians have several *foundational beliefs* about the Bible itself that develop out of our relationship with Christ and that we will not want to set aside each time we tackle a passage, as we do with our preunderstanding.

Several foundational beliefs about the Scriptures that evangelical Christians generally hold are as follows:

1. The Bible is the Word of God. Although God worked through people to produce it, it is nonetheless inspired by the Holy Spirit and is God's Word to us.
2. The Bible is trustworthy and true.
3. God has entered into human history; thus the supernatural (miracles, etc.) does occur.
4. The Bible is not contradictory; it is unified yet diverse. Nevertheless, God is bigger than we are, and he is not always easy to comprehend. Thus, the Bible also has tension and mystery to it.

Other foundational beliefs could perhaps be added,[5] but these are the central ones that must be mentioned here. These foundational beliefs have to do with how we view the entire Bible and serve as a starting point on which to build our method of study.

CONCLUSION—CAN WE BE OBJECTIVE?

Many writers have pointed out that total objectivity in interpretation is impossible, and we acknowledge this. However, total objectivity is not our goal. As Christians who have an intimate relationship with God through Jesus Christ, we are not striving for a neutral, objective viewpoint. We do not seek to be secular historians as we study the text (they are not objective either). We seek to hear what God has to say to us. Thus, we approach the text through faith and in the Spirit (see ch. 12). So we want objectivity within the framework of evangelical foundational beliefs like those listed above. This type of objectivity has to do with preventing *our* preunderstanding, *our* culture, *our* familiarity, or *our* laziness from obscuring the meaning that God has intended for us in the text.

This task also can be challenging; however, it is to this task that *Grasping God's Word* is devoted. Every chapter in this book deals with some aspect of correcting our preunderstanding or neutralizing the negative cultural influences on our

5. See the lists by William W. Klein, Craig L. Blomberg, and Robert L. Hubbard Jr., *Introduction to Biblical Interpretation*, 4th ed. (Grand Rapids: Zondervan, 2017), 237–41; and Roy B. Zuck, *Basic Bible Interpretation* (Wheaton, IL: Victor, 1991), 59–75. However, note that both books use slightly different terminology from ours.

understanding. The observation tools we learned in part 1 will help us to be objective. The method of reading carefully that was presented in those chapters requires that we submit our preunderstanding to the text while we scrutinize the text for details. Merely discovering the details of the text often corrects many of our preunderstandings and cultural misconstruals.

Part 2 stresses *context* because a proper study of context helps to clarify the actual meaning and corrects our preconceived ones. Part 3 deals with meaning and its origin. It will keep us searching to discover God's meaning from the text rather than trying to create novel understanding (overstanding?) from within our prideful selves. Finally, parts 4 and 5 will deal with the different specific types of literature found in the Bible. A clear understanding of different literary types will assist us greatly in avoiding the projection of contemporary literary/cultural norms onto the ancient literary texts of the Bible.

This chapter has merely delineated the problems we as readers bring to the text—the cultural baggage and preunderstandings that we must deal with as pre-text issues. The solution to the problem lies within the Interpretive Journey. We hope you find the trip rewarding. We certainly think it is worth all the hard work and effort you must exert as you travel through the following chapters!

ASSIGNMENT

Assignment 7–1

In three or four pages, describe your family background in regard to cultural influences. Discuss as well as you can both your mother (and her family) and your father (and his family). Include any other families that may have influenced you as well. For each, discuss attitudes and views toward religion, family, work, education, and wealth. Describe the socioeconomic location of your family and its religious context. Also, how do members of your family tend to relate to each other? Does your family tend to be warm and "huggy" or cold and distant? Finally, try to relate your family background to your own set of values and outlooks. What have you retained? What have you rejected?

Note: This assignment is not meant to pry into your personal life. Feel free to omit anything in the written assignment about which you are sensitive. But be sure to *think* about those things you omit so that you are aware of their influence on your study of the Bible. This exercise is a self-analysis; it is for your benefit and not ours.

CHAPTER 8

THE LITERARY CONTEXT

INTRODUCTION

Imagine that you are a college student strolling to class one day when a total stranger hits you with a one-liner: "Go for it!" How would you respond? Would you say, "Sure," and walk away thinking that he or she was one fry short of a Happy Meal? Or would you take the message with all religious seriousness and conclude that God must be speaking to you through that person, answering your prayers about your relationship dilemma or a decision you need to make or whether to take the job offer?

To unveil the meaning of "Go for it!" most of us would probably come back with a few questions of our own. "What exactly do you mean?" or "Go for what?" We would ask questions as part of our search for a context to give meaning to those three little words. Without a context, "Go for it!" can mean almost anything. Without a context, words become meaningless.

The most important principle of biblical interpretation is that *context determines meaning.*

When it comes to interpreting and applying the Bible, context is crucial. In fact, we would go so far as to say that the most important principle of biblical interpretation is that *context determines meaning*. When we ignore the context, we can twist the Scriptures and "prove" almost anything. Consider the example of a young man seeking advice from God's Word about whether to ask his girlfriend to marry him. As he dances around the Scriptures, he finds a couple of verses that provide the answer he so desperately wants, with a timetable to boot.

> 1 Corinthians 7:36c: "They should get married."
> John 13:27: "What you are about to do, do quickly."

The young man sees in the first verse a direct command to get married and in the second a timetable—get married now! God has spoken!

What keeps us from taking this ridiculous example seriously? *Context!* Apparently the young man did not bother to read the entire context of 1 Corinthians 7:36c, where the apostle Paul gives advice to engaged men in light of the distressing circumstances in Corinth (notice the italicized portions):

> [36]If anyone is worried that he might not be acting honorably toward the virgin he is engaged to, and if his passions are too strong and he feels he ought to marry, he should do as he wants. He is not sinning. *They should get married.* [37]But the man who has settled the matter in his own mind, who is under no compulsion but has control over his own will, and who has made up his mind not to marry the virgin—this man also does the right thing. [38]*So then, he who marries the virgin does right, but he who does not marry her does better.*

In light of the situation, Paul actually says that it's better not to marry. In the second verse (John 13:27), the phrase "what you are about to do" refers to Judas's betraying Jesus and has nothing at all to do with marriage. Under the spotlight of context, we see that these two verses give the young man no scriptural basis for proposing marriage.

Not all examples are this ridiculous, of course, but every violation of context is a dangerous matter. In contrast, by honoring the context of Scripture, we are saying that we would rather hear what God has to say than put words in his mouth. Context determines meaning!

To understand and apply the Bible, we need to be concerned with the two major kinds of context: historical and literary. *Historical context* is the historical-cultural background of a text, which we discussed in chapter 6. *Literary context* relates to the particular form a passage takes (the *literary genre*) and to the words, sentences, and paragraphs that surround the passage you are studying (the *surrounding context*). Literary context is the topic of this chapter.

WHAT IS LITERARY GENRE?

For every passage of Scripture, we must first notice the form it takes (i.e., *how* did it mean?) before we look at its content (i.e., *what* did it mean?).[1] The word *genre* is a French word meaning "form" or "kind." When applied to biblical interpretation, the expression *literary genre* simply refers to the different categories or *types* of literature found in the Bible. In the Old Testament you will encounter narrative, law, poetry, prophecy, and wisdom. The New Testament forms include gospel, history, letter, and apocalyptic literature. Both Old and New Testaments feature a number of subgenres (e.g., parables, riddles, sermons). We will discuss all the major literary genres in the last part of *Grasping God's Word*. For now, we will settle for why we need to recognize the literary genre to read a passage "in context."

***Literary genre* simply refers to the different categories or *types* of literature found in the Bible.**

The metaphor that many linguists use to describe literary genre is that of a game. You can think of each genre as a different kind of game complete with its own set of rules. This insightful analogy shows how we as readers have to play by the rules when it comes to recognizing literary genre.

> Think for a moment of a European soccer fan attending his first (American) football and basketball games. In football the offensive and defensive players can use their hands to push their opponents. In basketball and soccer they cannot. In basketball players cannot kick the ball, but they can hold it with their hands. In soccer the reverse is true. In football everyone can hold the ball with his hands but only one person can kick it. In soccer everyone can kick the ball but only one person can hold it. Unless we understand the rules under which the game is played, what is taking place is bound to be confusing.
>
> In a similar way, there are different "game" rules involved in the interpretation of the different kinds of biblical literature. The author has "played his game," that is, has sought to convey his meaning, under the rules covering the particular literary form he has used. Unless we know those rules, we will almost certainly misinterpret his meaning.[2]

For communication to occur, the reader must be on the same page as the author in terms of genre. When the stranger said, "Go for it!" you could have responded with

1. Sidney Greidanus, *Preaching Christ from the Old Testament: A Contemporary Hermeneutical Method* (Grand Rapids: Eerdmans, 1999), 229.

2. Robert H. Stein, *A Basic Guide to Interpreting the Bible: Playing by the Rules* (Grand Rapids: Baker, 1994), 75–76.

questions to clarify the meaning. But how can we clarify the meaning of the ancient authors when they are not around to answer our questions? The answer is by investigating literary genre. As Vanhoozer puts it, "What writing pulls asunder—author, context, text, reader—genre joins together."[3] Even though the author and reader cannot have a face-to-face conversation, they meet in the text where they are able to communicate because they subscribe to a common set of rules—the rules of the particular genre.

"Literary genre acts as a kind of *covenant of communication*, a fixed agreement between author and reader about how to communicate."
—Kevin Vanhoozer

In this way, literary genre acts as a kind of *covenant of communication*, a fixed agreement between author and reader about how to communicate.[4] To "keep the covenant," we must let the author's choice of genre determine the rules we use to understand his or her words. To disregard literary genre in the Bible is to violate our covenant with the biblical author and with the Holy Spirit who inspired his message.

If you stop and think about it, you are constantly encountering different genres in the course of ordinary life. In a single day you might read a political blog post, search for someone's phone number, order from a menu, reflect on a poem, enjoy an encouraging text from a friend, wade through instructions on how to complete an assignment, or meditate on a devotional book. When you meet these different genres, you know (whether you are conscious of it or not) that you need to play by certain rules of communication, the rules established by the genre itself. If you fail to play by its rules, you run the risk of misreading.

Each literary genre in the Bible comes with its own set of built-in rules for interpretation.

You run dangerous risks if you confuse a poem with assignment instructions or mistake a menu for a political blog. Obviously we don't read all these different genres in exactly the same way. We know instinctively that the various genres evoke certain interpretive expectations on the part of the reader. The genre game determines the rules for interpretation. Just as we know that the kind of game determines the rules we play by, so we know that each literary genre in the Bible comes with its own set of built-in rules for interpretation. When readers pay attention to those rules, they have a much greater chance of reading the passage as it was intended. Genres shape our expectations about how to approach a particular text. The form, or genre, of the text really is connected to its message, and for this reason, we should take literary genre seriously. The very meaning of the Bible is at stake!

3. Kevin J. Vanhoozer, *Is There a Meaning in This Text? The Bible, the Reader, and the Morality of Literary Knowledge* (Grand Rapids: Zondervan, 1998), 339.

4. Vanhoozer, 346.

WHAT IS SURROUNDING CONTEXT?

Surrounding context simply refers to the texts that surround the passage you are studying. You can think of it as the textual world in which your text lives. This includes the words, sentences, paragraphs, and discourses that come before and after your passage. The surrounding context of Romans 12:1–2, for instance, includes the first eleven chapters of Romans as well as Romans 12:3 through the end of the book. In a broader sense, the surrounding context of Romans 12:1–2 is the rest of the books in the New Testament and even the entire Old Testament. These various contexts form circles around your passage.

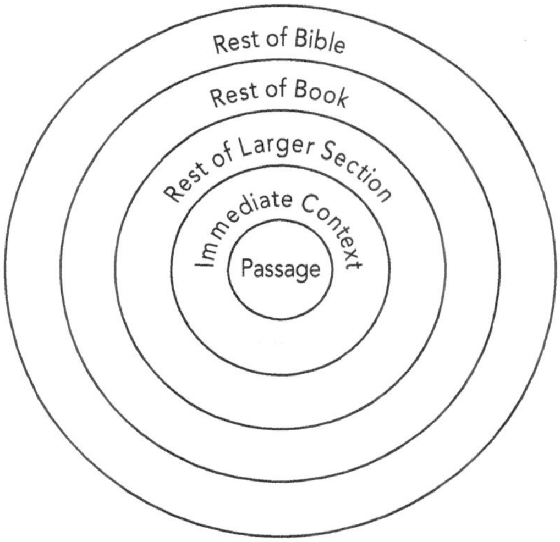

The *immediate context* circle is closest to the center since it describes what comes immediately before and after your passage. Do you remember the encouraging verse from 1 Peter 5:7: "Cast all your anxiety on him because he cares for you"? Do you recall its immediate context? The immediate context includes at least verses 5–9, perhaps more.

> 5In the same way, you who are younger, submit yourselves to your elders. All of you, clothe yourselves with humility toward one another, because,
>
> "God opposes the proud
> but shows favor to the humble."
>
> 6Humble yourselves, therefore, under God's mighty hand, that he may lift you up in due time. 7**Cast all your anxiety on him because he cares for you.**

> [8]Be alert and of sober mind. Your enemy the devil prowls around like a roaring lion looking for someone to devour. [9]Resist him, standing firm in the faith, because you know that the family of believers throughout the world is undergoing the same kind of sufferings.

We encourage you to give highest priority to the immediate context when determining the meaning of your passage. As the circles of the context diagram illustrates, the closer the circle is to the center, the greater influence it usually has on the meaning of your passage.

A careful look at the immediate context of 1 Peter 5:7 reveals that casting our cares on the Lord is strongly tied to humbling ourselves before him. This relationship grows even stronger when we realize that the word "cast" (v. 7) is actually a participle in the Greek text and should be translated "casting"; note the CSB translation of verses 6–7:

Give highest priority to the immediate context when determining the meaning of your passage.

> [6]Humble yourselves, therefore, under the mighty hand of God, so that he may exalt you at the proper time, [7]**casting** all your cares on him, because he cares about you.

The immediate context reveals that humbling ourselves before God means that we entrust our concerns and troubles to God because we know that God loves us and will take care of us. Pride says to God, "I can take care of this burden by myself," whereas humility involves casting our cares on our caring God. What a positive definition of humility! And that insight comes from a careful reading of the immediate context.

The next step is learning to *identify* the surrounding context of your passage. Before we do that, however, we should first discuss a couple of dangers associated with disregarding context.

DANGERS OF DISREGARDING LITERARY CONTEXT

You have probably heard it said that you can make the Bible say anything you want. That is true *only* if you disregard the literary context. When you honor the literary context (including the covenant of communication implicit in the genre), you cannot make the Bible say just anything. Cults are famous for Scripture twisting, and most of their misreadings stem from a violation of literary context.[5] Just because we approach

5. James W. Sire, *Scripture Twisting: 20 Ways the Cults Misread the Bible* (Downers Grove, IL: InterVarsity Press, 1980).

Scripture as Bible-believing Christians does not make us immune to misinterpretations should we decide to neglect literary context. A number of dangers are associated with disregarding literary context. Here we will discuss only two of the most common problems—the first associated with individual interpreters, the second with preachers.

> You can make the Bible say anything you want. That is true *only* if you disregard the literary context.

Ignoring the Surrounding Context

The first danger is simply ignoring the surrounding context. This usually happens when people focus on a single verse without paying attention to how the surrounding verses might affect its meaning. For example, the following verses are quotable favorites. Do you know their contexts?

- "Here I am! I stand at the door and knock. If anyone hears my voice and opens the door, I will come in and eat with that person, and they with me" (Rev. 3:20).
- "For where two or three gather in my name, there am I with them" (Matt. 18:20).
- "Flee the evil desires of youth and pursue righteousness, faith, love and peace, along with those who call on the Lord out of a pure heart" (2 Tim. 2:22).

Revelation 3:20 is commonly used to describe Jesus' promise to anyone who might accept him as Savior and Lord; that is, it is seen as an evangelistic promise: "If you will open the door of your heart, Christ promises to enter." But in context, Revelation 3:20 is a promise from the risen Christ to a congregation of "lukewarm" Christians. He assures these disobedient believers that he is ready and waiting to renew fellowship with them (standing at the door knocking) if they will repent (open the door). This verse applies directly to Christians living out of fellowship with Christ. As a believer, have you ever strayed so far from Christ that you wondered if he would ever take you back? Revelation 3:20 promises that he loves you and is waiting to restore you if you will turn back to him.

Matthew 18:20 is commonly quoted to remind everyone that group prayer is especially effective. But we rarely stop to think about what we are actually saying. Is Jesus with us only when we are with other Christians? The context of Matthew 18:20 is that of church discipline, as verses 15–17 make clear:

> [15]"If your brother or sister sins, go and point out their fault, just between the two of you. If they listen to you, you have won them over. [16]But if they will not

> listen, take one or two others along, so that 'every matter may be established by the testimony of two or three witnesses.' [17]If they still refuse to listen, tell it to the church; and if they refuse to listen even to the church, treat them as you would a pagan or a tax collector."

In other words, Jesus is saying that if congregations (even small ones with only a few believers) follow God's guidelines for corporate discipline, they will have his blessings.

Second Timothy 2:22 is a favorite verse for fighting off sexual temptation. But how does the surrounding context define "evil desires of youth"? Paul is writing to Timothy, who is facing the problem of false teachers within the leadership of the church at Ephesus. The previous unit (2:14–19) makes it clear that Timothy must resist the false teachers. This is supported by an analogy from the household (2:20–21). Likewise, 2:23–26 speaks of false teaching. In verse 22 Paul tells Timothy to run away from foolish discussions, arguments, and theological novelties so attractive to young ministers (i.e., "evil desires of youth") and to run instead after righteousness, faith, love, and peace with the true people of God. Much to the surprise of some, this verse has little (if anything) to do with sexual temptation. The Bible certainly addresses this issue, just not here.

These three examples illustrate the problem of ignoring the context that surrounds individual verses. The way our Bibles have been divided into chapters and verses doesn't help matters much. The chapter and verse numbers help us find passages quickly, but they can also lead us to believe that each verse stands alone as an independent unit of thought, like a number in a phone book.[6] Just because we attach numbers to the sentences in a paragraph doesn't mean that we can rip one particular sentence out of its context and disconnect it from what precedes or follows.

Chapter and verse divisions are not part of the original documents, but were added much later.

We also need to remember that the chapter and verse divisions are not part of the original documents, but were added much later. When we speak of the Holy Spirit's inspiring the Scriptures, we are talking about the text itself, not about the reference numbers. Don't let these later editorial additions cause you to lift individual sentences out of their surrounding context and give them a meaning never intended by their authors.

6. William W. Klein, Craig L. Blomberg, and Robert L. Hubbard Jr., *Introduction to Biblical Interpretation*, 4th ed. (Grand Rapids: Zondervan, 2017), 298.

Topical Preaching

A second danger associated with disregarding literary context is that of topical preaching. Topical preaching is a valid approach to preaching when the various passages are understood in context and the overall message doesn't violate those individual contexts. But far too often topical preaching distorts the meaning of Scripture by disregarding the literary context. Here is how that happens.

The diagram below shows how a biblical author's thought flows through a particular text. Expository preaching (in contrast to topical preaching) will follow an author's flow of thought through a particular text (e.g., John 10) in order to grasp the intended meaning and communicate that meaning to the congregation.

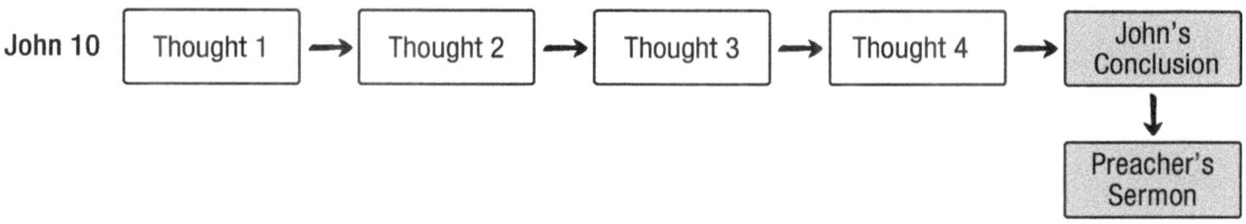

Topical preaching, by contrast, often jumps from one passage to another by stringing together a series of originally unrelated thoughts (see the resulting diagram below). That is the same as jumping from the blog post to the menu to the poem to the friend text, picking thoughts at random, to construct a message of your own choosing. You can see how this approach could easily violate the literary context and lead to all sorts of unbiblical conclusions.

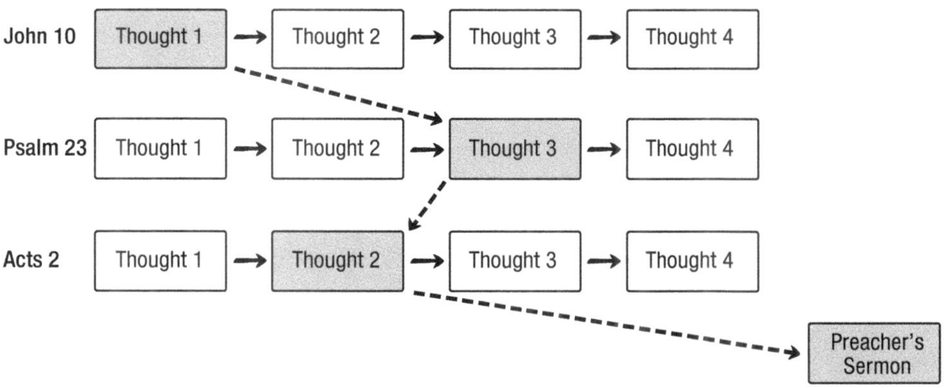

Quoting Bible passages out of context may make for an entertaining sermon, but it will mask God's true message. Misreading the Bible ultimately hurts people by enslaving them rather than setting them free with truth. What if the young man we mentioned at the beginning of the chapter really believed God had told him to marry his girlfriend when in fact God had done no such thing? The young man's failure to consider the context would cause a misreading with serious relational consequences. Who would want to enter such an important relationship without the Lord's blessing? Of course, his girlfriend might say no to his proposal and encourage him to take a class on interpreting the Bible. That would take care of everything.

Quoting Bible passages out of context may make for an entertaining sermon, but it will mask God's true message.

HOW TO IDENTIFY THE SURROUNDING CONTEXT

Up to this point in *Grasping God's Word*, we have spent a lot of time teaching you how to observe details and analyze parts of a passage. Reading a text closely and carefully is a good place to enter the world of biblical interpretation, but it is certainly not the final stopping place. The Bible is more than a collection of unrelated parts. The Holy Spirit moved the biblical writers to connect their words, sentences, and paragraphs into a literary whole in the normal way that people use language to communicate. Just imagine how a document would appear if the sentences were not linked together to form a unified message. Better yet, read the following paragraph:

> I heard an interesting story on the news the other night. The quarterback faded back to pass. Carbon buildup was keeping the carburetor from functioning properly. The two-inch steaks were burned on the outside but raw on the inside. Ten-feet-high snow drifts blocked the road. The grass needed mowing. The elevator raced to the top of the one-hundred-story building in less than a minute. The audience booed the poor performance.[7]

We typically don't string together randomly selected ideas when we are trying to communicate. Normally, sentences build on previous sentences and lead into later sentences to produce a coherent message. As God's communication to us, the parts of the Bible connect to form a whole, while the whole in turn provides guidelines or boundaries for understanding the parts. Our understanding of a specific text will always be shaped by the overall message of the book. If a reader fails to take into account what the author has already said or is about to say, he or she is in danger of missing the point of the passage.

7. Klein, Blomberg, and Hubbard, 296.

When we ask you to identify the surrounding context, we are asking you to see how these sentences (the parts) fit together in a book to communicate the larger message (the whole). We cannot read the author's mind, but we can trace his thought as it flows through each sentence and paragraph to form the whole book. We want to see how the smaller units connect to form the larger units. This will allow us to interpret our specific passage in light of its place in a larger section (i.e., in its original literary context). Knowing the surrounding context will answer questions such as the following:

- What is this unit's role or function or purpose in the book?
- What would happen if we removed this section from the book?
- Why did the author include this section as a crucial part of the whole?

Moreover, it is safe to say that the most accurate interpretation of a passage is the one that best fits that passage's surrounding context (i.e., one that best accounts for how the smaller sections fit into the larger sections). When our interpretation contradicts literary context (including literary genre and surrounding context), we violate the way people normally use language to communicate and our interpretation is invalid.

When it comes to surrounding context, our main goal is to identify how an author's thought flows through each part of the book to form the whole.

We are going to use the short New Testament book of Philemon to illustrate how to identify the surrounding context of a passage. Suppose that you are trying to interpret Philemon 4–7 (since there is only one chapter in the entire book, we will only use verse numbers after the book name). Your passage is highlighted in the letter below:

> [1]Paul, a prisoner of Christ Jesus, and Timothy our brother,
> To Philemon our dear friend and fellow worker—[2]also to Apphia our sister
> and Archippus our fellow soldier—and to the church that meets in your home:
> [3]Grace and peace to you from God our Father and the Lord Jesus Christ.
> [4]I always thank my God as I remember you in my prayers, [5]because I hear
> about your love for all his holy people and your faith in the Lord Jesus. [6]I pray
> that your partnership with us in the faith may be effective in deepening your
> understanding of every good thing we share for the sake of Christ. [7]Your love
> has given me great joy and encouragement, because you, brother, have refreshed
> the hearts of the Lord's people.
> [8]Therefore, although in Christ I could be bold and order you to do what
> you ought to do, [9]yet I prefer to appeal to you on the basis of love. It is as none

other than Paul—an old man and now also a prisoner of Christ Jesus—[10]that I appeal to you for my son Onesimus, who became my son while I was in chains. [11]Formerly he was useless to you, but now he has become useful both to you and to me.

[12]I am sending him—who is my very heart—back to you. [13]I would have liked to keep him with me so that he could take your place in helping me while I am in chains for the gospel. [14]But I did not want to do anything without your consent, so that any favor you do would not seem forced but would be voluntary. [15]Perhaps the reason he was separated from you for a little while was that you might have him back forever—[16]no longer as a slave, but better than a slave, as a dear brother. He is very dear to me but even dearer to you, both as a fellow man and as a brother in the Lord.

[17]So if you consider me a partner, welcome him as you would welcome me. [18]If he has done you any wrong or owes you anything, charge it to me. [19]I, Paul, am writing this with my own hand. I will pay it back—not to mention that you owe me your very self. [20]I do wish, brother, that I may have some benefit from you in the Lord; refresh my heart in Christ. [21]Confident of your obedience, I write to you, knowing that you will do even more than I ask.

[22]And one thing more: Prepare a guest room for me, because I hope to be restored to you in answer to your prayers.

[23]Epaphras, my fellow prisoner in Christ Jesus, sends you greetings. [24]And so do Mark, Aristarchus, Demas and Luke, my fellow workers.

[25]The grace of the Lord Jesus Christ be with your spirit.

As you read the passage, you ask, Why did Paul say this about Philemon? Is he just praying for Philemon as we would pray for a friend, or is there more to it? Does Paul thank God for Philemon simply because Philemon is a highly respected spiritual leader? Obviously Paul is praising Philemon for something. Why the glowing description?

You won't really know the answers to these questions until you know the surrounding context. To grasp what Paul really means in verses 4–7, you need to examine what Paul says before and after this passage. This is what we mean by "surrounding context"—how a section fits with what comes before and after it. If you don't know the surrounding context of your passage, you will probably just skim the surface and miss the real meaning. You need to discover the surrounding context of verses 4–7 to grasp Paul's message in that section. Remember, context determines meaning!

Finding the surrounding context of any passage consists of three steps. (1) Identify how the book is divided into paragraphs or sections. (2) Summarize the main idea of each section. (3) Explain how your particular passage relates to the surrounding sections. Let's continue with our Philemon example.

1. *Identify how the book is divided into paragraphs or sections.* Look at several different Bible translations to see how the translators have divided the book and the chapters into smaller units. Note how the following translations have divided Philemon.

NIV	KJV	CSB	RSV	ESV
1–3	1–3	1–3	1–3	1–3
4–7	4–7	4–7	4–7	4–7
8–11	8–25	8–16	8–16	8–16
12–16		17–22	17–21	17–20
17–21		23–24	22	21–22
22		25	23–25	23–25
23–25				

As you can tell, there is some agreement about how the book should be divided, but the translations are certainly not uniform. Remember that editorial decisions such as dividing the book into units are intended to help the reader, but they are not inspired. If you want to do the work yourself, you need to *look for changes in the text* as clues to a shift in the author's flow of thought. Items that mark changes or transitions include the following:

- conjunctions (e.g., *therefore*, *then*, *but*)
- change of genre (e.g., from a greeting to a prayer)
- changes of topic or theme (main idea)
- changes in time, location, or setting
- grammatical changes (e.g., subject, object, pronouns, verb tense, person, or number)

You will notice some of these transition points in Philemon. There is a change in topic between verses 3 and 4 as Paul switches from a greeting to a prayer. Don't miss the conjunction "therefore" in verse 8 and the "so" in verse 17, both beginning new sections. You will also find other change markers in the last few verses of the book: "one thing more" (v. 22), change to a greeting (v. 23), a final blessing (v. 25).

In our example, all the translations agree that verses 4–7 form a section, and most agree that verses 8–16 constitute another section. Although the translations will rarely agree 100 percent on how to divide the book, make some tentative decisions and move on to step 2. Writing the summaries in step 2 is one way of checking the validity of your section divisions in step 1.

2. *Summarize the main idea of each section in about a dozen words or less.* For each summary statement you write, make sure to summarize the point of the whole section and not just a portion of the section. After writing a summary, you might want to read the section again and see if your summary truly captures the entire section. When writing your summary, think about two things: (a) the topic or main idea of the section, and (b) what the author says about the topic or main idea. As you do this, you will have to resist the temptation to get lost in all the details. Stick with the main point, the big idea. Take a look at our summaries for each section of Philemon:

- vv. 1–3: Paul identifies the letter senders/recipients and offers a greeting.
- vv. 4–7: Paul thanks God for Philemon's faith and love and prays for him.
- vv. 8–16: Paul appeals to Philemon for his "son" Onesimus and offers Philemon perspective on God's plan.
- vv. 17–20: Paul urges Philemon to receive Onesimus as he would receive Paul himself.
- v. 21: Paul expresses confidence that Philemon will do even more than he asks.
- v. 22: Paul shares his hope to come in person and visit Philemon.
- vv. 23–24: Paul shares greetings from his fellow workers.
- v. 25: Paul closes the letter with a benediction of grace.

As you write a summary for each paragraph or section, you will be able to evaluate your decisions about section divisions. Don't be afraid to reconfigure the units as you try to summarize the main point of each.

3. *Explain how your particular passage relates to the surrounding sections.* Now that you can see the author's flow of thought through the entire book by reading your section summaries, it is time to look at how your passage fits into its surroundings. We tell our students, "If you do nothing else besides read what comes before and what comes after your passage, you will eliminate about 75 percent of all interpretive mistakes." The heart of identifying the surrounding context is to observe how your section relates to what comes before it and what comes after it. Let's try to identify the surrounding context of Philemon 4–7 (this serves as an example of the kind of explanation that you need to write in this step).

Our section (vv. 4–7) is sandwiched between the opening of the letter (vv. 1–3) and the body of the letter (vv. 8–22). Almost everything Paul says in the thanksgiving and prayer passage prepares the reader for what he is about to say in the body of the letter. In this case, the thanksgiving becomes the basis for the request that follows. Paul attributes a number of qualities to Philemon in verses 4–7, the very qualities that will enable Philemon to respond positively to Paul's request. Paul thanks God that Philemon trusts the Lord and loves people. This love, Paul goes on to say, "has given me great joy and encouragement." He also commends Philemon for refreshing the hearts of the saints. Now Paul has a favor to ask about one believer in particular, Onesimus. Thus, the thanksgiving and prayer section (vv. 4–7) prepares the way for the body of the letter. Philemon's good qualities that are highlighted in verses 4–7 provide the character anchor that will motivate him to do what Paul is about to request in the rest of the letter. When we study Philemon 4–7 with its surrounding context in view, we can truly grasp the meaning of the passage.

CONCLUSION

We study literary context because the interpretation that best fits the context is the most valid interpretation. When we disregard literary context, we run the risk of forcing the Bible to say what we want it to say. This may appear to satisfy people's immediate needs, but ultimately, this approach hurts people by robbing them of God's liberating truth. People are seeking time-tested answers to problems that are staring them in the face, answers that contemporary culture simply cannot supply. When we take the literary context seriously, we are saying, "We want to hear what God is trying to say to us."

Ultimately, disregarding the literary context of the Bible hurts people by robbing them of God's liberating truth.

In this chapter we have learned that literary context consists of both literary genre and the context surrounding your passage. Literary genre functions like a covenant of communication between the author and the reader. As readers, our job is to be faithful to this covenant by playing by the game rules established by the author. The surrounding context shows us that every passage lives in a world surrounded by other passages. We ourselves communicate by connecting our words, sentences, and paragraphs into a coherent message, and the Bible does the same. We reviewed two of the most common dangers associated with disregarding literary context and underscored the importance of knowing the immediate context of a passage. We concluded the chapter by suggesting three steps to identifying surrounding context, using Philemon as our example. As you honor the literary context of a passage of Scripture, you will be saying through your actions that above all you want to hear what God has to say to you through his Word.

ASSIGNMENTS

Assignment 8–1

Write a paragraph describing the surrounding context of the following passages: Acts 1:7–8 and 1 Corinthians 11:27–32.

Assignment 8–2

Turn to the Old Testament book of Jonah and do the following:

1. Read the entire book of Jonah and identify how the book is divided into paragraphs or sections.
2. Summarize the main idea of each section in about a dozen words or less.
3. Explain how your particular passage (use Jonah 1:13–16 for this exercise) relates to the surrounding context.

CHAPTER 9

WORD STUDIES

INTRODUCTION

Have you ever tried to put together one of those thousand-piece puzzles? The box cover features a majestic mountain scene or a picture of three cute kittens in a basket. Then you dump out all one thousand pieces and start to reconstruct the picture. Again and again you pick up a puzzle piece, look at its shape and its colors, and try to fit it into the larger scheme of things. Every piece contributes something to the picture even as the larger picture gives definition to each individual piece.

Words are like pieces of a puzzle. They fit together to form a story or a paragraph (i.e., the big picture). Until you know the meaning of certain words, you will not be able to grasp the meaning of the whole passage. Not knowing the meaning of certain words in a passage of Scripture can be compared to the frustrating discovery that you don't have all the pieces to your puzzle. Like individual pieces of a puzzle, words bring the larger picture to life. Words are worth studying!

> "[The aim of word study] is to try to understand as precisely as possible what the author was trying to convey by his use of *this* word in this context."
> —*Gordon Fee*

New Testament scholar Gordon Fee says that the aim of word study "is to try to understand as precisely as possible what the author was trying to convey by his use of *this* word in this context."[1] As readers we do not determine the meaning of biblical words; rather, we try to discover what the biblical writer meant when he used a particular word. We should always keep in mind this distinction between *determining* meaning and *discovering* meaning. In addition to serving as a purpose statement, Fee's definition also highlights the importance of context.

This chapter is all about studying the words of Scripture. Even if you don't know the original biblical languages, Hebrew and Greek, you can still learn to use interpretive tools to do a word study properly, and we will show you how. We start the chapter by warning you of common mistakes people make when studying words of Scripture. Then we will explain how to identify words in a passage that need further study, how to determine what a word could mean, and finally how to decide what a word does mean in context. In each phase we ask you to interact with us and practice the necessary steps. Since most people learn a great deal by having a model to imitate, we will close the chapter with a full example of how to do a word study. Again, you don't have to know Greek or Hebrew to do a word study properly. You can do this, but you need to know the proper procedure. Your reward for studying words carefully will often be a breathtaking view of a majestic biblical scene.

COMMON WORD-STUDY FALLACIES[2]

Before we show you how to do a word study properly, we want to point out a few of the more common mistakes interpreters make when studying words. The list could be much longer, but this should give you some idea of what to avoid when studying words.

English-Only Fallacy

Because the Bible was not originally written in English, it must be translated into English from the original biblical languages, Hebrew and Greek. This fact can complicate word studies for students who do not know the original languages. Here are two examples of problems that may develop. (1) You may not realize that a *word in Hebrew or Greek is often translated into English by a number of different English words.* For example, the Greek word *paraklēsis* is translated in the NIV with the following English words: "comfort, encouragement, appeal, be encouraged, consolation,

1. Gordon D. Fee, *New Testament Exegesis: A Handbook for Students and Pastors*, 3rd ed. (Louisville: Westminster John Knox, 2002), 79.

2. For more on word-study fallacies, see the thorough treatment by D. A. Carson in *Exegetical Fallacies*, 2nd ed. (Grand Rapids: Baker, 1996), 27–64, along with the brief survey by Darrell Bock in "Lexical Analysis: Studies in Words," in *Interpreting the New Testament Text*, ed. Darrell L. Bock and Buist M. Fanning (Wheaton, IL: Crossway, 2006), 149–52.

encourage, encouraged, encouraging message, exhortation, greatly encouraged, preaching, urgently." You will immediately notice that English words like "comfort" and "exhortation" can mean different things depending on the context.

(2) English-language students may not be aware that *different words in Hebrew or Greek can be translated into English using the same English word.* For instance, the NIV translates these different Greek words—*parakaleō*, *paraklēsis*, *paramytheomai*, *paramythia*, *paramythion*, and *parēgoria*—as "comfort."

The English-only fallacy occurs when you base your word study on the English word rather than the underlying Greek or Hebrew word and, as a result, draw unreliable or misleading conclusions. This chapter teaches you how to study words so that you don't make this mistake.

The English-only fallacy occurs when you base your word study on the English word rather than on the underlying Greek or Hebrew word.

Root Fallacy

One of the more common fallacies is the notion that the real meaning of a word is found in its original root (i.e., in the etymology of the word). Think about how silly this can be even in English. Is a *butterfly* actually a *fly* that has lost control and crash-landed into a tub of *butter*? Is a *pineapple* a certain kind of *apple* that grows only on *pine* trees? What in the world is a *sawhorse*?

Switching from English to a biblical language doesn't automatically change things. Just because someone can spout off the component parts of a Greek word doesn't mean that he or she has discovered the "real meaning" of the word. For example, the verb *ginōskō* means "to know, understand, or recognize" (e.g., Eph. 6:22), while the verb *anaginōskō* means "to read or read aloud" (e.g., Luke 4:16).[3] It is true that a word's individual parts *may* accurately portray its meaning, but only if the context supports such a meaning.[4] Give context priority over etymology, and you will be on solid ground.

Time-Frame Fallacy

The time-frame fallacy occurs when we latch onto a late word meaning (usually a meaning popular in our own time) and read it back into the Bible, or when we insist that an early word meaning still holds when in fact it has since become obsolete.

---

3. William D. Mounce, *Mounce's Complete Expository Dictionary of Old and New Testament Words* (Grand Rapids: Zondervan, 2006), 560–61.

4. Etymology becomes more important when we are trying to understand the meaning of words that are used only once in Scripture (we refer to such words as *hapax legomena*). You will find this to be the case more in the Hebrew Old Testament than in the Greek New Testament.

You will encounter the first instance of this fallacy far more than the second. D. A. Carson uses the English word *dynamite* and the Greek word *dynamis* (sometimes translated "power") to illustrate a particular form of the time-frame fallacy:

> I do not know how many times I have heard preachers offer some such rendering of Romans 1:16 as this: "I am not ashamed of the gospel, for it is the *dynamite* of God unto salvation for everyone who believes"—often with a knowing tilt of the head, as if something profound or even esoteric has been uttered. . . . Did Paul think of dynamite when he penned this word?[5]

Most certainly Paul was not thinking of the English word *dynamite* when he wrote the Greek word *dynamis*, since the English word originated centuries later. The two words may sound alike (a temptation many preachers find irresistible), but they are two words with very different meanings. Confusing the meaning of two words like this is misleading and dangerous. Do we really want to read this late word meaning back into the New Testament and conclude that God's power destroys like a devastating bomb when Paul himself says in this verse that God's power leads to salvation for everyone who believes? Carson concludes, "Of course, what preachers are trying to do when they talk about dynamite is give some indication of the greatness of the power involved. Even so, Paul's measure is not dynamite, but the empty tomb."[6]

Overload Fallacy

Most words can mean several different things. The overload fallacy is the idea that a word will include all of those meanings every time it is used. For example, the English word *spring* can refer to a season, a metal coil, an act of jumping, or a source of water. You would be overloading *spring* (pun intended . . . perhaps) to assume that in every passage in which it occurs, the word carries not just one, but *all*, of those senses. Which meaning for *spring* does the context demand in the sentence "Spring is my favorite season of the year"? If you said "all of the above," or even if you chose any meaning except a season of the year, you would be guilty of the overload fallacy.

Word-Count Fallacy

The word-count fallacy is a mistake we make when we insist that a word must have the same meaning every time it occurs. For example, if we are confident that a word carries a certain meaning in seven of its eight occurrences in Scripture, we might

5. Carson, *Exegetical Fallacies*, 34.
6. Carson, 34.

be tempted to conclude that it must have that same meaning in its eighth occurrence. Yet, as Darrell Bock maintains, "word meanings are determined by context, not word counts."[7]

Later in this chapter we will use the example of a word translated "suffer," which seems to carry the sense of negative experience every time it is used in Paul's letters, with one possible exception. In Galatians 3:4 the context suggests that the word refers to a positive rather than a negative experience and should be translated "experience" (rather than "suffer"). All this is to say that the word's immediate context should take priority over secondary contexts in determining the meaning of the word.

"Word meanings are determined by context, not word counts."
—*Darrell Bock*

Word-as-Concept Fallacy

We fall prey to the word-concept fallacy when we assume that once we have studied one word, we have studied an entire concept. If, for example, you want to discover what the New Testament says about the church, you should certainly study the word translated "church" (*ekklēsia*). Yet it would be a mistake to conclude that once you have studied *ekklēsia*, you will know all that the New Testament teaches about church. A concept is bigger than any one word. To see what the New Testament says about the church, you need to broaden your study to include ideas like "body of Christ," "temple of the Holy Spirit," and "household of faith." The concept of church is much broader than the one word *ekklēsia*.

Selective-Evidence Fallacy

When we cite just the evidence that supports our favored interpretation or when we dismiss evidence that seems to argue against our view, we commit the selective-evidence fallacy. This error is particularly dangerous because here we are intentionally tampering with the biblical evidence, whereas in other fallacies the mistakes may be unintentional. Although we want the Bible to support our convictions in every case, there will be times when its message confronts us for our own good. When that happens, we should change our view rather than twist Scripture to advance our own agenda. Before you begin studying a word in the Bible, make up your mind to accept all the evidence.

7. Bock, "Lexical Analysis," 151.

We have discussed seven common word-study fallacies. These mistakes are easy to make, but being aware of them will help you to avoid them. Now it is time to learn how to do a word study. The process consists of three steps: (1) choosing your words, (2) determining what the word *could* mean, and (3) determining what the word *does* mean in context.

CHOOSE YOUR WORDS CAREFULLY

Doing a word study properly takes time. Be realistic and admit that you cannot possibly study every word in your passage and still have any time for your friends. In fact, you don't need to study every word. Most biblical passages are filled with words whose meanings are clear and plain to the average reader. But some words do demand more in-depth study, and you need wisdom to know which ones. What should you do at this point? Use the following guidelines to help you choose the words you need to study.

1. Look for *words that are important or crucial to the passage*. Everything in the passage depends on the meaning of these words. They are loaded with historical or theological significance. They bear the weight of the passage. Often the crucial words in a passage will be the key nouns and/or verbs.
2. Look for *repeated words*. Usually the author will signal theme words by repeating them, so pay close attention to words that are repeated (e.g., "comfort" in 2 Cor. 1:3–7, "blessed" in Matt. 5:1–12, or "remain" in John 15:1–11). Study these words for sure.
3. Look for *figures of speech*. Here words are used not in a literal sense but as word pictures or images. When you read Jesus' statement "I am the gate" (John 10:9) or read about trees clapping their hands (Isa. 55:12), you are looking at figures of speech. Since the intended meaning of many figures or images is not automatically obvious, you may need to study them further. For example, the image of a lion refers to Jesus Christ in Revelation 5:5 and to Satan in 1 Peter 5:8.[8]
4. Look for *words that are unclear, puzzling, or difficult*. Perhaps you don't understand the English definition of a word. Or you may find that English translations differ widely when it comes to this particular word. Or a writer may be using a word in a technical or specialized sense. A good rule of thumb here is that "the most important words are those that give you trouble," and if a word gives you trouble, study it some more.[9]

8. See Leland Ryken, James C. Wilhoit, and Tremper Longman III, *Dictionary of Biblical Imagery* (Downers Grove, IL: InterVarsity Press, 1998), for help with figures of speech.

9. Mortimer J. Adler and Charles Van Doren, *How to Read a Book*, rev. ed. (New York: Simon & Schuster, 1972), 102.

Now you give it a try. Photocopy this page and circle the words in Romans 12:1–2 and Matthew 28:18–20 (below) that you think merit further study. In the margin explain why you chose each word. Remember, look for crucial words, repeated words, images, and difficult words.

Romans 12:1–2

1Therefore, I urge you, brothers and sisters, in view of God's
mercy, to offer your bodies as a living sacrifice, holy
and pleasing to God—this is your true and proper
worship. 2Do not conform to the pattern
of this world, but be transformed by the renewing of
your mind. Then you will be able to test and approve
what God's will is—his good, pleasing and perfect will.

Matthew 28:18–20

18Then Jesus came to them and said, "All authority
in heaven and on earth has been given to me.
19Therefore go and make disciples of all nations,
baptizing them in the name of the Father and of the
Son and of the Holy Spirit, 20and teaching them to
obey everything I have commanded you. And surely
I am with you always, to the very end of the age."

Now take a look at how we dealt with these same passages.

Romans 12:1–2

Key Verbs

Figure of Speech

Key Noun

[1]Therefore, I urge you, brothers and sisters, in view of God's
mercy, to offer your bodies as a living sacrifice, holy
and pleasing to God—this is your true and proper
worship. [2]Do not conform to the pattern
of this world, but be transformed by the renewing of
your mind. Then you will be able to test and approve
what God's will is—his good, pleasing and perfect will.

Difficult

Key Noun

Key Verbs

Difficult

Matthew 28:18–20

[18]Then Jesus came to them and said, "All authority
in heaven and on earth has been given to me.
[19]Therefore go and make disciples of all nations,
baptizing them in the name of the Father and of the
Son and of the Holy Spirit, [20]and teaching them to
obey everything I have commanded you. And surely
I am with you always, to the very end of the age."

Key Nouns

Key Verbs

Puzzling

Don't be surprised if you didn't pick the same words we picked, and don't be alarmed if you picked fewer. We intentionally selected a lot of words to illustrate why a reader might choose to study them. What's most important is that you think through *why* you would want to study certain words.

DETERMINE WHAT THE WORD COULD MEAN

Why do we need to determine what the word *could* mean before we decide what it *does* mean? Because most words can mean several different things (e.g., spring), but will usually carry only *one* of those meanings in a particular context.[10] By clarifying what a word could mean, we will not confuse the various meanings of a word when interpreting a particular passage of Scripture.

Consider this scenario. If, in the dead of winter, your friend says, "It's so cold, I can't wait until spring gets here," he would be referring to the arrival of the much warmer season that immediately follows winter, not the arrival of a metal coil or an improved jumping ability. Imagine the absurdity of the statement, "It's so cold, I can't wait until my jumping ability improves." You might begin to wonder if the cold had made your friend a little too sleepy.

Semantic Range

Once we see all the possible meanings of a word—what we refer to as a word's *range of meaning* or *semantic range*—we will be in a better position to decide what the word actually does mean in a specific context. For example, let's look at the semantic range of the English word *hand*. To find the range of meaning for an English word, just look it up in a standard English dictionary (also called a lexicon). A glance at the dictionary entry for *hand* reveals a range of meaning that looks something like this:

- the terminal part of a vertebrate forelimb (my right *hand*)
- a personal possession (It fell into the *hands* of the enemy.)
- a side (on the one *hand* . . . on the other *hand*)
- a pledge (I give you my *hand* in marriage.)
- a style of penmanship (This letter was written in my own *hand*.)
- a skill or ability (She tried her *hand* at sailing.)

10. The exception is when the biblical author intentionally makes a play on words. You see this occasionally in John's gospel. When Jesus tells Nicodemus that he "must be born again" (John 3:7 NIV), the expression could also mean "born from above" (NRSV). Is Jesus telling this Pharisee that he must be born a second time (i.e., experience a spiritual birth) or that he must be born from above (i.e., from God), or perhaps both? We could be looking at a wordplay here since the semantic range of the underlying Greek word *anōthen* includes both senses.

- a unit of measure (The horse is fifteen *hands* high.)
- aid or assistance (Please lend me a *hand*.)
- cards in a card game (I was dealt a bad *hand*.)
- one who performs a particular work (They employ more than fifty *hands*.)
- workmanship or handiwork (the work of the master's *hand*)

A word's range of meaning (or semantic range) is a list of all the possible meanings of a word—that is, a list of what the word *could* mean. Some of these meanings may be very closely related.

You might be thinking, *Okay. All I need to do to find my word's range of meaning is look it up in an English dictionary, right?* No, not really. You see, your word is an English translation of a Hebrew or Greek word, and that fact changes things. Since the Bible was not originally written in English, you are really trying to find the range of meaning for a Greek or Hebrew word, not the English word used in translation. You should use an English dictionary to find the meaning of an English word, but going straight to your English dictionary to find the range of meaning for a Greek or Hebrew word is a potentially big mistake.

Both the original-language word (Hebrew or Greek) and the English word used to translate it will have a semantic range. There will be some overlap between the semantic ranges of the two words; that's what makes translation possible. But the ranges will not be identical. We must remember that they are different words and will almost always have different (but overlapping) ranges of meaning.

As an example, let's look at a word Jesus uses in the parable of the talents: "Again, it will be like a man going on a journey, who called his servants and *entrusted* his wealth to them" (Matt. 25:14; cf. also 25:20, 22). If you look up the word *entrust* in your English dictionary, you will find a fairly narrow range of meaning:

a. to confer a trust on; to deliver something in trust to
b. to commit to another with confidence

You may be surprised to learn that the Greek word *paradidōmi*, the word the NIV translates "entrust," has a much broader range of meaning:

a. to hand over something to someone
b. to deliver someone into the control of someone else; to betray
c. to commend or commit
d. to pass on traditional instruction
e. to grant someone the opportunity to do something; to allow or permit

The NIV can translate the Greek word *paradidōmi* as "entrust" because the semantic ranges of the two words overlap. In Jesus' parable the master is "entrusting" in the sense of (A) in both lists above—he is handing over (or entrusting) his property to the servants while he is away on a journey. In spite of this essential overlap between the two words, they are different words with different ranges of meaning.

Here things get tricky. We could get into interpretive trouble if we were to say, for example, that the English word *entrust* could mean "betray" (which it cannot) or that the Greek word *paradidōmi* could never mean "betray" (which it can). We don't want you to misinterpret by confusing the semantic ranges for different words. Avoid the temptation to pick just any meaning from a list of possible meanings and read that meaning back into the passage. Always keep in mind as well that the original-language word and the translation word are different words with different ranges of meaning that overlap to some degree. The overlap is what makes translation possible. Your task is to locate the point of overlap (something we will teach you how to do soon). Before that, how about one more example of a word's range of meaning?

Suppose you want to study the word "confidence" in Hebrews 4:16: "Let us then approach God's throne of grace with *confidence*, so that we may receive mercy and find grace to help us in our time of need." If you go to the English dictionary, you will find a range of meaning for the word *confidence* similar to this:

a. a feeling of one's ability or power
b. a belief that a person will act in a proper or effective way
c. being certain about something
d. a relation of trust or intimacy (i.e., to take someone into confidence)
e. a secret (i.e., a communication made in confidence)

The NIV selects the word "confidence" in Hebrew 4:16 to translate the underlying Greek word *parrēsia*. Have a look at the range of meaning for *parrēsia*:

a. plainness, frankness (e.g., Jesus tells his disciples "plainly" [John 11:14])
b. openness to the public (e.g., Jesus speaks "publicly" to the crowds in the temple courts [John 7:26])
c. boldness, courage, confidence (when the rulers, elders, and teachers of the law saw the "courage" of Peter and John [Acts 4:13])

Most likely the English word *confidence* and the Greek word *parrēsia* overlap in the sense of (C) in both lists (it's a little harder to tell in this case). What is clear from the context is that the author of Hebrews does not want his readers to approach the throne of grace with a feeling of their own power or a trust in their own ability (sense [A] in the English-meaning list). Such a word-study blunder would suggest a rejection of Christ's work in favor of mere human effort. No, our confidence is more of a certainty about what our High Priest has accomplished rather than a reliance on what we have done. Because of the work that Jesus, our High Priest, has performed, we may approach God's throne for help when we face temptation.

Now back to our main task: determining what the word—the Greek or Hebrew word, not the English word—*could* mean. How do we find the range of meaning for the original-language word that underlies our English translation? We suggest you do two things.

Concordance Work

The first step is to use a concordance of the Bible to locate the original Hebrew or Greek word. A concordance is a listing of all the words used in a book, often with a summary of how those words are translated into English. As you see the different ways the word has been translated into English, you will begin to get a feel for what the word could mean (i.e., its semantic range). In this section you will learn how to use an English-language resource to find the original Hebrew or Greek word. We are going to use the online resource developed by the scholars at Tyndale House, Cambridge—the STEP program (**S**cripture **T**ools for **E**very **P**erson), available to use for free at www.stepbible.org.[11] The STEP program is tied to the ESV, so we will illustrate word studies below using the ESV.

Let's say you want to study the expression "press on" in Philippians 3:12, where Paul announces, "Not that I have already obtained this or am already perfect, but I *press on* to make it my own, because Christ Jesus has made me his own" (ESV). Go to www.stepbible.org and you will see in the "Find" box (or search bar) at the top "ESV" and "Gen 1." Close out the Gen 1 box and type Philippians 3 beside "ESV" and hit return or click on "Find." You should be looking at the ESV text of Philippians 3 in the box below. Now, put your cursor on "press on" in verse 12 and click on it. You will see a box appear to the right with some important information. This is what you should see in the Vocab panel to the right:

11. If you prefer the NIV translation, you could use *The Strongest NIV Exhaustive Concordance*, ed. Edward W. Goodrick and John R. Kohlenberger III (Grand Rapids: Zondervan, 1999). The online STEP Bible program is tied to the ESV translation. The main thing is that you use a concordance that matches the version of the Bible you are using.

Vocab

διώκω (*diōkō*) 'to pursue' (G1377)

to pursue, persecute, to systematically oppress and harass a person or group, as an extended meaning of pursuing a person on foot in a chase; also from the image of the chase comes the meaning of striving and pressing on to a goal with intensity: to press on

Search for this word (~47 occurrences)

Meaning

to put in rapid motion; to pursue; to follow, pursue the direction of, Lk. 17:23; **to follow eagerly, endeavor earnestly to acquire,** Rom. 9:30, 31; 12:13; **to press forwards,** Phil. 3:12, 14; **to pursue** with malignity, **persecute,** Mt. 5:10, 11, 12, 44

This tells you a lot about how this word is used in the New Testament. First, the underlying Greek word is διώκω, transliterated into English as *diōḵō*. The "G1377" number is the concordance number, but you don't need to worry about that for now. Second, you will see how the word is defined and what it means. The "Meaning" section is very helpful in providing a semantic range for your word. As you do your own study of the original word, you may refine its range of meaning, so don't feel bound by the "meaning" options provided here. They are simply a good place to begin. Finally, you will see how many times the word occurs in the New Testament (47).

Let's run through how to use the STEP Bible program once more, this time with an Old Testament word. Do you remember how Joseph got to Egypt? His brothers sold him to a band of Ishmaelite merchants, who took him there. In Egypt, Potiphar purchased Joseph from the Ishmaelites and eventually made Joseph his personal attendant. The story takes a sordid twist at this point. Potiphar's wife wanted Joseph to go to bed with her, but he kept refusing.

On one occasion when he was attending to his household duties and there were no other servants around, Potiphar's wife grabbed Joseph's cloak and demanded that he sleep with her. Joseph ran for his life, leaving his cloak in her hand. She then called the other servants and accused Joseph of laughing at her (Gen. 39:14–15): "She called to the men of her household and said to them, 'See, he has brought among us a Hebrew to laugh at us. He came in to me to lie with me, and I cried out with a loud voice. And as soon as he heard that I lifted up my voice and cried out, he left his garment beside me and fled and got out of the house" (ESV).

To know more about the expression "laugh," go the STEP Bible program and close out the Gen 1 box up top and type "Genesis 39" and hit return or find. Click on "laugh" in verse 14 and see the Vocab panel appear to the right with more information. You will see that the Hebrew word transliterated "*tsa.chaq*" is sometimes translated "to laugh, mock, play, to jest, to sport, play, make sport, toy with, or make a toy of" and is used twelve times in the Old Testament. By using the STEP Bible program, you can discover the underlying Hebrew or Greek word, get some information about its range of meaning, and find out how many times it is used in the Old or New Testament. You now have a better idea about what the word could mean.

Remember, however, that while a concordance will show a line of context for each occurrence, this may not be enough. You may need to open your Bible and have a look at the larger context.

Context Studies

We need to take the process one step further by looking more closely at context. The one rule in doing word studies that overrules all other rules is this: *Context determines word meaning.* If you take any word out of its context, you cannot really tell what it means. For example, what does the word *nice* mean? Something like *kind* or *considerate*? Maybe in certain contexts, such as "He is nice." But a change of context may change the meaning of the word (e.g., "He is nice and fat"). If the speaker is referring to a hog rather than a man, the meaning may be different. We cannot simply study a word by itself (e.g., *flesh*); we have to study a word in a particular context (e.g., "flesh" in Phil. 3:4).[12] Consequently, to be confident about knowing a word's range of meaning, you must see how it is used in context and not just how it has been translated into English.

To check the context, you need to know where the Greek or Hebrew word actually occurs in Scripture, and then you need to look up each occurrence. Checking the context takes time, but it is a crucial step in determining what the word *could* mean. The STEP Bible program is a huge help here. Let's look again at *diōkō*, translated "press on" in Philippians 3:12.

Using the STEP Bible program again, type in Philippians 3:12 in the search bar above. Then click on "press on" in the verse itself. Then click on "search for this word" in the Vocab panel to the right, and a list of all the occurrences of *diōkō* in the New Testament appears in a box to the left with the translations of this word highlighted. How cool! Now, take some time and check the word's range of meaning. If you need more context, you can click on the "Options" button in the bar above and expand the context by clicking on the + sign to add a verse of context.

12. Fee, *New Testament Exegesis*, 79.

As you consider the uses of *diōkō* in context, you begin to see a semantic range come into view:

a. to persecute (e.g., Matt. 5:10, 11, 12)
b. to follow or pursue in a physical sense (e.g., Luke 17:23; Matt. 23:34)
c. to pursue (in a figurative sense), strive for, seek after (e.g., Rom. 9:30, 31; 1 Cor. 14:1)

Although the range of meaning you have found is very similar to the "Meaning" information provided in the Vocab panel to the right, you now have a better sense of what the word could mean by looking at the context yourself.

While we are at it, let's check the context of our Old Testament example, "laugh" ("*tsa.chaq*") in Genesis 39:14. When you type in Genesis 39:14 in the STEP Bible search bar and click on "laugh" in the verse, then "search for this word," you now see all the occurrences of "*tsa.chaq*" in the Old Testament.

As you check the context for this Hebrew word, you might come up with a semantic range similar to what you see below:

a. to express doubt and disbelief by laughing (Gen. 17:17; 18:12, 13, 15)
b. to express joy by laughing (Gen. 21:6)
c. to caress physically (Gen. 26:8; 39:14, 17?)
d. to ridicule or mock (Gen. 21:9; 39:14, 17?)
e. to revel or play, perhaps in an immoral way (Ex. 32:6)
f. to joke (Gen. 19:14)
g. to entertain (Judg. 16:25)

By looking closely at the context, you pick up on something that you might not see in the "meanings" provided. You may have noticed that we added meaning "C. to caress physically (Gen. 26:8; 39:14, 17?)" to the list. This comes from comparing translations. In the STEP Bible when you have the word "*tsa.chaq*" and the ESV in the search bar with all twelve occurrences below, you can simply type "NIV" in the search bar also, then hit return, and this translation will be added to the list below. The ESV and NIV line up pretty well until you get to Genesis 26:8, where the NIV reads, "When Isaac had been there a long time, Abimelek king of the Philistines looked down from a window and saw Isaac caressing his wife Rebekah." Now, that's certainly different from "laughing with Rebekah." When you add context, you see that Abimelek realized from watching them that Rebekah really was Isaac's wife and not his sister (see 26:9). This strongly suggests they were doing more than laughing together. It also makes you wonder, in light of the context of Genesis 39 if there is something a bit more sexual about the use of the term in 39:14, 17. Comparing translations and looking more closely at the context can add a lot to our study of a word.

In summary, before you decide what your word does mean, you need to determine what it could mean. You can use the STEP Bible program to find the original Hebrew or Greek word and see its definitions and its translations into English. Then you must use the program again to check the context surrounding your word, perhaps even comparing the ESV with other translations. Now for the final step—it's time to decide what your word actually *does* mean in the context of the passage.

DECIDE WHAT THE WORD DOES MEAN IN CONTEXT

In light of the context, the first thing you must do is to select from the possible meanings the one meaning that best fits your word. What we said earlier about the importance of context bears repeating: *context determines word meaning!* Context includes everything that surrounds your word, such as the paragraph containing the word, the subject matter, the author's argument or flow of thought, as well as external factors such as the historical situation of the author and the original audience.

One of the most reliable ways to let the context guide your decision is through a concept known as "circles of context" (the diagram below illustrates the circles of context for a New Testament word; the same principle would also apply to the study of Old Testament words).

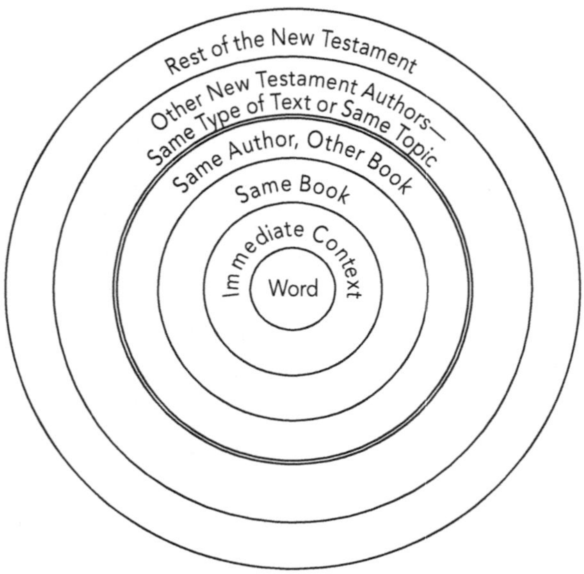

Generally speaking, the closer the circle is to the center, the greater influence it should normally have on your decision about the word's meaning. When trying to decide the meaning of a New Testament word, for example, you would usually give more weight to writings by the same author (and especially to the word's immediate context) than to other parts of the New Testament. All of this is based on the notion that we should look first and foremost to the original author to discover the meaning of the word.

Your goal when using the circles of context is to start with the immediate context and work your way out until you find your answer. Rarely will you have to move beyond the "same author" circle to answer the question about the meaning of the word. (The double lines in the diagram signal the priority you should give to everything written by the same author.)

Start with the immediate context and work your way out until you find your answer.

You should expect to spend most of your time working in the smaller circles of context. Remember that our purpose in doing word studies is to try to understand as precisely as possible what the author meant when he used a certain word in a specific context. We cannot stop our analysis when we know the possible meanings of the word. We must go on to choose the meaning that is most likely. As you struggle to decide the most likely meaning of the word in its context, you may find the following questions helpful.

- *Is there a contrast or a comparison that seems to define the word?* For example, Ephesians 4:29 reads, "Do not let any *unwholesome* talk come out of your mouths, but only what is helpful for building others up according to their needs, that it may benefit those who listen." The contrast in the immediate context between "unwholesome" talk and words that build up and benefit people helps us understand "unwholesome" talk as any kind of speech (not just profanity) that damages relationships.
- *Does the subject matter or topic of the passage dictate a word meaning?* Back to our Genesis 39 example (NIV "make sport of" or ESV "laugh"). Which category did you choose of the various possibilities? Although "make sport of" sounds very much like sense (D) ("to ridicule or mock"), the subject matter in the immediate context is clearly sexual in nature. Could it be that sense (C) ("to caress physically") is the more likely choice? Read 39:14–15 again in light of the topic of the passage and see what you think.
- *Does the author's usage of the same word elsewhere in a similar context help you decide which meaning best fits the word?* If you are studying the word "world" in the all-time favorite verse John 3:16 ("For God so loved the *world* . . ."),

for instance, you would be interested to know how John uses this word elsewhere in his writings. To save you time, we can tell you that John uses the term *world* in a variety of ways, but he often uses the word in the sense of human beings in rebellion against God, of people opposed to God and his purposes. John probably uses "world" in this sense in John 3:16 also. When we read that God so loved the "world," we are not merely to think of God's affection for his physical creation, but of God's willingness to send his Son to die for those who despise him. Knowing John's use of "world" here gives you a glimpse into the self-giving heart of God.

- *Does the author's argument in the book suggest a meaning?* At times the author's argument (or train of thought) will affect your decision about what the word means. In Galatians 3:4 Paul asks the Galatians a pointed question: "Did you suffer so many things in vain—if indeed it was in vain?" (ESV). The Greek word translated "suffer" (*paschō*) can mean (a) negative experiences (i.e., suffering) or (b) positive experiences. Most of the time in the New Testament the word carries this negative sense of suffering, as it does the other six times Paul uses the word (1 Cor. 12:26; 2 Cor. 1:6; Phil. 1:29; 1 Thess. 2:14; 2 Thess. 1:5; 2 Tim. 1:12). But his argument in Galatians seems to call for meaning (b). If you were to study Galatians thoroughly, you would see that in this section Paul recalls the Galatians' positive experience of the Spirit, speaking in the surrounding context of God's gift of his Spirit and miracles. Paul then asks them if they are giving up all their great spiritual experiences for nothing. Because of the author's argument in the immediate context, the NIV 2011 translation of *paschō* as "experience" seems preferable: "Have you experienced so much in vain . . . ?"
- *Does the historical situation tilt the evidence in a certain direction?* Occasionally the historical context will strongly favor a particular option. To the Philippian Christians, Paul writes in 1:27, "Whatever happens, conduct yourselves in a manner worthy of the gospel of Christ" (NIV). The key verb translated "conduct yourselves" (*politeuomai*; "let your manner of life be" in the ESV) probably carries political overtones that Paul uses to connect with the Philippians. The citizens of Philippi took great pride in their status as citizens of a Roman colony. The Christians in Philippi would likely have shared in this civic pride. Paul seems to be telling the believers there to make sure they live like citizens of heaven in Philippi and not merely like citizens of a Roman colony. After all, the real Lord is not Caesar but Jesus! Knowing the historical background can often help you discern a word's meaning.

Now, using these questions and others like them, select the meaning that best fits. Sometimes you will discover that more than one sense is possible, maybe even several are possible. But you need to decide which one *best* fits the context. Resist the temptation to select a word meaning only because it is more exciting than the other options or because it will "preach" better than the rest. What good is a captivating word meaning if it is not true to the text of Scripture? As you make your decision, remember that interpretation always involves an element of subjectivity. Therefore, we need to make our interpretive choices and hold our interpretive convictions with humility. We could be wrong. It has happened before.

Before moving on to our actual word study of "present" in Romans 12:1, there is one more thing you can do to select from the possible meanings the one that best fits—get advice from the experts. To check your own work and deepen your understanding of a word, consult the standard word-study resources as a final step in the process. We recommend the following as resources worth consulting for beginning students:

For Word Studies in the Old Testament

Brown, Francis, S. R. Driver, and Charles A. Briggs, eds. *Brown-Driver-Briggs Hebrew and English Lexicon*. Peabody, MA: Hendrickson, 1996.

Harris, R. Laird, Gleason L. Archer Jr., and Bruce K. Waltke, eds. *Theological Wordbook of the Old Testament*. 2 vols. Chicago: Moody Press, 1980.

Holladay, William L., ed. *A Concise Hebrew and Aramaic Lexicon of the Old Testament*. Grand Rapids: Eerdmans, 1971.

Jenni, Ernst, and Claus Westermann, eds. *Theological Lexicon of the Old Testament*. Translated by Mark E. Biddle. Peabody, MA: Hendrickson, 1997.

Mounce, William D. *Mounce's Complete Expository Dictionary of Old and New Testament Words*. Grand Rapids: Zondervan, 2006.

VanGemeren, Willem, gen. ed. *New International Dictionary of Old Testament Theology and Exegesis*. 5 vols. Grand Rapids: Zondervan, 1997.

For Word Studies in the New Testament

Balz, Horst, and Gerhard Schneider, eds. *Exegetical Dictionary of the New Testament*. 3 vols. Grand Rapids: Eerdmans, 1990–93.

Brown, Colin, ed. *New International Dictionary of New Testament Theology*. 4 vols. Grand Rapids: Zondervan, 1975–78.

Danker, Frederick W. *The Concise Greek-English Lexicon of the New Testament*. Chicago: University of Chicago Press, 2009.

Danker, Frederick W., Walter Bauer, William F. Arndt, and F. Wilbur Gingrich, eds. *A Greek-English Lexicon of the New Testament and Other Early Christian Literature.* 3rd ed. Chicago: University of Chicago Press, 2000.

Kittel, Gerhard, and Gerhard Friedrich. *Theological Dictionary of the New Testament.* 1 vol. Translated, edited, and abridged by Geoffrey W. Bromiley. Grand Rapids: Eerdmans, 1985.

Louw, Johannes P., and Eugene A. Nida. *A Greek-English Lexicon of the New Testament: Based on Semantic Domains.* 2nd ed. 2 vols. New York: United Bible Societies, 1989.

Mounce, William D. *Mounce's Complete Expository Dictionary of Old and New Testament Words.* Grand Rapids: Zondervan, 2006.

Spicq, Ceslas, ed. *Theological Lexicon of the New Testament.* 3 vols. Translated by James D. Ernest. Peabody, MA: Hendrickson, 1995.

Verbrugge, Verlyn D., ed. *The New International Dictionary of New Testament Theology.* Abridged ed. Grand Rapids: Zondervan, 2003.

Note on Computer Tools

A variety of software packages include standard resources for studying words. The Logos Bible Software package is particularly good. Having fingertip access to these kinds of tools is a wonderful time-saver, but it will not guarantee reliable results. We strongly encourage you to follow the same method of study in any case. Choose your words carefully, determine what the underlying Greek or Hebrew word *could* mean (i.e., its semantic range), then decide what it *does* mean in its particular context. Since context rather than a dictionary definition determines the meaning of a word, we hope you will consult the standard resources only as a final step. If you have access to computer resources, the process should go much faster.

A WORD STUDY: "PRESENT" IN ROMANS 12:1

The purpose of this section is to give you a complete example of what we have just talked about doing.

1. Choose your words carefully.

As we read through Romans 12:1–2, we select the word "present" for further study because it is crucial to our understanding of the passage. In view of God's mercy, what are we supposed to do? We are to "present" our bodies to God. Knowing more about the meaning of this key verb will help us see how we are to respond to God in light of all he has done for us.

2. Determine what the word could mean.

Using the STEP Bible program, look up the word "present" used in Romans 12:1. This entry shows the variety of ways that the original Greek word παρίστημι (transliterated *paristēmi*) is used in the New Testament:

> **Meaning**
>
> pluperfect, παρειστήκειν, also formed as παριστάνω, trans. **to place beside; to have in readiness, provide, put at disposal** Acts 23:24; **to range beside, to place at the disposal of,** Mt. 26:53; Acts 9:41; **to present** to God, **dedicate, consecrate, devote,** Lk. 2:22; Rom. 6:13, 19; **to prove, demonstrate, show,** Acts 1:3; 24:13; **to commend, recommend,** 1 Cor. 8:8; intrans. perf. παρέστηκα, part. παρεστώς, pluperf. παρειστήκειν, 2 aor. παρέστην, and mid., **to stand by** or **before,** Acts 27:24; Rom. 14:10; **to stand by, to be present,** Mk. 14:47, 69, 70; **to stand in attendance, attend,** Lk. 1:19; 1:24; of time, **to be present, have come,** Mk. 4:29; **to stand by** in aid, **assist, support,** Rom. 16:2

This helps you identify the word's range of meaning:

a. to make available, to put at someone's disposal, to provide (e.g., Matt. 26:53)
b. to arrive, to come (e.g., Mark 4:29)
c. to stand by, to be present (e.g., Mark 14:47)
d. to dedicate or devote to God (e.g., Luke 2:22)
e. to stand against, to appear as an enemy (e.g., Acts 4:26)
f. to prove or demonstrate (e.g., Acts 24:13)
g. to appear before a judge (e.g., Acts 27:24)
h. to help (e.g., Rom. 16:2)
i. to bring close or near, to commend (e.g., 1 Cor. 8:8)

3. Decide the most likely meaning of the word in context.

We must look carefully at the use of *paristēmi* in Romans 12:1. Beginning in 12:1 Paul shifts his focus to how Christians should respond to the mercy of God explained in chapters 1–11. The word "therefore" signals this transition from the theological foundation in chapters 1–11 to the exhortation in chapters 12–15. We are urged to respond to God by presenting or offering our bodies as a sacrifice.

Of the possible meanings for *paristēmi* listed above, the context suggests either sense (A) "to make available, to put at someone's disposal, to provide," or sense (D) "to dedicate or devote to God" as the best options. These are closely related meanings, and it is difficult to determine which one is best. We turn again to the context.

This word is used elsewhere in Romans in 6:13, 16, 19; 14:10; and 16:2. The parallels between the use of the word in chapter 12 and the uses in chapter 6 are strong. In both cases people are giving their bodies in service to some power. Since "body" probably refers here to the whole person and not just to the physical body, sense (D) seems preferable: we are giving ourselves to God.

We should also pay particular attention to the imagery of sacrifice in chapter 12, imagery not present in chapter 6. In 12:1 we are exhorted to present our bodies *as a sacrifice*. Since Christ has fulfilled the Old Testament sacrificial system, Christians no longer present literal sacrifices as part of our worship. Instead, we present ourselves totally and continuously to God as a sacrifice—a living, holy, and pleasing sacrifice.

God gave himself to us through the once-for-all sacrifice of his Son, Jesus Christ. We worship God by giving all of ourselves (bodies included) to him. Two kinds of sacrifice are involved: he died for us, and we are to live for him! Our lives become living sacrifices of worship.

As a matter of checking our work, examine what a leading word-study resource says about the word "present" (*paristēmi*). The entry shown here is from *The New International Dictionary of New Testament Theology: Abridged Edition*, edited by Verlyn D. Verbrugge (Grand Rapids: Zondervan, 2003), 439.

CONCLUSION

Words are the building blocks of language, connecting small pieces of a puzzle to bring the larger picture to life. As we grasp the meaning of individual words, we are able to comprehend the meaning of an entire passage. Yet, as we have seen in this chapter, the meaning of a word is determined by the context surrounding that word. Context determines word meaning just as word meaning helps form the context. When doing word studies, you can clearly see the dynamic interplay between the parts and the whole.

We began the chapter by making you aware of a number of the most common word-study fallacies. We hope the information in this chapter will help you avoid such mistakes. Next, you learned how to locate words that need further study and how to study the underlying Hebrew or Greek word using the STEP Bible program. The process is simple, even though it takes time: (1) choose your words carefully, (2) determine what the word could mean, and (3) decide the most likely meaning of the word in context. Finally, we encouraged you to check your work by consulting the experts. We left you with the example of "present" in Romans 12:1. Now it's your turn to give it a try using one or more of the assignments.

whose spiritual ideals cause them to live as virgins; but since Paul describes this situation in 7:1–7 and does not use *parthenos* there, that interpretation is unlikely. In 7:25–38, the couples in question are not married. More likely Paul has in mind the relation of a man to his betrothed, who is a virgin in the ordinary sense.

(c) Where the NT speaks of Mary as a virgin, it has in mind the period up to the birth of Jesus. Statements regarding Jesus' supernatural conception are limited to the nativity narratives in Matt. 1 and Lk. 1. Jesus' divine sonship is based on a miracle that went beyond the experience of Elizabeth (Lk. 1:36). Matt. adds a quotation from Isa. 7:14 and indicates Jesus' conception as fulfilling OT prophecy. Matt.'s genealogy denotes Mary's legal relation to Joseph, since for the sake of his Davidic sonship Jesus must pass legally for a son of Joseph (1:16; cf. Lk. 3:23). In spite of its importance in Christian theology, Paul makes no explicit reference to the virgin birth (see Rom. 1:3; Gal. 4:4, for his references to the birth of Jesus).

See also *gynē*, woman (*1222*); *mētēr*, mother (*3613*); *chēra*, widow (*5939*).

4225 παρίστημι

παρίστημι (*paristēmi*), place, put at the disposal of, present (*4225*).

CL & OT The basic meaning of *paristēmi* is (trans.) place beside, (intrans.) stand beside, and (mid.) place before oneself. Various nuances developed, such as: (trans.) put down, place at someone's disposal, bring (a sacrifice); (intrans.) approach (the emperor or an enemy), help someone, wait on (as a servant), be present.

The word is used in the LXX about 100x. It could refer to a foreigner entering God's service (Isa. 60:10), a servant standing before a master (a position of honor, cf. 1 Sam. 16:21; 2 Ki. 5:25), and angels (Job 1:6) and martyrs (4 Macc. 17:18) standing before God. The word also expresses God's standing by someone to reveal himself (Exod. 34:5), to help that person (Ps. 109:31), or to charge someone with sin (50:21).

NT 1. In the NT *paristēmi* is used intrans. of Paul's standing before Caesar (Acts 27:24) or humanity's standing before God's judgment (Rom. 14:10). God supported Paul by standing at his side (2 Tim. 4:17), an angel stood beside Paul (Acts 27:23), and Phoebe was to be supported by the local church (Rom. 16:2). Gabriel stands before God (Lk. 1:19) (note that in heaven, only God sits; all created beings must stand before him).

2. The trans. use is found primarily in Acts and Paul's letters. In Lk. 2:22 it denotes the presentation of Jesus to the Lord in the temple (cf. Exod. 13:2). Passages where *paristēmi* is used in the sense of make or present are of special importance. Col. 1:22 implies that because of Jesus' death, a new, holy community is being presented to God. Since Christ is perfect, the church can also be presented perfect to God (1:28). Just as Jesus presented himself as alive after Easter to his apostles in various appearances (Acts 1:3), so God will present believers raised to a new life with Jesus in his presence (2 Cor. 4:14). By his self-sacrifice Christ has presented the church in the splendor of a bride (Eph. 5:27; cf. 2 Cor. 11:2; Col. 1:22). Similarly, we should do our best to present ourselves as approved to God (2 Tim. 2:15).

Neither the supposed freedom of those who think themselves strong nor the scrupulous self-denial of those weak in faith will "bring us near to God" (1 Cor. 8:8). Rather, the members that were once yielded to impurity are now to be offered to God in the service of righteousness (Rom. 6:13–19). Those who have been justified by faith "offer" their bodies to God as living sacrifices (12:1). Paul may be adopting Hel. sacrificial terminology here for Christian service to Jesus as Lord.

See also *kathistēmi*, bring, appoint (*2770*); *horizō*, determine, appoint (*3988*); *procheirizō*, determine, appoint (*4741*); *tassō*, arrange, appoint (*5435*); *tithēmi*, put, place, set, appoint (*5502*); *prothesmia*, appointed date (*4607*); *cheirotoneō*, appoint (*5936*); *lanchanō*, obtain as by lot (*3275*).

4228 (*paroikeō*, inhabit as a stranger, live beside), → *4230*.

4229 (*paroikia*, the stay of a noncitizen in a strange place), → *4230*.

4230 πάροικος

πάροικος (*paroikos*), stranger, alien (*4230*); παροικέω (*paroikeō*), inhabit as a stranger, live beside (*4228*); παροικία (*paroikia*), the stay of a noncitizen in a strange place (*4229*).

CL & OT 1. *paroikos* is a compound of *para* (by) and *oikos* (house). It was originally an adj. but was later used as a noun meaning neighbor, noncitizen, one who lives among citizens without having citizen rights yet enjoying the protection of the community. The vb. *paroikeo* means to live beside, inhabit as a stranger. *paroikia* means sojourning.

2. In the LXX *paroikos* occurs over 30x, translating *gēr* and *tôšāb*, both words meaning an alien or stranger. *paroikeō* occurs over 60x, esp. as the equivalent of *gûr*, to sojourn. *paroikia* is found 16x. Words in this group designate non-Israelites who lived in Israel (2 Sam. 4:3; Isa. 16:4). The Israelites had definite obligations to resident aliens. For example, an adequate living should be made possible for them (Lev. 25:35–47). They were allowed to share the food of the Sabbath year (25:6), although they were prohibited from eating the Passover lamb (Exod. 12:45) or the sacrificial gift (Lev. 22:10). They had the right of asylum (Num. 35:15), and, like widows and orphans, they stood under the protection of the law (cf. Exod. 22:21). The devout, even if aliens, could live in the tent of Yahweh (Ps. 15) and so experience fellowship with him. Ezek. 47:22–23 promises the equality of Israelites and resident aliens. Still, resident aliens also had obligations. For example, they were required to keep the Sabbath (Exod. 20:10).

Repeated stress in the OT was laid on the fact that the patriarchs were aliens (Gen. 12:10; 17:8; 19:9; 20:1; 23:4; 35:27; 47:4; Exod. 6:4). Moses was an alien in Midian (2:22), as was the entire nation of Israel in Egypt. Israel's attitude toward aliens was to be motivated by this fact (cf. 22:21; 23:9). In one sense the Israelites were always aliens, even when they lived in the promised land (1 Chr. 29:15; Ps. 39:12; 119:19, 54; 120:5; 3 Macc. 7:19). The earth and soil of Palestine, as indeed the whole earth (cf. Ps. 24:1), belongs to Yahweh. For this reason the land could not be sold (Lev. 25:23).

3. For Philo, the godly man is a *paroikos*, for he lives far off from his heavenly home. Philo combined the ancient world's denial of the world with OT ideas.

NT The words of this group are found only in Lk., Acts, Eph., Heb., and 1 Pet. Each passage contains a quotation or reference to the history of Israel (cf. Acts 7:29 with Exod. 2:15; Acts 7:6 with Gen. 15:13). In Acts 13:16–17 Paul recalls Israel's *paroikia* in Egypt, while Heb. 11:9–10 stresses that Abraham lived as an alien in the promised land as in a foreign country, since by faith he was a citizen of the heavenly city. The same thought occurs in the use of *xenos* (→ *3828*) and *parepidēmos* (→ *4215*) in 11:13. In Jesus Christ Gentile believers are no longer *xenoi* and *paroikoi*, but fellow citizens with the saints and members of God's household. Consequently, the promises made to Israel and the call to the kingdom of God are also valid for them (Eph. 2:19).

From this point of view, Christians are also in a new sense *paroikoi* and *parepidēmoi* here on earth—hence the warning to abstain from sinful desires (1 Pet. 2:11). They are to live in their time of sojourning in the fear of God (1:17). *paroikeō* means "live" only in Lk. 24:18. Perhaps even here the thought is that the "visitor" in question is a member of the Jewish dispersion living at Jerusalem, or that he is a pilgrim temporarily staying in the city to attend the Passover.

See also *allotrios*, alien, hostile (*259*); *diaspora*, dispersion (*1402*); *xenos*, foreign; stranger, alien (*3828*); *parepidēmos*, staying for a while in a strange place; stranger, resident alien (*4215*).

ASSIGNMENTS

Assignment 9–1

Use the STEP Bible program as your concordance to answer the following questions:

1. Use the concordance to answer the following questions about Acts 1:8.
   a) Write out the English transliterated form of the word translated "power" in Acts 1:8: ______________.
   b) How many times does this word occur in the New Testament? _______
   c) List the passages in Acts that translate this word as "power":
   d) List the passages in Acts that translate this word as "miracles" or "mighty works":
2. Use the concordance to answer the following questions about Exodus 4:21.
   a) Write out the English transliterated form of the word translated "power" in Exodus 4:21: ______________.
   b) How many times does this word occur in the Old Testament? _______
   c) List the passages in Exodus that translate the word as "power":
3. The ESV uses the word "judge" in 1 Corinthians 4:3; 5:12; and Revelation 20:4. Are these the same Greek words? Write out the English transliteration of the three Greek words translated as "judge" in these three passages.
4. Use the concordance to answer the following questions about the word "hope":
   a) Paul uses the word "hope" in Romans 4:18. How many times total does Paul use this same Greek word in his letters? (Do not assume that Paul wrote Hebrews.) ________
   b) How many times is the word used in Matthew, Mark, and Luke? ________
   c) Is this the same word for "hope" that is used in 1 Corinthians 13:13?

Assignment 9–2

You are studying the Sermon on the Mount (Matt. 5–7) and the word "anxious" in Matthew 6:25 catches your eye. You decide to study the word "anxious" more in depth. Use the STEP Bible program as your concordance to answer the following questions:

1. What is the Greek word for "anxious" in Matthew 6:25? Write out the word in transliterated English form: ________________
2. How many times is it used in the New Testament? __________
3. Now do some more concordance work to decide what the word "anxious" *could* mean in the New Testament. Make a list of the "meanings" provided in the box to the right in the STEP Bible program. This gives you a good sense of what the word could mean. But you need to look a bit more closely at the context. There is an art to identifying a word's semantic range. Don't give up. Keep working at it and you'll find that it gets easier

with practice. Answer the following questions about how the word is used in each context as a way of getting at its range of meaning:

a) What things are we told not to be anxious about in Matthew 6:25, 27, 28, 31, 34; Luke 12:22, 25, 26?
b) What is the context of Matthew 10:19 and Luke 12:11? Is this a different kind of anxiety than that prohibited in Matthew 6:25?
c) What stands in contrast to Martha's anxiety (Luke 10:41)? How does this contrast help to define Martha's anxiety?
d) In 1 Corinthians 7 Paul uses the word four times. Describe the context of this usage.
e) What do the contexts of 1 Corinthians 12 and Philippians 2 have in common?
f) What kind of anxiety is Paul describing in Philippians 4? How do you know?

4. As you survey the word in context, do you want to add to or take away from the list of meanings? Based on your brief study of the word as used in context, describe as best you can the semantic range of the word. There are at least two major senses of the word and perhaps a couple more.
5. Now decide what the Greek word used in Matthew 6:25 and translated "be anxious" actually means in this verse. Select one of the semantic-range options that you identified in step 2 and explain why you think the word carries that meaning in Matthew 6:25.
6. To check your work, see Verbrugge, *New International Dictionary of New Testament Theology: Abridged Edition*, 364.

Assignment 9–3

You want to study the word "meditate" in Joshua 1:8, where God tells Joshua: "This Book of the Law shall not depart from your mouth, but you shall meditate on it day and night, so that you may be careful to do according to all that is written in it" (ESV). Use the STEP Bible program to answer the following questions:

1. Click on the word "meditate" in Joshua 1:8 What is the transliteration of the Hebrew word that appears in the Vocab panel to the right? _______________
2. How many times is it used in the Old Testament? _______
3. List out the meanings provided in the Vocab panel as a way to begin establishing a range of meaning. Now click on the phrase "Search for this word" in the Vocab panel to generate a list of its occurrences in the Old Testament. Now look at each occurrence as a means of clarifying the word's range of meaning. Based on your brief study of the word as used in context, describe as best you can the semantic range of this word.

4. Now decide what the Hebrew word used in Joshua 1:8 means. Select one of the semantic-range options that you identified in step 2 and explain why you think the word carries that meaning in Joshua 1:8.
5. To check your work, see VanGemeren, *New International Dictionary of Old Testament Theology and Exegesis*, 1:1006–8.

Assignment 9–4

Complete the following word study of the word "trials" in James 1:2 using the STEP Bible program. The example of our study of the word "present" in Romans 12:1 in this chapter may prove helpful.

1. First, why do you think it is important to study this word?
2. What *could* this word mean? In other words, identify the word's semantic range.
3. What *does* this word mean in context? Be sure to discuss your choice.

Assignment 9–5

Complete the following word study of the word "sick" in James 5:14 using the STEP Bible program. The example of our study of the word "present" in Romans 12:1 in this chapter may prove helpful.

1. First, why do you think it is important to study this word?
2. What *could* this word mean? In other words, identify the word's semantic range.
3. What *does* this word mean in context? Be sure to discuss your choice.

PART 3

MEANING AND APPLICATION

So far you have learned about Bible translations (ch. 1), the Interpretive Journey (ch. 2), reading texts carefully (chs. 3–5), and understanding the context of a biblical passage (chs. 6–9). In part 3 we concentrate on a few theoretical issues you must understand to cross the river of differences and grasp the meaning of the text in our town. Then we will be ready to take the Interpretive Journey through specific literary types within the Old and New Testaments.

In chapter 10 we ask an important question with two parts: What is meaning, and who controls it, the reader or the author? In all likelihood, what you believe about the Bible will determine your answers to this question. We highlight the crucial role that communication plays in the meaning of meaning. In chapter 11 we ask another meaning-related question: Does the Bible have different levels of meaning? Are there deeper levels of spiritual meaning beyond what the text seems to say on the surface? Here we will address the issues of spiritualizing, allegorizing, typology, and more.

At this stage of *Grasping God's Word*, some might ask: If we have the Holy Spirit, do we really need to worry about all these interpretive steps and procedures? That's a fair question. Thus, in chapter 12 we look at how the Spirit relates to the task of biblical interpretation. Can people without the Spirit grasp God's Word? How exactly does the Spirit help the Christian interpret and apply the Bible? What should we not expect the Spirit to do?

We wrap up part 3 by looking at application (ch. 13). What is the difference between meaning and application? How do we go about applying the meaning of the text in our lives? How do we move from head knowledge to life-changing action? We will suggest specific ways for doing just that. This chapter serves as a reminder that we study the Bible not just to learn more about God but to know and love God more.

CHAPTER 10

WHO CONTROLS THE MEANING?

INTRODUCTION

In chapter 2 we outlined our basic approach to reading, interpreting, and applying the Scriptures—to grasping God's Word. We begin by reading carefully to determine the meaning for the biblical audience. Next we identify the river of barriers that separates us from the biblical audience. Then we derive a theological principle from the text and cross over the river on that principlizing bridge. We ask how that theological principle fits with the rest of the Bible. Finally, we apply that principle to our specific life situation.

However, there are some fundamental questions that we need to answer before we get too far into the Interpretive Journey. These questions will have a profound effect on how we actually implement that journey. The most important question is this: *What is meaning, and who controls it, the author or the reader?* This chapter will address this basic issue.

WHO CONTROLS THE MEANING, THE READER OR THE AUTHOR?

When Danny's kids were small, one of their favorite videos was the old movie *The Wizard of Oz*. This movie is based on the book by L. Frank Baum.[1] To Danny's young children this delightful tale was about a young girl named Dorothy and her cute dog, Toto, who overcame the odds and defeated the powerful and scary "bad guys" (the wicked witches) with some help from Dorothy's nice new friends. To the young children, the story had this simple meaning.

If we observe the story closely, however, and if we start to poke around into the historical background of the time Baum wrote the book, a different meaning surfaces. One of the hottest political debates going on in America when Baum wrote this story was over the issue of whether America should continue to use the gold standard as the basis for the US dollar or switch to silver. This historical context suggests that the main line of the book ("Follow the yellow brick road!") may be a reference to the central political issue of the day. Remember that although the yellow brick road led to the great wizard of Oz, once Dorothy arrived there, she discovered he was a fraud. Dorothy's real hope lay in her shoes. In Baum's book the shoes are *silver*. Hollywood changed them to ruby so they would show up better in color for the movie. So, perhaps the book falls into the classification of political satire.

According to this line of interpretation, the characters in the story then probably represent different segments of American society. The Scarecrow represents the farmers (supposedly, no brains). Who would the Tin Woodsman represent? The factory workers (no heart). And the cowardly lion perhaps represents the political leadership of the country. We also meet the Wicked Witch of the East (the East Coast establishment?) and the Wicked Witch of the West (the West Coast establishment?). And who is the heroine? Middle America—Dorothy from Kansas.

So, who is right? Are Danny's kids *wrong* to interpret the story as a simple tale of good triumphing over evil? Did not the author intend it to be read as political satire? Are we wrong if we understand it otherwise? What *is* the meaning of the story? And *who* determines that meaning?

This question has prompted a lively and sometimes heated debate, not only in secular literary circles but also among students and scholars of the Bible. Throughout the first half of the twentieth century, the traditional approach to interpreting any literature, biblical or secular, was to assume that the author determines the meaning

1. L. Frank Baum, *The Wonderful Wizard of Oz*, illus. W. W. Denslow (Chicago and New York: George M. Hill, 1900).

and the reader's job is to find that meaning. Within the world of secular literary criticism, however, this approach came under attack throughout the latter half of the twentieth century, and many literary critics today argue that it is the *reader*, and not the *author*, who determines what a text *means*.

This view has drifted over from secular literary criticism into the field of biblical interpretation. Many biblical scholars began probing into the question "What is meaning?" They concluded that the term *meaning* applies only as a reader interacts with a text—that it takes both reader and text to produce *meaning*. The author, they argue, is no longer involved.[2]

Of course, there remain those who maintain that the original author still controls the meaning. As an author writes, they argue, he or she intends to convey a certain meaning in the text. This intended meaning of the author's is the true meaning of the text.

Authorial intention: Meaning is determined by the intention of the author.
Reader response: Meaning is determined by the reader or by a community of readers.

The position that stresses the author in the determination of meaning is called *authorial intention*. The opposing view, which focuses on the reader as the main character in the determination of meaning, is called *reader response*. Both positions have strong arguments. Which approach should we take?

COMMUNICATION—THE CENTRAL ISSUE

Certainly the reader has the freedom to interpret a text any way he or she chooses. No one will force you to read *The Wonderful Wizard of Oz* as political satire. So the author has control of the meaning only so far as the reader allows him to. But suppose, for example, that you receive a mushy love poem written to you by your girlfriend or boyfriend (remember the email from Kaitlyn in chapter 3?). As you read each word and line of the poem, you will be searching for the meaning that your girlfriend or boyfriend intended. You will want to know what she or he is trying to say *to you*. In this situation you will be following the *authorial-intention* approach, because you are viewing the text as *communication* between the author and yourself. You know the author and you want to know what the author is saying to you. You will be asking the interpretive question, *What does the author mean?*

2. The issue is actually much more complex than we have described, and numerous scholars from a wide range of philosophical positions are dismissing the author's authority over meaning in texts. Some say that each culture and community determines its own meaning apart from the author. Others would say that language is incapable of objectively describing reality; thus, there is no real meaning at all in any text. For further reading on this subject, we recommend Kevin J. Vanhoozer, *Is There a Meaning in This Text? The Bible, the Reader, and the Morality of Literary Knowledge* (Grand Rapids: Zondervan, 1998).

Let's assume, however, that one day as you walk through the woods, you find a piece of paper on the ground with a love poem written on it. The author is not even identified. The poem, however, is beautiful, and you enjoy it as you read. In this situation you may not care what the author intended or what the author meant. You do not even know who the author is. You have the freedom in this situation to read and interpret according to *reader response*. Your interpretive question will change to *What does this mean to me?* In the woods with an anonymous poem you are free to ignore the author and his or her intended meaning.

Sometimes we even consciously change the meaning that the author intended because we do not like that meaning. For example, John Lennon of the Beatles wrote a song back in the sixties titled, "With a Little Help from My Friends." This is a good song for singing in the shower. The opening line is especially appropriate for us ("What would you think if I sang out of tune?"). The song has a catchy melody and nice wholesome lyrics, if one interprets it literally as referring to the people whom we call *friends*.

However, if we study the historical context and probe into the likely intent of the author, we realize that Lennon is probably using the term "friends" to refer to drugs. Of course, this connection ruins the song for us, so we *intentionally* change Lennon's meaning for the term "friends," when we sing the song, to refer to people. In that situation, we don't really care what Lennon is trying to say in this song. We do not look to him for any philosophical guidance. So the song does not function as communication between us. Once the song loses its status as a communication medium, then we, as readers, are free to interpret it as we like. But we can only do this because we are uninterested in Lennon's thoughts and his attempts to convey them to us through his songs. Also, there are no negative consequences of changing Lennon's meaning; in fact, the consequences are positive.

Police interpret a STOP sign according to authorial intent.

In many situations, however, it is extremely important that we search for the author's meaning because of serious negative consequences that will come if we misunderstand or intentionally ignore the meaning the author intended. For example, one of the most common literary texts in America is the big word STOP painted on the red octagonal signs at many street intersections across the country. If you choose to, you can follow a *reader response* approach and interpret the text to mean: *slow down just a bit, look for cars, and then speed on through the intersection*. The police, however, believe strongly in *authorial intent* for the determination of meaning, so they will respond to your interpretation with a traffic ticket and fine.

Likewise, suppose you get a bill from the electric company, charging you $111 for the electricity you used in the previous month. Do you have the option to determine the meaning of that text (the bill)? Can you say that what the text means to you is that you should pay *eleven dollars*, not *one hundred and eleven*? Certainly you can *say* that. But you will soon start reading your texts in the dark, because the electric company will shut off your power! Some texts are obviously written to communicate important messages to their readers. To ignore the author's intention in these texts can produce serious consequences for the reader!

The issue of communication, therefore, lies at the heart of one's decision about how to interpret a text. If you, the reader, see the text as a communication between the author and yourself, then you should search for the meaning the *author intended*. If, however, you as the reader do not care to communicate with the author, then you are free to follow *reader response* and interpret the text without asking what the author meant. In some cases, however, there may be negative consequences for such a reading.

> If we view the text as communication, then we must seek the meaning the author intended.

Can you see how this discussion applies to reading and interpreting the Bible? This is an important issue—one that lies at the foundation of our approach to interpreting Scripture. If you read the Bible merely as great literature, merely for its aesthetic value, or merely for its suggestive moral guidance, not as communication from God, then you can interpret the text in any way you choose. Your main interpretive question will be *What does this text mean to me?* If, however, you believe that the Bible is God's revelatory word to you and that the Scriptures function as communication from God to you, you should interpret the Bible by looking for the meaning that God, the author, intended. Your interpretive question should be *What is the meaning God intended in this text?*

> We do not create the meaning. Rather, we seek to discover the meaning that has been placed there by the author.

We believe that the Bible is a revelation from God to us. God's purpose is to *communicate* with us about himself and his will for us. We can choose to ignore his message and interpret biblical texts according to our feelings and desires, but if we do, we will suffer the consequences of disobedience—traffic fines will appear and the lights will go out. We will also miss out on knowing God in the way he desires. So it is essential that we follow the *authorial intent* approach to interpreting the Bible. In biblical interpretation, the reader does not control the meaning; the author controls the meaning. This conclusion leads us to one of the most basic principles of our interpretive approach: *We do not create the meaning. Rather, we seek to discover the meaning that has been placed there by the author.*

DEFINITIONS

The first term that needs defining is *author*. When discussing nonbiblical literature, the term *author* refers to the person who wrote the literature. When we use the term *author* in conjunction with the Bible, however, we are referring to both the human author and the divine Author. Ultimately, when we study the Bible, we are looking for the meaning God intended.

However, although the biblical text is divinely inspired,[3] it certainly has human fingerprints all over it. God chose to work through human writers to deliver his message to us. The languages he chose to use were human languages. The divine and the human elements in the Scriptures are frequently difficult to distinguish. Thus, we propose to lump them together under the term *author*.

At this juncture it is also important that we define the terms *meaning* and *application*. We will use the term *meaning* to refer to *that which the author wishes to convey with his signs*.[4] Signs are simply the different conventions of written language—grammar, syntax, word meanings, and so on. Thus, in biblical interpretation meaning is not determined by the reader. Meaning is what the author intended to communicate when he wrote the text.

It would be incorrect for us to ask in a Bible study, "What does this passage *mean* to you?" The correct question sequence is, "What does this passage *mean*? How should you *apply* this meaning to your life?"

What the reader does with the meaning is *application*. Once we identify the meaning in the text that God is trying to communicate to us, we must respond to that meaning. We use the term *application* to refer to the response of the reader to the meaning of the text. Thus, it would be incorrect for us to ask in a Bible study, "What does this passage *mean* to you?" The correct question sequence is, "What does this passage *mean*? How should you *apply* this meaning to your life?"

Adhering to this order may seem picky at this point, but you will see that it is an important sequence to maintain. *Meaning* is something we can validate. It is tied to the text and the intent of the author, not to the reader. Therefore, the *meaning* of the text is the same for all Christians. It is not subjective and does not change from reader to reader. *Application*, on the other hand, reflects the impact of the text on the reader's life. It is much more subjective, and it reflects the specific life situation of the reader.

3. For more on the biblical doctrine of inspiration and its relationship to the Christian notion of canon as well as modern challenges to these topics, see appendix 1, "Inspiration and Canon."

4. This definition is based on that suggested by E. D. Hirsch Jr., *Validity in Interpretation* (New Haven, CT: Yale University Press, 1967), 8.

The *application* of the meaning will vary from Christian to Christian, but it will still have some boundaries influenced by the author's meaning (see ch. 13).

How do these definitions fit into the Interpretive Journey we discussed in chapter 2? We have reproduced the sketch of the journey below for your review:

Step 1: Grasp the text in their town. What did the text mean to the original audience?

Step 2: Measure the width of the river to cross. What are the differences between the biblical audience and us?

Step 3: Cross the principlizing bridge. What is the theological principle in this text?

Step 4: Consult the biblical map. How does this theological principle fit with the rest of the Bible?

Step 5: Grasp the text in our town. How should individual Christians today live out the theological principles?

In the Interpretive Journey, both steps 1 and 3 (the expression of meaning for the biblical audience and the theological principle) are part of the *meaning* of the text. Through Scripture God communicates to his people both the immediate concrete expression for the biblical audience and the theological principle for future audiences.

As God directed the writers of Scripture to compose the biblical texts, certainly he was conscious of future audiences. When Paul penned his letter to the Romans, for example, certainly the Holy Spirit, working within him, intended for this letter to have meaning for future Christians as well. Paul himself, the human author, was probably aware of this; but without doubt, God, the divine Author, had future congregations in mind as well as the Romans when he directed Paul to write.

Thus, both the specific details of the letter and the theological principle underlying each text are intended by the author. This is the meaning we seek to find in our Bible study. After we have identified this meaning, then we can begin to ask what we should do about the text. How do we live out God's Word (i.e., the application phase)?

DETERMINING WHAT THE AUTHOR MEANT

Our presuppositions about authorial intent will affect our approach of study. *Meaning*, remember, we defined as *that which the author wishes to convey with his signs*. The *signs* that we referred to are the conventions of language—syntax, grammar, word meaning, and so on. The author used these signs to communicate his message with us. Our goal is to use the signs as indicators for what the author was trying to convey. Contexts, both literary and historical-cultural, are also helpful indicators of what the signs meant for the author.

You will recall that meaning is tied to context and is not determined solely by grammar and dictionary definitions. That is, you cannot simply look up words in the dictionary and grammar in the grammar book and determine meaning. Meaning is tied to the one who produced the signs and to the context in which he produced them. Suppose, for example, that we ask a five-year-old what is under the hood of his or her parent's car. Most five-year-olds could tell us that under the hood is the engine. However, what does the child envision by the term *engine*? The child probably uses the word to mean something big, noisy, and somewhat mysterious that makes the car go. We cannot determine the meaning of the word *engine* in the child's dialogue by going to a dictionary. Likewise, if we ask a mechanic what is under the hood of the same car, he may also say "the engine," but what he envisions is a Chrysler 5.7L V8 Hemi. His use of the term *engine* has no connotations of being something mysterious. We would be misunderstanding the two people if we used the mechanic's definition of *engine* to interpret the child's statement or if we used the child's definition of *engine* to understand the mechanic. For proper interpretation (communication) to take place, we must ask what the author meant by the word used.

For another example, consider a humorous story that an African evangelist from Liberia once shared with Danny. He was visiting the United States, speaking in several churches along the way as he traveled across the country. One Sunday night in Tennessee, as he was driving to his next speaking engagement, he reflected on how beautiful the big, full harvest moon was. At the church later that evening, in the introduction to his sermon he commented on how much he liked the *moonshine* they had in that part of the country. He assumed that in English if you had *sunshine* during the day, then you should have *moonshine* at night. An easy mistake to make! No doubt he drew quite a few chuckles from the congregation in Tennessee.

This story provides us with a good illustration of authorial intent and meaning. Lexically, *moonshine* refers to an illegal, homemade, strong alcoholic beverage. One could interpret the evangelist's statement, if taken out of context, as reflecting his enjoyment of this alcoholic drink. But is that what he meant? Obviously not. If we examine the author and the context—a teetotaling African evangelist speaking English as a second language, preaching in the United States on a night with a full moon—then the meaning is clear. Furthermore, because of context, everyone in the congregation understood what he meant. Yet if we ignore the evangelist's expression as a vehicle of communication, and if we allow his statement to be an independent text that can be interpreted by detached readers, then it is unlikely that we would come up with the same meaning the author intended. As we study Scripture, remembering that meaning is determined by the intent of the author is important.

Authors cannot always express exactly what they want to say in literature. Language has its limitations, and some things, such as feelings, are difficult to convey accurately. Indeed, this limitation provides the basis for one of the arguments that is made against authorial intent. However, a vast range of reality, including many feelings, is sharable with others, and we generally use language to express those concepts and feelings. It is not a perfect medium, but it is nonetheless effective for communicating meaning from one person to another. Both the speaker and the listener (author and reader) usually realize the limitations of language and, in good communication, they both work hard to overcome those limitations. Our languages are complex precisely because we need to express a variety of complex nuances to each other as clearly as possible. We use grammar, syntax, and word meaning to convey to others what we want to communicate. We also use figures of speech, idioms, direct quotations, and a host of other literary devices to get our meaning across.

God has worked through human authors to convey his meaning through the conventions of language.

The writers of the Bible (including both the human author and the divine Author) likewise encoded their meaning into the normal conventions of the language they used. The writers used grammar, syntax, word meanings, literary context, historical context, and a host of literary devices to communicate God's message to us. This is why we spent so much time in part 1 stressing the importance of learning to read carefully and to observe, observe, and observe. If meaning lies within us—that is, if *we* create the meaning—then casual reading and study may suffice. However, as we have argued above, this is not the case. Meaning is being conveyed to us through the text.

In other words, God has worked through human authors to convey his meaning through the conventions of language. Sometimes his meaning is simple and clear; sometimes it is complex or subtle. We will find it as we prayerfully dig into the text and search diligently for the meaning God has placed there.

MORE ON THE JOURNEY AND HOW TO DETERMINE THEOLOGICAL PRINCIPLES

Back in chapter 2 we introduced you to the Interpretive Journey and to the concept of theological principles (step 3). Now, close on the heels of our discussion on the importance of trying to find the author's intended meaning, we want to expand on step 3 of the journey and give some additional guidelines, explanations, and helps for how to determine an author's intended theological principles.

First of all, understanding the relationship between *general, universal* theological truths and *context-specific* theological truths is key. Context-specific theological truths are based on the general, universal theological truths, yet are more narrowly focused into a specific setting. That is, undergirding the specific theological truths that we see in biblical passages playing out in the lives (context) of specific people are basic, general, and universal truths about God, his character, and his actions.

For example, one of the most foundational *general and universal* theological truths is that *God is holy*. This is a broad and universal theological principle. Furthermore, as God reveals himself to people and as he enters into close relationship with them, he wants them to understand and to respect his holiness as well as to grasp the implications of his holiness. Throughout the biblical story, however, the specific context of how people relate to God and his holiness is not always the same. This is particularly true as we move from the Old Testament, where God's holiness is manifested in his presence dwelling in Israel's midst in the tabernacle or temple, into the New Testament, where God's holiness is manifested through the indwelling presence of the Holy Spirit within believers' lives.

Thus, as God takes this general and universal principle (his holiness) and begins teaching it to his people, this generalized theological truth (God is holy) will take on different concrete and *context-specific* expressions, depending on the situation. When the river of differences is wide, the difference in the *context-specific* expression will be more significant. When the river of differences is narrow, the differences of the *context-specific* expression will be small. We have attempted to illustrate this in the diagram below:

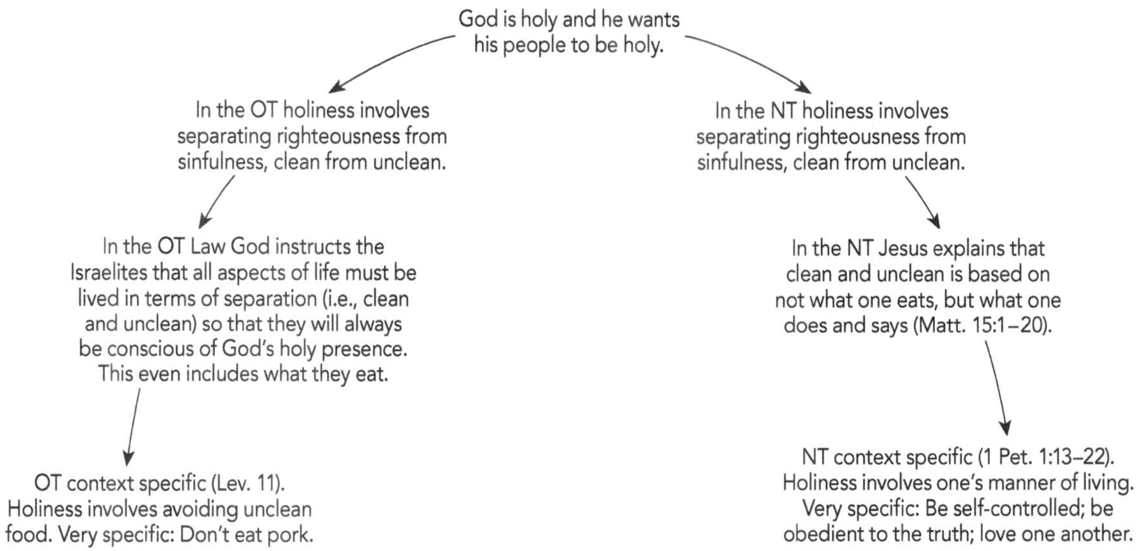

As you can see, behind (or above) each context-specific theological truth that we find in step 1 (what did it mean in their town?) lies a more general theological truth or even a series of theological truths that becomes more general as we move away from the specific context and closer toward the basic character of God that lies behind that truth.

It is in step 2 (define the river of differences) that we identify how far from the context-specific theological truth (what it meant for them) we need to move. That is, in step 2 we not only identify the differences between their context and ours but also the similarities. For example, regarding the food laws and separation laws in Leviticus, the differences are that we are not the Israelites, and we are not living under the old Mosaic covenant with God's presence residing in the tabernacle right down the street from us. The similarities are that we are still God's people, he is still holy, he still demands holiness (and separation from sin) from his people, and we still enjoy his presence (now through the Holy Spirit).

So with the differences from step 2 in mind, in step 3 we then seek to identify the more general and universal theological truths that lie behind the context-specific truth of step 1, looking for that level where the similarities let us know that the truth is now general enough to apply to us as well as to them.

When we explained the Interpretive Journey in chapter 2, we presented the steps as sequential actions, suggesting that after we finish one step, we then proceed to the next step. As we fine-tune the process, it is important to recognize that in reality steps 2, 3, and 4 are closely interrelated and need to happen somewhat concurrently. That is, the differences and similarities in step 2 are critical in helping identify valid theological principles in step 3. Likewise, as we move away from context-specific meaning toward more generalized universal truths, we will be fudging over into step 4, because our determination of general theological truth comes from our understanding of God as revealed in the rest of the Bible.

Another important factor to explore as we seek to determine theological principles is that of purpose. As we identify the meaning for the biblical audience in step 1, we need to ask, "Why?" That is, what is the purpose of the truth in step 1? Identifying the purpose is often instrumental in helping us move from context-specific theological meaning to more general theological meaning (principles). Leviticus 11 defines specifically what Israel (now under the Mosaic covenant) could eat and what they could not eat (step 1). As we probe into the purpose, we realize that these food laws (as well as other laws of separation) have to do with God's holiness and his insistence that Israel incorporate the implications of his holiness into all aspects of their lives. It is this purpose that helps us develop the theological principle that lies behind Leviticus 11, but one that also connects to our similarities (as the people of God still coming to grips with his presence and the demands of holiness).

The criteria we provided in chapter 2 for determining principles are still valid:

- The principle should be reflected in the text.
- The principle should be timeless and not tied to a specific situation.
- The principle should not be culturally bound.
- The principle should correspond to the teaching of the rest of Scripture.
- The principle should be relevant to both the biblical audience and the contemporary audience.

To these criteria we now add some additional and complementary guidelines and helps:

1. As part of step 1 (What did it mean to them?), be sure to identify *where this passage fits within the large, overarching story of the Bible.* This will help with identifying similarities and differences in step 2.
2. Related to question 1, as you move from step 1 to steps 2 and 3, be sure to identify *the purpose of the passage.* That is, what is the purpose of the context-specific meaning you identified in step 1?

3. With the similarities and the differences in your hand, use the purpose as a guide to *move from the context-specific meaning to the less context-specific and more general theological truths from that passage.* As in the example above, identify several possibilities, moving from mildly context-specific to broadly general and universal. At the most general and most universal level, you are usually identifying basic characteristics of God (God is love; God is holy and just; God is a God who saves and delivers; etc.). Right below this are general statements about the implications of these truths for God's people. Then these general truths take on more specific form as they are applied in the Scriptures to specific people in specific contexts.
4. Select the theological principle that is as specific as possible while still general enough to apply to us as New Testament believers.

CONCLUSION

Our approach to interpreting the Bible focuses on *authorial intent* rather than *reader response.* God has communicated with us through the Scriptures. He has worked through human authors to convey his meaning to us through the text. As readers we do not create the meaning; rather, we seek to find the meaning that has already been placed into the text by the author (both divine and human). This is why careful reading, context, historical background, word studies, translations, and genre are so important. These are the items we must grapple with if we are to grasp the intended meaning of the author.

ASSIGNMENTS

Assignment 10–1

Explain the difference between *reader response* and *authorial intent.*

Assignment 10–2

Why is the issue of *communication* important to the discussion of authorial intent?

Assignment 10–3

Discuss several situations whereby a reader may intentionally change an author's intended meaning.

CHAPTER 11

LEVELS OF MEANING

INTRODUCTION

Does the Bible have different *levels* of meaning? That is, after we have seen the so-called surface meaning or literal meaning, are there any other, deeper levels of spiritual meaning? This chapter will explore this question. This is not an esoteric issue of concern only to scholars. Every Christian who reads the Bible and seeks to find God's will for his or her life will encounter this issue.

Are there other, deeper levels of spiritual meaning?

For example, imagine yourself at a Bible study with a dozen other college students. This is your first time at this study and you are a bit uncomfortable. You have devoured several chocolate chip cookies, and now you are concentrating on your lemon LaCroix. A tall, skinny guy sitting to your right opens with prayer. You're pretty sure his name is Josh, but you've only met him once. After prayer he reads the passage to be discussed that evening:

> 8"Or suppose a woman has ten silver coins and loses one. Doesn't she light a lamp, sweep the house and search carefully until she finds it? 9And when she finds it, she calls her friends and neighbors together and says, 'Rejoice with me; I have found my lost coin.' 10In the same way, I tell you, there is rejoicing in the presence of the angels of God over one sinner who repents." (Luke 15:8–10)

"Okay," continues Josh. "There are more cookies in the kitchen if you need them, and I think we have another bag of SunChips around here somewhere. So, what do you think this passage means? What is God trying to teach us here?"

"I don't know," begins a girl with blond hair, wearing a Passion Conference T-shirt. "But my study Bible says that the houses in those days had low roofs and few windows, so it was kind of hard to see in there. That's why she needed the lamp."

Jared, a guy you know from your English class last semester, is sitting across from you eating Doritos. He sits up and chimes in, "Yeah, and she has to sweep out the house because it's dirty. So we have a dark, dirty house with not much light. I think this is like the world, you know? I mean, when we drift back into the world, it's like being that coin . . . not able to see clearly . . . lost in the dark and in the dirt . . . unable to see Jesus. So the house stands for the world, and we are the coin when we backslide. Jesus, of course, is the one who comes and looks for us and finds us in the dark."

You are thinking that Jared makes pretty good sense. And he is a smart guy, you remember from the English class. You nod your head like you knew this all the time.

"So you're saying that the woman is Jesus," objects a big guy named Matt. "I can't go for that." Matt is a macho kind of guy. He lived down the hall from you in the dorm during your freshman year. Drives a nice pickup but is not really a rocket scientist. You think maybe he is kidding, but he looks serious about it.

"It's a parable," answers Jared. "It doesn't matter if they portray Jesus as a woman."

"I don't have any problem with Jesus being played by a woman," offers Jessica. She is really cute—short with big, brown eyes and long, pretty, brown hair. In fact, you took her out once last year. You could kick yourself for not asking her out again. She seems to be interested in Jared now, however. Too bad.

"But Jared," Jessica continues, "I never thought of the house as referring to the *world*. When I think of a dark place where people can get lost, I think of the church today. I mean, just look at all the churches today that are not really following Jesus and just preaching psychology and stuff. You know, it's like that church in the book of Revelation that Jesus says is lukewarm—the one he will spit out of his mouth. The church really needs the light of the gospel today. And remember that all of those early churches were *house* churches, weren't they? I mean, they met in houses instead of churches like we do. So the house could be referring to the churches. It makes sense to me, anyway."

It's making sense to you too, especially since she looked right at you and smiled as she finished. You nod your head in agreement. Any moron can see that she is right.

"But then what would the coin be?" asks Brian, a sleepy-looking kid wearing long, ragged, tan-colored shorts, worn-out sandals, and a faded, black, long-sleeved T-shirt that reads Romans OneOneSix. He has been texting on his cell phone for the last five minutes, so everyone is a bit surprised that he was actually following the discussion. "And is there any more picante sauce for these Doritos?" he asks.

"Well," responds Jessica. "Maybe the coin represents the true, faithful congregations that just seem to get lost amid all those other churches who don't know what's going on. At least, that's the way it looks to me. The picante sauce is right there on the counter in the kitchen, Brian, in the red bowl."

"Thanks," says Brian. He gets up and lumbers into the kitchen.

"And then maybe the woman in the story really represents the pastor of a true church," suggests Jared. "He is sweeping out all of the false doctrine, trying to find the true believers."

"What's with all this woman stuff?" blurts out Matt again. "First she is Jesus, and now she is the pastor. Come on, now. We're not a bunch of radical feminists. And hey, Brian," he shouts toward the kitchen, "if there are any more Cokes in there, bring me one."

Brian saunters back in with a Coke for Matt and a red bowl of picante sauce. "Watch out," he warns, "this stuff is hot."

"I never really thought about the house as being churches," offers the Passion Conference girl. "If the house is dark and dirty, it is probably referring to our hearts. Isn't that what is dark and dirty in our lives? We try and try to follow Christ, but we fail because our hearts are not clean. However, Jesus comes and cleans our hearts, just like the woman in this story. He sweeps them out and then forgives us of all our sins. I like to think of Jesus as sweeping out my heart and making me clean. Isn't that neat?" She smiles brightly and then looks down at her Bible as she continues. "And look at this! This is really awesome. My study Bible says that the brooms they had in the Bible days were made of numerous two-foot-long straws bundled together and tied at the top. Wow! You know, like one straw can't do anything, but when they are bundled together, then they are really strong. The broom is kind of like the Bible. I mean, like Jesus sweeps out our hearts, right? What does he use to cleanse us? The Bible, right? The Bible is also composed of lots of individual books, sixty-six to be exact, and they are all bound up together so that they will be strong. Jesus cleanses our hearts with the Bible. Isn't that awesome?"

You're thinking that the Passion Conference girl is pretty insightful. You wish that you could see something so deep and spiritual. You look down at your Bible, but you can't come up with anything profoundly spiritual about the house or the woman or the coin. You find yourself a bit confused as well. Can the house refer to all of these things? Can it be the world, the backslidden churches, and also our hearts? Or maybe it just refers to a house. The woman had to live somewhere, after all. You wonder which one of these meanings Jesus intended. Should you just randomly choose one of the meanings? You're thinking that Jessica made a lot of sense, and you notice that she smiles at you again as she reaches for a cookie. You are trying to recall which meaning was hers. Oh well, you pick up another cookie and decide that perhaps you'll give Jessica a call tomorrow to discuss this some more.

SPIRITUALIZING

Did you notice how arbitrary the various interpretations were in the story above? The members of the Bible study felt free to develop whatever meaning struck their fancy. None of them seemed overly concerned to determine the meaning Jesus intended when he spoke the words or what Luke intended when he wrote down the episode under the guidance of the Spirit.

In addition, none of these Bible study participants seemed to notice the context of the story. The preceding story, for example, deals with the parable of the shepherd who loses one of his sheep, leaves his other ninety-nine, and searches until he finds the lost one, at which time he rejoices. The following story is the parable of the lost son, in which the father rejoices when his lost son returns. We will discuss parables in more detail in chapter 15, but for now it is fairly clear that these three parables go together and that they all speak of the joy God feels when someone who was lost comes to faith and is saved. They also stress God's concern over the lost and show the effort he exerts to find and restore that which is lost. Indeed, the last verse of the parable of the woman and the coin explicitly states as much: "In the same way, I tell you, there is rejoicing in the presence of the angels of God over one sinner who repents."

None of these Bible study participants seemed to notice the context of the story.

So Jesus is not using the *house* to represent *anything* specific in our lives. He is simply making a comparison. The woman is concerned over losing the coin because the coin is important to her. God feels the same way toward us. The woman goes to great lengths to find the coin. God likewise goes to great lengths to bring you and me into the kingdom. Finally, she rejoices after finding the coin. God also rejoices after we are "found" and restored. This seems to be the meaning intended by the author. Keep in mind the lessons from the last chapter. We do not seek to create meaning; rather, we seek to discover the meaning that is already there.

The students, however, have missed the obvious meaning of this text because they want to find a deep, hidden, "spiritual" meaning. Their desire to find this deeper meaning drives them right past the actual meaning that Luke (and the Spirit) intended. Thus, in their search for the spiritual, they miss what the Spirit is saying through the text! Christ searches for the lost and rejoices when they are found. This is the spiritual meaning. However, it is communicated through literary conventions (grammar, context, and so on); it is not created by the whims of our imaginations. The Bible is a spiritual book dealing with spiritual issues. We do not have to spiritualize it with our fertile imaginations.

Furthermore, when we attempt to find a deeper, hidden, "superspiritual" meaning, we usually find ourselves moving into an area of reader response, where *we* are the ones determining the meaning rather than the text. In our zeal for "superspiritual" meaning, we often miss completely the message God has intended for us—in essence substituting our word for his.

Occasionally in discussions on biblical interpretation a dichotomy is presented between *literal* meaning and *spiritual* meaning. Sometimes the reader is exhorted to search for the literal meaning and not the spiritual. We are uncomfortable with this dichotomy; indeed, we think that the term *literal* does more to confuse than to clarify. Many people use the term *literal interpretation* to stress that they believe the actual historical details of the Bible, especially the miracles. We certainly affirm the historicity of the Bible, including the miracles. But we think that the term *literal* is a bit too fuzzy. The Bible, as we mentioned earlier, is full of figures of speech and symbolic language. The determination of meaning has to take this into account. Such figures and symbols reflect a *nonliteral* usage of language.

In our zeal for "superspiritual" meaning, we often miss completely the message God has intended for us—in essence substituting our word for his.

For this reason we prefer the term *literary meaning. Literary meaning* refers to the meaning the authors have placed in the text. It reflects the type of literature used, the context, the historical background, the grammar, word meanings—basically everything we have been studying. This literary meaning does not preempt or replace spiritual meaning. Because the Bible is basically about God and his relationship with us, this literary meaning will be a spiritual meaning as well.

In other words, the dichotomy is not between literary meaning and spiritual meaning. The dichotomy is between the meaning the authors intended and the meaning a reader dreams up and projects onto the text. This reader-based "spiritualizing" is the danger. Such "spiritualizing" occurs when we "discover" deep, secret meanings that the authors never intended. This kind of "spiritualizing" is not based on this specific text or the Spirit of God; it is a product of our imaginations or a retrojection of other biblical truth back into this passage. That is, inaccurate, "spiritualized" meanings can be true, but they are true because of other biblical texts.

Not too long ago, an acquaintance shared with me a "deep insight" into Joshua 3–4 that he was very proud of. Joshua 3–4 is the story of how God stopped the waters of the Jordan River so that the Israelites could cross over easily into the promised land and attack Jericho. The Israelites were to memorialize this event by taking twelve stones from the dry riverbed and forming a monument out of these stones on the riverbank.

This acquaintance of mine, however, noticed that when God stopped up the water, the Israelites crossed over on "dry" ground (Josh. 3:17). Ignoring the context, he then proceeded to come up with a spiritualized meaning by running with the word "dry." The "dry riverbed," he proclaimed, shows us that God cares for us in the "dry times of life." From this connection (dry riverbed to dry times in life), he developed an entire sermon about how God cares for us even in the dry times of life when we don't feel his presence.

Will we seek the literary meaning intended by the authors and inspired by the Spirit or the meaning created in our own fanciful imagination?

This sermon thesis is true. God does care for us in the "dry" times of our lives. But this truth does not come from Joshua 3–4! In fact, Joshua 3–4 is teaching something very different. This is not a "dry" time for Israel! Quite to the contrary, it is one of the most dramatic and powerful interventions by God into Israel's history that ever occurs. The stone memorial is not to celebrate God's care in "dry times" but to celebrate how God brought his people into the promised land with power! It is a memorial of a "mountaintop" experience with God, not a "dry time." This friend had followed the "dry" trajectory right out of the literary context into whatever loose theological connection he could come up with for the word "dry." His meaning is not the one the author intended. Therefore, it is not a valid meaning for this text. In his attempt to be "spiritually insightful," this friend actually missed the important meaning that does emerge from this passage: we should take time and effort to remember and to celebrate the times when God works in our lives in dramatic ways.

The question is not whether we will seek literal meaning or spiritual meaning; the question is whether we will seek the literary meaning intended by the authors and inspired by the Spirit or the meaning created in our own fanciful imaginations.

ALLEGORY

Discussions on the purported difference between "spiritual" meaning and "literal" meaning date back to the first few centuries after Christ. Numerous early Christian scholars felt that the Old Testament would be relevant only if it spoke directly of Christ. Thus, they developed a system of interpretation that acknowledged a "literal" meaning of the text, but then encouraged the interpreter to look for the deeper, fuller, spiritual meaning below the surface of the text.[1] Indeed, some of these writers advocated a two-level system (literal and spiritual), while others expanded it into multileveled systems—either three (corresponding to body, soul, and spirit) or four (literal, allegorical, moral, and anagogical).

For example, the fourfold system would see four levels of meaning for the city of Jerusalem: (1) literal: the actual Israelite/Jebusite city; (2) allegorical: the church of Christ; (3) moral: the soul of a person; and (4) anagogical: the heavenly city of God. By the fourth century this interpretive approach, although not without its critics, was popular among many writers of the church, and allegorical interpretation, as this overall approach is now known, became the normal way of approaching the Old Testament.[2] This style of interpretation remained popular until the Reformation (sixteenth century), when the Reformers (primarily John Calvin and Martin Luther) led the new Protestant church away from the allegorical approach.

Although the Reformers occasionally still used allegorical interpretation, in general they returned the church to the literary context of the Bible for the determination of meaning. Contemporary evangelical scholarship has followed in the footsteps of the Reformers and has tried to caution the church against using fanciful allegorical interpretations that are often based more on imagination than on the text itself. However, allegorical interpretation was still used by numerous popular preachers throughout the twentieth century, and it is still around in various forms. It has also been brought back to life through some of the newer interpretive approaches, such as reader response. Once the author loses control of the meaning, many readers will naturally drift into overspiritualizing the text through fanciful allegorical interpretation.

Contemporary evangelical scholarship has tried to caution the church against using fanciful allegorical interpretations that are often based more on imagination than on the text itself.

What do we mean by allegory? An allegory is a story that uses an extensive amount of symbolism. It is similar to a parable but generally has a greater degree of correspondence—that is, most or many of the details in the story represent something or carry some specific nuance of meaning. Greidanus defines it as "an extended metaphor—that is, a number of elements in a story make up a string of metaphors which have a deeper unified meaning."[3] Allegory is a literary technique. Sometimes an entire book can employ the technique of allegory to convey its message. Bunyan's *Pilgrim's Progress* is such a

1. This fuller, deeper meaning is referred to as the *sensus plenior*, which is Latin for "fuller sense."

2. See the excellent discussion in Sidney Greidanus, *Preaching Christ from the Old Testament* (Grand Rapids: Eerdmans, 1993), 69–107.

3. Greidanus, 88.

book. Thus, when one reads and interprets *Pilgrim's Progress,* he or she must read it as allegory and not as history or as a historical novel.

The Bible also uses allegory occasionally. Isaiah 5:1–7 would qualify as an allegory. Read this text and note the extended use of metaphor:

> [1]I will sing for the one I love
>   a song about his vineyard:
> My loved one had a vineyard
>   on a fertile hillside.
> [2]He dug it up and cleared it of stones
>   and planted it with the choicest vines.
> He built a watchtower in it
>   and cut out a winepress as well.
> Then he looked for a crop of good grapes,
>   but it yielded only bad fruit.
>
> [3]"Now you dwellers in Jerusalem and people of Judah,
>   judge between me and my vineyard.
> [4]What more could have been done for my vineyard
>   than I have done for it?
> When I looked for good grapes,
>   why did it yield only bad?
> [5]Now I will tell you
>   what I am going to do to my vineyard:
> I will take away its hedge,
>   and it will be destroyed;
> I will break down its wall,
>   and it will be trampled.
> [6]I will make it a wasteland,
>   neither pruned nor cultivated,
>   and briers and thorns will grow there.
> I will command the clouds
>   not to rain on it."
>
> [7]The vineyard of the Lord Almighty
>   is the nation of Israel,
> and the people of Judah
>   are the vines he delighted in.

And he looked for justice, but saw bloodshed;
for righteousness, but heard cries of distress.

Isaiah preaches this passage to Israel to warn them that God will judge them for their lack of justice and righteousness. Isaiah uses an extended metaphor with numerous elements of correspondence. Fortunately, in verse 7 Isaiah himself identifies the meaning of the allegory and tells us what the corresponding elements are. God is the owner of the vineyard. Israel is the vineyard. The good grapes that the owner couldn't find are justice and righteousness.

So *allegory* itself is not a bad thing; it is merely another literary device used occasionally in the Bible to convey a message in a colorful way. However, *allegorical interpretation* as an interpretive method is quite different from *allegory*, and it can mislead us completely if we use it to interpret a nonallegorical text. *Few texts in the Bible are allegorical.* Therefore, you will find few opportunities to use it. Do not use it randomly on all Old Testament stories! Do not fall into the habit of trying to "spiritualize" the Old Testament through allegorical interpretation. Keep your meanings tied to the literary and historical-cultural context. Use the Interpretive Journey to arrive at meaning and application, not imaginative allegorical approaches.

Perhaps a few illustrations of improper allegorical interpretation will help. Greidanus cites the popular radio preacher M. R. DeHaan's interpretation of Genesis 2:18–25 as a good example. The passage reads as follows:

18The LORD God said, "It is not good for the man to be alone. I will make a helper suitable for him."

19Now the LORD God had formed out of the ground all the wild animals and all the birds in the sky. He brought them to the man to see what he would name
them; and whatever the man called each living creature, that was its name. 20So the
man gave names to all the livestock, the birds in the sky and all the wild animals.
But for Adam no suitable helper was found. 21So the LORD God caused
the man to fall into a deep sleep; and while he was sleeping, he took one of the
man's ribs and then closed up the place with flesh. 22Then the LORD God made a
woman from the rib he had taken out of the man, and he brought her to the man.

23The man said,

"This is now bone of my bones
and flesh of my flesh;
she shall be called 'woman,'
for she was taken out of man."

> [24]That is why a man leaves his father and mother and is united to his wife, and they become one flesh.
>
> [25]Adam and his wife were both naked, and they felt no shame.

DeHaan allegorized the passage with the following interpretation:

> While Adam slept, God created from his wounded side a wife, who was part of himself, and he paid for her by the shedding of his blood. . . . Now all is clear. Adam is a picture of the Lord Jesus, who left His Father's house to gain His bride at the price of His own life. Jesus, the last Adam, like the first, must be put to sleep to purchase his bride, the Church, and Jesus died on the cross and slept in the tomb for three days and three nights. His side too was opened after He had fallen asleep, and from that wounded side redemption flowed.[4]

DeHaan was rather imaginative with his connections between this text and the death of Christ. Greidanus correctly observes that although DeHaan was trying to be Christ-centered in his preaching, he was doing so at the cost of missing the meaning of the text. DeHaan's meaning has been read back into the text rather than developed from the text. "It has nothing whatsoever to do with the author's intended message," writes Greidanus. "And sadly," Greidanus continues,

> in the process of allegorizing the text, its real message is left behind. For the text is about God in the beginning making a partner for the lonely man. The author's message for Israel is about God's wonderful gift of marriage. Since Israel lived in a culture where polygamy was normal and where women were not valued as true partners, this message of God's original design for marriage taught Israel about God's norm for marriage. That message should have been preached, for it is still good news for women and men today. And it could have been reinforced by Jesus' own teaching based on this passage, "Therefore what God has joined together, let no one separate" (Mk. 10:9).[5]

So by trying to find a deep, "spiritual" meaning in Genesis 2, DeHaan ignored the context of the chapter and missed an important teaching about marriage. God's message to us on marriage is a *spiritual* message, and we do not need to search our imaginations for some strained connections to the death of Christ in order to make

4. M. R. DeHaan, *Portraits of Christ in Genesis* (Grand Rapids: Zondervan, 1966), 32–33; cited by Greidanus, *Preaching Christ*, 37.

5. Greidanus, *Preaching Christ*, 37.

this passage relevant. Everything DeHaan said about the significance of Christ and his death is true. Christ did die for his bride, the church, and redemption does "flow" from his side. However, simply because one understands the significance of Christ's death does not mean that he or she understands Genesis 2. We do not evaluate interpretations of Genesis 2 merely on the basis of correct New Testament theology. We evaluate it on the basis of whether or not we have evidence that it is the intended meaning that the Holy Spirit has placed in the passage. "Jesus died on the cross to save sinners like me" is an important biblical truth. However, that does not qualify it to be the meaning of every Old Testament text.

One area of the Old Testament that seems to elicit particularly imaginative allegorical interpretations is the description of the tabernacle in the book of Exodus. In this book, after God leads the Israelites out of Egypt and into the desert, he enters into a covenant with them. At the heart of the covenant is God's threefold statement: "I will be your God, you will be my people, and I will dwell in your midst." If he is to dwell physically in their midst, then he needs a place to stay. God tells them to construct a tabernacle (a portable temple) as the place where he will reside in their midst. Most of the latter half of the book of Exodus deals with the details of how to construct this tabernacle.

The significance of the tabernacle is that it was the physical location of the presence of God. As such it definitely has numerous New Testament connections. The presence of God is still a critical doctrine for New Testament believers, but now we experience the presence of God within us through the Spirit instead of experiencing his presence through worship at the tabernacle, as did the people in the days of Moses. Also, the Old Testament sacrificial system connects to Israelite worship in the tabernacle and provides valuable background to help us understand the sacrifice of Christ. Thus, in some sense the sacrifices do point us to Christ.

The book of Hebrews underscores numerous *comparisons* between Christ and the Old Testament system connected with the tabernacle. It tells us that the sacrifice of Christ is better than the old sacrifices, because he was blameless, and because his sacrifice is not repeated over and over as the Old Testament ones were. Christ is also better as a high priest than the Israelite priests, because he is a superior mediator, being without sin and better able to understand us. So there is much about the tabernacle and its associated sacrificial system that does have New Testament parallels. However, this affirmation does not give us license to make imaginative connections between Christ and every minute detail of the tabernacle.

Allegorical interpreters seem to search for any loose semantic or thematic connection between the details of the tabernacle and Jesus' life. Almost any connection is acceptable to this approach as long as it somehow relates to Jesus. Without taking time to validate their conclusions, these interpreters often proclaim this connection, however far-fetched, as *the* meaning.

For example, when you read in Exodus 27:19 a reference to *tent pegs* (*pins* in the KJV), the popular allegorical approach would lead you to search for some type of connection between Christ and the tent pegs. Think for a minute and see what you can dream up. Any ideas? Of course, if the pegs were made of wood, we could say that they represent the cross, but, alas, they are made of bronze (KJV "brass"). Maybe we can come up with something for *bronze*. Bronze doesn't decay and rot as wood does, and the salvation we find in Jesus doesn't decay or rot either, so maybe the bronze pegs represent our enduring relationship with Christ. How about that? Moreover, the tent pegs also hold up the sides of the curtain walls. This *holding up* idea should give us some fertile fields to work with. Jesus holds us up and supports us. He is our firm anchor as these pegs are firm anchors. So the pegs must represent Jesus and his strength in holding us up, right?

Much about the tabernacle has New Testament parallels, but this does not give us license to make imaginative connections between Christ and every minute detail of the tabernacle.

Do such meanings seem far-fetched to you? Is this how Christians should interpret the Bible? Are we going to find the message God has placed in the text through this kind of random speculation? What restricts our imaginations here? With this method we can dream up dozens of meanings for the tent pegs, none of which is the meaning intended by the author—if there even is any significance to the tent pegs beyond their role of holding up the tent walls.

Yet allegorical interpreters are able to find christological meaning in all of the details, even the tent pegs. For example, using the KJV translation of *pins* rather than *tent pegs*, Louis T. Talbot wrote,

> The pins, or nails, [tent pegs] of the Tabernacle were made of brass; therefore, they did not rust. As they withstood every desert storm, even so Christ's holy life withstood every onslaught of Satan. How minutely the details of the God-given pattern for the tabernacle in the wilderness foreshadow the glories of our crucified and risen Lord![6]

DeHaan outdid Talbot. He was able to move even beyond the outlandish suggestions we made above. First he agreed with Talbot that the corrosion resistance of the brass/bronze material of the pegs represents the "incorruptible life and death of our

6. Louis T. Talbot, *Christ in the Tabernacle* (Wheaton, IL: Van Kampen, 1942), 89.

Lord Jesus." But then he drew deep significance from the fact that the pegs were half buried in the ground. He wrote,

> We repeat, the pins were buried in the ground, but also emerged from the ground, and it speaks of the death and the resurrection, that which is buried, and that which is above the ground. The part of the pins beneath the ground becomes a symbol of the death of the Lord Jesus Christ; the part above the ground suggests His resurrection. And this is the Gospel, the "good news" of salvation, the finished work that makes us secure. If the pins were driven all the way into the ground, they would be worthless. Part of them must be above the ground in order that the ropes may be attached to them. So, too, the death of the Lord Jesus Christ by itself could not save a single sinner. The good news of the Gospel is not only the Cross, not only the death of Christ for sinners, but it is the death plus the resurrection of our Savior. The pins are buried, but also rise above the ground in order to make us secure.[7]

Notice the leap that DeHaan had taken from the text into sheer speculation. None of the passages in Exodus that mention the tent pegs alludes to the ground (Ex. 27:19; 35:18; 38:20, 31; 39:40). The ground is not even mentioned! Yet DeHaan created an entire level of spiritual meaning from this questionable connection between the unmentioned partial burial of tent pegs and the resurrection of Christ. Is this not far-fetched? What are the controls or limits of such interpretation? Are his readers free to pursue this line of reasoning, or did only DeHaan have this insight?

Tent pegs have dozens of connotations. Are we free to draw theology from *all* of them? And how did DeHaan know that the pegs were buried half in and half out like our modern tent pegs are? Those of you who have pitched tents in soft sand also know that normal tent pegs are useless in the soft sand unless the entire peg is buried (called a dead man). Did the priests in Exodus ever do this? In addition, in Numbers 3:36–37 and 4:32 the Merarite clan of the Levite tribe was given responsibility for maintaining and carrying the tent pegs. What does this do to DeHaan's Christology? Did the Old Testament priesthood care for Christ and carry him on their backs as these priests carried the tent pegs? Do you see how absurd this line of interpretation can become? There is no connection between the tent pegs in the tabernacle and the resurrection of Jesus Christ. Fabricating such a connection does not honor Christ.

Was there *symbolism* in the tabernacle? Absolutely! But the symbolism should be sought against the ancient Near Eastern background in which the people of the exodus

7. Martin R. DeHaan, *The Tabernacle* (Grand Rapids: Zondervan, 1955), 65.

lived. Throughout the Bible God communicated to his people using forms they were familiar with. The Bible uses symbols frequently. One of the problems with allegorical interpretation of symbols is that the interpreters tend to use their creative imagination to find deep theological connections to the New Testament without even asking what the symbol might have meant to the biblical audience. In their zeal to find symbolic representations of Christ, they often skip over the real meanings of significant symbols.

For example, the four major colors found in the tabernacle were red, white, purple, and blue. Without doing any apparent research into the significance of these colors in religious settings in the ancient Near East, Talbot concluded that "the blue speaks to us of our Lord's deity, for blue is the heavenly color."[8] DeHaan and A. B. Simpson concurred, writing that the blue color points to Christ's heavenly origin.[9]

Allegorical interpretation of symbols tend to depend on imaginative theological connections to the New Testament without paying attention to what the symbol might have meant to the biblical audience.

Note their apparent line of reasoning. Blue is the color of the sky. Another term for sky in the Bible is *the heavens*. Jesus is from heaven. Blue must refer to his heavenly origin. Thus, they came up with a "spiritual" meaning for the symbol *blue*. They were in the ballpark but not exactly on target. They had simply relied on their intuition and imagination instead of research into the background of color symbolism in the world of ancient Israel.

What did blue symbolize in the ancient Near East? How can we find out what it meant? Let's do some research. A good reference work to check when studying symbolic words is the *Dictionary of Biblical Imagery*, edited by Ryken, Wilhoit, and Longman. Their discussion of the symbolic use of blue in the ancient Near East is significant:

> In ancient thought the sky was believed to separate the place of the gods from the human realm. Therefore, blue, the color of the sky, could appropriately suggest the boundary between God and his people and symbolize his majesty. Like purple, blue was an expensive dye and thus connoted wealth and prestige. Blue was the dominant color of the vestments of ancient Israel's high priest (Ex 28). The high priest wore an outer garment of solid blue over the white robe of the priesthood. He was the boundary between the human and divine realms, moving in both as he ministered in the Holy of Holies.[10]

8. Talbot, *Christ in the Tabernacle*, 38.

9. DeHaan, *Tabernacle*, 36–37, 49. A. B. Simpson, *Christ in the Tabernacle* (Harrisburg, PA: Christian Publications, n.d.), 15. DeHaan could not resist the fact that there were four colors, which must, he assumed, refer to the four gospels.

10. Leland Ryken, James C. Wilhoit, and Tremper Longman III, eds., *Dictionary of Biblical Imagery* (Downers Grove, IL: InterVarsity Press, 1989), 158.

As you can see from this explanation, we do not have to allegorize or use our imaginations to find significant spiritual symbolism from the color blue in the tabernacle. The tabernacle was the location of the presence of God; he lived among his people like a king lived in his palace. Thus, to use the most expensive dyed material (blue and purple) to signify his majesty seems appropriate. The sky connotations are also significant. The point of using the large amount of blue material in the tabernacle was not to point to Jesus' heavenly origin, but rather to underscore the concept of the boundary between the holy God and sinful humanity—a boundary that normally *separates* humanity from the divine, but a boundary that is *crossed* by God through his dwelling in the tabernacle. This was the place where Israel approached God himself. The blue color reminded them of his majesty, and it reminded them that they were crossing over a mystical threshold to encounter the living God, who chose to dwell among them. There is no need to allegorize such a significant meaning as this.

Avoid the temptation to allegorize.

What can we conclude from this? As you seek to determine the meaning of a biblical passage, avoid the temptation to allegorize. Don't try to read Christ back into every rock and tent peg in the Old Testament lest you miss the actual meaning that God is trying to convey to you. Use the Interpretive Journey; it will help you to stay on track.

We certainly want to affirm that there are numerous legitimate connections between Christ and the Old Testament. These generally fall into the categories of prophecy and typology. We will discuss prophecy in chapter 21. Let's turn here to typology.

TYPOLOGY

Numerous passages in the Old Testament describe things that *point to* or *foreshadow* what Christ ultimately fulfills. For example, the entire sacrificial system of Israel *foreshadows* the sacrifice of Christ. As the book of Hebrews tells us, Christ is the ultimate sacrifice, eliminating forever the need for any other sacrifices. However, to view the Old Testament sacrificial system as a whole to be a foreshadowing of the sacrifice of Christ is much different from interpreting every aspect of the sacrificial system allegorically. The sacrificial system involved doves, goats, cows, grain, ashes, smoke, fire, knives, and a host of other details. Allegorical interpretation projects christological significance onto each of the minute details. The concept of foreshadowing, by contrast, suggests general connections (death, blood, without blemish, etc.) and does not speculate on the minute details.

Furthermore, most of the foreshadowing of Christ in the Old Testament is identified in the New Testament. Thus, we can rely on the guidance of the New Testament to help us discern whether a passage is a foreshadowing of Christ. We are, we should remember, trying to determine the meaning that God has placed in the text. We must not seek to be creative or clever, nor should we try to derive some hidden connection that no one else ever saw before. Thus, we advise you to use the New Testament as a guide to determining the foreshadowing passages in the Old Testament. Do not try to force Christ into every passage, as the allegorizers do.

Some scholars prefer to use the term *typology* instead of *foreshadowing*. The two terms are similar in meaning, although *typology* generally requires a correspondence of the New Testament fulfillment that is closer to the Old Testament representation than foreshadowing suggests. A *type* can be defined as "a biblical event, person or institution which serves as an example or pattern for other events, persons or institutions."[11] The Old Testament flows into the New Testament as part of a continuous salvation-history story. What is promised in the Old is fulfilled in the New. *Typology* is part of the promise-fulfillment scheme that connects the two testaments.[12]

In typology it is critical that this prophetic meaning be the one that was intended by the divine Author.

Thus, we view *typology* as being prophetic—a historical event or person in the Old Testament that serves as a prophetic pattern or example of a New Testament event or person. However, it is critical that this prophetic meaning be the one that was intended by the divine Author. Thus, the identification must be in the Bible and not merely in our imaginations. Also, we do not think that the human author was always cognizant of the complete fulfillment that was to come, although we acknowledge that there is much disagreement among scholars on this point.

Psalm 22 provides us with a good example of *typology*. Although David wrote Psalm 22 about a thousand years or so before the coming of Christ, note the close correspondence between the selected verses below and the suffering of Christ on the cross.

> [1]My God, my God, why have you forsaken me?
> Why are you so far from saving me,
> so far from my cries of anguish? . . .
> [7]All who see me mock me;

11. David Baker, "Typology and the Christian Use of the Old Testament," *Scottish Journal of Theology* 29.2 (1976): 153 (cited by Douglas J. Moo, "The Problem of Sensus Plenior," in *Hermeneutics, Authority, and Canon*, ed. D. A. Carson and John D. Woodbridge [Grand Rapids: Zondervan, 1986], 195).

12. Moo, "Problem of Sensus Plenior," 196.

they hurl insults, shaking their heads:
8"He trusts in the LORD," they say,
"let the LORD rescue him.
Let him deliver him,
since he delights in him. . . ."
14I am poured out like water,
and all my bones are out of joint.
My heart has turned to wax;
it has melted within me.
15My mouth is dried up like a potsherd,
and my tongue sticks to the roof of my mouth;
you lay me in the dust of death.

16Dogs surround me,
a pack of villains encircles me;
they pierce my hands and my feet.
17All my bones are on display;
people stare and gloat over me.
18They divide my clothes among them
and cast lots for my garment.

David apparently wrote this psalm during a time of intense suffering in his life. We doubt that David actually envisioned the future crucifixion of Christ (although it is possible). We believe that the Spirit led him in his choice of words as he wrote this psalm of lament. David used figures of speech (common in Hebrew poetry) to describe his physical suffering. Thus, his description in Psalm 22 is a figurative picture of a real time of suffering in his life. Jesus, however, lived out many of the descriptive aspects of this psalm on the cross. In his case, moreover, the language tends to describe his suffering in a literal manner rather than a figurative manner.

We see definite prophetic elements in Psalm 22 regarding the cross. David's suffering in this psalm is thus a *type* of the suffering of Christ on the cross. The figurative description of David's sufferings finds literal fulfillment in the suffering of Christ. Of course, clinching this *typological* connection is the fact that Jesus quotes Psalm 22 from the cross (Matt. 27:46; Mark 15:34), and John explicitly states that as the Roman soldiers cast lots for Jesus' clothes, they fulfilled Psalm 22:18. The New Testament guides us to the fact that Psalm 22 is fulfilled in the death of Christ. Since it also applies to a historical situation in David's life, we categorize the psalm as *typology*.

In our opinion an Old Testament passage usually cannot be confirmed as typological unless the New Testament identifies it as such. Therefore, while other Old Testament texts may bear some similarities to New Testament realities, they cannot be confidently classified as *typology* unless the New Testament indicates the fulfillment.

CONCLUSION

Let us return to the original question: "Does the Bible have different levels of meaning?" We do not believe it does. There is one level of meaning—the one tied to the historical-cultural and literary contexts. This meaning includes its meaning for the biblical audience and the theological principles behind that meaning. There can be different aspects of a text's meaning and even a number of principles behind those aspects. But there are not deep, "spiritual" meanings hidden in the text that are unrelated to the historical and literary context.

Typology is the only thing that comes close to being an exception. However, even though we affirm the predictive aspects of typology, we do not think typology opens the door for creating different, nonhistorical, "spiritualized" levels of meaning. Furthermore, Old Testament typology is limited to that which is identified in the New Testament; it is not something we are able to find or create through our cleverness. Likewise, we have argued that the popularized practice of allegorical interpretation is not indicative of deeper, spiritual levels of meaning, but more often indicative of the creative speculation of the reader.

We have encouraged you in this chapter to avoid the temptations of "spiritualizing" or allegorizing. Keep your search for meaning within the historical and literary contexts of your passage. Do not be a "tent-peg allegorizer." Seek the meaning of the divine Author and human author instead of the creative fantasies of human speculation. Use the Interpretive Journey to interpret the Bible. Throughout this book we will do our best to provide you with the proper skills to dig deeply into the Bible—skills that will help you to grasp God's Word for your life. We want you to find spiritual meaning, but we want you to find the spiritual meaning that lies within the text, not the meaning that people have projected back onto the text.

What role does the Holy Spirit play in all of this? Can the Holy Spirit lead us into a deeper, spiritual meaning that goes beyond the text? This is the topic of the next chapter.

ASSIGNMENT

Assignment 11–1

Read 1 Kings 17:1–6 below and use your imagination to develop a far-fetched allegorical interpretation. Ignore the context completely and try to come up with a "superspiritual" meaning for as many of the details as possible. Keep in mind that the point of this exercise is to misinterpret the passage intentionally. Don't be concerned with the real meaning of the passage. Be as creative (and wrong) as you can.

1 Now Elijah the Tishbite, from Tishbe in Gilead, said to Ahab, "As the LORD, the God of Israel,
lives, whom I serve, there will be neither dew nor rain in the next few years except at my word."
2 Then the word of the LORD came to Elijah: 3 "Leave here, turn eastward and hide in the Kerith
Ravine, east of the Jordan. 4 You will drink from the brook, and I have directed the ravens to supply
you with food there."
5 So he did what the LORD had told him. He went to the Kerith Ravine, east of the Jordan, and
stayed there. 6 The ravens brought him bread and meat in the morning and bread and meat in the
evening, and he drank from the brook.

Your far-fetched allegorical interpretation:

CHAPTER 12

THE ROLE OF THE HOLY SPIRIT

INTRODUCTION

Have you ever played a musical instrument—the piano, the trumpet, or perhaps the guitar? Learning to play an instrument entails taking time to master the basics—a tedious process. You learn where the notes are and how to play them correctly. You repeat the same exercises over and over . . . and over, until you get them right. You will never outgrow the basics, but there is more to playing the piano than reading notes, finding the correct hand position, and playing scales. You will eventually think less about mechanics and begin to experience the wonder and beauty of the musical piece. When we talk about the role of the Spirit in interpreting the Bible, we move beyond mere mechanics to the dynamic nature of a relationship. God gave us his Word to communicate with us; he gives us his Spirit to help us understand what he has said and is saying.

> Some of you may be asking yourself, *Is my relationship to the Bible being reduced to a set of interpretive steps?*

Our purpose in *Grasping God's Word* is to teach you how to discover the meaning of the biblical text and apply that meaning to your life. We spend a lot of time talking about methods, steps, procedures, and the like. We encourage you to analyze words, sentences, and paragraphs and discourses. We emphasize thinking and digging and searching. Some of you may be asking yourself, *Is this all there is to Bible study? Is my relationship to the Bible being reduced to a set of interpretive steps?* Jesus tells his disciples in John 16:13 that the Holy Spirit will "guide you into all the truth." "If we have the Spirit," you may ask, "why do we need to worry about proper procedures?" In other words, what role does the Holy Spirit play in biblical interpretation? This is what the present chapter is all about.

THE SPIRIT AS THE DIVINE AUTHOR

In chapter 10 we noted that when we speak about the *author* of the Bible, we are speaking about both the human author and the divine Author. The term *inspiration* refers to the Holy Spirit's work in the lives of the human authors of Scripture with the result that they wrote what God wanted to communicate (i.e., the Word of God). In 2 Timothy 3:16–17 the apostle Paul says that "all Scripture is *God-breathed* [sometimes translated *inspired*] and is useful for teaching, rebuking, correcting and training in righteousness, so that the servant of God may be thoroughly equipped for every good work." The Spirit of God has breathed the character of God into the Scriptures.

Inspiration refers to the Holy Spirit's work in the lives of the human authors of Scripture with the result that they wrote what God wanted to communicate (i.e., the Word of God).

The Greek word for "inspired" (*theopneustos*) is even related to the Greek word for "spirit" (*pneuma*). The Bible has the power and authority to shape our lives because it comes from God himself. We hold to the authority of the Scriptures because they are inspired ("God-breathed"). Paul's statement in 2 Timothy also reminds us that the Spirit and the Scriptures go together—the Word of God originated from the Spirit of God.

The Spirit's work of inspiration is finished, but his work of bringing believers to understand and receive the truth of Scripture continues. Theologians use the term *illumination* to refer to this ongoing work of the Spirit. On the night before he was crucified, Jesus promised his followers that the Holy Spirit would guide them into all truth:

> [12]"I have much more to say to you, more than you can now bear. But when he, the Spirit of truth, comes, he will guide you into all the truth. [13]He will not speak on his own; he will speak only what he hears, and he will tell you what is yet to come. [14]He will glorify me because it is from me that he will receive what he will make known to you." (John 16:12–14)

Notice how Jesus stresses that the work of the Spirit is directly related to Jesus' teachings (i.e., the Word of God).

Because of the Spirit's work of *inspiration* and *illumination*, we know that the Spirit and the Word work together and must never be set against one another. Since the Spirit inspired Scripture in the first place, we should not expect him to contradict himself when he illuminates it. This means, for example, that we should not allow personal experience, religious tradition, or community consensus to stand above the Spirit-inspired Word of God. The Spirit does not add new meaning to the biblical text; instead, he helps believers understand and apply the meaning that is already there.

Since the Spirit inspired Scripture in the first place, we should not expect him to contradict himself when he illuminates it.

In this regard Kevin Vanhoozer writes that the "Spirit may blow where, but not *what*, he wills." Vanhoozer goes on to describe the Spirit as the "*Word's empowering presence*."[1] This description is helpful because it reminds us that the Spirit's role is not to author a new Bible (i.e., revealing new meaning through personal experience or community tradition) but to bring home to us the meaning of the Scripture he has already authored.

CAN WE GRASP GOD'S WORD APART FROM THE SPIRIT?

Looking at the role of the Holy Spirit in biblical interpretation raises the question of whether people without the Spirit can grasp God's Word. We would answer this important question in three different ways.

"Yes"

If unbelievers use valid interpretive methods, they are able to comprehend much of the Bible (e.g., the sense of words, the rules of grammar, and the logic of a passage). People who are able to read literature effectively will certainly be able to detect a contrast or a command or a figure of speech in the Bible when they see one. The Bible does not insist that an unbeliever is incapable of understanding any of its basic grammatical or historical content. At the level of cognitive understanding, the Spirit appears to play a minimal role.

1. Kevin J. Vanhoozer, *Is There a Meaning in This Text?* (Grand Rapids: Zondervan, 1998), 429 (emphases original). He is using Jesus' words about the Spirit in John 3:3–8 as his backdrop.

"Yes, but Only to a Degree"

Going a step further, can persons without the Spirit understand the meaning of a biblical passage? Here we answer "Yes, but only to a degree." We would say that their understanding is limited (i.e., "only to a degree") for at least three reasons. First, sin has had an effect on the whole person, including the human mind. We are not suggesting that sin prevents us from recognizing prepositional phrases or locating literary themes. We do, however, believe that sin has dulled our ability to discern or perceive scriptural truth.

An unbeliever's ability to understand the meaning of a biblical text is limited by the effects of the "unbelieving" preunderstanding that he or she brings to the text.

Second, an unbeliever's ability to understand the meaning of a biblical text is limited by the effects of the "unbelieving" preunderstanding that he or she brings to the text. As Vanhoozer observes, pre-text baggage has the power to distort the way people understand the Scriptures: "We should recall how common it is for readers to let their prejudices or ideologies distort their reading. Distortion is a real possibility whenever readers are faced with texts that require behavioral change, not to mention the death of the old self and the end of self-love. Interpretation never takes place in a cognitively and spiritually clean environment."[2] Since the Spirit plays a crucial role in helping Christian interpreters deal with the baggage of their preunderstanding, a person who does not have the Spirit will encounter an even greater degree of distortion.

Third, we say that a person without the Spirit can understand the meaning of a biblical passage "only to a degree" because understanding involves more than just taking in information with your mind. Understanding the meaning of a biblical passage involves the whole person—mind, emotions, body, and so on. Unbelievers, by definition, do not accept the things of the Spirit of God.

"No"

Will people without the Spirit accept the truth of the Bible and apply it to their lives? The Bible itself says no. In 1 Corinthians 2:14 the apostle Paul says that "the person without the Spirit does not accept the things that come from the Spirit of God but considers them foolishness, and cannot understand them because they are discerned only through the Spirit." Paul does not mean that a person without the Spirit will have no intellectual comprehension of what the Bible is saying. Rather, he means that an unbeliever will understand its basic message but reject it.[3]

2. Vanhoozer, 428.

3. Note, too, that a person must have some understanding of the message to reject it as foolishness.

When Paul goes on to say that a person without the Spirit "cannot understand" the things of God, he is referring to a personal, experiential kind of understanding. People without the Spirit do not know the things of God because they have not experienced them.[4] Without the Spirit, although people may understand some of the Bible's meaning, they will not be persuaded of its truth and will not live it out. They may grasp the meaning of the biblical text, but they refuse to allow the text to grasp them. We cannot apply the Word of God without the help of the Spirit of God.

When it comes to biblical interpretation, the Spirit appears to work *little* in the cognitive dimension, *more* in the area of discerning truth, and *most* in the area of application.

Can we grasp God's Word apart from the Holy Spirit? Perhaps now you can see why we have three different answers to this important question. When it comes to biblical interpretation, the Spirit appears to work *little* in the cognitive dimension, *more* in the area of discerning truth, and *most* in the area of application. Since many of you do have the Spirit of God living in you, let's turn our attention to the role the Spirit plays in your life as you interpret the Bible.

THE SPIRIT AND THE CHRISTIAN INTERPRETER

As a believer, what can you expect the Spirit to do for you (or enable you to do) when it comes to interpreting the Bible? What should you not expect the Spirit to do? In the observations below about the role of the Spirit, we talk in terms of what the Spirit does and does not do. Please know up front that we are not trying to tell God what he can or cannot do. We are simply describing a few of the main ways the Spirit seems to work in relationship to the Scriptures.

1. a. When it comes to biblical interpretation, having the Holy Spirit does not mean that the Spirit is all you need. The Spirit does not make valid interpretation automatic. At first this observation may sound irreverent or even sacrilegious, but that is not our intention.

Perhaps an illustration will help. When children learn to walk, they usually want their parents involved in the experience. Usually the parents will sit a few feet apart facing each other, and one parent will point the wobbly child in the direction of the outstretched arms of the other parent. After playing "catch" with the child for a few days, the child finally gets the hang of it and begins to walk on his or her own. For the

4. On this common reading of 1 Corinthians 2:14, see Daniel P. Fuller, "The Holy Spirit's Role in Biblical Interpretation," in *Scripture, Tradition, and Interpretation*, ed. W. Ward Gasque and William Sanford LaSor (Grand Rapids: Eerdmans, 1978); Roy B. Zuck, "The Role of the Holy Spirit in Hermeneutics," *Bibliotheca Sacra* 141 (1984): 120–30; more recently, Vanhoozer, *Is There a Meaning in This Text?*, 428.

sake of illustration, what if the child thought, *Since my parents are here, I don't have to do anything. I don't have to move one foot in front of the other or stumble backward or fall down. I can stop trying to walk. With Mom and Dad close by, walking will come automatically.*

Although this illustration borders on the absurd, many people reason just like this child when it comes to the Spirit's role in biblical interpretation, saying, as it were, "Because I am a Christian and have the Spirit of God living in me, I don't have to do anything when it comes to interpreting the Bible; it will happen automatically." It simply doesn't work that way. Having the Holy Spirit in your life does not mean that the Spirit will do all the interpreting for you. The Spirit works *through* a careful exegesis of the text.

b. The Spirit does expect us to use our minds, proper interpretive methods, and good study helps to interpret the Bible accurately. Roy Zuck points out a helpful parallel between the process of inspiration and the process of interpretation: "In the inspiration of the Bible the Holy Spirit was working but so were the human authors. In a similar way in the interpretation of the Bible, human work is involved."[5] God gave us minds, and he expects us to use them when it comes to Bible study.[6] He wants us to think clearly and reason soundly. He wants us to study the Scriptures diligently and faithfully. Since God created us to think, study is "spiritual" (i.e., in line with the Spirit's will). We can also learn much from other believers by making use of good study helps such as Bible dictionaries and commentaries. As our heavenly Helper, the Spirit wants to hold our hand and guide us as we learn to walk, but he will not walk for us.

The Spirit does not create new meaning or provide new information.

2. a. The Spirit does not create new meaning or provide new information. The canon of Scripture is closed. This means that we should not expect the Spirit to add another book to the Bible or anything new to the sixty-six books we have. The Spirit does not provide new revelation on a par with Scripture, but he does give us a deeper understanding of the truth that is already there. Similarly, we should not expect the Spirit to whisper in our ears new insights that have been kept hidden from other believing interpreters for centuries.

b. We can rely on the Spirit to help us grasp the meaning of God's Word. The Spirit and the Word work together. The Spirit enables us to grasp the meaning of the Scriptures at a deeper level. Certainly this includes the ability to apply the meaning

5. Zuck, "Role of the Holy Spirit in Hermeneutics," 126.

6. We heartily recommend that you read the little book by John R. W. Stott titled *Your Mind Matters* (Downers Grove, IL: InterVarsity Press, 1973).

of the Bible, but it also includes the ability to discern the theology of a passage (what we refer to as "theological principles"). The Spirit gives us "ears to hear" what God is saying to us in his Word. This insight from the Spirit may come after hours of study and reflection (normally the case), or it may come suddenly. Either way the insight comes not as new revelation but as fresh understanding of the meaning of the Bible.

3. a. The Spirit does not change the Bible to suit our purposes or to match our circumstances. Much like the rapids of a river for the person in a kayak, life is constantly presenting us with a new set of challenges—some good, others bad. In the midst of this dynamic environment, we are tempted to adjust the meaning of a passage to fit our situation, our purposes, or our feelings. We may even find ourselves ignoring or violating context as we desperately search for a biblical connection to our situation. It is especially easy for new believers to confuse their own feelings with the voice of the Holy Spirit. But we cannot expect the Spirit to change the meaning of the Bible to correspond to our feelings. (The Spirit always agrees with himself.) The Spirit does, however, work with the Word to transform the life of the interpreter.

b. The Spirit brings the meaning of the Bible to bear on the reader. Vanhoozer sees three ways in which the Spirit works in the life of the Christian interpreter.[7] (i) The Spirit convicts us that the Bible is divinely inspired. We come to believe that the Bible is God's Word because of the work of the Holy Spirit. (ii) The Spirit works in our minds to impress on us the full meaning of the Scriptures (see [2] above). We come to understand that a command really is a command, a promise is a promise, and so on, and we are empowered to grasp the importance of each. (iii) The Spirit works in our hearts so that we are able to receive the Word of God (application).

Our spiritual maturity affects our ability to hear the voice of the Spirit (the divine Author) in the Scriptures.

The Spirit's ongoing work is to transform our character to the character of God (Rom. 12:1–2). Do you ever have the feeling as you study the Bible that while you are interpreting the text, the text is also interpreting you? That is the work of the Holy Spirit. As Vanhoozer puts it, "The Spirit's work in interpretation is not to change the sense [i.e., the meaning of the text] but to restore us to our senses."[8]

Being restored to our senses is crucial because *our spiritual maturity affects our ability to hear the voice of the Spirit (the divine Author) in the Scriptures.* What often separates an effective Christian interpreter from an ineffective one is his or her level of spiritual maturity. The zealous but immature believer is typically the one who will

7. Vanhoozer, *Is There a Meaning in This Text?*, 413.

8. Vanhoozer, 428.

come up with the most off-the-wall interpretations. He or she loves the Lord and means well, but such a person is spiritually immature, and it shows up in the way he or she interprets the Bible. Spiritual maturity includes learning how to listen to the divine Author by submitting to his Word.[9]

PRAYER AND DEVOTIONAL READING

In addition to all that we have just said about how the Spirit works through our thinking as we interpret Scripture, the Spirit often uses *devotional reading* and prayer to encourage spiritual growth. When you sit down with your Bible and listen to the Lord with your heart, you are engaging in devotional reading. The focus is less on analysis and study and more on a personal, intimate time of communing with the Lord. During such times the Spirit uses the Word to renew your soul. Don't think that every time you pick up your Bible you have to do an in-depth word study or observe fifty details in the text. Sometimes you need to be still and enter into the living presence of God, where you can drink deeply of his Word and respond in heartfelt worship. Eugene Peterson reminds us that all reading and study of the Bible is relational or participatory: "The authorial character of the Holy Scriptures was established as personal in the persons of Father, Son, and Holy Spirit. Because it was personal it was also relational, which meant that all reading/listening of Holy Scripture required personal, relational, participatory reading/listening. . . . Christian reading is participatory reading."[10]

One ancient way of reading the Bible that focuses attention on prayerfully listening to God and allowing him to transform us is known as *lectio divina* (Latin for "holy reading" or "prayerful reading"). This approach to the Bible complements the journey approach to biblical interpretation we are teaching you in *Grasping God's Word*; both are important. Traditionally, *lectio divina* consists of five phases:[11]

- *Silencio*—Prepare your heart to hear from God by slowing down. Get settled in one place and begin to quiet yourself before the Lord. As you cast your

9. For much more on the Spirit and the Christian interpreter, see Craig S. Keener, *Spirit Hermeneutics: Reading Scripture in Light of Pentecost* (Grand Rapids: Eerdmans, 2016).

10. Eugene H. Peterson, *Eat This Book: A Conversation in the Art of Spiritual Reading* (Grand Rapids: Eerdmans, 2006), 27–28.

11. For more on devotional reading, see Thelma Hall, *Too Deep for Words: Rediscovering Lectio Divina* (New York: Paulist, 1988); Evan B. Howard, *Praying the Scriptures: A Field Guide for Your Spiritual Journey* (Downers Grove, IL: InterVarsity Press, 1999); Mariano Magrassi, *Praying the Bible: An Introduction to Lectio Divina* (Collegeville, MN: Liturgical, 1998); M. Robert Mulholland Jr., *Shaped by the Word: The Power of Scripture in Spiritual Formation*, rev. ed. (Nashville: Upper Room, 2000); Peterson, *Eat This Book*; James W. Sire, *Learning to Pray through the Psalms* (Downers Grove, IL: InterVarsity Press, 2005).

cares on him, intentionally begin to let go of the hurry and noise that often prevent us from listening to God. Now is the time to slow down.

- *Lectio*—Select a passage of Scripture and read it slowly and out loud. Forget about reading quickly. Slow down. Use your imagination to picture yourself as part of the setting. Resist the temptation to analyze or judge the text or use the text to develop a message for someone else. Focus on listening as if God were speaking directly to you.
- *Meditatio*—Read the passage again, pausing to let the words sink deeply into your mind and heart. As a particular word or phrase catches your attention, repeat it several times. Without trying to overspiritualize the meaning, ponder what God seems to be saying to you through these words. How does this word or phrase connect with your life right now?
- *Oratio*—Respond by praying the passage as you read it a third time. Enter into a conversation with God. Honestly and truthfully talk with God about what he seems to be saying to you through this passage. Now is the time to respond to God. How does the passage make you feel? What action or attitude is God calling you to embrace? Respond from your heart to what God is saying.
- *Contemplatio*—Rest and wait patiently in God's presence. As you give God's Spirit time to work in your life, yield to him. Entrust your past, present, and future to the Lord in light of what he has spoken. Ask the Lord to continue to do his transforming work throughout the day as you continue to listen. Conclude with a prayer of thanksgiving.

When approaching the Bible, whether using the Interpretive Journey approach or devotional reading, we strongly encourage you to do so prayerfully.[12] As Fred Klooster notes, Paul repeatedly prayed that believers would grow in their understanding through the work of the Holy Spirit (e.g., Phil. 1:9–11; Col. 1:9–14).[13] Notice the relationship between prayer, the Spirit, and understanding in Ephesians 1:17–19:

> [17]I keep asking that the God of our Lord Jesus Christ, the glorious Father, may give you the Spirit of wisdom and revelation, so that you may know him

12. For more on prayer, see Richard J. Foster, *Prayer: Finding the Heart's True Home* (San Francisco: HarperSanFrancisco, 1992); Henri J. M. Nouwen, *The Only Necessary Thing: Living a Prayerful Life* (New York: Crossroad, 1999); and Philip Yancey, *Prayer: Does It Make Any Difference?* (Grand Rapids: Zondervan, 2006).

13. Fred H. Klooster, "The Role of the Spirit in the Hermeneutics Process," in *Hermeneutics, Inerrancy, and the Bible*, ed. Earl D. Radmacher and Robert D. Preus (Grand Rapids: Zondervan, 1984), 460.

> better. [18]I pray also that the eyes of your heart may be enlightened in order that you may know the hope to which he has called you, the riches of his glorious inheritance in his holy people, [19]and his incomparably great power for us who believe.

There is really no substitute for prayer when reading, interpreting, and applying the Bible. Communing with the divine Author through prayer can only help us understand what he is saying to us through his Word.

Devotional reading focuses less on analysis of details and more on a personal, intimate time of listening to the Lord with your heart.

In summary, when it comes to biblical interpretation, having the Holy Spirit does not mean that the Spirit is all we need, since he will not make biblical interpretation automatic. He expects us to use our minds, valid interpretive methods, and good study helps. The Spirit does not create new meaning or provide new information, but he does enable us to accept the Bible as God's Word and grasp its meaning. The Spirit will not change the Bible to fit our situation or match our circumstances, but he will work in our lives as interpreters. He restores us to our senses and helps us grow up spiritually so we can hear his voice in the Scriptures more clearly.

CONCLUSION

Much of *Grasping God's Word* is concerned with proper interpretive methodology, and we make no apologies for this. The methods and procedures needed to understand the Bible will always be important. There is no such thing as *autopilot interpretation*, where we flip a "spiritual" switch and God does it all for us. Nevertheless, we don't want to leave you with the impression that grasping God's Word involves nothing more than the application of a particular method. There is a real danger of overintellectualizing what it means to hear the divine Author. The interpretive task is not simply an intellectual one; it involves our entire being and the help of the Holy Spirit. Consequently, spiritual preparation becomes crucial for perceiving the truth of the Scriptures and receiving that truth into your life.[14]

When we truly grasp God's Word, we go beyond a series of steps to a dynamic interaction with the Spirit of God. We listen more intently than we listen even to our best friend. We throw off pride and laziness and study diligently and submissively, not because we love study for study's sake but because we love God. Rather than being a

14. For further study, see Gordon D. Fee, *Listening to the Spirit in the Text* (Grand Rapids: Eerdmans, 2000).

burden, studying God's Word becomes an act of joyful worship as we enter into a heavenly conversation. As you study the Bible, remember to pray that the Spirit will work in your mind and heart so that you will have ears to hear what he is saying through his Word.

ASSIGNMENTS

Assignment 12–1

Once upon a time there was a man with two PhDs in New Testament studies, both from prestigious universities. His academic credentials were impeccable, and he constantly devoted himself to the study of the New Testament. The Gospels were his specialty. He did not, however, claim to follow Jesus Christ as Lord and Savior. The professor's wife was a mature believer, with "only" an MA in biblical studies. They had a nine-year-old daughter who had just returned from a Christian children's camp, where she made the decision to give her life to Christ.

In light of what you have learned in this chapter about the Spirit's role in biblical interpretation, describe how each member of the family might approach John 3:16: "For God so loved the world that he gave his one and only Son, that whoever believes in him shall not perish but have eternal life." Write at least one paragraph from the perspective of each family member.

Assignment 12–2

Select one of the following passages and walk through the *lectio divina* exercise described in this chapter. Write a one- to two-page reflection of what this experience meant to you.

Worship: Psalm 100
Worry: Matthew 6:31–33 or 1 Peter 5:6–7
Temptation: 1 Corinthians 10:12–13
Sin and confession: Psalm 51:1–10
Freedom from condemnation: Romans 8:1–4
Abiding: John 15:1–5
Rest: Psalm 62:5–8
Renewing of the mind: Romans 12:1–2

CHAPTER 13

APPLICATION

INTRODUCTION

In his book *Applying the Bible*, Jack Kuhatschek tells an amazing story about a man who knew his Bible:

> While studying in the Holy Lands, a seminary professor of mine met a man who claimed to have memorized the Old Testament—in Hebrew! Needless to say, the astonished professor asked for a demonstration. A few days later they sat together in the man's home. "Where shall we begin?" asked the man. "Psalm 1," replied my professor, who was an avid student of the psalms. Beginning with Psalm 1:1, the man began to recite from memory, while my professor followed along in his Hebrew Bible. For two hours, the man continued word for word without a mistake as the professor sat in stunned silence. When the demonstration was over, my professor discovered something even more astonishing about the man—he was an atheist! Here was someone who knew the Scriptures better than most Christians ever will, and yet he didn't even believe in God.[1]

This man certainly knew the Bible—in Hebrew no less—but he did not really *grasp* God's Word. When we grasp God's Word, we not only understand its meaning; we also take the final step and live out that meaning. Jesus said plainly,

1. Jack Kuhatschek, *Applying the Bible* (Grand Rapids: Zondervan, 1990), 15–16.

"Whoever has my commands and keeps them is the one who loves me" (John 14:21a). There you have it in a nutshell:

have + keep = love

We cannot apply the Bible without knowing what it means, but we can know the Bible without living it. We can investigate context, analyze words, and even memorize chapters, but unless we act on what we know, we do not truly *grasp* the Word. Knowledge by itself is not enough; it should lead to action.

We cannot apply the Bible without knowing what it means, but we can know the Bible without living it.

We began the Interpretive Journey by discovering the meaning of the text in the town of the biblical audience. Then we measured the width of the river of differences and crossed the principlizing bridge. Next we looked at the larger biblical map to see how the passage fits into the rest of Scripture. Now it is time to ask, "How can we live out the meaning of the text in our town?"

Keep in mind that there is vast difference between knowing how to live out a biblical text and actually living out that text. Once you know how a text could be applied, it is up to you to submit to the Spirit of God and live out the application. For example, in Ephesians 4:26 we are told not to let the sun go down while we are still angry. We find in this verse the *theological principle* of putting a fairly short time limit on dealing with anger. As a volatile emotion, if anger goes unchecked for long, it can do major damage. One way to live out this principle would be to make sure that when you get angry with your friend or spouse, you deal with the problem as soon as possible (e.g., before the end of the day).

When we come to the point of truly grasping God's Word, we will find God's Word grasping us.

But again, knowing the theological principle and how to live it out is not the same thing as actually living it out. All we can possibly do in this chapter is explain to you how to apply a text. You will have to make the actual application as you yield to the Holy Spirit, rely on the power of prayer, and receive help from other Christians. God certainly wants us to know biblical principles and valid ways of living out those principles, but his ultimate goal in communicating with us is to transform our thinking and acting so that we are conformed to the image of his Son, Jesus Christ. When we come to the point of truly grasping God's Word, we will find God's Word grasping us. In the end, it's much more than just applying the Bible to our lives; it's about adjusting and conforming our lives to the Bible.[2]

2. For more on conforming our lives to God's great story, see J. Scott Duvall and J. Daniel Hays, *Living God's Word: Discovering Our Place in the Great Story of Scripture* (Grand Rapids: Zondervan, 2012).

MEANING AND APPLICATION

Do you remember how we defined the terms *meaning* and *application* in chapter 10? *Meaning* refers to what the author intended to communicate through the text. Because a text's meaning is tied to the author, it will be the same for all Christians. The reader does not determine meaning, nor does meaning change from reader to reader. As readers, however, we do need to respond to the meaning God has placed in the text. We use the term *application* to refer to the response of the reader to the meaning of the inspired text. Application reflects the specific life situation of the reader and will vary from Christian to Christian, although it will still have some boundaries influenced by the author's meaning. Thus, we should ask, "What does this passage *mean*, and how do I live out or *apply* this meaning to my life?" rather than "What does this passage mean to me?" The distinction between meaning and application is an important one.

Let's make sure we understand where meaning and application fit into the Interpretive Journey.

Step 1: Grasp the text in their town. What did the text mean to the biblical audience?

Step 2: Measure the width of the river to cross. What are the differences between the biblical audience and us?

Step 3: Cross the principlizing bridge. What is the theological principle(s) in this text?

Step 4: Consult the biblical map. How does our theological principle fit with the rest of the Bible?

Step 5: Grasp the text in our town. How should individual Christians today live out the theological principle(s)?

Steps 1–4 deal with the *meaning* of the text. Through Scripture God communicates to his people both the immediate concrete expression of his theological message for the biblical audience and the theological message or principle for future audiences. This is the meaning that we seek to find when we study the Bible responsibly. After we have identified this meaning, we can begin to ask how we should live out this meaning (step 5).

HOW TO APPLY (OR LIVE OUT) MEANING

In this section we will show you how to determine valid applications for theological principles you have discovered in a biblical text. Since applications may vary from reader to reader, we need a reliable method of making sure that the applications are within the boundaries established by the author's meaning. Our approach to applying biblical meaning follows the steps of the Interpretive Journey you are already familiar with (see above). We will expand step 5 below as we detail the application process.[3]

We will also illustrate the application of biblical principles using Philippians 4:13, a popular text that is often misapplied: "I can do all things through him [Christ] who strengthens me" (ESV). In each section, we will discuss each step and connect it to our example.

Step 1: Grasp the text in their town by summarizing the original situation (historical-cultural context) and the meaning of the text for the biblical audience.

In light of the historical-cultural context, summarize what you discovered about the original situation. Consider the book as a whole as well as the specific passage you are trying to apply. You can write a summary paragraph or simply list your observations about the situation. Either way, make sure that you have a clear picture of the original historical-cultural situation.

Regarding Philippians 4:13, we should note that Paul writes this letter while in prison awaiting trial (1:7, 13–14, 17). His faithfulness to Christ in the ministry of the gospel has landed him in prison. In this friendship letter to the church in Philippi, he exhorts the believers to stand firm in the face of external opposition and warns them against internal fighting. He reports about his own situation and thanks them for their ministry to him. In the section of 4:10–18, Paul acknowledges their monetary gift sent through their mutual friend Epaphroditus. He also wants to make it clear that while he is most grateful for their gift, his ministry is ultimately dependent on Christ.

As part of this step, write a statement of what the text meant for the biblical audience, keeping everything in past tense. From this past-tense statement, you will find it easy to transition to a theological principle. In this particular passage, you might write something like, "Paul told the Philippians that he had learned to be content in a variety of difficult circumstances through Christ, who gave him strength."

3. Some of the material in this section is drawn from George H. Guthrie and J. Scott Duvall, *Biblical Greek Exegesis: A Graded Approach to Learning Intermediate and Advanced Greek* (Grand Rapids: Zondervan, 1998), 154–60. Guthrie and Duvall rely on models suggested by Grant R. Osborne, *The Hermeneutical Spiral*, 2nd ed. (Downers Grove, IL: InterVarsity Press, 2006), 336–38; William W. Klein, Craig L. Blomberg, and Robert L. Hubbard Jr., *Introduction to Biblical Interpretation*, 4th ed. (Grand Rapids: Zondervan, 2017), 609–35; and Kuhatschek, *Applying the Bible*. More recently, see Craig L. Blomberg with Jennifer Foutz Markley, *A Handbook of New Testament Exegesis* (Grand Rapids: Baker, 2010); and Mark L. Strauss, *How to Read the Bible in Changing Times: Understanding and Applying God's Word Today* (Grand Rapids: Baker, 2011).

Step 2: Measure the width of the river to cross. What are the differences between the biblical situation and our situation?

The Christian today is separated from the biblical audience by a "river" of differences (e.g., language, culture, circumstances). This river hinders us from moving straight from meaning in their context to meaning in ours. We are certainly part of the same great story, but our place in the story is often different from that of our spiritual ancestors. Sometimes the river is wide, requiring a long bridge for crossing. At other times, it is a narrow creek, which we can cross easily. We need to know just how wide the river is before we start trying to construct a principlizing bridge across it.

When we interpret New Testament letters, normally the river is not very wide. There are exceptions, of course (e.g., dealing with the passage about meat offered to idols in 1 Corinthians), but usually this is the case. Regarding the Philippians passage, there are a few differences. Paul is an apostle and we are not apostles. Paul is in prison, and unlike Paul, most of us have not been imprisoned for our faith or for any other reason. Neither are we members of the Philippian church supporting Paul's ministry financially.

But there are also similarities. We are New Testament Christians under the same covenant. We are also members of Christ's body, the church. Moreover, many of us experience difficult situations as we seek to live out our faith. For the most part, the river of differences for Philippians 4:13 is not wide.

Step 3: Cross the principlizing bridge. List the theological principles communicated by the passage.

Simply write down the principle (or principles) the passage communicates. When you identify the theological truths or principles conveyed by a passage, you are discerning what is timeless in the passage and beginning to bridge the gap between the biblical text and the contemporary world. This will likely be similar to the meaning you identified in step 1 above but you will now use present- or future-tense verbs.

As for Philippians 4:13, you could say, "Believers can learn to be content in a variety of circumstances through Christ, who gives them strength." Or you might prefer, "Christ will give believers strength to be content in a variety of trying circumstances that come as a result of following him faithfully."

Step 4: Consult the biblical map. How does our theological principle fit with the rest of the Bible?

Here you need to see how the theological principle you have discovered fits with the rest of Scripture. Although the Bible is made up of sixty-six books, it tells a single overarching story, and we need to make sure that our principle isn't refuted by the clear teaching of the rest of the Bible. It's particularly important when interpreting the Old Testament to see how a principle derived from an Old Testament passage might be fulfilled or modified in the New Testament.

But consulting the biblical map also applies when interpreting New Testament passages. For example, Romans 13 and Revelation 13 offer two complementary perspectives on how believers should relate to the government: sometimes submitting to the state and at other times obeying God rather than the state. Both are important principles, but neither one can be made absolute so as to completely exclude the other one.

With Philippians 4:13 we don't see anything in the principle we have discovered that is refuted by the rest of the Bible.

Step 5: Grasp the text in our town. How should individual Christians today live out the theological principles? This step consists of several substeps.

a. Observe how the principles in the text address the original situation.

Look carefully at how the biblical principle addresses the historical-cultural situation. Here you are trying to see how the biblical author wanted his original audience to apply the meaning.[4] What you find in this intersection between the biblical text and the original situation lies at the center of the application process.

Application involves seeing how the principles in the text intersect with the original situation.

The intersection points between the principle in the biblical text and the original situation in Philippians 4:13 have to do with Paul. He is (1) a Christian, who is (2) experiencing a variety of trying circumstances as a result of following Christ faithfully, but is (3) able to endure difficult circumstances because of the strength provided by Christ. So, when Christians find themselves in difficult circumstances because they follow Jesus, they can rely on Jesus to give them the strength they need to endure faithfully.

Original Situation		Theological Principle in Text
Paul, a Christian, who is experiencing a variety of trying circumstances as a result of following Christ faithfully.	⟷	Christ will give Paul strength to endure such difficult situations.

4. See Blomberg with Foutz Markley, *Handbook of New Testament Exegesis*, 251–52.

b. Discover a parallel situation in a contemporary context.

In discovering how to apply or live out the Bible, we have to be students not only of the biblical world but also of our own world. Search for a situation in your life (or your world) that parallels the biblical situation.[5] In regard to Philippians 4:13, you would be looking for a situation where a Christian is facing difficult circumstances because of their faithful commitment to Christ.

Parallel Situation Today		Application of Theological Principle
Christians facing a variety of trying circumstances as a result of following Christ faithfully. [Notice that all the key points in the original situation are present in this parallel situation.]	→	Christ will give these Christians the strength to endure such difficult circumstances.

Below we provide three scenarios. The first is only an apparent parallel situation, since it does not include the element of a Christian facing hardships as a result of following Christ faithfully. The second and third scenarios are true parallels.

> **Example 1.** Philippians 4:13 has become a popular theme verse for Christian athletes in American society. The verse was even prominently displayed on the robe of a recent championship boxer. The phrase "I can do all things" no doubt motivated the boxer to defeat his opponent.
>
> Assuming that Paul and the boxer are both Christians, and that they both look to Christ for strength, we are still missing the idea that their difficulties are caused by their faithfulness to Christ. Paul and the boxer have radically different understandings of the expression "I can do all things." A close look at the literary context of Philippians 4:13 reveals that "all things" refers to enduring a variety of trying circumstances. At this point in his life, Paul is experiencing a trial caused by needs rather than a trial caused by an overabundance. When Paul says he can "do all things," he is referring to being content or enduring rather than defeating an opponent. There is a big difference between the "trials" of athletic competition and the trial of being imprisoned for your faith.

We misapply the Bible when we ignore the original situation and latch onto a situation that is not a genuine parallel. There may be a superficial connection, but one

5. Cf. Kuhatschek, *Applying the Bible*, 73; Blomberg with Foutz Markley, *Handbook of New Testament Exegesis*, 257–65.

or more of the important aspects of this intersection between the text and original situation is missing. This often happens by ignoring the original situation. As a result, you can then connect the principle in the biblical text to just about any situation, often twisting it to mean something very different from what is intended. It would be like taking something your employer or parents said to you (representing the biblical principle in this illustration) and applying it in a very different context so that even they wouldn't recognize their advice. You can imagine the resulting chaos.

Ultimately when we misapply the Bible, we hurt people by pointing them toward false realities. People put their hope in something they think is true when it is not, and they suffer for it. In our example from Philippians, the principle of contentment in Christ whatever the circumstances is replaced by a proof text calling on God to help us win a game or the contest. How does this misapplication affect the faith of a losing boxer? Couldn't the boxer actually apply this verse more appropriately after a serious defeat? What do you suppose God should do if this boxer fought another Christian boxer who also claimed the promise of Philippians 4:13?

Example 2. You are a Christian student experiencing financial difficulty. You had all your needs met when you lived at home, but circumstances changed when you answered God's call to prepare for ministry. Because of your parents' financial situation, you have to pay for your own education. You are struggling to make ends meet. The long hours of work turn into late nights and drowsy mornings in class. You believe God has called you to academic preparation, but you find yourself in a tough situation. You are tired most of the time, and your spiritual life even seems to be affected. In spite of it all, you are trusting Christ for strength to hang in there.

Example 3. You are a single mother whose non-Christian husband recently deserted you because of your commitment to Christ. Your two small children suddenly find themselves without a father. The sense of personal failure weighs heavy. The social pressure of what people will say lingers. You face overwhelming financial burdens and worry about how you will survive on your part-time job. As life seems to crumble around you, God has given you an unshakable peace that Jesus Christ is with you, that he understands, and that he will see you through.

In these last two scenarios, all the key points of the intersection between the text and the original situation are present: (1) a Christian (2) who is experiencing tough circumstances because of his or her commitment to Christ, and (3) looks to Christ for strength to endure. As you identify contemporary situations that are parallel, you can have confidence that you are applying the meaning of the biblical text rather than an invented meaning. The next step is to be even more specific with your application.

c. Make your applications specific.

Once you have identified a parallel situation—a genuine parallel—you should give some thought to specific ways the biblical principle(s) might apply. What should the student and the single mother be or think or do as they turn to Christ for strength? (We say *be* or *think* or *do* because applications may touch on our character and our thinking as well as our behavior.) Sometimes the best application relates to how we understand God and his ways. If we never suggest ways to make our applications specific, people may not know exactly how to live out the message of the Bible in the down and dirty of real life. Don't be afraid to make specific suggestions. People don't just need to know *what* to do; they also need to know *how* to do it. We not only have to offer people biblical insight; we also have to offer them skills and wisdom for living out that insight.

Application of Theological Principle (the same for all believers)		**Specific Applications (varies among individual believers)**
Christ will give these Christians the strength to endure such difficult circumstances.	→	We should think differently by. . . . We should do. . . . We should do something in this way. . . . We should pray for. . . .

Perhaps the best way to make your applications specific is by creating *real-world scenarios* or stories. These stories function as illustrations or examples of how a person might put the biblical principles into practice. They help us move beyond abstract principles to capture the color and emotion of the biblical text through stories. We are quick to admit that these real-world scenarios are not on the same level as inspired Scripture; they are merely analogies. But we intend for them to be guided by the Holy Spirit and faithful to the biblical principles (i.e., consistent with the author's intended meaning). We also want the contemporary audience to know that God's Word is eternally relevant. Real-world scenarios should be both faithful to the meaning of the text and relevant to the contemporary audience. Let's give it a try.

If we never make our applications specific, people may not know specifically how to live out the message of the Bible in the down and dirty of real life.

Example 1. A real-world scenario making specific applications for the student.

As a student you might gain encouragement and strength from a conversation with a pastor or a professor who knows the trials and rewards of preparing for ministry. Christ often works through his people to provide strength, and you could use a good conversation or two with someone who has been there. Ask them specifically about ways to manage your time and options for financing your education. They may suggest other people to consult. You could also do what Paul did and make your trust in Christ public by communicating your thoughts in writing, perhaps in a letter to a friend. As you confess Christ's ability to sustain you during the dark times, your faith will grow even stronger.

Also, do not hesitate to cry out to God in prayer and be honest with him about your tough situation. Make the heart prayers in the Psalms your own. Praying honestly may not change your circumstances, but it will make you more aware of God's empowering presence. God has called you to prepare for ministry. The work is hard, and the hours are long. It will be tougher than you ever imagined. But you can do it because Jesus Christ is there for you. He loves you and has plans for you. He will be there every minute of every day to give you strength to go on. You can do everything through Christ!

Example 2. A real-world scenario making specific applications for the single mother.

As a single mother, you could do many of the same things the student did—get counsel from a mature Christian, write down your thoughts, and pray honestly. You may also want to study other biblical passages that speak about husband-wife relations, divorce, remarriage, and so forth. God will give you wisdom as you search his Word. There may be businesspeople in your church who could assist you in making financial plans. Having a plan to provide for your kids will ease many of the day-to-day worries.

What about your husband? Throughout this entire ordeal, you have been a faithful wife. You have prayed constantly that your husband would allow the Lord to calm his restless spirit, but he made a decision to leave. He knew that your ultimate loyalty was to the Lord and that you would follow Christ above all, even him. While his leaving has been tougher than you ever expected, you have come to know God's grace and peace in ways that are beyond explanation. While you are frightened about the prospects of going it alone, you are not really alone. Of this one thing you are now sure: your Lord will never abandon you—never! He always keeps his promises. You can do all things through Christ.

Real-world scenarios furnish a wonderful way of making specific applications that are both faithful to the original meaning of the text and relevant to contemporary life. This approach works especially well when interpreting biblical stories, because you don't have to create entirely new scenarios. Instead, you just retell the biblical story for the contemporary audience (an approach sometimes referred to as *contemporization*). To contemporize a biblical story, you retell the story so that the effect on the contemporary audience is equivalent to the effect on the original audience. We translate the meaning of the story into our own context and reproduce its effects on the contemporary audience. Take a minute to read Jesus' parable of the lost son from Luke 15:11–24:

> [11]Jesus continued: "There was a man who had two sons. [12]The younger one said to his father, 'Father, give me my share of the estate.' So he divided his property between them.
>
> [13]"Not long after that, the younger son got together all he had, set off for a distant country and there squandered his wealth in wild living. [14]After he had spent everything, there was a severe famine in that whole country, and he began to be in need. [15]So he went and hired himself out to a citizen of that country, who sent him to his fields to feed pigs. [16]He longed to fill his stomach with the pods that the pigs were eating, but no one gave him anything.
>
> [17]"When he came to his senses, he said, 'How many of my father's hired servants have food to spare, and here I am starving to death! [18]I will set out and go back to my father and say to him: Father, I have sinned against heaven and against you. [19]I am no longer worthy to be called your son; make me like one of your hired servants.' [20]So he got up and went to his father.
>
> "But while he was still a long way off, his father saw him and was filled with compassion for him; he ran to his son, threw his arms around him and kissed him.
>
> [21]"The son said to him, 'Father, I have sinned against heaven and against you. I am no longer worthy to be called your son.'
>
> [22]"But the father said to his servants, 'Quick! Bring the best robe and put it on him. Put a ring on his finger and sandals on his feet. [23]Bring the fattened calf and kill it. Let's have a feast and celebrate. [24]For this son of mine was dead and is alive again; he was lost and is found.' So they began to celebrate."

In his book *What's So Amazing about Grace?* Philip Yancey contemporizes this parable. He retells the story in a contemporary setting so that when you hear the story, you feel just like Jesus' original audience must have felt. See what you think.

A young girl grows up on a cherry orchard just above Traverse City, Michigan. Her parents, a bit old-fashioned, tend to overreact to her nose ring, the music she listens to, and the length of her skirts. They ground her a few times, and she seethes inside. "I hate you!" she screams at her father when he knocks on the door of her room after an argument, and that night she acts on a plan she has mentally rehearsed scores of times. She runs away.

She has visited Detroit only once before, on a bus trip with her church youth group to watch the Tigers play. Because newspapers in Traverse City report in lurid detail the gangs, the drugs, and the violence in downtown Detroit, she concludes that is probably the last place her parents will look for her. California, maybe, or Florida, but not Detroit.

Her second day there she meets a man who drives the biggest car she's ever seen. He offers her a ride, buys her lunch, arranges a place for her to stay. He gives her some pills that make her feel better than she's ever felt before. She was right all along, she decides: her parents were keeping her from all the fun.

The good life continues for a month, two months, a year. The man with the big car—she calls him "Boss"—teaches her a few things that men like. Since she's underage, men pay a premium for her. She lives in a penthouse, and orders room service whenever she wants. Occasionally she thinks about the folks back home, but their lives now seem so boring and provincial that she can hardly believe she grew up there.

She has a brief scare when she sees her picture printed on the back of a milk carton with the headline "Have you seen this child?" But by now she has blond hair, and with all the makeup and body-piercing jewelry she wears, nobody would mistake her for a child. Besides, most of her friends are runaways, and nobody squeals in Detroit.

After a year the first sallow signs of illness appear, and it amazes her how fast the boss turns mean. "These days, we can't mess around," he growls, and before she knows it she's out on the street without a penny to her name. She still turns a couple of tricks a night, but they don't pay much, and all the money goes to support her habit. When winter blows in she finds herself sleeping on metal grates outside the big department stores. "Sleeping" is the wrong word—a teenage girl at night in downtown Detroit can never relax her guard. Dark bands circle her eyes. Her cough worsens.

One night as she lies awake listening for footsteps, all of a sudden everything about her life looks different. She no longer feels like a woman of the world. She feels like a little girl, lost in a cold and frightening city. She begins to whimper. Her pockets are empty and she's hungry. She needs a fix. She pulls her legs tight underneath her and shivers under the newspapers she's piled atop her coat. Something jolts a synapse of memory and a single image fills her mind: of May in Traverse City, when a million cherry trees bloom at once, with her golden retriever dashing through the rows and rows of blossomy trees in chase of a tennis ball.

God, why did I leave, she says to herself, and pain stabs at her heart. *My dog back home eats better than I do now.* She's sobbing, and she knows in a flash that more than anything else in the world she wants to go home.

Three straight phone calls, three straight connections with the answering machine. She hangs up without leaving a message the first two times, but the third time she says, "Dad, Mom, it's me. I was wondering about maybe coming home. I'm catching a bus up your way, and it'll get there about midnight tomorrow. If you're not there, well, I guess I'll just stay on the bus until it hits Canada."

It takes about seven hours for a bus to make all the stops between Detroit and Traverse City, and during that time she realizes the flaws in her plan. What if her parents are out of town and miss the message? Shouldn't she have waited another day or so until she could talk to them? And even if they are home, they probably wrote her off as dead long ago. She should have given them some time to overcome the shock.

Her thoughts bounce back and forth between those worries and the speech she is preparing for her father. "Dad, I'm sorry. I know I was wrong. It's not your fault; it's all mine. Dad, can you forgive me?" She says the words over and over, her throat tightening even as she rehearses them. She hasn't apologized to anyone in years.

The bus has been driving with lights on since Bay City. Tiny snowflakes hit the pavement rubbed worn by thousands of tires, and the asphalt steams. She's forgotten how dark it gets at night out here. A deer darts across the road and the bus swerves. Every so often, a billboard. A sign posting the mileage to Traverse City. *Oh, God!*

When the bus finally rolls into the station, its air brakes hissing in protest, the driver announces in a crackly voice over the microphone, "Fifteen minutes, folks. That's all we have here." Fifteen minutes to decide her life. She checks herself in a compact mirror, smooths her hair, and licks the lipstick off her teeth. She looks at the tobacco stains on her fingertips and wonders if her parents will notice. If they're there.

She walks into the terminal not knowing what to expect. Not one of the thousand scenes that have played out in her mind prepare her for what she sees. There, in the concrete-walls-and-plastic-chairs bus terminal in Traverse City,

> Michigan, stands a group of forty brothers and sisters and great-aunts and uncles and cousins and a grandmother and great-grandmother to boot. They're all wearing goofy party hats and blowing noise-makers, and taped across the entire wall of the terminal is a computer-generated banner that reads "Welcome home!"
>
> Out of the crowd of well-wishers breaks her Dad. She stares out through the tears quivering in her eyes like hot mercury and begins the memorized speech, "Dad, I'm sorry. I know . . ."
>
> He interrupts her. "Hush, child. We've got no time for that. No time for apologies. You'll be late for the party. A banquet's waiting for you at home."[6]

Wouldn't you agree that contemporization is a powerful tool for making specific applications of biblical principles? Yancey's retelling helps us experience Jesus' parable of the lost son in much the same way the biblical audience probably experienced it.

Real-world scenarios should accurately reflect the meaning of the biblical text and be relevant to contemporary life.

One word of caution is in order concerning real-world scenarios. You need to study the biblical passage carefully, especially the historical-cultural and literary contexts, so that the real-world scenario or story you create will accurately reflect the meaning of the biblical text. Otherwise you will be making a specific application for a biblical text that doesn't exist. Coming up with a scenario or retelling a story in a way that is both relevant and faithful to the original meaning takes discipline, hard work, and creativity. Please, please, please do your homework so that your scenario will reflect that meaning.

The best way to remain faithful when applying the biblical meaning is to stay tied to the intersection between the principle in the biblical text and the original situation, and then look for a true parallel so that the theological principle in the text will apply with the same truth, power and clarity. Ask yourself if your scenario includes the central aspects of this intersection between the text and the original situation. If not, revise your scenario. A real-world scenario or story must be tied to this intersection of text and situation, or you will be doing nothing more than reader response (see ch. 10).

CONCLUSION

This completes our approach to applying the meaning of the Bible. Because God's character and human nature do not change, his Word remains relevant! Our principlizing approach gives you a way to grasp the Bible's relevance for every generation—not

6. Philip Yancey, *What's So Amazing about Grace?* (Grand Rapids: Zondervan, 1997), 49–51.

only for us, but also for our children, our grandchildren, our great-grandchildren, and so on.

Some of you might be concerned that this method will restrict your freedom to apply the Scriptures. We remind you that as faithful readers our job is not to invent new meaning but to apply the meaning that has been inscribed in the biblical text by the Spirit of God working through the biblical authors. Don't worry. You'll be able to find a number of parallel situations in your life or in your world that are true parallels. And when you find a genuine parallel, you can be confident that you are applying the real meaning of the biblical text. Also, don't be afraid to make your applications specific by creating real-world scenarios or by contemporizing a biblical story. People need illustrations and examples of how the meaning might be lived out in real life. God wants his Word to sink deep into our hearts and minds and transform the way we live.

Before we move into the next unit of the book, where you will learn how to interpret the various literary types found in the New Testament, we need to remember the main reason we come to the Bible in the first place. We study Scripture not just to learn more *about God* but to *know and love God more.* He gave us his Word not just to fill our brains with biblical facts but to change our lives. The plain intention of the divine Author is that we would *grasp* his Word by understanding it and living it out. Or, as Jesus said in John 14:21, "Whoever has my commands and keeps them is the one who loves me."

ASSIGNMENTS

Assignment 13–1

We have written two real-world scenarios paralleling the biblical situation of Philippians 4:13 (the student and the single mother). Create another real-world scenario that parallels Philippians 4:13. Remember, when we say *parallel situation*, we mean a situation that contains the central elements of this intersection between the biblical text and the original situation.

Assignment 13–2

Read Jesus' parable of the good Samaritan in Luke 10:30–35. Contemporize the parable by writing a story of your own that retells the original story so that the effect on the contemporary audience is equivalent to the effect on the original audience.

Assignment 13–3

First Timothy 6:10a reads, "For the love of money is a root of all kinds of evil." Take this verse through the Interpretive Journey, including the application process:

1. Grasp the text in their town. Summarize the original situation and the meaning of the text for the biblical audience.
2. Measure the width of the river. What are the differences between the biblical situation and our situation?
3. Cross the principlizing bridge. List the theological principles communicated by the passage.
4. Consult the biblical map. How does our theological principle fit with the rest of the Bible?
    a) Grasp the text in our town. How should individual Christians today live out the theological principles?Observe how the principles in the text address the original situation.
    b) Discover a genuine parallel situation in your world.
    c) Make your applications specific by creating real-world scenarios or by contemporizing.

PART 4

THE INTERPRETIVE JOURNEY—*New Testament*

This marks the spot in *Grasping God's Word* where you will begin to learn how to take the Interpretive Journey through different literary genres within the Bible. You have learned to read carefully and have looked at a number of significant issues related to understanding the Bible. Now it's time to get practical again as we look at how to understand and live out different literary genres within God's Word.

Part 4 focuses on the New Testament. This order is different from what you might expect. We start with the New Testament because you're probably more familiar with it, and generally speaking, the river of differences is not as wide in the New. Throughout our book, we are more concerned with helping you learn than with maintaining a "logical neatness." For this reason, we will start with the New Testament.

There are four major genres in the New Testament. We will dedicate a chapter to each one. Chapter 14 will deal with letters, chapter 15 with the Gospels, chapter 16 with the book of Acts, and chapter 17 with Revelation. In each case you will learn practical and appropriate ways of reading the different genres.

CHAPTER 14

NEW TESTAMENT—LETTERS

INTRODUCTION

Buried in the top of a closet in the Duvall house are two shoeboxes filled with "mushies." For two years before Scott and Judy were married, they lived three hundred miles apart and survived by making frequent phone calls, taking occasional trips, and writing lots of letters. (This was back in the day before the invention of texting or email or cell phones.) The two shoeboxes are packed with love letters. Some are short, others long; some informative, others playful; some serious, others silly; but all are valuable pieces of communication between two people who loved (and continue to love) each other very much.

Letters (in all their modern technological forms) play an important role in all of our lives. How do you feel when you receive a personal note? Do you remember the letter informing you of your acceptance into a particular school? What about the long email advice from a parent or trusted friend? Have you ever received a "Dear John" letter or a DTR ("define the relationship") message? Have you ever written one? Then there are business letters, legal letters, medical letters, personal letters, and so on. Whether by a text or email, on official letterhead, on personal stationery, or on the back of a napkin, we write messages and notes and letters to communicate what we think and how we feel.

Of course, letters predate the Duvall romance. They were used widely in the ancient world and figure prominently in our New Testament. Twenty-one of the twenty-seven books of the New Testament are letters (about 35 percent of the entire New Testament).[1] Most evangelical scholars agree that Paul, James, Peter, John, Jude, and the author of Hebrews (who chose to write anonymously) are responsible for those twenty-one letters. (See the chart below.)

Scholars have traditionally made a distinction between the Pauline letters and the general or catholic (universal) letters. Each of Paul's thirteen letters takes its name from the individual (e.g., Timothy) or the group (e.g., "to all God's holy people in Christ Jesus at Philippi") to whom the letter is addressed. The general letters take their names not from the addressees (with Hebrews being the exception), but from their authors (e.g., James, John). While this distinction makes some sense, perhaps it is best to put them all in a basket labeled "New Testament letters" and evaluate them individually.

Paul	?	James	Peter	John	Jude
Romans	Hebrews	James	1 Peter	1 John	Jude
1 Corinthians			2 Peter	2 John	
2 Corinthians				3 John	
Galatians					
Ephesians					
Philippians					
Colossians					
1 Thessalonians					
2 Thessalonians					
1 Timothy					
2 Timothy					
Titus					
Philemon					

We will begin this chapter by looking inside the world of New Testament letters. What are some important characteristics of letters? What form do the letters take? Then we will explore how we should interpret the New Testament letters. The chapter concludes with an Interpretive Journey through a passage in a New Testament letter.

1. D. A. Carson, Douglas J. Moo, and Leon Morris, *An Introduction to the New Testament* (Grand Rapids: Zondervan, 1992), 231.

CHARACTERISTICS OF NEW TESTAMENT LETTERS

Comparable to Other Ancient Letters

How do New Testament letters compare to other ancient letters? To begin with, New Testament letters are typically longer than their ancient counterparts. E. Randolph Richards observes,

> In the approximately 14,000 private letters from Greco-Roman antiquity, the average length was about 87 words, ranging in length from about 18 to 209 words. Yet the letters of more literary men like Cicero and Seneca differed considerably. Cicero averaged 295 words per letter, ranging from 22 to 2,530 words, and Seneca averaged 995, ranging from 149 to 4,134. By both standards, though, Paul's letters were quite long. The thirteen letters bearing his name average 2,495 words, ranging from 335 (Philemon) to 7,114 (Romans).[2]

The added length makes sense when we consider how much space it took in a letter for these early Christian leaders to conduct their missionary work and shepherd their flocks from a distance. They needed room to say hello and goodbye, bring their readers up to date, encourage and instruct, tackle difficult issues, warn against false teaching, and much more.

Ancient letters tended toward two extremes. Many were informal, private letters—business contracts, civic records, letters between family members or friends, and the like. Such letters were a routine part of everyday life and were meant to be read only by the person to whom they were addressed. But others were formal, artistic, literary letters designed for public presentation. New Testament letters do not fit neatly into either category but fall somewhere between the two extremes. Within the New Testament we find informal, personal letters, such as Philemon, 2 John, and 3 John, as well as formal letters, such as Romans, Ephesians, Hebrews, James, and 1 Peter.

Authoritative Substitutes for Personal Presence

People in the ancient world wrote letters for much the same reason that we do today. We want to be with the people we care about but are unable to be there, so we write a letter (or send a text or email) as a substitute for our personal presence. The original audience would have viewed Paul's letters or Peter's letters, for example, as substitutes for the apostles themselves. When these apostles and other leaders were

2. E. Randolph Richards, *The Secretary in the Letters of Paul* (Tübingen: Mohr, 1991), 213. See also his more recent work, *Paul and First-Century Letter Writing: Secretaries, Composition and Collection* (Downers Grove, IL: InterVarsity Press, 2004).

unable to address a problem or deal with a situation in person, they did the next best thing: they wrote a letter. The letter provided a way for early Christian leaders to express their views and minister from a distance.

But New Testament letters were more than just substitutes for personal presence; they were *authoritative* substitutes. Often in the first verse of the letter the author identifies himself as an apostle of Jesus Christ:

> Paul, an apostle—sent not from men nor by a man, but by Jesus Christ and God the Father, who raised him from the dead . . . (Gal. 1:1)
>
> Paul, an apostle of Christ Jesus by the will of God . . . (Eph. 1:1)
>
> Simon Peter, a servant and apostle of Jesus Christ . . . (2 Peter 1:1)

Paul, Peter, and John write as more than just friends and acquaintances offering personal advice. They write as apostles (i.e., as witnesses of the resurrected Christ). Their letters of instruction, warning, and encouragement carry authority because they write as Christ's authentic representatives. Even those authors who are not apostles in the strict sense are closely connected to an apostle and are seen as God-appointed leaders of the congregations to whom they write. As a result, their letters carry authority.

Situational

New Testament letters are *occasional* or *situational*. This means that they were written to address specific situations or problems related to the author or (usually) to the readers. Those who wrote New Testament letters did so to meet the practical needs of those receiving the letters. They wrote to clarify an issue (e.g., Thessalonians), to address a doctrinal problem (e.g., Colossians), or to confront the readers about their behavior (e.g., James). The topics covered in a letter were usually dictated by the specific situations at work within the community to which the apostles wrote.

These letters were never meant to be exhaustive dictionaries of Christian doctrine. Rather than writing systematic theologies, the authors used their letters to apply theology in practical ways to specific situations in churches. Fee and Stuart rightly conclude that "one will go to the Epistles again and again for Christian theology; they are loaded with it. But one must always keep in mind that they were not primarily written to expound Christian theology. It is always theology applied to or directed toward a particular need."[3]

3. Gordon D. Fee and Douglas Stuart, *How to Read the Bible for All Its Worth*, 4th ed. (Grand Rapids: Zondervan, 2014), 61.

As a result, when interpreting New Testament letters we must be careful not to conclude too much from only one letter. Paul's letter to the Galatians emphasizes freedom in Christ for a church struggling with legalism. In 1 Corinthians, however, he stresses obedience for a church that is taking its freedom to immoral extremes. Neither letter, by itself, represents Paul's entire teaching on freedom or obedience. Both letters offer a corrective message tailored to the circumstances of those specific churches. We know from all of Paul's letters that he endorses both freedom and obedience, but he emphasizes freedom in Galatians and obedience in 1 Corinthians in order to correct the course of each church headed in the wrong direction.[4] If we fail to see the letters as occasional or situational, we will be tempted to conclude too much from one letter. This can easily lead us to misinterpret the letters.

Because the letters are occasional, we must try to reconstruct the situation that called for the letter in the first place. What was going on in Thessalonica or in Philippi, for example, that caused Paul to write 1 and 2 Thessalonians or Philippians? Knowing the original situation will help us when it comes time to identify theological principles within the letter itself. But reconstructing the original situation is not as easy as it sounds. Fee and Stuart explain the difficulty of reconstructing the situation of a letter by using the illustration of a telephone conversation.[5] Reading a New Testament letter, they say, is much like listening to one end of a phone conversation. We only hear what the New Testament letter writers, such as Peter or John, are saying. We don't hear what their audience is saying to them. We hear the response or the answer, but we are not quite sure what the questions are. Nevertheless, these authors are responding to real-life situations, and it is important for us to do our best to reconstruct the original situation. Later in this chapter we will talk about how to do that.

Carefully Written and Delivered

The process of composing and delivering a New Testament letter was more complex than we might imagine. The actual job of writing down a letter was normally assigned to a trained scribe or secretary (*amanuensis*). In Romans 16:22, the secretary even identifies himself: "I, Tertius, who wrote down this letter, greet you in the Lord." This does not mean that Tertius was the author of Romans, but he served as Paul's secretary in this instance. Some secretaries were given more freedom in the composition of a letter; others received less freedom.[6] In any case, the author (not the

4. The example of freedom and obedience in Galatians and 1 Corinthians is taken from Thomas R. Schreiner, *Interpreting the Pauline Epistles* (Grand Rapids: Baker, 1990), 43.

5. Fee and Stuart, *How to Read the Bible*, 60.

6. Sometimes an author would give a skilled and trusted secretary more freedom in composing a letter. Many scholars believe that Paul used his trusted coworker Luke as his secretary when writing the Pastoral Letters (1 and 2

secretary) was responsible for the final contents of the letter. At the end of a letter, it was customary for the author to "pick up the pen" and add a final greeting in his own handwriting.

> I, Paul, write this greeting in my own hand. (1 Cor. 16:21; Col. 4:18)

> I, Paul, write this greeting in my own hand, which is the distinguishing mark in all my letters. This is how I write. (2 Thess. 3:17)

These references indicate that a secretary wrote all but the last few lines of the letter. Most New Testament letters were probably produced in this way.

Along with secretaries, cosenders played an important part in New Testament letters. At the beginning of eight of his letters, Paul mentions a cosender. In six letters he mentions Timothy (2 Corinthians, Philippians, Colossians, 1 and 2 Thessalonians, Philemon); in 1 and 2 Thessalonians he includes Silas as well as Timothy. In Galatians he refers to "all the brothers and sisters with me," and in 1 Corinthians it is Paul and "our brother Sosthenes" who cosponsor the letter. We should probably envision Paul and his cosenders discussing, drafting, editing, and rewriting a letter until they were ready to produce a finished copy to send. These cosenders were not just mentioned as a formality. Along with Paul, they were significantly involved in ministry among the people to whom the letters were addressed.

After a finished copy of the letter had been prepared, it was delivered. The first-century postal system was available only for official government use (military reports, diplomatic letters, and the like). Wealthy citizens used slaves or employees to carry their letters, but the average citizen depended largely on people who happened to be traveling in the direction the letter needed to go. Paul used trusted friends such as Tychicus to carry his letters:

> Tychicus, the dear brother and faithful servant in the Lord, will tell you everything, so that you also may know how I am and what I am doing. I am sending him to you for this very purpose, that you may know how we are, and that he may encourage you. (Eph. 6:21–22)

> Tychicus will tell you all the news about me. He is a dear brother, a faithful minister and fellow servant in the Lord. I am sending him to you for the express

Timothy, Titus). If Paul gave Luke a greater degree of freedom in composing these letters, this may account for the differences between the vocabulary and style of the Pastorals and the rest of Paul's letters.

> purpose that you may know about our circumstances and that he may encourage your hearts. He is coming with Onesimus, our faithful and dear brother, who is one of you. They will tell you everything that is happening here. (Col. 4:7–9)

Letters were expensive endeavors, and faithful carriers were important not only to deliver the letter safely but also to elaborate on the details of the letter in person.

Intended for the Christian Community

New Testament letters were meant to be read aloud again and again to specific congregations. When we read New Testament letters, we normally read them silently to ourselves. But for a variety of reasons, people in the first century preferred to hear their letters read aloud. For one thing, letters were too valuable to loan out to families or individuals. Also, Jewish Christians were accustomed to hearing the Scriptures read aloud in services of worship from their days in the synagogue. And, of course, some Christians simply could not read. Consequently, letters were normally presented orally for the benefit of the group. We get a glimpse of this in the book of Revelation, where a blessing is pronounced on the person who reads (aloud) the words of the prophecy to the listening congregation:

> Blessed is the one who reads aloud the words of this prophecy, and blessed are those who hear it and take to heart what is written in it, because the time is near. (Rev. 1:3)

In a few places in Paul's letters, the apostle clearly refers to this common practice of having his letters read aloud:

> After this letter has been read to you, see that it is also read in the church of the Laodiceans and that you in turn read the letter from Laodicea. (Col. 4:16)

> I charge you before the Lord to have this letter read to all the brothers and sisters. (1 Thess. 5:27)

> So then, brothers and sisters, stand firm and hold fast to the teachings we passed on to you, whether by word of mouth or by letter. (2 Thess. 2:15)

Even Paul's more personal letter to Philemon was addressed not only to the slave owner himself, but also to the church that met in his house (Philem. 1–2). Everyone in the Christian community benefited from hearing the letters read aloud over and over.

In addition, New Testament letters were often meant to be exchanged with other churches. While writing to specific churches, these authors often saw their words as relevant and beneficial to the larger Christian community. From Colossians 4:16 (cited above), we know that Paul wanted his letter to the Colossians read also to the Laodiceans, and he wanted his letter to the Laodiceans (now lost) read to the Colossian church.

In summary, New Testament letters are generally longer than other ancient letters and fall between the two extremes of informal, private letters and the more formal, literary letters. Letters served as an authoritative substitute for the personal presence of their authors. They were occasional or situational, meaning that they were written to address specific situations in the communities that received the letter. The writers were most concerned with applying theology in practical ways to real-life situations.

THE FORM OF NEW TESTAMENT LETTERS

When we write a letter, we use a form or structure similar to that in the box below.

The ancient world also had a standard form, and most New Testament letters fit that mold. That form consists of an introduction, a body, and a conclusion. Let's look at each one in more detail.

Date

Name of addressee
Street address
City, state, zip code

Greeting,

Body of letter

Closing,

Signature

Introduction

There are four elements in a typical introduction—the name of the writer, the name of the recipients, a greeting, and an introductory prayer. In our letters we usually mention the writer's name at the end, whereas in ancient letters the name of the writer comes first, followed by the name of the recipients. Here are a few examples:

> Paul, an apostle—sent not from men nor by a man, but by Jesus Christ and God the Father, who raised him from the dead—and all the brothers and sisters with me, to the churches in Galatia. . . . (Gal. 1:1–2)

> Paul and Timothy, servants of Christ Jesus, to all God's holy people in Christ Jesus at Philippi, together with the overseers and deacons. . . . (Phil. 1:1)

> James, a servant of God and of the Lord Jesus Christ, to the twelve tribes scattered among the nations. . . . (James 1:1)

Often the writer and recipients are described in more detail in words that give us greater insight into the letter. For example, since Paul's apostleship is being called into question in Galatia, he begins the letter to the Galatians by emphasizing that his apostleship has a divine origin. Also, the lack of a term of affection in Galatians (such as Paul's usual "saints" or "beloved") sets a serious tone for the letter. When writing to the Philippian Christians, who are struggling with disunity, Paul does not call himself an apostle but a "servant." Perhaps he is trying to teach the Philippians from the start that to preserve unity they need the humility of a servant.

James doesn't say anything about being the half brother of Jesus (which he probably was), but instead describes himself as a "servant of God and of the Lord Jesus Christ." His authority to lead comes from his spiritual, not his physical, relationship to Jesus. Also, James writes to the "twelve tribes scattered among the nations," perhaps indicating that he is writing to Jewish Christians who have been dispersed because of persecution.

The *greeting* follows the identification of the writer and the recipients. Most ancient Greek letters began with the word *chairein* ("greetings"). Paul and Peter both replaced *chairein* with the word *charis* ("grace") and added the normal Jewish greeting "peace." In this way they completely transformed the standard greeting and filled it with Christian meaning. "Grace and peace to you" is a greeting, but it is also a prayer that the recipients might continue to experience God's unmerited favor and the peace that flows from it.

The final element in the introduction to a letter is the *prayer*. Ancient Greek letters usually began with a prayer to the gods. Almost all of Paul's letters begin with a prayer of thanksgiving to God for what he has done in the lives of the recipients. Here is Paul's opening prayer in 1 Corinthians:

> [4]I always thank my God for you because of his grace given you in Christ
> Jesus. [5]For in him you have been enriched in every way—with all kinds of
> speech and with all knowledge—[6]God thus confirming our testimony about
> Christ among you. [7]Therefore you do not lack any spiritual gift as you eagerly
> wait for our Lord Jesus Christ to be revealed. [8]He will also keep you firm to
> the end, so that you will be blameless on the day of our Lord Jesus Christ.
> [9]God is faithful, who has called you into fellowship with his Son, Jesus Christ
> our Lord. (1:4–9)

Along with expressing pastoral gratitude for all that God has done, Paul uses the prayer section to introduce important themes that will be developed later in the letter. For instance, in the 1 Corinthians passage above, he tells his readers that they have been enriched in all knowledge and that they "do not lack any spiritual gift." Later in 1 Corinthians, Paul will write extensively about knowledge and spiritual gifts—two problem areas for the Corinthians.

When changes are made to the prayer/thanksgiving section, we should pay attention. For example, when Paul omits the prayer of thanksgiving in Galatians and moves straight from the greeting into a rebuke, he sends a strong signal that he is deeply upset that they are deserting the gospel of Christ for legalism.

Body

Since the body of the letter is where the writer addresses specific situations facing the church community, it frequently makes up the largest part of a letter. There is no set format to the body of a New Testament letter. The different purposes of the writers and the different situations of their readers lead to different kinds of letter bodies. Within the body of the letter you will find instruction, persuasion, rebuke, exhortation, and much more.

Conclusion

A number of different elements appear in the conclusion or closing of a New Testament letter.[7]

- travel plans: e.g., Titus 3:12; Philemon 22
- commendation of coworkers: e.g., Romans 16:1–2
- prayer: e.g., 2 Thessalonians 3:16; Hebrews 13:20–21
- prayer requests: e.g., 1 Thessalonians 5:25; Hebrews 13:18–19
- greetings: e.g., Romans 16:3–16, 21–23; Hebrews 13:24; 2 John 13
- final instructions and exhortations: e.g., Colossians 4:16–17; 1 Timothy 6:20–21a
- holy kiss: e.g., 1 Thessalonians 5:26; 1 Peter 5:14
- autograph: e.g., Colossians 4:18; 2 Thessalonians 3:17
- benediction: e.g., 1 Corinthians 16:23–24; Ephesians 6:23–24
- doxology: e.g., 2 Peter 3:18; Jude 24–25

Not all the elements appear in every letter, of course, and the authors do not follow any set order. The final element, however, is normally the grace benediction ("Grace be with you"). What a great way to close a letter!

---

7. Schreiner, *Pauline Epistles*, 29–30.

Not all New Testament letters conform to the standard letter form described above. Hebrews doesn't start out like a typical letter, but it does have a letter-like ending. The anonymous author of Hebrews even refers to the book as a "word of exhortation" or a sermon (13:22). James opens like a letter, but it doesn't close like one, and it is organized more like a collection of short sermons aimed at a general audience. First John doesn't open or close like a normal letter, but it was written to specific group of people (1 John 2:7, 12–14, 19, 26).

Now that you have a general understanding of some important characteristics of New Testament letters and what form they take, let's turn our attention to how to interpret the letters.

HOW TO INTERPRET NEW TESTAMENT LETTERS

To interpret a New Testament letter, we return to the five steps of the Interpretive Journey discussed in chapter 1.

Step 1: Grasp the text in their town. What did the text mean to the biblical audience?

Begin by reading the whole letter in one sitting. This may take a while for longer letters, but it's the only way to see the big picture. Before you walk through the "land of the letter," you need to fly over it and see the terrain from above. You may want to make a note of main themes you encounter while moving through the letter, or you may prefer to wait until the end and summarize the main idea of the book in a sentence or two.

Both ancient and contemporary letters were meant to be read from start to finish. Don't let the chapter-and-verse divisions in your Bible tempt you to skip around and read only small sections of the letter in isolation. Kaiser and Silva explain how this pick-and-choose approach is not the way we read letters today and why it is not the best way to read a New Testament letter:

> What would one think of a man who receives a five-page letter from his fiancée on Monday and decides to read only the third page on that day, the last page on Thursday, the first page two weeks later, and so on? We are all aware of the fact that reading a letter in such piece-meal fashion would likely create nothing but confusion. The meaning of a paragraph on the third page may depend heavily on something said at the beginning of the letter, or its real significance may not become apparent until the next page is read. The more cogently the letter was written, the riskier it would be to break it up arbitrarily. Moreover, part of

> the meaning of a document is the total impact it makes on the reader, and that meaning is often more than the sum of its parts.[8]

We begin to understand what the text meant to the biblical audience by reading the whole letter from beginning to end, the way it was meant to be read.

Since letters are occasional or situational, the next step in discovering what the text meant to the biblical audience is to reconstruct the historical-cultural context of the biblical writer and his audience. Do you remember learning how to do this in chapter 6? Study tools such as Bible dictionaries and commentaries will help you find answers to the following questions:

- Who was the author?
- What was his background?
- When did he write?
- What was the nature of his ministry?
- What kind of relationship did he have with the audience?
- Why was he writing?
- Who was the biblical audience?
- What were their circumstances?
- How was their relationship to God?
- What about their relationship to the author and to each other?
- What was happening at the time the book was written?
- Are there any historical-cultural factors that might shed light on the book?

Reconstructing the original situation is not always easy. Because reading a New Testament letter is a lot like listening to one end of a telephone conversation, we have to read between the lines a bit to reconstruct the original situation. This can be dangerous if we invent a situation that is not supported by evidence from the letter itself, but we have little choice but to do at least some reading between the lines. How do we do this? The best approach is to read the letter carefully and gather bits and pieces of information that you can use to reconstruct the situation. (If you happen to be studying one of Paul's letters, you can also gain insight from the book of Acts.) Then use dictionaries, commentaries, and other study tools to see what scholars have to say about the historical-cultural context of the letter. Summarize your reconstruction of the situation in a paragraph or two.

8. Walter C. Kaiser Jr. and Moisés Silva, *Introduction to Biblical Hermeneutics: The Search for Meaning*, rev. and exp. ed. (Grand Rapids: Zondervan, 2007), 175.

After you have an idea about the situation of the author and the recipients, you need to identify the literary context of the specific passage you are studying. As we learned in chapter 8, the main goal when it comes to literary context is to trace the author's flow of thought. In the case of New Testament letters, remember to *think paragraphs*![9] Summarize the main point of the paragraph that comes before your passage, the one that contains your passage, and the one that comes right after your passage. Find out how these paragraphs link together to communicate the author's message. Specifically, look for the role your passage plays in the author's flow of thought. Summarize what you have found.

After reading the whole letter, reconstructing the historical-cultural situation, and tracing the author's flow of thought in the paragraphs surrounding your passage, determine what the passage meant to the biblical audience. Use your observation skills to read the text carefully. Look for details. Notice important connections. Study significant words. Finally, write out a statement of what the passage meant to the first-century audience.

Step 2: Measure the width of the river to cross. What are the differences between the biblical audience and us?

In New Testament letters, the river of differences is not usually wide. Letters were written to Christians (often Jewish Christians), not to the Old Testament people of Israel or to the Jewish leaders who opposed Jesus and the early church.

Nevertheless, even in the letters the river can sometimes present a challenge. Although they were written to Christians like us, they sometimes deal with situations foreign to us. Here the river becomes wider and more difficult to cross. For example, when Paul addresses the issue of eating food that has been sacrificed to idols in 1 Corinthians 8, the river is fairly wide. When was the last time you struggled with whether to eat meat offered as part of a sacrifice to idols? But when Paul writes about running away from sexual immorality (1 Cor. 6:18–20) or the priority of love (1 Cor. 13:1–13), the river is more like a narrow creek that we can easily jump over. After examining your passage, write a paragraph describing the differences that define the width of the river you need to cross.

Step 3: Cross the principlizing bridge. What are the theological principles in this text?

Here we are looking for theological principles reflected in the meaning of the text you identified in step 1. God not only gives specific expressions of meaning to biblical

9. Fee and Stuart, *How to Read the Bible*, 67.

audiences, but he also sends a broader, theological message through these same texts to all of his people. In light of how our situation compares to and differs from the situation of the biblical audience, try to identify the theological principles reflected in the text. Write out the principle (or principles) in a sentence or two, using present-tense verbs. For example, in chapter 2 we gave the following theological principle for Joshua 1:1–9: "To be effective in serving God and successful in the task to which he has called us, we must draw strength and courage from his presence. We must also be obedient to God's Word, meditating on it constantly."

In his book *Applying the Bible*, Jack Kuhatschek mentions three questions that can help us locate theological principles in a passage.[10] (1) Does the author state a principle? Often in New Testament letters the author will state his message in the form of a theological principle (e.g., Eph. 6:1: "Children, obey your parents in the Lord"). When this happens, you already have your principle.

(2) Does the broader context reveal a theological principle? Sometimes the author will supply a theological principle in the surrounding context. For example, in Ephesians 5:21 Paul writes, "Submit to one another out of reverence for Christ." He follows this general principle with specific examples of how people in the ancient household should submit to each other (wives/husbands, children/fathers, slaves/masters). If you happen to be studying any of the specific examples, you would want to be aware of the general principle given earlier in 5:21.

(3) We should ask why a particular command or instruction was given. Sometimes when you locate the reason behind the command or instruction, you will also find the theological principle. In Galatians 5:2 Paul writes, "I, Paul, tell you that if you let yourselves be circumcised, Christ will be of no value to you at all." When we ask why the apostle warns the Galatians against circumcision, we find the theological principle that people cannot achieve God's acceptance by keeping the law or by human effort alone (symbolized by circumcision). God's grace is given as a gift.

After you have written out your principle or principles in one or two sentences using present-tense verbs, test them against the criteria we mentioned in chapter 2 (see below). This will help you determine whether you have truly discovered a theological principle:

- The principle should be reflected in the biblical text.
- The principle should be timeless and not tied to a specific situation.
- The principle should not be culturally bound.[11]

---

10. Jack Kuhatschek, *Applying the Bible* (Grand Rapids: Zondervan, 1990), 57–61.

11. Sometimes determining what is cultural or time-bound in a text and what is normative or timeless presents a challenge. If you want to learn more about this issue, we recommend the following: Fee and Stuart, *How*

- The principle should be consistent with the teaching of the rest of Scripture.
- The principle should be relevant to both the biblical and the contemporary audience.

Theological principles provide a bridge across the river of historical and cultural barriers that separate the ancient text and the contemporary audience.

Step 4: Consult the biblical map. How does our theological principle fit with the rest of the Bible?

Here you need to see how the theological principle you have discovered fits with the rest of Scripture. Is it supported or refuted by the clear teaching of Scripture elsewhere?

Since New Testament letters are situational, you need to make sure that the way you formulate a principle from one letter doesn't contradict the clear teaching of another part of the Bible, even another New Testament letter. Take Galatians 2:16 and James 2:24 as an example:

> So we, too, have put our faith in Christ Jesus that we may be justified by faith in Christ and not by the works of the law, because by the works of the law no one will be justified. (Gal. 2:16b)

> You see that a person is considered righteous by what they do and not by faith alone. (James 2:24)

When interpreting one of these passages, you might be tempted to state a principle that, if taken absolutely, would clearly contradict the other passage. Paul and James are addressing two completely different situations in their letters. Both are contending for the importance of a genuine faith that results in obedience. In fact, they both use Abraham as their example of a faith that acts (see Gal. 3:6–9; James 2:21–24). So when writing out a principle for one of these passages, you need to be aware of the broader biblical teaching on the relationship between faith and works.

---

to Read the Bible, 84–90; William W. Klein, Craig L. Blomberg, and Robert L. Hubbard Jr., *Introduction to Biblical Interpretation*, 4th ed. (Grand Rapids: Zondervan, 2017), 613–32; Grant R. Osborne, *The Hermeneutical Spiral*, 2nd ed. (Downers Grove, IL: InterVarsity Press, 2006), 326–38.

Step 5: Grasp the text in our town. How should individual Christians today live out the theological principles?

In the last phase of interpreting a New Testament letter, we ask how Christians today can live out the theological principle or principles. Remember that while these principles are determined by the meaning of the text, they may be applied in a number of different ways today. In chapter 13 we learned how to apply theological principles and even used a passage from a New Testament letter to illustrate the process (Phil. 4:13).

There are three steps. (1) We observe how the theological principles in the biblical text address the original situation. We look closely at this intersection between the principle in the text and the historical situation. (2) We search for a situation in our lives or our world that parallels the ancient situation. (3) We need to make our applications specific by creating real-world scenarios that are both faithful to the meaning of the text and relevant to the contemporary audience. Remember, to truly grasp God's Word, we need to obey what we learn.

MAKING THE INTERPRETIVE JOURNEY

In the previous section we reviewed the five basic steps of the Interpretive Journey, steps that are essential for understanding and applying New Testament letters. If you are like most people, you need an example to go along with the explanation. In this section we want to take Hebrews 12:1–2 through the five steps of the Interpretive Journey. We hope this will clarify what you need to do when interpreting a letter in the New Testament.

Hebrews 12:1–2

> [1]Therefore, since we are surrounded by such a great cloud of witnesses, let us throw off everything that hinders and the sin that so easily entangles. And let us run with perseverance the race marked out for us, [2]fixing our eyes on Jesus, the pioneer and perfecter of faith. For the joy set before him he endured the cross, scorning its shame, and sat down at the right hand of the throne of God.

Step 1: Grasp the text in their town. What did the text mean to the biblical audience?

As you read Hebrews from start to finish, you will notice a rather serious tone as God speaks powerfully through the author about the cost of discipleship. The book actually reads more like a sermon and even admits to being a "word of exhortation" (13:22). You may also notice a central focus on Jesus Christ along with an extensive use of the Old Testament. When you consult the study tools to reconstruct the historical-cultural situation, you can easily see why Hebrews sounds a note of urgency.

The believers addressed by Hebrews probably came out of a Jewish background and formed a house church or a group of churches in or near Rome.[12] The letter was likely written during the mid-60s AD, just prior to a period of severe persecution under Emperor Nero. A small band of believers was facing the temptation to reject Christianity and return to Judaism to have an easier time of life. They were discouraged and appear to have been wavering in their commitment to Christ. No one knows for sure who wrote Hebrews, but the author's purpose seems clear enough. He writes *"to encourage a group of discouraged believers drifting away from real Christianity by bolstering their commitment to draw near to God and to endure in commitment to Christ."*[13] The book is filled with instruction about the superiority of Jesus Christ and warnings to persevere in faith.

The next step toward grasping the original meaning of Hebrews 12:1–2 is to identify its literary context. How does the author's thought run through this section of the letter/sermon? The word "therefore" in 12:1 shows us that our passage is closely connected to the preceding chapter. Hebrews 11—often called the great "Hall of Faith"—presents example after example of how the saints of old persevered in faith. In Hebrews 12:1–2 the author/preacher uses the image of a race and the example of Jesus himself to exhort his audience to endure in faith. In the paragraph that follows (12:3–11), the author/preacher uses the analogy of a parent's love for a child to explain why believers should embrace hardships as expressions of God's love. The theme of enduring difficult times binds these sections together.

After we come to grips with the context of the passage and before we summarize what the passage meant to the first-century audience, we need to observe the text carefully. It says that we are "surrounded by such a great cloud of witnesses," referring to the examples of faith listed in Hebrews 11. These models of faithfulness offer much-needed encouragement for the struggling house church(es). Knowing that many people have already walked the path of hardship and found God faithful, the biblical audience is called (1) to "throw off" what hinders and the sin that so easily entangles, (2) to run the race with perseverance, and (3) to fix their eyes on Jesus, the ultimate example of faith.

The author uses the image of a race to illustrate the nature of the Christian life. This image governs how we should understand many of the key words and expressions

---

12. Our summary of the historical-cultural situation is drawn from George H. Guthrie, *Hebrews*, NIV Application Commentary (Grand Rapids: Zondervan, 1998), 17–38. On pages 17–18, Guthrie makes the setting come to life with his fictitious account of a young man named Antonius.

13. Guthrie, 22 (italics in original).

in this passage. Running this kind of race requires both effort and endurance and suggests that the author has in mind a long-distance race such as a marathon rather than a short sprint. About the need for runners to "throw off everything that hinders," Keener writes:

> "Laying aside weights" (KJV) may refer to removing artificial weights used in training but not in races, but more likely it refers to the Greek custom of stripping off clothes to run unencumbered. The image would represent anything that would hinder his readers from winning their race.[14]

Runners are also challenged to run a race that is "marked out" or set before them, meaning that they must put their faith into action by making the right choices even though such choices may prove difficult. Yet those who run the race do not run in their strength alone. That is, in part, why they are urged to fix their eyes on Jesus, "the author and perfecter of our faith." Guthrie notes that the word translated "author" can communicate the idea of "champion, leader, forerunner, or initiator."[15] Both "champion" and "forerunner" fit the race imagery and, when paired with the idea of "perfecting," the word teaches that Jesus "has cleared the path of faith so that we may run it. The way is open, and although hurdles exist, the roadblocks have been removed."[16]

Jesus not only stands as the ultimate example of endurance, he also inspires endurance in those who follow because he himself focused on the reward that lay beyond the immediate obstacle of suffering. The future joy set before Jesus enabled him to endure the cross. Even more, he "scorned" the shame of the cross or considered it insignificant in comparison to the promised rewards to come. Having endured, he then "sat down at the right hand of the throne of God."

We can now summarize the meaning of Hebrews 12:1–2 for the biblical audience in the following way: The author of Hebrews uses the image of a long-distance race to challenge his audience to persevere in their commitment to Christ in spite of opposition. Rather than drifting away from Christ and reverting to Judaism, they need to run the race with endurance. For inspiration and encouragement, they should consider the scores of faithful saints who have already endured in faith. They are urged especially to focus on Jesus himself, the ultimate example of perseverance under pressure, rather than on the immediate circumstance of difficulty.

---

14. Craig S. Keener, *The IVP Bible Background Commentary: New Testament* (Downers Grove, IL: InterVarsity Press, 1993), 678.

15. Guthrie, *Hebrews*, 398.

16. Guthrie, 399.

Step 2: Measure the width of the river to cross. What are the differences between the biblical audience and us?

As with most situations in the letters, the river separating the biblical audience and us is not wide. As Christians living after the death and resurrection of Christ amid a hostile world, we, too, find ourselves in a long-distance race struggling to endure. We have a wealth of faithful examples who have gone before, and we must look to Jesus, the author and perfecter of our faith.

However, we must be aware of a few differences when interpreting this passage. Many of us do not face the same level of persecution confronting the original audience. We will have to familiarize ourselves with the suffering church in other parts of the world to feel the full impact of the challenge to endure. In addition, most of us are not tempted to revert to Judaism to avoid such opposition. But there certainly are religious practices or groups the world considers "acceptable" and to which Christians are tempted to turn for "safety" from trouble. These can serve as helpful parallels.

Step 3: Cross the principlizing bridge. What are the theological principles in this text?

We find at least three central theological principles in Hebrews 12:1–2:

- The Christian life is like a difficult long-distance race, which requires both effort and endurance.
- The saints who have gone before supply us with valuable examples of endurance. We should look to them for inspiration and encouragement.
- To run the race successfully, we need to reject things in life that hinder our progress and, most importantly, focus on Jesus and our relationship with him.

Step 4: Consult the biblical map. How does our theological principle fit with the rest of the Bible?

When you look at the three theological principles above, they all seem to fit well with the rest of Scripture. They are general enough not to contradict the clear teaching of the rest of the Bible. This will often be the case with principles from New Testament letters.

Step 5: Grasp the text in our town. How should individual Christians today live out the theological principles?

To illustrate the application step, let's use the first of the three theological principles mentioned above: "The Christian life is like a difficult long-distance race, which requires both effort and endurance." As we seek to grasp the text in our town, we must look closely at the intersection between the theological principle and the original situation. In this case, we find several important aspects of this intersection:

- The runners are Christians, and the race is life itself.
- The race is difficult, and we are tempted to take an easier route or even quit.
- Running a successful race requires both effort and endurance.

We continue the process by searching for a contemporary situation that truly parallels the original situation. In this case it will be easy to find a parallel situation. Any Christian who is tempted to give up because of the difficulty of staying faithful to Christ will need to be reminded that the race demands effort and endurance. To fully grasp the text in our town, we need to make our application specific.

In other parts of Scripture, the emphasis falls on the grace God gives. This passage, however, stresses how we should respond to God's grace. We must realize that life is not a sprint. Our instantaneous society does not view endurance as a virtue, but God calls us to lay aside impatience and to persevere. We need to think less in terms of minutes and even days and think more in terms of months and years. God wants us to remain steadfast under pressure and to stay the course. To run successfully means making the right choices today and the next day and the next week, month, year, and so on. God calls us to hang in there over the long haul.

In our teaching ministries, occasionally we encounter Christian students who have come out of difficult, non-Christian home situations. They come to Ouachita, a Christian liberal arts university, and end up in our classes. Over the course of the semester, we get to know them and some of what they are dealing with in life. They feel guilty and angry about their parents' divorce, if they even know their parents. Some have suffered verbal or physical abuse. Others are struggling financially because of lack of support. Nearly all of them have been wounded emotionally and continue to carry a lot of baggage. But these students are committed to the Lord and are running the race faithfully. We pray for them and love them and encourage them to endure. They know by experience that running a successful race means choosing Christ even when ridiculed, excluded, or treated unjustly at home. Running with endurance means staying on our feet and fixing our gaze on Christ, even if we feel exhausted and depleted and stressed to the breaking point. The race is not a sprint but a marathon. To endure is to win.

CONCLUSION

Life simply would not be the same without letters. We use them to communicate our deepest thoughts and feelings, some of which can be quite "mushy." When we turn to the twenty-one letters of the New Testament, we catch a glimpse of the practical, frontline work of early Christian disciple-makers. These letters serve as authoritative substitutes for leaders who could not always minister in person. They were written to address specific situations and meet the practical needs of their readers. The letters were carefully prepared and were meant to be read aloud to the congregation again and again.

When you approach a New Testament letter, remember that it is a letter and not a telephone directory. Letters are meant to be read from beginning to end, the same way you read a personal letter today. Take the historical-cultural situation seriously, and place a high priority on tracing the author's flow of thought (i.e., the literary context). Then use the principlizing bridge to cross the river of differences and apply the meaning of the biblical text to your life.

The letters of the New Testament offer a window into the struggles and victories of the early church. They provide inspired instruction and advice for living a godly life, for which we can be forever grateful. We close this chapter with a typical closing from a New Testament letter: "Grace be with you. Amen."

ASSIGNMENTS

Assignment 14–1

When it comes to letters, we need to be able to trace the author's flow of thought. The first step is to see how paragraphs relate to surrounding paragraphs. Write out your answer to the following questions as a way of gaining experience at tracing the author's flow of thought:

1. How does Philippians 2:1–4 relate to Philippians 2:5–11?
2. What is the connection between Ephesians 5:15–21 and Ephesians 5:22–6:9?
3. What role does 1 Corinthians 13 play in the larger unit of 1 Corinthians 12–14?

Assignment 14–2

Take one of the following passages through all five steps of the Interpretive Journey explained and illustrated in this chapter:

- Romans 8:26–27
- 1 Corinthians 11:27–32
- Galatians 5:16–18
- Colossians 3:1–4
- 2 Timothy 3:16–17
- Hebrews 4:12–13
- 1 Peter 5:6–7

CHAPTER 15

NEW TESTAMENT—GOSPELS

INTRODUCTION

At the very center of our faith stands a person—Jesus Christ. He performed miracles and spoke the very "words of eternal life" (John 6:68). One thing Jesus never did was publish his autobiography. Without a book from Jesus himself, how do we know anything about him?

We certainly have enough information about Jesus from sources outside the New Testament to know that he really existed, but our most direct witness to Jesus comes from the four canonical Gospels: Matthew, Mark, Luke, and John.[1] These four books comprise almost half of the New Testament in terms of percentage. In them the first followers of Jesus give us something similar to a biography of Jesus. The four Gospels are significant because they tell us the story of Jesus, the unique Son of God.[2]

In this chapter you can expect to learn two main things. First, we will answer the question "What are the Gospels?" Specifically, what kind of story did the gospel writers intend to tell? Are they like modern biographies? If so, why do they

1. See, for example, Peter J. Williams, *Can We Trust the Gospels?* (Wheaton, IL: Crossway, 2018).

2. For more on the life of Christ and the Gospels, see especially Mark L. Strauss, *Four Portraits, One Jesus: A Survey of Jesus and the Gospels* (Grand Rapids: Zondervan, 2007); Craig L. Blomberg, *Jesus and the Gospels: An Introduction and Survey*, 2nd ed. (Nashville: Broadman, 2009).

not tell us everything we want to know about Jesus, such as what happened during his teenage years? Why do these four books not always follow the same chronological sequence? We need to understand as much as possible about the genre of gospel in order to read the Gospels as intended.

Once we understand the nature of the Gospels, we can move on to our second concern: how to interpret the Gospels. Is there a way to approach the Gospels so that we can draw out the intended meaning of the text and apply it to our lives? We suggest that there is an appropriate way to read the story of Jesus. Let's begin by taking up our first concern, the genre of gospel.

WHAT ARE THE GOSPELS?

The term *gospel* translates the Greek word *euangelion*, which means "good news." Prior to the New Testament, this word usually referred to good news of a political or military victory. In the New Testament the word denotes the good news proclaimed by Jesus (Mark 1:14–15) or the good news about Jesus (1 Cor. 15:1). It is easy to see why the early Christians would eventually refer to Matthew, Mark, Luke, and John as the Gospels. But how did the Holy Spirit inspire the gospel authors (often called the "evangelists") to present or communicate this good news? Correct interpretation depends on correct identification of the kind of communication taking place.

The term *gospel* translates the Greek word *euangelion*, which means "good news."

First and foremost the Gospels are stories. Everybody loves a good story, but why? What is it about stories that captures our attention like nothing else does? Stories are interesting. We find ourselves "entering" the story and relating to the characters. In this way we participate in the story. We can use our imaginations to visualize how the story plays out. The Gospels are powerful because they are stories. But what kind of stories are they?

Matthew, Mark, Luke, and John were viewed early on as stories of Jesus drawn from the personal experience of the apostles. In his *First Apology*, the early church leader Justin Martyr (ca. AD 100–165) characterizes the Gospels as the "memoirs" of the apostles. This sounds like the authors were writing biographies of Jesus. But when you read the four Gospels, you immediately notice that they are somewhat different from modern biographies. Can you think of specific ways that the Gospels seem to differ from most modern autobiographies or biographies?

Unlike most modern biographies, the Gospels do not cover the whole life of Jesus, but rather jump from his birth to his public ministry. Matthew and Luke include accounts of Jesus' birth, while in Mark's account we first encounter Jesus when he arrives at the Jordan River as a full-grown adult to be baptized (Mark 1:9). Mark tells us nothing about Jesus' birth or boyhood.

Often the writers of the Gospels arrange Jesus' actions topically rather than chronologically and report what Jesus says in a variety of ways. Another difference between the Gospels and most modern biographies is the comparatively large percentage of space the Gospels devote to the last week of Jesus' life. For example, in John the last week of Jesus' life begins in chapter 12. Also, you will not find anything like a detailed psychological analysis of Jesus or any other main characters in the Gospels. It is easy to see that the four Gospels differ considerably from most modern biographies.

Yet just because the Gospels differ from modern biographies does not mean they are not biographies; it simply means they are not *modern* biographies. Ancient biographers followed a different set of rules. Ancient biographies normally had a simple outline, beginning with the birth or arrival of the main character and ending with his death. (The authors commonly devoted a large portion of their work to the character's death, since the way a person dies says a lot about the person.) The material between the main character's birth and death included stories and sayings selected and arranged by the author to tell the audience something important about the character. When we read Matthew, Mark, Luke, and John, it becomes obvious that they have a lot in common with the genre of ancient biography.[3]

The Gospels devote a large amount of space to the last week of Jesus' life.

If you have spent any time at all reading the Gospels, you will notice that while all four tell essentially the same story, the details vary from one Gospel to another. We really have four different versions of the one story of Jesus. For those of us who seem fixated on chronological strictness, the variety can cause problems. For example, how do we understand Matthew and Luke switching the order of the second and third temptations of Jesus (cf. Matt. 4:5–10 with Luke 4:5–13)?

On a larger scale, you will sometimes find considerable variation in the order of the same events as presented in the first three Gospels. Matthew, Mark, and Luke are commonly called the *Synoptic Gospels* since they can easily be "seen together" when placed side by side (*syn* means *together*, *optic* means *see*). John often takes a different course altogether. In the chart below, you can see how the gospel writers place the same events and stories in slightly different order in their respective Gospels.[4]

3. For a scholarly discussion of the genre of gospel as ancient biography, see Richard A. Burridge, *What Are the Gospels? A Comparison with Graeco-Roman Biography*, 2nd ed. (Cambridge: Cambridge University Press, 2004).

4. See Darrell L. Bock, "The Words of Jesus in the Gospels: Live, Jive, or Memorex?" in *Jesus Under Fire: Modern Scholarship Reinvents the Historical Jesus*, ed. Michael J. Wilkins and J. P. Moreland (Grand Rapids: Zondervan, 1995), 84–85.

Event	Matthew	Mark	Luke
Cleansing of leper	8:1–4	1:40–45	5:12–16
Centurion of Capernaum	8:5–13	no parallel	7:1–10
Peter's mother-in-law	8:14–15	1:29–31	4:38–39
Sick healed	8:16–17	1:32–34	4:40–41
Following Jesus	8:18–22	no parallel	9:57–62
Stilling the storm	8:23–27	4:35–41	8:22–25
Gadarene demoniac	8:28–34	5:1–20	8:26–39
Healing of the paralytic	9:1–8	2:1–12	5:17–26
Matthew's call	9:9–13	2:13–17	5:27–32
Fasting question	9:14–17	2:18–22	5:33–39
Jairus and the woman	9:18–26	5:21–43	8:40–56

You will also find variety in wording in the Gospels. Compare "Blessed are the poor in spirit" in Matthew 5:3 with simply "Blessed are you who are poor" in Luke 6:20. Notice the difference in the interchange between Jesus and the high priest at his trial:

> The high priest said to him, "I charge you under oath by the living God: Tell us if you are the Messiah, the Son of God."
>
> "You have said so," Jesus replied. (Matt. 26:63–64)

> Again the high priest asked him, "Are you the Messiah, the Son of the Blessed One?"
>
> "I am," said Jesus. (Mark 14:61–62)

> "If you are the Messiah," they said, "tell us."
>
> Jesus answered, "If I tell you, you will not believe me, and if I asked you, you would not answer. But from now on, the Son of Man will be seated at the right hand of the mighty God."
>
> They all asked, "Are you then the Son of God?"
>
> He replied, "You say that I am." (Luke 22:67–70)

It seems obvious that what we have in the four Gospels is not the result of four people following Jesus around with cell phones recording everything he says and does. What should we make of all this? We should begin by recognizing that the gospel writers (like any reporter or historian) could not tell all there was to tell about Jesus. John admits as much in the final sentence of his Gospel (21:25): "Jesus did many other things as well. If every one of them were written down, I suppose that even the whole world would not have room for the books that would be written." You can read Jesus' longest speeches (e.g., the Sermon on the Mount in Matt. 6) in a matter of minutes, yet he often spoke to the crowds for hours at a time. There was simply not enough time and not enough scroll space to tell the whole story. As a result, under the direction of the Spirit, the gospel writers chose what to include (and omit) as well as how to arrange it in a way that effectively communicated the good news to their contemporaries.

As ancient biographers, the gospel writers felt free to paraphrase or summarize what Jesus said and to arrange the events according to a particular theme rather than according to strict chronological sequence.

As ancient biographers, the gospel writers felt free to paraphrase or summarize what Jesus said and to arrange the events according to a particular theme rather than according to strict chronological sequence. In his prologue (Luke 1:1–4), Luke admits his use of eyewitness testimony and careful research in retelling the story of Jesus.[5] The goal of the gospel writers was to tell the story of Jesus in a faithful, yet relevant and persuasive manner for their readers. Rather than viewing the differences between accounts as errors in reporting, we should see them as illustrations of the different theological purposes and emphases of the gospel writers.

Once we realize that the evangelists were operating under ancient rather than modern literary rules, many of the so-called discrepancies between the Gospels fade away. Take the difference in the order of the second and third temptations of Jesus as an example. A central theme in Matthew's Gospel is the kingdom of God. It makes sense that Matthew would end his account of the temptations with Jesus seeing all the kingdoms of the world (Matt. 4:8–10). Because Jerusalem figures prominently in Luke's Gospel, you can easily understand why Luke would want to conclude with Jesus being tempted to jump off the temple in Jerusalem (Luke 4:9–12). Matthew and Luke vary the details in telling the story of Jesus to make a theological point. This leads us to make one last important point about gospel genre.

We have seen how the Gospels are similar in genre to ancient biography. But there is an added dimension to the Gospels that we need to emphasize. The Gospels are not just biography; they are Christ-centered biography.[6] The evangelists are telling

5. On the importance of eyewitness testimony, see Richard Bauckham, *Jesus and the Eyewitnesses: The Gospels as Eyewitness Testimony*, 2nd ed. (Grand Rapids: Eerdmans, 2017).

6. See Richard A. Burridge, "About People, by People, for People: Gospel Genre and Audiences," in *The Gospels for All Christians*, ed. Richard Bauckham (Grand Rapids: Eerdmans, 1998), 113–45.

us the story of Jesus, the Christ (or Messiah); they are not simply recording historical facts. They are telling the story to teach their readers something about the person and mission of Jesus. The gospel writers selected and arranged their material about Christ to communicate theological truth to their audience. All storytelling is storytelling for a particular purpose, and the purpose of Matthew, Mark, Luke, and John is thoroughly Christ-centered!

The Gospels are christological biography.

Where does all of this lead us? We need to grasp the genre of *gospel* in order to read the Gospels properly. The four Gospels are similar in many ways to ancient biography, but they are more than ancient biography. By focusing on Jesus' life and teachings, we may describe the Gospels accurately as *christological biography*. This brings us to the two primary purposes that the evangelists had in mind when writing their Gospels. (1) They have selected and arranged material to tell the story of Jesus. (2) Through the story of Jesus, they are saying something important to their first readers (and to us). Since the Holy Spirit saw fit to inspire the Gospels in this way, we need to adopt a way of reading them that matches the method used by the gospel writers.

HOW SHOULD WE READ THE GOSPELS?

Our method of reading the Gospels must respect the means God used to inspire them in the first place. The gospel writers are saying something about Jesus *in* each episode, and they are saying something *by the way* they link the smaller stories together to form the larger story.

To arrive at a method of reading the Gospels that matches the means of God's communication, let's transform these two central purposes cited above into two simple interpretive questions. (1) What does this small story tell us about Jesus? (2) What is the gospel writer trying to say to his readers by the way that he puts the smaller stories together? The chart below depicts the two central interpretive questions for reading the Gospels.

<table>
<tr><th>↓ Episode 1</th><th>↓ Episode 2</th><th>↓ Episode 3</th></tr>
<tr><td>What is this episode telling us about Jesus?</td><td>What is this episode telling us about Jesus?</td><td>What is this episode telling us about Jesus?</td></tr>
<tr><th colspan="3">→ Episodes 1, 2, and 3</th></tr>
<tr><td colspan="3">What is the gospel writer trying to communicate to his readers by the way he connects these stories?</td></tr>
</table>

Take the familiar story of Mary and Martha in Luke 10:38–42 as an example. Step 1 is to read the story and understand its message, usually a message that centers around Jesus.

↓Luke 10:25–37	↓Luke 10:38–42	↓Luke 11:1–13
	Here we discover the principle that doing good things for God can sometimes cause us to miss God himself. Martha's desire to put on a feast for Jesus causes her to miss the best thing: listening to Jesus.	

Before moving on, give this a try. Read Luke 10:25–37 and Luke 11:1–13 and ask, What is the main idea of each story? What does this story teach me about Jesus? What does Jesus teach in this story? What do I learn from Jesus' actions captured in this story? We will learn a lot more about how to read individual episodes later in this chapter, but for now we want you to summarize the main idea. Take a look at how we tried to capture Luke's message.

↓Luke 10:25–37	↓Luke 10:38–42	↓Luke 11:1–13
We see the principle that love for one's neighbor should transcend all human boundaries, such as nationality, race, religion, or economic status.	Here we discover the principle that doing good things for God can sometimes cause us to miss God himself. Martha's desire to put on a feast for Jesus causes her to miss the best thing: listening to Jesus.	Jesus teaches us how to communicate with God through prayer (vv. 1–4). This is followed by a parable on prayer (vv. 5–8) and an exhortation to pray (vv. 9–13).

Step 1, then, is to understand the main message of each story, a message usually focusing on the life and teachings of Jesus. In step 2 we need to put the episode of Mary and Martha alongside the surrounding episodes to see what Luke is trying to communicate to his readers (and to us) by the way he has arranged the material. Look at our summaries above and think about what these three stories have in common. Do you see any connections? Look below to see what we came up with.

→ Luke 10:25–37; 10:38–42; 11:1–13

The common theme seems to be relationships. In the first story, we are told that followers of Jesus should be loving neighbors to people in need. In our second story, we are taught that listening to Jesus should take priority over "religious activity." Finally, Luke emphasizes our relationship to God in 11:1–13. Followers of Jesus need to know how to relate to their neighbors (service), how to relate to their Lord (devotion), and how to relate to their Father (prayer).

We cannot be 100 percent sure we have captured Luke's intention here, and different readers may see different connections. Don't force anything. Try to stick with the main idea of each passage, and you will discover some great insights into the Gospels.

Up to this point we have seen that reading the Gospels consists of asking two main questions, questions that correspond to the two central purposes of the evangelists: (1) What is taught *in* each episode? (2) What is taught *by the way* the episodes are linked together to form the larger story? In the next part of this chapter, we will explore both questions in more detail, beginning with how to read individual episodes.

1. How to Read Individual Stories

There are some basic interpretive guidelines for discovering theological principles in specific stories. We will illustrate the rules using the story of Jesus calming the storm (Mark 4:35–41) and a few other texts.

> 35That day when evening came, he said to his disciples, "Let us go over to the
> other side." 36Leaving the crowd behind, they took him along, just as he was, in
> the boat. There were also other boats with him. 37A furious squall came up, and
> the waves broke over the boat, so that it was nearly swamped. 38 Jesus was in the
> stern, sleeping on a cushion. The disciples woke him and said to him, "Teacher,
> don't you care if we drown?"
>
> 39He got up, rebuked the wind and said to the waves, "Quiet! Be still!" Then
> the wind died down and it was completely calm.
>
> 40He said to his disciples, "Why are you so afraid? Do you still have
> no faith?"
>
> 41They were terrified and asked each other, "Who is this? Even the wind
> and the waves obey him!"

a. Ask the standard questions that you should ask of any story: Who? What? When? Where? Why? and How? We list a few observations of this passage to illustrate the process.

Who? (characters)	• Jesus (vv. 35, 36, 38, 39, 40, 41) • Disciples (vv. 35, 36, 38, 40, 41) • Crowd (v. 36)
What? (story line)	• While Jesus and the disciples are crossing the sea, a storm comes up, and the waves nearly swamp the boat. (v. 37) • The disciples wake Jesus, who is sleeping on a cushion in the stern of the boat. (v. 38) • Jesus rebukes the storm, then rebukes the disciples for their lack of faith. (vv. 39–40) • The disciples are terrified by Jesus' authority over the sea and ask, "Who is this?" (v. 41)
When? (time)	• When evening comes the disciples and Jesus begin to cross the sea. (v. 35) • During the storm Jesus the carpenter sleeps, and the fishermen disciples fear for their lives. (v. 38) • After Jesus rebukes the wind, the sea grows calm. (v. 39) • After stilling the storm, Jesus asks his disciples a couple of tough questions. (v. 40) • After the calming of the storm and Jesus' questions, the disciples are terrified. (v. 41)
Where? (place)	• Jesus and his disciples head to the other side of the sea. (v. 35) • They are in the boat. (v. 36) • The waves are breaking over the boat. (v. 37) • Jesus is in the stern, sleeping on a cushion. (v. 38)
Why? (reason)	• The disciples wake Jesus because they are angry at their teacher's indifference to their safety. (v. 38) • The wind and waves calm down because of Jesus' rebuke. (vv. 39, 41) • The disciples are terrified because they realize that Jesus has authority over the sea. (vv. 40–41)
How? (means)	• The disciples use a question to rebuke Jesus. (v. 38) • Jesus calms the stormy sea by his spoken word. (v. 39) • Jesus uses questions to rebuke the disciples. (v. 40) • The disciples verbalize their fear in the form of a question about Jesus' identity: "Who is this?" (v. 41)

From these simple questions, we make some significant discoveries about the story. Because Jesus and the disciples appear in almost every verse, we know the story focuses on Jesus' relationship to his disciples. What is Jesus trying to teach his followers? Will they learn the lesson? Also, by contrasting Jesus' response to the storm with that of the disciples, we see the difference between faith and fear. Jesus sleeps in trust while these professional fishermen frantically bail water in fear of drowning. We notice, too, the power of Jesus' spoken word. Even the stormy sea is subject to him. The role that questions play in this passage is interesting. The disciples question Jesus' indifference. Jesus questions the disciples' lack of faith. This causes the disciples in turn to question Jesus' identity: "Who is this guy who can control the sea?"

b. Look for interpretive instructions from the author himself. Often a gospel writer will help readers see his point by offering clues in the story's introduction. The author may say something like, "When he noticed how the guests picked the places of honor at the table, he told them this parable" (Luke 14:7). Without even hearing the parable, you can guess that it will have something to do with spiritual pride or humility or both.

The introduction to the Sermon on the Mount reads like this: "Now when Jesus saw the crowds, he went up on a mountainside and sat down. His disciples came to him, and he began to teach them. He said . . ." (Matt. 5:1–2). From this introduction we know to read the sermon that follows as teaching directed to people who are already following Jesus rather than to people who are considering discipleship.

Often the author's interpretive clue will appear in the conclusion to the story. In Mark 4 the story climaxes with the disciples' question in the final verse: "Who is this? Even the wind and the waves obey him!" We are left with the distinct impression that Mark wants his readers to know that Jesus is something more than your average rabbi (or "teacher"). He even possesses divine authority over the powerful forces of nature!

Look for interpretive instructions from the author himself.

In the story of Jesus' encounter with the rich young man in Matthew 19, the last line reads, "But many who are first will be last, and many who are last will be first" (v. 30). Jesus is turning the world's values upside down. Those who have given up everything to follow Jesus now should not worry; they will indeed be first in God's kingdom.

Occasionally a gospel writer will include a parenthetical remark to clarify the intended meaning of the story. In Mark 7:1–23 Jesus confronts the Pharisees and teachers of the law over the issue of ritual purity. Mark then adds these words: "In saying this, Jesus declared all foods clean" (v. 19). With this comment, Mark draws out the implication of the story for his readers. What makes a person clean or unclean is a matter of the heart, not the digestive tract.

As another example, remember when Peter and John ran to the empty tomb? Peter went inside first. Scripture says that when John finally entered the tomb, he "saw and believed" (John 20:8). The gospel writer tacks on this comment: "They still did not understand from Scripture that Jesus had to rise from the dead" (John 20:9). This remark makes it clear that at this point John's faith was based not on a particular reading of the Old Testament, but on his experience of seeing the grave clothes without the body; the tomb was empty, Jesus had risen, John saw and believed!

You can expect to find theological principles in stories by looking to the author himself for help. Often you will find such explicit instructions in the introduction or conclusion to a story or in the author's parenthetical comments.

c. Take special note of anything that is repeated in the story. Stories often use repetition to convey theological truth. As you read individual episodes in the Gospels, be alert for what shows up again and again. While reading John 15 you will notice that the word "remain" (or "abide") appears over and over. In Matthew 23 the repeated expression "Woe" conveys an unmistakable tone of warning to the reader. In Matthew 5 Jesus repeatedly highlights the uniqueness of his teaching, using the phrase "You have heard that it was said. . . . But I tell you. . . ."

Stories often use repetition to convey theological truth.

When the gospel writers repeat a word or theme or when a particular character figures prominently, pay attention! Authors use repetition to signal an important truth, and you don't want to miss it. What theme do you see repeated in Luke 12:22–34 below? (Underline words or phrases that repeat that particular theme.)

> [22]Then Jesus said to his disciples: "Therefore I tell you, do not worry about your life, what you will eat; or about your body, what you will wear. [23]For life is more than food, and the body more than clothes. [24]Consider the ravens: They do not sow or reap, they have no storeroom or barn; yet God feeds them. And how much more valuable you are than birds! [25]Who of you by worrying can add a single hour to your life? [26]Since you cannot do this very little thing, why do you worry about the rest?
>
> [27]"Consider how the wild flowers grow. They do not labor or spin. Yet I tell you, not even Solomon in all his splendor was dressed like one of these. [28]If that is how God clothes the grass of the field, which is here today, and tomorrow is thrown into the fire, how much more will he clothe you—you of little faith! [29]And do not set your heart on what you will eat or drink; do not worry about it. [30]For the pagan world runs after all such things, and your Father knows that you need them. [31]But seek his kingdom, and these things will be given to you as well.
>
> [32]"Do not be afraid, little flock, for your Father has been pleased to give you the kingdom. [33]Sell your possessions and give to the poor. Provide purses for yourselves that will not wear out, a treasure in heaven that will never fail, where no thief comes near and no moth destroys. [34]For where your treasure is, there your heart will be also."

d. Be alert for places where the story shifts to direct discourse. Direct discourse occurs when the characters speak directly, that is, when their words appear in quotation marks in the text. By isolating the direct discourse, you can usually see the heart of the story. Notice how the direct discourse in Mark 4:35–41 really does give you the story in a nutshell:

v. 35: "Let us go over to the other side."
v. 38: "Teacher, don't you care if we drown?"
v. 39: "Quiet! Be still!"
v. 40: "Why are you so afraid? Do you still have no faith?"
v. 41: "Who is this? Even the wind and the waves obey him!"

Another example that comes to mind is Jesus' transfiguration, where we hear God's voice: "This is my Son, whom I love; with him I am well pleased. Listen to him!" (Matt. 17:5). After Jesus had predicted his own death, God's reassurance must have meant a lot to disciples struggling with the notion of a crucified Messiah.

Some passages feature almost exclusively the dialogue between main characters. John 4:4–26 is a conversation between Jesus and a Samaritan woman. Perhaps the conversation between a Jewish man and a Samaritan woman was worth preserving for its shock value alone, since as John notes, "Jews do not associate with Samaritans" (4:9). By studying the contents of the conversation, you can see clearly what John intended to communicate to his readers about Jesus. Direct discourse generally offers an exceptionally clear window for gazing at the theological message of the story.

When trying to identify theological principles in individual stories, we must ask the standard narrative questions, pay attention to the author's own interpretive instructions, note what is repeated, and concentrate on direct discourse within the story. The story of Jesus calming the storm in Mark 4:35–41 might be summarized as follows:

> Jesus exerts his power over the sea and responds to the storm himself by trusting the Father during a difficult circumstance.

Now let's look at how this story connects to surrounding stories.

2. How to Read a Series of Stories

The second interpretive question for reading the Gospels expands the context beyond any one story or episode to the surrounding stories: "What is the gospel writer trying to say by the way he strings together the individual stories?" Since the gospel writers could not tell us everything about Jesus, they have selected material and arranged that material to send their first readers (and us) a powerful, life-changing message about Jesus.

Are there reliable guidelines for reading a series of stories or episodes? We believe there is one central guideline that can be applied in a number of different ways. *The most important thing to do when reading a series of stories is to look for connections.* This is exactly what you learned to do back in chapter 5 using scenes from Mark 8. Look for common themes or patterns. Search for logical connections like cause and effect. Pay attention to how episodes are joined together (e.g., transition statements or conjunctions). Notice how the stories differ at key points. Compare the characters, paying close attention to Jesus, the main character of the Gospels. Focus on his identity, his mission, his teaching, and responses to him. Seeing connections used by the author will help you discern the intended message.

The most important thing to do when reading a series of stories is to look for connections.

Let's search for connections between Mark 4:35–41 and surrounding stories. When we look at what occurs before 4:35–41, we find a large section consisting of Jesus' parables "by the lake" (4:1). The series of parables set off by the word "parables" at the beginning (4:2) and the end (4:33–34) indicates that 4:1–34 should be seen as a unit. Beginning in Mark 4:35 the parables stop, and we see a change in location (from beside the lake to the lake itself) as well as audience (from the crowds to the disciples). These changes strongly suggest that Mark is beginning another unit in 4:35. As a result, we should read the story of Jesus calming the storm (4:35–41) with the scenes that follow rather than the parables that precede.[7]

How, then, does Mark 4:35–41 connect with the larger unit beginning in 4:35 and ending in 5:43 (or maybe even 6:6a)? The following chart summarizes the message of the individual stories.

Mark 4:35–41	Mark 5:1–20	Mark 5:24b–34	Mark 5:21–24a Mark 5:35–43
Jesus exerts his power over the sea and responds with faith during a difficult circumstance.	Jesus casts out a legion of demons, restores a man to his right mind, and sends him out as a faithful follower.	Jesus heals the woman with the hemorrhage who, because of faith, touched him, then confessed him publicly.	Jesus raises the daughter of Jairus from the dead in the presence of Peter, James, John, and the girl's parents.

7. Here we have a good reminder that although chapter and verse numbers help us find our way around the Bible, they do not always accurately define the units intended by the biblical authors. In this case, the story of Jesus' calming the storm in Mark 4:35–41 clearly belongs with chapter 5 rather than chapter 4. Chapters and verses were not part of the original inspired text but were added hundreds of years later.

When we look for connections between the episodes in 4:35–5:43, we notice several common themes:

- Life is hard. People experience the threat of death, satanic attack, disease, and death itself.
- Jesus is sovereign over forces that are hostile to God. First-century people feared some of the same things that we fear: the sea, the demonic, disease, and death. Jesus has power over these.
- We should trust Jesus in the midst of the desperate situations of life. The water was threatening to swamp the boat, the demoniac could not be restrained, the bleeding had lasted twelve years, and the daughter was dead. The common thread running through this entire section is the hopelessness of the situation. Jesus calls us to faith. He scolds the disciples for failing to have faith in the middle of the storm (4:40). He commends the woman with the hemorrhage for her saving faith (5:34), and he tells Jairus not to fear but to believe (5:36).

Mark's message to his first-century audience and to us becomes clear (see the horizontal box below):

Mark 4:35–41	**Mark 5:1–20**	**Mark 5:24b–34**	**Mark 5:21–24a Mark 5:35–43**
Jesus exerts his power over the sea and responds with faith during a difficult circumstance.	Jesus casts out a legion of demons, restores a man to his right mind, and sends him out as a faithful follower.	Jesus heals the woman with the hemorrhage who, because of faith, touched him, then confessed him publicly.	Jesus raises the daughter of Jairus from the dead in the presence of Peter, James, John, and the girl's parents.
Through his mighty works, Jesus shows himself sovereign over the forces that are hostile to God. Demons, disease, and death strike fear and hopelessness into the hearts of people. Mark's first-century readers were facing persecution and hostility. Through this series of stories, he assures them that Jesus has power over everything they fear! He can calm the sea, he can cast out demons, he can heal diseases, and he can raise the dead. They should trust him in the midst of the desperate situations of life.			

As Mark's Gospel continues in 6:1–6a, Jesus returns to his hometown of Nazareth, where he faces rejection from those who assume that they know him best. "Isn't this the carpenter?" they ask (6:3). Mark's closing comment reveals the tragic irony of this cold and faithless reception: "He could not do any miracles there, except lay his hands on a few sick people and heal them. He was amazed at their lack of faith" (6:5–6a). What a sad contrast to the hopeful message of the four preceding stories (4:35–5:43).

3. Applying the Message of the Gospels

Part of grasping God's Word is moving beyond theological principles and truths to application. How does this work in real life? Much of what you learned in chapter 13 on application will apply here. One of the most important things to remember when seeking to apply truths from these stories is that we should always keep the larger context in view. Saying that Jesus has power over hostile forces does not guarantee that he will always deliver us from cancer or car wrecks or other disasters. We should trust Jesus in the midst of desperate situations in life, but the rest of Scripture and all of history make it clear that his deliverance can take different forms. Sometimes he delivers us from immediate danger by prevention or healing. At other times he delivers us from ultimate danger by resurrection from the dead. When Paul said in 2 Timothy 4:18 that "the Lord will rescue me from every evil attack and will bring me safely to his heavenly kingdom," he must have been speaking about ultimate and final deliverance, since, as tradition tells us, he himself died a martyr's death. Perhaps now you can see why we need to "consult the biblical map" after identifying the theological principle, since knowing how the principle relates to the rest of the Bible can help us apply the message responsibly.

One of the most important things to remember when seeking to apply truths from these stories is that we should always keep the larger context in view.

What would be a legitimate application of the stories in Mark 4–5? How can we live out these stories in our day? Just before the second edition of *Grasping God's Word* went to print, an airplane carrying a group of students and faculty members from Ouachita Baptist University (a Christian liberal arts school in Arkansas where we both teach) crashed when returning from a ministry trip. One student and the daughter of a professor were killed. How might this group of Christians live out the message of Mark 4–5? Remember, these stories teach that (1) life is hard, (2) Jesus is sovereign over forces hostile to God, and (3) we should trust Jesus in the desperate situations of life.

Living out the first principle is rather easy: Life is hard! Christians should not expect to be exempt from difficult situations such as disease and death.

The second principle is much more difficult to apply. If Jesus calmed the storm for the first disciples, why didn't he "calm the storm" for our friends? We return again to the larger context. Even while on earth Jesus did not heal every sick person or raise every dead person. (We assume that even Jairus's daughter eventually died again.)

The first readers of Mark's Gospel were facing intense hostilities associated with living faithfully in a fallen world. When Mark communicates that Jesus is sovereign over forces hostile to God, we believe that he intends for his audience to understand this in an ultimate sense. Jesus' miracles are previews of what is to come, glimpses of what life will be like when his kingdom comes in all its fullness at his return.

The message of the whole New Testament is clear for those who have a relationship with God through Jesus Christ: in time "there will be no more death or mourning or crying or pain" (Rev. 21:4). If you consider this to be an empty and irrelevant application, have you considered what it would be like to face the same trouble in this life without any help from the Spirit of God or the body of Christ and without any hope of a new heaven and new earth?

This brings us to the third principle: faith in Jesus. When we speak of faith, we are speaking about a wholehearted trust in Jesus. Faith means hanging on to Jesus even when the immediate circumstances look bleak. Whether the deliverance is immediate or ultimate, we should have faith in Jesus because Jesus has been, is, and always will be faithful.

Let's return to Luke 10 for two more examples of how to apply the message of the Gospels. One principle we found in Luke 10:25–37 is that love for one's neighbor should transcend all human barriers. Even on Christian college campuses there are outcasts created by barriers of appearance, race, economic status, intelligence, social skills, and so on. This story calls us to love our way through such barriers—befriending a "less attractive" person, tutoring a struggling classmate, reaching out to an international student, or forgiving an obnoxious roommate. Jesus teaches us in this story that not even religious excuses are acceptable when we refuse to love our neighbor.

In the story of Mary and Martha in Luke 10:38–42 we discover the principle that doing good things for God can sometimes cause us to miss God. The application of this one is not hard to see. Consider these questions. Do we take time to listen to the Lord on a regular basis? Are we obsessed with religious activities to such an extent that our relationship with God is drying up? Have we learned how to say no to some good things in order to say yes to God's best? Jesus desires our fellowship, and that takes time.

To summarize, we have learned that we should read the Gospels in a way that matches how they were written. The evangelists wrote (1) to tell individual stories about Jesus and (2) to send a message to their readers (e.g., trust rather than fear) by the way they put these individual stories together into a larger story. We now turn our attention to special literary forms that you will encounter as you read the Gospels. Our two rules remain central, but we have a few tips for understanding these special forms.

SPECIAL LITERARY FORMS IN THE GOSPELS

As a teacher, Jesus would never have been accused of being boring. One reason he was such an engaging teacher was that he conveyed his message through a wide array of literary forms and techniques.[8] We cannot discuss them all, but we want to give you some guidelines for understanding Jesus' use of exaggeration, metaphor and simile, narrative irony, rhetorical questions, parallelism, and parables.

Exaggeration

As a master teacher, Jesus commonly used exaggeration (also called hyperbole) to connect in a powerful way with his listeners and drive home his point. Exaggeration occurs when a truth is overstated for the sake of effect to such an extent that a literal fulfillment is either impossible or completely ridiculous. Statements like "I studied forever for that test" or "I'm so hungry I could eat a horse" are examples of exaggeration. The student didn't really study forever, and the person may be hungry, but not that hungry. In both cases, however, an urgent message comes through. Here are a few examples from the Gospels.

> "If your right eye causes you to stumble, gouge it out and throw it away. . . . And if your right hand causes you to stumble, cut if off and throw it away. It is better for you to lose one part of your body than for your whole body to go into hell." (Matt. 5:29–30)

> "If anyone comes to me and does not hate father and mother, wife and children, brothers and sisters—yes, even their own life—such a person cannot be my disciple." (Luke 14:26)

> "Children, how hard it is to enter the kingdom of God! It is easier for a camel to go through the eye of a needle than for someone who is rich to enter the kingdom of God." (Mark 10:24b–25)

When you see exaggeration in the Gospels, do not force a literal interpretation or you will miss the real meaning of the passage. Imagine the awful implications of thinking that gouging out your right eye would actually cure the problem of lust. We should take Scripture seriously but not always literally. Figurative language can carry a meaning (and corresponding application) every bit as radical as anything literal.

8. You will find an excellent discussion of the different forms and techniques of Jesus' teaching in Robert H. Stein, *The Method and Message of Jesus' Teachings*, rev. ed. (Louisville: Westminster John Knox, 1994), 7–32.

When you encounter exaggeration, ask the simple question: "What's the real point here?" In Matthew 5:29–30 Jesus is telling his followers to take drastic steps to avoid sexual sin. In Luke 14:26 Jesus is making the point that our love for him should be so strong that, by comparison, our natural affection for our family members, and even ourselves, will appear as hate. In Mark 10:24b–25 Jesus uses exaggeration to point out how difficult it will be for rich people to enter the kingdom of God—more difficult, we might say, than squeezing a school bus through a keyhole.

To interpret exaggeration literally is to miss the point.

Metaphor and Simile

When Jesus says to his disciples, "You are the salt of the earth" (Matt. 5:13), or to the teachers of the law and the Pharisees, "You are like whitewashed tombs" (Matt. 23:27), he is using metaphor and simile respectively. Both literary vehicles make comparisons. With metaphor the comparison is implicit; with simile it is made explicit with words such as "like" or "as." The Gospels are full of metaphors and similes. "Be as shrewd as snakes and as innocent as doves" (Matt. 10:16). "I am the bread of life" (John 6:35). "Jerusalem, Jerusalem . . . how often I have longed to gather your children together, as a hen gathers her chicks under her wings, and you were not willing" (Luke 13:34). The list goes on.

When interpreting metaphors and similes, locate the intended point of the comparison. Disciples are compared to salt to underscore their responsibility to permeate and stop the decay in society. Teachers of the law and Pharisees are compared to whitewashed tombs in the sense that their outward appearance covers up spiritual decay going on underneath. You get the idea. Find the comparison intended by the author, and you have found the meaning of the metaphor or simile. It may help you to visualize the figure of speech since the visual image usually carries the emotional impact.

Be careful not to press the details of the comparison too far. Whether implicit in metaphor or explicit in simile, the comparison is usually made between things that are different (e.g., Jesus to bread, Jesus to a hen). They are compared to make a point. When pressed too far, the comparison breaks down and the point itself is lost, or worse yet, a thousand points blossom in its place—all unintended by the author.

Narrative Irony

Irony is grounded in the principle of contrast—contrast between what is expected and what actually happens. You might say there is an unexpected twist to the story. Someone hearing the story of Mary and Martha for the first time might expect Jesus to tell Mary to get up and help her sister, but as you know, that is not how things turn out. When the dust settles in Mark 4–5, the uncontrollable, demon-possessed man has been restored to his right mind, while the demon-possessed pigs (an appalling combination especially for Jews) return to the sea, the same sea that produced the original storm.

You will see irony at work in many of Jesus' stories. Consider the following parable from Luke 12:16–21:

> 16 And he told them this parable: "The ground of a certain rich man yielded an abundant harvest. 17 He thought to himself, 'What shall I do? I have no place to store my crops.'
>
> 18 "Then he said, 'This is what I'll do. I will tear down my barns and build bigger ones, and there I will store my surplus grain. 19 And I'll say to myself, "You have plenty of grain laid up for many years. Take life easy; eat, drink and be merry."'
>
> 20 "But God said to him, 'You fool! This very night your life will be demanded from you. Then who will get what you have prepared for yourself?'
>
> 21 "This is how it will be with whoever stores up things for themselves but is not rich toward God."

The primary interpretive goal in the case of irony is to notice it in the first place. After you detect irony, take time to reflect on the unexpected turn of events. What contrasts are present? What if things had actually turned out as expected? What does the twist in the story reveal about our own expectations?

By the way, what is the supreme example of irony recorded in the New Testament?

Rhetorical Questions

Jesus is fond of rhetorical questions, questions designed to make a point rather than to retrieve an answer. Here are some examples:

> "If you love those who love you, what reward will you get?" (Matt. 5:46)
>
> "Can any one of you by worrying add a single hour to your life?" (Matt. 6:27)
>
> "Why are you so afraid? Do you still have no faith?" (Mark 4:40)
>
> "Do you think I came to bring peace on earth?" (Luke 12:51)

Sometimes when Jesus asks a question, he is really making a statement.

When Jesus asks a rhetorical question, you don't get the feeling that he wants an answer. Rather, he is making a strong statement in a creative way. The best way to approach rhetorical questions is to turn them into statements. Look at how we might transform the above examples into statements:

> "You don't get any reward for loving only those who love you." (Matt 5:46)
>
> "You can't add a single hour to your life by worrying." (Matt. 6:27)
>
> "You are afraid and you still have no faith." (Mark 4:40)
>
> "I did not come to bring peace on the earth." (Luke 12:51)

By transforming rhetorical questions into statements, you will clearly see what Jesus intended to communicate.

Parallelism

Poetic parallelism is an expression we use to describe a relationship between two or more lines of text. The use of parallelism reminds us to read the lines together as a unit of thought, never separating one line from the other. The lines belong together and should be read together. This is a major feature of Old Testament poetry, and we will discuss this feature in more detail in chapter 20. However, you will also encounter several types of parallelism in the Gospels.

Synonymous—the lines say basically the same thing in a similar way:

> "Ask and it will be given to you;
> seek and you will find;
> knock and the door will be opened to you." (Matt. 7:7)
>
> "For whatever is hidden is meant to be disclosed,
> and whatever is concealed is meant to be brought out into the open." (Mark 4:22)

Contrastive—the second line contrasts with the first line:

> "Whoever has will be given more;
> whoever does not have, even what they have will be taken from them." (Mark 4:25)
>
> "A good man brings good things out of the good stored up in him,
> and an evil man brings evil things out of the evil stored up in him." (Matt. 12:35)

Developmental—the second line repeats part of the first line, then advances the thought of the first line to a climax:

"Anyone who welcomes you welcomes me,
  and anyone who welcomes me welcomes the one who sent me." (Matt. 10:40)

"All those the Father gives me will come to me,
  and whoever comes to me I will never drive away." (John 6:37)

Parables

One of Jesus' favorite literary techniques was the parable. You're probably familiar with the stories about the good Samaritan, the lost son, the wheat and the weeds—a few of Jesus' most famous parables. A *parable* is a story with two levels of meaning, where certain details in the story represent something else (e.g., in the parable of the lost son, the father represents God). The difficulty is to know how many details in the story should stand for other things.

A *parable* is a story with two levels of meaning, where certain details in the story represent something else.

Throughout the centuries some Christians have taken great liberty with the parables by making almost every detail in each story stand for something. Perhaps the most famous example of such allegorization is the treatment of the parable of the good Samaritan by the early church leader Augustine.[9]

the man going down to Jericho	=	Adam
Jerusalem	=	the heavenly city from which Adam fell
Jericho	=	the moon (signifying Adam's mortality)
robbers	=	the devil and his angels
stripping him	=	taking away his immortality
beating him	=	persuading him to sin
leaving him half dead	=	as a man lives, but is dead spiritually; therefore, he is half dead
priest and Levite	=	priesthood and ministry of the Old Testament
the Samaritan	=	Christ himself
binding of the wounds	=	binding the restraint of sin
wine	=	exhortation to work with fervent spirit

9. Cited in Gordon D. Fee and Douglas K. Stuart, *How to Read the Bible for All Its Worth*, 4th ed. (Grand Rapids: Zondervan, 2014), 155.

beast	=	flesh of Christ's incarnation
the inn	=	the church
two denarii	=	promise of this life and life to come
innkeeper	=	the apostle Paul

You can see why this approach would prove problematic. Few, if any, interpreters would agree on exact details, resulting in a wide variety of interpretations, with some clearly contradicting others. Also, by ignoring the context, interpreters could read into almost any parable a meaning that would have nothing to do with what Jesus intended for his original audience. In Augustine's allegorization he misses Jesus' point to love your neighbor.

The one-point approach for parables appears to us to be inadequate.

Since the late nineteenth century, a majority of New Testament scholars have insisted that every parable makes essentially one point, which usually comes at the end. This has been a welcome corrective to the absurdity of unrestrained allegorization used by Augustine and others. But does the "one-point rule" restrict meaning more than Jesus would have intended? Take the parable of the lost son as an example. What is the one point? Does the one point that comes to your mind deal with the rebellious son, the resentful brother, or the forgiving father? Do you really want to pick just one and say that Jesus did not intend to make a point about the other two? The one-point approach appears to us to be inadequate. After all, not many stories of any kind make only one point.

Evangelical scholar Craig Blomberg offers a more balanced approach to interpreting the parables.[10] Jesus' parables are not to be allegorized down to the last microscopic detail, but neither are they to be limited to only one point. Following Blomberg, we suggest two principles for interpreting Jesus' parables.

(1) Look for one main point for each main character or group of characters. Most parables will make one, perhaps two, but usually not more than three main points. All the other details are there to enhance the story. Looking at the parable of the lost son (Luke 15:11–32), we can see how this interpretive guideline helps us identify three main points, one for each main character.

Rebellious son	Sinners may confess their sins and turn to God in repentance.
Forgiving father	God offers forgiveness for undeserving people.
Resentful brother	Those who claim to be God's people should not be resentful when God extends his grace to the undeserving.

10. Craig L. Blomberg, *Interpreting the Parables*, 2nd ed. (Downers Grove, IL: InterVarsity Press, 2012).

Here is how the same principle might apply to the parable of the good Samaritan (Luke 10:25–37):

Man beaten by robbers	Even enemies (here Samaritans) can show love.
Jewish religious leaders	Even religious duty is no excuse for lovelessness.
Samaritan	Even a "hated foreigner" can serve as a model of love.

(2) In addition, the main points you discover must be ones that Jesus' original audience would have understood. If we come up with a point that Jesus' audience would not grasp, we have probably missed his point. This guideline is intended to keep us from reading into Jesus' parables what he never intended in the first place.

Whenever we read the Gospels, we must reflect on how to apply their message to our lives. When we truly grasp God's Word, we will do more than read and interpret; we will allow the great truths taught by Jesus to penetrate our hearts and minds and make a real difference in how we live.

CONCLUSION

God chose to give us four accounts of the good news of Jesus Christ—Matthew, Mark, Luke, and John. As we take the Gospels through the Interpretive Journey, it is important to realize that we are dealing with *christological biography*—stories about Jesus told for a particular purpose. To get across the principlizing bridge, we should ask two basic questions: What is the main message of each episode? and What is the gospel writer trying to communicate by the way he puts the smaller stories together? Since you will be able to draw principles from both levels, we have looked at how to read individual stories and how to read a series of stories.

We also learned in this chapter that grasping God's Word does not stop when we cross the river of differences between the biblical audience and today. We must wrestle with how to relate the great truths of the Gospels to the rest of the Bible and learn how to live out Jesus' teachings ourselves. Developing legitimate applications of some principles will be straightforward and rather easy; for others it will be complex and difficult (as in the case of the tragedy of the fall). We close this chapter with gratitude that we have the good news of Jesus written down so that we may pick up the Book at any time and read and apply it. As we grasp God's Word, we also feel God taking hold of us and using us to bring glory to his name.

ASSIGNMENTS

Assignment 15–1: Interpreting a Story

Apply the two interpretive questions we used to read the Gospels to Matthew 24:43–25:13 or to another section of the Gospels selected by your teacher. Photocopy this page and record your findings in the chart below.

Matt. 24:43–44	Matt. 24:45–51	Matt. 25:1–13

Assignment 15–2: Interpreting a Parable

Interpret the parable of the great banquet in Luke 14:15–24 or the parable of the unjust judge and the persistent widow in Luke 18:1–8 according to the interpretive principles explained in this chapter in the section dealing with parables.

Assignment 15–3: Reading about the Kingdom of God

One of Jesus' most frequent teaching topics was the kingdom of God. By reading one or both of the following articles on the kingdom of God in the teachings of Jesus, your understanding of the Gospels will be greatly enhanced:

Fee, Gordon D., and Douglas Stuart. "A Final, Very Important Word." In *How to Read the Bible for All Its Worth*, 4th ed., 150–53. Grand Rapids: Zondervan, 2014.

Stein, Robert H. "The Content of Jesus' Teaching: The Kingdom of God." In *The Method and Message of Jesus' Teachings*, rev. ed., 60–81. Louisville: Westminster John Knox, 1994.

CHAPTER 16

NEW TESTAMENT—ACTS

INTRODUCTION

While we have four versions of the life and ministry of Jesus Christ (the four Gospels), we have only one account of the birth and growth of the early church. That makes Acts—our one story of the spread of Christianity across the New Testament world—unique and indispensable! Traditionally this book that bridges the gap between the Gospels and the New Testament letters has been known as the "Acts of the Apostles." Since Luke focuses on Peter and Paul and lesser-known characters like Stephen and Philip much more than the original twelve disciples/apostles, a more precise title might be "The Continuing Acts of Jesus by His Spirit through the Apostles and Other Early Christian Leaders." But that's far too long, and it's easy to see why most people prefer the name "Acts" (i.e., deeds or actions). The book of Acts shows us and tells us how God worked through the early church to change the world.

Acts: "The Continuing Acts of Jesus by His Spirit through the Apostles and Other Early Christian Leaders."

In Acts we read about the Holy Spirit's coming to empower believers, about Peter's Pentecostal sermon where thousands are saved, about signs and wonders, and about a vibrant Christian community. We read of Stephen's dying for his faith, of Philip's carrying the gospel to the Samaritans, and of Paul's famous missionary journeys, leading him eventually to Rome. In the gospel of Luke, Jesus had to go to Jerusalem to accomplish salvation for the entire world. In Acts the good news of that salvation goes forth from Jerusalem to the ends of the earth. As a record of how the gospel marched triumphantly from Jerusalem to Rome, Acts is packed with spiritual power and adventure. Who wouldn't want to read Acts?

Along with the adventure, Acts carries its own set of interpretive challenges. How does Acts relate to the Gospel of Luke (the two books were written by the same person)? Is Acts merely a record of what happened (history), or does it also promote the Christian belief about God (theology)? Why did Luke write Acts, and how does its message relate to us? How did Luke organize Acts? And most important, how do we grasp the message of Acts?

Is Acts normative or descriptive?

This last question is particularly timely because of our tendency to idealize the early church, thinking of it as bigger than life. We forget that the early church included people with sins, weaknesses, and problems—people just like us. We tend to look to Acts as the blueprint for the church of all ages. This raises the central interpretive question related to grasping the message of Acts: Should we take Acts as *normative*, so that the church in every age should imitate the experiences and practices of the early church? Or should we read Acts as merely *descriptive* of what was valuable and inspiring in the early church, but not necessarily binding on us today? In this chapter we will meet these interpretive questions head-on and offer you insight into reading one of the greatest real-life adventure stories of all time.

ACTS: A SEQUEL TO LUKE

Most scholars believe that the author of the Gospel of Luke also wrote Acts and that he intended to produce a single work in two parts: *Luke-Acts*. Originally these two volumes even circulated among the churches as a single work, but in the second century the Gospel of Luke joined the other three Gospels, and Acts began to circulate on its own. There are some strong indications that Luke intended to link these two books closely together in telling the story.

1. The opening verses of the two books imply a connection:

> [1]Many have undertaken to draw up an account of the things that have been fulfilled among us, [2]just as they were handed down to us by those who from the first were eyewitnesses and servants of the word. [3]With this in mind, since I myself have carefully investigated everything from the beginning, I too decided

> to write an orderly account for you, most excellent Theophilus, [4]so that you may know the certainty of the things you have been taught. (Luke 1:1–4)

> [1]In my former book, Theophilus, I wrote about all that Jesus began to do and to teach [2]until the day he was taken up to heaven, after giving instructions through the Holy Spirit to the apostles he had chosen. (Acts 1:1–2)

Luke's reference in Acts 1:1 to his "former book" obviously refers to the Gospel of Luke, where he "wrote about all that Jesus began to do and to teach." In the sequel (Acts), Luke continues the story by showing how Jesus acted by his Spirit through his church. In addition, you will notice that Luke dedicates both volumes to Theophilus (more on him later).

2. Thematic and structural parallels exist between the two books. Some of the prominent themes of Luke's Gospel reoccur in Acts (e.g., prayer, the work of the Spirit, the gospel for all people). Certain miracles in Acts closely resemble miracles in Luke (compare the healing of Aeneas in Acts 9:32–35 with the healing of the paralytic in Luke 5:17–26; the raising of Tabitha from the dead in Acts 9:36–43 with the raising of Jairus's daughter in Luke 8:40–42, 49–56).[1] Both Luke and Acts feature a journey motif. In the Gospel Jesus journeys to Jerusalem and the cross (Luke 9:51; 13:22, 33; 17:11; 18:31; 19:41). In Acts Paul makes a number of journeys, the climactic one being his journey from Judea to Rome for a trial before Caesar (Acts 27–28).

3. The ending of Luke overlaps the beginning of Acts. Jesus' words to his disciples in Luke 24:49—"I am going to send you what my Father has promised; but stay in the city until you have been clothed with power from on high"—are certainly fulfilled in Acts 1–2. When Jesus speaks about repentance and forgiveness of sins being preached in his name to all nations, beginning in Jerusalem (Luke 24:47), we automatically think of Acts 1:8. Perhaps the most noticeable overlap is the record of the ascension of Jesus in both Luke (24:51) and Acts (1:9–11), the only two places in the New Testament where this event is described.

Luke and Acts are really two parts of a single story.

Luke links his Gospel and Acts closely together as two parts of a single story. The God who acted in mighty ways in the Old Testament and revealed himself supremely in Jesus Christ is now at work by his Spirit. Luke presents to us the grand story of God's salvation. We should always remember, therefore, to read Acts as a continuation of the story that started in Luke's Gospel.

1. These examples are cited in William W. Klein, Craig L. Blomberg, and Robert L. Hubbard Jr., *Introduction to Biblical Interpretation*, 4th ed. (Grand Rapids: Zondervan, 2017), 536.

What Jesus began to do during his ministry on earth he now continues to do through his Spirit-empowered followers. As a practical matter, before you study Acts, you might take time to read through the Gospel of Luke.

WHAT KIND OF BOOK IS ACTS?

1. Acts Is a Story

Like the Gospels, Acts is a narrative. Does it differ from the Gospels? You will remember that we described the Gospels as *theological* (or more specifically *christological*) *biographies*. The evangelists wrote with two central purposes in mind: (1) to tell about Jesus, and (2) to send a message to their readers by the way they arranged the individual stories into a larger story. Because of the close connection between Luke and Acts, we can expect these two books to have much in common when it comes to literary type. That is indeed the case. Much of what we said about how to read the Gospels applies to Acts as well, including the two main interpretive questions. The primary difference is that the Gospels concentrate on one person, Jesus of Nazareth, while the story in Acts focuses on several key church leaders, mainly Peter and Paul.

2. Acts Is Theological History

As Luke widens his angle from Jesus to the early church leaders, he moves from *theological biography* in his Gospel to *theological history* in Acts. Luke is a *historian* who composes a reliable record of what happened in the outreach of the gospel. We should not assume, of course, that Luke approved of everything that happened. As in the Old Testament historical books, people sometimes did things God did not endorse. When Luke describes something that happens (e.g., Paul's quarrel with Barnabas in Acts 15:36–40), we need to resist the temptation to turn this into the approved plan of God.

As Luke widens his angle from Jesus to the early church leaders, he moves from *theological biography* in his Gospel to *theological history* in Acts.

As well as being a historian, Luke is also a *theologian* who tells his story for the purpose of advancing the Christian faith. Is it possible to be both a historian and a theologian? We believe it is. All history writing is selective (i.e., you can't possibly tell everything that happens) and is written from some faith perspective. Historians are not neutral observers without any belief system. They are human and have a point of view just like the rest of us. Their viewpoint (including some faith perspective) influences the way they interpret events, select what to include, and shape their story. In Acts, Luke gives us accurate, reliable history, but he has selected and arranged his material for theological purposes.

In the speeches of Acts, for example, Luke tells what really happened (history) for theological purposes. Speeches make up approximately one-fourth to one-third of the entire book, making Acts truly a continuation of "all that Jesus began to *do* and to *teach*" (Acts 1:1). We should not suppose that all of the speeches of Acts are verbatim accounts since (a) Luke was not present to hear every speech, (b) he possessed no tape recorder, and (c) they are far too short to be complete transcriptions. As an example of this last point, in Acts 3 Peter began preaching shortly after 3:00 p.m. (3:1) and quit sometime that evening (4:3), but Luke takes only fifteen verses to capture Peter's lengthy sermon (3:12–26). The speeches are reliable summaries of what was actually said. Luke does not create them out of thin air, but he does paraphrase in ways that advance his theological purpose of telling the story of God's salvation.

The single most helpful guideline for grasping the theological truths of Acts is to look for repeated themes and patterns.

Luke shapes his story for theological purposes, but how are we supposed to discern those purposes as we read the book of Acts? To put it more generally, how do we locate theology in a story? We use many of the same principles that we used to find theological principles in the Gospels. We ask the standard narrative questions, pay attention to instructions from the author, concentrate on direct discourse, and so on.

Perhaps the single most helpful guideline for grasping the theological truths of Acts is to look for repeated themes and patterns. In the major themes of Acts, you can see Luke working out his theological purposes. When you find Luke's theological purposes, you also find the heart of his message to his original audience and to us. We turn now to survey some of the major themes in Acts.

WHY DID LUKE WRITE ACTS?

Acts is a kind of comprehensive discipleship manual, designed to reinforce the Christian faith for new believers.

Luke states his purpose for Luke-Acts in the first few verses of his Gospel. Both volumes are addressed to the "most excellent Theophilus," likely a recent convert to Christianity of high social standing and perhaps the person who gave Luke the money to publish these two books. Luke writes his account "so that you [Theophilus] may know the certainty of the things you have been taught" (Luke 1:4). Presumably Theophilus has received instruction (*katēcheō*, meaning "to teach") that was not entirely adequate. Luke wants to encourage and establish Theophilus and others like him more fully in their new faith.

Perhaps we should think of Acts as a kind of comprehensive discipleship manual, designed to reinforce the Christian faith for new believers. Luke does this by showing these new believers that what God promised in the Old Testament and fulfilled in Jesus, he now continues to work out. In short, the *Holy Spirit* empowers the *church* (both Jewish and gentile believers) to take the *gospel* of Jesus Christ to the *world* (Acts 1:8).

Spirit → Church → Gospel → World

This is biblical history at its finest, painted in broad strokes to assure Christians that they are part of God's grand plan. We can hear Luke saying to believers, "You're on the right track. You're truly part of what God is doing. Don't give up!" Luke's overarching purpose surfaces in a number of subpurposes or themes. Let's look briefly at a few of them.

1. The Holy Spirit

The whole operation starts with the Spirit of God. In Acts 1 Jesus promises that the Father will send the Holy Spirit. At Pentecost (Acts 2) the Spirit descends to indwell and empower the disciples of Jesus. The rest of the book is a record of the acts or deeds of the Spirit through the church. The Spirit empowers believers for witness (4:8, 31), guides them (8:29, 39; 10:19; 16:6–7; 20:22), breaks down barriers (10:44–46), sets believers apart for mission (13:2), and so on. What Jesus began to do (the gospel), he continues to do through his Spirit.

2. God's Sovereignty

Closely related to the Spirit's role in guiding the church is the theme of God's sovereignty. When you read Acts, you are left with the strong sense that God is in control. The Old Testament Scriptures are fulfilled as God works out his plan (e.g., Acts 1:16; 2:16–21, 25–28, 34–35; 4:24–26; 13:32–37, 47). God's will has been accomplished through Jesus (2:23–24), and his purpose is being accomplished through his people. He overrules imprisonment (4:23–31), human travel plans (16:6–10), the powerful Jewish Sanhedrin (23:11), and even violent storms at sea (27:13–44) to advance his cause. The apostles perform signs and wonders by the power of God. But, as John Stott reminds us, God's sovereign work is for the sake of the gospel message, not always for the comfort and convenience of its messengers: "So by God's providence Paul reached Rome safe and sound. But he arrived as a prisoner! Christ's promise that he would testify in Rome had not included that information."[2]

2. John R. W. Stott, *The Spirit, the Church, and the World* (Downers Grove, IL: InterVarsity Press, 1990), 402.

3. The Church

The Spirit works chiefly through the church (the people of God) to accomplish his will. As the following summaries illustrate, the Spirit creates a healthy, thriving community where people worship God, care for each other, grow spiritually, and join in the mission:

> [42]They devoted themselves to the apostles' teaching and to fellowship, to the breaking of bread and to prayer. [43]Everyone was filled with awe at the many wonders and signs performed by the apostles. [44]All the believers were together and had everything in common. [45]They sold property and possessions to give to anyone who had need. [46]Every day they continued to meet together in the temple courts. They broke bread in their homes and ate together with glad and sincere hearts, [47]praising God and enjoying the favor of all the people. And the Lord added to their number daily those who were being saved. (Acts 2:42–47)

> [32]All the believers were one in heart and mind. No one claimed that any of their possessions was their own, but they shared everything they had. [33]With great power the apostles continued to testify to the resurrection of the Lord Jesus. And God's grace was so powerfully at work in them all [34]that there were no needy persons among them. For from time to time those who owned land or houses sold them, brought the money from the sales [35]and put it at the apostles' feet, and it was distributed to anyone who had need. (Acts 4:32–35)

The early Christians were marked as people of prayer, and you will find them praying in almost every chapter of Acts.

4. Prayer

As in the Gospel of Luke, prayer is a major theme in Acts. The early Christians were marked as people of prayer, and you will find them praying in almost every chapter of Acts. The church is born out of a prayer meeting (1:14). They pray when facing opposition and danger (4:24; 12:5; 16:25; 18:9, 10). They pray for God's guidance (1:24; 9:11; 22:17–18). They pray for each other's spiritual needs (8:15; 19:6). They minister to the sick and hopeless through prayer (9:40; 16:16; 28:8). They pray when they commission persons for special service (6:6; 13:3; 14:23). They pray when saying goodbye (20:36; 21:5). They pray when facing death (7:59–60). Prayer is central to the life of the early church.[3]

3. Robert E. Coleman, *The Master Plan of Discipleship* (Grand Rapids: Revell, 1987), 108.

5. Suffering

As we read about wonderful things that God is doing in Acts, we sometimes lose sight of the price paid by the early Christians. They suffer imprisonment, beatings, and rejection; they face angry mobs, violent storms, persecution, and even death (e.g., 5:41; 7:59–60; 9:15–16; 12:4; 14:22; 16:22–23; 20:23–24; 21:30–33; 27:13–44). Paul's words to the Ephesian elders are typical of the early Christian belief that suffering was the rule rather than the exception:

> [23]"I only know that in every city the Holy Spirit warns me that prison and hardships are facing me. [24]However, I consider my life worth nothing to me; my only aim is to finish the race and complete the task the Lord Jesus has given me—the task of testifying to the good news of God's grace." (Acts 20:23–24)

In spite of such hardships, the gospel advances.

6. Gentiles

In Acts the gospel comes first to the Jews, but it spreads quickly "to the ends of the earth" (Acts 1:8)—to gentile country. (A *gentile* is anyone who is not an ethnic Jew.) The true Israel of God is made up of Jews *and* gentiles who have accepted Jesus the Messiah. In his Pentecostal sermon, Peter quotes the prophet Joel, who says, "I will pour out my Spirit on *all people*. . . . And *everyone* who calls on the name of the Lord will be saved" (2:17b, 21). Peter later realizes that God is serious about a mission that includes gentiles. After seeing the Spirit come on the Samaritans (8:14–17) and the gentiles (10:1–48), he confesses: "I now realize how true it is that God does not show favoritism but accepts from every nation the one who fears him and does what is right" (10:34–35). The narrative movement in Acts is from Jerusalem to Rome, from Peter to Paul, from Jew only to Jew and gentile.

7. Witness

The apostles focus their witness on the resurrection of Jesus from the dead (e.g., 1:9, 22; 2:32–36; 4:2, 20, 33; 5:20, 32, 42; 10:39–41). Acts 3:15 is typical: "You killed the author of life, but God raised him from the dead. We are witnesses of this." The empowering of the Spirit for witness does not stop with the apostles. Stephen is faithful in his witness (*martys*) to the very end (6:8–8:1; 22:20). Philip preaches "the good news of the kingdom of God and the name of Jesus Christ" (8:12, 35, 40). Paul is charged by the risen Lord to carry the gospel to the gentiles (9:15), and his witness occupies the second half of the story. Luke's message in Acts is clear: to be a follower of Jesus Christ means to be a faithful witness.

HOW IS ACTS ORGANIZED?

Acts 1:8 holds the key to understanding how the entire book unfolds: "But you will receive power when the Holy Spirit comes on you; and you will be my witnesses in *Jerusalem*, and in all *Judea and Samaria*, and to the *ends of the earth*." The good news of Jesus is first preached to the Jews in and around Jerusalem (chs. 1–12) before spreading to the gentiles (chs. 13–28). The outline below illustrates Luke's account of the triumphant expansion of the gospel from Jerusalem (the heart of Israel) to Rome (the heart of the empire).

1–12	**The Christian Mission to Jews**	**Location**
1	Preparation for Pentecost	*in Jerusalem*
2	Pentecost: The Coming of the Holy Spirit	
3–4	The Spirit Works through the Apostles	
5–6	Threats to the Church	
6–8	Stephen the First Martyr	*in Judea and Samaria*
8	Philip the Evangelist	
9	The Conversion of Paul	
9–11	The Ministry of Peter beyond Jerusalem	
11	Christianity Comes to Antioch	
12	The Gospel Spreads in Spite of Obstacles	
13–28	**The Christian Mission to Gentiles**	
13–14	Paul's First Missionary Journey	*to the ends of the earth*
15	The Jerusalem Council	
15–18	Paul's Second Missionary Journey	
18–21	Paul's Third Missionary Journey	
21–23	Paul's Witness in Jerusalem	
24–26	Paul's Witness in Caesarea	
27–28	Paul's Witness in Rome	

While Peter is the leading figure in the mission to the Jews in Acts 1–12, the attention shifts to Paul in Acts 13–28 as the gospel moves to "the ends of the earth" (1:8). Actually the leading figure in all of Acts is the Spirit of God, who works in both

Peter and Paul in similar ways. We see this when we compare some of the parallels between Peter and Paul in the book of Acts. (Here we have another example of how a biblical author uses the technique of comparison to move a story forward.)

Peter	**Paul**
Peter's sermon at Pentecost (2:22–36)	Paul's sermon at Pisidian Antioch (13:26–41)
Healing of a lame man (3:1–10)	Healing of a lame man (14:8–11)
Shaking of a building by prayer (4:31)	Shaking of a building by praise (16:25–26)
Rebuke of Ananias and Sapphira (5:1–11)	Rebuke of Elymas (13:8–12)
Healing by the shadow of Peter (5:15–16)	Healing by the handkerchiefs of Paul (19:11–12)
Laying on of hands (8:17)	Laying on of hands (19:6)
Rebuke of Simon the sorcerer (8:18–24)	Rebuke of Jewish sorcerer (13:6–11)
Resuscitation of Tabitha (9:36–42)	Resuscitation of Eutychus (20:7–12)
Removal of chains in prison (12:5–7)	Removal of chains in prison (16:25–28)

In addition, Luke pauses throughout his story to summarize the progress of the gospel and the growth of the Christian community. There are five such summaries:

- 6:7: "So the word of God spread. The number of disciples in Jerusalem increased rapidly, and a large number of priests became obedient to the faith."
- 9:31: "Then the church throughout Judea, Galilee and Samaria enjoyed a time of peace and was strengthened. Living in the fear of the Lord and encouraged by the Holy Spirit, it increased in numbers.
- 12:24: "But the word of God continued to spread and flourish."
- 16:5: "So the churches were strengthened in the faith and grew daily in numbers."
- 19:20: "In this way the word of the Lord spread widely and grew in power."

In the very last verses of Acts (28:30–31), with Paul now in Rome, Luke writes:

> 30For two whole years Paul stayed there in his own rented house and welcomed all who came to see him. 31He proclaimed the kingdom of God and taught about the Lord Jesus Christ—with all boldness and without hindrance!

In the Greek text (and several major English translations) the word we translate "without hindrance" is actually the last word in the book. What a way to finish! Paul may be in prison, but the gospel of Jesus Christ marches on—"without hindrance"!

GRASPING THE MESSAGE OF ACTS

Since Acts is narrative, we should approach it in much the same way that we approached the Gospels. The two interpretive questions remain central. (1) What is the central message of each episode? (2) What is Luke telling his readers by the way he puts the individual stories and speeches together to form the larger narrative?

To find theological principles in the individual episodes of Acts, we should focus on the standard narrative questions: Who? What? When? Where? Why? and How? These provide a simple plan for understanding any story. When looking for theological principles in a series of episodes, look for connections between the stories. How are the stories positioned? What does the length of each episode tell us about what Luke thinks is important? Above all, what themes and patterns are repeated throughout Acts?

Still, when it comes to reading and applying Acts, we face one major interpretive challenge that we did not have to deal with when reading the Gospels, even though both are narrative. In the Gospels we read about Jesus and his original disciples without ever once thinking that we will be in that same situation. We will never get into a boat with Jesus to cross the Sea of Galilee or walk with him through the streets of Jerusalem. In Acts, however, the situation is different. From the Gospels to Acts there is a major shift in biblical history from the period of Jesus' ministry on earth to the period of the Spirit's ministry through the church. And as believing readers, we are part of that Spirit-driven church! Here comes the tricky part.

Should we take Acts as *normative*, so that the church of all times should imitate the experiences and practices of the early church? Or should we read Acts as merely *descriptive* of what was valuable and inspiring in the early church but not necessarily binding on us today? Without a doubt this is the most significant issue we face as we learn to interpret Acts.

On the one hand, if we read Acts as purely descriptive, then why bother reading it at all? Would a mere description of the way things were in the early church have anything at all to contribute to us? Besides, Luke gives us no clue that he understands the time of the early church as completely unique and unrepeatable. If, on the other hand, we take Acts as normative, do we have to repeat *all* the practices of the early church, including the rivalries, immoralities, and heresies? Do we have to make decisions by casting lots? Do we have to pool our possessions? Will God judge us like he judged Ananias and Sapphira (sudden death for lying)? Should we read Acts as normative or descriptive?

In making the Interpretive Journey in the book of Acts, we believe that a *both-and* approach works best (i.e., take some parts of Acts as normative and other parts as descriptive). This means that crossing the principlizing bridge in Acts is complicated by nature. The difficulty lies in knowing what is normative for the church today and what is not. On what basis should we make these decisions? Unless we think through this issue, we will almost certainly pick and choose based on how we feel at the time.

We offer the following guidelines for determining what in Acts is normative for today's church.

How do we know what in Acts is normative for the church today and what is not?

1. Look for what Luke intended to communicate to his readers. When we find the message Luke has intended, we find the normative meaning of the passage. In Acts 8, for example, we read about the conversion and baptism of the Samaritans and the Ethiopian eunuch during the ministry of Philip. After reading this account, we cannot help but ask several questions. What was the nature of sorcery? Why didn't the Spirit come on the Samaritans at the time they believed? Did Simon lose his salvation, or was he never really saved in the first place? How did the angel of the Lord speak to Philip? How much water is necessary for a proper baptism? When the text says, "the Spirit of the Lord suddenly took Philip away" (v. 39), what does that mean exactly?

These are fair questions, but they are not at the heart of what Luke intends to communicate in this chapter. We agree with Klein, Blomberg, and Hubbard concerning Luke's intent in Acts 8.

> This passage occurs in the section of his outline that concentrates on how the gospel began to leave exclusively Jewish territory. Thus, the two most striking features of Acts 8 become the reception of Philip's message first by *Samaritans* and then by a *eunuch*, both considered ritually unclean by orthodox Jews. The main applications of Acts 8 for Christian living today, therefore, should not center on the timing of the arrival of the Holy Spirit and its effects, nor on debates about how much water one needs for baptism, or how quickly it should follow on conversion. Rather, these texts should call all Christians today to determine who the Samaritans and eunuchs are in our world. Christian ministry must not neglect today's "untouchables" or outcasts—AIDS victims, the homeless, unwed mothers, drug addicts, gang members, and the like.[4]

4. Klein, Blomberg, and Hubbard, *Introduction to Biblical Interpretation*, 535.

We cannot always know Luke's intent for certain, but we can look for common themes and patterns that connect the stories. Here we will discover Luke's message to his readers (and to us). We might ask, ***What do Samaritans and eunuchs have in common?*** Samaritans were "half-breeds" and eunuchs were physical rejects; both groups were considered religious and social outcasts to one degree or another. The normative message from Luke is that the gospel of Jesus Christ destroys human barriers that are used to keep people from God. God accepts us not because we have developed a perfect body or have been born in a certain part of the world, but because of what he has done for us through his Son Jesus. The intent of the author should take precedence over our own curiosity when looking for what is normative in Acts.

2. Look for positive and negative examples in the characters of the story. It makes sense that Luke would want us to imitate positive characters like Stephen, Barnabas, Lydia, and Silas but not want us to follow in the footsteps of people like Ananias and Sapphira, Simon the sorcerer, and King Agrippa. Luke probably intends that most of what is done by the Christians in the story of Acts should be taken as normative for future generations of Christians.[5] This will not always be the case (e.g., John Mark's desertion of the mission team in 13:13; cf. 15:38), but it's a good rule of thumb.

This guideline of following positive role models and avoiding negative ones raises an important issue when it comes to the apostles. With the exception of Acts 14:4, 14, where Paul and Barnabas are called "apostles," Luke restricts the term *apostle* to the original twelve men chosen by Jesus.[6] Peter explains the qualifications for an apostle in Acts 1, where Matthias is chosen to replace Judas, who had abandoned his position:

> 21"Therefore it is necessary to choose one of the men who have been with us the whole time the Lord Jesus was living among us, 22beginning from John's baptism to the time when Jesus was taken up from us. For one of these must become a witness with us of his resurrection." (Acts 1:21–22)

In this sense apostleship is unique and not something we can repeat. Remember the phase of the Interpretive Journey where we identified the differences between the biblical audience and us? Apostleship is part of the river of differences. Simply put, we are not apostles. We would expect the Lord to do unusual signs and wonders through the apostles at this special stage of salvation history, and indeed this is the case, as most of the miracles in Acts come through the hands of the apostles.

5. Ben Witherington III, *The Acts of the Apostles: A Socio-Rhetorical Commentary* (Grand Rapids: Eerdmans), 99.

6. In Paul's letters, the range of meaning for *apostle* broadens to include those who have received a commission from the Lord for special service (e.g., Rom. 16:7; Eph. 4:11).

But the Lord also enabled Stephen (6:8), Philip (8:6), and Barnabas (14:3; 15:12) to perform signs and wonders, and these men were not members of the original Twelve (although Barnabas is called an apostle in the broader sense). Our aim here is not to restrict the work of the Spirit through an overly narrow interpretive method, but we do not see Luke demanding that every character in Acts must perform an "apostolic" miracle in order to qualify as a faithful follower of Christ. Many characters in Acts offer a positive (and we suggest normative) example without performing "signs and wonders." You also get the distinct impression when reading Acts that Luke views the greatest miracle as the supernatural work of the Spirit on the human heart, as people respond to the gospel of Jesus Christ.

When looking for what is normative, Luke's main emphasis should take precedence over our own fascination with details in the story.

3. Read individual passages in light of the overall story of Acts and the rest of the New Testament. In some cases the progression of the whole story will offer clear boundaries for determining what is normative in specific passages. We should not claim as normative any interpretation that fails to honor the overall movement of the story. Let's say, for example, that you are studying Acts 19:1–7 and are wondering about Paul's question in verse 2: "Did you receive the Holy Spirit when you believed?"

> [1]While Apollos was at Corinth, Paul took the road through the interior and arrived at Ephesus. There he found some disciples [2]and asked them, "Did you receive the Holy Spirit when you believed?"
>
> They answered, "No, we have not even heard that there is a Holy Spirit."
>
> [3]So Paul asked, "Then what baptism did you receive?"
>
> "John's baptism," they replied.
>
> [4]Paul said, "John's baptism was a baptism of repentance. He told the people to believe in the one coming after him, that is, in Jesus." [5]On hearing this, they were baptized in the name of the Lord Jesus. [6]When Paul placed his hands on them, the Holy Spirit came on them, and they spoke in tongues and prophesied. [7]There were about twelve men in all.

Should we interpret this text to support a two-stage conversion as normative for all Christians? In other words, should we expect all Christians first to believe in Jesus (stage 1) and later to receive the Holy Spirit (stage 2)?

The framework of the larger story suggested by Acts 1:8 (Jerusalem, Judea and Samaria, ends of the earth) argues that we should not interpret a two-stage conversion as normative. As you can see from the following diagram, the story of Acts shows the Spirit being poured out on believers in national and racial stages: first Jews, then Samaritans, and finally gentiles. This is simply the way the story of biblical history unfolds.

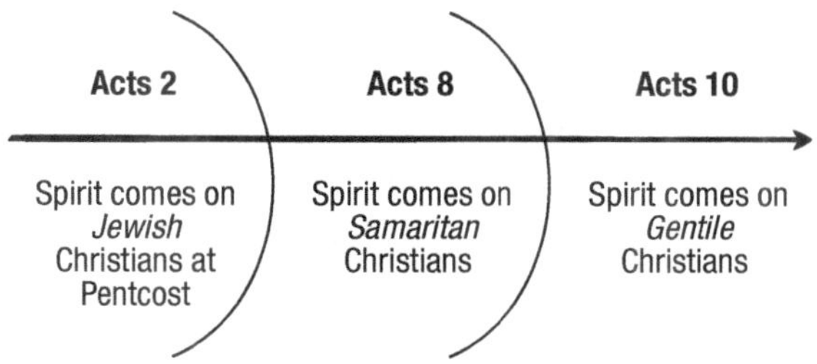

Once we move past Acts 10, there are no more ethnic barriers to overcome. From that point on, believing in Jesus and receiving the Spirit seem to be part of a single experience (Acts 11:17; Rom. 8:9b). On closer inspection, the same holds true for the passage in Acts 19. Paul's questions indicate that the "disciples" he encountered at Ephesus were not yet believers in Jesus, but rather followers of John the Baptist. They were unaware of Pentecost, and they had received John's baptism of repentance rather than Christian baptism. In short, they still needed to recognize Jesus as the true Messiah and receive the Holy Spirit—which is exactly what they did. We encourage you to let the overall story of Acts set the boundaries for what is normative in individual passages.

4. Look to other parts of Acts to clarify what is normative. When you read in Acts 2:42–47 and 4:32–35 about the early church selling their possessions and sharing the proceeds, you may wonder if Acts teaches that Christians should give up their individual property, pool their resources, and join a commune (a Christian one, of course). There is something about their sensitivity to the needs of others, their radical generosity, and their spirit of surrender that causes us to want to follow their example. Does Acts suggest that communal living should be normative for a *real* New Testament church in every age? Sometimes you will find your answer by looking in another part of Acts.

Walter Liefeld notes how Acts 5 sheds light on our questions about Acts 2 and 4.[7] In Acts 5:3–4 Peter confronts Ananias about lying to the Holy Spirit regarding the sale of some property:

7. Walter L. Liefeld, *Interpreting the Book of Acts* (Grand Rapids: Baker, 1995), 122.

> [3]Then Peter said, "Ananias, how is it that Satan has so filled your heart that you have lied to the Holy Spirit and have kept for yourself some of the money you received for the land? [4]Didn't it belong to you before it was sold? And after it was sold, wasn't the money at your disposal? What made you think of doing such a thing? You have not lied just to human beings but to God."

According to Peter, the property belonged to Ananias before the sale and the money belonged to Ananias after the sale. He didn't have to sell the property, nor did he have to give the money from the sale in order to be a full-fledged member of the community. Acts 5 makes it clear that sharing possessions in the early Christian community was completely voluntary. Consequently, we cannot conclude that communal living is normative for all churches. What does appear to be normative is the radical generosity that led to meeting physical needs of other members of the Christian community. Occasionally the context of Acts itself will clarify what is normative and what is merely descriptive.

Occasionally the context of Acts itself will clarify what is normative and what is merely descriptive.

5. *Look for repeated patterns and themes.* Perhaps the most important principle for identifying what is normative for the church today is to look for themes and patterns that remain constant throughout the changing story of Acts. Earlier we identified a number of general themes in Acts: the work of the Spirit, God's sovereignty, the role of the church, prayer, suffering, the gospel for Jews and gentiles, and the power of witness. These represent normative realities for the church throughout the ages. Let's look at a few examples of what is involved in looking for consistent patterns as a guide to what is normative.

Consider how the believers chose Judas's replacement in Acts 1:23–26:

> [23]So they nominated two men: Joseph called Barsabbas (also known as Justus) and Matthias. [24]Then they prayed, "Lord, you know everyone's heart. Show us which of these two you have chosen [25]to take over this apostolic ministry, which Judas left to go where he belongs." [26]Then they cast lots, and the lot fell to Matthias; so he was added to the eleven apostles.

Dare we say that since they chose Matthias by casting lots, we should choose church leaders using that same method? Since this method of discovering God's will shows up in the book of Acts, should we take it as normative for Christians today? According to our principle, casting lots would be a normative method of discerning God's will only if it is used consistently throughout Acts. In fact, this is not the case.

Acts 1:23–26 is the only place in the entire book that a church leader is chosen by casting lots. As the story of Acts progresses and the Spirit is poured out on the followers of Jesus, leaders are chosen in other ways (e.g., 6:1–6; 13:1–3; 14:23). This does not mean, we might add, that choosing Matthias was a mistake and that Paul should have been picked—a popular position without scriptural support. The fact that making decisions by casting lots does not appear in the rest of Acts (or the rest of the New Testament) does suggest, however, that it should not be considered a normative method for finding God's will.

How does God make his will known to believers in Acts? Is there any one repeated pattern? A careful reading of Acts reveals that God uses a variety of means to guide his people. He uses angels (8:26; 12:7), his Spirit (8:39; 10:19; 16:6–7), visions (9:10–12; 16:9–10), the Scriptures (1:20; 8:30–35; 18:24–26), circumstances (3:1–10; 8:1), prayer (13:1–3), discussion (15:1–21), and other believers (6:1–6; 9:17–19), just to name a few. What is normative is not so much *how* God guides his people, but *that* God guides his people. The one constant is that God directs our paths in a variety of ways—of this we can be confident!

Another example of looking for repeated patterns as a guide to what is normative relates to what happens when people receive the Holy Spirit. In Acts 2:4 we are told that after receiving the Holy Spirit the people spoke "in other tongues as the Spirit enabled them." Can we conclude that Acts teaches that a person who truly possesses the Holy Spirit must speak in tongues? Our interpretive principle reminds us to ask whether the pattern in question is repeated consistently throughout Acts. Here is what we find when we look at what happened to a person who received the Spirit:

1:8	witnessed of Jesus
2:4	spoke in other tongues (languages)
2:17–18	prophesied
4:31	spoke the word of God boldly
8:15–17	(no description)
9:17–20	preached that Jesus is the Son of God
10:44–46	spoke in tongues and praised God
19:6	spoke in tongues and prophesied

When people received the Spirit, they spoke about their experience, but they did not always speak in other tongues. They might witness or speak the word of God or preach or prophesy. The constant in this picture (with the possible exception of Acts 8:15–17, where no result is mentioned) is that people who received the Spirit of God spoke about their experience. We would say that Spirit-empowered speech of some kind is normative. People who experience God talk about it.

One final example of the principle of finding repeated patterns concerns the nature of evangelistic preaching in Acts.[8] Is there anything about the sermons of Acts that is normative for Christian missions and preaching today? Yes, we see three central features that appear consistently throughout Acts. (1) The message is constantly spreading. Like the ripples in a pond, the gospel progresses in ever-widening circles of influence. According to Acts we can expect that the one, true gospel of Jesus Christ will permeate societies and change lives.

(2) The gospel of Jesus Christ remains constant. The message remains the same: the life, death, and resurrection of Jesus Christ followed by an invitation to respond (2:22–24, 31–33, 36–39; 3:13–21; 8:34–35; 10:36–43; 13:23–39; 17:29–31). Acts 10:39–43 is typical:

> [39]"We are witnesses of everything he did in the country of the Jews and in Jerusalem. They killed him by hanging him on a cross, [40]but God raised him from the dead on the third day and caused him to be seen. [41]He was not seen by all the people, but by witnesses whom God had already chosen—by us who ate and drank with him after he rose from the dead. [42]He commanded us to preach to the people and to testify that he is the one whom God appointed as judge of the living and the dead. [43]All the prophets testify about him that everyone who believes in him receives forgiveness of sins through his name."

(3) The message is shaped to specific audiences. This does not entail changing the message, but tailoring it to ensure the greatest possible acceptance. In cross-cultural terms this is known as *contextualizing* the gospel. When preaching to Jews, the preachers usually use Scripture and the history of Israel as the basis of the appeal (chs. 2, 3, 13). When preaching to gentiles, the preachers build a bridge by appealing to God as Creator (chs. 14, 17). On the topic of evangelistic preaching, we can say that Acts teaches us to hold fast to the core message of the gospel, but we must be willing to tailor our presentation depending on the nature of our audience.

Acts teaches us to hold fast to the core message of the gospel, but we must be willing to tailor our presentation depending on the nature of our audience.

As important as it is to look for repeated patterns and themes when it comes to identifying normative principles

8. See the helpful analysis of "Evangelistic Preaching in Acts" on pp. 32–38 of Ajith Fernando, *Acts*, NIV Application Commentary (Grand Rapids: Zondervan, 1998).

in Acts, even this guideline can be abused. For example, some might say that since Paul traveled by ship on some of his missionary journeys, all missionaries should sail rather than fly. A closer look reveals that Paul did not always travel by ship; sometimes he walked. (Sometimes Paul had no choice in the matter—Acts 27:1.) Ship travel represented the fastest, most modern means of travel for the people of that time. The principle that emerges from Acts, then, is not that we must walk or sail, but that we should use the most appropriate form of travel in serving the Lord.

CONCLUSION

Acts really is a spiritual adventure! What Jesus began to do during his ministry on earth, he now continues to do as his Spirit empowers the church to take the gospel to the world. To grasp the message of Acts, we must first respect that it is a story told for theological purposes (i.e., theological history). This means we will interpret Acts in much the same way we learned to interpret the Gospels. The most difficult problem when reading Acts is knowing how to deal with the river of differences and identify what is normative for today's church. We suggest the following guidelines:

- Look for what Luke intended to communicate to his readers.
- Look for positive and negative examples in the characters.
- Read individual passages in light of the overall story.
- Look to other parts of Acts for clarification.
- Look for repeated patterns and themes.

The challenge of determining what is normative and what is merely descriptive is complex. As believers we want to grasp the full message of Acts, but we do not want to misrepresent what God intends. Striking the balance is not always easy. If you discover something from Acts that is not governed by one of these five guidelines, think carefully before you declare it normative. We admit that our guidelines are not handed down from heaven, and there are probably guidelines besides these five that may help you distinguish between the normative and the descriptive. Our prayer is that what we have said will encourage you to be a more faithful interpreter of this powerful story of the birth and growth of the early church.

ASSIGNMENT

Assignment 16–1

Take one of the following texts through all five steps of the Interpretive Journey as explained and illustrated in chapter 14. Do this by answering the following five questions:

- Acts 2:42–47
- Acts 6:1–7
- Acts 13:1–3
- Acts 15:1–21
- Acts 17:16–34

Step 1: Grasp the text in their town. What did the text mean to the biblical audience?
Step 2: Measure the width of the river to cross. What are the differences between the biblical audience and us?
Step 3: Cross the principlizing bridge. What are the theological principles in this text?
Step 4: Consult the biblical map. How does our theological principle fit with the rest of the Bible?
Step 5: Grasp the text in our town. How should individual Christians today apply the theological principles in their lives?

CHAPTER 17

NEW TESTAMENT—REVELATION

INTRODUCTION

Do you remember the first time that you read (or tried to read) Revelation? What kind of experience was it? Confusing? Intimidating? Exhilarating? Mind-boggling? You probably made sense of chapter 1 even with its unusual vision of one "like a son of man" (v. 13) at the end. You may have even felt comfortable with the messages to the seven churches in chapters 2 and 3. But how did you react to the four living creatures in chapter 4 or the Lamb with seven horns and eyes in chapter 5? Or what did you think about the moon turning red or the 144,000 or the talking eagle or Babylon, the mother of prostitutes? If you are like most people, when you finished the last page, you put down your Bible and concluded that Revelation is one bizarre book.[1]

---

1. For a responsible explanation of the most important theological themes in Revelation for a general audience, see J. Scott Duvall, *The Heart of Revelation: Understanding the Ten Essential Themes of the Bible's Final Book*, rev. ed. (Nashville: B&H Academic, 2019). Also, see J. Scott Duvall, *Revelation*, Teach the Text Commentary (Grand Rapids: Baker, 2014).

This last book of the Bible describes itself in 1:1 as a "revelation of Jesus Christ" (CSB), an expression that functions as a title for the entire book. The term *revelation* (*apokalypsis* in Greek) suggests that something once hidden is now being unveiled or displayed openly (i.e., from John's generation on). To speak about the book as a revelation "of Jesus Christ" could mean that it tells us something *about* Jesus Christ, or that it is communication *from* Jesus Christ, or (most likely) some of both.

In this "final chapter" of the story of salvation, God pulls back the curtain to give his people a glimpse of his plans for human history, plans that center around Jesus Christ.

In this "final chapter" of the story of salvation, God pulls back the curtain to give his people a glimpse of his plans for human history, plans that center around Jesus Christ. Revelation is powerful, difficult, perplexing, colorful, suspenseful, tragic, and amazing. It is like a raging river, a bloody battle, an enticing mystery, and a breathtaking wedding all rolled into one. You had better fasten your seat belt, because Revelation will take you on the interpretive ride of your life. Let's begin our ride with a look at the historical context of Revelation.

HISTORICAL CONTEXT

To understand why there is a need for such an unveiling, imagine yourself in the following situation:

> The first Christians lived in eager expectation of Christ's return. But sixty years after his death it still had not happened, persecution was increasing, and some were beginning to doubt. So Revelation's letters to the churches, and the book as a whole, were needed to encourage them to stand firm. God is in control, no matter how things may look. Christ, not the emperor, is Lord of history. He has the key of destiny itself. And he is coming again to execute justice. There is a glorious, wonderful future for every faithful believer—and especially for those who lay down their lives for Christ.[2]

There are indications within the book itself that Christians are being persecuted for their faith and that the persecution is growing more intense and widespread. John himself is suffering because of his commitment to Christ (1:9):

2. David Alexander and Pat Alexander, eds., *Zondervan Handbook to the Bible* (Grand Rapids: Zondervan, 1999), 764.

> I, John, your brother and companion in the suffering and kingdom and patient endurance that are ours in Jesus, was on the island of Patmos because of the word of God and the testimony of Jesus.

We are told that the church at Ephesus has persevered and endured hardship and has not grown weary (2:3). Note also what Jesus says to the church at Smyrna (2:9–10):

> [9]I know your afflictions and your poverty—yet you are rich! I know about the slander of those who say they are Jews and are not, but are a synagogue of Satan. [10]Do not be afraid of what you are about to suffer. I tell you, the devil will put some of you in prison to test you, and you will suffer persecution for ten days. Be faithful, even to the point of death, and I will give you life as your victor's crown.

Antipas, a faithful witness to Jesus, was put to death in the city of Pergamum (2:13).[3] The Philadelphian Christians have little strength, but they have kept Jesus' word and have not denied his name (3:8). At the opening of the fifth seal, John sees the souls of "those who had been slain because of the word of God and the testimony they had maintained" (6:9). Also, a number of places tell us that pagan powers have shed the blood of the saints (ch. 13; 16:5–6; 17:6; 18:24; 19:2; 20:4).

Much of this persecution was already taking place by the end of the first century during the reign of the Roman emperor Domitian (AD 81–96). The standard sources from that time period (e.g., Pliny, Tacitus, Suetonius) characterize Domitian as savage, cruel, devious, sexually immoral, mad, and evil. Pliny's description of the palace under Domitian doesn't sound like a place where you would want to hang out:

> [It is the] place where . . . that fearful monster built his defences with untold terrors, where lurking in his den he licked up the blood of his murdered relatives or emerged to plot the massacre and destruction of his most distinguished subjects. Menaces and horror were the sentinels at his doors . . . always he sought darkness and mystery, and only emerged from the desert of his solitude to create another (*Pan.* 48.3–5).[4]

3. For a creative yet accurate re-creation of the historical and cultural setting of Asia Minor in the first century, see Bruce W. Longenecker, *The Lost Letters of Pergamum: A Story from the New Testament World*, 2nd ed. (Grand Rapids: Baker Academic, 2016). Antipas plays a major role in Longenecker's fictitious story.

4. Quoted in Leonard L. Thompson, *The Book of Revelation: Apocalypse and Empire* (New York: Oxford University Press, 1990), 98.

Domitian wanted his subjects to address him as *dominus et deus noster* ("our lord and god"). Many of the titles given to first-century Roman emperors were similar to titles Christians gave to Jesus. For Christians, the earliest and most basic confession was "Jesus is Lord." When Christians refused to confess "Caesar is Lord" in worship of the emperor, they were considered disloyal to the state and were subject to persecution. At this time in history, the pressure to bow to the emperor was becoming more widespread and systematic.

When Christians refused to confess "Caesar is Lord" in worship of the emperor, they were considered disloyal to the state and were subject to persecution.

But don't get the impression that every Christian in Asia Minor was standing strong against persecution. When faced with the threat of suffering for their faith, many remained faithful and suffered, but some were openly denying Christ, and others were trying to strike a deal with the pagan powers.[5] Some Christians reverted to Judaism, a legal religion of the Roman Empire, to escape trouble. Others joined trade guilds to avoid economic difficulty, but in those trade guilds they often had to participate in idolatry. Still others were led astray by false teachers.

The messages to the seven churches are filled with warnings for those tempted to turn away from Christ and to compromise with the world system. Ephesus has forsaken her first love (2:4). Some in Pergamum and Thyatira are following false teachers (2:14–15, 20). Sardis has a reputation of being alive but is dead (3:1). Laodicea is lukewarm, and the Lord is about to spit her out of his mouth (3:16).

Revelation is filled with comfort for those who are being persecuted and warnings for those who are trying to avoid persecution. As Craig Keener puts it, "Revelation speaks to churches both alive and dead, but more of the churches are in danger of compromising with the world than of dying from it."[6] The historical context is one in which false religion has formed a partnership with pagan political power. One result is that those who claim to follow Christ are beginning to face tremendous pressure. Will they compromise with the world to avoid persecution, or will they openly confess Christ, knowing that it may cost them their lives? As we read Revelation in light of its historical context, we see that the book offers hope for those who are suffering and challenge for those who are complacent.

Revelation is a strange book because it combines three different literary genres: letter, prophecy, and apocalyptic.

A major part of interpreting the Bible properly is paying careful attention to the

5. See G. K. Beale, *The Book of Revelation: A Commentary on the Greek Text* (Grand Rapids: Eerdmans, 1999), 31–32.

6. Craig S. Keener, *Revelation*, NIV Application Commentary (Grand Rapids: Zondervan, 2000), 39.

literary genre. It is like playing a game by the right set of rules. If we really want to grasp this mysterious and captivating book, we need to understand the kind of book it is intended to be. Let's now look more closely at the literary genre of Revelation.

LITERARY GENRE

Revelation reads like a "normal" book of the Bible for the first few chapters before moving into unfamiliar territory. The book seems strange because it combines three different literary genres: letter, prophecy, and apocalyptic.

1. Revelation is a letter. The book opens and closes like a typical New Testament letter:

> [4]John,
>
> To the seven churches in the province of Asia:
>
> Grace and peace to you from him who is, and who was, and who is to come, and from the seven spirits before his throne, [5]and from Jesus Christ, who is the faithful witness, the firstborn from the dead, and the ruler of the kings of the earth. (Rev. 1:4–5)
>
> The grace of the Lord Jesus be with God's people. Amen. (Rev. 22:21)

This suggests that the whole book of Revelation is a single letter meant to be circulated among seven specific churches in Asia Minor: Ephesus, Smyrna, Pergamum, Thyatira, Sardis, Philadelphia, and Laodicea. The messages to the seven churches in chapters 2–3 are not so much separate "letters" as they are specific messages that introduce the rest of the book. Revelation is really a single letter addressed to all seven churches.[7]

As you look at the map below, you will notice that the churches are named in the order in which a letter carrier would visit them, starting from Patmos (John's location at the time of writing) and moving in a circle around Asia Minor.

Like other New Testament letters, Revelation is "situational." That is, it addresses specific problems or situations that occur in the local churches. We must read Revelation in light of the original situation faced by those churches (i.e., comfort for the persecuted and challenge for the complacent). If we choose to ignore the original situation, we will surely distort the meaning of the letter. We should not worry that Revelation will have no value for people like us who live at a different time and in a different place. As we take any New Testament letter through the steps of the Interpretive Journey (including Revelation), we are able to hear God speak a

7. Richard Bauckham, *The Theology of the Book of Revelation* (Cambridge: Cambridge University Press, 1993), 2.

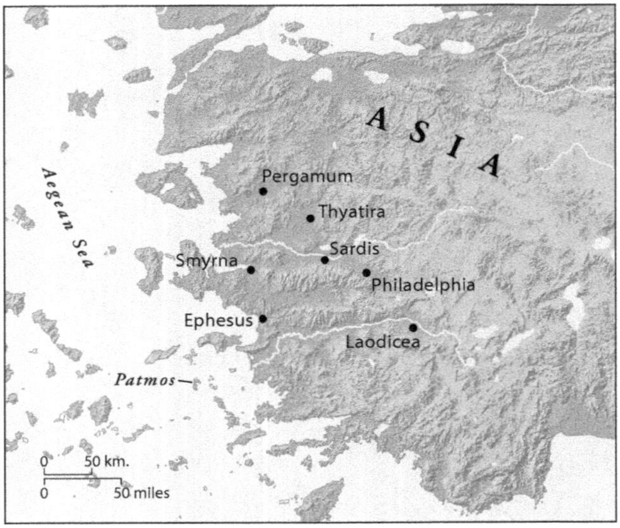

timeless word about how we should live in this world.

Often in the introduction portion of a New Testament letter you find main themes that are developed later in the body of the letter. The same is true with Revelation. If the messages to the seven churches are actually part of an extended introduction to Revelation (as many commentators believe), what should we expect from the rest of the book? Bauckham suggests that Christ's promises to the one who "overcomes" at the end of each of the seven messages provides a major clue (2:7, 11, 17, 26–29; 3:5–6, 12–13, 21–22).[8]

What it means to "overcome" (or "conquer") becomes clear only as the entire book unfolds. As just noted, the introduction to the letter shows us that the entire letter centers around overcoming. In the central section of the book, we read that true believers "triumphed over him [Satan] by the blood of the Lamb and by the word of their testimony; they did not love their lives so much as to shrink from death" (12:11). At the end of the book, in the vision of the new Jerusalem, we hear the promise that "those who are victorious will inherit all this, and I will be their God and they will be my children" (21:7). In other words, at the beginning of Revelation we are challenged to overcome; in the middle we see the struggle to overcome; at the end we see the inheritance that overcomers will receive.

A major theme of Revelation is overcoming.

2. Revelation also claims to be a prophetic letter:

> Blessed is the one who reads aloud the words of this *prophecy*, and blessed are those who hear it and take to heart what is written in it, because the time is near. (Rev. 1:3)

> 6The angel said to me, "These words are trustworthy and true. The Lord, the God who inspires the prophets, sent his angel to show his servants the things that must soon take place."
>
> 7"Look, I am coming soon! Blessed is the one who keeps the words of the *prophecy* written in this scroll." (Rev. 22:6–7)

8. Bauckham, 14. For more on this theme, see Mark Wilson, *The Victor Sayings in the Book of Revelation* (Eugene, OR: Wipf & Stock, 2007).

> Then he told me, "Do not seal up the words of the *prophecy* of this scroll, because the time is near. (Rev. 22:10)

> [18]I warn everyone who hears the words of the *prophecy* of this scroll: If anyone adds anything to them, God will add to that person the plagues described in this scroll. [19]And if anyone takes words away from this scroll of *prophecy*, God will take away from that person any share in the tree of life and in the Holy City, which are described in this scroll. (Rev. 22:18–19)

Biblical prophecy includes both *prediction* of the future and *proclamation* of God's truth for the present (usually the emphasis is on proclamation). In the very places where Revelation is described as a prophecy, the readers are exhorted to do what God has said (i.e., to respond to the proclamation). Those who hear this prophecy will be blessed if they take it to heart (1:3) and keep its words (22:7). We should remember that Revelation is not just about the future; it is also a book about what God wants to see happen in the here and now. Even in John's day, the book is said to be an "unsealed" or open book, whose message is available to all who have ears to hear (22:10).

Biblical prophecy includes both *prediction* of the future and *proclamation* of God's truth for the present.

As a prophetic letter, Revelation stands in the tradition of the Old Testament prophets. It is filled with allusions to the powerful language and imagery used by the Old Testament prophets. For example, John's prophecy against Babylon in Revelation 18–19 echoes every one of the prophecies against Babylon found in the Old Testament prophets.[9] The main difference, of course, between Revelation and the Old Testament prophets is that John's prophetic letter is for Christians who are living between the *already* of the cross and resurrection and the *not yet* of Christ's glorious return.

3. Revelation is a prophetic-apocalyptic letter. Already in 1:1 we are told that the book is a "revelation" or "apocalypse" that comes from God through Jesus Christ, through an angel, and through John to the servants of God:

> The revelation [*apocalypsis*] from Jesus Christ, which God gave him to show his servants what must soon take place. He made it known by sending his angel to his servant John. (Rev. 1:1)

The term *apocalyptic* refers to a group of writings that include a divine revelation, usually through a heavenly intermediary, to some well-known figure, in which God

9. Bauckham, *Theology of the Book of Revelation*, 5.

promises to intervene in human history and overthrow evil empires and establish his kingdom.[10] Most scholars believe that apocalyptic grew out of Hebrew prophecy and actually represents an intensified form of prophecy written during a time of crisis. We see other examples of apocalyptic literature in Ezekiel, Daniel, and Zechariah, and in noncanonical Jewish writings such as *1 Enoch* and *4 Ezra*. Although apocalyptic was well-known to people living from about 200 BC to AD 200, we are not as familiar with it in our day. We catch a glimpse of apocalyptic in certain movies and political cartoons, but even then the comparison leaves something to be desired.

Apocalyptic represents an intensified form of prophecy.

The chief characteristic that makes apocalyptic so unfamiliar to us is its use of images. In its abundant use of visual images, Revelation goes beyond any other apocalypse.[11] As Fee and Stuart point out, while we are familiar with picture language used in other parts of Scripture, apocalyptic literature uses images that are often forms of fantasy rather than reality—for example, locusts with scorpion tails and human heads (9:10), a woman clothed with the sun (12:1), and a beast with seven heads and ten horns (13:1).[12] When Jesus compares his followers to salt and light (Matt. 5:13–14), we know what he means. But who has ever seen a beast with seven heads and ten horns?

Often what makes the image fantastically strange is how the items are combined to form the image. For example, we know about women and we know about the sun, but we do not know much about a woman clothed with the sun. As a prophetic-apocalyptic letter, Revelation is full of strange visions and bizarre images. What is the purpose of all these images and symbols? That brings us to consider the purpose of the book as a whole.

WHAT IS THE PURPOSE OF REVELATION?

The purpose of Revelation is tied up with its literary type as a prophetic-apocalyptic letter, especially with its images. The images of Revelation create a symbolic world in which the readers may live as they read (or hear) the book. When they enter this symbolic world, its message affects them and changes their entire perception of the world in which they live.[13] They are able to see their own situation in this world from a heavenly perspective as they are transported by the visions of Revelation into the future. There they can see the present from the perspective of its final outcome—God's

10. Cf. the definition given by Robert H. Mounce, *The Book of Revelation*, rev. ed., New International Commentary on the New Testament (Grand Rapids: Eerdmans, 1998), 1.

11. Bauckham, *Theology of the Book of Revelation*, 9.

12. Gordon D. Fee and Douglas K. Stuart, *How to Read the Bible for All Its Worth*, 4th ed. (Grand Rapids: Zondervan, 2014), 260–61.

13. Bauckham, *Theology of the Book of Revelation*, 10.

ultimate victory.[14] In this way Revelation provides Christians with a set of "prophetic counterimages" to purge their imagination of the pagan view of the world and restore it with a view of what is real and how the world will be one day under God's rule.[15] Bauckham illustrates using Revelation 17:

> For example, in chapter 17 John's readers share his vision of a woman. At first glance, she might seem to be the goddess Roma, in all her glory, a stunning personification of the civilization of Rome, as she was worshipped in many a temple in the cities of Asia. But as John sees her, she is a Roman prostitute, a seductive whore and a scheming witch, and her wealth and splendour represent the profits of her disreputable trade. For good measure there are biblical overtones of the harlot queen Jezebel to reinforce the impression. In this way, John's readers are able to perceive something of Rome's true character—her moral corruption behind the enticing propagandist illusions of Rome which they constantly encountered in their cities.[16]

As Christians in hostile circumstances read the book again and again, they are continually reminded that "what they believe is not strange and odd, but truly normal from God's perspective."[17]

By using images in this way, Revelation answers the question "Who is Lord?" During times of oppression and persecution, the righteous suffer, and the wicked seem to prosper. This raises the question of whether God is on the throne and still in control. Revelation says that despite how things appear, Caesar is not Lord and Satan is not Lord. Jesus is Lord, and he is coming soon to set things right. Revelation provides that prophetic word from God that people need to remain faithful amid opposition.

The main message of Revelation is "God will win!"

God uses this prophetic-apocalyptic letter to pull back the curtain in his cosmic drama and show his people how things will turn out in the end. The main message of Revelation is "God will win!" Those who are not compromising with the pagan world should see God's future and be filled with hope in the present. Those who are compromising should be shocked out of their spiritual slumber and warned to repent. As the "last chapter" of the story of salvation, Revelation gives people a foretaste of God's ultimate victory and offers them the perspective and the encouragement they need to overcome.

14. Bauckham, 7.
15. Bauckham, 17.
16. Bauckham, 17–18.
17. Beale, *Book of Revelation*, 175.

INTERPRETING REVELATION

Interpreters have traditionally approached Revelation in four primary ways. The *preterist* approach takes the historical context of Revelation seriously and attempts to understand the book the way John's audience would have understood it. Many of the events of Revelation are seen as having been fulfilled in the first century. The *historicist* approach views Revelation as a map or outline of what has happened or will happen throughout church history from the first century until the return of Christ. The *futurist* approach views most of the book as related to future events immediately preceding the end of history. Finally, the *idealist* approach does not understand Revelation in terms of any particular reference to time, but rather relates it to the ongoing struggle between good and evil.

In this chapter, we opt for an *eclectic* approach to reading Revelation—an approach that seeks to combine the strengths of several of the above approaches. Revelation certainly seems to address the first Christians directly. We should read Revelation the same way we read every other book of the Bible—by taking its historical context seriously. Revelation also presents timeless truths for surviving the struggle between good and evil. The visions of Revelation challenge us to forsake our complacency and to stay faithful during times of persecution. Moreover, this book certainly has something to say about events still to come. Some events it describes await future fulfillment (e.g., the return of Christ, the great white throne judgment, and the arrival of the holy city).

In addition to these general approaches to Revelation, we need more specific principles for reading this prophetic-apocalyptic letter. Here are seven suggestions.[18]

1. Read Revelation with humility. We should resist "Revelation-made-easy" approaches. Revelation is not easy! People who must satisfy their curiosity or people who are unwilling to live with any uncertainty are those most likely to read into Revelation things that are not there. Beware of interpreters who appear to have all the answers to even the smallest of questions. "Experts" who claim absolute knowledge about every minute detail of Revelation should be held in suspicion. Reading with a humble mind means that we are willing to admit that our interpretation could be wrong and to change our view when the biblical evidence points in a different direction.

Reading with a humble mind means that we are willing to adjust our view to match the biblical evidence.

18. Many of the interpretive principles discussed below are drawn from Fee and Stuart, *How to Read the Bible*, 258–66.

2. Try to discover the message to the original readers. Discovering the message to the original audience is the top priority with any book of the Bible, but especially with this one. When it comes to reading Revelation, the tendency is to ignore the first Christians and jump directly to God's message for us. Some people use today's newsfeed as the key to interpreting Revelation. But, as Keener notes, this approach does not fit well with a high view of Scripture.[19] The "newsfeed" approach assumes that we must be living in the last Christian generation. It also implies that in Revelation God was not really speaking to the very first Christians. Doesn't that seem arrogant on our part as contemporary interpreters? What if Christ does not return until AD 4000? Would Revelation still have a message for us since we would not be the last generation? We must never forget that the first Christians were blessed for obeying Revelation (1:3) and that the book is described as an unsealed (or open) book, even for people living in John's day (22:10).

When it comes to reading Revelation, the tendency is to ignore the first Christians and jump directly to God's message for us.

The best place to begin is by asking, "What was John trying to communicate to his audience?" If our interpretation makes no sense for original readers, we have probably missed the meaning of the passage. Fee and Stuart remind us of how important it is to discover the message to the original audience: "As with the Epistles, *the primary meaning of the Revelation is what John intended it to mean, which in turn must also have been something his readers could have understood it to mean*."[20] The Interpretive Journey serves as a reminder that we must understand what Revelation *meant* in John's day in order to understand what it *means* today.

3. Don't try to discover a strict chronological map of future events. Don't look for Revelation to progress in a neat linear fashion. The book is filled with prophetic-apocalyptic visions that serve to make a dramatic impact on the reader rather than to present a precise chronological sequence of future events. For example, notice that the sixth seal (6:12–17) takes us to the end of the age.

> 12I watched as he opened the sixth seal. There was a great earthquake. The sun
> turned black like sackcloth made of goat hair, the whole moon turned blood red,
> 13and the stars in the sky fell to earth, as figs drop from a fig tree when shaken
> by a strong wind. 14The heavens receded like a scroll being rolled up, and every
> mountain and island was removed from its place.

19. Keener, *Revelation*, 21–22.

20. Fee and Stuart, *How to Read the Bible*, 263 (emphasis original).

> [15]Then the kings of the earth, the princes, the generals, the rich, the mighty,
> and everyone else, both slave and free, hid in caves and among the rocks of the
> mountains. [16]They called to the mountains and the rocks, "Fall on us and hide
> us from the face of him who sits on the throne and from the wrath of the Lamb!
> [17]For the great day of their wrath has come, and who can withstand it?"

But when the seventh seal is opened, we are given a whole new set of judgments—the trumpets—and the seventh trumpet (11:15–19) also takes us to the end of the age:

> [15]The seventh angel sounded his trumpet, and there were loud voices in heaven, which said:
>
> "The kingdom of the world has become
> the kingdom of our Lord and of his Messiah,
> and he will reign for ever and ever."
>
> [16]And the twenty-four elders, who were seated on their thrones before God,
> fell on their faces and worshiped God, [17]saying:
>
> "We give thanks to you, Lord God Almighty,
> the One who is and who was,
> because you have taken your great power
> and have begun to reign.
> [18]The nations were angry,
> and your wrath has come.
> The time has come for judging the dead,
> and for rewarding your servants the prophets
> and your people who revere your name,
> both great and small—
> and for destroying those who destroy the earth."
>
> [19]Then God's temple in heaven was opened, and within his temple was seen the ark of his covenant. And there came flashes of lightning, rumblings, peals of thunder, an earthquake and a severe hailstorm.

Then with the first bowl in 16:1–2 we are given another series of judgments. Revelation 19–22 paints the most colorful and detailed picture of the end, but, as you can see, this is not the first time the readers have been transported to the very end.

On a smaller scale, in Revelation 6:13–16 we are told that "the stars in the sky fell to earth. . . . The heavens receded like a scroll being rolled up, and every mountain and island was removed from its place." Yet in 7:3 the four angels are told not to "harm the land or the sea or the trees until we put a seal on the foreheads of the servants of our God." To attempt to force a strict chronological sequence on this wouldn't make sense. Rather than searching for a chronological map of future events in Revelation, we encourage you to grasp the main message in each vision about living in the here and now.

4. Take Revelation seriously, but don't always take it literally. Some who say that we should interpret Scripture symbolically do so to deny the reality of a scriptural truth or a historical event. When they say that something is figurative or symbolic, they mean that it is not real or that it never happened. That is not our intention in *Grasping God's Word.* We insist that picture language with its symbols, images, and figures is capable of conveying literal truth and describing literal events. Picture language is just another language vehicle, another way of communicating reality. In our way of thinking, Revelation uses picture language to *emphasize* historical reality rather than to deny or diminish it.

Picture language with its symbols, images, and figures is quite capable of conveying literal truth and describing literal events.

One of the ground rules of interpretation is that our method of interpretation should always match the literary genre used by the author. As a result, we should avoid taking picture language literally. When we try to force a literal method on the genre of picture language, we run the risk of perverting the author's intended meaning.

For example, what happens when we try to take the reference in Revelation 17:9 to the woman who sits on seven hills literally? To force this image into a literal mold results either in one very large woman or in seven very small hills. But when we say that the woman in 17:9 is not a literal woman, we do not deny the reality of Scripture at all. We do not take the image literally, but we do take it seriously. First-century Christians would naturally understand the woman to represent Rome, a city built on seven hills. The text probably also looks beyond Rome to powerful pagan empires opposed to God. We take picture language seriously but not literally.

We are told in Revelation 1:1 that God has "signified" (KJV) the book to John. The word translated "signify" (NIV "made it known") suggests that God has communicated the book to John by means of signs or symbols.[21] According to Beale, the background of this term is Daniel 2, where God "signifies" to the king what will occur in the latter days by showing him a pictorial revelation (v. 45). When interpreting

21. Beale, *Book of Revelation*, 50–55.

much of the Bible, the general rule is to interpret literally except where the context clearly calls for a symbolic reading. The word "signify" in Revelation 1:1 suggests that when we come to this book, the general rule is just the reverse: interpret symbolically unless the context calls for a literal reading.[22]

5. Pay attention when John identifies an image. When John himself provides a clue to the interpretation of an image, we should take notice. In other words, we should pay close attention when John identifies or defines the images for his readers. For example, in Revelation 1:17 the one "like a son of man" (1:13) is Christ, in 1:20 the golden lampstands are the churches, in 5:5–6 the Lion is the Lamb, in 12:9 the dragon is Satan, and in 21:9–10 the heavenly Jerusalem is the wife of the Lamb or the church. When images that John has identified are repeated elsewhere in the book, we should assume that they probably refer to the same things.

For example, the lampstands are clearly identified in 1:20 as the churches: "The seven stars are the angels of the seven churches, and the seven lampstands are the seven churches." When the image of the lampstand occurs later in 11:3–4, we should assume that it probably refers to the church there also, based on John's earlier identification:

> [3]"And I will appoint my two witnesses, and they will prophesy for 1,260 days, clothed in sackcloth." [4]They are "the two olive trees" and the two lampstands, and "they stand before the Lord of the earth."

In this case, the interpretive guideline suggests that the two witnesses of Revelation 11 represent the witnessing church.

You have to be careful not to confuse John's direct identification of an image (those mentioned above) with John's fluid use of images. In other words, John is not shy about using the same image to refer to different things. For example, the seven stars are the angels of the seven churches (1:16, 20; 2:1; 3:1). But John also uses the image of a star (not the seven stars) to refer to other things, such as God's agents of judgment (8:10–12) or even Jesus himself (22:16). In the same way, the image of a woman can be used for a false prophet (2:20), the messianic community (ch. 12), the harlot city or empire (ch. 17), and the bride of Christ (19:7; 21:9). Even though John is free to use images to refer to different things, when he identifies an image, we should pay attention.

Revelation contains more Old Testament references than any other New Testament book.

22. Beale, 52.

6. *Look to the Old Testament and historical context when interpreting images and symbols.* Revelation uses language at several different levels:

- Text level: words written on the page
- Vision level: the picture that the words paint
- Referent level: what the vision refers to in real life

One of the most difficult aspects of reading Revelation is knowing what the images and symbols refer to. Even when we understand what is happening at the text and vision levels, we may not know what is going on at the referent level. In other words, we usually know what Revelation is saying, but we are often not sure what it is talking about.

The two places to go for answers are to the first-century historical context and the Old Testament. Earlier in this chapter we discussed the historical context, but we have not talked much about how Revelation uses the Old Testament. Although there is no explicit Old Testament quotation in Revelation, the book is filled with echoes and allusions to the Old Testament. In fact, Revelation contains more Old Testament references than any other New Testament book, with the Old Testament appearing in almost 70 percent of Revelation's verses.[23] Psalms, Isaiah, Daniel, and Ezekiel make the most important contribution to Revelation.

Let's look briefly at how John draws on the Old Testament book of Daniel to describe his vision of Jesus in Revelation 1. Notice how many of Daniel's words and phrases John uses to depict Jesus as a glorious divine being (see the italicized words):

> 9"As I looked,
>
> thrones were set in place,
> and the Ancient of Days took his seat.
> His clothing was as white as snow;
> the hair of his head was *white like wool.*
> His throne was flaming with fire,
> and its wheels were all ablaze. . . .
>
> 13"In my vision at night I looked, and there before me was one *like a son of man, coming with the clouds* of heaven. He approached the Ancient of Days and was led into his presence. 14He was given authority, glory and sovereign power;

23. Keener, *Revelation*, 33.

> all nations and peoples of every language worshiped him. His dominion is an everlasting dominion that will not pass away, and his kingdom is one that will never be destroyed." (Dan. 7:9, 13–14)
>
> [5]I looked up and there before me was a man dressed in linen, with a *belt of fine gold* from Uphaz around his waist. [6]His body was like topaz, his face like lightning, his *eyes like flaming torches*, his *arms and legs like the gleam of burnished bronze*, and his *voice like the sound of a multitude*. (Dan. 10:5–6)

> [7]"Look, he is coming with the clouds,"
> and "every eye will see him,
> even those who pierced him";
> and all peoples on earth "will mourn because of him."
> So shall it be! Amen. . . .
>
> [12]I turned around to see the voice that was speaking to me. And when I turned I saw seven golden lampstands, [13]and among the lampstands was *someone like a son of man*, dressed in a robe reaching down to his feet and with a *golden sash* around his chest. [14]The hair on his head was *white like wool*, as white as snow, and his *eyes were like blazing fire*. [15]His *feet were like bronze glowing in a furnace*, and his *voice was like the sound of rushing waters*. (Rev. 1:7, 12–15)

Understanding Daniel helps us to understand Revelation here. John often uses the Old Testament language to describe what he has seen and heard. As we struggle to identify what the vision is about, we should turn to the historical context and to the Old Testament.

> With Revelation, we should start with the big picture and work toward an understanding of the details.

7. Above all, focus on the main idea and don't press all the details. This last interpretive guideline is perhaps the most important of all. With most literary genres in the Bible, we begin with the details and build our way toward an understanding of the whole. With Revelation, however, we should start with the big picture and work toward an understanding of the details. As we seek to identify theological principles in Revelation, we should focus on the main ideas. Try this: read a section of Revelation and capture the main idea in a short statement. For example, the main idea of Revelation 4–5 relates to the ascended and exalted Lord, who alone is worthy to execute the divine judgments.

The details of any particular section will heighten the impact on the reader but will not change the main idea. Resist the temptation to focus on the details so much that you miss the main idea. Don't let the main point of each section or vision fade from view. As has been said, when reading Revelation, the main thing is to make the main thing the main thing!

If the central interpretive rule is to grasp the main idea of each vision, it becomes important that we have a general understanding of how the book unfolds. We see the book unfolding in seven broad movements, bracketed by an introduction and a conclusion.

HOW DOES REVELATION UNFOLD?

Introduction (1:1–3:22)

The first few verses of this prophetic-apocalyptic letter tell us that there is a blessing for those who hear its message and take it to heart. The rest of chapter 1 introduces us to John and describes his vision of "one like a son of man" (Jesus) who walks among the seven golden lampstands (the churches). John has been selected to write the revelation of Jesus Christ on a scroll and to send it to these churches.

Chapters 2–3 contain the seven messages to the churches. These messages generally feature a description of Christ, followed by his commendation, complaint, warning, and promise for the church. At the end of this long introduction, the readers have a clear sense of who Jesus is (the Sovereign Lord) and what he expects of his followers.

Vision of God and the Lamb (4:1–5:14)

The seven messages set the scene on earth and clarify the dangers the church faces: persecution and compromise. In chapters 4–5 the scene shifts to heaven, where God reigns in majestic power from his throne. All of heaven worships the Creator. Also worthy of ceaseless praise is the Lion-Lamb (Jesus), who alone is able to open the scroll. By his sacrificial death the Lamb has redeemed a people to serve God.

Opening of the Seven Seals (6:1–8:1)

The stage has been set and the unveiling of God's ultimate victory formally begins. This section marks the first of a series of three judgment visions, each with seven elements:

- Seven seals (6:1–8:1)
- Seven trumpets (8:2–11:19)
- Seven bowls (15:1–16:21)

In the first two series—seals and trumpets—there is a dramatic interlude between the sixth and seventh elements.

Chapter 6 begins with the opening of the first four seals—the famous four horsemen of the apocalypse: conquest, war, famine, and death. The fifth seal consists of the martyrs' question, "How long, Sovereign Lord?" The sixth seal concludes with the question "Who can withstand it?" as the Lamb pours out his wrath.

Before the opening of this final seal, there is an interlude in chapter 7 consisting of two visions. In the first, the servants of God, numbering 144,000, are sealed with divine protection (vv. 1–8). The second describes a great multitude of believers standing before God's throne (vv. 9–17). Even as the seals are removed, God is careful to encourage and assure his people by revealing what awaits them in heaven. With the opening of the seventh seal in 8:1, there is a dramatic pause before the next series of seven.

Sounding of the Seven Trumpets (8:2–11:19)

The trumpets reveal God's judgment on a wicked world. They are patterned after the plagues of Egypt leading up to the exodus. Despite the ever intensifying judgments, the "earth-dwellers" (a common way in Revelation to refer to unbelievers [NIV: "rest of mankind"]) refuse to repent (9:20–21).

Once again, before the seventh element in the series, there is an interlude consisting of two visions: the angel and the little scroll (10:1–11) and the two witnesses (11:1–14). These visions once again offer the saints encouragement and instruction about what they should do as God carries out his purposes in history. With the seventh trumpet we return again to a scene of heavenly worship and are told that "the kingdom of the world has become the kingdom of our Lord and of his Messiah, and he will reign for ever and ever" (11:15).

The People of God versus the Powers of Evil (12:1–14:20)

Revelation 12 explains the real reason why God's people face hostility in this world: the conflict between God and Satan (the dragon). Satan attempted to destroy Christ (the male child) but was defeated decisively by Christ's death and resurrection. As a defeated enemy with a limited amount of time to do damage, Satan vents his rage on God's people. Fee and Stuart rightly observe that "chapter 12 is the theological key to the book."[24] Knowing the real reason for persecution and the certain outcome of victory encourages the people of God to persevere to the end.

Chapter 13 introduces Satan's two agents for waging war against God's people

24. Fee and Stuart, *How to Read the Bible*, 270.

—the beast out of the sea (vv. 1–10) and the beast out of the earth (vv. 11–18). Pagan political power joins forces with false religion. The dragon and the two beasts constitute a satanic or unholy trinity resolute on seducing and destroying God's people.

As a defeated enemy with a limited amount of time to do damage, Satan vents his rage on God's people.

But in chapter 14 the reader is once again given a glimpse of the blessings of the final future that God has in store for his people. In spite of the persecution they now face in this world, the followers of the Lamb will one day stand with him on Mount Zion and sing a new song of redemption. Following this heavenly scene, John records three angelic proclamations about God's judgment, followed by two visions of judgment using the images of a grain harvest and a winepress. This final part of chapter 14 reminds us that God's judgment of evil is certain and encourages the saints to remain faithful to Jesus.

Pouring Out of the Seven Bowls (15:1–16:21)

Chapter 15 features seven angels with seven golden bowls filled with the wrath of God. The bowls follow the seals and trumpets as the final series of seven. Chapter 16 describes the pouring out of these seven bowls on the unrepentant world. The plagues are devastating, uninterrupted, universal manifestations of God's anger toward sin and evil. God will make Babylon the Great (the Roman Empire in the first century) drink the "wine of the fury of his wrath" (v. 19). In response the earth-dwellers not only refuse to repent; they go so far as to curse God (vv. 9, 11, 21).

The bowl judgments are devastating, uninterrupted, universal manifestations of God's anger toward sin and evil.

Judgment of Babylon (17:1–19:5)

From this point on in the book of Revelation, John sets before us a "tale of two cities"—the city of humanity (earthly Babylon destined for destruction) and the city of God (heavenly Jerusalem, where God will dwell among his people forever).[25] Chapters 17–18 depict the death of Babylon, the great mother of prostitutes. Babylon undoubtedly represents Rome, a pagan power said to be "drunk with the blood of God's holy people, the blood of those who bore testimony to Jesus" (17:6). The funeral laments of chapter 18 give way to the explosive celebration in heaven as God's people rejoice over Babylon's downfall (19:1–5).

25. Mounce, *Book of Revelation*, 306.

God's Ultimate Victory (19:6–22:5)

This section of Revelation portrays God's ultimate victory over the forces of evil and the final reward for his people. The scene opens with the announcement of the wedding of the Lamb (19:6–10) and the return of Christ for his bride (19:11–16). The Warrior-Christ returns, captures the two beasts and their allies, and throws them into the fiery lake of burning sulfur (19:17–21). The dragon, or Satan, is bound (20:1–3), during which time Jesus' faithful followers reign with him (20:4–6). Satan is then released from his temporary prison only to join the two beasts in eternal torment (20:7–10). The dead are judged by him who sits on the great white throne. Anyone whose name is not found written in the Book of Life is also thrown into the lake of fire (20:11–15). At this point death itself is judged.

Having judged sin, Satan, and death, God ushers in the eternal state of glory. A general description of "a new heaven and a new earth" is provided in 21:1–8, followed by a more detailed presentation in 21:9–22:5. There will be no more crying or pain or death—God is making everything new (21:4–5). The Old Testament promise that God would live among his people finds its ultimate fulfillment here (21:3). There is no temple in this city of God because God Almighty and the Lamb are its temple (21:22).

God's victory is complete, and the fellowship he desired with Adam and Eve is now recovered in a restored garden of Eden complete with "the tree of life" (22:1–2). The curse of sin is removed, and redeemed humanity is once again able to walk with God and see his face (22:4).

Conclusion (22:6–21)

Revelation closes with a final blessing on those who keep "the words of the prophecy written in this scroll" (22:7) and a warning for those who practice sexual immorality, idolatry, and the like (22:15). This book is an authentic revelation from God and should be read faithfully to the churches (22:6, 16). Jesus assures his people that his return is imminent (22:7, 12, 20). And John responds with a prayer statement that Christians of all times can make their own—"Come, Lord Jesus." In the meantime, John writes, "The grace of the Lord Jesus be with God's people. Amen" (22:21).

REVELATION 12:1–17 AND THE INTERPRETIVE JOURNEY

Before we close this chapter, we want to show you how to take a passage in Revelation through the steps of the Interpretive Journey. Revelation 12:1–17 provides a useful example. We realize that not everyone will agree with our interpretations of this passage, but we will go through the process anyway so that you can see what is involved.

Step 1: Grasp the text in their town. What did the text mean to the biblical audience?

This step consists of understanding the context of chapter 12 so that we may be able to interpret the symbols ("signs" in 12:1, 3) in light of that context. The chapter opens with a woman who is about to give birth to a male child. An enormous red dragon is waiting to devour the child. But as soon as the child is born, he is snatched up to God, who also provides a safe place on earth for the mother. The scene then shifts to heaven, where the archangel Michael and his angels fight against the dragon and his angels. The dragon (now explicitly called "the devil, or Satan," 12:9) is defeated and thrown down to earth. As a defeated foe who has had to forfeit his place in heaven, the devil pursues the woman with a vengeance and makes war against the rest of her offspring.

How would the first-century audience have understood these characters in Revelation 12?

How would the first-century audience have understood these characters? Most likely they would not have identified the woman with Mary, the mother of Jesus (a much later interpretation). Instead, they likely would have thought of the woman as the true Israel, the faithful community who gives birth to both the Messiah and the church. Both the male child and the offspring (12:17) serve as keys for identifying the woman. Note that the prophets often portray righteous Israel as a mother and the symbols used in 12:1 confirm this interpretation (cf. Gen. 37:9).[26] After giving birth to the Messiah, the woman flees to a place of spiritual refuge for a period of 1,260 days, the time of persecution between the ascension and exaltation of Christ and his future return (cf. Rev. 11:2; 12:14; 13:5).

The dragon is explicitly identified in the passage as the devil, or Satan (12:9). This enemy of God attempts to devour the male child and lead the whole world astray. The detailed description of the dragon as red with seven heads, ten horns, and seven crowns only adds to the awesomeness of the image.

We are told that the male child "will rule all the nations with an iron scepter" (12:5), an allusion to Psalm 2 that is applied even more clearly to Jesus in Revelation 19:5. The male child most certainly represents Jesus Christ. After the child is born, he is taken up to God. By moving straight from Jesus' birth to his ascension and enthronement, John stresses that Satan's evil plot has been foiled by Jesus' incarnation, life, death, resurrection, ascension, and exaltation.

The original audience would have understood the war in heaven (12:7–12) and the subsequent rage of the devil (12:13–17) as an explanation of two significant realities. (1) God has defeated Satan and the victory is certain. (2) God's people on earth will

26. Keener, *Revelation*, 314.

continue to suffer as victims of the devil's rage. The heavenly perspective would help the original audience to understand their hostile environment and encourage them to persevere. They, too, can appropriate the victory and overcome the devil "by the blood of the Lamb and by the word of their testimony," that is, by bearing faithful witness to the gospel of Jesus Christ even if it costs them their lives (12:11).

Step 2: Measure the width of the river to cross. What are the differences between the biblical audience and us?

Like the original audience, we look back on the first coming of Christ and forward to his second coming. Both the biblical audience and the contemporary audience live between the already and the not yet. Because we share this situation with the original audience, we, too, can expect to suffer. As offspring of the woman (12:17), we will also encounter the anger of a defeated devil. Nevertheless, because we live in a different place and time (i.e., we are not part of Domitian's Roman Empire), our suffering may take different forms and may vary in intensity. In general, churches in North America are not being persecuted to the same degree that churches in Asia Minor were being persecuted, though that could change.

> Like the first-century Christians, we also feel the attack of the devil in our attempt to live consistently and faithfully in the midst of a world system opposed to God.

We do, however, struggle with many of the same temptations toward complacency and compromise that the churches of Asia Minor faced. Immorality, idolatry, false teaching, materialism, and other such sins are still alive and well in our day. Like our ancestors, we also feel the attack of the devil in our attempt to live consistently and faithfully in the midst of a world system opposed to God. We know what it means to be at war with the evil one. The comment in 12:11 that first-century believers "triumphed over him [Satan] by the blood of the Lamb and by the word of their testimony" and "did not love their lives so much as to shrink from death" will pose a strong challenge to North American Christians not accustomed to considering radical sacrifice for the cause of Christ, much less martyrdom.

Step 3: Cross the principlizing bridge. What are the theological principles in this text?

The theological principles are built on similarities between their situation and ours. Several principles or truths emerge from this passage:

- There is a real devil who is opposed to God and is bent on deceiving and destroying God's people. Spiritual warfare is real.

- Satan has been defeated by the life and redemptive work of Christ.
- Christians can overcome the devil by living and proclaiming the gospel of Jesus Christ faithfully.
- Christians can expect to suffer for being faithful in their witness to Christ.

Step 4: Consult the biblical map. How does our theological principle fit with the rest of the Bible?

The rest of the Bible clearly affirms all four principles identified above (i.e., the existence of Satan, his purposes of opposing God and his people, and how Christians triumph over him through faithfulness to Christ even to the point of being willing to suffer).

Step 5: Grasp the text in our town. How should individual Christians today live out this theological principle?

In chapter 13 of *Grasping God's Word*, we explained what is involved in the application of a biblical text. We need to see first how the principles in the text address the original situation. Let's use the third theological principle listed above as an example: "Christians can overcome the devil by living and proclaiming the gospel of Jesus Christ faithfully."

In this intersection between the biblical text and the original situation, we see Christians who are experiencing victory over the devil by living and proclaiming the gospel of Jesus Christ, even under threat of death.

Next we must discover a true parallel situation in a contemporary context. In the original context, the satanic attack takes the form of persecution. Consequently, we can say that any time Christians suffer persecution for their faithfulness to the gospel of Christ, we have a parallel situation.

Real-world scenarios should be both faithful to the meaning of the text and relevant to the contemporary audience.

Finally, we need to make our application specific so that people will know how to live out this part of the biblical story. In our example, persecuted Christians overcome the devil by living and proclaiming the gospel of Christ. As we mentioned in chapter 13, perhaps the best way to make an application specific is to create a real-world scenario to serve as an illustration or example of how a person might live out the biblical principles. Real-world scenarios or stories should be both faithful to the meaning of the text and relevant to the contemporary audience. You might create a scenario illustrating appropriate and mature strategies for overcoming the devil. Or you could come up with a scenario of how to engage the culture with the gospel of Christ rather than withdrawing to avoid persecution. Sometimes a real-life story serves as the best illustration of all.

Consider the gripping account of faithful Christians living on the Indonesian island of Buru:

> On the morning of December 23, 1999, a group of Muslims murdered scores of Christians, including women and children at a plywood factory on the Indonesian island of Buru, according to several Christian employees who survived the attack. Christians and Muslims have been fighting for more than a year and hundreds have been killed. Yoke Pauno, a factory worker who has taken refuge in Ambon, the capital, says she saw armed Muslims ask a woman holding a baby if she was "obed" or "achan," the local slang for Christian and Muslim, respectively. When the woman answered "obed," both she and her child were brutally killed.[27]

Real-life scenarios and stories help us to grasp the text in our town.

CONCLUSION

In the book of Revelation, God pulls back the curtain to give his people a glimpse of his plans for human history. Center stage in this cosmic drama is Jesus Christ, the Lion and the Lamb, who secures victory through sacrifice. Revelation is strange because of its blended literary genre (prophetic-apocalyptic letter), but it is not a closed book. We can grasp the meaning of Revelation and apply it to our lives, but we need to "play by its rules," not our own.

As we study the historical context of Revelation, we see a situation where Christians were increasingly being persecuted for their faith because they refused to join the pagan parade. The pressure to bow the knee to Caesar rather than to Jesus was spreading, and hope was beginning to fade. In addition, some Christians were growing comfortable with their pagan surroundings and compromising their faithfulness to Christ. Revelation encourages the persecuted and warns those who were selling out.

We might say that the purpose of Revelation is to answer the question "Who is Lord?" Historian Will Durant, in *The Story of Civilization*, concludes:

> There is no greater drama in human record than the sight of a few Christians, scorned and oppressed by a succession of emperors, bearing all trials with a fierce

27. Dr. Randy Richards, our former colleague at Ouachita who served as a missionary to Indonesia, has confirmed the report through his former mission chairman, who personally interviewed one of the eyewitnesses. The story was also reported in *The Christian Science Monitor*, January 24, 2000.

> tenacity, multiplying quietly, building order while their enemies generated chaos, fighting the sword with the word, brutality with hope, and at last defeating the strongest state that history has known. Caesar and Christ had met in the arena, and Christ had won.[28]

Revelation answers this question by creating a symbolic world in which readers may find the heavenly perspective they need to endure trying times. When we read about God on his throne or about the Lamb conquering the beast or about the garden where we will live in the presence of God, we are encouraged to hang in there, to remain faithful. The purpose of the book is to show us in picture language that Jesus rather than Caesar (any Caesar!) is Lord. As we read, we are reminded that God wins, and we can continue on in hope.

The purpose of Revelation is to show us in picture language that Jesus rather than Caesar is Lord.

Revelation is indeed an amazing book. As God paints a picture of his plans for history, he uses a rainbow of colors. He overwhelms our imaginations with his awesome strength.

As we bow down to worship the Lord God Almighty for all he has done to rescue us, the powers of this world lose their grip on our souls. We, too, pray the prayer, "Come, Lord Jesus!"

28. Will Durant, *The Story of Civilization, Part III: Caesar and Christ* (New York: Simon & Schuster, 1944), 652, as quoted in Philip Yancey, *The Jesus I Never Knew* (Grand Rapids: Zondervan, 1995), 248.

ASSIGNMENTS

Assignment 17–1

Read the entire book of Revelation and write a one-line description of the main idea of each chapter of the book. For example, for Revelation 1 you might write, "John's vision of the glorified Christ among the churches."

Assignment 17–2

In Revelation 2–3 we find messages from Jesus Christ to seven churches in Asia Minor. Make a chart showing the message to each of these churches in terms of the (1) command to write, (2) description of Jesus, (3) commendation or praise, (4) complaint or rebuke, (5) exhortation or warning, and (6) promise. Then add an eighth church to the chart—your home church. Write out the message you think Christ would speak to your church for each of the six areas.

Assignment 17–3

Read again the section in this chapter on Revelation 12:1–17 and the Interpretive Journey. In step 3 on crossing the principlizing bridge, we listed four theological principles or truths that emerge from Revelation 12:1–17. We used the third principle to illustrate the application process. Create a real-world scenario for the first, second, or fourth principle to make a specific application. Write out your real-world scenario.

PART 5

THE INTERPRETIVE JOURNEY—*Old Testament*

In 2 Timothy 3:16–17 the apostle Paul writes, "All Scripture is God-breathed and is useful for teaching, rebuking, correcting and training in righteousness, so that the servant of God may be thoroughly equipped for every good work." When Paul refers to "all Scripture," he is certainly including the Old Testament. Paul is teaching us that the Old Testament is also inspired by God and is filled with God's Word—important material from God that we need to know. These narratives, psalms, and prophecies from the Old Testament can teach us about God and equip us for Christian living. A truly mature Christian needs to be able to interpret and apply the Old Testament as well as the New Testament.

Now that you are a veteran of many Interpretive Journeys, you are ready to tackle the Old Testament. In part 5 you will take all that you have learned so far in this book and apply it to the various genres of the Old Testament. You will learn how to interpret and apply Old Testament narrative, legal material, poetry, prophetic writings, and wisdom literature. The interpretive river in the Old Testament is wider than the one in the New Testament, and the principlizing bridge becomes even more critical. The genre differences are also significant, as you will see. However, the stories and poems in the Old Testament are exciting and inspiring, and God reveals many things about himself through these texts. Without doubt, the time you spend in the Old Testament will be rewarding.

Also, keep in mind that we read and interpret the Old Testament as Christians. That is, although we believe that the Old Testament is part of God's inspired Word to us, we do not want to ignore the cross and thus interpret and apply this literature as if we were Old Testament Hebrews. We affirm that we are New Testament Christians, and we will interpret the Old Testament from that vantage point.

During step 1 (*Grasp the text in their town*), of course, we will focus on what the text meant to those living in the Old Testament era. However, it is critical that we not stop here! After we have defined the width of the river (step 2) and formulated a theological principle (step 3), it is especially critical that we give appropriate attention to step 4 (*Consult the biblical map*). In this step we ask how our theological principle fits with the rest of the Bible. When we are in the Old Testament, this means running our theological principle through the grid of the New Testament, looking for what the New Testament adds to that principle or how the New Testament modifies it. In essence we are expanding step 4 in our Journey.

The Old Testament Interpretive Journey, therefore, will now look like this:

Step 1: Grasp the text in their town. What did the text mean to the biblical audience?

Step 2: Measure the width of the river to cross. What are the differences between the biblical audience and us?

Step 3: Cross the principlizing bridge. What is the theological principle in this text?

Step 4: Consult the biblical map. How does our theological principle fit with the rest of the Bible? Does the New Testament teaching modify or qualify this principle, and if so, how?

Step 5: Grasp the text in our town. How should individual Christians today live out this modified theological principle?

1
CULTURE ~ LANGUAGE
2
TIME ~ SITUATION
3
PRINCIPLIZING BRIDGE
4
YOU ARE HERE
5

CHAPTER 18

OLD TESTAMENT—NARRATIVE

INTRODUCTION

Danny was watching the Super Bowl on TV a few years ago when a fascinating commercial came on the tube. The setting was in ancient days, and the scene portrayed two battle lines drawn up ready for war. The soldiers, armed with shields, spears, helmets, and swords, were taunting one another. Suddenly a gigantic soldier walked out from one battle line and issued a challenge to the other side. "Goliath?" Danny mused. Sure enough, about that time a small boy clad in sheepskin and armed with a sling stepped forward from the other side. Without ever telling us that this was David, the commercial continued. David ran forward and fired his rock at Goliath, striking him in the head and sending him to the ground in a crumpled heap. David then ran over to the fallen Goliath and retrieved his stone. He turned the stone around in his hand and looked at the inscription written on the back of the stone, the "*W*" logo for *Wilson Sporting Goods*. For the first and only time in the commercial, the narrator spoke: "The right equipment makes all the difference."

What interested Danny was the fact that this commercial only worked because everybody in America knows the story (the narrative) of David and Goliath. Later he saw another commercial with Samson and Delilah as the characters. Samson was clad in his *Hanes* underwear. Again the advertisement never identified the two people; they assumed that we could identify the story by the appearance of the characters. These advertisers had reached into the Bible and drawn out two of the best-known narratives in the Old Testament as the settings for their commercials.

These two commercials remind us of how powerful the stories of the Old Testament are and how much impact they make on people, both in and out of the Christian community. The stories of David and Goliath and of Samson and Delilah are not the only well-known stories from the first half of the Bible. Other equally well-known episodes include the account of Adam and Eve in the garden, Daniel in the lions' den, Jonah in the big fish, Job's trials, and Moses's crossing the Red Sea. Hollywood has also found these stories irresistible, and in recent years we have seen them produce numerous movies about the life and times of David, Moses, Abraham, and Noah.

Narratives (stories) comprise nearly half of the Old Testament.

Truly the Old Testament has some great stories in it. Of course, there are some lesser-known narratives in the Old Testament as well, some of which are interesting and some even a bit strange. What do you think of Abraham arguing with God about how many righteous people in Sodom it would take to spare the city (Gen. 18:22–33)? Or how about Balaam's donkey speaking to him and Balaam answering back (Num. 22:21–41)? Puzzling things happen in the Old Testament. For instance, God appears to send a *lying* spirit to the king's false prophets (1 Kings 22:19–23). Also, several grotesque events transpire, such as the account of the Levite in Judges 19:1–30, who cut up his raped and murdered concubine into twelve parts and sent one part to each tribe of Israel to call them to war.

Narratives (stories) comprise nearly half of the Old Testament, a hefty percentage of the Bible. Indeed, the following books all contain large chunks of narrative material: Genesis, Exodus, Numbers, Joshua, Judges, Ruth, 1 and 2 Samuel, 1 and 2 Kings, 1 and 2 Chronicles, Ezra, Nehemiah, Daniel, Jonah, and Haggai. Several other books have substantial amounts of narrative interspersed in the text as well: Job, Isaiah, Jeremiah, and Ezekiel. Obviously, narrative is an important genre.

We will use the terms *narrative* and *story* interchangeably to refer to the *genre* of this type of literature. Narrative is a literary form characterized by sequential time action and involving plot, setting, and characters. It is the *story* form of literature. The *meaning* of a narrative derives primarily from the actions of its characters. Rather than *telling* us how to live or how not to live, the narrative *shows* us how to live or how not to live by the actions of the characters. For example, rather than telling us to trust God and live by faith in his promises, Genesis presents us with the story of Abraham. Also keep in mind that God is one of the central characters in Old Testament narrative. We can learn much about him by studying his actions and his dialogue in the narratives. We will discuss God's role in the narrative in more detail below.

To some people, the terms *narrative* and *story* imply that the events described may not be true, historical events. We do not use the terms in this way, for we believe that the narrative does describe true events. However, this literature is much more than just *history*. The Old Testament is giving us much more than just the history of Israel. The purpose of these stories is theological—that is, God is using them to teach us theology. Again, this does not deny the historicity of the texts, and the term *theological history* is an accurate classification. However, this theological history comes in a *narrative* form, and we prefer to use that term. We will also use the term *narrator* as a synonym for *author*.

Narrative is a literary form characterized by sequential time action and involving plot, setting, and characters. It is the *story* form of literature.

Why did God choose narrative literature to communicate theological truth to us? Why didn't he communicate everything through essays or law? Think for a moment about these questions. Try to list some advantages of using narrative to communicate theological truth to us. Compare your list of advantages with ours below:

Advantages (Pros) of Using Narrative to Communicate Theological Truth

1. Narratives are interesting, both to children and to adults.
2. Narratives pull us into the action of the story.
3. Narratives usually depict real life and are thus easy to relate to. We find ourselves asking what we would have done in that situation.
4. Narratives can portray the ambiguities and complexities of life.
5. Narratives are easy to remember.
6. God can include himself as one of the characters in the narrative. Thus, he can teach us about himself by what he says and does in specific contexts.
7. Narratives are holistic; we see characters struggle, but we also often see resolution of their struggles. We see the entire character.
8. Narratives relate short incidents and events to a bigger overall story.

Are there negative aspects to narrative? Limitations? That is, are there some drawbacks to using narrative for conveying theological truth? See if you can add any cons to our list below:

Disadvantages (Cons) of Using Narrative to Communicate Theological Truth

1. The meaning of the narrative can be subtle or ambiguous and not clearly stated; the casual reader may miss it altogether.
2. The reader may get enthralled with the narrative as a story and miss its meaning.
3. The reader may assume that since the literature is narrative, it deals only with history and not theology.
4. The reader may read too much theology into the narrative (allegorizing).

The pros appear to outweigh the cons. Obviously the authors of the Bible thought so. At the core of the list of advantages are issues revolving around how the literature connects with people. In our opinion, God chose to use the literary device known as narrative as a major way to communicate his big story to us precisely because the biblical narratives engage us in such a powerful way. They challenge us, interest us, rebuke us, puzzle us, and entertain us. They stick in our memory. They make us think and reflect. They involve us emotionally as well as intellectually. They teach us about God and his plan for his people. They teach us about all kinds of people—good ones and bad ones, faithful, obedient ones and mule-headed, disobedient ones. They teach us about life in all its complexities and ambiguities.

The narrators of the Bible write with skill and power. Sometimes their meaning is clear, but sometimes the writers are subtle and the meaning of the text is not always obvious. We have a substantial interpretive river to cross when we read Old Testament narrative. The rest of this chapter will help you to cross that river and take the Interpretive Journey from the Old Testament narrative text to application today. We will focus on how to read narrative passages carefully and how to draw valid theological principles out of those passages—principles that can be applied to life today.

READING NARRATIVE

Fundamental to interpreting Old Testament narrative correctly is reading the passage carefully. Remember all the observation skills you learned back in part 1? You will need all of them as you read Old Testament narrative. Turn back to chapter 5 and review briefly. Do you remember how noticing all the small details in Mark 8:22–26 and in the surrounding passages helped you to interpret that passage? Likewise review our discussion in chapter 5 on Genesis 11:1–9. That passage was constructed as a *chiasm*, remember? That complicated chiastic structure should be an indication to us that the writers of the Old Testament narratives can be subtle in their writing, and they can use some sophisticated literary devices to tell their story.

Recall as well the skills you learned in chapter 15 on the Gospels. There are many similarities between reading the New Testament Gospels and reading Old Testament narrative. The skills you developed with the Gospels will also serve you well in tackling the stories of the Old Testament. One of the differences, however, is that the episodes in the Old Testament are usually longer than those in the New. In the Gospels most of the stories we looked at were only a few verses long. Furthermore, the context we analyzed was usually the paragraphs immediately preceding and immediately following. So our analysis of the Gospels was fairly compact. The episodes within Old Testament narrative, however, are usually longer, often involving entire chapters.

Moreover, the literary context that must be explored may be even longer, often involving numerous chapters. Don't take shortcuts! Do not assume that these Old Testament narratives are simple stories! Observe! Probe into the text like Sherlock Holmes or a CSI team does into a crime scene. Look for repetition, comparison, contrast, movement from general to specific, and so on. Notice the small details and ask why the details are there.

Let's look at a fascinating narrative text in Joshua 2 as an example. Open your Bible and read that chapter. In the early chapters of Joshua, the Israelites are beginning their conquest of the promised land. In chapter 1, God exhorts Joshua to be courageous and to lead Israel across the Jordan River to victory in the promised land. In Joshua 2, however, the story of the conquest slows down, interrupted by the episode about Rahab the harlot. This story is replete with details; the narrator (author) shares a tremendous amount of information about Rahab. We know her name and occupation (which should raise some questions). We are given numerous other details. For example, she hides the spies on the roof, where she dries flax; she talks to them about God, and she expresses faith in Israel's God based on what she has heard about him; her family members are mentioned twice (2:13, 18); she gives the spies advice about their best escape route; she deceives the king's soldiers (her own countrymen); in general she is a clever girl.

This in and of itself should set off some alarms in our heads, leading us to start asking a million observation questions. Why all the details? The roof? The red cord? Why even mention Rahab? Placed here at the beginning of the conquest story, the Rahab episode is given prominence. It seems to be stressed. Is this not unusual? The Israelites are ordered to annihilate everyone in the promised land, and yet the first story of the conquest is an exception—a Canaanite prostitute turns to God in faith and is saved. Certainly the location of this story and the emphasis placed on it by the amount of text assigned to it indicate that this is an important episode to understanding the conquest and the book of Joshua. Is Rahab an isolated individual, or does her character in the story represent a larger group—perhaps people of faith? Thus, we plunge into Joshua 2, observing closely and asking questions.

Next we begin to explore the surrounding chapters, looking for connections and clues. Joshua 3 through 5 describes the Israelites' preparations for their attack on Jericho (Rahab's city). Joshua 6 describes the actual miraculous capture of Jericho. Rahab appears again in Joshua 6 (vv. 17, 23, 25), so we need to slow down and take a look. Note that once again her family as well as her possessions are mentioned: "All who are with her in her house shall be spared" (v. 17), "her father and mother, her brothers and sisters and all who belonged to her" (v. 23), and "with her family and all who belonged to her" (v. 25). Also note how this deliverance contrasts with the fate of everyone else in Jericho, as described in 6:21: "They devoted the city to the LORD and destroyed with the sword every living thing in it—men and women, young and old, cattle, sheep and donkeys."

Joshua 7, however, introduces us to a new character named Achan. This man, an Israelite, steals some of the loot that was to be devoted to God. Because of his action, Israel loses the next battle. Joshua eventually finds out about Achan, and Israel executes him *and his family*, along with his cattle, donkeys, and sheep. Whoa! Alarms should start going off in your head. The cattle, donkeys, and sheep were also specifically mentioned in 6:21 regarding the destruction of Jericho. Is the death of Achan being compared to the destruction of Jericho? And what about the destruction of his family members? Recall that the *deliverance* of family members was stressed in the Rahab story. Is there a connection? Are Rahab and Achan perhaps being contrasted with each other?

Let's take a closer look at Achan—with Rahab in mind. As we read through Joshua 7 we realize that Achan is the *exact opposite* of Rahab. Indeed, Rahab and Achan are the only two new major characters who are introduced into the story in the first seven chapters of Joshua. Their stories form *bookends* around the chapters dealing with the fall of Jericho (remember that this is the literary technique called *inclusio*). As we explore the details of the Achan narrative, we realize that many of the details in his story *contrast* with the details of the Rahab story. It seems as though the narrator is intentionally contrasting the two, with the destruction of Jericho as the background. Read through Joshua 2 and Joshua 7 again and list as many contrasts as you can. Compare your list with ours below:

In essence, Rahab and Achan trade places. She becomes like an Israelite and lives among God's people. She even shows up in the genealogy of Christ. Achan, by contrast, a member of Israel, dies like the Canaanites. In fact, the destruction of Achan and his family parallel the destruction of Jericho. The major difference between Rahab and Achan is their attitude toward God. Rahab takes God seriously, placing her faith in him and risking her life to protect the two Israelite spies she is hiding. Achan treats God as if he does not exist and assumes that he can blatantly disobey God without suffering any consequences.

Rahab	Achan
Woman	Man
Canaanite	Hebrew (tribe of Judah, the best)
Prostitute (disrespectable)	Respectable
Should have died, but survived and prospered	Should have prospered, but died
Her family and all she owned survived	His family and all he owned perished
Nation perishes	Nation prospers
Hides the spies from the king	*Hides the loot* from God and Joshua
Hides the spies *on the roof*	Hides the loot *under his tent*
Fears the God of Israel	Does not fear the God of Israel
Has only *heard* of God yet believes	Has *seen* the acts of God but disobeys
Her house survives, while the city is burned	His tent is burned
Cattle, sheep, and donkeys of Jericho perish	Cattle, sheep, and donkeys of Achan perish
She becomes like an Israelite and lives	He becomes like a Canaanite and dies

These two narratives together bracket the destruction of Jericho. Note the irony. As we begin reading the story of the annihilation of the Canaanites by the Israelites (the conquest), the first two people we meet in the story are exceptions to the rule! The Canaanite Rahab lives and the Israelite Achan dies. The narrator is letting us know there is more to the conquest than just the destruction of the Canaanites. Critical issues of individual faith and obedience are involved. Likewise, there is more to faith in God than just nationality or respectability. A Canaanite harlot can find it and a respectable Israelite can miss it. Thus, you can see much of the theological meaning and application for us comes out of critical contrasting observations that these two characters present.

Read carefully. Note the details. Observe! Read through surrounding chapters. Look for connections. Use all of the skills you developed in part 1. Ask questions of the text. Ask why the details are there. Keep reading and digging.

LITERARY FEATURES OF NARRATIVE

In part 1 we learned techniques for reading literature carefully. Several of the literary features we learned to look for are also important features of narrative. We will revisit a few of these in this chapter, but we will also add a few new special features to search for while observing Old Testament narrative.

Four important elements of narrative that we did not discuss in part 1 are: (1) plot, (2) setting, (3) characters, and (4) the viewpoint of the narrator. In our discussion of the Gospels (ch. 15), we encouraged you to ask the standard story questions of Who? What? When? Where? Why? and How? These questions will get you started into your study of narrative, but we need to expand on these for each of the four elements mentioned above.

1. Plot

Exploring the plot is an expansion of the *What?* and the *How?* questions. Plot is the organizing structure that ties narrative together. The sequence of events, along with the rise and fall of dramatic action, outlines the structure of the plot and moves the story forward. Plot is also the feature that ties individual episodes into a larger coherent story. For example, in the narrative about Abraham (Gen. 12–25) we encounter numerous short episodes about his life (he receives the promise, he goes to Egypt, he rescues Lot, he sends Hagar away, etc.). All of these shorter episodes are part of the larger plot of the story that deals with God's promise to Abraham and the fulfillment of that promise.

Plot is the organizing structure that ties narrative together.

Most narrative plots have three basic components. The story starts off with *exposition*, in which the basic setting is described and the main series of events begins. Next is *conflict*. Usually something in the exposition part of the story is characterized by incompleteness, disorder, or unfilled desire, and this shortcoming leads to conflict. The conflict can be internal (within a character) or external (between two characters or groups). Often in the Old Testament the central conflict is between God and his hardheaded people. The story next usually intensifies, rising to a climax, which is followed by the final element, plot *resolution*, where the conflict is resolved.[1] As you read narrative, be sure to identify the main plot. Ask, "*What* is this story about?" Try to trace which events move the story along: What is the main conflict? How does tension develop? How is the conflict resolved?

2. Setting

Setting deals with the questions *When?* and *Where?* The writers of the Old Testament do not provide nearly the same amount of descriptive material about the

1. Much of this material is based on Danna Nolan Fewell and David M. Gunn, "Hebrew Narrative," in *The Anchor Bible Dictionary*, ed. David Noel Freedman (New York: Doubleday, 1992), 4:1024–25.

setting as modern authors do, but they do still usually identify the setting. The stories of the Bible do not occur against a blank backdrop, nor are they presented against a mythical or imaginary backdrop. The settings of the Old Testament are concrete places and scenes: in Pharaoh's magnificent court in Egypt, in the desert of Sinai, inside a cave, on a trail in the mountains, or on the threshing floor in the dark. The setting is important. The events of the narrative take place against a backdrop, and the backdrop affects how we understand the story. Be certain to identify the setting. Note any setting changes in the narrative. Note particularly when anyone leaves the promised land. Remember that this area of land was a special place to the Israelites of the Old Testament, for it was connected to their covenant relationship with God.

For example, Ruth 1:1 states:

> In the days when the judges ruled, there was a famine in the land. So a man from Bethlehem in Judah, together with his wife and two sons, went to live for a while in the country of Moab.

Several aspects of the setting are presented in this first verse of Ruth and are important for understanding the rest of the book. The *time setting*, "in the days when the judges ruled," ties the story to the setting of the book of Judges. When we skim back through Judges, we realize that this was a terrible time period. Chaos and disorder filled the land. Lawlessness, disobedience to God, and raids by foreigners were common. This setting underscores how dangerous it was for Ruth and Naomi to travel alone and how dangerous it was for Ruth, a foreigner, to venture out into a field alone when the fields were full of men. It also underscores how unusual it was for her to meet someone as pious and honest as Boaz.

The *place setting* is also important, especially since it changes several times in the story. The man from Bethlehem leaves the land and goes to Moab. In the Old Testament, leaving the land generally indicated a lack of trust in God. Total disaster befalls this family in the next few verses. Is it because they have left the land? Later in the story Naomi and Ruth will return to the land. Are the ensuing blessings related to their return? Probably so. Notice also that the setting described in the opening verse of the story sets the ironic tone of the book. The name of the town, Bethlehem, means "house of bread." There was a "famine" in "the house of bread."

3. Characters

Characters are the answer to the *Who?* question, and they are critical to narrative. They carry out the action and move the plot forward. Usually the meaning being conveyed in the text is tied to the behavior of one or more characters in the story.

However, true to life, characters are complex. Furthermore the narrators (authors) do not always let us know what each character is thinking or feeling. They often leave gaps or ambiguities regarding their characters, and we as readers struggle to suggest possibilities for filling in these gaps. Like the participants of the story themselves, we as readers frequently do not have all the information we would like to have. The narrators tease us, pulling us along slowly and revealing only critical pieces of information that keep us enthralled with the story and reading on. This is part of good story writing.

Consider, for example, the character of Uriah, who was the unfortunate husband of Bathsheba. In 2 Samuel 11, while Uriah is off fighting for his king, King David commits adultery with Uriah's wife, Bathsheba. After she becomes pregnant, David brings Uriah back from the war, hoping he will sleep with his wife and thus conclude that he is the father of the forthcoming child. David's scheme, of course, does not work, and he finally has Uriah killed. The central scene of the story—one could say the climax—is an encounter between David and Uriah, described in 2 Samuel 11:10–12. Uriah has refused to go home to see his wife, and that refusal is spoiling David's plan.

Here is where we as readers would like some more information. Does Uriah know about the affair? Would it really have been possible for David to keep it hushed up? As we read back through the narrative, we realize that a lot of people are involved in the cover-up. Has a court insider leaked this scandal to Uriah, who undoubtedly knows many of the people in the court? In verse 10 David asks Uriah, "Why didn't you go home?" We listen to Uriah's answer and wonder if he is naive and honest, giving a straightforward answer, or whether perhaps his answer is subtle and sly, indicating that he knows more than he reveals. His answer is ironic in any case, but if he knows about the affair, his answer contains an indictment on David: "The ark and Israel and Judah are staying in tents, and my commander Joab and my lord's men are camped in the open country. How could I go to my house to eat and drink and make love to my wife? As surely as you live, I will not do such a thing!" (v. 11).

David, who has not gone to war as he should, has been doing the very thing Uriah refuses to do. Uriah plays an important role in the story. The way we fill in the gaps of Uriah's knowledge and behavior affects how we understand his answer. The narrator never gives us this information, leaving us intentionally in the dark, perhaps to let us identify with the confusion and fear in the heart of David, who also probably is uncertain about whether Uriah knows.[2]

2. See the extended discussion in Meir Sternberg, *The Poetics of Biblical Narrative* (Bloomington: Indiana University Press, 1987), 186–222.

4. Viewpoint of the Narrator

The narrator (author) is the one responsible for conveying the meaning to the readers through the story. Sometimes the narrator expresses his view to us clearly by using summary statements or judgment statements. For example, in 2 Kings 17:7 the narrator interprets the preceding events for us and explains, "All this took place because the Israelites had sinned against the Lord their God, who had brought them up out of Egypt." However, the narrator often stays maddeningly neutral. The meaning he conveys through the story is an implicit meaning, not an explicit one. He does not come right out and tell us the meaning; rather, he lets the characters and their actions speak for themselves. He expects the reader to be sophisticated enough to discern the good from the bad.

The narrator often seems to stay neutral when readers would really like for him to express his opinions.

In the latter part of Judges, for example, Israel commits disgustingly sinful acts. The worst judgment statement that the narrator actually says directly is found in 21:25, "In those days Israel had no king; everyone did as they saw fit." What an understatement! In those last few chapters of Judges, the nation, which had been spiraling downward theologically and morally, hits the moral and theological bottom. Not only have they failed to drive out the Canaanites as God commanded them at the beginning of the book, but (1) other nations have moved in; (2) the Israelites are killing each other instead of the inhabitants of the land; (3) they have turned to other gods; (4) a Levitical priest leads the tribe of Dan into pagan worship; (5) an Israelite town attempts to molest a priest, raping his concubine instead, and so on. You get the picture. The situation is terrible.

Does the narrator completely pass up the opportunity of making a moral judgment on this mess? Not at all. However, he presents his judgment with finesse through the artful way he tells the story. His judgment is there, but it is subtle. For example, in Judges 19 he tells the horrendous story of how the Israelite mob in the city of Gibeah threatens to molest a Levitical priest, shouting to the man protecting him, "Bring out the man who came to your house so we can have sex with him" (v. 22). Does this episode sound familiar? Does it bring to mind an earlier event? Most certainly! Back in Genesis 19 the people in Sodom did exactly the same thing. Do you perceive what the narrator of Judges is doing? He does not comment directly on the episode in Gibeah, but he certainly does indirectly. He presents the story in a way that highlights the obvious parallel between the event in Gibeah and the event in Sodom, and he lets the reader draw the obvious conclusion.

God severely judged the sin of Sodom in Genesis 19, and all its people were destroyed. The Old Testament portrays this episode as the epitome of sinful behavior.

The extreme sinfulness of the Canaanites, as illustrated by the city of Sodom, justifies the conquest. "See how sinful the Canaanites are!" the story in Genesis proclaims. But note the incredible irony in Judges 19. The people at Gibeah are not Canaanites. These people are Israelites! They are supposed to stay faithful to God and drive the sinful Canaanites out of the land. Instead, as the narrator shows us, the Israelites have become as Canaanites, forsaking God and committing the same horrendous sin that was committed in Sodom. Should God not judge the Israelites as well? What right does Israel now have, the narrator asks between the lines, to stay in the promised land when they are no different than the Canaanites?

Read carefully. Watch for details that indicate the viewpoint of the narrator. Be aware that the narrative may be subtle in its manner of presentation. However, if you observe closely and read carefully, you will be able to see the subtle details and clues the narrator has placed to keep us on the right track and to allow us to grasp his intended meaning.

As you can see, plot, setting, characters, and the viewpoint of the narrator are four important features of narrative. There are two other critical features that we addressed briefly in part 1, but they are worth repeating here. These are comparison/contrast and irony.

5. Comparison/Contrast

This literary technique is a major device used in Old Testament narrative to develop plot and to move the story forward. We noted above the contrast between Rahab and Achan. However, numerous other comparisons and contrasts appear in the Old Testament narratives. The opening chapters of 1 Samuel, for example, are structured around the contrast between Hannah and Eli. Likewise, Hannah's good son, Samuel, is contrasted with Eli's rotten sons, Hophni and Phinehas. The fortunes of each are reversed as Hannah's life is blessed through Samuel while Eli's life is troubled by Hophni and Phinehas. Ultimately, Eli dies, as do his two sons. Hannah prospers, and Samuel rises to prominence in the country, eventually replacing Eli as priest.

Perhaps the longest running contrast in the Old Testament is between Saul and David. This contrast is detailed, extending over numerous chapters in 1 Samuel. Some of the contrasting details are obvious, but many are subtle, to be seen only by those who read carefully. For example, consider the way in which each character is introduced into the story. Saul is introduced in 1 Samuel 9:1–2, where the narrator tells us that Saul was "as handsome a young man as could be found anywhere in Israel, and he was a head taller than anyone else." In contrast, David, introduced in 1 Samuel 16, is not even brought to Samuel for examination at first because of his youth and his unimposing size. Samuel sees Eliab, David's older brother, and thinks to himself that this impressive man must be the one whom God has chosen to be king. God, however, corrects Samuel's thinking by saying, "Do not consider his appearance or his height. . . . The LORD does not look at the things people look at. People look at the outward appearance, but the LORD looks at the heart" (v. 7).

The contrast in size between David and Saul surfaces again in 1 Samuel 17, the Goliath episode. In 17:8–9 the giant Goliath challenges the Israelites to send forth their champion to fight him. Who is the champion of Israel? Who would the logical candidate be? Who is taller by a head than everyone else? Saul, of course! Saul is the biggest Israelite, and he is the king. He is the obvious choice. However, the towering king shirks his responsibility and tries to buy his way out (v. 25). David, the diminutive youth, is different. He accepts the task of fighting Goliath even though he has no responsibility to do so; indeed, he is not even part of the army. Big, tall Saul hides in his tent while the small, young David defeats the giant who threatens Israel.

These contrasts are fairly obvious. Now let's look at a few that are subtler. When Saul is introduced in 1 Samuel 9, he is searching for his father's lost donkeys. The narrator does not tell us who lost the donkeys, but since Saul is out looking for them, there is the possibility that he has lost them. The text stresses this event, providing numerous details that describe the journey Saul and his servant make looking for these lost donkeys. How heroic is this introduction? How valiant does Saul appear to be? He cannot find his father's donkeys and he suggests to the servant that they give up and return home. Saul's servant, however, persuades Saul to travel to the next town and ask Samuel, the man of God, about the donkeys. Saul follows the advice of his servant, but when he encounters Samuel by chance in the town, he does not even recognize him as the man of God.

All of this is a bit humorous. The future king of Israel is introduced to us as a stumbling, bumbling lout, looking hopelessly for his dad's lost donkeys and following the initiative of his servant. He does not appear to be very bright or bold. But how is David introduced? The narrator stresses that David is keeping his father's sheep. This is mentioned no less than six times in 1 Samuel 16–17, the chapters that introduce him. Moreover, he defends his father's sheep from lions and bears. He is not one who loses sheep or who roams around aimlessly looking for lost donkeys, of all things.

David faithfully watches over his father's sheep while Saul searches vainly for his lost donkeys.

Likewise, David explodes on the scene in chapter 17, fighting and killing Goliath. David is everything Saul is not, and the narrator stresses this with the details he presents. Saul is wishy-washy and shirks responsibility. He is frightened by Goliath (v. 11) and probably runs from him with the rest of the Israelite army (v. 24). David is decisive, accepting responsibility. He does not run from the lions that attacked his father's sheep; neither will he ignore the insulting words of Goliath (the figurative lion attacking the figurative sheep of David's figurative father) and run from him. David is not frightened by Goliath. Rather than run from the giant, David actually runs to meet him in battle (v. 48). During this episode, David, in essence, switches flocks. He changes from watching his fathers' sheep to watching over God's sheep, the nation of Israel. He accepts the responsibility for this, regardless of the danger. Saul, by contrast, is someone who searches for lost donkeys, shirks his responsibilities, and runs from danger. Next to David, Saul is pathetic. The contrast continues for many chapters, and much of 1 Samuel revolves around it. Recognizing this contrast is critical to understanding 1 Samuel.

6. Irony

Irony is the literary term used to describe situations where the literal or surface meaning of an event or episode is quite different—indeed, sometimes opposite—of the narrator's real intended meaning. This is not done to hide the meaning from the reader but to present the meaning with more force. It allows the narrator to sneak up on the readers and surprise them with the unexpected. Occasionally it also provides some humor. In irony, actions and events may have multiple implications. When it occurs, usually one or more characters in the story (and sometimes the reader) miss out on some knowledge and fail to see anything other than the surface implication. The authors of Old Testament narrative love to use this technique, and their frequent use of irony enhances their stories, making them fascinating to study and enjoyable to read.

A good example of irony occurs in 1 Samuel 5–6. Without consulting God, the foolish, wicked sons of Eli, Hophni and Phinehas, carry the ark of the covenant (i.e., the presence of the Lord) into battle as a good-luck omen. The Philistines, however, defeat the Israelites and capture the ark. They think that they have defeated not only the Israelites, but also the Israelites' God. They treat the ark as the idol of a conquered nation and place it at the feet of their god Dagon. We, the readers, are anxious. Has the Lord been defeated? How can the ark be captured by pagan Philistines?

The Lord, however, is playing ironic tricks on the Philistines (and the narrator is playing tricks on us as well). The idol of Dagon falls to its face each day before the ark in submission to the Lord. Eventually his hands and head are cut off (a common fate executed on defeated kings). A plague of tumors breaks out in the Philistine city, and in terror they transfer the ark to another Philistine city. God strikes that city with the plague as well, throwing all of Philistia into a panic. The Philistines then give gold gifts to God to placate him and allow the ark of the covenant to return to Israel.

On the surface the Philistines think that they have won the war, defeating the Israelites and carrying off the Israelite God as a trophy. In reality the Lord invades Philistia. He destroys the Philistine god Dagon and continues to move through the country of Philistia, smiting city after city, as if on a military campaign. Finally, the Philistines capitulate and pay tribute to God. He returns to Israel victoriously and with gold tribute. The two clods Hophni and Phinehas may have been defeated by the Philistines, but the God of Israel was not; he was victorious. The irony is rich.

LITERARY CONTEXT—THE BIG STORY

In chapter 8 we discussed the importance of literary context. We reiterated this point in chapter 15 on the Gospels. So it should come as no surprise that we bring up this issue again in this chapter. Obviously, it is important to locate the episode you are studying in the context of the narratives that surround it. Likewise, it is important to keep relating the parts to the whole. That is, when studying a small story within a particular book, it is imperative that you relate that story to the overall plot of the book. What role does your episode play in the big narrative of the entire book? The parts/whole interaction is important to keep in mind as you attempt to interpret individual stories accurately. Interpretations that do not fit into the overall story line are probably incorrect. Furthermore, a proper understanding of many events is only possible when they are read in light of the bigger story.

For instance, the smaller narrative of Numbers 14 describes the rebellion of the Israelites and their refusal to go into the promised land and conquer it as God had commanded them through Moses. How does this event relate to the larger narrative? God has promised this land to Abraham's descendants way back in Genesis 12. All throughout Genesis this promise is repeated. In Exodus God delivers the Hebrews out of Egyptian slavery for the explicit purpose of taking them to the promised land. So, after he strikes the Egyptians with plagues, parts the Red Sea, enters into covenant relationship with the Israelites to dwell among them, and then miraculously leads them through the desert to the special land he has given to them, they refuse it. They do not want the land if they have to fight for it.

When we view the Israelites' refusal in light of the overall narrative instead of just the smaller narrative, their behavior becomes outrageous. How could they refuse the land? Moving in to possess the land was the whole point of the exodus from Egypt! Possessing the land was the culmination of a plan God had been developing for centuries. Their refusal to enter, then, was not just another everyday episode of Israelite disobedience to God, such as we find throughout Numbers. It is the climax of their disobedience in this book.

Another passage illustrating the importance of literary context is the episode recorded in 2 Samuel 11–12 that we discussed in chapter 5, that of David and Bathsheba. After David commits his terrible sins of adultery and murder, Nathan his prophet comes to him and rebukes him. David acknowledges his sin and repents sincerely. God forgives him, and he marries Bathsheba. At the end of 2 Samuel 12 David musters his army and returns to battle (where he should have been at the beginning of the story). If we stay in this chapter, all seems to be well. David has been forgiven and everything has returned to normal.

All the king's horses and all the king's men could not put David together again.

The overall story of 2 Samuel, however, throws a different light on this episode. The first ten chapters of 2 Samuel present David's rise to power. He is continually victorious. He is the hero of the land, both militarily and theologically. He has corrected the disastrous situation described in the book of Judges, and he has the nation back on track. The narrator sums up the situation in 2 Samuel 8:15: "David reigned over all Israel, doing what was just and right for all his people."

The second half of the book, however, is quite different. Starting in 2 Samuel 13 things start to go sour for David. His son Amnon rapes his half sister Tamar, only to be killed by another son, Absalom. Later Absalom leads a rebellion against David, and most of the country deserts their "hero." At the low point of the story, as David flees, he is pelted with stones by a single man along the road (contrast with the earlier Goliath episode!). Absalom is killed, breaking David's heart, but rebellion and political intrigue continue to plague David for the rest of his reign. Humpty Dumpty has indeed fallen, and no one in the story is able to put him back together again.

In other words, the first half of the book is wonderful for David, but the second half is disastrous. What lies in the middle? Adultery with Bathsheba and the murder of Uriah! How does the larger story help us understand David's life-changing choices? What principle is the narrator really trying to present to us? God forgives David, but God does not return everything back to the way it was. David finds out that his sin has serious consequences for his relationship with his children and his nation. When one repents of sin, God will forgive him or her of the sin, but the consequences of that sin will likely continue.

What application can we draw from this? Suppose that a Christian, under pressure from old friends, spends an evening drinking. Later, while drunk, he is driving home in his car and hits a four-year-old child who lives next door, killing the child. In the morning, realizing what he has done, he sincerely confesses his sin and repents. Will God forgive him of this sin? Most certainly! But the child is still dead, and the child's parents will mourn that child for a long, long time.

Literary context is important. Placing the smaller narratives that we study into proper context within the overall story is crucial to developing a correct understanding of the passage. How is this done? How much text should we read in order to place an episode in proper context? We suggest the following guidelines, moving from the larger context to the smaller context:

- Be aware of the overall story of the Old Testament. Explore how the character or episode that you are studying fits into the big picture.
- Study the overall themes and message of the book of the Bible that your episode is in. Read a summary statement of the book in a good Bible dictionary. If possible read the entire book yourself. Look for connections between the episode you are studying and the rest of the book. What role does your episode play in the overall plot of the book?
- We recommend that you read the entire larger episode. For example, if you are studying an event in Abraham's life, then read all of the Abraham narrative (Gen. 12–25). Try to determine how the event you are studying fits into the larger episode. Remember to read carefully and look for connections.
- As a minimum, read three chapters: the entire chapter in which your episode occurs, the chapter that precedes it, and the chapter that follows it.

DO THE "GOOD GUYS" ALWAYS WEAR WHITE HATS?

When we were children, many of the movies and television shows we watched, especially Westerns, had simple, basic plots. There were only two types of characters, the "good guys" and the "bad guys," and it was not difficult to tell them apart. To make it even simpler for us to grasp, sometimes the good guys wore white hats and the bad guys wore black ones. However, this simplistic world was mythical, existing only on the screen. As time passed, movies became more complex. Characters became more complex. Sometimes the bad guys had the audacity to wear white hats! Audiences were confused. A friend once complained, "I didn't like that movie at all, because I couldn't tell who were the good guys and who were the bad guys." The problem was that some of the good guys had a few bad traits, while some of the bad guys had a few good traits. The distinction between good and bad was still there, but it now required some thought and reflection to discern it.

The Bible deals with real life and with real people. People are complex, and so are the great stories about them.

The Old Testament is not like the old Westerns. Those old movies portrayed a mythical world with simple characters and no gray areas. The Bible deals with real life and with real people. People are complex, and so are the great stories about them. We should not be surprised to find complicated personalities in the Old Testament.

This observation is important, because as we make the Interpretive Journey, we will derive many of the theological principles from the behavior of the main characters. Many of the characters will become models for us, providing patterns and examples of faithful living before God. It is essential, then, that we be able to discern the good guys from the bad guys. One of the most common errors made in interpreting Old Testament narrative is to assume that everyone in the story is a hero, a model for us to copy. This is simply not true. Many of the people are negative characters, and we need to be aware of this. If we mistake a bad guy for a good guy, we will be missing the point of the story.

Also keep in mind that most of the main characters (excluding God) exemplify mixtures of good and bad traits. Few characters emerge from the story as squeaky-clean. The narrator expects us to read with sophistication and discernment. He does not identify his characters with white hats and black hats.

Solomon is a good example. Is he a good guy or bad guy? He seems to start out well. At times he appears to be a good model, trusting God. However, much of the time his behavior is questionable so that the narrator, as mentioned above, seems to be criticizing him rather than promoting him as a model. Ultimately, of course, Solomon's standing is clear. He turns away from God and follows idols. He is a tragic character. For all of his great wisdom and wonderful building projects, he ends up a failure. He leaves a legacy of idolatry to his descendants, and the nation continues to follow his lead as they chase after idols.

What about Samson? Is he a hero or a bum? We should look for clues from the narrator. He tells us that God strengthens Samson, and he does some great feats of physical strength. Militarily he has some significant personal victories over the Philistines. He whups on the bad guys (the Philistines). Doesn't that make him a hero? The narrator answers in the negative. The entire moral and theological life of Samson is rotten. He ignores his call as a Nazirite and violates all of the Nazirite requirements. He blatantly violates the law and intentionally feeds unclean meat to his parents. He spends most of his time chasing after foreign women. He is self-centered and driven only by the pursuit of his own pleasure. He is not a positive model. He is perhaps a picture of squandered potential, one who wasted the power and opportunity that God had given to him by pursuing self-gratification.[3]

3. The fact that Samson appears in Hebrews 11:32 does not mean that we should completely reinterpret the narrative about him in Judges and "sanitize" the Old Testament text. Hebrews 11:32 and the surrounding verses are not citing the so-called "heroes of faith" as exemplary models in all aspects of life. Rahab the prostitute is cited in 11:31. Clearly her life as a prostitute is not the exemplary aspect of her life that the author is stressing; rather, the

As mentioned above, another important procedure to follow in interpreting these characters is to relate their story to the larger context. What is taking place in the larger story, and what role does the specific individual under consideration play in the big picture? How does Samson fit into the overall story of Judges? The book of Judges, remember, is basically a book chronicling the downward theological and moral spiral of Israel after they settle in the land. Samson is part of the downward spiral. Although God empowers him, Samson does not seem to care about serving or obeying God. The understanding of Samson as one who was gifted with great things from God but who nonetheless squandered everything through his self-centeredness fits into the context of Judges fairly well. Although Samson accomplished a few good things for Israel, he is not one of the "good guys"; he is a negative model.

Throughout most of the Old Testament narrative literature, *God is a central character.* God is not aloof in the Old Testament, speaking only in shadows through the narrator. He is a major player in the story. A central feature of narrative is dialogue, and God is involved in more than two hundred separate dialogues in the Old Testament! If we miss God in the story, then we have missed the story. Narrative is powerful and effective at revealing the character of the participants to us. One of the central purposes of this material is to reveal God to us. We have the opportunity to see God at work in numerous situations, dealing with various human-related problems.

Let God be God, and don't try to fit him into a neat, small box.

This leads us to another important point. *Let God be God.* Too often we seek to systematize God. We fit him into neat theological or philosophical categories (God is omnipotent, omniscient, omnipresent, etc.). Certainly these doctrines are true, but they are abstract concepts, and if they are not balanced with the personal aspects of God, they tend to isolate us from God. If we are not careful, God will become an impersonal, distant abstraction for us, like the Force in Star Wars movies. The narratives of the Old Testament reject this view of God. The Lord is not something abstract that you feel, but rather a person who speaks, relates, gets angry, hurts, changes his mind, argues, and loves. He relates to people on a human level, but he continues to be more than us, still above us. He is the hero of the story.

Many Christians come to Old Testament narratives with their God in a neat, small theological box. As they learn to read carefully, however, they are often stunned

author stresses the one central event of faith that led to her deliverance. Likewise, the self-centered character of Samson can hardly be seen as exemplary in his day-to-day lifestyle (i.e., visiting prostitutes, etc.). However, Samson does, by the power of God, crush Israel's enemies, especially in his final suicidal act. Hebrews 11 cites him for this reason, but that fact does not override the book of Judges to establish that Samson somehow lived a *life* of faith. God can work great miracles of deliverance through bums too, as Samson demonstrates. Our response should be to glorify God for using such an unworthy individual and not to whitewash Samson to somehow make him appear to be worthy.

by his behavior, because he does not act according to their preunderstanding of him. In Exodus 32:10, for example, following Israel's construction of the golden calf idol, God says to Moses, "Now leave me alone so that my anger may burn against them and that I may destroy them." In the next three verses Moses *argues* with God and convinces him to *change his mind*. Exodus 32:14 records the results: "Then the LORD relented and did not bring on his people the disaster he had threatened." How do we deal with a text like this? How can God, who sees all and knows all, change his mind?

We suggest that you let God be God. He has chosen to reveal himself to us in these narratives. Apparently there are aspects of his nature and personality that he wishes to convey to us through these stories. As you read Old Testament narrative, do not get bogged down with explaining away these troubling passages. Take them at face value and study them carefully to see what they reveal to us about the character of God. Do not try to keep God in a small box.

We have found that it is tough to keep God in the box if you read a lot of Old Testament narrative. He just keeps poking out of the box and refusing to be defined in a simplistic way. If people in real life are complex characters, how much more so is God! However, this complex God has chosen to relate to us personally and to reveal his character to us through these passages. If our goal is to know God, then it is imperative that we seek to hear what he is trying to tell us about himself in these narrative texts.

SUMMARY—MAKING THE JOURNEY

All of the material above will help us as we make the Interpretive Journey. Let's review the steps of this journey for Old Testament narrative, summarizing the issues from this chapter as we move through each step. We will use the Rahab and Achan story (Josh. 2:1–24; 7:1–26) as an example.

Step 1: Grasp the text in their town. What did the text mean to the biblical audience?

Use all of your observation skills to read the text carefully. Note all of the details. Search for connections. Analyze the literary and historical contexts. Be sure that you identify the overall story line for the book you are in and try to fit your narrative into the larger story. Write out a statement of what the text meant to the biblical audience.

For the Rahab and Achan story: Rahab, the Canaanite prostitute, is contrasted with Achan, the Israelite. She believes in the God of Israel and trusts him with her life, resulting in the deliverance of her and her family from the destruction of Jericho. Achan, however, trivializes God and ignores his strict commands, resulting in his death and that of his family. The two trade places.

Step 2: Measure the width of the river to cross. What are the differences between the biblical audience and us?

Identify the differences between the biblical audience and us. Be sure to remember the change in covenants (we are no longer under the law). Other significant differences that you may encounter may relate to the land, the monarchy, the conquest of Canaan, sacrifices, and direct conversation with God.

For the Rahab and Achan story: We are under a different covenant than Achan. Our situation is different. We are not in the conquest and we are not involved in any type of literal holy war. Nor are we Canaanites (or prostitutes) living in a city about to be conquered. God has not given us the same specific commands as he gave Achan.

Step 3: Cross the principlizing bridge. What is the theological principle in this text?

Identify possible similarities between the situation of the biblical audience and us. Search for theological principles that relate to both but that are derived from the text. Do not allegorize! Do not ignore the Old Testament meaning and simply zoom off into the New Testament. Remember the guidelines for developing theological principles we discussed earlier:

- The principles should be reflected in the text.
- The principles should be timeless and not tied to a specific situation.
- The principles should not be culturally bound.
- The principles should correspond to the teaching of the rest of Scripture.
- The principles should be relevant to both the biblical and the contemporary audiences.

For the Rahab and Achan story: God sees past superficial externals and saves unusual people who place their faith in him. This is because deliverance is based on true faith (demonstrated by action) and not mere externals, such as ethnicity or religious tradition. God is a God of grace. But judgment comes on those who trivialize God and treat him as if he does not exist.

Step 4: Consult the biblical map. How does our principle fit with the rest of the Bible? Does the New Testament teaching modify or qualify this principle, and if so, how?

Try to determine whether the New Testament addresses the issues raised by the text. Does the New Testament modify the theological principle in any way, or does it make the principle more specific? Do not abandon the Old Testament in this step.

We are still striving to grasp the meaning in the Old Testament text that was intended by the author. We are seeking to determine how that meaning plays out in the New Testament context. The meaning we determine in this step should be applicable to any New Testament believer.

For the Rahab and Achan story: the New Testament reaffirms that God looks beyond superficial externals and saves people based on faith in Jesus Christ. That God chooses some unusual people is likewise reaffirmed in the New Testament. Mere association with the church, rather than true faith, will not result in salvation.[4]

Step 5: Grasp the text in our town. How should individual Christians today live out this modified theological principle?

Be as specific as possible. Remember that there can be numerous individual applications of the theological principles.

For the Rahab and Achan story: We tend to judge people based on externals. We meet a clean-cut, middle-class American and think what a great Christian he or she would make. Likewise, when we see people involved in open sinful activity (drugs, prostitution, gambling, stealing), we tend to write them off and assume that *they* could never become Christians. This attitude is wrong, because God delights in saving the most unusual people. He wants us to have the same attitude toward these people as he does. There are no *unlikely candidates* for coming to salvation in Christ.

4. Note that the story of Ananias and Sapphira in Acts 5:1–11 has a certain affinity with the Achan story. In the New Testament, God still takes lying to him (and his appointed leaders) seriously and will judge those who blatantly try to deceive him. We cannot hide our sin from God.

ASSIGNMENTS

Assignment 18–1

First, study 1 Samuel 3:1–21, printed below, and make as many observations as you can. Mark the observations on a photocopy of the text. Use additional paper as needed. Then identify the literary context and the historical context. That is, explain how this narrative fits into the overall story of the book. Use a Bible dictionary or commentary if necessary to help you determine the main story line of the book. Next, take the Interpretive Journey. Complete each of the five steps above, writing out one or more statements for each step.

1The boy Samuel ministered before the Lord under Eli. In those days the word of the Lord was rare; there were not many visions.

2One night Eli, whose eyes were becoming so weak that he could barely see, was lying down in his usual place. 3The lamp of God had not yet gone out, and Samuel was lying down in the house of the Lord, where the ark of God was. 4Then the Lord called Samuel.

Samuel answered, "Here I am." 5And he ran to Eli and said, "Here I am; you called me."

But Eli said, "I did not call; go back and lie down." So he went and lay down.

6Again the Lord called, "Samuel!" And Samuel got up and went to Eli and said, "Here I am; you called me."

"My son," Eli said, "I did not call; go back and lie down."

7Now Samuel did not yet know the Lord: The word of the Lord had not yet been revealed to him.

8A third time the Lord called, "Samuel!" And Samuel got up and went to Eli and said, "Here I am; you called me."

Then Eli realized that the Lord was calling the boy. 9So Eli told Samuel, "Go and lie down, and if he calls you, say, 'Speak, Lord, for your servant is listening.' " So Samuel went and lay down in his place.

10The Lord came and stood there, calling as at the other times, "Samuel! Samuel!"

Then Samuel said, "Speak, for your servant is listening."

11And the Lord said to Samuel: "See, I am about to do something in Israel that will make the ears of everyone who hears about it tingle. 12At that time I will carry out against Eli everything I spoke against his family—from beginning to end. 13For I told him that I would judge his family forever because of the sin he knew about; his sons blasphemed God, and he failed to restrain them. 14Therefore, I swore to the house of Eli, 'The guilt of Eli's house will never be atoned for by sacrifice or offering.' "

15Samuel lay down until morning and then opened the doors of the house of the Lord. He was afraid to tell Eli the vision, 16but Eli called him and said, "Samuel, my son."

Samuel answered, "Here I am."

17"What was it he said to you?" Eli asked. "Do not hide it from me. May God deal with you, be it

ever so severely, if you hide from me anything he told you." [18]So Samuel told him everything, hiding
nothing from him. Then Eli said, "He is the LORD; let him do what is good in his eyes."

[19]The LORD was with Samuel as he grew up, and he let none of Samuel's words fall to the ground.
[20]And all Israel from Dan to Beersheba recognized that Samuel was attested as a prophet of the LORD.
[21]The LORD continued to appear at Shiloh, and there he revealed himself to Samuel through his word.

Assignment 18–2

First, study Genesis 22:1–19, printed below, and make as many observations as you can. Mark the observations on a photocopy of the text. Use additional paper as needed. Then identify the literary context and the historical context. That is, explain how this narrative fits into the overall story of the book. Use a Bible dictionary or commentary if necessary to help you determine the main story line of the book. Next, take the Interpretive Journey. Complete each of the five steps above, writing out one or more statements for each step.

1Some time later God tested Abraham. He said to him, "Abraham!"

"Here I am," he replied.

2Then God said, "Take your son, your only son, whom you love—Isaac—and go to the region of Moriah. Sacrifice him there as a burnt offering on a mountain I will show you."

3Early the next morning Abraham got up and loaded his donkey. He took with him two of his servants and his son Isaac. When he had cut enough wood for the burnt offering, he set out for the place God had told him about. 4On the third day Abraham looked up and saw the place in the distance. 5He said to his servants, "Stay here with the donkey while I and the boy go over there. We will worship and then we will come back to you."

6Abraham took the wood for the burnt offering and placed it on his son Isaac, and he himself carried the fire and the knife. As the two of them went on together, 7Isaac spoke up and said to his father Abraham, "Father?"

"Yes, my son?" Abraham replied.

"The fire and wood are here," Isaac said, "but where is the lamb for the burnt offering?"

8Abraham answered, "God himself will provide the lamb for the burnt offering, my son." And the two of them went on together.

9When they reached the place God had told him about, Abraham built an altar there and arranged the wood on it. He bound his son Isaac and laid him on the altar, on top of the wood. 10Then he reached out his hand and took the knife to slay his son. 11But the angel of the LORD called out to him from heaven, "Abraham! Abraham!"

"Here I am," he replied.

12"Do not lay a hand on the boy," he said. "Do not do anything to him. Now I know that you fear God, because you have not withheld from me your son, your only son."

13Abraham looked up and there in a thicket he saw a ram caught by its horns. He went over and took the ram and sacrificed it as a burnt offering instead of his son. 14So Abraham called that place The LORD Will Provide. And to this day it is said, "On the mountain of the LORD it will be provided."

15The angel of the LORD called to Abraham from heaven a second time 16and said, "I swear by myself, declares the LORD, that because you have done this and have not withheld your son, your only son, [17]I will surely bless you and make your descendants as numerous as the stars in the sky and as the sand on the seashore. Your descendants will take possession of the cities of their enemies, [18]and through your offspring all nations on earth will be blessed, because you have obeyed me."

[19]Then Abraham returned to his servants, and they set off together for Beersheba. And Abraham stayed in Beersheba.

Assignment 18–3

As background, read Deuteronomy 17:14–17 (rules for the king) and 1 Samuel 8:10–18 (warnings about the king). Now read the story of Solomon (1 Kings 1–11). Discuss the ways in which Solomon violates the rules for the king and how he fulfills the warnings. Contrast his good deeds with his bad deeds. In the narrator's mind, is Solomon a good character or a bad character? Is he a hero or a bum?

CHAPTER 19

OLD TESTAMENT—LAW

INTRODUCTION

A large portion of the Pentateuch (the first five books of the Bible) is comprised of *laws*. Indeed, there are over six hundred commandments in these books. We find this legal material throughout most of Leviticus and most of Deuteronomy. Also, about half of Exodus, along with a portion of Numbers, presents various laws that God gave to Israel. Obviously, these laws are important. But many of them seem strange to us. Consider the following laws:

> Exodus 34:26: "Do not cook a young goat in its mother's milk."
> Leviticus 19:19: "Do not wear clothing woven of two kinds of material."
> Leviticus 12:2: "A woman who becomes pregnant and gives birth to a son will be ceremonially unclean for seven days."
> Leviticus 13:40: "A man who has lost his hair and is bald is clean."
> Deuteronomy 22:12: "Make tassels on the four corners of the cloak you wear."

Furthermore, there are numerous Old Testament laws that we as modern Christians violate with some regularity. Which of the following have you violated?

> Deuteronomy 22:5: "A woman must not wear men's clothing, nor a man wear women's clothing."

Leviticus 19:32: "Stand up in the presence of the aged."
Leviticus 19:28: "Do not . . . put tattoo marks on yourselves."
Deuteronomy 14:8: "The pig is also unclean; although it has a divided hoof, it does not chew the cud. You are not to eat their meat or touch their carcasses."

While we tend to ignore such laws, there are other Old Testament commands that we latch onto as the moral underpinnings of Christian behavior. These will be more familiar to you:

Leviticus 19:18: "Love your neighbor as yourself."
Exodus 20:13: "You shall not murder."
Deuteronomy 5:18: "You shall not commit adultery."

So, why do we adhere to some laws and ignore others? Which laws are valid, and which are not? Many Christians today are baffled by the interpretive problem of the law. Some of us take the approach of simply skimming through the legal texts, skipping over all of the laws that do not seem to apply to us. These laws we choose to ignore altogether. Then when we encounter one that does seem to make sense in today's world, we grab it, underline it, and use it as a guideline for living. Surely this willy-nilly approach to interpreting the Old Testament law is inadequate. But how *should* we interpret the law?

In this chapter you will learn a consistent approach to interpreting the Old Testament law. We will first discuss a popular traditional approach that we consider inadequate. We will then present the method we feel is most valid for interpreting the law. As part of our suggested approach, we will first explore the narrative and covenant context of the Old Testament legal material and discuss the implications of that context to interpretation. Then we will apply the Interpretative Journey to the task of interpreting the law, providing several examples.

TRADITIONAL APPROACH

For many years the traditional approach to interpreting the Old Testament law has been to emphasize the distinction between *moral*, *civil*, and *ceremonial* laws. *Moral laws* were defined as those that dealt with timeless truths regarding God's intention for human behavior. "Love your neighbor as yourself" is a good example of a so-called moral law. *Civil laws* were those describing aspects that we normally see in a country's legal system. These laws dealt with the courts, economics, land, crimes, and punishment. An example of a civil law can be found in Deuteronomy 15:1: "At the end of every seven years you must cancel debts." *Ceremonial laws* were defined as those that dealt with sacrifices, festivals, and priestly activities. For example, Deuteronomy 16:13 instructed the Israelites to "celebrate the Festival of Tabernacles for seven days after you have gathered the produce of your threshing floor and your winepress."

Under this approach, these distinctions between *moral*, *civil*, and *ceremonial* laws were critically important, because this identification allowed believers to know whether the law applied to them. Moral laws, according to this system, were universal and timeless. They still applied *as law* to Christian believers today. Civil and ceremonial laws, however, applied only to ancient Israel, not to believers today. This system has been helpful to many, providing a methodology whereby texts such as "Love your neighbor as yourself" can still be claimed as law for the Christian while all the texts dealing with sacrifices and punishments can be dismissed.

The distinctions between moral, civil, and ceremonial laws appear to be arbitrary.

However, in recent years many Christians have become uncomfortable with this approach. First, the distinctions between moral, civil, and ceremonial laws appear to be arbitrary. There is no such distinction in the text. For example, "Love your neighbor as yourself" (Lev. 19:18) is followed in the very next verse by the law, "Do not wear clothing woven of two kinds of material" (19:19). Should we see verse 18 as applicable to us but dismiss verse 19 as nonapplicable? The text gives no indication whatsoever that any kind of interpretive shift has taken place between the two verses.

In addition, it is often difficult to determine whether a law falls into the moral category or into one of the others. Because the law defined the covenant relationship between God and Israel, the law, by nature, was *theological*. *All* of the law had theological content. The question then becomes, *Can a law be a* theological law *but not a* moral law?

For example, consider the commandment in Leviticus 19:19, "Do not plant your field with two kinds of seed. Do not wear clothing woven of two kinds of material." One of the central themes running throughout Leviticus is the holiness of God. Part of this theme is the teaching that *holy* things must be kept separate from *profane* or *common* things. While we may not understand all the nuances of the command against mixing cloth material or mixing seed, we do know that it relates back to the holiness of God. Indeed, all of the laws relating to separation appear to connect to the overarching principle of God's holiness and separation. So what kind of law would Leviticus 19:19 be? Civil? Unlikely. It is unrelated to the needs of society. Ceremonial? Perhaps, although the

All of the law, by nature, was *theological*.

law does not appear to apply to ceremonies or sacrifice. The way the Israelites planted seed and the way they wove cloth had *theological* significance to it. How can this *not* be a moral issue?

Another good example of a law that is difficult to classify with this system occurs in Numbers 5:11–28:

> [11]Then the LORD said to Moses, [12]"Speak to the Israelites and say to them: 'If a man's wife goes astray and is unfaithful to him [13]so that another man has sexual relations with her, and this is hidden from her husband and her impurity is undetected (since there is no witness against her and she has not been caught in the act), [14]and if feelings of jealousy come over her husband and he suspects his wife and she is impure—or if he is jealous and suspects her even though she is not impure—[15]then he is to take his wife to the priest. He must also take an offering of a tenth of an ephah of barley flour on her behalf. He must not pour olive oil on it or put incense on it, because it is a grain offering for jealousy, a reminder-offering to draw attention to wrongdoing.
>
> [16]" 'The priest shall bring her and have her stand before the LORD. [17]Then he shall take some holy water in a clay jar and put some dust from the tabernacle floor into the water. [18]After the priest has had the woman stand before the LORD, he shall loosen her hair and place in her hands the reminder-offering, the grain offering for jealousy, while he himself holds the bitter water that brings a curse. [19]Then the priest shall put the woman under oath and say to her, "If no other man has had sexual relations with you and you have not gone astray and become impure while married to your husband, may this bitter water that brings a curse not harm you. [20]But if you have gone astray while married to your husband and you have made yourself impure by having sexual relations with a man other than your husband"—[21]here the priest is to put the woman under this curse—"may the LORD cause you to become a curse among your people when he makes your womb miscarry and your abdomen swell. [22]May this water that brings a curse enter your body so that your abdomen swells or your womb miscarries."
>
> " 'Then the woman is to say, "Amen. So be it."
>
> [23]" 'The priest is to write these curses on a scroll and then wash them off into the bitter water. [24]He shall make the woman drink the bitter water that brings a curse, and this water that brings a curse and causes bitter suffering will enter her. [25]The priest is to take from her hands the grain offering for jealousy, wave it before the LORD and bring it to the altar. [26]The priest is then to take a handful of the grain offering as a memorial offering and burn it on the altar; after that, he is to have the woman drink the water. [27]If she has made herself impure and been

> unfaithful to her husband, this will be the result: When she is made to drink the water that brings a curse and causes bitter suffering, it will enter her, her abdomen will swell and her womb will miscarry, and she will become a curse.
> [28]If, however, the woman has not made herself impure, but is clean, she will be cleared of guilt and will be able to have children.' "

The passage describes how a woman suspected of adultery is to be tried by the priest. Surely adultery is a moral issue. Is this law, then, a timeless universal for us? To determine guilt or innocence, the priest makes a suspected adulteress drink some bitter water. If she gets sick, she is guilty. If she does not get sick, she is innocent. Should this be practiced today?

Surely adultery is a moral issue.

In our opinion this traditional approach to understanding Old Testament law is too ambiguous and too inconsistent to be a valid approach to interpreting Scripture. We simply do not see a clear distinction in Scripture between these different categories of law. The vagueness of this distinction thus makes us uncomfortable about using such a distinction to determine whether a particular law is to be obeyed or can be ignored. We also question the validity of dismissing the so-called civil and ceremonial laws as not being applicable. *All* Scripture is applicable to the New Testament believer.

We maintain, therefore, that the best method of interpreting the law is one that can be used consistently with all legal texts. It should be one that does not make arbitrary *nontextual* distinctions between verses and their applicability. The traditional approach to interpreting the law will, no doubt, continue to be a standard methodology for many Christians. It is a method with a long history, and it is a method we should respect. However, in the pages that follow, we suggest an alternative approach to the Old Testament law—one that can help us to be consistent in studying and applying the Old Testament law.

THE NARRATIVE CONTEXT

The Old Testament legal material does not appear by itself in isolation. This is an important observation. The Old Testament law, therefore, is different in the way it is presented than, for example, a book such as Proverbs. The book of Proverbs appears somewhat in isolation from other texts. It is not connected to a story. There are a few vague historical connections, but the book largely stands by itself within the Old Testament canon. True, it is connected theologically to the other *wisdom* books (Job, Ecclesiastes, Song of Songs), but the connection is loose and the relationship of Proverbs to the theological history of Israel is vague.

By contrast, the Old Testament law is firmly embedded in the story of Israel's theological history. It is part of the narrative that runs from Genesis 12 to 2 Kings 25. The law is not presented by itself as some sort of timeless universal code. Rather, it is presented as part of the theological narrative that describes how God delivered Israel from Egypt and established them in the promised land as his people.

This is true for each of the books that contain elements of the Old Testament law. For example, the main legal material in Exodus is found in Exodus 20–23. This section also contains the Ten Commandments. But notice the narrative context. The first nineteen chapters of Exodus tell the story of the Israelites' bondage in Egypt and their deliverance by the mighty works of God. It describes the call of Moses and his powerful encounters with Pharaoh. It presents the story of the plagues on Egypt, culminating in the visit by the death angel. Next, Moses leads the Israelites out of Egypt and through the sea. The book of Exodus then describes their journey in the desert until, in chapter 19, the Israelites arrive at Mount Sinai, where God calls them into covenant relationship.

The Old Testament law is firmly embedded in the story of Israel's theological history. It is part of the narrative that runs from Genesis 12 to 2 Kings 25.

The Ten Commandments in Exodus 20 and the laws that follow in Exodus 21–23 are part of this story. This passage is textually tied into the story of God's encounter with Moses and Israel at Mount Sinai. Note, for example, that the Ten Commandments are listed in Exodus 20:1–17, but they flow immediately back into the narrative in verse 18, "When the people saw the thunder and lightning and heard the trumpet and saw the mountain in smoke, they trembled with fear." Likewise, God presents numerous laws to Israel in Exodus 21–23, but these are also part of the narrative. They are part of the dialogue between God and Israel, with Moses as the intermediary. Notice the reaction of the people in Exodus 24:3 to God's presentation of the law: "When Moses went and told the people all the Lord's words and laws, they responded with one voice, 'Everything the Lord has said we will do.'"

The book of Leviticus is likewise painted on a narrative canvas against the backdrop of the encounter with God at Mount Sinai (26:46; 27:34). The laws in Leviticus are presented as part of a dialogue between God and Moses. Dialogue is a standard feature of narrative. The book begins, "The Lord called to Moses and spoke to him from the tent of meeting." The phrase "The Lord said to Moses" occurs over and over throughout the book. In addition, Leviticus contains numerous time-sequence phrases, an indication of a story line time movement, another characteristic of narrative:

"Then Moses took . . ." (8:10)
"He then presented . . ." (8:14)
"Moses then said . . ." (8:31)
"On the eighth day Moses summoned . . ." (9:1)
"So Aaron came to the altar . . ." (9:8)
"So fire came out from the presence of the LORD and consumed them . . ." (10:2)
"The LORD spoke to Moses after the death of the two sons of Aaron . . ." (16:1)

The book of Numbers picks up the story in the second year after the exodus (1:1) and describes the Israelites' journeys and wanderings for the next forty years (33:38). Central to this book is Israel's rejection of the promised land in chapters 13–14. This disobedience results in the forty years of wandering that the book recounts. At various points during the story, God presents Israel with additional laws. As in Exodus and Leviticus, the laws in Numbers are firmly tied into the narrative material.

The narrative setting for the book of Deuteronomy is in the eleventh month of the fortieth year after the exodus (1:3), just prior to Israel's entry into Canaan. The place is likewise specified—just east of the Jordan River (1:1, 5). In the overall story, Israel has completed the forty years of wandering that God specified as a punishment for their refusal to enter the land. A new generation has grown up, and God presents them with a restatement of the covenant he made with their parents forty years earlier (in Exodus).

Most of Deuteronomy consists of a series of speeches that Moses delivers to the Israelites on God's behalf. These speeches are connected to the narrative because they are tied to the same time and place, and they have a specific speaker and a specific audience, both of whom are main characters in the overall story. Also, the end of the book contains some nonlegal material: the appointment of Joshua as leader (31:1–8), the song of Moses (32:1–47), a blessing of Moses on the tribes (33:1–29), and the death of Moses (34:1–12). These events are likewise presented in a narrative setting. Furthermore, the events of Deuteronomy flow right into the book of Joshua, where the story continues without interruption.

The Old Testament law, therefore, is firmly embedded in the story of Israel's exodus, wandering, and conquest. Our interpretive approach to the law should take this into account. Remember the importance of *context* that you learned back in chapters 6 and 8. The law is part of a story, and this story provides an important context for interpreting the law. Indeed, our methodology for interpreting Old Testament law should be similar to our methodology for interpreting Old Testament narrative, for the law is contextually part of the narrative.

THE COVENANT CONTEXT

God introduces the law in a covenant context, saying, "Now if you obey me fully and keep my covenant, then out of all nations you will be my treasured possession" (Ex. 19:5). The people agree to keep the terms of the covenant (24:3), and Moses seals the agreement in blood: "Moses then took the blood, sprinkled it on the people and said, 'This is the blood of the covenant that the LORD has made with you in accordance with all these words' " (24:8).

Part of this covenant was God's promise to dwell in Israel's midst. This is stressed several times in the latter half of Exodus (25:8; 29:45; 33:14–17; 40:34–38). Associated with God's presence are the instructions for constructing the ark and the tabernacle, the place where God will dwell (chs. 25–31; 35–40). Leviticus is thus the natural sequence to the latter half of Exodus, for it addresses how Israel is to live with God in their midst. How do they approach him? How do they deal with personal and national sin before a holy God living among them? How do they worship and fellowship with this holy, awesome God in their midst? Leviticus provides the answers to these questions, giving practical guidelines for living with God in their midst under the terms of the Mosaic covenant.

The law is tightly intertwined with the Mosaic covenant.

After Israel's refusal to obey God and enter the promised land (Num. 13–14), God sends them into the desert for thirty-eight more years to allow that disobedient generation to die out. God then leads the people back toward Canaan. Before they enter, however, he calls them to a covenant renewal. With this new, younger generation, the Lord reinstates the Mosaic covenant that he originally made with their parents in the book of Exodus. Deuteronomy describes this renewed call to covenant that God is making with Israel just prior to their entering the promised land. Indeed, in Deuteronomy God elaborates and gives even more details about the covenant than he did in Exodus. Deuteronomy describes in detail the terms by which Israel will be able to live in the promised land successfully and be blessed by God.

Since the Old Testament law is tightly intertwined into the Mosaic covenant, it is important to make several observations about the nature of this covenant. (1) *The Mosaic covenant is closely associated with Israel's conquest and occupation of the land.* The covenant provides the framework by which Israel can occupy and live prosperously with God in the promised land. The close connection between the covenant and the land is stressed over and over in Deuteronomy. Indeed, the Hebrew word for "land" occurs 197 times in Deuteronomy. A selection of passages that directly connect the terms of the covenant with life in the land includes 4:1, 5, 14, 40; 5:16; 6:1, 18, 20–25; 8:1; 11:8; 12:1; 15:4–5; 26:1–2; 27:1–3; 30:5, 17–18; and 31:13.

(2) *The blessings from the Mosaic covenant are conditional.* A constant warning runs throughout Deuteronomy, explaining to Israel that obedience to the covenant will bring blessing, but that disobedience to the covenant will bring punishment and curses. Deuteronomy 28 is particularly explicit in this regard: verses 1–14 list the blessings for Israel if they obey the terms of the covenant (the law) while verses 15–68 spell out the terrible consequences if they do not obey those terms. The association of the covenant with the land and the conditional aspect of the covenant blessings are likewise linked tightly together, as illustrated in Deuteronomy 30:15–18:

> [15]See, I set before you today life and prosperity, death and destruction. [16]For I command you today to love the LORD your God, to walk in obedience to him, and to keep his commands, decrees and laws; then you will live and increase, and the LORD your God will bless you in the land you are entering to possess.
>
> [17]But if your heart turns away and you are not obedient, and if you are drawn away to bow down to other gods and worship them, [18]I declare to you this day that you will certainly be destroyed. You will not live long in the land you are crossing the Jordan to enter and possess.

(3) *The Mosaic covenant is no longer a functional covenant.* New Testament believers are no longer under the old, Mosaic covenant. Hebrews 8–9 makes it clear that Jesus came as the mediator of a *new* covenant that replaced the *old* covenant. "By calling this covenant 'new,' he has made the first one obsolete" (Heb. 8:13). The Old Testament law presented the terms by which Israel could receive blessings in the land under the old (Mosaic) covenant. If the old covenant is no longer valid, how can the laws that made up that covenant still be valid? If the old covenant is obsolete, should we not also view the system of laws that make up the old covenant as obsolete?

(4) *The Old Testament law as part of the Mosaic covenant is no longer applicable over us as law.* Paul makes it clear that Christians are not under the Old Testament law. For example, in Galatians 2:15–16 he writes, "We . . . know that a person is not justified by the works of the law, but by faith in Jesus Christ." In Romans 7:4 Paul states that "you also died to the law through the body of Christ." Likewise, in Galatians 3:24–25 he declares, "So the law was our guardian until Christ came that we might be justified by faith. Now that this faith has come, we are no longer under a guardian." Paul argues forcefully against Christians returning to the Old Testament law. In our interpretation and application of the law, we must be cautious to heed Paul's admonition. Now that we are freed from the law through Christ, we do not want to put people back under the law through our interpretive method.

But what about Matthew 5:17, where Jesus states, "Do not think that I have come to abolish the Law or the Prophets; I have not come to abolish them but to fulfill them"? Is Jesus contradicting Paul? We do not think so. First of all, note that the phrase "the Law and the Prophets" is a reference to the entire Old Testament. So Jesus is not just speaking about the Mosaic law. Also note that the antithesis is not between *abolish* and *observe*, but between *abolish* and *fulfill*. Jesus does not claim that he has come to *observe* the law or to *keep* the law; rather, he has come to *fulfill* it.

Matthew uses the Greek word translated "fulfill" numerous times; it normally means "to bring to its intended meaning." Jesus is *not* stating that the law is eternally binding on New Testament believers. If that were the case, we would be required to keep the sacrificial and ceremonial laws as well as the moral ones. This is clearly against New Testament teaching. What Jesus is saying is that he did not come to sweep away the righteous demands of the law, but that he came to fulfill these righteous demands. Furthermore, the law as well as the Old Testament prophets had prophetic elements, particularly in pointing to the ultimate demands of holiness because of the presence of God. Jesus is the climax of this aspect of salvation history. He fulfills all of the righteous demands and the prophetic foreshadowing of "the Law and the Prophets."

In addition, Jesus has become the final interpreter of the law—indeed, the authority over the meaning of the law, as other passages in Matthew indicate (many of which follow immediately on the heels of Matt. 5:17). Some Old Testament laws Jesus restates (19:18–19), but some he modifies (5:31–32). Some laws he intensifies (5:21–22, 27–28), and some he changes significantly (5:33–37, 38–42, 43–47). Furthermore, some laws he appears to abrogate entirely (Mark 7:15–19). Jesus is not advocating the continuation of the traditional Jewish approach of adherence to the law. Nor is he advocating that we dismiss the law altogether. He is proclaiming that we must *reinterpret* the meaning of the law in light of his coming and in light of the profound changes the new covenant has brought. This leads us to our last principle.

(5) *We must interpret the law through the grid of New Testament teaching.* Second Timothy 3:16 tells us that "all Scripture is God-breathed and is useful for teaching, rebuking, correcting and training in righteousness." Paul certainly is including the law in his phrase "all Scripture." As part of God's Word, the value of the Old Testament law is eternal. We should study and seek to apply all of it. However, the law no longer functions as the terms of the covenant for us, and thus *it no longer applies as direct, literal law for us.* The coming of Christ as the fulfillment of the law has changed that forever. However, the Old Testament legal material contains rich *principles* and *lessons* for living that are still relevant when interpreted through New Testament teaching.

How do we discover these lessons and principles? What method should we use to interpret the Old Testament law for New Testament believers, who are no longer under the law? The best approach is to use the Interpretive Journey.

THE INTERPRETIVE JOURNEY

We introduced the Interpretive Journey to you in chapter 2, and we discussed how it specifically relates to Old Testament interpretation in the introduction to part 5. In chapter 18 we learned how to use the Interpretive Journey to interpret Old Testament narrative. As we have been maintaining, our approach to the Old Testament law should be similar to our approach to Old Testament narrative. Look back through these sections and quickly review the Interpretive Journey. It gives us a consistent, valid approach to interpreting the Old Testament law. It also allows us to apply the same method to all passages dealing with the law.

We can interpret and apply all of the Old Testament law through the Interpretive Journey.

The Old Testament Interpretive Journey is presented below, followed by a discussion of how to use it to interpret and apply the Old Testament law.

Step 1: Grasp the text in their town. What did the text mean to the biblical audience?
Step 2: Measure the width of the river to cross. What are the differences between the biblical audience and us?
Step 3: Cross the principlizing bridge. What is the theological principle in this text?
Step 4: Consult the biblical map. How does our theological principle fit with the rest of the Bible? Does the New Testament teaching modify or qualify this principle, and if so, how?
Step 5: Grasp the text in our town. How should individual Christians today live out this modified theological principle?

Now let's walk through the process of using the Interpretive Journey to interpret and apply Old Testament laws.

Step 1: Grasp the text in their town. What did the text mean to the biblical audience?

Using the observation skills you developed in part 1, read carefully the text you are studying and observe as much as you can. Remember that the Old Testament law is part of a larger narrative. Read and study it as you would a narrative text. Identify the historical and literary contexts. Are the Israelites on the bank of the Jordan, preparing to enter the land (Deuteronomy)? Or are they back at Mount Sinai just after the exodus (Exodus, Leviticus)?

Has the law you are studying been given as a response to a specific situation, or is it describing the requirements for Israel after they move into the land? What other laws are in the immediate context? Is there a connection between these laws? Probe into the nature of the particular law you are studying. Try to identify how this particular law relates to the old covenant. Does it govern how the Israelites approach God? Does it govern how they relate to each other? Does it relate to agriculture or commerce? Is it specifically tied to life in the promised land? Now determine what this specific, concrete expression of the law meant for the Old Testament audience. Identify clearly what the law demanded of them. Do not generalize in step 1, but be specific to their town.

Step 2: Measure the width of the river to cross. What are the differences between the biblical audience and us?

Determine the differences between us today as Christians and the Old Testament audience. For example, we are under the new covenant and not under the old covenant as they were. Thus, we are no longer under the law as the terms of the covenant. Also, we are not Israelites preparing to live in the promised land with God dwelling in the tabernacle or temple; we are Christians with God living within each of us. We do not approach God through the sacrifice of animals; we approach God through the sacrifice of Jesus Christ. We live under a secular government and not under a theocracy, as ancient Israel did. We do not face pressure from Canaanite religion, but rather from non-Christian worldviews and philosophies. Most of us do not live in an agrarian society, but in an urban setting. What other differences can you note?

Step 3: Cross the principlizing bridge. What is the theological principle in this text?

Behind the expression of the meaning for the original audience lies a theological principle. Each of the Old Testament laws presents a concrete, direct meaning for the Old Testament audience, a meaning tied up with the old covenant context. But that meaning is usually based on a broader universal truth, a truth that is applicable to all of God's people, regardless of when they live and which covenant they live under. In this step we will cross over the bridge and ask, "What is the theological principle that is reflected in this specific law? What is the broad principle that God has behind this text that allows for this specific ancient application?"

What is the broad principle that God has behind this text that allows for this specific ancient application?

Remember that in developing this theological principle we must use the following criterion:

- The principle should be reflected in the text.
- The principle should be timeless.
- The principle should correspond to the teaching of the rest of Scripture.
- The principle should not be culturally tied.
- The principle should be relevant to both the biblical and contemporary audiences.

In legal passages, these principles will often be directly related to the character of God and his holiness, the nature of sin, or concern for other people.

Step 4: Consult the biblical map. How does our theological principle fit with the rest of the Bible? Does the New Testament teaching modify or qualify this principle, and if so, how?

Now pass through the New Testament with the theological principle and filter it through the New Testament teaching regarding the principle or the specific law being studied. For example, if you are interpreting Exodus 20:14, "You shall not commit adultery," your theological principle will relate to the sanctity of marriage and the need for faithfulness in marriage. As you pass into the New Testament, you must incorporate Jesus' teaching on the subject. In Matthew 5:28 Jesus states, "But I tell you that anyone who looks at a woman lustfully has already committed adultery with her in his heart." Jesus has expanded the range of this law. He applies it not only to *acts* of adultery but also to *thoughts* of adultery. Thus, the commandment not to commit adultery for us becomes, "You shall not commit adultery, in act or in thought."

There is also something of a culture barrier with regard to the commandment on adultery. In the Old Testament culture, girls married at a very young age. There was little opportunity for premarital sex. The major sexual temptation for that culture was extramarital affairs. Our culture, however, has both temptations, and both fall into the category of violating the sanctity of marriage and faithfulness in marriage. The expression of the principle for today's audience, therefore, should address both categories of temptation and challenge to marriage sanctity (premarital and extramarital sexual relations). The expression of this principle for us, therefore, is something like this: "Do not have sexual relations outside of marriage, in act or in thought."

Remember that this step develops a concrete expression of the theological principle for today's Christian audience. This concrete expression should be one that is broad enough to address an entire Christian *community* or *church*, but one that is specific for New Testament believers today.

Step 5: Grasp the text in our town. How should individual Christians today live out this modified theological principle?

Take the expression developed in step 4 and apply it to specific situations that *individual* Christians encounter today.

Example 1: Leviticus 5:2

We will now take a look at two examples of how we might use the Interpretive Journey to interpret and apply specific Old Testament laws. We begin with Leviticus 5:2:

> "'If anyone becomes aware that they are guilty—if they unwittingly touch anything ceremonially unclean (whether the carcass of an unclean animal, wild or domestic, or of any unclean creature that moves along the ground) and they are unaware that they have become unclean, but then they come to realize their guilt. . . .'"

The action required to correct the ***unclean*** status in this verse is described later in Leviticus 5:5–6. Thus, we should also include verses 5–6 with our study of verse 2:

> [5]"'When anyone becomes aware that they are guilty in any of these matters, they must confess in what way they have sinned. [6]As a penalty for the sin they have committed, they must bring to the LORD a female lamb or goat from the flock as a sin offering; and the priest shall make atonement for them for their sin.'"

Step 1: Grasp the text in their town. What did the text mean to the biblical audience?

The broader context of Leviticus deals with how the Israelites are to live with the holy, awesome God dwelling in their midst. How are they to approach God? How should they deal with sin and unclean things in light of having the holy God living among them? These verses fall into the smaller literary context of Leviticus 4:1–5:13. This unit deals with purification offerings—how to make oneself pure again after becoming ritually unclean. Leviticus 4 deals primarily with the leaders; Leviticus 5 focuses on regular people. Leviticus 5:2 is declaring to the Israelites that if they touch any unclean thing (dead animals or unclean animals), they are defiled. This is true even if they touch it by accident. As part of their unclean status, they are unable to approach God and worship him. To be purified (made clean), they must confess their sin and bring the priest a lamb or a goat for a sacrifice (5:5–6). The priest will sacrifice the animal on their behalf, and they will be clean again, able to approach and worship God.

Step 2: Measure the width of the river to cross. What are the differences between the biblical audience and us?

Remember that we are not under the old covenant and that our sin is now covered by the death of Christ. Also, we have direct access to the Father through Christ and no longer need human priests as mediators.

Step 3: Cross the principlizing bridge. What is the theological principle in this text?

The theological principle behind these verses is the concept that *God is holy.* When he dwells among his people, his holiness demands that his people keep separate from sin and unclean things. If they fail and become unclean, they must be purified by a blood sacrifice.

Note that this principle is reflected in the text of Leviticus 5:2, 5–6, but it is much more general than the concrete expression found in the text and described in step 1. Also, this general principle takes into account the overall theology of Leviticus and the rest of Scripture. It is expressed in a form that is universally applicable to both Old and New Testament people.

Step 4: Consult the biblical map. How does our theological principle fit with the rest of the Bible? Does the New Testament teaching modify or qualify this principle, and if so, how?

As we cross into the New Testament, we must examine what the New Testament teaches on this subject. God no longer dwells among us by residing in the tabernacle; he now lives within each of us through the indwelling of the Holy Spirit. His presence, however, still makes demands of holiness on us. He demands that we do not sin and that we stay separate from unclean things. But the New Testament clearly redefines the terms *clean* and *unclean*. Look at the words of Jesus in Mark 7:15, 20–23:

> [15]"Nothing outside a person can defile them by going into them. Rather, it is what comes out of a person that defiles them. . . ."
>
> [20]He went on: "What comes out of a person is what defiles them. [21]For it is from within, out of a person's heart, that evil thoughts come—sexual immorality, theft, murder, [22] adultery, greed, malice, deceit, lewdness, envy, slander, arrogance and folly. [23]All these evils come from inside and defile a person."

In other words, we who are under the new covenant are not made unclean by touching dead animals. We become unclean by impure thoughts or by sinful actions. The text in Leviticus also stresses that the individual is unclean even if he or she contacted the unclean item by accident. This principle does not appear to change in the New Testament. Sinful actions and thoughts that are unintentional, if there are such things, still make us unclean.

The new covenant has also changed the way that we as God's people deal with sin and uncleanness. No longer do we bring a lamb or goat to atone for our sin and to restore us to clean status. Now our sins are covered by the sacrifice of Christ. The death of Christ washes away our sin and changes our status from unclean to clean. Confession of sin, however, is still important to us under the new covenant (1 John 1:9), just as it was under the old covenant.

Thus, a concrete expression of the theological principle for today's New Testament audience would be: Stay away from sinful actions and impure thoughts because the holy God lives within you. If you do commit unclean acts or think unclean thoughts, then confess this sin and receive forgiveness through the death of Christ.

Step 5: Grasp the text in our town. How should individual Christians today live out this modified theological principle?

In step 5 we try to identify specific individual applications of the expression we developed in step 4. There are numerous applications possible. One application, for example, would be regarding the issue of internet pornography. Many Christians now have easy access to pornographic material in the privacy of their homes or dorm rooms. This text teaches us that the holiness of God, who dwells within us, demands that we lead clean lives. Viewing pornography falls clearly into the category the New Testament defines as unclean. Such action is a violation of God's holiness and hinders one's ability to approach and worship or fellowship with God. Therefore, we are to stay away from internet pornography, realizing that it makes us unclean, offends the holy God who dwells within us, and disrupts our fellowship with him. However, if you do fall into this sin, you must confess the sin, and through the death of Christ you will be forgiven and your fellowship with God will be restored.

Other applications are possible. What about greed? Envy? Slander? Take a look at your own situation. What unclean things are in your life?

Example 2: Deuteronomy 8:6–18

Is the Interpretive Journey making sense to you? Are you able to follow the procedure in the example above? Will you be able to apply this method to other passages? Let's look at another text, Deuteronomy 8:6–18, just to be sure that this method is sinking in.

> 6Observe the commands of the LORD your God, walking in obedience to him
> and revering him. 7For the LORD your God is bringing you into a good land—a
> land with brooks, streams, and deep springs gushing out into the valleys and
> hills; 8a land with wheat and barley, vines and fig trees, pomegranates, olive oil
> and honey; 9a land where bread will not be scarce and you will lack nothing; a
> land where the rocks are iron and you can dig copper out of the hills.
>
> 10When you have eaten and are satisfied, praise the LORD your God for the
> good land he has given you. 11Be careful that you do not forget the LORD your
> God, failing to observe his commands, his laws and his decrees that I am giving
> you this day. 12Otherwise, when you eat and are satisfied, when you build fine
> houses and settle down, 13and when your herds and flocks grow large and your
> silver and gold increase and all you have is multiplied, 14then your heart will
> become proud and you will forget the LORD your God, who brought you out
> of Egypt, out of the land of slavery. 15He led you through the vast and dreadful
> wilderness, that thirsty and waterless land, with its venomous snakes and scorpions. He brought you water out of hard rock. 16He gave you manna to eat in the
> wilderness, something your ancestors had never known, to humble and test you
> so that in the end it might go well with you. 17You may say to yourself, "My power
> and the strength of my hands have produced this wealth for me." 18But remember
> the LORD your God, for it is he who gives you the ability to produce wealth, and
> so confirms his covenant, which he swore to your ancestors, as it is today.

Remember that these interpretation steps must be preceded with a thorough observation step. Don't forget to observe, observe, and observe! Study the context. Study the words. Observe some more.

Step 1: Grasp the text in their town. What did the text mean to the biblical audience?

Israel must continue to obey the commands of God. As they enter the promised land, they must not become proud, thinking that they are the ones who have brought about the blessings of the promised land rather than God. They must not forget that God is the source of blessing and that he is the one who delivered them from Egypt.

Step 2: Measure the width of the river to cross. What are the differences between the biblical audience and us?

We are not under the old covenant. Also, we are not about to enter the promised land and to receive the material blessings of the promised land.

Step 3: Cross the principlizing bridge. What is the theological principle in this text?

God's people should obey God. We must not become proud and think we are the ones responsible for the blessings we receive from God. We must always remember God and how he has delivered us.

Step 4: Consult the biblical map. How does our theological principle fit with the rest of the Bible? Does the New Testament teaching modify or qualify this principle, and if so, how?

Obedience to God is still stressed, but the New Testament shifts the focus from law obedience to obedience in following Christ. Jesus also stresses obedience to the "new command," that of loving each other (John 13:34). Pride and the attitude of self-sufficiency are condemned in the New Testament as well as in the Old Testament. Blessings in the New Testament, however, tend to be spiritual rather than material (Eph. 1). Finally, God does not deliver us out of Egypt, but he saves us from sin through Jesus Christ. All of the blessings we receive flow out of our relationship with Christ. We must continue to follow Christ and his commandments. We must never think that we have produced the blessings in our lives; all the fantastic blessings in our lives are from God, flowing out of our relationship with Christ. We should always remember God and praise him for saving us in Christ.

The New Testament shifts the focus from law obedience to obedience in following Christ.

Step 5: Grasp the text in our town. How should individual Christians today live out this modified theological principle?

Success or blessings in a Christian's life can produce pride in a variety of ways, leading to a memory lapse regarding who is actually responsible for the blessing. If one succeeds in business, for example, the temptation is to think that he or she is the one responsible for the success rather than God. Affluence can be a real danger today in leading us to forget God. Likewise, students who are smart and do well in school are prone to credit themselves for their success rather than to realize that God is the one who has provided them with the brains and background that enable them to succeed. All our real blessings in life come from our relationship with Christ.

CONCLUSION

In this chapter we have seen that the traditional way of interpreting the Old Testament law was to classify the law into the categories of moral, civil, or ceremonial law. However, we have concluded that this approach is inadequate, and we have suggested an alternative approach. We noted the narrative context of the law and discussed the covenant context of the law. Out of these two contexts, we then applied the Interpretive Journey to interpret the Old Testament law. This method is the best approach to the law.

After the observation phase of study, we determine what the text meant to the biblical audience. Then we identify the differences between the biblical audience and us. Next we cross the principlizing bridge and draw out theological principles. We take the theological principles and filter them through the grid of New Testament teaching as we cross over into the New Testament to identify the meaning for today's Christian audience. Finally, we determine specific applications of this meaning that will apply to specific individuals today.

This approach allows us to interpret all Old Testament legal texts with the same methodology. It provides us with a step-by-step system by which we can find valid application for a wide range of Old Testament laws. Are you ready to tackle the Old Testament law on your own?

ASSIGNMENTS

For each of the passages below, first study the text and make as many observations as you can. Mark the observations on a photocopy of the text. Be sure you understand the meanings of all the words. Do background study and word studies as needed to understand each term. Next, identify the historical-cultural context and the literary context. When and where is this law given? What does the surrounding text discuss? Finally, take the Interpretive Journey, completing the following five steps:

Step 1: Grasp the text in their town. What did the text mean to the biblical audience?
Step 2: Measure the width of the river to cross. What are the differences between the biblical audience and us?
Step 3: Cross the principlizing bridge. What is the theological principle in this text?
Step 4: Consult the biblical map. How does our theological principle fit with the rest of the Bible? Does the New Testament teaching modify or qualify this principle, and if so, how?
Step 5: Grasp the text in our town. How should individual Christians today live out this modified theological principle?

Assignment 19–1

Leviticus 26:1: "Do not make idols or set up an image or a sacred stone for yourselves, and do not place a carved stone in your land to bow down before it. I am the LORD your God."

Assignment 19–2

Leviticus 23:22: "When you reap the harvest of your land, do not reap to the very edges of your field or gather the gleanings of your harvest. Leave them for the poor and for the foreigner residing among you. I am the LORD your God."

Assignment 19–3

Numbers 15:17–21: "The LORD said to Moses, 'Speak to the Israelites and say to them: "When you enter the land to which I am taking you and you eat the food of the land, present a portion as an offering to the LORD. Present a loaf from the first of your ground meal and present it as an offering from the threshing floor. Throughout the generations to come you are to give this offering to the LORD from the first of your ground meal." ' "

Assignment 19–4

Deuteronomy 22:8: "When you build a new house, make a parapet around your roof so that you may not bring the guilt of bloodshed on your house if someone falls from the roof."

Assignment 19–5

Leviticus 23:3: "There are six days when you may work, but the seventh day is a day of sabbath rest, a day of sacred assembly. You are not to do any work; wherever you live, it is a sabbath to the LORD."

CHAPTER 20

OLD TESTAMENT—POETRY

INTRODUCTION

> Lord, our Lord,
> how majestic is your name in all the earth! (Ps. 8:1)

Over one third of the Bible consists of poetry. The books of Psalms, Job, Proverbs, Song of Songs, and Lamentations are almost entirely poetic. Furthermore, the prophetic books also incorporate poetry as a major literary feature. Indeed, practically every Old Testament book has some poetry in it. Even many narrative texts have poems embedded in them. Because poetry comprises such a large portion of the Old Testament, it is important that we learn how to read and interpret it. We hope that you learn how to enjoy poetry as well!

Over one third of the Bible consists of poetry.

Some of the most beautiful and beloved passages in the Bible are found in the poetic sections of the Old Testament. Christians throughout the ages have turned to Psalms, for example, for encouragement in difficult times, and their spirits have been lifted and their hearts refreshed by the colorful and powerful poetry of the Psalter. Believers have soared on the wings of eagles with Isaiah, and they have viewed the tragic, heartrending devastation of Jerusalem with Jeremiah. Indeed, the poetry of the Old Testament has a way of resonating within us—it can reach right down inside and vibrate within our souls, speaking to us quietly but powerfully. This phenomenon is universal. Regardless of age, education, or culture, Christians around the world cherish Old Testament poetry, especially the Psalms.

Shortly after Danny arrived as a missionary in southern Ethiopia, a new translation of the New Testament was introduced into the area where he worked. But the Christians in the area bought few copies of the new translation, and the translators, who had worked hard on the project, were disappointed. However, the missionaries continued their translation project by translating the book of Psalms next. After a few years, they printed a special edition of the new translation, one that contained the New Testament *and Psalms*. This edition sold like hotcakes.

Why? What is it in the Psalms (and other Old Testament poetry) that attracts us? Why do *you* enjoy Psalms? Is it because this book leads you into a deeper worship of God? Is it the wonderful imagery and powerful figures of speech? Perhaps it is because the psalms have a way of connecting to real-life situations and of reflecting a refreshing honesty that we in real-life situations can relate to. In many contemporary pious Christian circles, believers are discouraged from expressing doubt, despair, or pain in public. Apparently, the assumption is that such emotions are reflective of immature faith. The psalmists, by contrast, do not hesitate from expressing a wide variety of emotions. They come right out and express what bothers them.

"Why, LORD, do you reject me and hide your face from me?"
—*Psalm 88:14*

The psalmist in Psalm 88:14, for example, feels free to cry out, "Why, LORD, do you reject me and hide your face from me?" If you stood up in church and prayed that verse as a prayer, we suspect your church would not call on you to pray anymore! Such declarations simply are not accepted in many Christian circles, and this leaves us without any biblical way to deal with despair.

The Christian church today sometimes tends to minimize the emotional dimension of the Christian's spiritual life. We believe this stunts the believer's growth as badly as minimizing the intellectual dimension does. The poetry of the Old Testament actually *focuses* on our emotional response to God as well as on our emotional response to those who are hostile to God and his people. The poetry of the Old Testament connects with us deep down, both in joy and in despair. It resounds in our hearts and stirs us spiritually and emotionally. We should not minimize it. Instead, we should drink deeply of it.

In this chapter we will explore the nature of Old Testament poetry. We will discuss how and why it affects us so powerfully. We will delve into some of the mechanics and features of Old Testament poetry in an attempt to gain an appreciation of the artistry employed by these poets. We hope this study will help you see and appreciate the poetry in the Old Testament even more than you do now. We will also explore issues of interpretation and application in order to give you some guidelines for reading and grasping God's poetic word in the Old Testament.

JET ENGINES AND PAINTINGS

One summer Danny and his family visited Washington, DC. One morning, while at the Smithsonian Institute, they spent a few hours puttering around in the Air and Space Museum. They looked with interest at the many fascinating airplanes and rockets. They lingered for a while at an exhibit that explains jet propulsion. This exhibit features numerous models and cross-sectional drawings, all with interesting written explanations and all fascinating to scientific novices who are curious to understand jet engines. The mystery of jet propulsion is explicated logically and historically.

Next, however, the Hays family crossed the mall and visited the National Gallery of Art. What a contrast! No models or rational, scientific explanations are on display here. Only paintings—life conveyed through brushstrokes of color on pieces of canvas. Danny and his son spent the next several hours roaming from room to room, captivated by the paintings and the messages these works of art portrayed. Here they saw the emotions of human life—fear, love, hate, despair, triumph, beauty, and disgust. In the painting titled *The Repentant Magdalen*,[1] for example, they observed the ex-harlot Mary Magdalene gazing meditatively into a dimly lit mirror (Reflecting on her past?). A skull (Her past? Her mortality?) sits before her on the table on top of a book (The Bible?). The mirror is angled so that the viewer of the painting sees the skull (and the book) reflected in the mirror rather than Mary. Does she also look in the mirror and see the skull? What a fascinating yet complex work of art! It reached right out and grabbed them as they walked by, pulling them in emotionally and demanding that they likewise ponder the complicated and deeply personal issue of repentance and forgiveness. Does our past haunt us even after forgiveness comes?

Moving from New Testament letters to Old Testament poetry is like crossing the mall from the Air and Space Museum and entering the National Gallery of Art.

The different genres of the Bible are similar to the different museums that make up the Smithsonian Institute. Moving from New Testament letters to Old

1. Georges de La Tour (1593–1652). Church tradition at the time of the painting identified Mary Magdalene as the "sinful" woman in Luke 7:36–50 and thus viewed her as a repentant harlot. However, there is no biblical evidence to connect Mary Magdalene with a life of immorality, even though Jesus does exorcise her of seven demons (Luke 8:2).

Testament poetry is like crossing the mall from the Air and Space Museum and entering the National Gallery of Art. Much of the New Testament, especially the letters, is presented rationally and logically, appealing to our Western minds like the exhibits in the jet propulsion room of the Air and Space Museum.

The genre of New Testament letters tends to focus on propositional truth (see chapter 14). Paul, for example, argues point by point in the book of Romans. He builds his theme logically and propositionally, supporting his main points with subpoints and supporting examples. He appeals primarily to logic and rational thought. The kind of language Paul uses in letters like Romans indicates that he is building his argument in such a fashion. Note, for example, the sequence in Romans 1:24–28: "therefore" (v. 24), "because of this" (v. 26), and "furthermore" (v. 28).

The Old Testament poets, however, write much differently than Paul. Like the paintings in the National Gallery of Art, they appeal primarily to our emotions. Furthermore, they do not build complex grammatical arguments, but rather use images (like paintings) to convey their meanings. They paint colorful pictures with words to convey messages loaded with emotional impact. This doesn't mean that they ignore logic or write illogically. It simply means that they focus on emotional aspects more than on logical aspects. True, Paul is not devoid of emotion in his letters, but his focus is on reasoning.

This comparison can be summed up in the following chart:

Paul and New Testament Letters	Old Testament Poets
Appeals to logic	Appeals to emotion
Rational arguments are central	Images are central
Syntax/grammar are critical to analyze	Figures of speech are critical to analyze

One of the problems many Christians today encounter when they tackle Old Testament poetry is that they attempt to interpret these texts with methods that are geared for New Testament letters. These interpretive methods are inadequate, sometimes even misleading, for interpreting Old Testament poetry. If we approach a painting by Raphael and study it by analyzing the light-wave frequencies of the colors he uses, we will most likely miss much of the message he intended to communicate. Likewise, we cannot approach Psalm 51 with the same method we use in Romans 3. Therefore, we need to handle the interpretation of Old Testament poetry with a method that acknowledges the function of images and the connection these images make to the emotional dimension of our relationship to God and to humanity. Such a method should also incorporate an understanding of the various other elements of Old Testament poetry.

ELEMENTS OF OLD TESTAMENT POETRY

Old Testament poetry, by its artistic nature, is not easy to define precisely. Indeed, prose and poetry are not totally separate, and in some Old Testament texts it is not clear whether the text is prose or poetry. We agree with Klein, Blomberg, and Hubbard's suggestion that poetry and prose be viewed as opposite ends of a literary continuum. Poetry is characterized by *terseness, a high degree of structure*, and *figurative imagery*. The more a literary work reflects these three elements, the further it moves to the poetry end of the literary spectrum.[2] Let us define these elements that serve as central features of Old Testament poetic texts.

Terseness

Terseness simply means that poetry uses a minimum number of words. The words are chosen carefully for their impact and their power. Narrative texts frequently have long, descriptive sentences, but poetic texts consist of short, compact lines of verse with few words. Consider Psalm 25:4:

> Show me your ways, Lord,
> teach me your paths.

In the Hebrew text, the first line has only three words and the second line has but two. Yet even in the English translation, we can catch a feel for the short number of words that are used. Prose texts, by contrast, tend to use many more words. Contrast the poetic terseness of Psalm 25:4 above with the wordiness of a prose text such as Genesis 12:10:

> Now there was a famine in the land, and Abram went down to Egypt to live there for a while because the famine was severe.

Structure

1. Parallelism

One of the most obvious features of Old Testament poetry is that the text is structured around poetic lines of verse rather than around sentences and paragraphs. Punctuation is not nearly as important in poetry as it is in narrative or in New Testament letters. But don't despair; the line represents more of the thought unit

2. William W. Klein, Craig L. Blomberg, and Robert L. Hubbard Jr., *Introduction to Biblical Interpretation*, 4th ed. (Grand Rapids: Zondervan, 2017), 362–64.

than the sentence does. So train your eye to read line by line rather than sentence by sentence.

Furthermore, the lines are usually grouped in units of two or three. That is, two lines of Old Testament poetry are grouped together to express one thought. Most of the verses in Psalms are structured this way. For example, take a look at Psalm 3:1–2:

> [1]Lord, how many are my foes!
> How many rise up against me!
> [2]Many are saying of me,
> "God will not deliver him."

This feature is called *parallelism*, and it is the dominant structural characteristic of Old Testament poetry.[3] Usually one thought is expressed by two lines of text (although occasionally the poets use three or even four lines of text to convey one thought). Often the verse notations follow this pattern, and each verse will consist of two lines of text. Such verse notations help us as we read because we need to interpret the text by reading each parallel construction together. That is, we look for two lines to convey one idea or thought.

In Old Testament poetry, the line represents the thought unit better than the sentence does. So train your eye to read line by line rather than sentence by sentence.

The two lines of parallelism usually relate to one another in one of several different ways, explained below. For clarity, in the examples we will designate the first line as A and the second line as B.

a. Synonymous. This involves a close similarity between lines using words with similar meanings. That is, the second line repeats much the same idea as the first line, using similar terminology. For example, consider Psalm 2:4:

> (A) The One enthroned in heaven laughs;
> (B) the Lord scoffs at them.

Note that "the One enthroned in heaven" from line A is paralleled by "the Lord" in line B. Likewise, "laughs" in line A is paralleled by "scoffs" in line B. The two lines are saying the same thing. They should be read as a unit and interpreted as a unit.

3. Much of the material on parallelism has been taken from Allen Ross's class notes at Dallas Theological Seminary and from James Limburg, "Psalms, Book of," in *The Anchor Bible Dictionary*, ed. David Noel Freedman (New York: Doubleday, 1992), 5:528–30.

Sometimes synonymous parallelism can involve four lines of text. Psalm 19:8 illustrates this feature well:

> (A) The precepts of the Lord are right,
> (B) giving joy to the heart.
> (A′) The commands of the Lord are radiant,
> (B′) giving light to the eyes.

In this verse the line "The precepts of the Lord are right" (A) is paralleled, not by the next line (B), but by line (A′), "The commands of the Lord are radiant." Likewise, line (B), "giving joy to the heart" is paralleled by (B′), "giving light to the eyes." So the thought expressed in A + B is paralleled synonymously by lines A′ + B′.

b. Developmental.[4] In developmental parallelism the second line develops further the idea of the first; for example:

> (A) He will not let your foot slip—
> (B) he who watches over you will not slumber. (Ps. 121:3)

Line B can relate to line A in numerous ways to further develop the thought of A. For example, A can make a statement and B give a reason:

> (A) Praise be to the Lord,
> (B) for he showed me the wonders of his love. (Ps. 31:21)

Or A can ask a question and B provide the answer:

> (A) How can a young person stay on the path of purity?
> (B) By living according to your word. (Ps. 119:9)

Both of the relationships above can be inverted as well. The reason can come first in line A with the main statement following in B. Likewise, the question is not restricted to line A but can occur in line B as well.

c. Illustrative. In illustrative parallelism line A conveys the idea and line B illustrates it with an example or a symbol.

---

4. Often this type of parallelism is called synthetic parallelism.

(A) Sovereign LORD, my strong deliverer,
(B) you shield my head in the day of battle. (Ps. 140:7)

In line A David calls God a strong deliverer. In line B he illustrates how this is true—God, like a helmet, shields David's head in battle.

d. Contrastive. This type of parallelism employs the use of contrast, in that line B is contrasted with line A.

(A) For the LORD watches over the way of the righteous,
(B) but the way of the wicked leads to destruction. (Ps. 1:6)

This type of parallelism is common in the book of Proverbs. For example, read Proverbs 10:12:

(A) Hatred stirs up conflict,
(B) but love covers over all wrongs.

e. Formal. The formal category is simply a "miscellaneous" category to catch the remaining types of parallelism that do not fall into the categories listed above. In this type of parallelism two lines or phrases are joined solely by metric considerations:

(A) "I have installed my king
(B) on Zion, my holy mountain." (Ps. 2:6)

Thus, we have listed five types of parallelism to watch for in Hebrew poetry: synonymous, developmental, illustrative, contrastive, and formal. But remember that we are dealing with poetry! Poets are not constrained to follow conventional forms or rules. The types of parallelisms that we have presented are representative of the most common types of parallelism, but this discussion is by no means exhaustive. The Hebrew poets are creative, and they use parallelism in many complicated ways, many of which are difficult to define precisely.

Parallelism is the dominant structural characteristic of Old Testament poetry.

2. Acrostics

Another fascinating structural feature of Old Testament poetry is the occasional use of *acrostics*. An acrostic is a poem in which each successive line of poetry starts with the next letter of the Hebrew alphabet. If this occurred in English, for example, the first line would start with *a*, the second line with *b*, the third with *c*, and so forth.

If you scanned down the margin of the poem, looking at the first letters of each line, you would see the alphabet.

As an example, we have created an acrostic in English. Although we have used only the first eight letters of the alphabet instead of all twenty-six, we think you will get the general idea. We know it is corny; forgive us.

> **A**h, acrostics. What wonderful artistry
> **B**efore us lies!
> **C**an you not see the beauty?
> **D**o you not sense the wonder?
> **E**ach one of us should marvel
> **F**or acrostics are marvelous things
> **G**iven to delight us.
> **H**ow wonderful and delightful they are!

There are numerous acrostics in the poetic sections of the Old Testament. Psalms 25, 34, 111, 112, and 145 are all acrostics. In Psalms 25, 34, and 145 the acrostic is in the first letter of each *verse*. Thus, these psalms each have twenty-two verses, matching the twenty-two letters in the Hebrew alphabet.[5] In Psalms 111 and 112, however, the acrostic is in the first letter of each *line*. Thus, they have twenty-two lines of acrostic text, each starting with successive letters of the Hebrew alphabet (actually there are twenty-three lines of text, but the opening phrase, "Praise the LORD," is not part of the acrostic).

Several other acrostic texts are scattered across the Old Testament. In the book of Lamentations, chapters 1, 2, 3, and 4 are acrostic, but not chapter 5. The popular text describing the noble wife, Proverbs 31:10–31, is also an acrostic. Note that the editors of most modern Bibles, such as the NIV, inform us in footnotes when acrostics occur. Look at the footnotes in your Bible for notations regarding the acrostic passages mentioned above.

Perhaps the most interesting acrostic in the Old Testament is Psalm 119. Every first word in each of the first eight verses starts with the beginning letter of the Hebrew alphabet, *aleph*. Likewise verses 9 to 16 all start with *beth*, the second letter of the Hebrew alphabet. This continues eight lines at a time, all the way through Psalm 119 and all the way through the Hebrew alphabet. Again, note that the editors of most Bibles indicate this for you by writing the Hebrew letters prior to each unit.

---

5. Actually the Hebrew alphabet has twenty-three letters, but in acrostics the writers combine the letters for "s" and "sh" into a single letter.

For example, if you look in a NIV Bible at Psalm 119:1, you will see "א Aleph" written above the line. Thus, you can actually read the Hebrew alphabet if you scan through Psalm 119 reading these headings.

Figurative Imagery

The major medium through which the Old Testament poets communicate is figurative imagery. They do not write essays; they paint pictures. The colors with which they paint these pictures are figures of speech and wordplays. We are not strangers to this type of language. English is rich in figurative language. We use figures of speech all the time.[6] Consider the following student monologue, poetically proclaimed to a sympathetic friend in a university hallway:

> My chemistry professor is an absolute psycho. He just gave us the hardest test in the entire world. He asked the stupidest and most ridiculous questions that have ever been written. I studied forever for that test, yet I really bombed it. I had no idea what he was asking. Nobody knows the answers to some of those questions. He must have dreamed them up. It was absolutely the most ridiculous thing in the world. Everybody in the class bombed it. Is he from outer space or what? I could strangle him. He expects us to study chemistry twenty-four hours a day. I do have a life, you know. But if I get a D in chemistry, my GPA will drop right through the floor. Mom and Dad will be mad as hornets—and all because of a psycho professor.

Every sentence in the student's diatribe contains figurative language. Read back through the paragraph and try to identify each figure of speech. Explore the figure and try to determine why it works. Figures of speech can be simple (comparing Mom and Dad to mad hornets), but they can also be quite complex. For example, what does the student mean by the phrase "I do have a life"?

Old Testament poets do not write essays; they paint pictures.

The sympathetic friend listening to this in the hallway likely understands her fellow student clearly and probably never even stopped to consider that multiple figures of speech were being used. The figures used were commonplace, and the friend easily interpreted the colorful figures and grasped the speaker's intended meaning. The friend realized instantly that little of what her moaning colleague said was to be understood literally.

However, suppose that walking behind these two American students is an

6. Note that *all the time* is also a figure of speech, falling into the category of exaggeration (hyperbole).

international student. He has studied English for numerous years at home, but he is unfamiliar with American figures of speech. He understands all of the words, but he is puzzled about the conversation. As he struggles to interpret the conversation, his mind ponders the following:

> What do "bombs" and "hornets" have to do with chemistry tests? And how did the American student drop her GPA "through the floor"? Are the bombs related to the idea of dropping GPAs? Is this angry student really planning to kill the professor? Should I alert the police? And does "psycho" mean "psychopathic"? Is the professor psychopathic? Is he the dangerous type? Is that why the student is concerned about having a life? Oh no! I am signed up to take chemistry under this professor next semester. Is this professor dangerous? Crazy? Will exam questions come from the professor's dreams? Will he expect me to study twenty-four hours every day? That's quite impossible. Maybe I should change majors.[7]

Old Testament poetry employs figures of speech as freely as the American student does in the example above. In a book like Psalms, practically every verse contains a figure of speech. As readers, we are like the international student. We come to the conversation from outside the literary world of the immediate audience. If we take the figures of speech literally, we will misunderstand the text as badly as the international student misunderstood the chemistry student. If we want to understand the authors of the Old Testament, it is critical that we recognize figures of speech when they are used and that we interpret them as figures of speech and not as literal realities.

Keep in mind that this does not in any way deny the literal reality behind the figure of speech. In the example above, a literal student took a literal chemistry test. In the student's mind, the test was too hard, and the student was upset with the professor. All of this is literally true. Furthermore, the real emotional distress of the student is part of the meaning, and the figures of speech she used reflect this. Reading and interpreting poetry are similar. The authors are conveying real thoughts, events, and emotions to us—that is, *literal* truth—but they express this truth figuratively. Our job as readers is to grapple with the figures and to strive to grasp the reality and the emotion that the poets are conveying by their figurative language.

The authors are conveying real thoughts, events, and emotions to us—that is, *literal* truth—but they express this truth figuratively.

7. We have, of course, exaggerated this example. Most international students are well aware that Americans use figures of speech frequently, just as they probably do in their own language. However, figures of speech remain one of the most difficult aspects of a foreign language (especially English!) to learn.

Some figures of speech can be subtle and complex. However, most of them can be readily recognized and interpreted. In general, the figures of speech in the Old Testament poetic texts can be placed into two major categories: figures involving *analogy* and figures involving *substitution*. A few figures of speech, however, do not really fall into either category, and we will discuss them as a separate, *miscellaneous* category. Finally, we will discuss *wordplays*, a category that has some similarity to figures of speech, but which is nonetheless distinctive enough to warrant a separate discussion.

1. Figures of Speech Involving Analogy

Many figures of speech involve drawing analogies between two different items. When the student above, for example, said, "Mom and Dad will be mad as hornets," the student was drawing an analogy between the angry, buzzing attack mode of disturbed hornets and the expected attitude of her parents over her bad grade. However, analogies also fall into several distinct subclassifications. That is, there are numerous ways of making figurative analogies. The Old Testament employs a wide range of these analogies as figures of speech. The most common ones are *simile*, *metaphor*, *indirect analogy*, *hyperbole*, and *personification/anthropomorphism/zoomorphism*.

a. Simile. This figure of speech makes a comparison by using the words *like* or *as* to explicitly state that one thing resembles another. The chemistry student's statement that "Mom and Dad will be mad *as* hornets" is a simile. This is a common figure of speech, both in English and in Old Testament poetry.

> *Like* a gold ring in a pig's snout
> is a beautiful woman who shows no discretion. (Prov. 11:22)

> "Though your sins are *like* scarlet,
> they shall be as white *as* snow." (Isa. 1:18)

> *As* the deer pants for streams of water,
> so my soul pants for you, my God. (Ps. 42:1)

b. Metaphor. Metaphors make the analogy between items by direct statement without the use of *like* or *as*.

> The LORD is my shepherd. (Ps. 23:1)

> A father to the fatherless, a defender of widows,
> is God in his holy dwelling. (Ps. 68:5)

A cheerful heart is good medicine. (Prov. 17:22)

c. Indirect analogy (also known as *hypokatastasis*). This is a literary device that uses the analogous item without directly stating the comparison. It assumes that the reader can make the comparison without it being explicitly stated. Suppose, for example, that the writers wish to make an analogy between the Lord's wrath and a storm. A *simile* would say, "The wrath of the Lord is like a storm." A *metaphor* would express the analogy by saying, "The wrath of the Lord is a storm." *Indirect analogy* skips the identification of the analogy and states, "The storm of the Lord will burst out in wrath, a driving wind swirling down on the heads of the wicked" (Jer. 30:23). Other examples include the following:

Roaring lions that tear their prey
open their mouths wide against me. (Ps. 22:13)[8]

He drew me out of deep waters. (Ps. 18:16)[9]

His faithfulness will be your shield and rampart. (Ps. 91:4)

In each of these examples, note the difference between indirect analogy and similes or metaphors. In Psalm 22:13, for example, the psalmist does not say that his enemies are *like* lions or even that they *are* lions. He simply says that lions tearing their prey open their mouths against him. He is drawing the analogy between his enemies and lions by implication. The meaning is much the same as if he had used a metaphor or simile, but the straightforward use of indirect analogy intensifies the image. David skips right to the image that he wants his readers to have in their heads, and he describes that image.

d. Hyperbole. Leland Ryken defines *hyperbole* as a "conscious exaggeration for the sake of effect." As an expression of strong feeling, hyperbole intentionally exaggerates: "It advertises its lack of literal truth." Indeed, as Ryken notes, it makes no pretense at all of being factual.[10] The struggling chemistry student above uses hyperbole throughout her monologue: "He gave us the *hardest* test in the world. . . . I studied *forever*. . . . It was the *most ridiculous* thing in the world. . . . *Everybody* in the class bombed it." None of these statements is literally true, but the listening friend would not have understood

8. This is a reference to the psalmist's enemies.
9. This is a reference to deliverance from enemies.
10. Leland Ryken, *How to Read the Bible as Literature* (Grand Rapids: Zondervan, 1984), 99–100.

them as true either. To make an emotional point, the chemistry student overstates her case, poetically exaggerating the details. This is allowed in figures of speech. It does not reflect on the honesty of the speaker. When the student says, for example, that she studied forever, the meaning is simply that she studied for a long time.

The poets of the Old Testament likewise employ hyperbole frequently. They consciously exaggerate to express deep emotion. For example, consider the following:

> My tears have been my food day and night. (Ps. 42:3)

> I beat them [enemies] as fine as windblown dust;
> I trampled them like mud in the streets. (Ps. 18:42)

> For troubles without number surround me. (Ps. 40:12)

In each of the examples, the psalmist consciously overstates or exaggerates his point to underscore the deep emotion he feels. To interpret the passage in Psalm 40:12 as meaning that David's troubles are, in reality, too numerous to count (we can count really high) is to misunderstand David. He is overwhelmed by his trouble, and he wants to stress the magnitude of his trouble. He is not suggesting that his troubles number more than one million or one billion or some other such number.

e. Personification/anthropomorphism/zoomorphism. These three figures of speech are similar in that they attribute to one entity the characteristics of a totally different kind of entity. *Personification* involves attributing human features or human characteristics to nonhuman entities.

> Lift up your heads, you gates. (Ps. 24:7)

> Burst into song, you mountains,
> you forests and all your trees. (Isa. 44:23)

> Hear me, you heavens! Listen, earth! (Isa. 1:2)

> Out in the open wisdom calls aloud,
> she raises her voice in the public square. (Prov. 1:20)

Anthropomorphism is the representation of God with human features or human characteristics. God is described as having hands, arms, feet, a nose, breath, a voice, and ears. He walks, sits, hears, looks down, thinks, talks, remembers, gets angry, shouts, lives in a palace, prepares tables, anoints heads, builds houses, and pitches tents. He has a rod, staff, scepter, banner, garment, tent, throne, footstool, vineyard, field, chariot, shield, and sword. He is called a father, husband, king, and shepherd. All these human actions or human features are used figuratively to describe God and his actions. A few examples are listed below:

> Your face, LORD, I will seek. (Ps. 27:8)
>
> God looks down from heaven on all mankind. (Ps. 53:2)
>
> The voice of the LORD is powerful. (Ps. 29:4)
>
> In the heavens God has pitched a tent for the sun. (Ps. 19:4)

Do all representations of God in human terms involve figures of speech? This is an interpretive issue that takes us into broader areas of theology. What is God really like? Since we are created in the image of God (Gen. 1:27), how similar are we to God? Clearly, if God is spirit, then the description of God as "looking down" or the mention of his hands would be a figure of speech (anthropomorphism). However, what about God's anger, love, patience, mercy, hurt, and compassion? These are probably literal realities and not figures of speech. We understand these emotions in human terms because we experience these same emotions, but that does not necessarily qualify them as figures of speech. On the other hand, does God have ears? Probably not. We suspect that all of the physical human references to God are figurative.

Do all representations of God in human terms involve figures of speech?

Zoomorphism. Other, nonhuman images for God are also used. When animal imagery is used, the figure is called *zoomorphism*. Consider the following poetic text:

> He will cover you with his *feathers*,
> and under his *wings* you will find refuge. (Ps. 91:4)

Certainly Psalm 91:4 does not imply that God is a bird or that he resembles a bird in any physical aspect. But there is a definite analogy being suggested by the text between God and birds—the image of a mother hen (or other bird) surrounding her chicks with her wings to protect and comfort them. God comforts and protects his people in the same fashion.

Keep in mind that an anthropomorphism or a zoomorphism can also be a simile, metaphor, or indirect analogy (*hypokatastasis*). For example, in Psalm 23:1, David states, "The Lord is my shepherd." This is both a metaphor (direct comparison using *is*) and an anthropomorphism (attributing human characteristics to God). Likewise, the verse mentioned above from Isaiah 44:23, "Burst into song, you mountains," is both personification and hyperbole.

2. Figures of Speech Involving Substitution

a. Effects and causes (also known as *metonymy*). Imagine that you are at Truist Park in Atlanta, sitting in the fourth row behind the hometown dugout, watching the Atlanta Braves play the Los Angeles Dodgers. Atlanta is down by three runs in the bottom of the ninth. With two outs and the bases loaded, the Braves send their best home-run hitter to the plate. The count runs full, and as the pitcher winds up to throw the final pitch, the rabid Braves fan in front of you jumps to his feet and pleads at the top of his lungs with the hitter, "Please make me happy! Make me happy! Make me happy!"

The poets of the Old Testament are as colorful and emotional as baseball fans are.

Perhaps this fan doesn't realize it, but he is employing a figure of speech (substitution) involving *cause and effect*. What he wants is for the batter to hit a home run, but what he says is "Make me happy!" If the batter hits a home run, the fan will be happy because his team will have won. He could simply say, "Hit a home run!" However, in an attempt to express himself colorfully, he substitutes the *effect* (his happiness) for the *cause* (hitting a home run).

The poets of the Old Testament are certainly as colorful and emotional as the Braves fan, and they will often employ the same literary device. For example, in Psalm 51:8 David states, "Let me hear joy and gladness." This is the effect. The cause, the action that David really is asking for, is forgiveness for his sin with Bathsheba. Yet what he states is the result of that forgiveness—joy and gladness. So David has used a figure of speech, substituting the effect for the cause.

Likewise, Proverbs 19:13 reads, "A foolish child is a father's ruin." The phrase "a father's ruin" is an effect, substituted for the intended cause (the things the foolish child does that lead to the ruin). Jeremiah 14:17 follows the same pattern: "Let my eyes overflow with tears." The prophet's tears are the effect. What he is really talking about is the coming Babylonian invasion (the cause). Rather than say, "The Babylonians are coming, and it will be awful," Jeremiah states the emotional effect the invasion will have on him: "Let my eyes overflow with tears."

This figure can be used in reverse as well—the cause can be stated when the effect is intended—but this usage is not common.

b. Representation (also known as *synecdoche*). Often the poets will substitute a representative part of an entity instead of the entity itself. We do this in English if we use the city of Washington, DC, to represent the entire United States. For example, a newscaster could say, "If Washington and Tokyo cannot work out these trade differences, there may be difficult times ahead." Both Washington and Tokyo are used figuratively to represent their respective nations. In similar fashion the Old Testament poets will use cities and/or individual tribes to represent entire nations figuratively. Thus, "Ephraim" (the largest northern tribe) and "Samaria" (the capital city) are used to refer to the northern kingdom Israel while "Judah" (the main southern tribe) and "Jerusalem" (the capital city) can refer to the southern kingdom of Judah.

Numerous other representative figures of speech occur. Psalm 44:6 uses the words "bow" and "sword" to represent weapons of war in general: "I put no trust in my bow, my sword does not bring me victory." Psalm 20:7 uses "chariots" and "horses" to represent military power: "Some trust in chariots and some in horses, but we trust in the name of the Lord our God." Bows, swords, chariots, and horses belong to a larger group of military weapons. Citing only one or two of them as figures brings into mind the entire category of weapons or military power.

"Feet" can be used to represent the entire person (Pss. 40:2; 44:18; 122:2), especially in contexts of moving or standing firm. "Bones" also represent the entire person, usually in contexts of suffering or pain (Pss. 6:2; 31:10; 32:3; 42:10). Likewise, the poets use "lips" as a frequent figurative substitute for one's speech (Pss. 12:2; 17:1; 31:18; 63:3).

3. Miscellaneous Figures of Speech

Since figures of speech are artistic and fluid, it is difficult to categorize them into nice, neat packages. Although most figures fall into the broad categories of analogy or substitution, a few fall outside of those categories. Two of these miscellaneous figures of speech that are fairly common are *apostrophe* and *irony*.

a. Apostrophe. Writers use apostrophe when they address as if present a person or entity not actually present. They do this to express strong feeling or to stress a particular point.[11] Apostrophes appear without warning, as if the writer suddenly visualizes the absent addressee and immediately speaks to him. Apostrophe is also often combined with personification, for the poets frequently address inanimate objects (heavens, earth, gates). Note the following examples of apostrophe. Who is addressed in each example?

11. Ryken, 98–99.

Therefore, you kings, be wise;
be warned, you rulers of the earth. (Ps. 2:10)

Away from me, all you who do evil. (Ps. 6:8)

Lift up your heads, you gates;
be lifted up, you ancient doors,
that the King of glory may come in. (Ps. 24:7)

Why was it, sea, that you fled?
Why, Jordan, did you turn back? (Ps. 114:5)

Occasionally, one of the poets will address himself (or his soul) as if he is also present as a separate entity. This is also a type of apostrophe. Consider the following:

Praise the Lord, my soul;
all my inmost being, praise his holy name. (Ps. 103:1)

Why, my soul, are you downcast? (Ps. 42:5)

b. Irony. When using irony, the writer says the exact opposite of what he really means. For example, suppose a student stops her friend Fred in the hall to tell him that a garbage truck just backed into Fred's new candy-apple-colored Corvette. In despair Fred replies, "Oh, that's just *great*!" Obviously the situation is not *great*, but quite the contrary. Fred states the opposite of the real situation to underscore how bad the news really is. Sometimes irony is also used in sarcasm, as when Fred tells the driver of the truck, "Mister, backing into my car was really smart! You are a great driver if ever I saw one." Old Testament poetry likewise often combines irony with sarcasm. Note God's use of sarcastic irony as he chides Job for challenging his divine wisdom:

18 Have you comprehended the vast expanses of the earth?
Tell me, if you know all this.
19 What is the way to the abode of light?
And where does darkness reside?
20 Can you take them to their places?
Do you know the paths to their dwellings?
21 *Surely you know, for you were already born!*
You have lived so many years! (Job 38:18–21)

Note, too, the sarcasm in the irony of Amos 4:4, where God in essence tells Israel to "go to Bethel and sin." Likewise, catch the sarcasm in Isaiah 41:22–23, as God speaks with irony of the idols that Israel worships:

> 22Tell us, you idols,
> what is going to happen.
> Tell us what the former things were,
> so that we may consider them
> and know their final outcome.
> Or declare to us the things to come,
> 23tell us what the future holds,
> so we may know that you are gods.
> Do something, whether good or bad,
> so that we will be dismayed and filled with fear.

4. Wordplays

Wordplays are fairly common in English, and many of them are quite clever. For example, as he signed the Declaration of Independence, Ben Franklin is credited with quipping, "Let us all *hang together* or else we may all *hang separately*." Franklin was making a play of two very different meanings of the word "hang."

Many Hebrew wordplays in Old Testament poetry follow the patterns of these two examples. They either play off variant possible meanings of a word, or else they play off sound similarities. Unfortunately, the wordplays rarely translate into English. We want to present a few of these wordplays to enable you to appreciate the rich, literary artistry of Old Testament poetry.

"Let us all *hang together* or else we may all *hang separately.*" —*Ben Franklin*

The prophet Jeremiah employs an extended wordplay throughout his book with his usage of the Hebrew word *shub*. (Don't forget chapter 9, "Word Studies," and how to use the STEP Bible!) This word basically means "to turn." It can mean "to turn to something" or "to turn away from something." Thus, it can be used of turning to God (repentance) or of turning away from God (backsliding), meanings that are opposite. Jeremiah could not resist using it in both senses. He outdoes Ben Franklin's use of "hang" by using *shub* eleven times from Jeremiah 3:1 to 4:1 alone. He uses the word three times in a single verse (Jer. 3:22)! In English this verse reads:

> "*Return, faithless* people;
> I will cure you of *backsliding*."

A quick look in our concordance shows that "return," "faithless," and "backsliding" are all English renderings of the Hebrew word *shub*. A literal translation would read:

> "*Turn*, you sons of *turning*
> I will cure your *turning*."

INTERPRETING OLD TESTAMENT POETRY

As with any text in the Old Testament, the interpretation of poetry involves making the Old Testament Interpretative Journey. You haven't forgotten the steps of the journey, have you? Let's apply them to a representative Old Testament poetic text, Psalm 116:1–4.

Step 1: Grasp the text in their town. What did the text mean to the biblical audience?

Our first step is to ask what the text meant to the biblical audience. We begin with a close reading of the passage. Remember what you learned in chapters 2–4! Don't forget how to read carefully and make observations! As part of your close observation in Psalm 116:1–4, *identify each parallelism in the passage* as we discussed earlier in this chapter (synonymous, developmental, illustrative, contrastive, formal). Combine the parallel passages into thoughts or images and then study the passage thought by thought. As described earlier in this chapter, this will often involve reading two lines as one thought rather than reading one line at a time or reading one sentence at a time.

The opening verses of Psalm 116 can be divided into the following basic thoughts, based on parallelism:

Thought 1	I love the LORD, for he heard my voice; he heard my cry for mercy.
Thought 2	Because he turned his ear to me, I will call on him as long as I live.
Thought 3	The cords of death entangled me, the anguish of the grave came over me; I was overcome by distress and sorrow.
Thought 4	Then I called on the name of the LORD: "LORD, save me!"

Next, *locate and visualize each figure of speech*. First, try to visualize the image. For example, explore the image in thought 2 of Psalm 116 above ("Because he turned his ear to me"). People will often tilt their head or turn their head toward the source of a sound to hear well. Can you visualize the psalmist crying out to God, who, in response, turns his head to listen carefully?[12] What about thought 3? We see ropes coming up out of an open grave, wrapping around the psalmist's legs and pulling him down into the grave.

Then be sure to *enter into the emotional world of the image*. Feel the comfort the psalmist has when he sees God turn his head to listen to him. Imagine the nightmare conveyed by the cords of death image! Ropes are wrapped around you and are pulling you down into a creepy, shadowy, open grave. You fall into the grave and scream for help! Death has a hold on you, but God hears your cry and reaches down to pull you out. This could come right out of a Stephen King movie!

Try to enter the emotional world that the imagery of the poet portrays.

As your heartbeat slows back down, *try to identify each figure of speech* based on the categories listed earlier in this chapter (simile, metaphor, indirect analogy, hyperbole, personification, anthropomorphism, zoomorphism, substitution, representation, apostrophe, and irony). Remember that many figures of speech fall into more than one category. Referring to God's ear is an anthropomorphism. However, the figure of God's turning his ear is also a substitution. The turning of God's ear (cause) leads to his action of deliverance (effect), and it is God's delivering action to which the psalmist really points.

Now we are ready to *summarize what the text meant for the biblical audience*. Keep in mind that these figures of speech were figures of speech for the ancient readers as well. Don't try to make the images literal for them but figurative for us. The writer of Psalm 116 was not being pulled down into a grave by cords literally. We could grasp the text of Psalm 116:1–4 in their town by summarizing as follows:

> The writer is facing an immediate, scary, difficult situation. He may even be close to death itself.[13] He calls out to God, who listens to him and then delivers him from the situation. Because of this, he expresses his love for God.

12. Also remember the ancient Near East context. Stone idols, by contrast, do not turn their heads to hear. They are impersonal and distant. The Lord, by contrast, is concerned. He is personal; he turns his head to hear.

13. It is difficult to determine whether he is actually facing death and thus using the cords as a figure of how death tries to pull him into the grave, or if he is using the entire image of death to represent figuratively all other difficult, frightening, and hopeless situations as well. This is poetry, and exact analysis will often elude us.

Step 2: Measure the width of the river to cross. What are the differences between the biblical audience and us?

Of course, one of the central differences to remember when crossing the river from the Old Testament is that we as New Testament believers are under a different covenant. While this is not a critical difference for the message of Psalm 116, it is always a factor to keep in mind. What other differences are there? We may not be in as frightening or difficult a situation as the psalmist was. (Yet some of us probably are.) We may not be facing imminent death.

Another important difference is that the Old Testament focuses on a different view of death than the New Testament does. There is little in the Old Testament about the afterlife (resurrection and heaven). The Old Testament doctrine on death is vague and shadowy. The assurance of eternal life is a doctrine that blossomed after Jesus' life, death, and resurrection.

Step 3: Cross the principlizing bridge. What is the theological principle in this text?

Remember the criteria for developing theological principles:

- The principle should be reflected in the text.
- The principle should be timeless and not tied to a specific situation.
- The principle should not be culturally bound.
- The principle should correspond to the teaching of the rest of Scripture.
- The principle should be relevant to both the biblical and the contemporary audiences.

A theological principle that can be seen in Psalm 116:1–4 is that God's people should express their love to God when he hears them and delivers them from difficult and frightening situations such as death.

Step 4: Consult the biblical map. How does our theological principle fit with the rest of the Bible? Does the New Testament teaching modify or qualify this principle, and if so, how?

The New Testament reaffirms the principle that we should express our love to God for having delivered us from difficult situations. In addition, the New Testament has much to say about our deliverance from death (and sin). First Corinthians 15 discusses this at length, explaining how God through Jesus has given us victory over death. We are promised resurrection and given eternal life. Those without Christ are staring death in the face, and the "cords of death" do indeed pull them in.

We also were in this predicament before we came to Christ, but God heard our cry and delivered us.

Note, however, that neither the New Testament nor the Old Testament teaches that God always intervenes to save us from all difficult physical situations. God's people suffer and die physically throughout the Bible. Christians still get cancer and die. Car accidents still occur. For Christians, however, death never really wins. The cords never really get us in the grave. Christ has defeated the power of death, and he gives us victory over death.

Step 5: Grasp the text in our town. How should individual Christians live out this modified theological principle?

Applications vary, depending on our situation. For Christians actually facing death, this text should give assurance that God will deliver us from the power of death through resurrection and eternal life. These Christians should express their love to God for such deliverance. The rest of us should likewise express our love to God for saving us from eternal death. We should also remember the times when he responded and delivered us from other difficult situations. We should express our love to him for hearing us and delivering us from those situations.

UNIQUE ASPECTS OF PSALMS

Poetry is used often in prophetic literature, wisdom literature, and in the Psalms. Prophetic literature and wisdom literature are discussed in the next two chapters. They reflect distinct genre types and require specific interpretive approaches. These approaches will build on the discussion of poetry presented here. Likewise, the Psalms are also unique, and interpreting them involves some special aspects that we will discuss here.

First of all, we agree with Fee and Stuart that the Psalms "do not function primarily for the teaching of doctrine or moral behavior."[14] We caution you strongly against interpreting Psalms in the same fashion as one would the book of Romans, which does focus on the teaching of doctrine and moral behavior. The Psalms definitely have doctrinal components, and they also speak to moral behavior (Ps. 1), but those elements are corollaries or subpoints and not generally the intended focal point. Fee and Stuart write:

14. Gordon D. Fee and Douglas K. Stuart, *How to Read the Bible for All Its Worth*, 4th ed. (Grand Rapids: Zondervan, 2014), 212–13.

> The difficulty with interpreting the Psalms arises primarily from their nature—what they are. Because the Bible is God's Word, many Christians automatically assume that all it contains are words *from* God *to* people. Thus they fail to recognize that the Bible also contains words spoken *to* God or *about* God—which is what the psalms do—and that these words, too, are God's Word.[15]

The function of the Psalms, therefore, is to "give us inspired models of how to talk and sing to God."[16] In addition, the Psalms provide us with inspired models of how to meditate about God—that is, how to think reflectively about God and what he has done for us. This interactive communication in Psalms between people and God can take place in numerous different contexts, reflecting the wide variety of life experiences from which people encounter God. Brueggemann has suggested that the Psalms can be categorized roughly into three main contexts of human life: (1) "seasons of well-being that evoke gratitude for the constancy of blessing," (2) "anguished seasons of hurt, alienation, suffering, and death," and (3) seasons of "surprise when we are overwhelmed with the new gifts of God, when joy breaks through the despair."[17]

The Psalms give us inspired models of how to talk and sing to God.

So we see that even though the book of Psalms is God's Word to us, it does not present specific doctrinal guidelines to us, but rather examples of how to communicate our deepest emotions and needs to God. When a psalmist cries out in anguish and despair, for example, the point or lesson is not that we also should cry out in despair. Rather, the lesson is that when we find ourselves in despair, it is right and proper for us, like the psalmist, to cry out in anguish and pain to God. As we do so, we can begin to experience his comfort and indeed be lifted "out of the slimy pit, out of the mud and mire" (Ps. 40:2).

Honesty with God is an important lesson that we can learn from the Psalms. The psalmists tell God exactly how they feel, and it often does not sound very spiritual or mature. Christians today tend to pressure each other into suppressing any emotional outpouring about God. The Christian model for many is that of a hard stoic, like Spock on *Star Trek*. The Psalms shatter this false image of Christian behavior and provide us with wonderful models of frank, honest communication with God, full of emotion, bubbling up out of good and bad times alike.

---

15. Fee and Stuart, 212.
16. Robert B. Chisholm Jr., *From Exegesis to Exposition* (Grand Rapids: Baker, 1998), 225.
17. Walter Brueggemann, *The Message of the Psalms* (Minneapolis: Augsburg, 1984), 19.

To summarize, the Psalms help us in our Christian lives in several areas. First, they give us a guide to serious worship. Second, they help us to relate honestly to God. Finally, they lead us into reflection and meditation on what God has done for us.[18]

CONCLUSION

One thing we know for certain about God—he is not boring. He has decided to communicate his Word to us through several fascinating and interesting literary forms. Truly, poetry is one of the most dynamic and emotive literary genres available. God wants to connect with our minds, but he also wants to connect with our hearts ("all my inmost being," Ps. 103:1). Thus, we have seen how Old Testament poetry differs from New Testament letters. We are dealing with paintings instead of scientific exhibits. The stress of the poets is on the emotional impact that the poetry makes in the life of the reader. Poetry is characterized by terseness, a high degree of structure (parallelism), and figurative imagery.

Recognizing these elements will assist us greatly in appreciating and interpreting the powerful messages that the Old Testament poets present to us. In addition, to grasp these words fully, we must still travel along the Interpretive Journey, starting with their world and crossing over the river of differences on the principlizing bridge. Finally, we must open our hearts to the message and let it transform us and change us more and more into the image of Christ.

18. Fee and Stuart, *How to Read the Bible*, 231.

ASSIGNMENTS

Assignment 20–1: Parallelism (Psalm 20)

Based on the discussion of parallelism in this chapter, classify each of the couplets (verses) in Psalm 20. That is, identify each set of parallel lines as *synonymous*, *developmental*, *illustrative*, *contrastive*, or *formal*. Note that verses 5 and 6 each have three lines instead of two. Either classify all three lines together as one category, or classify the first two as one category and then relate the last line to the first two as a category. Verse 1 has been completed as an example for you.

1 May the LORD answer you when you are in distress;
may the name of the God of Jacob protect you. *Developmental*
2 May he send you help from the sanctuary
and grant you support from Zion. ________
3 May he remember all your sacrifices
and accept your burnt offerings. ________
4 May he give you the desire of your heart
and make all your plans succeed. ________
5 May we shout for joy over your victory
and lift up our banners in the name of our God. ________
May the LORD grant all your requests. ________
6 Now this I know:
the LORD gives victory to his anointed.
He answers him from his heavenly sanctuary ________
with the victorious power of his right hand. ________
7 Some trust in chariots and some in horses,
but we trust in the name of the LORD our God. ________
8 They are brought to their knees and fall,
but we rise up and stand firm. ________
9 LORD, give victory to the king!
Answer us when we call! ________

Assignment 20–2: Figures of Speech (Psalm 102:1–14)

For each of the figures of speech listed below, (1) classify the figure according to the categories discussed in this chapter, and (2) explain what the figure or image means. The first entry has been completed for you.

102:1b: cry	Classification—indirect analogy Explanation—The psalmist is comparing his prayer to a cry.
102:2a: face	Classification Explanation
102:2b: ear	Classification Explanation
102:3a: days/smoke	Classification Explanation
102:3b: bones/embers	Classification Explanation
102:4a: heart/grass	Classification Explanation
102:5b: skin and bones	Classification Explanation
102:6: owl	Classification Explanation
102:7: bird	Classification Explanation
102:9a: ashes/food	Classification Explanation
102:9b: drink/tears	Classification Explanation
102:11a: days/shadow	Classification Explanation
102:11b: grass	Classification Explanation
102:13a: arise	Classification Explanation
102:14a: stones	Classification Explanation
102:14b: dust	Classification Explanation

Assignment 20–3: Take the Interpretive Journey with Psalm 1

Follow the directions below, completing all three parts of the assignment.

1. Read through Psalm 1 several times. Find and mark as many observations as you can on a photocopy of the text below.

> 1 Blessed is the one
> who does not walk in step with the wicked
> or stand in the way that sinners take
> or sit in the company of mockers,
> 2 but whose delight is in the law of the LORD,
> and who meditates on his law day and night.
> 3 That person is like a tree planted by streams of water,
> which yields its fruit in season
> and whose leaf does not wither—
> whatever they do prospers.
>
> 4 Not so the wicked!
> They are like chaff
> that the wind blows away.
> 5 Therefore the wicked will not stand in the judgment,
> nor sinners in the assembly of the righteous.
> 6 For the LORD watches over the way of the righteous,
> but the way of the wicked leads to destruction.

2. Describe and define the figures of speech in each verse.
3. Make the Interpretive Journey by completing the following:

Step 1: *Grasp the text in their town. What did the text mean to the biblical audience?* Give a one- or two-sentence summary of what the text meant to the biblical audience.

Step 2: *Measure the width of the river to cross. What are the differences between the biblical audience and us?* Identify the major differences between the psalmist and us.

Step 3: *Cross the principlizing bridge. What is the theological principle in this text?* Synthesize the passage into one basic principle.

Step 4: *Consult the biblical map. How does our theological principle fit with the rest of the Bible? Does the New Testament teaching modify or qualify this principle, and if so, how?* Describe any ways in which the New Testament adds to, reaffirms, or modifies the issue this psalm is speaking about.

Step 5: Grasp the text in our town. How should individual Christians live out this modified theological principle? Describe a specific way of applying this psalm in your own life.

CHAPTER 21

OLD TESTAMENT—PROPHETS

INTRODUCTION

The Prophets! What a fantastic collection of books! The prophetic books of the Old Testament contain some of the most inspiring passages in the Bible. Isaiah is a favorite of many Christians. Recall his uplifting words in 40:31:

> But those who hope in the Lord
> will renew their strength.
> They will soar on wings like eagles;
> they will run and not grow weary,
> they will walk and not be faint.

Christians love that verse. Does it not lift your heart? Or ponder the profound truth expressed in Isaiah 53:6 concerning Jesus Christ and us:

> We all, like sheep, have gone astray,
> each of us has turned to our own way;

> and the LORD has laid on him
>   the iniquity of us all.

We could go on and on, citing wonderful, beloved prophetic passages. The prophets, however, also contain some rather unusual and difficult verses. For example, there are some gruesome texts, as in Amos 3:12:

> As a shepherd rescues from the lion's mouth
>   only two leg bones or a piece of an ear,
> so will the Israelites living in Samaria be rescued.

Some passages were extremely insulting to their original audiences, such as Jeremiah 2:23b–24:

> 23 See how you behaved in the valley;
>   consider what you have done.
> You are a swift she-camel
>   running here and there,
> 24 a wild donkey accustomed to the desert,
>   sniffing the wind in her craving—
>   in her heat who can restrain her?
> Any males that pursue her need not tire themselves;
>   at mating time they will find her.

And there are strong passages of judgment, as reflected in Jeremiah 15:1–2:

> Then the LORD said to me: "Even if Moses and Samuel were to stand before me, my heart would not go out to this people. Send them away from my presence! Let them go! And if they ask you, 'Where shall we go?' tell them, 'This is what the LORD says:
>
> " 'Those destined for death, to death;
> those for the sword, to the sword;
> those for starvation, to starvation;
> those for captivity, to captivity.' "

Some of the Old Testament prophetic passages are wonderful and easy to grasp, but some texts are bewildering and troubling. In this chapter we will teach you how to tackle this fascinating portion of Scripture. We will first discuss the nature of the Old Testament prophetic literature. Next we will explore the important theological and historical contexts in which the prophets wrote. With these contexts under our belt, we will then discuss the overall message of the prophets to determine exactly what they were trying to say to the people of their time. Once we have understood what the text meant to the biblical audience, then we will be ready to complete the Interpretive Journey and begin to interpret and apply specific prophetic passages. We will then wrap up the chapter with a summary discussion and end with a few assignments.

THE NATURE OF OLD TESTAMENT PROPHETIC LITERATURE

The prophetic books include the four *major prophets* (Isaiah, Jeremiah, Ezekiel, and Daniel), as well as the twelve *minor prophets* (Hosea, Joel, Amos, Obadiah, Jonah, Micah, Nahum, Habakkuk, Zephaniah, Haggai, Zechariah, and Malachi).[1] The terms *major* and *minor* have nothing to do with importance. Rather, they refer to the length of the books. The first four prophetic books are much longer than the twelve that follow.

A large percentage of the latter half of the Old Testament consists of this prophetic literature. Indeed, the prophets take up as much space in the Bible as the New Testament does! Clearly, then, this material is an important part of God's message to us.

Yet of all the genre types in the Bible, prophetic literature is perhaps the most difficult for us to understand. Why? The main reason is probably related to the fact that we have nothing similar to this genre in English literature. Think about it for a moment. We are familiar with narrative because we read stories all the time. Likewise, we are comfortable with Psalms because we are familiar with hymns and choruses. The letters in the New Testament bear some similarities with modern letters, so we are not lost when confronted with the genre of letter.

There is, however, little in the literature of our language and culture that resembles the prophetic literature of the Old Testament. The world of the prophets can seem strange and baffling. However, even though we are not overly familiar with this type of literature, we can learn to recognize the elements of prophetic genre, and we can learn interpretive principles for this genre. Furthermore, as we mention below, there is perhaps a hint of genre similarity between Old Testament prophecy and some of our music. So let's begin!

1. In the Hebrew Bible, Daniel is included with the Writings (along with Psalms, Job, Ecclesiastes, Ruth, etc.) rather than with the Prophets. Some scholars would not classify Daniel as a prophet because both his literary style and his message are different.

The prophetic books contain primarily numerous, short spoken or preached messages, usually proclaimed by the prophet to either the nation of Israel or the nation of Judah. They also contain visions from God, as well as short narrative sections and symbolic acts.

Only a small percentage of Old Testament prophecy deals with events that are still future to us. This may surprise you. Many people assume that the term *prophecy* only refers to events of the end times and that the prophets of the Old Testament are primarily concerned with predicting the end times. Note what Fee and Stuart write: "Less than 2 percent of Old Testament prophecy is messianic. Less than 5 percent specifically describes the new-covenant age. Less than 1 percent concerns events yet to come in our time."[2] The vast majority of the material in the prophetic books addresses the disobedience of Israel and/or Judah and the consequential impending judgment. The role of the prophet included the proclamation of this disobedience and the imminent judgment as much as it did the prediction of things to come in the more distant future.

Only a small percentage of the Old Testament prophetic literature deals with future events. The vast majority addresses the disobedience of Israel/Judah and the consequential impending judgment.

The prophets use poetry for much of their message, and it is the poetic aspect of their message that is the most foreign to us. In chapter 20 we explored the fascinating topic of Hebrew poetry. Be sure to apply the lessons of that chapter to the poetic sections of the prophetic writings as well. A central feature of Hebrew poetry, remember, is the extensive use of *figures of speech*. These figures of speech are some of the main weapons in the literary arsenal of the prophets. Such language is what makes the prophetic books so colorful and fascinating.

- Amos does not simply say, "God is mad." Rather, he proclaims, "The lion has roared" (Amos 3:8).
- Isaiah does not analytically contrast the awfulness of sin and the amazing wonder of forgiveness; he uses figurative language, announcing, "Though your sins are like scarlet, they shall be as white as snow" (Isa. 1:18).
- Jeremiah is disgusted with Judah's unfaithful attitude toward God and wants to convey the pain the Lord feels because Judah has left him for idols. Thus, throughout the book he compares Judah to an unfaithful wife who has become a prostitute. "You have lived as a prostitute with many lovers" (Jer. 3:1), Jeremiah proclaims, referring figuratively to Judah's idolatry.

2. Gordon D. Fee and Douglas K. Stuart, *How to Read the Bible for All Its Worth*, 4th ed. (Grand Rapids: Zondervan, 2014), 188.

Remember that the power of poetry lies in its ability to affect the emotions of the reader or listener. Without doubt, prophetic literature is some of the most emotional literature in the Bible. The prophets express the deep, deep love of the Lord toward his people and the intense pain he feels as a result of their rejection of him. Nevertheless, the prophets are also explicit in their description of how horrible the coming judgment (invasion by the Assyrians or Babylonians) will be. They are scathing in their critique and criticism of society, especially of the king and the corrupt priesthood.

The prophets express the deep, deep love of the Lord toward his people and the intense pain he feels as a result of their rejection of him.

There is little in American literature or culture that resembles the scathing, poetic critiques that the prophets deliver against the nations Israel and Judah. The closest genre we could locate is that of protest songs of the 1960s, and those of Bob Dylan (the "prophet of the '60s") in particular. Of course, we are not suggesting that Dylan is at all similar to the prophets theologically, but the *form* of some of his songs has strong points of similarity—the scathing, poetic critique of the status quo in society, the attack on the authority structures of that society, and the prediction of impending judgment or destruction if the message falls on deaf ears. Consider, for example, Dylan's popular song "The Times They Are A-Changin'." He exhorts the listeners to "admit that the waters around you have grown," and then he warns, "you'd better start swimmin' or you'll sink like a stone."

Dylan uses the colorful, poetic imagery of an impending flood. This is similar to the figurative imagery used of judgment in the prophetic books. The prophets will criticize the king, the false prophets, and the corrupt priests. In the second verse of "The Times They Are A-Changin'," Dylan addresses writers. Verse 3 is aimed at senators and congressmen, and verse 4 contains a strong warning for parents. Keep in mind that we are not elevating Dylan to the status of a prophet, but we believe that it is helpful to connect the biblical genre that you are studying to something similar in form within your own culture and language, if possible.

"You'd better start swimmin' or you'll sink like a stone."
—*Bob Dylan*

Another important feature to note about the prophets is that their books are primarily *anthologies*. By this we mean that the prophetic books are collections of shorter units, usually oral messages that the prophets have proclaimed publicly to the people of Israel or Judah. Other literary units, such as narrative, oracles, and visions, are mixed in. Sometimes the delivered oral message is the vision or oracle.

It is important to note the *collection* nature of the books. Like a contemporary collection of a writer's poetry, the prophetic books contain relatively independent, shorter units. These units are not always arranged chronologically, and often they do not appear to have thematic order either (see especially Jeremiah). Occasionally a broad overall theme (judgment, deliverance) unites a large section of text, but for the most part, tight thematic unity is absent.

The prophetic books are primarily *anthologies*.

Because of this anthology feature, most prophetic books are almost impossible to outline satisfactorily. We can, by contrast, outline each of the New Testament letters, and our understanding of each book is usually enhanced by the outline. Even the narratives of the Bible can be outlined beneficially. Outlines of the prophetic books, however, are normally useless. As anthologies they focus on a few major themes that they repeat over and over, so there is also much repetition.

But don't despair. Just because we cannot outline the message of the prophets does not mean that we cannot understand the message. Anthologies can be crystal clear in communicating their message. While Jeremiah, for example, is impossible to outline in any detail, his message comes across loud and clear. And just because the genre or literary form of the prophets is not one we are readily familiar with, this does not mean that we cannot feel the emotion of the text and grasp what God is saying through the prophets. However, we simply cannot approach Old Testament prophetic literature in the same way we would approach a modern essay.

Outlines of the prophetic books are normally useless.

THE HISTORICAL-CULTURAL AND THEOLOGICAL CONTEXT

In chapters 6 and 8 we learned how important historical-cultural and literary contexts are to proper interpretation. Since the Old Testament prophetic literature is unique, to attempt to interpret it out of context is to invite confusion and error. First of all, we must identify the historical-cultural context in which the prophets preached. To do this, let's review Israel's history and locate the prophets in their proper time within the biblical story.

A continuous story runs from Genesis 12 to 2 Kings 25. In Genesis God calls Abraham and promises him descendants, a land, and blessings. This promise is repeated to Abraham's son Isaac and to Isaac's son Jacob, who, in turn, has twelve sons. One of these sons is Joseph, whom the other sons sell into slavery. He is taken to Egypt, and the family later follows, settling there. Genesis thus ends with this special family in Egypt.

Sometime during the next four hundred years the Hebrews are forced into slavery by the Egyptians. God comes to them and raises up Moses to deliver them miraculously from Egypt (the book of Exodus). God then enters into covenant relationship with them, stating, "I will be your God; you will be my people. I will dwell in your midst." God presents them with the various laws of Exodus, Leviticus, and Numbers, which define the terms by which they can live in the promised land with God in their midst and be blessed by him in the land.

However, that first generation refuses to enter the land, and God allows them to die off in the desert. He then takes the next generation back to the perimeter of the promised land and recommits them to a covenant relationship. As before, the terms of the covenant define how they are to live in the land with God in their midst. This relationship is defined specifically by the laws in Deuteronomy. This book clearly shows the people that if they obey God and keep the law, they will be immensely blessed. However, the book also stresses that if they disobey the law and turn away from God, they will be punished; and if they do not repent, they will eventually even lose the promised land.

The themes of Deuteronomy are woven into the fabric of the prophetic books.

The rest of the story up to the end of 2 Kings deals with the issue of whether the Israelites are going to keep the terms of this agreement. In Joshua, the next book after Deuteronomy, the Israelites remain faithful to the Lord. But in Judges they turn away from him and backslide into idolatry. Ruth introduces David, who dominates the story in 1 and 2 Samuel. David is faithful to God, and he brings the nation back to covenant obedience. However, even David is unable to stay completely faithful, as his sin with Bathsheba demonstrates. David's son Solomon is able to coast for a while on his father's relationship with God, but soon he turns to idols, setting the pattern for future kings and people alike.

The books of 1 and 2 Kings tell the story of how the two nations of the Hebrews, Israel and Judah, continually fall away from the Lord, turning instead to the idols of their neighbors. Ultimately the Lord punishes them, and they lose the right to live in the promised land. The northern kingdom, Israel, falls into idolatry very early and is destroyed by the Assyrians (722 BC). Later the southern kingdom, Judah, likewise turns away and is destroyed by the Babylonians (587 BC). The book of 2 Kings ends with the destruction of Jerusalem and the exile of the southern kingdom's inhabitants to Babylon.

The prophets preach primarily within the context of the latter part of this story. As the nation turns away from the Lord, thus forgetting the covenant agreement they made with God in Exodus and Deuteronomy, the prophets emerge as God's spokesmen to call the people back to covenant obedience. Thus, in regard to the historical context, most of the prophets preach in one of two contexts: just prior to the

Assyrian invasion, which destroyed the northern kingdom, Israel; or just prior to the Babylonian invasion, which destroyed the southern kingdom, Judah.

These contexts are extremely important to understand the prophets. We must constantly keep them before us as we read and interpret the Old Testament prophetic literature. Theologically the prophets proclaim their message from the context of the Mosaic covenant, primarily as defined in Deuteronomy. They tell the people to repent, to turn from idols, and to return to the covenant they agreed to keep in Deuteronomy. They warn the Israelites of the terrible punishments God threatened in Deuteronomy. The ultimate punishment, which they announce with sorrow, is the loss of God's presence and the loss of the promised land.

Theologically the prophets proclaim their message from the context of the Mosaic covenant, primarily as defined in Deuteronomy.

THE BASIC PROPHETIC MESSAGE

We have seen that the prophets write in the theological context of Deuteronomy and in the historical context of an imminent invasion by either the Assyrians (against Israel) or the Babylonians (against Judah). What is their message in this context?

The prophets serve as the Lord's prosecuting attorneys. They stand before the Lord, accusing and warning the people of the consequences of covenant violation. While there are numerous nuances and subpoints to their proclamation, their overall message can be boiled down to three basic points, each of which is important to the message of the prophets:

1. You have broken the covenant; you had better repent!
2. No repentance? Then judgment!
3. Yet there is hope beyond the judgment for a glorious future restoration.

Under point 1, the prophets stress how serious the nation's covenant violation has become and the extent to which the people have shattered the covenant. The prophets present a tremendous amount of evidence validating this charge. Evidence of this violation falls into three categories, all of which are explicitly listed in Deuteronomy. These categories reflect three major types of indictments against Israel or main areas of covenant violation: idolatry, social injustice, and religious ritualism.

Idolatry is perhaps the most flagrant violation of the covenant, and the prophets preach continuously against it. Israel engages in idolatry from their political beginning, with the golden calves in Bethel and Dan. But even Judah falls into serious idolatrous worship. Syncretism (the blending of religions) was in vogue with her neighbors, and

Judah feels free to create a pantheon, worshiping Baal, Asherah, and other gods along with the Lord God. They attempt to maintain the ritual of worshiping the Lord in the temple while also sacrificing to the other regional gods and participating in their festivals.

This syncretistic idolatry climaxes in Ezekiel 8. The Spirit takes Ezekiel on a tour to the temple in Jerusalem. There he sees an idol at the entrance to the north gate, drawings and carvings of idols and unclean animals on the walls, women burning incense to the Babylonian vegetation god Tammuz, and the elders with their backs to the presence of the Lord, facing the east and bowing to the sun. "This," the Lord declares, "will drive me far from my sanctuary" (8:6). Indeed, in Ezekiel 10 the glory of the Lord departs. The old Mosaic covenant as defined in Deuteronomy comes to an end with the departure of the Lord's presence in Ezekiel 10.

The prophets indict Israel on the charges of idolatry, social injustice, and religious ritualism.

Idolatry is not merely a violation of the law. It strikes at the heart of the relationship between the Lord and his people. The central covenant formula in the Old Testament is the statement by the Lord that "I will be your God; you will be my people. I will dwell in your midst." Idolatry rejects this relationship. Several of the prophets stress the emotional hurt that God feels at this rejection. For God the issue is as much an emotional issue as a legal one.

To aptly illustrate this, several of the prophets use the faithful husband/unfaithful wife image. This is perhaps the central imagery that paints the seriousness of the idolatry charge. The prostitute/unfaithful wife image runs throughout Jeremiah as one of his central images. Ezekiel also uses this relational picture in chapter 16. And poor Hosea lives out the heartbreaking drama in his own life.

The prophets use the image of the unfaithful wife to underscore the pain God feels when his people are unfaithful.

The prophets not only proclaim that idolatry violates the relational and legal aspects of the covenant, but they also deliver scathing polemical diatribes against the idols, demonstrating how irrational and foolish it is to worship them. "Tell us, you idols," Isaiah taunts, "what is going to happen. Tell us what the former things were. . . . Or declare to us the things to come . . . so we may know that you are gods. Do something," the prophet challenges, "whether good or bad, so that we will be dismayed and filled with fear" (Isa. 41:22–23). Jeremiah also jeers at the idols and their impotence, mocking them with his imagery: "Like a scarecrow in a cucumber field, their idols cannot speak; they must be carried because they cannot walk" (Jer. 10:5).

The covenant in Deuteronomy, however, bound the people to more than just the worship of the Lord. Relationship with God required proper relationship with people. The Lord was concerned with *social justice* for all, and he was especially concerned with how weaker individuals in society were treated. Deuteronomy demanded fair treatment of workers (24:14–15), justice in the court system (19:15–21), and special care for widows, orphans, and foreigners (24:17–22). As Israel and Judah turn from the Lord, they also turn from the Lord's demands for social justice. The prophets consistently condemn this and cite it as a central part of the covenant violation. They frequently cite the treatment of orphans and widows as examples of the social failure of the people. They also state that this lack of social justice invalidates the sacrifices.

A proper relationship with God requires proper relationship with people.

For example, in his opening salvo in chapter 1, Isaiah proclaims that the Lord will hide his eyes and not listen as they sacrifice because of their social injustice. Likewise, Jeremiah proclaims, "'They do not promote the case of the fatherless; they do not defend the just cause of the poor. Should I not punish them for this?' declares the Lord" (Jer. 5:28–29). In similar fashion Micah underscores that justice is more important to God than the ritual of sacrifice. In Micah 6:7–8 he states:

> 7Will the Lord be pleased with thousands of rams,
> with ten thousand rivers of olive oil?
> Shall I offer my firstborn for my transgression,
> the fruit of my body for the sin of my soul?
> 8He has shown you, O mortal, what is good.
> And what does the Lord require of you?
> To act justly and to love mercy
> and to walk humbly with your God.

The nation is relying on *religious ritualism* instead of relationship. The people have forgotten that ritual is the means to the relationship, not a substitute for relationship. As Israel becomes more enamored with formalized ritual, they lose the concept of relationship with the Lord. They trivialize the significance of God's presence in their midst. They think that only ritual is required of them. They draw the illogical conclusion that proper ritual will cover over other covenant violations like social injustice and idolatry. They rationalize their social injustice and their syncretism by focusing on the cultic ritual. This is hypocritical, the prophets declare, and not at all what God wants. Micah states this clearly in 6:7–8 (quoted above). Likewise, in Isaiah 1:11–13a the Lord asks, "The multitude of your sacrifices—what are they to me? . . .

Who has asked this of you, this trampling of my courts? Stop bringing meaningless offerings!"

Sacrifice is not the only cultic ritual that the prophets critique. In Isaiah 58 the prophet criticizes fasting as well. "You cannot fast as you do today and expect your voice to be heard on high," Isaiah quotes God as stating. He continues:

> [6]"Is not this the kind of fasting I have chosen:
> to loose the chains of injustice
> and untie the cords of the yoke,
> to set the oppressed free
> and break every yoke?
> [7]Is it not to share your food with the hungry
> and to provide the poor wanderer with shelter—
> when you see the naked, to clothe them,
> and not to turn away from your own flesh and blood?" (Isa. 58:6–7)

Idolatry, social injustice, and religious ritualism—these are the three interrelated indictments that make up point 1 of the prophetic message: *You have broken the covenant; you had better repent!* The call to repent is the other aspect of this point. The prophets beg the people to repent and to restore their relationship with the Lord. Even after the prophets proclaim that the judgment is imminent, they continue to plead for repentance. Jeremiah is the classic example, proclaiming the inevitability of the victorious Babylonian conquest, but all the while saying that it can be averted if only the people will repent.

As Israel became more enamored with formalized ritual, they lost the concept of relationship with the Lord.

The second point of the prophetic message is *No repentance? Then judgment!* The prophets plead with the people to repent and to turn back to covenant obedience. However, neither Israel nor Judah repents, and the prophets acknowledge that obstinacy, proclaiming the severe consequences. Much of the material in the prophetic books delineates the terrible imminent judgment about to fall on Israel or Judah. The major judgments predicted by the prophets are the horrific invasions by first the Assyrians and later the Babylonians. The most serious aspect of this is the loss of the promised land. The Lord is about to drive them out of the promised land, as he warned them in Deuteronomy.

The third and final point of the prophetic message is: *Yet there is hope beyond the judgment for a glorious future restoration*. The messianic promises and future predictions of the prophets comprise a large portion of point 3. The prophets do not proclaim a restoration after the destruction that simply returns to the current status quo.

The theological and relational picture of God's people in the future is different . . . and better. In the future, the prophets proclaim, there will be a new exodus (Isaiah), a new covenant (Jeremiah), and a new presence of the Lord's indwelling Spirit (Ezekiel and Joel). Forgiveness and peace will characterize this new system. Relationship will replace ritual.

All the wonderful prophecies of Christ fall into this category. The prophets announce that the people have failed miserably to keep the law and the Mosaic covenant. Thus, judgment is coming. However, after the destruction there will be a glorious restoration that includes the non-Jewish peoples (gentiles). The Messiah will come and inaugurate a new and better covenant. Furthermore, the prophets stress, these events are not haphazard, nor are they driven by chance or by the determination of world nations. Quite to the contrary, the prophets proclaim boldly, all of these events, including the judgment and the restoration, are part of God's plan, and the unfolding of these events provides clear evidence that God is the Lord over history.

The prophets do not proclaim a restoration after the destruction that simply returns to the current status quo. The theological and relational picture of God's people in the future is different . . . and better.

Most of the prophets can be summarized by the three points discussed above. For example, Isaiah, Jeremiah, Ezekiel, Hosea, Micah, and Zephaniah contain all three points. Amos, however, focuses primarily only on the first and second points (broken covenant and judgment). Not until chapter 8 does he mention any future hope and restoration. Joel, by contrast, virtually skips the first point, apparently assuming that the people understand that they have broken the covenant. He goes straight into judgment (point 2) and then into the future restoration (point 3). Obadiah and Nahum do not follow the typical pattern at all. They are different because they preach against foreign nations (Edom and Nineveh, respectively) rather than against Israel or Judah. They play a minor role in the overall prophetic picture. The postexilic prophets (Zechariah, Haggai, Malachi) likewise have a different message because they write after the exile.

Jonah, however, is much more important to the basic prophetic message, even though he also preaches against a foreign city (Nineveh) and not against Israel or Judah. Our understanding of Jonah is that while the actual historical preached message is to the Ninevites, the literary message is an indictment against Israel and Judah. Jonah, one of the earliest prophets, sets up a foil for the ones that follow. The repentance of the Ninevites stands in stark contrast to the obstinacy of the Israelites. What happens in Nineveh is what should be happening in Jerusalem and Samaria, but is not.

For example, Jeremiah preaches in Jerusalem for decades, and the response is only one of hostility. No one repents, from the greatest to the least of them. Jonah, by contrast, preaches a short, reluctant sermon in Nineveh (of all places!), and the entire city repents, from the greatest to the least. The book of Jonah underscores how inexcusable the response of Israel and Judah is to the prophetic warning.

INTERPRETATION AND APPLICATION

Having a good grasp of the central message of the prophets as discussed above is important, because most of the prophetic texts you will encounter present one of the three major points or expound on one of the three main indictments. Familiarity with these overall emphases will assist you in determining step 1 of the Interpretive Journey: *Grasp the text in their town. What did the text mean to the biblical audience?* Remember the historical-cultural and theological context. Read carefully and observe, observe, observe!

Next, you must identify the differences between the biblical audience and us (step 2 of the Interpretive Journey). We are not under the old covenant, nor are we facing the covenant curses in Deuteronomy. Likewise, we are not facing invasion from the Babylonians or Assyrians. We are also not a theocracy. The United States is not equivalent to ancient Israel.

Step 3 is crossing the principlizing bridge and developing one or more theological principles. Let's suppose for a moment that you are studying a passage in which one of the prophets is proclaiming the first point of the prophetic message: *You have broken the covenant; you had better repent!* The obvious and most common theological truth from this is that disobedience to God is sin and that sin brings punishment if not dealt with properly. However, it is imperative that we consult the biblical map (step 4) and pass this theological truth through the filter of New Testament teaching. In this step we will understand anew this truth in light of the cross.

Be sure to consult the biblical map, bringing the Old Testament principles through the filter of the New Testament.

In teaching about sin and covenant violation, we must be careful lest we forget Paul and grace and become Judaizers. Remember our discussion in chapter 19 concerning the law. We are no longer under the covenant of law, so we must be careful in translating this principle down to today's audience. We see two different situations for how this principle translates to concrete expression for people today, one for believers and one for unbelievers. Sin against God by the unbeliever does result in terrible judgment. However, when a believer sins, he or she is still covered by the atonement of Christ.

In attempting to grasp the meaning of these texts that announce covenant violation, we often find it more helpful to focus on the relational aspects that our sin, or covenant violation, affects. In the prophetic books, God used the marriage analogy and the unfaithful spouse image to convey the emotional pain he felt when Israel and Judah were unfaithful. However, most people, even Christians, in the broader culture of America tend to view sin against God in the same fashion as they view breaking secular laws—speeding laws, for example. If you break the law, you pay a price, but no one is hurt emotionally. Certainly, Uncle Sam couldn't care less about our speeding tickets.

One of the most important theological truths coming out of the prophetic message is that when we are unfaithful to God, we damage our relationship with him, causing him to hurt emotionally.

This particular attitude reflects a popular theology, that is, a theology arising out of our culture rather than out of the Bible. It is a theology that has a detached, emotionally neutral, impassive God, and it is a theology that is propagated through the culture both in and out of the church. In contrast, one of the most important theological truths coming out of the prophetic message is that when we are unfaithful to God, we damage our relationship with him, causing him to hurt emotionally. When one loves someone deeply, they open themselves up and become vulnerable. God has made himself vulnerable to our unfaithfulness, and we find ourselves in the incredible situation of being able to hurt God when we are unfaithful to our relationship with him. For the New Testament believer, the consequence of unconfessed sin is not a Babylonian invasion and exile, but rather a strained and damaged relationship with God, who has been hurt by our unfaithfulness.

To complete the Interpretive Journey, we must move on to the application level (step 5). This truth must be translated into specific real-life situations of individual Christians. A Christian today, for example, who attends church and professes Jesus but who regularly indulges in sexual promiscuity is not far from the eighth-century BC Hebrew who regularly offered sacrifices to the Lord but also participated in Baal worship. Both actions hurt God and damage the relationship. True repentance and a change of heart are called for in both situations.

As you read and study the prophets, you will also frequently encounter passages that contain one of the three indictments (idolatry, social injustice, religious ritualism). Each of these can be carried along on the Interpretive Journey across the river and through the New Testament into a contemporary context fairly well.

The charge of idolatry, for example, translates for us today into whatever it is that draws our worship and focus away from our relationship with God. For many American adults, this is often a job, success, or the need to make more money.

For younger adults, the more common idols are popularity, clothes, movies, TV, cars, sports, and even grades.

Social injustice, however, is more difficult to transpose into today's context. Or perhaps the expression of this concept is simply more difficult to accept once it has been transposed. The prophets preached often against social injustice, and they considered violations of social justice as serious as idolatry. They addressed numerous cases of social injustice, such as judicial bribery, marketplace dishonesty, or failure to pay just wages. One of the major social issue themes running throughout the prophets, however, is the abuse, oppression, or even the neglect of the underclass, whom the prophets identify as the widow, the orphan, and the alien or foreigner. Deuteronomy mentions this triad eight times, commanding that the people of God give them both legal justice and food (10:18; 24:17, 19, 20, 21; 26:12, 13; 27:19). Apparently this group did not have enough political and economic clout in the society to fend for themselves, so the Lord commands his people to pay specific attention to caring for them. Both Israel and Judah failed miserably at keeping this commandment, and the prophets made this one of their major indictments against them.

The prophets proclaimed social injustice to be as serious a sin as idolatry.

The theological principle for this indictment would be related to the fact that God is concerned for those who are weak, either physically or socioeconomically. Furthermore, he expects his people, since they have him living in their midst, to be actively helping and defending such people. Certainly, bringing this truth through the New Testament filter (step 4) does not alter the demand for social justice. Jesus' application of the Levitical commandment, "Love your neighbor as yourself," in the story of the good Samaritan indicates that Jesus continues to exhort us to care for those in need, even if, or especially if, the one in need is racially or culturally different from us.

Application of this truth is often difficult today, because frequently political affiliation and regional cultural outlook play greater roles in shaping the North American Christian's view of social justice than biblical theology does. If one were to stop Americans on the street at random, finding out their party affiliation would likely be a more accurate predictor of their views on social issues than finding out whether they are evangelical believers. This is troubling to us, and it lies at the root of the problem we face when we try to apply the prophetic exhortation on social justice. When biblical theology conflicts with strongly held cultural views, the tendency is to modify or conform the theology to the culture. This is, of course, backward, but it is also precisely what the culture in Jerusalem did to Jeremiah, and it resulted in the exile.

It is important to note that the prophets were in direct conflict with commonly held attitudes of their culture. Part of their message was that the social views of God's people should be driven by the Word of God, not by the culture. One of the challenges for us, as mentioned in chapter 7, is to realize that we bring a lot of cultural-political baggage with us on this issue. The biblical interpretive challenge for us is not to have Republican views or Democrat views, but rather Christian views—views anchored in biblical theology rather than in secular culture.

The biblical interpretive challenge for us is not to have Republican views or Democrat views, but rather Christian views—views anchored in biblical theology rather than in secular culture.

Thus, we need to ask several application questions. Who today does not have enough political and economic clout to get justice or food? Minorities? Illegal immigrants? The poor? The elderly? Children? Abused women? The unborn? The application process is not complete until we come to grips with the seriousness of the issue and until we realize that God holds us (his people) responsible for caring for those who do not have the political or economic power to care for themselves.

Finally, you will also encounter many passages that relate to the third indictment of the prophets, the charge of religious ritualism. Especially in Judah, the people believed that maintaining the rituals of worship was all that God required. They believed that ritual activity such as sacrifice fulfilled their obligation to God and therefore freed them to do anything else outside the covenant they chose. The prophets condemn this attitude unequivocally. Remember, of course, that ritual in and of itself was not bad. The Lord himself ordained many of the rituals that the prophets critique. So the prophetic message is not a blanket repudiation of ritual. The problem for Judah was that they used the ritual to *replace* the relationship rather than to *enhance* the relationship.

God desires relationship over ritual.

The theological principle emerging from this indictment is that God desires relationship over ritual. Rituals have validity only in that they assist in developing the relationship. As we cross into the New Testament, this principle is reaffirmed. The Pharisees of Jesus' day were more concerned with Sabbath observance than with the needs and hurts of people. Jesus rebukes them strongly for this. Most of the rituals of the Old Testament were dropped in the New Testament, but the church quickly began to develop its own rituals. The goal of faith, however, then as now, is to develop a relationship with God. Ritual, then as now, can help God's people in the development of that relationship.

However, without the relationship the ritual is meaningless. Once the ritual becomes the end rather than the means to the end, it becomes meaningless—or worse.

Once it becomes the rationalized cover for a life devoid of social justice and true relationship with God, then the ritual is on the same level as idolatry. The expression of this principle for us today is that our Christian rituals (how we do church) are valid as long as they enhance the development of our relationship with God. The rituals are the means to an end (relationship), not the end themselves. Likewise, the observance of ritual, without the underpinning of relationship, is hardly a substitute for living a life characterized by social justice and authentic worship of God.

Spend a few moments evaluating the rituals of your religious life. Do your rituals function as tools to assist you in the development of your relationship with God? Have the rituals helped you to inherit the faith and relationship of the preceding generation, and will they help you to pass faith and relationship on to the next one? Or have your rituals degenerated into a replacement of a relationship with God? Is your goal on Sunday to relate to God or simply to attend church?

Do your rituals function as tools to assist you in the development of your relationship with God?

Now let's give some thought to point 2 of the prophetic message: *No repentance? Then judgment.* In the discussion above, we indicated that for the biblical audience, this judgment took the form of an invasion by a foreign army, the destruction of the nation, the loss of God's presence, and the loss of the right to live in the promised land. The theological principle behind this prophetic message should reflect the fact that sin is an offense against God's holiness. Furthermore, sin demands appropriate judgment. Also, because of God's holiness, continued sin places a barrier between God's people and their relationship with him as he dwells in their midst.

As we carry the principle through the New Testament, we recognize that sin has not changed and that the consequences of sin have not changed. What has changed is that God has now transferred the judgment of death for the Christian's sin onto Christ. However, sin in the New Testament believer's life is still an affront to God's holiness. God indwells each believer, and sin in the believer's life offends the holy God dwelling within us. If we fail to repent and turn from our sin, our relationship with God will be damaged. We will lose the right to fellowship closely with him, and numerous negative consequences will follow.

Finally, let's look at interpreting and applying point 3: *Yet there is hope beyond the judgment for a glorious future restoration.* Numerous Old Testament passages proclaim this point. It is imperative, of course, that we see the ultimate fulfillment of these promises in Christ, but the spectacular prophetic message of forgiveness and restoration can also be transposed up from the national level of the ancient Hebrews to a theological principle and then back down to us today. The theological principle expresses the reality that God is in the business of forgiving and restoring people.

As we move into the New Testament, we see that forgiveness and restoration find their ultimate expression in Jesus Christ. There is no sin or situation in our lives that God will not forgive and restore if we turn to him humbly through Christ.

The specific applications of this expression are numerous. Many Christians struggle with depression. Many come out of horrendous family situations. Many are scarred deeply by the events in their past. These passages apply to them by demonstrating that God can completely restore what has been damaged or destroyed. God can renew anyone and give people hope. God is in the business of forgiving and restoring to newness of life.

As we move into the New Testament, we see that forgiveness and restoration find their ultimate expression in Jesus Christ. There is no sin or situation in our lives that God will not forgive and restore if we turn to him humbly through Christ.

For example, if we are applying Ezekiel 37, we need to stand with Ezekiel and gaze out over the valley of bleached and scattered bones as God breathes new life into them and restores them to wholeness of life. How hopeless was that situation? How dead were those people? How hopeless is your situation? Cannot the God whom Ezekiel describes breathe new life into you as well? If we leave the study of the prophets with a pessimistic, depressed outlook on life, we have failed to grasp one of the most critical elements of the prophetic message.

SPECIAL PROBLEMS—THE PREDICTIVE PASSAGES

While most of the prophets' words are directed to the events of their time, a small portion of their message points to events that are still future to us. We, of course, are extremely interested in that portion of prophecy that still lies ahead of us. These passages, however, present us with a unique set of interpretive challenges, especially as we try to interpret the *details* of those future things. Indeed, today there is substantial disagreement over the correct interpretive approach to such texts.

One of the major problems that surfaces when we attempt to interpret the predictive prophecies is the *near view–far view* problem. When the prophets looked into the future, they saw clearly the destruction of Israel or Judah by the Assyrians or Babylonians. However, they also saw glimpses of destruction on other nations; indeed, they saw judgment on the entire world (the day of the Lord). The *near* judgment (Assyrian or Babylonian) is easy for us to identify historically, but the *far* judgment is much vaguer.

Likewise, when the prophets paint the images of the events related to future hope and restoration, they can be referring to one of three things: (1) the return of the

Jewish exiles to Israel under Ezra and Nehemiah, (2) the first coming of Christ, or (3) the second coming of Christ. The interpretive problem for us is that the prophets are not always clear as to when they are looking at near events and when they are looking at far events. The prophets will slide back and forth from describing events that will occur soon within their lifetimes (the near view) to events that will occur during the first advent of Christ (the far view) to events that are still future even for us (the even farther view). These events often seem to be blurred together in the images they present.

This *near view–far view* is similar to the visual image we encounter when we look at a mountain range from a distance. Suppose, for example, you are standing on a flat prairie and looking at a mountain range in the distance. What you see is a landscape similar to the sketch below:

When we peer at the landscape from a distance, the mountains seem two-dimensional; that is, they all appear to be the same distance away from us. The mountains in front do not look any closer than the mountains in back. In reality, however, there are large valleys that separate the mountains from each other. The mountains in the back of our landscape view may be miles and miles away from the mountains in the front. Yet from our vantage point, they all look to be equally distant.

The prophets paint their images of future events in a similar fashion. Their picture of the return of the exiles under Ezra and Nehemiah is like the mountain in front; the mountains behind are the events relating to the first and second comings of Christ. To the prophets these events are all future and distant, and so they do not always indicate which event they are describing. Indeed, often they seem to shift from one future event to another even within the same passage, and sometimes within the same verse.

This phenomenon leads us to be cautious about being overly dogmatic in interpreting the specific details of future events. We need to be aware of the *near view–far view* characteristics of these texts. However, this manner of describing the future events should not hinder us from taking the Interpretive Journey and developing theological principles as normal. The broad, sweeping themes we discussed above are still clear. Furthermore, it is possible that the prophets have intentionally blurred these events together so that their readers would in fact focus more on the larger, broader principles rather than on the details (e.g., trying to determine exactly when the Messiah will return).

Often it is difficult to determine whether the picture the prophets paint is a literal prediction of the future or a figurative, symbolic one.

Another interpretive problem that we will encounter occasionally is that some biblical prophecies appear to have aspects of conditionality attached to their fulfillment. God himself states this clearly in Jeremiah 18:7–10:

> 7"If at any time I announce that a nation or kingdom is to be uprooted, torn down and destroyed, 8and if that nation I warned repents of its evil, then I will relent and not inflict on it the disaster I had planned. 9And if at another time I announce that a nation or kingdom is to be built up and planted, 10and if it does evil in my sight and does not obey me, then I will reconsider the good I had intended to do for it."

God seems to be saying that in many cases the final outcome of a prophecy is conditioned by the response of people to the prophetic word. This does not indicate any kind of failure on the part of God's Word; indeed, he indicates that this conditionality is part of his sovereign will and is related to his sovereign right to decide such things (Jer. 18:6).

A good illustration of a conditional biblical prophecy can be found in the book of Jonah. In Jonah 3:4 the prophet declares, "Forty more days and Nineveh will be overthrown." However, the people of Nineveh respond to Jonah by believing him, repenting of their deeds, putting on sackcloth, and fasting. God then responds to the actions of the Ninevites with compassion, canceling the prophesied imminent destruction (3:10). Therefore, as stated in Jeremiah 18:7–10, God is free to exercise his sovereign choice and modify the fulfillment of a prophetic word as a consequence of his great compassion and the repentance and prayer of the people under judgment.

A literary feature in the prophetic books that presents us with interpretive challenges is the prophets' use of imagery and figures of speech to describe future events. Remember that the prophets use poetic language continuously! They paint visual pictures with their imagery and use wonderful, colorful figures of speech to convey their predictions of the future. Often it is difficult to determine whether the picture they paint is a literal prediction of the future or a figurative, symbolic one. Certainly, their predictive imagery represents firm future realities, but determining with certainty whether their image is literal or symbolic can be difficult.

For example, consider Isaiah 11:6:

> The wolf will live with the lamb,
> the leopard will lie down with the goat,
> the calf and the lion and the yearling together;
> and a little child will lead them.

Clearly this text is talking about peace, but how literal is it? Are the "wolf" and the "lamb" figures of speech representing traditional enemies? That is, does this passage speak primarily of a time when nations will no longer war with each other? Or is it completely literal? In the coming kingdom age, will wolves and lambs literally live together in peace? What is the intent of the author in this text?

Or consider Isaiah 65:17–20. The Lord states in 65:17 that he will "create new heavens and a new earth." In 65:20 he adds:

> "Never again will there be in it
> an infant who lives but a few days,
> or an old man who does not live out his years;
> the one who dies at a hundred
> will be thought a mere child;
> the one who fails to reach a hundred
> will be considered accursed."

Is this all to be understood literally or figuratively? Is this passage saying that God will literally create a new physical earth? Will it be an earth in which people literally live quite long but still die? Or is it all symbolic?

Christians remain divided on how best to interpret this type of predictive passage. Even among believers who approach the Bible with the same "evangelical" presuppositions, there is disagreement concerning the interpretation of many of these predictive texts of the prophets. The disagreement revolves around two central questions. The first question is the broad one: How literal are the images that the prophets use to predict the future? That is, do we interpret the figures of speech in a literal sense or a symbolic sense? The second question, arising from the details of the first, grapples with a related issue: Does the New Testament church fulfill the Old Testament prophecies that refer to Israel?

The issues involved in this debate are lengthy and complex, and they are beyond the scope of this book. We are striving to teach you an interpretive method; we are not trying to convince you of any particular theological position. However, on this issue, one's broad theological understanding of future events and of the relationship between the church and Israel usually determines one's methodological answer to the two interpretive questions above. This is not necessarily bad; remember that as we interpret, we must move back and forth between the parts and the whole. We must interpret particular passages within the context of the entire Bible.

However, we have also cautioned you against allowing your fixed theological preunderstandings to dictate how you interpret a particular passage even before you begin to struggle with it. The correct balance is maintained as we allow the parts and the whole to inform each other. That is, we do bring our overall theological understanding with us into these predictive texts, but we also seek constantly to update and mature our overall theological understanding (the whole) precisely by our study of particular texts (the parts).

In the Interpretive Journey, this issue arises during both step 3 (the theological principle) and step 4 (How does our theological principle fit with the rest of the Bible?). Remember that the theological principle developed in step 3 must be faithful to the text, but it must also correspond to the teaching of the rest of Scripture. Likewise, we must next pass through the filter of New Testament teaching (step 4). The New Testament also has much to say about future events, providing us with numerous passages that address the nature of God's kingdom, the relationship between Israel and the church, the second coming of Christ, and the events of the end times. So our understanding of these New Testament teachings will necessarily influence the way we translate the expression of meaning for the Old Testament audience into an expression of meaning for the church today.

The prophets soar like eagles, painting their images of the future with big broad strokes. They appear to have little concern for presenting an organized, structured, detailed description of the end times.

A few suggested guidelines may be helpful. First, do not overlook the poetic aspect of prophecy. That is, do not allow your theological preunderstanding to ride roughshod over your appreciation and understanding of imagery and figures of speech. You should spend more time struggling to grasp the images that the prophets paint than trying to fit the events they describe into some overall future time schedule. Yet keep in mind that grappling with the imagery and the figures of speech certainly does not suggest a negation of the literal reality behind the image. Jesus Christ came to earth as a literal, physical fulfillment of Old Testament prophetic imagery. The way in which he fulfilled prophecy in his first advent on earth is perhaps suggestive of how he may fulfill prophecy during his future coming.

We also suggest that you focus more on translating and applying the broader theological principles than on trying to fit all the details into a system. The prophets soar like eagles, painting their images of the future with big broad strokes. They appear to have little concern for presenting an organized, structured, detailed description of the end times.

Finally, do not forget the way in which the prophets use the *near view–far view*. The future events are often blurred together.

CONCLUSION

Whew! The prophetic books are full of wonderful material. Certainly the Lord's spokesmen give us rich and deep teachings about the character of God. They also speak powerfully to us about our character and our behavior, using incredibly colorful and gripping poetic language that both sears and soars. Yet their basic message can be summarized into three simple points:

- You have broken the covenant; you had better repent!
- No repentance? Then judgment!
- Yet there is hope beyond the judgment for a glorious future restoration.

At the heart of their message, intertwined into all the different aspects of the prophetic word, we find the constant theme of God's relationship with his people. Studying the prophets can help you to understand better the character of God and to grasp for yourself what God expects of you in your relationship with him and with your fellow human beings.

ASSIGNMENTS

For each of the passages below, apply the Interpretive Journey. Study the text and make as many observations as you can. Mark the observations on a photocopy of the text and in the margins. Be sure that you understand the meanings of all of the words. Do background study and word studies as needed to understand each term. Be sure to identify all figures of speech. Then answer the specific questions listed under step 1 and write a paragraph for each of the other steps.

Step 1: Grasp the text in their town. What did the text mean to the biblical audience? Identify the historical-cultural context and the literary context. When and where does this prophecy occur? (Use a Bible dictionary or commentary to help you with this, if necessary.) What does the surrounding text discuss? Does this passage fall into one of the three main points of the prophetic message or one of the indictments discussed above? If so, which one? Review the discussion above regarding the point of the prophetic message that relates to your passage.

Step 2: Measure the width of the river to cross. What are the differences between the biblical audience and us?

Step 3: Cross the principlizing bridge. What is the theological principle in this text?

Step 4: Consult the biblical map. How does our theological principle fit with the rest of the Bible? Does the New Testament teaching modify or qualify this principle, and, if so, how?

Step 5: Grasp the text in our town. How should individual Christians today live out this modified theological principle?

Assignment 21–1: Micah 6:6–8

6 With what shall I come before the LORD

and bow down before the exalted God?

Shall I come before him with burnt offerings,

with calves a year old?

7 Will the LORD be pleased with thousands of rams,

with ten thousand rivers of olive oil?

Shall I offer my firstborn for my transgression,

the fruit of my body for the sin of my soul?

8 He has shown you, O mortal, what is good.

And what does the LORD require of you?

To act justly and to love mercy

and to walk humbly with your God.

Assignment 21–2: Jeremiah 7:1–7

1This is the word that came to Jeremiah from the LORD: 2"Stand at the gate of the LORD's house and there proclaim this message:

" 'Hear the word of the LORD, all you people of Judah who come through these gates to worship the LORD. 3This is what the LORD Almighty, the God of Israel, says: Reform your ways and your actions, and I will let you live in this place. 4Do not trust in deceptive words and say, "This is the temple of the LORD, the temple of the LORD, the temple of the LORD!" 5If you really change your ways and your actions and deal with each other justly, 6if you do not oppress the foreigner, the fatherless or the widow and do not shed innocent blood in this place, and if you do not follow other gods to your own harm, 7then I will let you live in this place, in the land I gave your ancestors for ever and ever.' "

Assignment 21–3: Jeremiah 31:10–14

10"Hear the word of the LORD, you nations;

proclaim it in distant coastlands:

'He who scattered Israel will gather them

and will watch over his flock like a shepherd.'

11For the LORD will deliver Jacob

and redeem them from the hand of those stronger than they.

12They will come and shout for joy on the heights of Zion;

they will rejoice in the bounty of the LORD—

the grain, the new wine and the olive oil,

the young of the flocks and herds.

They will be like a well-watered garden,

and they will sorrow no more.

13Then young women will dance and be glad,

young men and old as well.

I will turn their mourning into gladness;

I will give them comfort and joy instead of sorrow.

14I will satisfy the priests with abundance,

and my people will be filled with my bounty,"

declares the LORD.

CHAPTER 22

OLD TESTAMENT—WISDOM

INTRODUCTION

Well, you have persevered to the end of the book. This is the last chapter. The writer of Ecclesiastes, one of the wisdom books, has a word that is perhaps applicable both to you, the reader, and to us, the authors: "Of making many books there is no end, and much study wearies the body" (Eccl. 12:12b).

We conclude our study of the various biblical genres with a venture into the Old Testament wisdom books (Proverbs, Job, Ecclesiastes, and Song of Songs).[1] Without a doubt, these books contain some of the most interesting material in the Bible. On the one hand, the wisdom books have some material that is extremely easy to interpret and grasp—verses for which the interpretive river is shallow and easy to cross. Such proverbs as "A gossip betrays a confidence, but a trustworthy person keeps a secret" (Prov. 11:13), or "Hatred stirs up conflict, but love covers over all wrongs" (10:12) seem straightforward and simple to understand.

1. In many scholarly discussions, Song of Songs (or Song of Solomon) is not considered to be part of the wisdom literature. However, we agree with Gordon D. Fee and Douglas K. Stuart, *How to Read the Bible for All Its Worth*, 4th ed. (Grand Rapids: Zondervan, 2014), 233, 238, 254–57, that it should be included as one of the wisdom books, and that it plays a significant role in balancing the picture of wisdom presented in the other books.

On the other hand, numerous passages in the wisdom literature raise questions. For example, Proverbs 22:4 seems to promise wealth to those who fear God and are humble: "Humility is the fear of the LORD; its wages are riches and honor and life." Does this teach that if Christians are poor, either they must not be humble or they don't fear God? Does it mean that rich Christians are humbler and more God-fearing than poor Christians?

Likewise, the book of Job has some puzzling texts. Look at Job 3:1, "After this, Job opened his mouth and cursed the day of his birth." How do we interpret and apply this verse? Is this to be a model for how we respond to adversity? And the book of Ecclesiastes is really strange, with all manner of unusual verses. Consider the following:

> A feast is made for laughter,
> wine makes life merry,
> and money is the answer for everything. (Eccl. 10:19)

Is the author recommending partying, drinking, and the pursuit of money?

Furthermore, the Song of Songs seems to be the mushy, intimate words of two young lovers to each other. "How beautiful you are, my darling! Oh, how beautiful! . . . Your teeth are like a flock of sheep just shorn, coming up from the washing. Each has its twin; not one of them is alone" (Song 4:1–2). Apparently this young man's girl has white teeth and none of them are missing, but how does this relate to us? Is the Bible teaching us about the importance of dental hygiene?

Is Song of Songs 4:1–2 teaching us about the importance of dental hygiene?

Obviously, there are some interpretive issues for us to tackle in the wisdom books. By now you are well aware of how important context is for the proper interpretation of any passage. Indeed, in the silly examples above you were probably shouting, "Context! Context!" as the solution to our confusion over these examples. You are correct, of course, because placing the wisdom literature into the proper context will be a critical step along the way to grasping what God has for us in these books.

In this chapter, therefore, we will first discuss the purpose of the wisdom books, for purpose is a critical aspect of the wisdom genre and its literary context. Next we will look at the big picture—what the major thrust of each book is and how the books relate to each other. Following that, we will discuss the poetic aspects of the literature. Then we will actually take the Interpretive Journey in each of the wisdom books, pointing out the varying widths of the river and suggesting principles that span the river and make the text applicable to us today. Finally, we will wrap up the chapter with a concluding summary and the ever-present assignments.

THE PURPOSE OF THE WISDOM BOOKS

Although the wisdom books are definitely different from the rest of the Old Testament, they do seem to play a special role in God's revelation to us. In comparing the wisdom books to the rest of the Old Testament, Kidner makes this insightful comment:

> In other words, in the Wisdom books the tone of voice and even the speakers have changed. The blunt "Thou shalt" or "shalt not" of the Law, and the urgent "Thus saith the LORD" of the Prophets, are joined now by the cooler comments of the teacher and the often anguished questions of the learner. Where the bulk of the Old Testament calls us simply to obey and to believe, this part of it (chiefly the books we have mentioned, although wisdom is a thread that runs through every part) summons us to think hard as well as humbly; to keep our eyes open, to use our conscience and our common sense, and not to shirk the most disturbing questions.[2]

It is important that we not misunderstand Kidner's quote. He is not denying the intellectual component of the rest of the Old Testament, nor is he denying the spiritual dimension of the wisdom literature. He is merely observing that the law, the narratives, and the prophets stress the imperatives of "Believe!" and "Obey!" while the wisdom books stress the imperative "Think!" However, just as believing and obeying result in action, the challenge to think likewise results in action.

The imperative of the wisdom literature is "Think!"

While the wisdom books do not stress the standard elements of the salvation story (covenant, promise, redemption, forgiveness), they do nonetheless *assume* the theological underpinnings of the rest of the Old Testament. Proverbs 1:7 states, "The fear of the LORD is the beginning of knowledge." The wisdom books start with this theological basis and then use the salvation story as a foundation on which to build a practical theology for living a day-to-day godly life in a complicated world.

The imperatives of the wisdom literature—listen, look, think, reflect—combine to focus on the overarching purpose of these books: to develop character in the reader.

2. Derek Kidner, *The Wisdom of Proverbs, Job and Ecclesiastes: An Introduction to Wisdom Literature* (Downers Grove, IL: InterVarsity Press, 1985), 11.

The wisdom books are not a collection of universal promises. Rather, they are a collection of valuable insights into godly living, which, if taken to heart (and head), will develop godly character, a character that will make wise choices in the rough-and-tumble marketplace of life.[3] Wisdom literature makes the subtle suggestion that godly living involves solid, commonsense choices. Thus, living in a foolish, naive, or cynical fashion is a reflection of ungodly living.

The wisdom books present a practical theology for living a day-to-day godly life in a complicated world.

Wisdom thus has a strong practical tone. The character to be developed is not a hypothetical or idealistic one, but a real, down-to-earth, commonsense character. R. B. Y. Scott summarized by writing that wisdom "has to do with how men [and women] ought to act in the workaday world, with personal character, and with a way of life that can be called good because it has coherence, value, and meaning."[4] So wisdom can be defined as that combination of knowledge and character that allows one to live in the real world in a right and godly manner.

THE BIG PICTURE

Each of the four wisdom books (Proverbs, Job, Ecclesiastes, and Song of Songs) is different in its contribution to our education in wise living. It is important to see the different roles of each, but we must also be able to see how they integrate to form the broad literary context of wisdom. The four books balance each other theologically, and any one of them read out of the context of the others can be easily misunderstood. Basically, Proverbs presents the rational, ordered norms of life, while the other three books present the exceptions and limitations to the rational, ordered approach to life. This basic summary is further clarified below.

The goal of wisdom is to develop character.

The Basic Approach to Life (Proverbs)

Proverbs presents the rational, ordered norms of life. The many proverbs in the book are *not* universals (i.e., things that are always true), but rather norms of life (i.e., things that are normally true). God has set in place an ordered, rational world, and it all makes sense. If you work hard, you will prosper; if you don't, you will be poor. Wise, righteous, hardworking people can expect a blessed, prosperous life, while foolish, sinful, lazy people can expect a hard life.

3. William P. Brown, *Character in Crisis: A Fresh Approach to the Wisdom Literature of the Old Testament* (Grand Rapids: Eerdmans, 1996).

4. R. B. Y. Scott, *The Way of Wisdom in the Old Testament* (New York: Macmillan, 1971), 5.

Exception 1: The Suffering of the Righteous (Job)

The book of Job demonstrates that often events occur that humans cannot grasp or understand through the wisdom approach delineated in Proverbs. Sometimes tragedy strikes those who are wise, righteous, and hardworking, and God does not disclose the reasons behind such tragedy. Proverbs teaches us that life is rational and that the wise person can understand it. Job qualifies this with some real-world experience. If we take both books together, we conclude that *most* of life is rational and can be understood. *Some* events in life, however, are inexplicable to us as mere humans. Our wisdom approach of Proverbs fails us in these situations, and we are forced to rely on faith in the Creator. This is what we learn from Job.

Exception 2: The Failure of the Rational, Ordered Approach to Provide Ultimate Meaning to Life (Ecclesiastes)

The book of Ecclesiastes is an intellectual search for meaning in life. While the author acknowledges that being wise is better than being stupid, he concludes that wisdom does not by itself provide meaning to life. Also, while Job tells the story of one exception to the norms of Proverbs, the cynical analysis in Ecclesiastes chronicles numerous exceptions to the thesis of an ordered, rational universe. The ultimate conclusion in Ecclesiastes, not disclosed until the final verses, is that the only way to find meaning in life is to be in relationship with God. Logic and rational thought (wisdom) can help you on a day-to-day basis, but ultimate meaning in life requires relationship with God.

Proverbs presents the rational, ordered norms of life, while the other three books present the exceptions and limitations to the rational, ordered approach to life.

Exception 3: The Irrationality of Romantic Love between a Husband and Wife (Song of Songs)

Proverbs gives good, practical, wise advice about marriage. It advises men not to marry women who are quarrelsome or ill-tempered (21:9, 19), and it depicts clearly for women the fate of lazy fools and drunkards, thus implicitly warning against marrying such men. Throughout Proverbs the picture of a good, wise man of character is presented, and in the final section (31:10–31) the picture of a good, wise, and noble wife is presented. All this advice is good and rational.

However, it is difficult to build a great love relationship in marriage with only logic and rational thought. The Song of Songs celebrates the wild, irrational, mushy, and corny aspects of true love. This book suggests to us that in the marketplace husbands and wives may need to be the quiet, discerning, hardworking people of Proverbs, but that once the lights go out in the privacy of their home, they need to be the crazy, madly-in-love, slightly irrational couple in Song of Songs.

WISDOM AS POETRY

A large majority of the wisdom literature is poetry. There are some short narrative sequences in Job and a moderate amount of prose reflection in Ecclesiastes, but the rest of the material is painted with poetry. It is important, therefore, to remember the principles of interpreting poetry that we learned back in chapter 20.

A large majority of the wisdom literature is poetry.

Thus, we find that the wisdom books use *parallelism* as their standard structural feature. This is obvious in Proverbs, where each verse consists of two lines that clearly combine to form one thought. However, it is important to note that the rest of the wisdom material also follows this pattern. Thus, the form of Job's complaint in 6:2 is that of synonymous parallelism:

> If only my anguish could be weighed
> and all my misery be placed on the scales!

Even God's response to Job at the end of the book is poetic, following the standard literary format of parallelism (synonymous parallelism in this example):

> Have you journeyed to the springs of the sea
> or walked in the recesses of the deep? (Job 38:16)

Likewise, many of the verses in Ecclesiastes and most of the verses in Song of Songs exhibit parallelism.

> For with much wisdom comes much sorrow;
> the more knowledge, the more grief. (Eccl. 1:18, synonymous parallelism)

> Your cheeks are beautiful with earrings,
> your neck with strings of jewels. (Song 1:10, synonymous parallelism)

Another characteristic feature of Hebrew poetry is the frequent use of figurative imagery. In chapter 20 we noted that figurative imagery is effective especially when the author is trying to connect emotionally with the reader. However, the stress of wisdom literature, particularly the book of Proverbs, is on thinking, not on feeling. Thus, the use of poetry and figurative imagery would be surprising. In fact, the book of Proverbs rarely uses figurative imagery. While figures of speech occur throughout the book, they do not do so with the same frequency as in other poetic books. The form we find throughout the book defined as *proverb* is a type of poetry, but it is distinct, and it differs from traditional Hebrew poetry on some points, such as in its minimal use of figurative language. This concurs with the low level of emotional appeal in Proverbs.

The Song of Songs, however, is completely different. It is highly emotional and attempts to connect with the audience at an emotional level. It is not surprising, therefore, to find this book replete with figurative imagery. Job, also an emotionally charged book, is likewise characterized by figures of speech, while Ecclesiastes, lying somewhere between Proverbs and Job in its emotional orientation, likewise uses figures of speech more frequently than Proverbs but less than Job. Thus, if we can place the books in an order of increasing emotional orientation (Proverbs, Ecclesiastes, Job, and Song of Songs), we recognize that this same order also reflects a corresponding increasing use of figurative imagery.

GRASPING THE WISDOM BOOKS

In this section we will discuss each wisdom book, noting the unique features of each and the impact such features have on interpretation. We will relate these features to the Interpretative Journey, providing you with broad principles for studying and applying the wisdom books. The wisdom books are fascinating and fun. We think you will enjoy your study.

Proverbs

The book of Proverbs is perhaps the easiest of the wisdom books to understand because it speaks to such common, everyday aspects of life: work, friendship, marriage, speech, money, and integrity. The proverbs also make sense to us because we are familiar with the literary form. In America we have dozens of old proverbs, and we use them in much the same way as the ancient Hebrews used their collection. Do you remember the following proverbs?

> Look before you leap.
> The early bird gets the worm.
> You can lead a horse to water, but you can't make him drink.

One bad apple spoils the entire barrel.
If you can't stand the heat, get out of the kitchen.
All that glitters is not gold.
Don't count your chickens before they're hatched.

How many other American proverbs can you think of? There are dozens. Proverbs are common in many other cultures as well. Usually they are short, pithy statements that teach practical wisdom about life. The proverbs in the Bible are similar. Usually they consist of two lines of parallel poetry (as discussed above). They are brief and phrased to be "catchy" for easy memorization.

Don't count your chickens before they're hatched.

The practical nature of these proverbs makes them applicable to almost anyone. Indeed, the ancient Hebrews borrowed many of their individual proverbs from the wisdom literature of their neighbors. Nevertheless, the book of Proverbs subordinates all of this borrowed wisdom to faith in God. Ross writes,

> Finally, many specific emphases in Proverbs find parallels in the wisdom literature of the ancient Near East. But even though the collections share some of the same interests, the biblical material is unique in its prerequisite of a personal faith in a personal God. To the Hebrews the success of wisdom did not simply require a compliance with wise instructions, but trust in, reverence for, and submission to the Lord (Prov. 1:7; 3:5–6; 9:10) who created everything and governs both the world of nature and human history (3:19–20; 16:24; 21:1). Any ancient wisdom used by the Hebrews had to harmonize with this religious worldview, and any ancient wisdom used in this collection took on greater significance when subordinated to the true faith.[5]

Perhaps the most critical thing to remember when interpreting and applying the book of Proverbs is that the individual proverbs reflect general nuggets of wisdom and not universal truths. To interpret the proverbs as absolute promises from God is to misunderstand the intent of the author. Proverbs gives guidance for life, addressing situations that are *normally* true.

For example, consider Proverbs 10:4:

5. Allen P. Ross, "Proverbs," in *Expositor's Bible Commentary*, ed. Frank Gaebelein (Grand Rapids: Zondervan, 1991), 5:885.

> Lazy hands make for poverty,
>   but diligent hands bring wealth.

This proverb is generally true. If you work hard, you will most likely prosper; but if you are lazy, you will most likely not prosper. This lesson was true especially in ancient Israel, where most people were involved in farming. To succeed in farming required a tremendous amount of hard work, and laziness was a disaster. The same is good advice for any person today in his or her job: Don't be lazy! Be a hard worker! However, in today's economy there is hardly a direct correlation between how hard one works and how much money one makes. Farmers, factory workers, construction workers, and loggers work every bit as hard as lawyers, doctors, and stockbrokers, but their blue-collar income is but a fraction of that enjoyed by white-collar workers. In our current world of e-commerce and stock trading, millionaires can be made overnight, and while hard work often plays a role, it is not always the major ingredient. We have to be careful not to interpret Proverbs 10:4 as a universal promise that applies to every work situation at all times.

Proverbs gives guidance for life, addressing situations that are *normally* true.

Likewise, think about the wisdom in Proverbs 3:9–10:

> 9Honor the LORD with your wealth,
>   with the firstfruits of all your crops;
> 10then your barns will be filled to overflowing,
>   and your vats will brim over with new wine.

This proverb tells people (farmers) that if they honor God and tithe out of their produce, they will prosper and always have a good harvest. Certainly, this proverb reflects good, practical wisdom. It teaches us that tithing should be part of a lifestyle based on wisdom. However, is this a promise? Is it a universal, automatic cause and effect? Danny was working in Ethiopia as a missionary in the mid-1980s when a terrible drought and famine hit that country. In the region of Wolayta there were over nine hundred churches with thousands of strong, faithful believers who had honored God with their harvest each year. Yet for several years there was not enough rain to grow crops, and these Christians were hit with a devastating famine instead of "barns filled to overflowing." They found the wisdom in Job to be more directly applicable to them than verses such as this from Proverbs.

Step 1: Grasp the text in their town. What did the text mean to the biblical audience?

Thus, as we move into step 1, it is important to remember that these proverbs are never universal promises. They were (and are today) guidelines and sound advice for character formation and decision-making. The book of Proverbs deals with the norms of life, not the exceptions.

As part of step 1, we need to explore the literary context. First, as mentioned above, note the overall connection of Proverbs with the rest of wisdom literature and keep in mind that occasionally there are exceptions to many of the individual proverbs.

Next, it is helpful to note the structure of the book itself. Proverbs 1–9 introduces the book with fatherly exhortations to youth. It is perhaps significant to note that younger people are the primary audience of this introductory section of Proverbs. Indeed, Daniel Estes suggests that the primary role of the entire book of Proverbs may have been to educate youth.[6]

Daniel Estes suggests that the primary role of the entire book of Proverbs may have been to educate youth.

This orientation will affect how we view other proverbs outside this section as well. For example, Proverbs 25:24 states:

> Better to live on a corner of the roof
> than share a house with a quarrelsome wife.[7]

The lesson of this proverb is *not* directed to men who have quarrelsome wives, supposedly telling them that living on the roof would be better than living in the house with a grouchy wife. Rather, the proverb is directed at young men who have not married yet, and it gives wisdom about what kind of woman to avoid in marriage.[8]

Proverbs 1–9 consists of longer poetic units than just the two-line parallelism of ordinary proverbs. So while this section is part of the book of Proverbs, it does not really contain any of the small, individual two-line units we call *proverbs*. Rather, it contains reflections on life, usually followed by examples and admonitions. For example, all of Proverbs 5 must be taken together, for it comprises a complete unit—one that warns its readers of the dangerous consequences of sexual immorality. Thus, while reading in this section, you must note the larger literary unit (usually about a chapter long) as part of our context.

---

6. Daniel J. Estes, *Hear, My Son: Teaching and Learning in Proverbs 1–9*, New Studies in Biblical Theology (Grand Rapids: Eerdmans, 1997), 18.

7. Proverbs 21:19 states the same proverb in a stronger fashion: "Better to live in a *desert* than with a quarrelsome and nagging wife."

8. Fee and Stuart, *How to Read the Bible*, 248.

Proverbs 10–29 contains the literary form that we traditionally call *proverb*—usually two short lines of poetry expressing one general truth of wisdom. Note that most of these proverbs are somewhat random in their placement. There is no apparent order throughout most of this section. Therefore, the larger unit (chapter, paragraph, etc.) does not play a role in literary context for this section. These proverbs each stand by themselves against the context of the entire book and the rest of the wisdom books; they do not relate to the verses immediately preceding and following. Because the literary context is so limited in these verses, the historical-cultural context takes on an important role.

Note the balance in Proverbs regarding men and women. The book begins with a father speaking primarily to young men (chs. 1–9) and closes with words from a mother (31:1–9), followed by the model of a noble wife (31:10–31).

The next section, Proverbs 30:1–31:9 (the sayings of Agur and King Lemuel's mother), has slightly longer units of text, stretching to several verses. It is followed by the unique closing to the book, Proverbs 31:10–31. This final section is an acrostic, with each verse beginning with the next successive letter of the Hebrew alphabet (remember our discussion of acrostics in chapter 20). These verses, describing the wife of true, wise character, must also be taken as a unit.

Step 2: Measure the width of the river to cross. What are the differences between the biblical audience and us?

We move now to step 2 of the Interpretive Journey. As mentioned above, each proverb usually presents a generalized principle to start with. It addresses practical aspects of everyday life. Therefore, the river before us in Proverbs is usually quite narrow and shallow. We have to note the agrarian context of those proverbs that deal with work and occasional references to the king, but most proverbs speak to situations that have not changed much throughout human history.

Step 3: Cross the principlizing bridge. What is the theological principle in this text?

Because the river is narrow, moving to step 3 is not difficult. Usually the proverb is already worded as a fairly general principle. However, remember our warnings about misinterpreting the proverbs as constant, universal promises. We must keep the exceptions from the other wisdom books in mind, and we must remind ourselves that the principles from Proverbs are guidelines to develop character and to help with life's choices. The principles are normally true but not universally so.

Step 4: Consult the biblical map. How does our theological principle fit with the rest of the Bible? Does the New Testament teaching modify or qualify this principle, and if so, how?

Many of the themes in Proverbs are likewise reflected in the New Testament (humility, concern for the poor, warnings about gossip and foolish speech, truth, hard work, selflessness and concern for others, living righteously rather than wickedly, etc.), and the principles from the verses in Proverbs relating to these themes generally translate over through the New Testament teaching without change.

Note, however, that the theme of wealth as a blessing from God does undergo some changes in the New Testament. Proverbs exhorts the wealthy to support the poor, and the New Testament echoes this same attitude. However, the Old Testament in general, and Proverbs in particular, presents material wealth as a blessing from God and a reward for righteous living. It is a blessing that happens now in this world. In the New Testament, however, the wealth blessing becomes an eschatological blessing, one that is enjoyed in the world to come. "Store up for yourselves treasures in heaven," Jesus exhorts in Matthew 6:20.

In the New Testament, the wealth blessing becomes an eschatological blessing, one that is enjoyed in the world to come.

Blomberg notes that "the [Old Testament] covenant model that assumes material reward for piety never reappears in Jesus' teaching and is explicitly contradicted throughout."[9] Likewise, Paul in his letters promises a multitude of blessings for those who faithfully serve the Lord, but nowhere does he promise material wealth as a blessing. In fact, the New Testament warns us that following Jesus may very well result in a *loss* of material wealth. So we cannot take the notion from Proverbs that faithfulness to God will result in material wealth and apply this directly to New Testament believers as some type of "health and wealth" theology.

Step 5: Grasp the text in our town. How should individual Christians live out this modified theological principle?

Remember that one of the goals of wisdom is to develop character. So while we are concerned with *doing* what the book of Proverbs advises, we want to be sure we catch the larger picture of *being* what the text tells us to be. As our character changes, so will our behavior.

For example, numerous individual proverbs tell us to speak gently, using our

9. Craig L. Blomberg, *Neither Poverty nor Riches: A Biblical Theology of Material Possessions*, New Studies in Biblical Theology (Grand Rapids: Eerdmans, 1999), 145.

speech as a means of healing relationships and not as a means of hurting people (Prov. 12:18, 25; 15:4). Proverbs 15:1, for example, reads:

> A gentle answer turns away wrath,
> but a harsh word stirs up anger.

The river is narrow here, and the principle for us is the same as it was for the ancient readers. We should speak gently and not harshly, especially in heated situations. The New Testament reconfirms the importance of gentleness and of controlling our speech (Eph. 4:2; James 1:19–26). For application, each of us should examine our own speech habits and our reaction to heated situations. Is gentleness of speech a characteristic of your life? What would your friends say? Your parents? Your husband/wife or children? Grasping the text means that we must make a conscious effort to change our character for the better in this regard.

Job

The story of Job is one of the better known stories in the Bible. People throughout the centuries have been able to relate to this book because it deals honestly with tragic suffering. Practically everyone in the world, including God's children, is touched at some point in life by inexplicable tragedy. Indeed, during the time that we worked on this book the students and faculty of the university where we teach have been shaken by two terrible, fatal boating accidents and one tragic airline crash. We have buried several wonderful, dynamic young Christians who loved the Lord dearly and served him wholeheartedly. The haunting question that continues to lurk in the minds of those of us who have been slapped in the face by such a harsh reality is, "How do we make sense out of what has happened?" It is for these situations that Job was written.

Practically everyone in the world, including God's children, is touched at some point in life by inexplicable tragedy.

As mentioned above, the book of Job is a strong counterbalance to the book of Proverbs. In Proverbs the world is rational and ordered. If we serve God faithfully, work hard, and treat others correctly, we will have a blessed and prosperous life. Job's experience, however, contrasts sharply with Proverbs. He does all the good things that Proverbs commands, but instead of receiving blessing, he enters a nightmarish world of dead children, economic ruin, endless physical suffering, and harsh criticism from close friends. Most of the time we live in the world that Proverbs describes; inevitably we also spend some of our lives hurting and questioning in the world of Job.

Although the story of Job is well-known, actually grasping the book is not all that easy. The principles to be learned from this book do not lie out on the surface as in Proverbs. Job is much subtler. Keep in mind also that the book is forty-two chapters long, so there is a lot of material to deal with.

Of utmost importance for our interpretation and application is the literary context. The book of Proverbs is comprised largely of short, unrelated proverbial statements. The book of Job, by contrast, is a story. The book has movement, time sequence, and plot. As we seek to understand various passages in it, it is critical to place those smaller passages into the context of the complete story. Major misinterpretations will emerge if we pull verses from Job out of context and try to interpret them as we do the independent verses in Proverbs. While the book is fairly long, the story is not overly complicated and can be outlined as follows:

1:1–2:10: Job is afflicted. The first two chapters are in prose (narrative). Because of a challenge from Satan (and unknown to Job), God allows Satan to remove all of the earthly blessings in Job's life. Job loses his children and his material wealth. Furthermore, Job is stricken with painful sores. Job's wife criticizes him, but he maintains a stoic faith, stating, "Shall we accept good from God, and not trouble?" (2:10).

2:11–37:24: Job and his friends search unsuccessfully for a rational answer. These chapters make up the bulk of the book, but they are the least well-known. Note also that the author switches to poetry for this unit instead of narrative. In this section Job and his friends grope for an explanation of his terrible tragedy. Working off of the theology reflected in Proverbs, they try to explain Job's situation. In 2:11–31:40 Job interacts with three friends, all of whom are "wise" individuals, seeking to apply wisdom to life's events. They observe that Job's afflictions seem divine in origin. Since God is moral and just, it is obvious that Job is being punished by God for some great sin. They accuse Job of this and tell him to repent.

Job challenges the way God runs the universe.

Job, however, knows he has not committed any great sin. He is puzzled by God's actions and irritated by his friends' accusations. Job turns bitter and accuses God of injustice in the way he runs the universe. He demands his day in court, wanting to stand before God and present the case for his innocence. In 32:1–37:24 another, younger acquaintance (Elihu) spouts off his wisdom as well, indignant that Job would question God's justice. Elihu argues that God "repays everyone for what they have done; he brings on them what their conduct deserves" (34:11).

38:1–42:6: God answers Job's accusations. In the previous chapters Job demanded an audience with God to question him about what has happened and how he runs the universe. In this section God appears and Job gets his audience before the divine Judge, but he soon discovers that God is the one who asks all the questions. "Just what do you know about running the universe, Job?" God asks with a tinge of sarcasm. God does not answer Job's earlier accusations but rather stresses his limitless divine knowledge and power in contrast to Job's narrow, human limitations. Job realizes his bigmouthed mistake and repents. This section is also poetic.

42:7–17: Job's friends are rebuked and Job is restored. The literary style returns to narrative, thus balancing with the opening section. God rebukes Job's three critical friends and Job is vindicated before them. Note, however, that God ignores the young Elihu (32:1–37:24) altogether, dismissing him without comment. Job is then restored, but God never explains to him the background reason for the entire ordeal.

Now that we have introduced the book and presented an overview of the literary context, let's look at Job in light of the Interpretive Journey.

Step 1: Grasp the text in their town. What did the text mean to the biblical audience?

Be sure to place the passage you are studying into the proper literary context, noting the role that your particular passage plays within the overall story. It is critical to remember that the central lessons of the book are not evident until the last two sections (38:1–42:17), where God himself pronounces the lessons of the book. Those lessons are in stark contrast to the ramblings of Job and his friends in the middle of the book. Most passages from the middle of the book reflect the misguided search of Job and his friends. Don't interpret this misguided search as guidelines for us! Also keep in mind that the prevailing theology of the time appears similar to that of Proverbs, so this book would have been quite shocking to the initial audience. Nonetheless, numerous lessons emerge from the story.

First of all, there are several lessons to be learned from the misguided friends of Job. They try to explain the tragedy through the misapplication of traditional wisdom. Thus, they make two central assumptions: (1) Through wisdom they have access to all the information they need to analyze the problem; and (2) through wisdom, and based on this information, they can correctly understand the problem. *Both assumptions are wrong!* Thus, the limitations of wisdom are underscored. Working off of wrong assumptions, the friends make numerous mistakes. Kidner writes, "They overestimate their grasp of truth, misapply the truth they know, and close their minds to any facts that contradict what they assume."[10]

After some initial sympathy, Job's friends place themselves above Job and his sufferings. They do not seek to comfort; rather, they seek to explain. Comforting and explaining are quite different. The basic theology of the friends is not bad, but their application of it is incorrect. As Kidner notes, the rebuke of the friends by God

10. Kidner, *Wisdom of Proverbs, Job and Ecclesiastes*, 61.

does not dismiss the basic theology of Proverbs as much as it "attacks the arrogance of pontificating about the *application* of these truths, and of thereby misrepresenting God and misjudging one's fellow men."[11] The friends are thus negative characters and not models of behavior for the audience. Much of what they say is true, but they say it at the wrong time and apply it to the wrong situation.

> "[Job's friends] overestimate their grasp of truth, misapply the truth they know, and close their minds to any facts that contradict what they assume."
>
> —*Derek Kidner*

Note also that God chides Job quite gently in Job 38–41. Then in Job 42:7 God tells the three friends that they "have not spoken the truth about me, *as my servant Job has*." God does not seem to be overly upset with Job's wondering, questioning, and challenging. He does, however, seem aggravated at the three friends for misreading Job's suffering as a punishment for sin and for trying to explain rather than comfort.

Step 2: Measure the width of the river to cross. What are the differences between the biblical audience and us?

In this step, we realize that the differences between the ancient audience and us are not great. True, we are under different covenants, but the covenants play a negligible role in Job. We still have the same desire to want a simple and rational explanation for all the terrible things that happen, and we tend to misapply the theology of Proverbs in much the same way as Job's friends did. We cannot assume that all our tragedy is due to satanic involvement, and thus we differ from Job. However, Job did not know the origin of his troubles either, and in our shared ignorance of cosmic cause and effect we are similar to Job.

Step 3: Cross the principlizing bridge. What is the theological principle in this text?

Because the river is narrow and shallow, we can easily cross over it with much the same principles as those listed above in step 1. The principles are as follows:

1. God is sovereign, and we are not.
2. God knows all, and we know little.
3. God is always just, but he does not disclose his explanations to us.
4. God expects us to trust in his character and his sovereignty when unexplained tragedy strikes.

---

11. Kidner, 61.

Step 4: Consult the biblical map. How does our theological principle fit with the rest of the Bible? Does the New Testament teaching modify or qualify this principle, and if so, how?

As mentioned above in the discussion of Proverbs, the New Testament does not repeat the Old Testament picture of peace and prosperity as a result of righteous living. Indeed, the New Testament predicts in numerous places that those who live in obedience to Christ will suffer persecution. Jesus warns his disciples, "You will be hated by everyone. . . . When you are persecuted in one place, flee to another. . . . Do not be afraid of those who kill the body but cannot kill the soul" (Matt. 10:22, 23, 28).

Likewise, consider the "reward" Paul received in this world for his faithful service: "Five times I received from the Jews the forty lashes minus one. Three times I was beaten with rods, once I was pelted with stones, three times I was shipwrecked" (2 Cor. 11:24–25). Paul also spent several years in prison, and tradition tells us he ultimately was executed by the Romans. So, unlike the Old Testament, the New Testament presents suffering as a *normal* feature of the godly life, not as an aberration. James cites Job himself (along with the prophets) as an example of patient suffering (James 5:11).

Furthermore, the New Testament suggests that the righteous believer glorifies God by enduring unjust hardship. Paul reminds us that we conquer suffering and hardship through our experience of the love of Christ (Rom. 8:35–39).

However, we want to be careful that we do not repeat the mistake of Job's friends and misuse biblical truth, perhaps adding to a friend's grief instead of comforting them. Recall Romans 8:28, "And we know that in all things God works for the good of those who love him, who have been called according to his purpose." It would be terribly insensitive for us to tell a couple who has just lost their four-year-old child to a drunk driver that all things work together for good and then piously to cite this verse. It is true that much of Romans 8:28 resonates with the theology of Job (the universe is bigger than our private ash heap, with purposes that we cannot imagine). Eventually people who are struck with senseless tragedy may come to grasp this aspect of God's sovereignty. But hitting people with this in the midst of their grief as if this solution should somehow answer their questions and ease their pain reflects the same self-righteous, heartless pontificating of Job's friends. Comforting is different from explaining. When your friends suffer inexplicable tragedy, your role is to suffer and weep with them.

The New Testament presents suffering as a *normal* feature of the godly life, not as an aberration.

Step 5: Grasp the text in our town. How should individual Christians today live out this theological principle?

When the slats are kicked out from under our lives and senseless, heartrending tragedy crashes into our private world, the book of Job provides us with a place of refuge and a word of comfort. It tells us that it is not wrong to cry out in anger and frustration to God (Psalms told us this as well, remember?). It tells us that there probably is no answer in the human realm to the "Why?" question. Our focus in our grief should not be on the "why" but rather on God and his character. Acknowledging that we do not understand tragedy, we should strive to trust in God's ability to run the universe, reaffirming that in the world to come such suffering will not occur.

As mentioned above, another area of application is that of comforting others who are grieving because of tragedy. We should hurt and suffer with them. We should acknowledge along with Job that our understanding of the universe is limited. Thus, we should avoid the glib explanations that seek to rationalize and justify a tragedy. Our role as friends is not to explain or try to make sense of tragic events. Our role is to share in the grief and to remind our friends by our actions that we, along with their Savior, love them deeply and feel their pain.

Ecclesiastes

"Of all the books of the Bible," William Brown writes insightfully, "Ecclesiastes is perhaps the least straightforward (although Job may come a close second)."[12] Ecclesiastes is similar to Job in that the literary context of the entire book must be considered in analyzing any of its smaller parts. Ecclesiastes must be interpreted as a whole. The book is not a collection of guidelines for living, as Proverbs is. Rather, the book is an intellectual search for meaning in life. Most of the search is futile; the true meaning is not discovered until the end of the book. Therefore, the interpretation of any of the intermediate parts of the book must be understood in light of the entire search and the ultimate answer found at the end.

Ecclesiastes must be interpreted as a whole.

The autobiographical character in Ecclesiastes who embarks on this search is called "the Teacher" (NIV) or "the Preacher" (NASB).[13] Using the tools of wisdom

12. William P. Brown, *Ecclesiastes*, Interpretation (Louisville: Westminster John Knox, 2000), 17.

13. The Hebrew word behind "Teacher" or "Preacher" is *qōhelet*, literally meaning "the one who assembles." The name probably referred to the speaker in an assembly. It may have been the author's nickname. When this book was translated into Greek (the Septuagint), the translators used the Greek word *ecclēsiastēs*, referring to "one who speaks in the assembly [*ecclēsia*]." The title given the book in our English Bibles comes from this Greek translation.

(serious, rational, logical reflection), he attempts to analyze life itself and grasp the meaning of his existence. The book presents observations on life, followed by comments and conclusions. Ecclesiastes is filled with satire and sarcasm. Up until the end the tone is cynical in nature, even bordering on bitter.

One of the key words in this book is the word "meaningless" (NIV). Behind this English translation is the Hebrew word *hebel*—a word that occurs thirty-eight times (five times in the Hebrew of 1:2 alone!). The word is normally used to describe breath, mist, or vapor—things that look as if they have substance but in reality do not. Ecclesiastes 1:2 sets the cynical tone of the book. The Teacher discovers that if one attempts to understand life from a strictly rational approach, the meaning of life becomes like the mist, an illusion of a reality that does not exist.

After the brief opening summary of futility, the Teacher begins his quest for meaning. Wright summarizes the first six chapters by writing:

> Can purpose of life be found in nature, money, self-indulgence, property, position, intelligence, philosophy, and religious observances? Obviously, some of these pursuits are better than others, but all encounter some crowning frustration that invalidates them as solutions to the problem of living. The world does not contain the key to itself.[14]

The Teacher then explores the nature and limitations of wisdom itself (chs. 7–11). He concludes in 8:17, "No one can comprehend what goes on under the sun. Despite all their efforts to search it out, no one can discover its meaning. Even if the wise claim they know, they cannot really comprehend it." Yet the Teacher suggests that life should be enjoyed, even if it cannot be understood. The Teacher next bemoans the fact that the common fate of death overtakes all, both the righteous and the wicked. He does not dismiss wisdom as worthless; it is still better to be wise than to be foolish. But wisdom is limited and futile as a means for ultimate understanding. Finally, in chapter 12 the Teacher comes to his conclusion: "Fear God and keep his commandments" (v. 13), implying that obedience to God is better than continuously striving after understanding.

The Teacher discovers that if one attempts to understand life from a strictly rational approach, the meaning of life becomes like the mist, an illusion of a reality that does not exist.

14. J. Stafford Wright, "Ecclesiastes," in *Expositor's Bible Commentary*, ed. Frank E. Gaebelein (Grand Rapids: Zondervan, 1991), 5:1145.

Step 1: Grasp the text in their town. What did the text mean to the biblical audience?

What did this strange book mean to the original audience? Three main conclusions emerge from the Teacher's search:

1. Apart from God, life is meaningless. Wisdom is not bad, but it does not provide meaning in life.
2. Wisdom does not explain the contradictions of life; it only points them out. Therefore, people should simply trust God (the same meaning as Job).
3. Life, therefore, is not a puzzle to be completely understood, but a gift to be enjoyed (similar to Song of Songs).

Most of the proverbs the Teacher quotes, the reflections he shares, the observations he makes, and the experiences he discusses point to one of these three conclusions.

Step 2: Measure the width of the river to cross. What are the differences between the biblical audience and us?

The tendency to search for meaning through sheer intellectual avenues is also common in our day and time, so the river is not wide on this issue. The human need to find meaning in life and our futile attempt to find meaning through wealth, entertainment, work, philosophy, and so on, is also fairly universal, so the river is shallow at that point as well.

The Teacher seems to have a limited understanding of death, with almost no concept of an afterlife. We Christians, by contrast, live with a confident assurance of resurrection.

One significant difference does exist, however. The Teacher seems to have a limited understanding of death, with almost no concept of an afterlife. We Christians, by contrast, live with a confident assurance of resurrection. Likewise, the Teacher is concerned with meaning in relation to this life only. As New Testament believers, we know that meaning for people is tied to the kingdom of Christ and that a significant dimension of this is spiritual, not physical. Also, keep in mind that we are under a different covenant. The conclusion of the Teacher to "fear God and keep his commandments" will have slightly different nuances to us who know Jesus Christ and are therefore under the new covenant.

Step 3: Cross the principlizing bridge. What is the theological principle in this text?

Because the river is narrow, most theological principles that can be developed from various texts in Ecclesiastes will be similar to those listed in step 1.

Step 4: Consult the biblical map. How does our theological principle fit with the rest of the Bible? Does the New Testament teaching modify or qualify this principle, and if so, how?

The New Testament stresses that relationship with God under the new covenant must center on the life, death, and resurrection of his Son, Jesus Christ. Thus, all life outside of Jesus Christ is futile and meaningless. Therefore, the first conclusion from step 1 above should be modified to read, "Apart from a relationship with Jesus Christ, life is meaningless. Rational, logical thought is not bad, but it does not provide meaning in life."

Likewise, as discussed in step 2, in contrast to the cloudy understanding of the Teacher reflected in his search, the New Testament presents a clear picture of a glorious, victorious afterlife, when all wrongs will be corrected and all suffering will pass away. Therefore, it is imperative that we see the cynicism and bitterness of the Teacher as a result of the fruitless part of his search and not as part of the final principles we come away with. There is nothing bitter or cynical about the gospel!

As you may have noticed, the book of James addresses many of the issues brought out in the Old Testament wisdom literature. Without doubt, James draws much of his thought from the Old Testament wisdom books, including Ecclesiastes. James sounds much like the Teacher of Ecclesiastes as he blasts those misguided people who acquire wealth as a means of guaranteeing the future (James 5:1–6).

Step 5: Grasp the text in our town. How should individual Christians live out this modified principle?

As we have mentioned frequently, application will vary somewhat with the situation of each believer who seeks to apply the passage. However, most of us need to be constantly reminded that "apart from a relationship with Jesus Christ, life is meaningless." The world around us (movies, TV, literature) offers us the illusion (***hebel***) that meaning can be found in education, work, wealth, or pleasure. The Teacher points out, however, that a close, rational scrutiny of the situation reveals that such a search is meaningless, a chasing after the wind. Only a relationship with our Creator gives us meaning. We as believers would do well to focus our lives on this aspect of life in our quest for meaning.

Song of Songs

The Song of Songs[15] is perhaps one of the most shocking books in the Bible because it speaks openly and joyfully of human sexuality. It could be called an R-rated

15. This book is also called Song of Solomon (KJV) or Canticles (the Latin Vulgate).

book because of sexually explicit passages. It is in essence a collection of love poems between a young man and a young woman (called the Shulamite).

Unlike Proverbs, the Song of Songs is organized into three logical, sequential units: the Courtship (1:2–3:5), the Wedding (3:6–5:1), and the following Life of Love (5:2–8:14).[16] In some sections the man and woman are describing their love for each other; in other sections they are describing how beautiful or handsome their mate is. The woman, who does most of the talking, also describes the dreams she has of her husband while he is away and shares how much she misses him. The book is highly emotional and is full of figurative imagery as the man and woman use a wide range of colorful analogies to describe their wonderful mates and the wild and crazy love they have for each other.

The Song of Songs is perhaps one of the most shocking books in the Bible because it speaks openly and joyfully of human sexuality.

The church has struggled through the years with how to interpret and apply such an unusual book. Starting from the third century AD and continuing on throughout much of church history, the prevailing approach to Song of Songs has been to explain it as an allegory. (Do you remember? We discussed allegory back in chapter 11, "Levels of Meaning.") Keep in mind that after the apostolic period and prior to the Reformation (sixteenth century), most biblical interpretation was done by unmarried priests and monks. We suspect they had difficulty in relating to the literal aspects of this book. Also, the early church frequently used the allegorical method to interpret other Old Testament texts. Because they desired to find Christ in every text, they abandoned literal meanings and literary context and spiritualized practically all Old Testament passages.

As a result, the man and woman in Song of Songs became symbolic of Christ and the church (cf. Eph. 5:23–33), and the book was transformed from a wisdom book about love and marriage into a theological tract on the love of Christ for his bride, the church. This certainly made the book easier to preach on Sunday mornings. Echoes of such allegorical interpretation are still around,[17] especially in our songs. Indeed, many Christians today sing the familiar lines "He leads me up to his banqueting table; his banner over me is love" (cf. Song 2:4), and they interpret "he/his" allegorically as Christ, an understanding that differs significantly from the context of Song of Songs 2.

However, the allegorical method of interpreting Song of Songs breaks down when we read the text closely and pay attention to context. Scholars today are virtually

16. The major features of this outline are taken from Dennis F. Kinlaw, "Song of Songs," in *Expositor's Bible Commentary*, ed. Frank E. Gaebelein (Grand Rapids: Zondervan, 1991), 5:1214.

17. Many commentaries and study Bibles prior to 1950 followed the allegorical method of interpreting Song of Songs.

unanimous in rejecting the allegorical interpretation. Christians today also recognize that sexuality in marriage is a big part of life, and if the wisdom literature is to address the major issues of life, we should not be shocked to see a frank discussion of the joys associated with marital intimacy. Undoubtedly sexuality in marriage was also an issue when the book was composed.

Step 1: Grasp the text in their town. What did the text mean to the biblical audience?

Thus, as we approach step 1, we are reminded of Roland Murphy's conclusion that "ancient Israel perceived the wonders of human sexuality, fulfilled in marital love, to be a divine blessing."[18] Kinlaw concurs:

> The Bible does not see marriage as an inferior state, a concession to human weakness. Nor does it see the normal physical love within that relationship as necessarily impure. Marriage was instituted before the Fall by God with the command that the first couple become one flesh. Therefore physical love within that conjugal union is good, is God's will, and should be a delight to both partners.
>
> The prospect of children is not necessary to justify sexual love in marriage. Significantly, the Song of Solomon makes no reference to procreation. It must be remembered that the book was written in a world where a high premium was placed on offspring and a woman's worth was often measured in terms of the number of her children. Sex was often seen with reference to procreation; yet there is not a trace of that here. The Song is a song in praise of love for love's sake and for love's sake alone. This relationship needs no justification beyond itself.[19]

We do not know for certain the settings in which the book was used by ancient Israel, but we suspect it was read (or sung) at weddings. Just as the psalmist praised God for the wonders of nature, so the Song of Songs praises God for the wonders of marital intimacy.

Of course, it is also important to note that the lyrics of the Song of Songs are addressed to the man or the woman in the story and not to God. If we assume this to be part of wisdom and part of the teachings about character and living rightly, we conclude that the book also provided a model for

The Song of Songs also provided a model for how a husband and his wife were to feel toward one another and how they were to express their feelings.

18. Roland E. Murphy, *A Commentary on the Book of Canticles or Song of Songs*, Hermeneia (Minneapolis: Fortress, 1990), 99.

19. Kinlaw, "Song of Songs," 5:1207.

how a husband and his wife were to feel toward one another and how they were to express their feelings. As mentioned above, the wisdom of Proverbs presented a model to ancient Israel of a quiet, thoughtful, somewhat reserved wise person who acted dignified in the public world. This image changes in the Song of Songs. The wise, righteous person is now seen as madly in love with his or her spouse, spouting out line after line of mushy compliments and praises about the lover's sexuality.

Step 2: Measure the width of the river to cross. What are the differences between the biblical audience and us?

Although the authorship of the book is attributed to Solomon, the book itself does not seem to describe any specific historical relationship in his life. We suspect it was written as a description of an idealized relationship, one to which any young couple in Israel could relate. With the exception of the mention of Solomon's wedding carriage in 3:7–10, there is little in the book reflecting the unique status of Solomon that would create a wide area of the interpretive river for us to cross. The joy and irrationality of a couple madly in love has not really changed much.

We do, however, encounter trouble in appreciating the imagery that is used. We suspect that our wives would not be too flattered if we told them their hair looked like a flock of goats descending from Mount Gilead (4:1) or their noses resembled the tower of Lebanon looking toward Damascus (7:4)! Compliments to the opposite sex are extremely culture specific. We may smile at the idioms and figures of speech used in Song of Songs, but keep in mind that the ancient readers would likewise laugh at translations of our compliments "She's a babe!" or "He's a hunk!" So the figurative language does create a wide spot in the river of differences to cross. We would not suggest transposing the compliments from Song of Songs literally into the intimate moments of your marriage. A little modern updating of the language is needed!

We suspect that our wives would not be too flattered if we told them their hair looked like a flock of goats descending from Mount Gilead (4:1) or their noses resembled the tower of Lebanon looking toward Damascus (7:4)!

Also, most readers will be struck by how corny or mushy the sentimental language in this book can be. However, we are not convinced that this is a big difference if the passages are placed in the right context. A Christian couple today, if they are as madly and crazily in love as the one in the Song, will also say some overly sweet and dopey things to each other when they are alone. Most loving couples we know would die of embarrassment if their private words to each other were published for the entire church to read. The private, mushy, sentimental stuff one whispers to his or her spouse in the dark is inherently corny to all outsiders yet delightful and wonderful to the spouse. The dignified, wise person modeled for us in Proverbs does not say intimate, mushy things about his or her spouse in public. However, Song of Songs tells us that that wise person had better shift gears when he or she gets home, set the straitlaced wisdom of Proverbs[20] aside, and become a sappy romantic.

Step 3: Crossing the principlizing bridge. What is the theological principle in this text?

As mentioned above, any theological principles must be built on similarities between their situation (that of the biblical audience) and ours. One of the main theological principles that emerges from many passages in Song of Songs is that the person seeking to live a wise, godly life should be madly in love with her husband or his wife and should express this love in strong, emotional (sappy and mushy?) terms.

Step 4: Consult the biblical map. How does our theological principle fit with the rest of the Bible? Does the New Testament teaching modify or qualify this principle, and if so, how?

The New Testament does not really modify the principle from step 3. In Ephesians 5:21–33 Paul's advice to husbands and wives (love, submission) corresponds well with the main principle in step 3.

Step 5: Grasp the text in our town. How should individual Christians live out this modified principle?

As mentioned earlier in the book, applications will vary with the situation of various believers. However, note that the celebration of sexuality in Song of Songs is apparently directed to married couples or those approaching marriage. It is especially appropriate for those who are newly married. We suggest that newly married couples read Song of Songs to each other on their honeymoon. Yes, it's corny, but also fun and appropriate.

We do not think that this book has much application for those who are not married. However, married couples can apply it by verbally expressing their love to their spouses with lots of romantic, sentimental compliments, dopey as they may be to outsiders. We *grasp the text* as this wisdom book shapes our character, that is, as we become a little bit wild and crazy in our love affair with our marriage partner. We balance our way of life with both Proverbs and Song of Songs. In public we follow the pattern of the quiet, thoughtful, frugal, hardworking, wise person. But when alone

20. Proverbs hints at the joys of Song of Songs in Proverbs 5:15–19, but only in the context of warning against adultery.

with our wives/husbands, we follow the wild and crazy pattern of the two lovers in Song of Songs. This, too, is wisdom.

CONCLUSION

One thing we hope you have observed is that the wisdom books are extremely applicable to Christians today. Many of the principles flowing out of these books deal with everyday issues that believers today struggle with. Don't ignore these books! The wisdom books are rich and deep with practical help for us in our day-to-day life. They will help us to be wise and to develop godly character—a character that is able to make right decisions in life.

ASSIGNMENTS

Assignment 22–1

Take the Interpretive Journey with each of the proverbs listed below. That is, take the first proverb and write a short paragraph for each of the five steps regarding that proverb. Then turn to the next proverb and complete the five steps for it, followed by the same procedure for the last proverb. Try to make the application in step 5 a real application for your life.

Hatred stirs up conflict,
    but love covers over all wrongs. (Prov. 10:12)

The LORD detests dishonest scales,
    but accurate weights find favor with him. (Prov. 11:1)

One who has unreliable friends soon comes to ruin,
    but there is a friend who sticks closer than a brother. (Prov. 18:24)

Assignment 22–2

Take the Interpretive Journey with the passage below from Job 38:18–21. That is, write a short paragraph for each of the five steps of the journey. Be sure that you include a discussion of literary context as part of step 1—that is, identify where in the overall story of Job this passage occurs. Identify who is speaking to whom in this text and what is occurring in the chapters that surround this text. Then complete the rest of the journey.

18 "Have you comprehended the vast expanses of the earth?
    Tell me, if you know all this.
19 What is the way to the abode of light?
    And where does darkness reside?
20 Can you take them to their places?
    Do you know the paths to their dwellings?
21 Surely you know, for you were already born!
    You have lived so many years!"

APPENDIX 1

INSPIRATION AND CANON

INTRODUCTION

Throughout *Grasping God's Word* we have been operating on the presupposition that the Bible is the inspired Word of God and that the term *Bible* is limited to the sixty-six books of the Protestant canon. In this appendix we will discuss the basis for such a presupposition. This topic is not generally included in textbooks dealing with hermeneutics (how to study and interpret the Bible), but in recent years there has been such a proliferation of popular literature challenging the traditional understanding of the nature and scope of the Bible that we felt it was important to address the issue at least briefly in this book.

INSPIRATION

The reason we study the Bible is that we want to hear God's Word to us. The Bible was written by numerous human authors, but the divine aspect of it is inseparably and mysteriously interwoven into every verse. The term we use to describe this relationship between the divine role and the human role is *inspiration*. Inspiration can be defined as the process by which God directed individuals, incorporating their abilities and styles, to produce his message to humankind.

Paul addresses the concept of inspiration in 2 Timothy 3:16–17:

> All Scripture is *God-breathed* and is useful for teaching, rebuking, correcting and training in righteousness, so that the servant of God may be thoroughly equipped for every good work. (NIV)

> All Scripture is *inspired by God* and profitable for teaching, for reproof, for correction, for training in righteousness; so that the man of God may be adequate, equipped for every good work. (NASB)

The key Greek word Paul uses in verse 16 is *theopneustos.* Traditionally, translators have translated this word as "inspired," as the NASB has rendered it. Literally, this word means "God-breathed," which is the translation the NIV has chosen. This verse tells us much about how the Scriptures came into being. The origin of the action is God, and the method is "God-breathed." The scope of the inspiration extends to *all Scripture.* Paul's use of "all Scripture" certainly includes all of the canonical Old Testament books, and it likewise extends to all verses in those books. In addition, by the time Paul writes 2 Timothy, the church has probably started to use the term "Scripture" to apply as well to those New Testament writings that had been completed and were in circulation.

Note also that it is the *Scriptures* that are described as inspired, not the *writers.* This is an important distinction to make. Sometimes the term inspiration is used to describe something that happened to the author of a text. In this verse Paul is stating that it is the final written product that is God-breathed and thus of infinite value to us as we seek to follow Christ.

Another central verse is 2 Peter 1:20–21:

> Above all, you must understand that no prophecy of Scripture came about by the prophet's own interpretation of things. For prophecy never had its origin in the human will, but prophets, though human, spoke from God as they were carried along by the Holy Spirit.

This verse also stresses the divine origin of the Scriptures. How were the human authors involved? They were "carried along" by the Holy Spirit. The Greek word used here often refers to the moving of a ship's sails by the wind.

Thus, the Bible itself describes the inspiration process as one in which the human authors are "carried along" by the Holy Spirit to produce a document that is "God-breathed." So human authors are involved, the Holy Spirit is involved, and the final product (the Bible) is inspired by God.

The implications of an inspired Bible are enormous. It is doubtful that you would be reading *Grasping God's Word* if you (or least your professor) did not believe in the divine inspiration of the Bible, and certainly we would not have taken the time to write this book if we did not believe it. The point of inspiration is that it gives the biblical text the same authority over us as if the words came from the mouth of God.

It should be our goal in life to try to understand him correctly and to search for his meaning in the text and not our imagined meaning.

THE CHICKEN OR THE EGG?

Some have raised the question of which comes first, faith in Christ or belief in the inspiration of the Bible? Do Christians believe in Jesus because they believe the Bible is inspired, or do they believe the Bible is inspired because they believe in Jesus? On the one hand, we (Scott and Danny) believed in Jesus Christ at an early age, long before we pondered the question of whether the Bible was true or not. Later, as we grew up and began to read the Bible in a more serious manner, it resonated with our faith, reaffirming it and strengthening it. From our faith perspective, the Bible seemed to us to be obviously trustworthy and true, and it still does after all of our years of academic study. So did faith in Christ come first? On the other hand, when we were children, everything that we accepted by faith about Jesus actually came from the Bible, so by believing in him we were believing in the biblical account of him. So did belief in the Bible come first? Is it the chicken or the egg?

In actuality, it seems to us that the two go together and are inseparable. We believe in the divine inspiration and trustworthiness of the Bible because we know Jesus Christ, and we know Jesus Christ through the testimony of the Bible. In this appendix we present a brief defense of why the Scriptures are trustworthy and true. But our belief in the trustworthiness of the Bible can never be reduced to an intellectual argument that rationally proves that the Bible is absolutely true and therefore forces us, if we are rational, to believe in Jesus as the Son of God. It is good to be able to present a clear, logical defense of the inspiration and trustworthiness of the Bible, but our relationship with Jesus Christ does not depend on our ability to create a rational defense for biblical inspiration.

INERRANCY

How accurate is the Bible? How extensive is the truth in the Bible? Is it completely without error? Even within evangelicalism, among people who affirm inspiration, there is some disagreement over some of the issues relating to inerrancy. We find it helpful to examine some New Testament passages in which Jesus uses the Scriptures (i.e., the Old Testament). How does he view the Bible?

In Matthew 5:18 Jesus declares, "For truly I tell you, until heaven and earth disappear, not the smallest letter, not the least stroke of a pen, will by any means disappear from the Law until everything is accomplished." Jesus will fulfill the Law down to the smallest of details—not only to the smallest of letters but even to small strokes of the pen that distinguish one letter from another. Even if Jesus is speaking figuratively, the point of his figure of speech is that he will fulfill the Old Testament down to the smallest of details. This implies that the Scriptures can be trusted down to tiniest details.

Likewise, in Matthew 22:31–32 Jesus says, "But about the resurrection of the dead—have you not read what God said to you, 'I am the God of Abraham, the God of Isaac, and the God of Jacob'? He is not the God of the dead but of the living." In these verses Jesus argues from verb tenses. In refuting those who said there was no resurrection, Jesus points out the present tense statement made by God in the Old Testament, "*I am* the God of . . ."

Finally, note that in Matthew 22:41–46 Jesus argues from the use of the pronoun "my." The text reads,

> [41]While the Pharisees were gathered together, Jesus asked them, [42]"What do you think about the Messiah? Whose son is he?"
>
> "The son of David," they replied.
>
> [43]He said to them, "How is it then that David, speaking by the Spirit, calls him 'Lord'? For he says,
>
> [44]" 'The Lord said to my Lord:
"Sit at my right hand
until I put your enemies
under your feet." '
>
> [45]If then David calls him 'Lord,' how can he be his son?" [46]No one could say a word in reply, and from that day on no one dared to ask him any more questions.

Thus, it appears that Jesus treated the Old Testament as if it were accurate and without error down to the level of verb tenses and pronouns. To us this looks like a good model to follow. However, keep in mind that this level of accuracy only extends to the biblical books as they were written. Mistakes made by people in copying the manuscripts or mistakes made by translators in translating lie outside the parameter of "God-breathed."

Actually, we do not think that the term *inerrancy* is the best one to use in this discussion because not everyone defines "error" in the same manner. If we are to talk about errors or absence of errors, then it is critical to define exactly what an "error" is.

Indeed, often the arguments over inerrancy become somewhat muddled because of the imprecise definition of the term. If Matthew tells a story of Jesus in a different way than Luke does, is this an error? We certainly don't think so (see chapter 15, "New Testament—Gospels"). Sometimes, however, the Bible can be complex and contain what we term "tensions." We would argue that these "tensions" are intentional, placed in the text not by mistake but by design; they hardly count as "errors." Thus, we would prefer to speak of the trustworthiness, reliability, and inspiration of the Bible rather than focus on the somewhat imprecise term *inerrancy*.

However, *inerrancy* has become a common term used by evangelical scholars in the discussion of the accuracy of Scripture. Within this discussion we certainly affirm inerrancy. But we feel it is important to carefully define the term, and we offer the following simple working definition of *inerrancy*: the Bible (in the original autographs) says exactly what God wants it to say and has not been corrupted by human mistakes.

A much more comprehensive definition was developed in 1978 by a large group of evangelical scholars as part of the International Council on Biblical Inerrancy. They wrestled with the complexity of issues regarding the definition and the implications of the term inerrancy, and they incorporated their results into a document titled "The Chicago Statement on Biblical Inerrancy." This document continues to be one of the best discussions and definitions of biblical inerrancy. You can read this document online from one of the many websites that offers it. Simply do a search for "The Chicago Statement on Biblical Inerrancy."

OLD TESTAMENT CANON

Our English word *canon* is a translation of a Greek word that originally referred to a "straight rod" or a "measuring rod." It was literally used to measure "straightness," but the term was used figuratively to denote the rules or norms of the Christian faith. By the fourth century AD, it was used regularly to refer to the collection of books that were considered authoritative or inspired. Today we still use the term *canon* or *canonical* to refer to the collection of books the church accepts as inspired and authoritative.

The thirty-nine books in our Old Testament were fairly well set as the authoritative Scriptures of the Jews prior to the coming of Christ. The order of the books was different, and this is reflected in the title Jews use today for their "Bible." They refer to their Scriptures (our Old Testament) as the *Tanaḳ*. This is an acronym for the threefold division of their Bible: T for Torah, N for Nebi'im (the Prophets), and K for Ketubim (the Writings). The arrangement of the books in the Jewish Tanak differs from that of the Protestant Old Testament, but the actual books are the same.

The early church accepted the books of the Jewish canon. Indeed, the writers of the New Testament clearly treat the books of the Old Testament as authoritative and as God's Word for Christians, as seen in the discussion above regarding 2 Timothy 3:16–17. Marcion, a writer in the second century AD, challenged the canonical status of the Old Testament and tried to convince the church to abandon it. However, the New Testament writers had clearly embraced the Old Testament books, and the gospel tradition handed down to the church from the apostles had clearly affirmed the Old Testament as the Word of God. Thus, Marcion was not able to sway the church away from its belief that the Old Testament books were inspired, authoritative, and canonical.

But what is the *Apocrypha*? Although the Jewish canon was probably fixed by the year 200 BC, other Jewish theological works were written during the time period from 200 BC to AD 100. Many of these "books" were read, circulated, and highly respected in Jewish synagogues, but they were never accepted by the Jews as equal to the authoritative books within the canon.

During this same time period the Jewish Scriptures were translated from Hebrew into Greek (the Septuagint), and this Greek version of the Old Testament became popular with the emerging early Christian church. Several of the noncanonical Jewish theological works were also translated into Greek (some may have been written in Greek to begin with) and were included in the collection of sacred writings known as the Septuagint. While the Jewish rabbis were able to make it clear in their synagogues that these extra books were helpful but not authoritative or canonical—like our modern study notes perhaps—some in the new Christian church began to assume that if these works were included in the biblical volume, then they must be part of inspired Scripture.

Most of the scholars in the early church tried to help the church maintain this important distinction—that these apocryphal books were helpful but not inspired or canonical. In the fourth century, Jerome produced a Latin translation known as the Vulgate. He included the Apocrypha but noted clearly that these books were not to be viewed with the same status as the canonical books. As the years passed, however, Jerome's notes were dropped, and the readers of this Latin Bible started to accept these books as part of the Bible. When Latin became the major theological language of the Western church, the apocryphal books in the Vulgate became accepted as canonical.

An important part of the Protestant Reformation in the 1500s was the translation of the Bible into the common languages of Europe (English, German, French, etc.). Driven by a high regard for the original languages, Hebrew, Aramaic, and Greek, these translators bypassed the Latin Vulgate and returned to the Hebrew, Aramaic, and Greek manuscripts. Observing that the Hebrew Bible did not include the Apocrypha and recalling all the scholarly rejection of the Apocrypha in earlier church history, the Reformers either placed the Apocrypha in the appendix of their new Bibles or dropped it altogether. In response to the action taken by the Protestant Reformers, at the Council of Trent (1545–64) the Roman Catholic Church declared that the Latin Vulgate was the official Bible of the true church and that the Apocrypha within the Vulgate was therefore canonical and equally authoritative.

Since that time Protestant Bibles have usually omitted the apocryphal books while Catholic Bibles have included them. These books include Tobit, Judith, 1 Maccabees, 2 Maccabees, Wisdom of Solomon, Ecclesiasticus (also known as Ben Sirach), Baruch, and several additions to the books of Daniel (e.g., Susanna and Bel and the Dragon) and Esther.

There is really nothing profoundly unusual in these books if they are viewed as Jewish religious writings. The Catholic Church does make appeal to texts in these books for their doctrine of purgatory and the practice of prayer for the dead, but in actuality the texts appear to be vague regarding these doctrines. At the same time, the Apocrypha (along with other Jewish writings of this time period) provides us with a tremendous wealth of information about what Jews understood and believed during the two hundred years prior to Christ and throughout the first century of the church. The two books of Maccabees are our primary historical source for the intertestamental period. Along with other significant Jewish writings of the period (such as *Jubilees*, *Sibylline Oracles*, *Assumption of Moses*, and *1 Enoch*), these books help us understand the Jewish theology with which Jesus and Paul collided. These books are ancient and interesting, and they provide a wealth of historical background material that can help us understand the New Testament better. But they are not inspired and should not be viewed as authoritative or as part of the Christian canon.

NEW TESTAMENT CANON

The early Christians inherited the Old Testament canon from the Jews and embraced the canonical Old Testament books from the beginning. However, the New Testament books were being written, copied, and disseminated at the same time the church was being planted and formed. The books we now know as the New Testament were not produced all at once but were written during the years AD 49–95, at exactly the same time the gospel was spreading rapidly across the Mediterranean world. Indeed, throughout the latter half of the first century the spread of Christianity was probably outrunning the copying and dissemination of the New Testament literature. At the close of the first century, these early churches were reading and collecting the various New Testament books (especially the four Gospels and the letters of Paul), but few churches would have had all of the New Testament books.

By the close of the first century (AD 100) there appears to have been widespread acceptance among the early churches of the four Gospels (Matthew, Mark, Luke, and John), the book of Acts, and the letters of Paul as authoritative "canonical" literature (although they were not using the word *canon* in this sense yet). Because the other books were either written late in the first century (Revelation), were smaller and not circulated as much (2 John, 3 John), or had questions about their authorship (Hebrews), they were accepted in some regions but not in others. That is, in some regions they were acknowledged as authoritative and were read in the churches, while in other areas the church was either unfamiliar with them or had questions about their authority.

Thus, as the second century AD began, the theology of the church (i.e., the "gospel") was defined primarily by the four canonical Gospels and the letters of Paul, for these were the books that had been universally accepted. The churches were still disseminating the other books and evaluating them. As time passed, more and more churches began accepting the other books of the New Testament. The decision (beyond the Gospels and Paul) regarding which books were canonical was a fairly slow process. The criteria used by the churches included authorship (connection to an apostle), widespread acceptance and use, and conformance to the "gospel" tradition as received orally from the first century and as defined in the four written Gospels and the letters of Paul.

In addition, as the second century progressed (and into the third century as well), numerous other works of "Christian" literature appeared and were read in some Christian churches. Among the more popular books were the *Shepherd of Hermas*, the *Apocalypse of Peter*, the *Epistle of Barnabas*, and the *Didache*. Opinions varied on the validity of these books, and the church likewise began discussing and evaluating them.

During the second century and into the third, however, several heretical individuals and groups (Marcionites, Montanists, Gnostics) also began to produce written literature—works that attempted to revise significantly the traditional Christian theology of the first century (defined in the four Gospels and letters of Paul) to accommodate current philosophical trends of the second century. These works (such as the *Gospel of Thomas*, written around AD 150) challenged the theology of early Christianity, and the proponents of these works appeared to be trying to lead the church down a different path from the one proclaimed by Paul in his letters and Jesus in the four Gospels. Church leaders responded strongly to these works, noting the heretical theology they espoused and clearly identifying them as a dangerous challenge to the true gospel.

Thus, although the church took some time in deciding universally whether to accept 2 John and the *Shepherd of Hermas*, it nonetheless responded fairly quickly and strongly to heretical works such as the Gnostic "gospels" like the *Gospel of Thomas*. Likewise, other Gnostic literary works, such as the *Gospel of Truth*, the *Gospel of Philip*, the *Gospel of the Hebrews*, and the *Gospel of Mary Magdalene* (second- to third-century compositions), were never seriously considered as authoritative or canonical by significant numbers of churches. They were simply labeled as heretical and removed from serious consideration by the churches.

From the end of the second century AD and into the third century, we find actual lists of "canonical" books. Writers such as Origen (early third century) had three categories: accepted books, disputed books, and rejected books. According to this church father, accepted by the entire church without controversy were the four Gospels (Matthew, Mark, Luke, and John), Acts, the thirteen letters of Paul, Hebrews, 1 Peter, 1 John, and Revelation. Disputed were 2 and 3 John, 2 Peter, James, and Jude. Rejected firmly were the Gnostic "gospels," including the *Gospel of Thomas*.

Eusebius, a church historian writing in the early fourth century, followed a threefold pattern similar to Origen. His list is similar to Origen's, accepting the four Gospels, the letters of Paul, 1 Peter, 1 John, and Revelation. Disputed are James, Jude, 2 Peter, and 2 and 3 John. Rejected as heretical are the Gnostic "gospels," including the *Gospel of Thomas*.

Finally, in AD 367, Athanasius, bishop of Alexandria, provided a list of canonical books that conformed exactly to the twenty-seven books we have in our New Testaments today. At the end of the fourth century, Jerome produced the Latin Vulgate, with a New Testament that contained the same twenty-seven books. During this same time period, Augustine wrote clearly that these twenty-seven, and only these, were canonical and to be used in the church. Although the canon for the churches in Syria continued to stay open regarding a few books for a few more centuries, for the Western church the issue was settled and the canon was closed by the end of the fourth century.

Keep in mind, however, that the four Gospels and the letters of Paul were never at issue; they were accepted as authoritative and "canonical" soon after they were written and first copied. Indeed, widespread acceptance of these core New Testament books had occurred by the end of the first century. What was debated for the next two hundred to three hundred years were the other New Testament books and other religious documents, such as the *Shepherd of Hermas*. Rejected quickly and firmly by the early churches were the works of heretics, such as the Gnostic gospels (*Gospel of Thomas*, *Gospel of Mary*, etc.).

CURRENT CHALLENGES TO THE CHRISTIAN NEW TESTAMENT CANON

Many of the noncanonical writings discussed above have been in print and available for centuries to scholars (and students) to study. There is nothing mysterious or "hidden" (*apocryphal* means hidden) in them, and they are helpful for understanding early church history. As the church grew and spread, by necessity it was constantly engaging with local non-Christian religious and philosophical ideas. Many of these works reflect this engagement.

The *Gospel of Thomas*, however, while referred to numerous times by early Christian writers as heretical, was available to historians only in fragments until the mid-twentieth century. In 1945, near the Egyptian village of Nag Hammadi, some local Bedouins discovered a buried jar containing old leather-bound papyri books. These books were a collection of Gnostic writings dating to the second half of the fourth century AD. This collection of Gnostic literature has come to be known as the Nag Hammadi texts. Included is a complete copy of the *Gospel of Thomas*.

Over the last few years, a tremendous popular interest in the Nag Hammadi texts and, in particular, the *Gospel of Thomas* has emerged in North America. Indeed, several books based on these and other Gnostic writings have jumped to the top of the *New York Times* bestseller list. In the last twenty years, dozens of books have been written on the Gnostic "gospels." Still popular are the novel *The Da Vinci Code* by Dan Brown, *Lost Christianities* by Bart Ehrman, and *Beyond Belief: The Secret Gospel of Thomas* by Elaine Pagels.

Although these modern books differ in numerous details, one of the themes they all put forward is that the Gnostic "gospels" (especially the *Gospel of Thomas*, but also the *Gospel of Mary Magdalene* and the *Gospel of Philip*) should be viewed as a valid early alternative expression of Christianity. They argue that Christianity was diverse in the second and third centuries and that the Gnostic literature reflects one of the valid branches of Christianity. Often the suggestion is made that the Gnostic writings may be even more authentic than one or more of the four Gospels of the New Testament. These "gospels," they argue, fell from popularity because certain politically powerful Christian leaders and church councils in the fourth century opposed them and had all copies of these "gospels" destroyed.

Elaine Pagels, for example, in her bestseller *Beyond Belief: The Secret Gospel of Thomas*, argues that the *Gospel of Thomas* did indeed go back to the apostle Thomas in the first century and reflects a special collection of authentic sayings of Jesus that he entrusted to Thomas. The canonical Gospel of John, she argues, was written later to refute the more authentic *Gospel of Thomas*. Thus, what Pagels proposes is that

Christians today should adopt the *Gospel of Thomas instead of* the Gospel of John. At issue is the divinity of Jesus Christ. Pagels (and several other pro-Gnosticism advocates) maintains that Jesus is merely human and not divine. Indeed, she argues, this is precisely the Christology that would emerge if people today would substitute the *Gospel of Thomas* for the Gospel of John. She argues that the Gnostic gospels demonstrate that such a view reflects an authentic alternative expression of historic Christianity valid for believers today.

Dan Brown propagates a similar point in his novel *The Da Vinci Code*. Although this is a novel, Brown has stated clearly in national television interviews that he believes his book is historically accurate and is based on the best scholarship available in regard to its discussions of early Christian literature and history. His characters tell the audience that the current canon, which stresses the divinity of Christ, was only determined by a close church council vote in the fourth century, a vote that resulted in the destruction and suppression of the then-popular Gnostic gospels, which stressed only the humanity of Christ. Brown's characters, and also a few other writers who speculate on the *Gospel of Mary Magdalene*, further state that Jesus was married to Mary Magdalene and fathered children by her. Also, Brown argues, Jesus told Mary deeper and more mature revelations than he told the apostles.

Brown and Pagels converge again in their insistence that, as the Gnostic "gospels" teach, revelation of God does not come through biblical revelation but rather through the individual. Pagels makes this point crystal clear, attempting to shift the focus of divine revelation away from the Bible to the individual, in accordance with the *Gospel of Thomas*.

What should we make of these new claims? First of all, although we cannot cover all of the details in a short appendix like this, it is important to underscore that both Pagels and Brown have seriously distorted the historical data. While history shows that the final closing of the canon was a slow process, it also shows that the Gnostic "gospels" were *never* considered canonical by a large number of churches. The truth is not that they were "deleted" from the canon, as Pagels and Brown argue, but that they were never part of the authoritative works of the early churches.

It is also important to note that absent from the collection of Gnostic texts found at Nag Hammadi are *any* of the other New Testament canonical books. This observation has strong implications regarding the nature of the religion that was being followed by the writers of the Nag Hammadi material. The religion reflected by those documents may have referred to Jesus Christ, but it apparently was not Christianity, and without stronger, authenticated connections to Jesus and the apostles of the first century, this literature cannot claim to represent Christianity.

The four canonical Gospels (Matthew, Mark, Luke, and John) and the letters of

Paul were widely accepted by the church by the end of the first century and the beginning of the second. The divinity of Christ as well as the importance of his life, death, and resurrection are firmly established by these documents. Pagels and others have no texts or evidence that the *Gospel of Thomas* is any earlier than the mid-second century (about AD 150). By contrast, we have an actual Greek manuscript fragment from a copy of the Gospel of John that dates firmly to at least AD 120, and the implication is that the original was written much earlier, probably toward the end of the first century (most evangelical Johannine scholars date the Gospel of John at AD 80–85, and the majority of other Johannine scholars favor AD 90–100). The evidence points to the conclusion that the Gospel of John predates the *Gospel of Thomas* by probably more than fifty years. Thus, the argument of Pagels that the Gospel of John is a rebuttal of the *Gospel of Thomas* is difficult to maintain.

Throughout the history of Christianity, various distortions and heresies have appeared. Indeed, Christians have always needed to study their Bibles to discern between the truth of Jesus Christ and the false doctrines suggested by those not faithful to the revealed Scriptures. Throughout history the church has often had to identify heretical documents and teachings and to separate them from the trustworthy and inspired books of the Bible that Christians have lived by for nearly two thousand years. Second-century heresies such as Gnosticism are ancient and interesting, but in the end they are still heresies.

FURTHER READING

The issues relating to inspiration, inerrancy, and canon development are complex, and the brevity of this appendix has forced us to try to synthesize and simplify some complicated issues. Indeed, this discussion is but a brief overview. We encourage you to read further on these issues.

On Inspiration and Inerrancy

Dockery, David S. *Christian Scripture: An Evangelical Perspective on Inspiration, Authority and Interpretation*, 37–60. Nashville: B&H, 1995.

Grudem, Wayne. *Systematic Theology: An Introduction to Biblical Doctrine*, 73–104. Grand Rapids: Zondervan, 1994.

Marshall, I. Howard. *Biblical Inspiration*. Grand Rapids: Eerdmans, 1982.

Regarding the Old Testament Canon

Beckwith, Roger. *The Old Testament Canon of the New Testament Church and Its Background in Early Judaism*. Grand Rapids: Eerdmans, 1985.

Hill, Andrew E., and John H. Walton. *A Survey of the Old Testament*. 3rd ed. Grand Rapids: Zondervan, 2009.

Kaiser, Walter C., Jr. *The Old Testament Documents: Are They Reliable and Relevant?* Downers Grove, IL: InterVarsity Press, 2001.

Kitchen, Kenneth A. *On the Reliability of the Old Testament*. Grand Rapids: Eerdmans, 2003.

Regarding the Development of the New Testament Canon

Barnett, Paul. *Is the New Testament Reliable?* 2nd ed. Downers Grove, IL: InterVarsity Press, 2005.

Bruce, F. F. *The Canon of Scripture*. Downers Grove, IL: InterVarsity Press, 1988.

Carson, D. A., Douglas J. Moo, and Leon Morris. *An Introduction to the New Testament*, 487–500. Grand Rapids: Zondervan, 1992.

Metzger, Bruce M. *The Canon of the New Testament: Its Origin, Development, and Significance*. Oxford: Oxford University Press, 1997.

Patzia, Arthur G. *The Making of the New Testament: Origin, Collection, Text and Canon*. 2nd ed. Downers Grove, IL: InterVarsity Press, 2011.

Wallace, Daniel B. *Revisiting the Corruption of the New Testament: Manuscript, Patristic, and Apocryphal Evidence*. Grand Rapids: Kregel, 2011.

Gnostic Gospels

To read the primary sources (in English translation) of early noncanonical Christian literature and Gnostic literature, see the following:

Schneemelcher, Wilhelm, ed. *New Testament Apocrypha*. 2 vols. Rev. ed. Cambridge and Louisville: James Clark and Westminster John Knox, 1991.

Critiques of the Gnostic Gospel Advocates

Bock, Darrell L. *Breaking the Da Vinci Code*. Nashville: Nelson, 2004.

Eddy, Paul Rhodes, and Gregory A. Boyd. *The Jesus Legend: A Case for the Historical Reliability of the Synoptic Jesus Tradition*. Grand Rapids: Baker, 2007.

Jones, Timothy Paul. *Misquoting Truth: A Guide to the Fallacies of Bart Ehrman's "Misquoting Jesus."* Downers Grove, IL: InterVarsity Press, 2007.

Komoszewski, J. Ed, M. James Sawyer, and Daniel B. Wallace. *Reinventing Jesus: What the Da Vinci Code and Other Novel Speculations Don't Tell You*. Grand Rapids: Kregel, 2006.

Pate, C. Marvin, and Sheryl Pate. *Crucified in the Media: Finding the Real Jesus amidst Today's Headlines*. Grand Rapids: Baker, 2005.

Roberts, Mark D. *Can We Trust the Gospels? Investigating the Reliability of Matthew, Mark, Luke, and John*. Wheaton, IL: Crossway, 2007.

Witherington, Ben, III. *The Gospel Code: Novel Claims about Jesus, Mary Magdalene, and Da Vinci*. Downers Grove, IL: InterVarsity Press, 2004.

———. *What Have They Done with Jesus? Beyond Strange Theories and Bad History*. New York: HarperSanFrancisco, 2006.

APPENDIX 2

WRITING AN EXEGETICAL PAPER

These guidelines assume that you are using *Grasping God's Word* to learn how to read, interpret, and live out the Bible. As a result, we will focus here on how to present the results of your interpretive work. Teachers have personal preferences when it comes to writing exegetical papers (e.g., footnotes or endnotes?). Our guidelines present the basics related to form and content that should prove helpful.

FORM

The paper is to be typed, using double spacing, a twelve-point font, and one-inch margins. The minimum length is nine pages; the maximum is thirteen pages (excluding the title page and the bibliography).

Citations should be referenced in accordance with the guidelines of the style manual that your teacher prefers. Commonly used style manuals for writing exegetical papers include these:

Hudson, Robert, gen. ed. *The Christian Writer's Manual of Style*. 4th ed. Grand Rapids: Zondervan, 2016.

Turabian, Kate. *A Manual for Writers of Research Papers, Theses, and Dissertations*. 9th ed. Chicago: University of Chicago Press, 2018.

Vyhmeister, Nancy J., and Terry Robertson. *Quality Research Papers: For Students of Religion and Theology*. 3rd ed. Grand Rapids: Zondervan, 2014.

CONTENT

1. Title Page (1 page)

The title page should clearly state the passage that you are exegeting, the course title, the professor's name, the date submitted, and your name.

2. Main Idea and Outline (1 page)

Identify your passage, then summarize the main idea of the passage in one sentence. Next, present a full outline of your passage, showing how the main idea unfolds. For each main point of your outline, show in parentheses the corresponding verses. All the verses of your passage should be included in the main points of your outline.

3. Introduction (½–1 page)

This paragraph should gain the reader's attention and introduce the main idea of your passage.

4. Context (1–2 pages)

This part consists of two sections. First, include a brief discussion of the historical-cultural context of the book. What do your readers need to know about the biblical author, the original audience, and their world in order to grasp the meaning of the passage?

Second, discuss the literary context of your passage. Describe the author's flow of thought in the book and discuss how your passage fits into and contributes to the flow of thought. Pay particular attention to how your passage relates to the passage that precedes it and the one that follows it.

5. Content (5–8 pages)

This represents the body of your paper and the heart of your exegetical work. You should let the main points of your outline function as subheadings. Include under each subheading a detailed explanation of your passage.

Explain what the text says and what it means in context. Be sure to include significant elements that you discovered as you observed the text and studied the passage's historical-cultural context. Also, explain the meaning of critical words and concepts. Synthesize your own observations with those of the commentaries.

Speaking of commentaries, you must consult and cite at least four sources. Allow these commentaries to assist you, but be careful not to let them dictate what you conclude about the passage. Be critical of your sources and do not be afraid to disagree with commentators. As always, cite your sources so as not to plagiarize.

Keep in mind that the goal of this section is to explain the meaning of the text in context. Discuss the details of the text, but be sure to move beyond mere description of details to show how they come together to convey meaning.

6. Application (1 page)

Discuss several applications of this passage to contemporary audiences. Be as practical and realistic as possible.

7. Bibliography (1 page)

Present a formal bibliography of the sources you cite in your paper in accordance with your teacher's preferred style manual.

CHECKLIST

- I have double-spaced the paper with a twelve-point font and one-inch margins.
- The paper has a title page.
- The paper is between nine and thirteen pages long.
- I have cited sources in accordance with the preferred style manual.
- My main idea summarizes the entire passage in one sentence.
- All verses in the passage are included in my outline.
- My introduction gains the reader's attention and introduces the main idea.
- I discuss both the historical-cultural and literary contexts.
- The main points of my outline serve as subheadings in the body of my paper.
- I explain the meaning of critical words and concepts in my passage.
- I have consulted at least four reputable sources.
- I discuss several applications of this passage for a contemporary audience.
- I include a bibliography of sources cited in the paper.
- I have proofread the paper.

GRADING

Grading will be based on the following:

- Form and style (typing, spelling, grammar, etc.) _____%
- Research (use of sources) _____%
- Main idea and outline _____%
- Context (historical-cultural and literary) _____%
- Content _____%
- Application _____%

APPENDIX 3

BUILDING A PERSONAL LIBRARY

Because our funds are limited and not all study tools are created equal, most of us need a strategy for building a personal library. We don't want to throw our money away on resources we will never use. You might consider a two-phase strategy for building a personal library.

PHASE ONE

Get something dependable on every book of the Bible. We suggest purchasing a less expensive but quality series such as Bible Speaks Today, Expositor's Bible Commentary, or Tyndale Old/New Testament Commentaries. If this is not possible, then start out with a good one- or two-volume commentary. In addition, you will need a few basic reference tools, such as a concordance, a Bible dictionary, an atlas, and a dictionary of theology. This small library will give you at least some place to turn for advice when you study the Scriptures.

PHASE TWO

In this phase we suggest that you add a top-notch evangelical commentary on each book of the Bible. Next, try to expand your reference section by adding tools mentioned in the first part of our recommended list below. Finally, you will want to add additional commentaries. We suggest that you add other evangelical works before moving to nonevangelical works.

You may want to approach this second phase in a systematic fashion, starting with Genesis or Matthew and working forward. Or you may decide it would be best to purchase resources on a particular book when you find yourself studying that book.

To help you make informed choices, we offer the following recommendations on study tools. In the lists below, we have placed an asterisk (*) beside works that we consider most appropriate for our students. We are not necessarily saying that these are the definitive works in the field, but we think our students would profit most from them at this point in their journey.

Recommending study tools, especially commentaries, can be a dangerous business. Since we cannot list every book, choices must be made. We hope you realize that our suggestions are somewhat subjective. Nevertheless, we offer the following as a suggested guide for building a library of your own.

Concordances

Goodrick, Edward W., and John R. Kohlenberger III, eds. *The Strongest NIV Exhaustive Concordance*. 2nd ed. Grand Rapids: Zondervan, 1999.

Kohlenberger, John R., III. *The NRSV Concordance Unabridged*. Grand Rapids: Zondervan, 1991.

Kohlenberger, John R., III, Edward W. Goodrick, and James A. Swanson. *The Greek-English Concordance to the New Testament*. Grand Rapids: Zondervan, 1997.

Kohlenberger, John R., III, and James A. Swanson, *The Hebrew-English Concordance to the Old Testament*. Grand Rapids: Zondervan, 1998.

Mounce, William D. *The Crossway Comprehensive Concordance of the Holy Bible: English Standard Version*. Wheaton, IL: Crossway, 2002.

Strong, James. *The New Strongest Strong's Exhaustive Concordance of the Bible*. Revised by John R. Kohlenberger III and James A. Swanson. Grand Rapids: Zondervan, 2001.

Thomas, Robert. *NAS Exhaustive Concordance, Revised*. LaHabra, CA: Lockman Foundation, 1998; Grand Rapids: Zondervan, 2000.

Bible Handbooks

Alexander, Pat, and David Alexander, eds. 5th ed. *Zondervan Handbook to the Bible*. Grand Rapids: Zondervan, 2017.

B&H Editorial Staff, eds. *Holman Illustrated Bible Handbook*. Nashville: B&H, 2012.

Hays, J. Daniel, and J. Scott Duvall. *The Baker Illustrated Bible Handbook*. Grand Rapids: Baker, 2011.

Old Testament Surveys and Introductions

Arnold, Bill. *Introduction to the Old Testament*. Cambridge: Cambridge University Press, 2014.

Arnold, Bill, and Bryan Beyer. *Encountering the Old Testament*. 3rd ed. Grand Rapids: Baker, 2015.

Dearman, J. Andrew, and Robert L. Hubbard Jr. *Introducing the Old Testament*. Grand Rapids: Eerdmans, 2018.

DeRouchie, Jason, ed. *What the Old Testament Authors Really Cared About*. Grand Rapids: Kregel, 2012.

Goldingay, John. *An Introduction to the Old Testament: Exploring Text, Approaches and Issues*. Downers Grove, IL: InterVarsity Press, 2015.

Harrison, R. K. *Introduction to the Old Testament*. Peabody, MA: Hendrickson, 2004.

Hess, Richard S. *The Old Testament: A Historical, Theological, and Critical Introduction*. Grand Rapids: Baker Academic, 2016.

*Hill, Andrew E., and John H. Walton. *A Survey of the Old Testament*. 3rd ed. Grand Rapids: Zondervan, 2009.

House, Paul R., and Eric Mitchell. *Old Testament Survey*. 2nd ed. Nashville: B&H, 2007.

*Longman, Tremper, III, and Raymond B. Dillard. *An Introduction to the Old Testament*. 2nd ed. Grand Rapids: Zondervan, 2006.

Van Pelt, Miles V., ed. *A Biblical-Theological Introduction to the Old Testament: The Gospel Promised*. Wheaton, IL: Crossway, 2016.

Walton, John H., and Andrew E. Hill. *Old Testament Today*. 2nd ed. Grand Rapids: Zondervan, 2014.

New Testament Surveys and Introductions

Achtemeier, Paul, Joel Green, and Marianne Meye Thompson. *Introducing the New Testament*. Grand Rapids: Eerdmans, 2001.

Berding, Kenneth, and Matt Williams, eds. *What the New Testament Authors Really Cared About*. Grand Rapids: Kregel, 2008.

*Burge, Gary M., and Gene L. Green. *The New Testament in Antiquity*. 2nd ed. Grand Rapids: Zondervan Academic, 2020.

*Carson, D. A., and Douglas J. Moo. *An Introduction to the New Testament*. 2nd ed. Grand Rapids: Zondervan, 2005.

*DeSilva, David. *An Introduction to the New Testament: Contexts, Methods & Ministry Formation*. 2nd ed. Downers Grove, IL: InterVarsity Press, 2018.

Elwell, Walter A., and Robert W. Yarbrough. *Encountering the New Testament*. 2nd ed. Grand Rapids: Baker, 2005.

*Gundry, Robert H. *A Survey of the New Testament*. 5th ed. Grand Rapids: Zondervan, 2012.

Guthrie, Donald. *New Testament Introduction*. Rev. ed. Downers Grove, IL: InterVarsity Press, 1990.

*Hagner, Donald A. *The New Testament: A Historical and Theological Introduction*. Grand Rapids: Baker, 2012.

*Köstenberger, Andreas J., L. Scott Kellum, and Charles L. Quarles. *The Cradle, the Cross, and the Crown: An Introduction to the New Testament*. 2nd ed. Nashville: B&H, 2016.

Kruger, Michael J. *A Biblical-Theological Introduction to the New Testament: The Gospel Realized*. Wheaton, IL: Crossway, 2016.

Lea, Thomas D., and David Alan Black. *The New Testament: Its Background and Message*. 2nd ed. Nashville: B&H, 2003.

Powell, Mark Allan. *Introducing the New Testament: A Historical, Literary, and Theological Survey*. 2nd ed. Grand Rapids: Baker, 2018.

*Wright, N. T., and Michael F. Bird. *The New Testament in Its World: An Introduction to the History, Literature, and Theology of the First Christians*. Grand Rapids: Zondervan Academic, 2019.

Bible Atlases

Aharoni, Yohanan, et al. *The Carta Bible Atlas*. 5th ed. Jerusalem: Carta, 2011.

Beck, John A. *Discovery House Bible Atlas*. Grand Rapids: Discovery House, 2015.

*Beitzel, Barry J. *The New Moody Atlas of the Bible Lands*. Chicago: Moody, 2009.
*Brisco, Thomas V. *Holman Bible Atlas: A Complete Guide to the Expansive Geography of Biblical History*. Nashville: B&H, 2014.
Currid, John D., and David P. Barrett. *Crossway ESV Bible Atlas*. Wheaton, IL: Crossway, 2010.
Curtis, Adrian. *Oxford Bible Atlas*. 4th ed. Oxford: Oxford University Press, 2007.
Rasmussen, Carl G. *Zondervan Atlas of the Bible*. Rev. ed. Grand Rapids: Zondervan, 2009.

Bible Dictionaries and Encyclopedias

Alexander, T. Desmond, and David W. Baker, eds. *Dictionary of the Old Testament: Pentateuch*. Downers Grove, IL: InterVarsity Press, 2003.
Arnold, Bill T. and H. G. M. Williamson, eds. *Dictionary of the Old Testament: Historical Books*. Downers Grove, IL: InterVarsity Press, 2005.
Boda, Mark J., and J. Gordon McConville, eds. *Dictionary of the Old Testament Prophets*. Downers Grove, IL: InterVarsity Press, 2012.
Brand, Chad, Charles W. Draper, and Archie England, eds. *Holman Illustrated Bible Dictionary*. Rev. and exp. ed. Nashville: B&H, 2015.
Douglas, J. D., Merrill C. Tenney, and Moisés Silva, eds. *Zondervan Illustrated Bible Dictionary*. Grand Rapids: Zondervan, 2011.
Elwell, Walter, ed. *Baker Encyclopedia of the Bible*. 2 vols. Grand Rapids: Baker, 1988.
Elwell, Walter, and Philip Comfort, eds. *Tyndale Bible Dictionary*. Wheaton, IL: Tyndale, 2001.
Evans, Craig A., and Stanley E. Porter, eds. *Dictionary of New Testament Background*. Downers Grove, IL: InterVarsity Press, 2000.
Freedman, David Noel, ed. *The Anchor Bible Dictionary*. 6 vols. Garden City, NY: Doubleday, 1992.
Green, Joel B., Jeannine K. Brown, and Nicholas Perrin, eds. *Dictionary of Jesus and the Gospels*. 2nd ed. Downers Grove, IL: InterVarsity Press, 2013.
Green, Joel B., Scot McKnight, and I. Howard Marshall, eds. *Dictionary of Jesus and the Gospels*. Downers Grove, IL: InterVarsity Press, 1992.
Hawthorne, Gerald F., Ralph P. Martin, and Daniel G. Reid, eds. *Dictionary of Paul and His Letters*. Downers Grove, IL: InterVarsity Press, 1993.
*Longman, Tremper, III, ed. *The Baker Illustrated Bible Dictionary*. Grand Rapids: Baker, 2013.
Longman, Tremper, III, and Peter Enns, eds. *Dictionary of the Old Testament: Wisdom, Poetry and Writings*. Downers Grove, IL: InterVarsity Press, 2008.
*Marshall, I. Howard, A. R. Millard, J. I. Packer, and D. J. Wiseman, eds. *New Bible Dictionary*. 3rd ed. Downers Grove, IL: InterVarsity Press, 1996.
Martin, Ralph P., and Peter H. Davids, eds. *Dictionary of the Later New Testament and Its Developments*. Downers Grove, IL: InterVarsity Press, 1997.
Powell, Mark Allan, gen. ed. *HarperCollins Bible Dictionary*. Rev. and updated ed. San Francisco: HarperSanFrancisco, 2011.
Reid, Daniel G., ed. *The IVP Dictionary of the New Testament*. Downers Grove, IL: InterVarsity Press, 2004.
*Ryken, Leland, James C. Wilhoit, and Tremper Longman III, eds. *Dictionary of Biblical Imagery*. Downers Grove, IL: InterVarsity Press, 1998.

Sakenfeld, Katharine D., ed. *The New Interpreter's Dictionary of the Bible*. 5 vols. Nashville: Abingdon, 2006–9.

Tenney, Merrill C., and Moisés Silva, eds. *The Zondervan Encyclopedia of the Bible*. Rev. ed. 5 vols. Grand Rapids: Zondervan, 2009.

Wordbooks and Lexicons

Balz, Horst, and Gerhard Schneider, eds. *Exegetical Dictionary of the New Testament*. 3 vols. Grand Rapids: Eerdmans, 1990–93.

*Brown, Colin, ed. *New International Dictionary of New Testament Theology*. 4 vols. Grand Rapids: Zondervan, 1975–78.

Brown, Francis, S. R. Driver, and Charles A. Briggs, eds. *Brown-Driver-Briggs Hebrew and English Lexicon*. Peabody, MA: Hendrickson, 1996.

Danker, Frederick W., Walter Bauer, William F. Arndt, and F. Wilbur Gingrich, eds. *A Greek-English Lexicon of the New Testament and Other Early Christian Literature*. 3rd ed. Chicago: University of Chicago Press, 2000.

Harris, R. Laird, Gleason L. Archer Jr., and Bruce K. Waltke, eds. *Theological Wordbook of the Old Testament*. 2 vols. Chicago: Moody Press, 1980.

Jenni, Ernst, and Claus Westermann, eds. *Theological Lexicon of the Old Testament*. Translated by Mark E. Biddle. Peabody, MA: Hendrickson, 1997.

Kittel, Gerhard, and Gerhard Friedrich. *Theological Dictionary of the New Testament*. 1 vol. Translated, edited, and abridged by Geoffrey W. Bromiley. Grand Rapids: Eerdmans, 1985.

*Louw, Johannes P., and Eugene A. Nida. *A Greek-English Lexicon of the New Testament: Based on Semantic Domains*. 2 vols. New York: United Bible Societies, 1989.

Mounce, William D., ed. *Mounce's Complete Expository Dictionary of Old and New Testament Words*. Grand Rapids: Zondervan, 2006.

*Silva, Moisés, ed. *New International Dictionary of New Testament Theology and Exegesis*. 5 vols. 2nd ed. Grand Rapids: Zondervan, 2014.

Spicq, Ceslas, ed. *Theological Lexicon of the New Testament*. 3 vols. Translated by James D. Ernest. Peabody, MA: Hendrickson, 1995.

*VanGemeren, Willem A. *New International Dictionary of Old Testament Theology and Exegesis*. 5 vols. Grand Rapids: Zondervan, 1997.

*Verbrugge, Verlyn, ed. *The New International Dictionary of New Testament Theology*. Abridged ed. Grand Rapids: Zondervan, 2003.

Old Testament Histories

Arnold, Bill T., and Richard S. Hess, eds. *Ancient Israel's History: An Introduction to Issues and Sources*. Grand Rapids: Baker Academic, 2014.

Bright, John A. *A History of Israel*. 4th ed. Philadelphia: Westminster John Knox, 2000.

*Kaiser, Walter, Jr., and Paul D. Wegner. *A History of Israel: From the Bronze Age through the Jewish Wars*. Rev. ed. Nashville: B&H Academic, 2017.

Long, V. Philips, David Baker, and Gordon Wenham, eds. *Windows into Old Testament History*. Grand Rapids: Eerdmans, 2002.

Merrill, Eugene H. *Kingdom of Priests: A History of Old Testament Israel.* 2nd ed. Grand Rapids: Baker, 2008.

Provan, Iain, V. Philips Long, and Tremper Longman III. *A Biblical History of Israel.* Louisville: Westminster John Knox, 2003.

New Testament Histories

Barnett, Paul. *The Birth of Christianity: The First Twenty Years.* Grand Rapids: Eerdmans, 2005.

*———. *Jesus and the Rise of Early Christianity: A History of New Testament Times.* Downers Grove, IL: InterVarsity Press, 1999.

Bruce, F. F. *New Testament History.* Garden City, NY: Doubleday, 1972.

Carter, Warren. *Seven Events That Shaped the New Testament World.* Grand Rapids: Baker Academic, 2013.

*Ferguson, Everett. *Backgrounds of Early Christianity.* 3rd ed. Grand Rapids: Eerdmans, 2003.

*Jeffers, James S. *The Greco-Roman World of the New Testament Era.* Downers Grove, IL: InterVarsity Press, 1999.

Lohse, Eduard. *The New Testament Environment.* Translated by John Steely. Nashville: Abingdon, 1976.

Niswonger, Richard L. *New Testament History.* Grand Rapids: Zondervan, 1988.

*Witherington, Ben, III. *New Testament History: A Narrative Account.* Grand Rapids: Baker, 2001.

Special Studies in Ancient Life and Culture

Arnold, Bill T., and Brent A. Strawn, eds. *The World around the Old Testament: The People and Places of the Ancient Near East.* Grand Rapids: Baker Academic, 2016.

Bailey, Kenneth E. *Jesus through Middle Eastern Eyes: Cultural Studies in the Gospels.* Downers Grove, IL: IVP Academic, 2008.

Barton, John, ed. *The Biblical World.* New York: Routledge, 2002.

Bauckham, Richard. *The Christian World around the New Testament.* Grand Rapids: Baker Academic, 2017.

———. *The Jewish World around the New Testament.* Grand Rapids: Baker Academic, 2010.

Clements, Ronald. *The World of Ancient Israel.* Cambridge: Cambridge University Press, 1989.

*DeSilva, David A. *Honor, Patronage, Kinship and Purity: Unlocking New Testament Culture.* Downers Grove, IL: InterVarsity Press, 2000.

DeVries, LaMoine F. *Cities of the Biblical World.* Peabody, MA: Hendrickson, 1997.

Evans, Craig A. *Ancient Texts for New Testament Studies: A Guide to the Background Literature.* Peabody, MA: Hendrickson, 2005.

Green, Joel B., and Lee Martin McDonald, eds. *The World of the New Testament: Cultural, Social, and Historical Contexts.* Grand Rapids: Baker Academic, 2013.

Greer, Jonathan S., John W. Hilber, and John H. Walton, eds. *Behind the Scenes of the Old Testament: Social, Cultural, and Historical Contexts.* Grand Rapids: Baker Academic, 2018.

Helyer, Larry R. *Exploring Jewish Literature of the Second Temple Period.* Downers Grove, IL: InterVarsity Press, 2002.

Hoerth, Alfred J., Gerald L. Mattingly, and Edwin M. Yamauchi, eds. *Peoples of the Old Testament World*. Grand Rapids: Baker, 1994.
*Jeremias, Joachim. *Jerusalem in the Time of Jesus*. Philadelphia: Fortress, 1969.
King, Philip, and Lawrence Stager. *Life in Biblical Israel*. Louisville: Westminster John Knox, 2001.
Malina, Bruce. *Handbook of Biblical Social Values*. Peabody, MA: Hendrickson, 1998.
———. *The New Testament World*. Louisville: Westminster John Knox, 1993.
*Matthews, Victor H. *Manners and Customs in the Bible*. 3rd ed. Peabody, MA: Hendrickson, 2006.
Matthews, Victor H., and Don C. Benjamin. *Social World of Ancient Israel 1250–587 B.C.E.* Peabody, MA: Hendrickson, 1993.
Scott, J. Julius. *Customs and Controversies*. Grand Rapids: Baker, 1995.
Shanks, Hershel, ed. *Ancient Israel*. Rev. and exp. ed. Washington, DC: Biblical Archaeology Society, 1999.
Skarsaune, Oskar. *In the Shadow of the Temple: Jewish Influences on Early Christianity*. Downers Grove, IL: InterVarsity Press, 2002.
Vos, Howard. *Nelson's New Illustrated Bible Manners and Customs*. Nashville: Thomas Nelson, 1999.
Walton, John H. *Ancient Near Eastern Thought and the Old Testament: Introducing the Conceptual World of the Hebrew Bible*. 2nd ed. Grand Rapids: Baker, 2018.

Old and New Testament Theologies

Barr, James. *The Concept of Biblical Theology*. Minneapolis: Fortress, 1999.
*Beale, G. K. *A New Testament Biblical Theology: The Unfolding of the Old Testament in the New*. Grand Rapids: Baker, 2011.
*Blomberg, Craig L. *A New Testament Theology*. Waco, TX: Baylor University Press, 2018.
Boda, Mark. *The Heartbeat of Old Testament Theology: Three Creedal Expressions*. Grand Rapids: Baker, 2017.
Brueggemann, Walter. *Old Testament Theology: An Introduction*. Nashville: Abingdon, 2008.
Caird, George B. Completed and edited by L. D. Hurst. *New Testament Theology*. Oxford: Clarendon, 1994.
Childs, Brevard S. *Biblical Theology of the Old and New Testaments*. Minneapolis: Fortress, 1993.
———. *Old Testament Theology in a Canonical Context*. Philadelphia: Fortress, 1985.
Dunn, James D. G. *New Testament Theology: An Introduction*. Nashville: Abingdon, 2009.
*Duvall, J. Scott, and J. Daniel Hays. *God's Relational Presence: The Cohesive Center of Biblical Theology*. Grand Rapids: Baker, 2019.
*Goldingay, John. *Old Testament Theology*. 3 vols. Downers Grove, IL: InterVarsity Press, 2003–9.
Goldsworthy, Graeme. *According to Plan*. Downers Grove, IL: InterVarsity Press, 2002.
Guthrie, Donald. *New Testament Theology*. Downers Grove, IL: InterVarsity Press, 1981.
Hafemann, Scott, ed. *Biblical Theology: Retrospect and Prospect*. Downers Grove, IL: InterVarsity Press, 2002.

Helyer, Larry W. *The Witness of Jesus, Paul and John: An Exploration in Biblical Theology*. Downers Grove, IL: InterVarsity Press, 2008.

House, Paul R. *Old Testament Theology*. Downers Grove, IL: InterVarsity Press, 1998.

Kaiser, Walter. *Toward an Old Testament Theology*. Grand Rapids: Zondervan, 1978.

Kessler, John. *Old Testament Theology: Divine Call and Human Response*. Waco, TX: Baylor University Press, 2013.

*Ladd, George Eldon. *A Theology of the New Testament*. Rev. ed. Grand Rapids: Eerdmans, 1993.

*Marshall, I. Howard. *New Testament Theology: Many Witnesses, One Gospel*. Downers Grove, IL: InterVarsity Press, 2004.

Martens, Elmer A. *God's Design: A Focus on Old Testament Theology*. 4th ed. Eugene, OR: Wipf & Stock, 2015.

Matera, Frank J. *New Testament Theology: Exploring Diversity and Unity*. Louisville: Westminster John Knox, 2007.

Merrill, Eugene H. *Everlasting Dominion: A Theology of the Old Testament*. Nashville: B&H, 2006.

Moberly, R. W. L. *Old Testament Theology: Reading the Hebrew Bible as Christian Scripture*. Grand Rapids: Baker, 2013.

Morris, Leon. *New Testament Theology*. Grand Rapids: Zondervan, 1986.

Pate, C. Marvin, et al. *The Story of Israel*. Downers Grove, IL: InterVarsity Press, 2004.

Routledge, Robin. *Old Testament Theology: A Thematic Approach*. Downers Grove, IL: InterVarsity Press, 2008.

Sailhamer, John H. *Introduction to Old Testament Theology*. Grand Rapids: Zondervan, 1994.

Schnelle, Udo. *Theology of the New Testament*. Grand Rapids: Baker, 2009.

*Schreiner, Thomas R. *New Testament Theology: Magnifying God in Christ*. Grand Rapids: Baker, 2008.

Scobie, Charles. *An Approach to Biblical Theology*. Grand Rapids: Eerdmans, 2002.

Thielman, Frank. *Theology of the New Testament: A Canonical and Synthetic Approach*. Grand Rapids: Zondervan, 2005.

*Waltke, Bruce, with Charles Yu. *An Old Testament Theology: An Exegetical, Canonical, and Thematic Approach*. Grand Rapids: Zondervan, 2007.

Walton, John H. *Old Testament Theology for Christians: From Ancient Context to Enduring Belief*. Downers Grove, IL: InterVarsity Press, 2017.

Witherington, Ben, III. *The Indelible Image: The Theological and Ethical Thought World of the New Testament*. 2 vols. Downers Grove, IL: InterVarsity Press, 2009–10.

Youngblood, Ronald. *Heart of the Old Testament*. 2nd ed. Grand Rapids: Baker, 1998.

Zuck, Roy, and Darrell Bock, eds. *A Biblical Theology of the New Testament*. Chicago: Moody Press, 1994.

Dictionaries of Theology

*Alexander, T. Desmond, Brian S. Rosner, D. A. Carson, and Graeme Goldsworthy, eds. *New Dictionary of Biblical Theology*. Downers Grove, IL: InterVarsity Press, 2000.

*Elwell, Walter A., ed. *Baker Theological Dictionary of the Bible*. Grand Rapids: Baker, 2001.

*________, ed. *Evangelical Dictionary of Theology*. 2nd ed. Grand Rapids: Baker, 2001.

Ferguson, Sinclair B., David F. Wright, and J. I. Packer, eds. *New Dictionary of Theology*. Downers Grove, IL: InterVarsity Press, 1988.

Vanhoozer, Kevin J., gen. ed. *Dictionary for Theological Interpretation of the Bible*. Grand Rapids: Baker, 2005.

Systematic Theologies

Bloesch, Donald G. *Christian Foundations*. 7 vols. Downers Grove, IL: InterVarsity Press, 1992–.

*Erickson, Millard. *Christian Theology*. 2nd ed. Grand Rapids: Baker, 1998.

Garrett, James Leo. *Systematic Theology*. 2 vols. Grand Rapids: Eerdmans, 1990, 1995.

*Grenz, Stanley J. *Theology for the Community of God*. Grand Rapids: Eerdmans, 2000.

Grudem, Wayne. *Systematic Theology*. Grand Rapids: Zondervan, 1994.

Horton, Michael. *The Christian Faith: A Systematic Theology for Pilgrims on the Way*. Grand Rapids: Zondervan, 2011.

Lewis, Gordon R., and Bruce Demarest. *Integrative Theology*. 3 vols. Grand Rapids: Zondervan, 1987–94.

McGrath, Alister E. *Christian Theology*. 3rd. ed. Oxford: Blackwell, 2001.

Preaching Helps

Brown, H. C., Jr., H. Gordon Clinard, Jesse J. Northcutt, and Al Fasol. *Steps to the Sermon*. Rev. ed. Nashville: B&H, 1996.

*Bryson, Harold T. *Expository Preaching: The Art of Preaching through a Book of the Bible*. Nashville: B&H, 1995.

*Carter, Terry G., J. Scott Duvall, and J. Daniel Hays. *Preaching God's Word*. Grand Rapids: Zondervan, 2005.

*Chapell, Bryan. *Christ-Centered Preaching: Redeeming the Expository Sermon*. 2nd ed. Grand Rapids: Baker, 2005.

Edwards, J. Kent. *Effective First-Person Biblical Preaching: The Steps from Text to Narrative Sermon*. Grand Rapids: Zondervan, 2005.

Goldsworthy, Graeme. *Preaching the Whole Bible as Christian Scripture*. Grand Rapids: Eerdmans, 2000.

Greidanus, Sidney. *The Modern Preacher and the Ancient Text: Interpreting and Preaching Biblical Literature*. Grand Rapids: Eerdmans, 1988.

________. *Preaching Christ from the Old Testament*. Grand Rapids: Eerdmans, 1999.

Johnston, Graham. *Preaching to a Postmodern World: A Guide to Reaching Twenty-First Century Listeners*. Grand Rapids: Baker, 2001.

Kent, Grenville J. R., Paul J. Kissling, and Laurence A. Turner. *Reclaiming the Old Testament for Christian Preaching*. Downers Grove, IL: InterVarsity Press, 2010.

MacArthur, John F., Jr., Richard L. Mayhue, and Robert L. Thomas. *Rediscovering Expository Preaching*. Dallas: Word, 1992.

Mathewson, Steven D. *The Art of Preaching Old Testament Narrative*. Grand Rapids: Baker, 2002.

Mathews, Alice P. *Preaching That Speaks to Women*. Grand Rapids: Baker, 2003.

Miller, Calvin. *Preaching: The Art of Narrative Exposition*. Grand Rapids: Baker, 2010.

Mitchell, Henry H. *Celebration and Experience in Preaching*. Nashville: Abingdon, 1990.

Moseley, Allan. *From the Study to the Pulpit: An 8-Step Method for Preaching and Teaching the Old Testament*. Bellingham, WA: Lexham, 2017.

Piper, John. *The Supremacy of God in Preaching*. Rev. ed. Grand Rapids: Baker, 2004.

Quicke, Michael J. *Preaching as Worship: An Integrative Approach to Formation in Your Church*. Grand Rapids: Baker, 2011.

———. *360-Degree Preaching: Hearing, Speaking, and Living the Word*. Grand Rapids: Baker, 2003.

*Robinson, Haddon W. *Biblical Preaching*. 2nd ed. Grand Rapids: Baker, 2001.

*Robinson, Haddon W., and Craig Brian Larson, gen. ed. *The Art and Craft of Biblical Preaching: A Comprehensive Resource for Today's Communicators*. Grand Rapids: Zondervan, 2005.

Smith, Steven W. *Recapturing the Voice of God: Shaping Sermons Like Scripture*. Nashville: B&H, 2015.

Stott, John R. W. *Between Two Worlds: The Challenge of Preaching Today*. Grand Rapids: Eerdmans, 1982.

Sunukjian, Donald R. *Invitation to Biblical Preaching: Proclaiming Truth with Clarity and Relevance*. Grand Rapids: Kregel, 2007.

Walton, Benjamin H. *Preaching Old Testament Narratives*. Grand Rapids: Kregel, 2016.

Wright, Christopher J. H. *How to Preach and Teach the Old Testament for All Its Worth*. Grand Rapids: Zondervan, 2016.

Spiritual Growth

Barnes, M. Craig. *Searching for Home: Spirituality for Restless Souls*. Grand Rapids: Brazos, 2003.

Barton, Ruth Haley. *Invitation to Solitude and Silence: Experiencing God's Transforming Presence*. Downers Grove, IL: InterVarsity Press, 2010.

———. *Sacred Rhythms: Arranging Our Lives for Spiritual Transformation*. Downers Grove, IL: InterVarsity Press, 2006.

*———. *Strengthening the Soul of Your Leadership: Seeking God in the Crucible of Ministry*. Downers Grove, IL: InterVarsity Press, 2018.

Boa, Kenneth. *Conformed to His Image: Biblical and Practical Approaches to Spiritual Formation*. Grand Rapids: Zondervan, 2001.

Buchanan, Mark. *Spiritual Rhythm: Being with Jesus Every Season of Your Soul*. Grand Rapids: Zondervan, 2010.

Calhoun, Adele Ahlberg. *Spiritual Disciplines Handbook: Practices That Transform Us*. Rev. and exp. ed. Downers Grove, IL: InterVarsity Press, 2015.

Demarest, Bruce. *Satisfy Your Soul*. Colorado Springs: NavPress, 1999.

*Duvall, J. Scott. *Experiencing God's Story of Life and Hope: A Workbook for Spiritual Formation*. Grand Rapids: Kregel, 2008.

*Foster, Richard J. *Celebration of Discipline*. 20th anniversary ed. San Francisco: HarperCollins, 1998.

Foster, Richard J., and Emilie Griffin, eds. *Spiritual Classics: Selected Readings on the Twelve Spiritual Disciplines*. San Francisco: HarperSanFrancisco, 2000.

Howard, Evan. *The Brazos Introduction to Christian Spirituality*. Grand Rapids: Brazos, 2008.
*———. *A Guide to Christian Spiritual Formation: How Scripture, Spirit, Community, and Mission Shape Our Souls*. Grand Rapids: Baker Academic, 2018.
Kelly, Thomas R. *A Testament of Devotion*. New York: Harper & Brothers, 1941.
Larsen, David L. *Biblical Spirituality: Discovering the Real Connection between the Bible and Life*. Grand Rapids: Kregel, 2001.
Lovelace, Richard. *Dynamics of Spiritual Life*. Downers Grove, IL: InterVarsity Press, 1979.
McGrath, Alister. *Beyond the Quiet Time: Practical Evangelical Spirituality*. Grand Rapids: Baker, 1995.
*Mulholland, M. Robert, Jr. *Invitation to a Journey: A Road Map for Spiritual Formation*. Rev. and exp. ed. Downers Grove, IL: InterVarsity Press, 2016.
———. *Shaped by the Word: The Power of Scripture in Spiritual Formation*. Rev. ed. Nashville: Upper Room, 2000.
Nouwen, Henri J. M. *In the Name of Jesus*. New York: Crossroad, 1992.
*———. *The Return of the Prodigal Son*. New York: Doubleday, 1992.
*Ortberg, John. *The Life You've Always Wanted*. Grand Rapids: Zondervan, 1997.
*Peterson, Eugene H. *A Long Obedience in the Same Direction: Discipleship in an Instant Society*. Downers Grove, IL: InterVarsity Press, 1980.
———. *Subversive Spirituality*. Grand Rapids: Eerdmans, 1997.
Stevens, R. Paul. *Down-to-Earth Spirituality: Encountering God in the Ordinary, Boring Stuff of Life*. Downers Grove, IL: InterVarsity Press, 2003.
Thomas, Gary. *Sacred Pathways: Discover Your Soul's Path to God*. Rev. ed. Grand Rapids: Zondervan, 2010.
Whitney, Donald S. *Spiritual Disciplines for the Christian Life*. Colorado Springs: NavPress, 1991.
*Wilhoit, James C. *Spiritual Formation as If the Church Mattered: Growing in Christ through Community*. Grand Rapids: Baker, 2008.
*Wilkins, Michael J. *In His Image: Reflecting Christ in Everyday Life*. Colorado Springs: NavPress, 1997.
Willard, Dallas. *Divine Conspiracy*. San Francisco: HarperSanFrancisco, 1998.
*———. *Renovation of the Heart: Putting on the Character of Christ*. Colorado Springs: NavPress, 2002.
*———. *The Spirit of the Disciplines*. San Francisco: Harper, 1988.

One- and Two-Volume Commentaries

*Barker, Kenneth L., and John R. Kohlenberger III, eds. *Zondervan NIV Bible Commentary*. Vol. 1: Old Testament. Vol. 2: New Testament. Grand Rapids: Zondervan, 1994.
*Beale, G. K., and D. A. Carson, eds. *Commentary on the New Testament Use of the Old Testament*. Grand Rapids: Baker, 2007.
Brown, Raymond E., Joseph Fitzmyer, and Roland Murphy, eds. *The New Jerome Biblical Commentary*. 2nd ed. Englewood Cliffs, NJ: Prentice-Hall, 1999.
Dunn, James D. G., and John W. Rogerson, eds. *Eerdmans Commentary on the Bible*. Grand Rapids: Eerdmans, 2003.

Elwell, Walter A., ed. *Evangelical Commentary on the Bible*. Grand Rapids: Baker, 1989.
Mays, James, ed. *HarperCollins Bible Commentary*. Rev. ed. San Francisco: HarperSanFrancisco, 2000.
*Wenham, G. J., J. A. Motyer, D. A. Carson, and R. T. France, eds. *New Bible Commentary*. 21st-Century Edition. Downers Grove, IL: InterVarsity Press, 1994.

Background Commentaries

*Arnold, Clint, gen. ed. *Zondervan Illustrated Bible Backgrounds Commentary: New Testament*. 4 vols. Grand Rapids: Zondervan, 2002.
Hays, J. Daniel, and J. Scott Duvall, eds. *The Baker Illustrated Bible Background Commentary*. Grand Rapids: Baker, 2020.
*Keener, Craig S. *The IVP Bible Background Commentary: New Testament*. Downers Grove, IL: InterVarsity Press, 1993.
*Walton, John H., gen. ed. *Zondervan Illustrated Bible Backgrounds Commentary: Old Testament*. 5 vols. Grand Rapids: Zondervan, 2009.
Walton, John H., Mark W. Chavalas, and Victor H. Matthews. *The IVP Bible Background Commentary: Old Testament*. Downers Grove, IL: InterVarsity Press, 2000.

Commentary Series

Apollos Old Testament Commentary. Leicester: Apollos.
Baker Exegetical Commentary. Grand Rapids: Baker.
Bible Speaks Today. Downers Grove, IL: InterVarsity Press.
Expositor's Bible Commentary. Grand Rapids: Zondervan.
International Biblical Commentary. Peabody, MA: Hendrickson.
Interpretation. Louisville: Westminster John Knox.
IVP New Testament Commentary. Downers Grove, IL: InterVarsity Press.
New American Commentary. Nashville: B&H.
New International Commentary on the New Testament. Grand Rapids: Eerdmans.
New International Commentary on the Old Testament. Grand Rapids: Eerdmans.
New International Greek Testament Commentary. Grand Rapids: Eerdmans.
New Interpreter's Bible. Nashville: Abingdon.
NIV Application Commentary. Grand Rapids: Zondervan.
Pillar New Testament Commentaries. Grand Rapids: Eerdmans.
Story of God Bible Commentary. Grand Rapids: Zondervan Academic.
Tyndale New Testament Commentaries. Downers Grove, IL: InterVarsity Press.
Tyndale Old Testament Commentaries. Downers Grove, IL: InterVarsity Press.
Word Biblical Commentary. Grand Rapids: Zondervan Academic.
Zondervan Exegetical Commentary on the New Testament. Grand Rapids: Zondervan Academic.

Commentaries on Books of the Bible

Genesis

Arnold, William T. *Encountering the Book of Genesis*. Grand Rapids: Baker, 1998.

Atkinson, David J. *The Message of Genesis 1–11*. Bible Speaks Today. Downers Grove, IL: InterVarsity Press, 1990.

Baldwin, Joyce G. *The Message of Genesis 12–50*. Bible Speaks Today. Downers Grove, IL: InterVarsity Press, 1986.

Brueggemann, Walter. *Genesis*. Interpretation. Louisville: John Knox, 1982.

*Hamilton, Victor P. *The Book of Genesis*. New International Commentary on the Old Testament. 2 vols. Grand Rapids: Eerdmans, 1990, 1995.

Hartley, John E. *Genesis*. New International Biblical Commentary. Peabody, MA: Hendrickson, 2000.

Kidner, Derek. *Genesis*. Tyndale Old Testament Commentaries. Downers Grove, IL: InterVarsity Press, 1967.

Longman, Tremper, III. *Genesis*. The Story of God Bible Commentary. Grand Rapids: Zondervan, 2016.

Mathews, Kenneth A. *Genesis*. New American Commentary. 2 vols. Nashville: B&H, 1996, 2005.

Ross, Allen P. *Creation and Blessing: A Guide to the Study and Exposition of Genesis*. Grand Rapids: Baker, 1988.

Sailhamer, John H. "Genesis." In *Expositor's Bible Commentary*, 1:21–331. Rev. ed. Grand Rapids: Zondervan, 2008.

Sarna, Nahum M. *Genesis*. JPS Torah Commentary. Philadelphia: Jewish Publication Society, 1989.

*Waltke, Bruce K., and Cathi Fredericks. *Genesis: A Commentary*. Grand Rapids: Zondervan, 2001.

*Walton, John. *Genesis*. NIV Application Commentary. Grand Rapids: Zondervan, 2001.

*Wenham, Gordon J. *Genesis*. Word Biblical Commentary. 2 vols. Nashville: Nelson/Word, 1987, 1994.

Westermann, Claus. *Genesis*. 3 vols. Minneapolis: Augsburg, 1984–86.

Exodus

*Childs, Brevard. *The Book of Exodus*. Old Testament Library. Louisville: Westminster John Knox, 1974.

Cole, R. Alan. *Exodus*. Tyndale Old Testament Commentaries. Downers Grove, IL: InterVarsity Press, 1973.

Currid, John D. *Exodus*. 2 vols. Evangelical Press Study Commentary. Auburn, MA: Evangelical Press, 2000.

Dozeman, Thomas B. *Exodus*. Eerdmans Critical Commentary. Grand Rapids: Eerdmans, 2009.

*Durham, John. *Exodus*. Word Biblical Commentary. Waco, TX: Word, 1987.

*Enns, Peter. *Exodus*. NIV Application Commentary. Grand Rapids: Zondervan, 2000.

Fretheim, Terence E. *Exodus*. Interpretation. Louisville: John Knox, 1991.

Kaiser, Walter C., Jr. "Exodus." In *Expositor's Bible Commentary*, 1:333–561. Rev. ed. Grand Rapids: Zondervan, 2008.

Propp, William H. C. *Exodus*. Anchor Yale Bible Commentary. 2 vols. New York: Doubleday, 1998, 2006.

Sarna, Nahum. *Exodus*. JPS Torah Commentary. Philadelphia: Jewish Publication Society, 1991.
*Stuart, Douglas K. *Exodus*. New American Commentary. Nashville: B&H, 2006.

Leviticus

Gane, Roy. *Leviticus, Numbers*. NIV Application Commentary. Grand Rapids: Zondervan, 2004.
Harrison, R. K. *Leviticus*. Tyndale Old Testament Commentaries. Downers Grove, IL: InterVarsity Press, 1980.
Hartley, John E. *Leviticus*. Word Biblical Commentary. Dallas: Word, 1992.
Hess, Richard S. "Leviticus." In *Expositor's Bible Commentary*, 1:563–832. Rev. ed. Grand Rapids: Zondervan, 2008.
Kaiser, Walter C., Jr. "The Book of Leviticus." In *The New Interpreter's Bible*. Nashville: Abingdon, 1994.
Kiuchi, Nobuyoshi. *Leviticus*. Apollos Old Testament Commentary. Downers Grove, IL: InterVarsity Press, 2007.
Levine, Baruch A. *Leviticus*. JPS Torah Commentary. Philadelphia: Jewish Publication Society, 1989.
Milgrom, Jacob. *Leviticus*. Anchor Bible. 3 vols. New York: Doubleday, 1991–2000.
Rooker, Mark F. *Leviticus*. New American Commentary. Nashville: Broadman and Holman, 2000.
*Ross, Allen P. *Holiness to the Lord: A Guide to the Exposition of the Book of Leviticus*. Grand Rapids: Baker, 2002.
Sprinkle, Joe M. *Leviticus and Numbers*. Teach the Text Commentary. Grand Rapids: Baker, 2015.
*Wenham, Gordon J. *The Book of Leviticus*. New International Commentary on the Old Testament. Grand Rapids: Eerdmans, 1979.

Numbers

Allen, Ronald B. "Numbers." In *Expositor's Bible Commentary*, 2:655–1008. Grand Rapids: Zondervan, 1990.
*Ashley, Timothy R. *The Book of Numbers*. New International Commentary on the Old Testament. Grand Rapids: Eerdmans, 1993.
*Bellinger, W. H., Jr. *Leviticus, Numbers*. New International Biblical Commentary. Peabody, MA: Hendrickson, 2001.
Cole, R. Dennis. *Numbers*. New American Commentary. Nashville: B&H, 2000.
Harrison, R. K. *Numbers*. Wycliffe Exegetical Commentary. Chicago: Moody, 1990.
Levine, Baruch A. *Numbers*. Anchor Bible. 2 vols. New York: Doubleday, 1993, 2000.
Milgrom, Jacob. *Numbers*. JPS Torah Commentary. Philadelphia: Jewish Publication Society, 1990.
Olson, Dennis T. *Numbers*. Interpretation. Louisville: Westminster John Knox, 1996.
Wenham, Gordon J. *Numbers*. Old Testament Guides. Sheffield: Sheffield Academic Press, 1997.
———. *Numbers*. Tyndale Old Testament Commentaries. Downers Grove, IL: InterVarsity Press, 1981.

Deuteronomy

*Block, Daniel. *Deuteronomy*. NIV Application Commentary. Grand Rapids: Zondervan, 2012.

Christensen, Duane L. *Deuteronomy*. Word Biblical Commentary. 2 vols. Nashville: Nelson, 2001–2.

Craigie, Peter C. *The Book of Deuteronomy*. New International Commentary on the Old Testament. Grand Rapids: Eerdmans, 1976.

Lundbom, Jack R. *Deuteronomy: A Commentary*. Grand Rapids: Eerdmans, 2013.

*McConville, J. G. *Deuteronomy*. Apollos Old Testament Commentary. Downers Grove, IL: InterVarsity Press, 2002.

Merrill, Eugene. *Deuteronomy*. New American Commentary. Nashville: Broadman, 1994.

Miller, Patrick D. *Deuteronomy*. Interpretation. Louisville: John Knox, 1990.

Nelson, Richard D. *Deuteronomy*. Old Testament Library. Louisville: Westminster John Knox, 2003.

Thompson, J. A. *Deuteronomy*. Tyndale Old Testament Commentaries. Downers Grove, IL: InterVarsity Press, 1974.

Tigay, J. H. *Deuteronomy*. JPS Torah Commentary. Philadelphia: Jewish Publication Society, 1996.

Weinfeld, Moshe. *Deuteronomy 1–11*. Anchor Bible. New York: Doubleday, 1991.

*Wright, Christopher J. H. *Deuteronomy*. New International Biblical Commentary. Peabody, MA: Hendrickson, 1996.

Joshua, Judges, Ruth

Atkinson, David. *The Message of Ruth*. Bible Speaks Today. Downers Grove, IL: InterVarsity Press, 1983.

Auld, A. Graeme. *Joshua, Judges, and Ruth*. Daily Study Bible. Philadelphia: Westminster, 1984.

Beal, Lissa M. Wray. *Joshua*. The Story of God Bible Commentary. Grand Rapids: Zondervan, 2019.

*Block, Daniel. *Judges, Ruth*. New American Commentary. Nashville: B&H, 1999.

Boling, Robert G. *Judges: Introduction, Translation, and Commentary*. Anchor Bible. Garden City, NY: Doubleday, 1975.

Bush, Frederic. *Ruth, Esther*. Word Biblical Commentary. Dallas: Word, 1996.

Butler, Trent. *Joshua*. Word Biblical Commentary. Waco, TX: Word, 1983.

Campbell, Edward F., Jr. *Ruth*. Anchor Bible. Garden City, NY: Doubleday, 1975.

*Chisholm, Robert B., Jr. *A Commentary on Judges and Ruth*. Kregel Exegetical Library. Grand Rapids: Kregel, 2013.

Cundall, Arthur E., and Leon Morris. *Judges and Ruth*. Tyndale Old Testament Commentaries. Downers Grove, IL: InterVarsity Press, 1968.

Gow, Murray D. *The Book of Ruth: Its Structure, Theme and Purpose*. Leicester: Apollos, 1992.

*Hess, Richard S. *Joshua*. Tyndale Old Testament Commentaries. Downers Grove, IL: InterVarsity Press, 1996.

*Howard, David, Jr. *Joshua*. New American Commentary. Nashville: Broadman, 1998.

*Hubbard, Robert L., Jr. *Joshua*. NIV Application Commentary. Grand Rapids: Zondervan, 2009.

———. *The Book of Ruth*. New International Commentary on the Old Testament. Grand Rapids: Eerdmans, 1988.

Huey, F. B., Jr. "Ruth." In *Expositor's Bible Commentary*, 3:507–49. Grand Rapids: Zondervan, 1992.

Mathews, Kenneth A. *Joshua*. Teach the Text Commentary. Grand Rapids: Baker, 2016.

Nelson, Richard D. *Joshua*. Old Testament Library. Louisville: Westminster John Knox, 1997.

Niditch, Susan. *Judges*. Old Testament Library. Louisville: Westminster John Knox, 2008.

Nielsen, Kirsten. *Ruth*. Old Testament Library. Louisville: Westminster John Knox, 1997.

Pitkänen, Pekka M. A. *Joshua*. Apollos Old Testament Commentary. Downers Grove, IL: InterVarsity Press, 2010.

Way, Kenneth C. *Judges and Ruth*. Teach the Text Commentary. Grand Rapids: Baker, 2016.

Woudstra, Marten. *The Book of Joshua*. New International Commentary on the Old Testament. Grand Rapids: Eerdmans, 1981.

*Younger, K. Lawson Jr. *Judges and Ruth*. NIV Application Commentary. Grand Rapids: Zondervan, 2002.

First and Second Samuel

Anderson, A. A. *2 Samuel*. Word Biblical Commentary. Dallas: Word, 1989.

Arnold, William T. *1 and 2 Samuel*. NIV Application Commentary. Grand Rapids: Zondervan, 2003.

Auld, A. Graeme. *I and II Samuel*. Old Testament Library. Louisville: Westminster John Knox, 2011.

*Baldwin, Joyce G. *1 and 2 Samuel*. Tyndale Old Testament Commentaries. Downers Grove, IL: InterVarsity Press, 1988.

*Bergen, Robert D. *1, 2 Samuel*. New American Commentary. Nashville: Broadman, 1996.

Brueggemann, Walter. *First and Second Samuel*. Interpretation. Louisville: Westminster John Knox, 1990.

*Chisholm, Robert B., Jr. *1 and 2 Samuel*. Teach the Text Commentary. Grand Rapids: Baker, 2013.

Evans, Mary J. *1 and 2 Samuel*. New International Biblical Commentary. Peabody, MA: Hendrickson, 2000.

Evans, Paul S. *1–2 Samuel*. The Story of God Bible Commentary. Grand Rapids: Zondervan, 2018.

*Firth, David G. *1 and 2 Samuel*. Apollos Old Testament Commentary. Downers Grove, IL: InterVarsity Press, 2009.

Gordon, Robert P. *1 and 2 Samuel*. Grand Rapids: Zondervan, 1988.

Klein, Ralph W. *1 Samuel*. Word Biblical Commentary. Waco, TX: Word, 1983.

McCarter, P. Kyle, Jr. *I Samuel*. Anchor Bible. Garden City, NY: Doubleday, 1980.

———. *II Samuel*. Anchor Bible. Garden City, NY: Doubleday, 1984.

Tsumura, David Toshio. *The First Book of Samuel*. New International Commentary on the Old Testament. Grand Rapids: Eerdmans, 2007.

*Youngblood, Ronald F. "1, 2 Samuel." In *Expositor's Bible Commentary*, 3:21–614. Rev. ed. Grand Rapids: Zondervan, 2009.

First and Second Kings

Brueggemann, Walter. *1 and 2 Kings*. Smyth & Helwys Bible Commentary. Macon, GA: Smyth & Helwys, 2000.

Cogan, Mordechai. *1 Kings*. Anchor Bible. New York: Doubleday, 2001.

Cogan, Mordechai, and Hayim Tadmor. *II Kings*. Anchor Bible. Garden City, NY: Doubleday, 1988.

DeVries, Simon J. *1 Kings*. Word Biblical Commentary. Waco, TX: Word, 1985.

Hobbs, T. R. *2 Kings*. Word Biblical Commentary. Waco, TX: Word, 1985.

*House, Paul R. *1, 2 Kings*. New American Commentary. Nashville: B&H, 1995.

*Konkel, August H. *1 and 2 Kings*. NIV Application Commentary. Grand Rapids: Zondervan, 2006.

Nelson, Richard. *First and Second Kings*. Interpretation. Louisville: Westminster John Knox, 1987.

Patterson, Richard D., and Hermann J. Austel. "1, 2 Kings." In *Expositor's Bible Commentary*, 3:615–960. Rev. ed. Grand Rapids: Zondervan, 2009.

*Provan, Iain W. *1 and 2 Kings*. New International Biblical Commentary. Peabody, MA: Hendrickson, 1995.

Seow, Choon-Leong. "The First and Second Books of Kings." In *New Interpreter's Bible*, 3:1–296. Nashville: Abingdon, 1999.

Sweeney, Marvin A. *I and II Kings*. Old Testament Library. Louisville: Westminster John Knox, 2007.

Walsh, Jerome T. *1 Kings*. Berit Olam. Collegeville, MN: Liturgical, 1996.

*Wiseman, Donald J. *1 and 2 Kings*. Tyndale Old Testament Commentaries. Downers Grove, IL: InterVarsity Press, 1993.

First and Second Chronicles

Allen, Leslie C. "The First and Second Books of Chronicles." In *New Interpreter's Bible*, 3:297–660. Nashville: Abingdon, 1999.

Braun, Roddy. *1 Chronicles*. Word Biblical Commentary. Waco, TX: Word, 1986.

Dillard, Raymond B. *2 Chronicles*. Word Biblical Commentary. Waco, TX: Word, 1987.

*Hill, Andrew E. *1, 2 Chronicles*. NIV Application Commentary. Grand Rapids: Zondervan, 2003.

Japhet, Sara. *I and II Chronicles*. Old Testament Library. Louisville: Westminster John Knox, 1993.

*Knoppers, Gary N. *1 Chronicles*. Anchor Bible. 2 vols. New York: Doubleday, 2003–4.

McConville, J. G. *I and II Chronicles*. Daily Study Bible. Philadelphia: Westminster, 1984.

Payne, J. Barton. "1, 2 Chronicles." In *Expositor's Bible Commentary*, 4:301–562. Grand Rapids: Zondervan, 1988.

*Selman, Martin J. *1 Chronicles*. Tyndale Old Testament Commentaries. Downers Grove, IL: InterVarsity Press, 1994.

———. *2 Chronicles*. Tyndale Old Testament Commentaries. Downers Grove, IL: InterVarsity Press, 1994.

*Thompson, J. A. *1, 2 Chronicles*. New American Commentary. Nashville: Broadman, 1994.

Tuell, Steven S. *First and Second Chronicles*. Interpretation. Louisville: John Knox, 2001.

Wilcock, Michael. *The Message of Chronicles*. Bible Speaks Today. Downers Grove, IL: InterVarsity Press, 1987.

Williamson, H. G. M. *1 and 2 Chronicles*. New Century Bible. Grand Rapids: Eerdmans, 1982.

Ezra, Nehemiah, Esther

Allen, Leslie C. *Ezra, Nehemiah, Esther*. New International Biblical Commentary on the Old Testament. Peabody, MA: Hendrickson, 2003.

*Baldwin, Joyce G. *Esther*. Tyndale Old Testament Commentaries. Downers Grove, IL: InterVarsity Press, 1984.

Blenkinsopp, Joseph. *Ezra–Nehemiah*. Old Testament Library. Louisville: Westminster John Knox, 1988.

Breneman, Mervin. *Ezra, Nehemiah, Esther*. New American Commentary. Nashville: Broadman, 1993.

Bush, Frederic. *Ruth, Esther*. Word Biblical Commentary. Dallas: Word, 1996.

Clines, David J. A. *Ezra, Nehemiah, Esther*. New Century Bible. Grand Rapids: Eerdmans, 1984.

Davies, Gordon F. *Ezra and Nehemiah*. Berit Olam. Collegeville, MN: Liturgical Press, 1999.

Fensham, F. Charles. *The Books of Ezra and Nehemiah*. New International Commentary on the Old Testament. Grand Rapids: Eerdmans, 1982.

Fox, Michael. *Character and Ideology in the Book of Esther*. 2nd ed. Grand Rapids: Eerdmans, 2001.

Huey, F. B., Jr. "Esther." In *Expositor's Bible Commentary*, 4:773–839. Grand Rapids: Zondervan, 1988.

*Jobes, Karen H. *Esther*. NIV Application Commentary. Grand Rapids: Zondervan, 1999.

Kidner, Derek. *Ezra and Nehemiah*. Tyndale Old Testament Commentaries. Downers Grove, IL: InterVarsity Press, 1979.

Klein, Ralph. "The Books of Ezra and Nehemiah." In *New Interpreter's Bible*, 3:661–852. Nashville: Abingdon, 1999.

Levenson, Jon D. *Esther*. Old Testament Library. Louisville: Westminster John Knox, 1997.

McConville, J. G. *Ezra, Nehemiah, and Esther*. Daily Study Bible. Philadelphia: Westminster, 1985.

*Nykolaishen, Douglas J. E., and Andrew J. Schmutzer. *Ezra, Nehemiah, and Esther*. Teach the Text Commentary. Grand Rapids: Baker, 2018.

Throntveit, Mark A. *Ezra–Nehemiah*. Interpretation. Louisville: Westminster John Knox, 1992.

*Williamson, H. G. M. *Ezra, Nehemiah*. Word Biblical Commentary. Waco, TX: Word, 1985.

*Yamauchi, Edwin. "Ezra and Nehemiah." In *Expositor's Bible Commentary*, 4:563–771. Grand Rapids: Zondervan, 1988.

Job

*Alden, Robert L. *Job*. New American Commentary. Nashville: Broadman, 1993.

Andersen, Francis I. *Job*. Tyndale Old Testament Commentaries. Downers Grove, IL: InterVarsity Press, 1976.

Balentine, Samuel E. *Job*. Smyth & Helwys Bible Commentary. Macon, GA: Smyth & Helwys, 2006.
Clines, David J. A. *Job 1–20*. Word Biblical Commentary. Dallas: Word, 1989.
———. *Job 21–42*. Word Biblical Commentary. Nashville: Nelson, 2002.
*Estes, Daniel J. *Job*. Teach the Text Commentary. Grand Rapids: Baker, 2013.
Fyall, Robert. *Now My Eyes Have Seen You: Images of Creation and Evil in the Book of Job*. Downers Grove, IL: InterVarsity Press, 2002.
*Hartley, John E. *The Book of Job*. New International Commentary on the Old Testament. Grand Rapids: Eerdmans, 1988.
Janzen, J. Gerald. *Job*. Interpretation. Louisville: Westminster John Knox, 1985.
Smick, Elmer B. "Job." In *Expositor's Bible Commentary*, 4:841–1060. Grand Rapids: Zondervan, 1988.
*Walton, John H. *Job*. NIV Application Commentary. Grand Rapids: Zondervan, 2012.

Psalms

Allen, Leslie C. *Psalms 101–150*. Word Biblical Commentary. Waco, TX: Word, 1983.
Broyles, Craig C. *Psalms*. New International Biblical Commentary. Peabody, MA: Hendrickson, 1999.
*Brueggemann, Walter, and William H. Bellinger, Jr. *Psalms*. New Cambridge Bible Commentary. New York: Cambridge University Press, 2014.
*Bullock, C. Hassell. *Psalms*. Teach the Text Commentary. 2 vols. Grand Rapids: Baker, 2015, 2017.
*Craigie, Peter C. *Psalms 1–50*. Word Biblical Commentary. Waco, TX: Word, 1983.
*deClaissé-Walford, Nancy, Rolf A. Jacobson, and Beth LaNeel Tanner. *The Book of Psalms*. New International Commentary on the Old Testament. Grand Rapids: Eerdmans, 2014.
Futato, Mark D. *Interpreting the Psalms: An Exegetical Handbook*. Handbooks for Old Testament Exegesis. Grand Rapids: Kregel, 2007.
*Goldingay, John. *Psalms*. Baker Commentary on the Old Testament. 3 vols. Grand Rapids: Baker, 2006–8.
Kidner, D. *Psalms*. Tyndale Old Testament Commentaries. 2 vols. Downers Grove, IL: InterVarsity Press, 1973, 1975.
Limburg, James. *Psalms*. Westminster Bible Companion. Louisville: Westminster John Knox, 2000.
Mays, J. L. *Psalms*. Interpretation. Louisville: Westminster John Knox, 1994.
*Ross, Allen P. *A Commentary on the Psalms: Volume 3 (90–150)*. Kregel Exegetical Library. Grand Rapids: Kregel, 2016.
Tate, Marvin E. *Psalms 51–100*. Word Biblical Commentary. Dallas: Word, 1990.
Terrien, Samuel L. *The Psalms: Strophic Structure and Theological Commentary*. Eerdmans Critical Commentary. Grand Rapids: Eerdmans, 2002.
VanGemeren, Willem A. "Psalms." In *Expositor's Bible Commentary*, 5:21–1024. Rev. ed. Grand Rapids: Zondervan, 2008.
Westermann, Claus. *The Living Psalms*. Grand Rapids: Eerdmans, 1989.
Wilcock, Michael. *The Message of Psalms 1–72: Songs for the People of God*. Bible Speaks Today. Downers Grove, IL: InterVarsity Press, 2001.

———. *The Message of Psalms 73–150: Songs for the People of God*. Bible Speaks Today. Downers Grove, IL: InterVarsity Press, 2001.

Wilson, Gerald. *Psalms* (1–72). NIV Application Commentary. Grand Rapids: Zondervan, 2002.

Proverbs

Alden, Robert L. *Proverbs: A Commentary on an Ancient Book of Timeless Advice*. Grand Rapids: Baker, 1983.

Clifford, Richard. *Proverbs*. Old Testament Library. Louisville: Westminster John Knox, 1999.

Fox, Michael V. *Proverbs*. Anchor Bible. 2 vols. New York: Doubleday, 2000, 2003.

*Garrett, Duane A. *Proverbs, Ecclesiastes, Song of Songs*. New American Commentary. Nashville: Broadman, 1993.

*Kidner, D. *Proverbs*. Tyndale Old Testament Commentaries. Downers Grove, IL: InterVarsity Press, 1964.

Koptak, Paul E. *Proverbs*. NIV Application Commentary. Grand Rapids: Zondervan, 2003.

*Longman, Tremper, III. *Proverbs*. Baker Commentary on the Old Testament. Grand Rapids: Baker, 2006.

McKane, W. *Proverbs: A New Approach*. Old Testament Library. Louisville: Westminster John Knox, 1970.

Murphy, Roland E. *Proverbs*. Word Biblical Commentary. Nashville: Nelson, 1998.

O'Dowd, Ryan P. *Proverbs*. The Story of God Bible Commentary. Grand Rapids: Zondervan, 2017.

Perdue, Leo G. *Proverbs*. Interpretation. Louisville: John Knox, 2000.

Ross, Allen P. "Proverbs." In *Expositor's Bible Commentary*, 6:21–252. Rev. ed. Grand Rapids: Zondervan, 2008.

Van Leeuwen, Raymond C. "The Book of Proverbs." In *New Interpreter's Bible*, 5:17–624. Nashville: Abingdon, 1997.

*Waltke, Bruce. *The Book of Proverbs*. New International Commentary on the Old Testament. 2 vols. Grand Rapids: Eerdmans, 2004–5.

Ecclesiastes

*Bartholomew, Craig G. *Ecclesiastes*. Baker Commentary on the Old Testament. Grand Rapids: Baker, 2009.

Crenshaw, James L. *Ecclesiastes*. Old Testament Library. Philadelphia: Westminster, 1987.

Eaton, Michael A. *Ecclesiastes: An Introduction and Commentary*. Tyndale Old Testament Commentaries. Downers Grove, IL: InterVarsity Press, 1983.

*Fredericks, Daniel C., and Daniel J. Estes. *Ecclesiastes and the Song of Songs*. Apollos Old Testament Commentary. Downers Grove, IL: InterVarsity Press, 2010.

Kidner, Derek. *A Time to Mourn and a Time to Dance*. Bible Speaks Today. Downers Grove, IL: InterVarsity Press, 1976.

*Longman, Tremper, III. *The Book of Ecclesiastes*. New International Commentary on the Old Testament. Grand Rapids: Eerdmans, 1998.

Murphy, Roland E. *Ecclesiastes*. Word Biblical Commentary. Dallas: Word, 1992.
*Provan, Iain. *Ecclesiastes and Song of Songs*. NIV Application Commentary. Grand Rapids: Zondervan, 2001.
Seow, C. L. *Ecclesiastes*. Anchor Bible. New York: Doubleday, 1997.
Whybray, R. N. *Ecclesiastes*. New Century Bible. Grand Rapids: Eerdmans, 1988.

Song of Songs

Carr, G. Lloyd. *The Song of Solomon*. Tyndale Old Testament Commentaries. Downers Grove, IL: InterVarsity Press, 1984.
*Garrett, Duane, and Paul R. House. *Song of Songs/Lamentations*. Word Biblical Commentary. Nashville: Nelson, 2004.
Gledhill, Tom. *The Message of the Song of Songs*. Bible Speaks Today. Downers Grove, IL: InterVarsity Press, 1994.
*Hess, Richard S. *Song of Songs*. Baker Commentary on the Old Testament. Grand Rapids: Baker, 2005.
Keel, Othmar. *The Song of Songs*. Continental Commentary. Minneapolis: Fortress, 1994.
Kinlaw, Dennis F. "Song of Songs." In *Expositor's Bible Commentary*, 5:1199–244. Grand Rapids: Zondervan, 1991.
*Longman, Tremper, III. *Song of Songs*. New International Commentary on the Old Testament. Grand Rapids: Eerdmans, 2001.
Murphy, Roland E. *The Song of Songs*. Hermeneia. Minneapolis: Fortress, 1990.
Pope, Marvin H. *Song of Songs*. Anchor Bible. Garden City, NY: Doubleday, 1977.
*Provan, Iain. *Ecclesiastes and Song of Songs*. NIV Application Commentary. Grand Rapids: Zondervan, 2001.

Isaiah

Blenkinsopp, Joseph. *Isaiah 1–39*. Anchor Bible. New York: Doubleday, 2000.
Brueggemann, Walter. *Isaiah*. Westminster Bible Companion. 2 vols. Louisville: Westminster John Knox, 1998.
*Childs, Brevard S. *Isaiah*. Old Testament Library. Louisville: Westminster John Knox, 2001.
Goldingay, John. *Isaiah*. New International Biblical Commentary. Peabody, MA: Hendrickson, 2001.
Goldingay, John, and David Payne. *Isaiah 40–55*. International Critical Commentary. 2 vols. Edinburgh: T&T Clark, 2007.
Grogan, Geoffrey W. "Isaiah." In *Expositor's Bible Commentary*, 6:433–864. Rev. ed. Grand Rapids: Zondervan, 2008.
Motyer, J. Alec. *The Prophecy of Isaiah*. Downers Grove, IL: InterVarsity Press, 1993.
*Oswalt, John. *Isaiah*. New International Commentary on the Old Testament. 2 vols. Grand Rapids: Eerdmans, 1986, 1998.
———. *Isaiah*. NIV Application Commentary. Grand Rapids: Zondervan, 2003.
Seitz, Christopher R. "The Book of Isaiah 40–66." In *New Interpreter's Bible*, 6:307–552. Nashville: Abingdon, 2001.
*Smith, Gary V. *Isaiah 40–66*. New American Commentary. Nashville: B&H, 2009.

Sweeney, Marvin A. *Isaiah 1–39*. The Forms of the Old Testament Literature. Grand Rapids: Eerdmans, 1996.

Watts, John D. W. *Isaiah*. Word Biblical Commentary. 2 vols. Rev. ed. Nashville: Nelson, 2006.

Westermann, Claus. *Isaiah 40–66*. Old Testament Library. Philadelphia: Westminster, 1969.

Williamson, H. G. M. *Isaiah 1–5*. International Critical Commentary. Edinburgh: T&T Clark, 2006.

Jeremiah, Lamentations

Allen, Leslie C. *Jeremiah*. Old Testament Library. Louisville: Westminster John Knox, 2008.

Brown, Michael L. "Jeremiah." In *Expositor's Bible Commentary*, 7:21–572. Rev. ed. Grand Rapids: Zondervan, 2010.

Brueggemann, Walter. *A Commentary on Jeremiah: Exile and Homecoming*. Grand Rapids: Eerdmans, 1998.

Clements, Ronald E. *Jeremiah*. Interpretation. Atlanta: John Knox, 1988.

Craigie, Peter C., Page H. Kelley, and Joel F. Drinkard Jr. *Jeremiah 1–25*. Word Biblical Commentary. Dallas: Word, 1991.

*Dearman, J. Andrew. *Jeremiah and Lamentations*. NIV Application Commentary. Grand Rapids: Zondervan, 2002.

Ferris, Paul W., Jr. "Lamentations." In *Expositor's Bible Commentary*, 7:573–640. Rev. ed. Grand Rapids: Zondervan, 2010.

Fretheim, Terence. *Jeremiah*. Smyth & Helwys Bible Commentary. Macon, GA: Smyth & Helwys, 2002.

Garrett, Duane, and Paul R. House. *Song of Songs/Lamentations*. Word Biblical Commentary. Nashville: Nelson, 2004.

*Hays, J. Daniel. *Jeremiah and Lamentations*. Teach the Text Commentary. Grand Rapids: Baker, 2016.

Hillers, Delbert R. *Lamentations*. Anchor Bible. 2nd ed. New York: Doubleday, 1992.

Holladay, William Lee. *Jeremiah*. Hermeneia. 2 vols. Minneapolis: Fortress, 1986–89.

Huey, F. B. *Jeremiah, Lamentations*. New American Commentary. Nashville: Broadman, 1993.

Keown, Gerald L., Pamela J. Scalise, and Thomas G. Smothers. *Jeremiah 26–52*. Word Biblical Commentary. Dallas: Word, 1995.

*Longman, Tremper, III. *Jeremiah, Lamentations*. New International Biblical Commentary on the Old Testament. Peabody, MA: Hendrickson, 2008.

*Lundbom, Jack. *Jeremiah*. Anchor Bible. 3 vols. New York: Doubleday, 1999, 2004.

McKane, William. *Jeremiah*. International Critical Commentary. 2 vols. Edinburgh: T&T Clark, 1986–96.

*Provan, Iain. *Lamentations*. New Century Bible. Grand Rapids: Eerdmans, 1991.

*Thompson, J. A. *The Book of Jeremiah*. New International Commentary on the Old Testament. Grand Rapids: Eerdmans, 1980.

Ezekiel

Alexander, Ralph H. "Ezekiel." In *Expositor's Bible Commentary*, 7:641–928. Rev. ed. Grand Rapids: Zondervan, 2010.

Allen, Leslie C. *Ezekiel*. Word Biblical Commentary. 2 vols. Dallas: Word, 1990, 1994.
Blenkinsopp, Joseph. *Ezekiel*. Interpretation. Louisville: John Knox, 1990.
*Block, Daniel I. *The Book of Ezekiel*. New International Commentary on the Old Testament. 2 vols. Grand Rapids: Eerdmans, 1997–98.
Cooper, Lamar E. *Ezekiel*. New American Commentary. Nashville: Broadman, 1994.
*Duguid, Iain M. *Ezekiel*. NIV Application Commentary. Grand Rapids: Zondervan, 1999.
Greenberg, Moshe. *Ezekiel*. Anchor Bible. 2 vols. Garden City, NY: Doubleday, 1983, 1997.
Odell, Margaret S. *Ezekiel*. Smyth & Helwys Bible Commentary. Macon, GA: Smyth & Helwys, 2005.
Wright, Christopher. *The Message of Ezekiel: A New Heart and a New Spirit*. Bible Speaks Today. Downers Grove, IL: InterVarsity Press, 2001.
Zimmerli, Walther. *Ezekiel*. Hermeneia. 2 vols. Philadelphia: Fortress, 1979, 1983.

Daniel

Archer, Gleason L., Jr. "Daniel." In *Expositor's Bible Commentary*, 7:1–157. Grand Rapids: Zondervan, 1985.
*Baldwin, Joyce G. *Daniel*. Tyndale Old Testament Commentaries. Downers Grove, IL: InterVarsity Press, 1978.
*Goldingay, John. *Daniel*. Rev. ed. Word Biblical Commentary. Grand Rapids: Zondervan, 2019.
Hill, Andrew E. "Daniel." In *Expositor's Bible Commentary*, 8:19–212. Rev. ed. Grand Rapids: Zondervan, 2008.
*Longman, Tremper, III. *Daniel*. NIV Application Commentary. Grand Rapids: Zondervan, 1999.
*Lucas, Ernest C. *Daniel*. Apollos Old Testament Commentary. Downers Grove, IL: InterVarsity Press, 2002.
Miller, Stephen R. *Daniel*. New American Commentary. Nashville: Broadman, 1994.
Pierce, Ronald W. *Daniel*. Teach the Text Commentary. Grand Rapids: Baker, 2015.
Wallace, Ronald S. *The Message of Daniel*. Bible Speaks Today. Downers Grove, IL: InterVarsity Press, 1984.
Widder, Wendy L. *Daniel*. The Story of God Bible Commentary. Grand Rapids: Zondervan, 2016.

Minor Prophets

Alden, Robert L. "Haggai" and "Malachi." In *Expositor's Bible Commentary*, 7:567–91, 699–725. Grand Rapids: Zondervan, 1985.
*Alexander, Desmond, David W. Baker, and Bruce K. Waltke. *Obadiah, Jonah, Micah*. Tyndale Old Testament Commentaries. Downers Grove, IL: InterVarsity Press, 1988.
*Allen, Leslie C. *The Books of Joel, Obadiah, Jonah, and Micah*. New International Commentary on the Old Testament. Grand Rapids: Eerdmans, 1976.
Andersen, Francis I., and David N. Freedman. *Amos*. Anchor Bible. New York: Doubleday, 1989.
———. *Hosea*. Anchor Bible. Garden City, NY: Doubleday, 1980.

Armerding, Carl E. "Obadiah," "Nahum," and "Habakkuk." In *Expositor's Bible Commentary*, 8:421–50, 553–648. Rev. ed. Grand Rapids: Zondervan, 2008.

Bailey, Waylon. *Nahum*. New American Commentary. Nashville: B&H, 1999.

Baker, David W. *Joel, Obadiah, Malachi*. NIV Application Commentary. Grand Rapids: Zondervan, 2006.

———. *Nahum, Habakkuk, Zephaniah*. Tyndale Old Testament Commentaries. Downers Grove, IL: InterVarsity Press, 1988.

Baldwin, Joyce G. *Haggai, Zechariah, Malachi*. Tyndale Old Testament Commentaries. Downers Grove, IL: InterVarsity Press, 1972.

*Barker, Kenneth L. *Micah, Nahum, Habakkuk, Zephaniah*. New American Commentary. Nashville: B&H, 1998.

Berlin, Adele. *Zephaniah*. Anchor Bible. New York: Doubleday, 1994.

Block, Daniel I. *Obadiah: The Kingship Belongs to YHWH*. Hearing the Message of Scripture. Grand Rapids: Zondervan, 2013.

*Boda, Mark J. *The Book of Zechariah*. New International Commentary on the Old Testament. Grand Rapids: Eerdmans, 2016.

*———. *Haggai, Zechariah*. NIV Application Commentary. Grand Rapids: Zondervan, 2004.

*Bruckner, James. *Jonah, Nahum, Habakkuk, Zephaniah*. NIV Application Commentary. Grand Rapids: Zondervan, 2004.

*Carroll R., M. Daniel. "Hosea." In *Expositor's Bible Commentary*, 8:213–306. Rev. ed. Grand Rapids: Zondervan, 2008.

Craigie, Peter C. *Twelve Prophets*. Daily Study Bible. Philadelphia: Westminster, 1984.

Crenshaw, James L. *Joel*. Anchor Bible. New York: Doubleday, 1995.

*Dearman, J. Andrew. *The Book of Hosea*. New International Commentary on the Old Testament. Grand Rapids: Eerdmans, 2010.

*Fuhr, Richard Alan, Jr., and Gary E. Yates. *The Message of the Twelve: Hearing the Voice of the Minor Prophets*. Nashville: B&H, 2016.

*Garrett, Duane. *Hosea, Joel*. New American Commentary. Nashville: B&H, 1997.

Hill, Andrew E. *Malachi*. Anchor Bible. New York: Doubleday, 1998.

Hubbard, David Allan. *Hosea*. Tyndale Old Testament Commentaries. Downers Grove, IL: InterVarsity Press, 1989.

———. *Joel and Amos*. Tyndale Old Testament Commentaries. Downers Grove, IL: InterVarsity Press, 1989.

Jeremias, Jörg. *The Book of Amos*. Old Testament Library. Louisville: Westminster John Knox, 1998.

Kidner, Derek. *The Message of Hosea*. Bible Speaks Today. Downers Grove, IL: InterVarsity Press, 1981.

Macintosh, A. A. *A Critical and Exegetical Commentary on Hosea*. International Critical Commentary. Edinburgh: T&T Clark, 1997.

Mays, James L. *Amos*. Old Testament Library. Philadelphia: Westminster, 1969.

———. *Hosea*. Old Testament Library. Philadelphia: Westminster, 1969.

*McComiskey, Thomas E., ed. *The Minor Prophets: An Exegetical and Expository Commentary*. Vol. 1: *Hosea–Amos*. Grand Rapids: Baker, 1992.

*———. *The Minor Prophets: An Exegetical and Expository Commentary*. Vol. 2: *Obadiah–Habakkuk*. Grand Rapids: Baker, 1993.

*McComiskey, Thomas E., and Tremper Longman III. "Amos" and "Micah." In *Expositor's Bible Commentary*, 8:347–420, 491–552. Rev. ed. Grand Rapids: Zondervan, 2008.

Merrill, Eugene H. "Haggai" and "Malachi." In *Expositor's Bible Commentary*, 8:697–720, 835–64. Rev. ed. Grand Rapids: Zondervan, 2008.

Meyers, Carol L., and Eric M. Meyers. *Haggai, Zechariah*. Anchor Bible. Garden City, NY: Doubleday, 1987, 1993.

Nixon, Rosemary. *The Message of Jonah*. Bible Speaks Today. Downers Grove, IL: InterVarsity Press, 2003.

Paul, Shalom. *Amos*. Hermeneia. Minneapolis: Fortress, 1991.

Petersen, David L. *Haggai and Zechariah 1–8*. Old Testament Library. Philadelphia: Westminster, 1984.

———. *Zechariah 9–14 and Malachi*. Old Testament Library. Louisville: Westminster John Knox, 1995.

Roberts, J. J. *Nahum, Habakkuk, and Zephaniah*. Old Testament Library. Louisville: Westminster John Knox, 1991.

*Robertson, O. Palmer. *The Books of Nahum, Habakkuk, and Zephaniah*. New International Commentary on the Old Testament. Grand Rapids: Eerdmans, 1990.

*Ross, Allen P. *Malachi Then and Now: An Expository Commentary Based on Detailed Exegetical Analysis*. Wooster, OH: Weaver, 2016.

Sasson, Jack M. *Jonah*. Anchor Bible. New York: Doubleday, 1990.

Smith, Gary V. *Amos*. Grand Rapids: Zondervan, 1998.

*———. *Hosea, Amos, Micah*. NIV Application Commentary. Grand Rapids: Zondervan, 2001.

Smith, Ralph L. *Micah–Malachi*. Word Biblical Commentary. Waco, TX: Word, 1984.

*Stuart, Douglas K. *Hosea–Jonah*. Word Biblical Commentary. Waco, TX: Word, 1987.

Verhoef, Pieter A. *The Books of Haggai and Malachi*. New International Commentary on the Old Testament. Grand Rapids: Eerdmans, 1987.

*Waltke, Bruce K. *A Commentary on Micah*. Grand Rapids: Eerdmans, 2008.

Walton, John H. "Jonah." In *Expositor's Bible Commentary*, 8:451–90. Rev. ed. Grand Rapids: Zondervan, 2008.

Wolff, Hans W. *Joel and Amos*. Hermeneia. Philadelphia: Fortress, 1977.

———. *Micah*. Philadelphia: Fortress, 1981.

Youngblood, Kevin J. *Jonah: God's Scandalous Mercy*. Hearing the Message of Scripture. Grand Rapids: Zondervan, 2013.

Matthew

Allison, D., and W. D. Davies. *A Critical and Exegetical Commentary on the Gospel according to St. Matthew*. International Critical Commentary. 3 vols. Edinburgh: T&T Clark, 1988–97.

*Blomberg, Craig L. *Matthew*. New American Commentary. Nashville: Broadman, 1992.

Brown, Jeannine. *Matthew*. Teach the Text Commentary. Grand Rapids: Baker, 2015.

Brown, Jeannine, and Kyle Roberts. *Matthew*. Two Horizons New Testament Commentary. Grand Rapids: Eerdmans, 2018.

*Carson, D. A., "Matthew." In *Expositor's Bible Commentary*, 9:23–670. Rev. ed. Grand Rapids: Zondervan, 2010.

France, R. T. *The Gospel of Matthew*. New International Commentary on the New Testament. Grand Rapids: Eerdmans, 2007.

Green, Michael. *The Message of Matthew*. Bible Speaks Today. Downers Grove, IL: InterVarsity Press, 2000.

Hagner, Donald A. *Matthew*. Word Biblical Commentary. 2 vols. Dallas: Word, 1993, 1995.

Keener, Craig S. *The Gospel of Matthew: A Socio-Rhetorical Commentary*. 2nd ed. Grand Rapids: Eerdmans, 2009.

Morris, Leon. *The Gospel according to Matthew*. Pillar New Testament Commentary. Grand Rapids: Eerdmans, 1992.

Nolland, John. *The Gospel of Matthew*. New International Greek Testament Commentary. Grand Rapids: Eerdmans, 2005.

*Osborne, Grant R. *Matthew*. Zondervan Exegetical Commentary on the New Testament. Grand Rapids: Zondervan, 2010.

Reeves, Rodney. *Matthew*. Story of God Bible Commentary. Grand Rapids: Zondervan, 2017.

Turner, David L. *Matthew*. Baker Exegetical Commentary on the New Testament. Grand Rapids: Baker, 2008.

*Wilkins, Michael. *Matthew*. NIV Application Commentary. Grand Rapids: Zondervan, 2004.

Mark

*Edwards, James R. *The Gospel according to Mark*. Pillar New Testament Commentary. Grand Rapids: Eerdmans, 2001.

Evans, Craig. *Mark 8:27–16:20*. Word Biblical Commentary. Nashville: Nelson, 2001.

France, R. T. *The Gospel of Mark: A Commentary on the Greek Text*. New International Greek Testament Commentary. Grand Rapids: Eerdmans, 2002.

*Garland, David E. *Mark*. NIV Application Commentary. Grand Rapids: Zondervan, 1996.

Geulich, Robert A. *Mark 1–8:26*. Word Biblical Commentary. Dallas: Word, 1989.

Hooker, Morna D. *The Gospel according to Saint Mark*. Peabody, MA: Hendrickson, 1991.

Hurtado, Larry W. *Mark*. New International Biblical Commentary. Peabody, MA: Hendrickson, 1989.

*Lane, William L. *The Gospel of Mark*. New International Commentary on the New Testament. Grand Rapids: Eerdmans, 1974.

Schnabel, Eckhard J. *Mark*. Tyndale New Testament Commentaries. Downers Grove, IL: IVP Academic, 2018.

Stein, Robert H. *Mark*. Baker Exegetical Commentary on the New Testament. Grand Rapids: Baker, 2008.

*Strauss, Mark L. *Mark*. Zondervan Exegetical Commentary on the New Testament. Grand Rapids: Zondervan, 2014.

Witherington, Ben, III. *The Gospel of Mark: A Socio-Rhetorical Commentary*. Grand Rapids: Eerdmans, 2001.

Luke

*Bock, Darrell L. *Luke*. Baker Exegetical Commentary on the New Testament. 2 vols. Grand Rapids: Baker, 1994, 1996.

*———. *Luke*. NIV Application Commentary. Grand Rapids: Zondervan, 1996.

*Edwards, James. *The Gospel according to Luke*. Pillar New Testament Commentary. Grand Rapids: Eerdmans, 2015.

Evans, Craig A. *Luke*. New International Biblical Commentary. Peabody, MA: Hendrickson, 1990.

Fitzmyer, Joseph A. *The Gospel according to Luke*. Anchor Bible. 2 vols. New York: Doubleday, 1981, 1985.

France, R. T. *Luke*. Teach the Text Commentary. Grand Rapids: Baker, 2013.

*Garland, David E. *Luke*. Zondervan Exegetical Commentary on the New Testament. Grand Rapids: Zondervan, 2011.

*Green, Joel B. *The Gospel of Luke*. New International Commentary on the New Testament. Grand Rapids: Eerdmans, 1997.

Johnson, Luke T. *The Gospel of Luke*. Sacra Pagina. Wilmington, DE: Michael Glazier, 1991.

Liefeld, Walter L., and David Pao. "Luke." In *Expositor's Bible Commentary*, 10:19–355. Rev. ed. Grand Rapids: Zondervan, 2007.

Marshall, I. Howard. *The Gospel of Luke*. New International Greek Testament Commentary. Grand Rapids: Eerdmans, 1978.

Nolland, John. *Luke*. Word Biblical Commentary. 3 vols. Grand Rapids: Zondervan, 1990–93.

Stein, Robert A. *Luke*. New American Commentary. Nashville: Broadman, 1992.

John

Beasley-Murray, George R. *The Gospel of John*. Word Biblical Commentary. 2nd ed. Nashville: Nelson, 1999.

Blomberg, Craig. *The Historical Reliability of John's Gospel*. Downers Grove, IL: InterVarsity Press, 2002.

Borchert, Gerald L. *John*. New American Commentary. 2 vols. Nashville: B&H, 1996, 2002.

Brown, Raymond. *The Gospel according to John*. Anchor Bible. 2 vols. Garden City, NY: Doubleday, 1966, 1970.

Bruce, F. F. *The Gospel of John*. Grand Rapids: Eerdmans, 1983.

*Burge, Gary M. *John*. NIV Application Commentary. Grand Rapids: Zondervan, 2000.

*Carson, D. A. *The Gospel according to John*. Pillar New Testament Commentary. Grand Rapids: Eerdmans, 1991.

Keener, Craig S. *The Gospel of John: A Commentary*. 2 vols. Grand Rapids: Hendrickson, 2003.

Klink, Edward W., III. *John*. Zondervan Exegetical Commentary on the New Testament. Grand Rapids: Zondervan, 2016.

*Kruse, Colin. *John*. Tyndale New Testament Commentaries. Downers Grove, IL: IVP Academic, 2017.

*Michaels, J. Ramsey. *The Gospel of John*. Rev. ed. New International Commentary on the New Testament. Grand Rapids: Eerdmans, 2010.

Ridderbos, Herman. *The Gospel of John*. Grand Rapids: Eerdmans, 1997.
Thompson, Marianne Meye. *John: A Commentary*. Louisville: Westminster John Knox. 2015.
Whitacre, Rodney. *John*. IVP New Testament Commentary. Downers Grove, IL: InterVarsity Press, 2007.

Acts

Barrett, C. K. *A Critical and Exegetical Commentary on the Acts of the Apostles*. International Critical Commentary. 2 vols. Edinburgh: T&T Clark, 1994, 1998.
*Bock, Darrell L. *Acts*. Baker Exegetical Commentary on the New Testament. Grand Rapids: Baker, 2007.
Bruce, F. F. *The Book of Acts*. New International Commentary on the New Testament. Rev. ed. Grand Rapids: Eerdmans, 1988.
*Fernando, Ajith. *Acts*. NIV Application Commentary. Grand Rapids: Zondervan, 1998.
Fitzmyer, Joseph A. *The Acts of the Apostles*. Anchor Bible. New York: Doubleday, 1999.
Garland, David E. *Acts*. Teach the Text Commentary. Grand Rapids: Baker, 2017.
Johnson, Luke Timothy. *The Acts of the Apostles*. Sacra Pagina. Collegeville, MN: Liturgical, 1992.
Keener, Craig S. *Acts: An Exegetical Commentary*. 4 vols. Grand Rapids: Baker Academic, 2012–15.
Larkin, William J., Jr. *Acts*. IVP New Testament Commentary. Downers Grove, IL: InterVarsity Press, 2011.
*Longenecker, Richard N. "Acts." In *Expositor's Bible Commentary*, 10:663–1102. Rev. ed. Grand Rapids: Zondervan, 2007.
Marshall, I. Howard. *Acts*. Tyndale New Testament Commentaries. Downers Grove, IL: IVP Academic, 2008.
*Peterson, David G. *The Acts of the Apostles*. Pillar New Testament Commentary. Grand Rapids: Eerdmans, 2009.
*Polhill, John B. *Acts*. New American Commentary. Nashville: Broadman, 1992.
Schnabel, Eckhard J. *Acts*. Zondervan Exegetical Commentary on the New Testament. Grand Rapids: Zondervan, 2012.
*Stott, John R. W. *The Spirit, the Church, and the World: The Message of Acts*. Downers Grove, IL: InterVarsity Press, 1990.
Wall, Robert W. "The Acts of the Apostles." In *New Interpreter's Bible*, 10:1–368. Nashville: Abingdon, 2002.
*Witherington, Ben, III. *The Acts of the Apostles: A Socio-Rhetorical Commentary*. Grand Rapids: Eerdmans, 1998.

Romans

Bird, Michael F. *Romans*. Story of God Bible Commentary. Grand Rapids: Zondervan, 2016.
Bruce, F. F. *The Epistle of Paul to the Romans*. Tyndale New Testament Commentaries. Downers Grove, IL: IVP Academic, 2008.
Cranfield, C. E. B. *The Epistle to the Romans*. International Critical Commentary. 2 vols. Edinburgh: T&T Clark, 1975, 1979.

Dunn, James D. G. *Romans*. Word Biblical Commentary. 2 vols. Dallas: Word, 1988.
Kruse, Colin G. *Paul's Letter to the Romans*. Pillar New Testament Commentary. Grand Rapids: Eerdmans, 2012.
*Longenecker, Richard N. *The Epistle to the Romans*. The New International Greek Testament Commentary. Grand Rapids: Eerdmans, 2015.
*Moo, Douglas J. *Encountering the Book of Romans*. 2nd ed. Grand Rapids: Baker, 2014.
———. *The Epistle to the Romans*. New International Commentary on the New Testament. 2nd ed. Grand Rapids: Eerdmans, 2018.
*———. *Romans*. NIV Application Commentary. Grand Rapids: Zondervan, 2000.
Morris, Leon. *The Epistle to the Romans*. Pillar New Testament Commentary. Grand Rapids: Eerdmans, 1988.
Mounce, Robert H. *Romans*. New American Commentary. Nashville: B&H, 1995.
Osborne, Grant R. *Romans*. IVP New Testament Commentary. Downers Grove, IL: InterVarsity Press, 2004.
*Schreiner, Thomas R. *Romans*. Baker Exegetical Commentary on the New Testament. 2nd ed. Grand Rapids: Baker, 2018.
*Stott, John R. W. *Romans: God's Good News for the World*. Downers Grove, IL: InterVarsity Press, 1994.
Thielman, Frank S. *Romans*. Zondervan Exegetical Commentary on the New Testament. Grand Rapids: Zondervan, 2018.
Witherington, Ben, III, and Darlene Hyatt. *Paul's Letter to the Romans: A Socio-Rhetorical Commentary*. Grand Rapids: Eerdmans, 2004.
*Wright, N. T. "The Letter to the Romans." In *New Interpreter's Bible*, 10:393–770. Nashville: Abingdon, 2002.

First Corinthians

Barrett, C. K. *A Commentary on the First Epistle to the Corinthians*. Harper's New Testament Commentary. New York: Harper, 1968.
*Blomberg, Craig L. *1 Corinthians*. NIV Application Commentary. Grand Rapids: Zondervan, 1994.
*Ciampa, Roy E., and Brian S. Rosner. *The First Letter to the Corinthians*. Pillar New Testament Commentary. Grand Rapids: Eerdmans, 2010.
*Fee, Gordon D. *The First Epistle to the Corinthians*. New International Commentary on the New Testament. Rev. ed. Grand Rapids: Eerdmans, 2014.
Garland, David E. *1 Corinthians*. Baker Exegetical Commentary on the New Testament. Grand Rapids: Baker, 2003.
Hays, Richard B. *First Corinthians*. Interpretation. Louisville: Westminster John Knox, 1997.
Morris, Leon. *1 Corinthians*. Tyndale New Testament Commentaries. Downers Grove, IL: IVP Academic, 2008.
Prior, David. *The Message of 1 Corinthians*. Bible Speaks Today. Downers Grove, IL: InterVarsity Press, 1985.
Thiselton, Anthony C. *First Corinthians: A Shorter Exegetical and Pastoral Commentary*. Grand Rapids: Eerdmans, 2006.

———. *The First Epistle to the Corinthians: A Commentary on the Greek Text*. New International Greek Testament Commentary. Grand Rapids: Eerdmans, 2000.

Vang, Preben. *1 Corinthians*. Teach the Text Commentary. Grand Rapids: Baker, 2014.

Verbrugge, Verlyn D. "1 Corinthians." In *Expositors' Bible Commentary*, 11:239–414. Grand Rapids: Zondervan, 2008.

Witherington, Ben, III. *Conflict and Community in Corinth: A Socio-Rhetorical Commentary*. Grand Rapids: Eerdmans, 1995.

Second Corinthians

*Barnett, Paul. *The Second Epistle to the Corinthians*. New International Commentary on the New Testament. Grand Rapids: Eerdmans, 1997.

*Belleville, Linda L. *2 Corinthians*. IVP New Testament Commentary. Downers Grove, IL: InterVarsity Press, 2011.

Garland, David E. *2 Corinthians*. New American Commentary. Nashville: B&H, 1999.

*Guthrie, George H. *2 Corinthians*. Baker Exegetical Commentary on the New Testament. Grand Rapids: Baker Academic, 2015.

*Hafemann, Scott J. *2 Corinthians*. NIV Application Commentary. Grand Rapids: Zondervan, 2000.

*Harris, Murray J. *The Second Epistle to the Corinthians*. New International Greek Testament Commentary. Grand Rapids: Eerdmans, 2005.

Kruse, Colin G. *The Second Epistle of Paul to the Corinthians*. Tyndale New Testament Commentaries. Downers Grove, IL: IVP Academic, 2015.

Martin, Ralph P. *2 Corinthians*. Word Biblical Commentary. 2nd ed. Grand Rapids: Zondervan, 2014.

Galatians

Bruce, F. F. *Commentary on Galatians*. New International Greek Testament Commentary. Grand Rapids: Eerdmans, 1982.

deSilva, David A. *The Letter to the Galatians*. New International Commentary on the New Testament. Rev. ed. Grand Rapids: Eerdmans, 2018.

*Fung, R. Y. K. *The Epistle to the Galatians*. New International Commentary on the New Testament. Grand Rapids: Eerdmans, 1988.

George, Timothy. *Galatians*. New American Commentary. Nashville: Broadman, 1994.

*Hansen, G. Walter. *Galatians*. IVP New Testament Commentary. Downers Grove, IL: InterVarsity Press, 1994.

Hays, Richard B. "The Letter to the Galatians." In *New Interpreter's Bible*, 11:181–348. Nashville: Abingdon, 2000.

*Keener, Craig S. *Galatians: A Commentary*. Grand Rapids: Baker, 2019.

*Longenecker, Richard N. *Galatians*. Word Biblical Commentary. Dallas: Word, 1990.

Martyn, J. Louis. *Galatians*. Anchor Bible. New York: Doubleday, 1997.

Matera, Frank J. *Galatians*. Sacra Pagina. Collegeville, MN: Liturgical, 1992.

McKnight, Scot. *Galatians*. NIV Application Commentary. Grand Rapids: Zondervan, 1995.

Moo, Douglas J. *Galatians*. Baker Exegetical Commentary on the New Testament. Grand Rapids: Baker Academic, 2013.

Morris, Leon. *Galatians*. Downers Grove, IL: InterVarsity Press, 1996.

*Schreiner, Thomas R. *Galatians*. Zondervan Exegetical Commentary on the New Testament. Grand Rapids: Zondervan, 2010.

Stott, John. *The Message of Galatians*. Bible Speaks Today. Downers Grove, IL: InterVarsity Press, 1968.

Witherington, Ben, III. *Grace in Galatia*. Grand Rapids: Eerdmans, 1998.

Ephesians

*Arnold, Clinton E. *Ephesians*. Zondervan Exegetical Commentary on the New Testament. Grand Rapids: Zondervan, 2010.

*Bruce, F. F. *The Epistles to the Colossians, to Philemon, and to the Ephesians*. New International Commentary on the New Testament. Grand Rapids: Eerdmans, 1984.

Cohick, Lynn H. *Ephesians*. New Covenant Commentary Series. Eugene, OR: Cascade, 2010.

*Hoehner, Harold. *Ephesians: An Exegetical Commentary*. Grand Rapids: Baker, 2002.

Klein, William W. "Ephesians." In *Expositor's Bible Commentary*, 12:19–173. Rev. ed. Grand Rapids: Zondervan, 2006.

Liefeld, Walter L. *Ephesians*. IVP New Testament Commentary. Downers Grove, IL: InterVarsity Press, 1997.

Lincoln, A. T. *Ephesians*. Word Biblical Commentary. Dallas: Word, 1990.

Roberts, Mark. *Ephesians*. Story of God Bible Commentary. Grand Rapids: Zondervan, 2016.

Schnackenburg, R. *The Epistle to the Ephesians*. Edinburgh: T&T Clark, 1991.

*Snodgrass, Klyne. *Ephesians*. NIV Application Commentary. Grand Rapids: Zondervan, 1996.

*Stott, John R. W. *The Message of Ephesians*. Bible Speaks Today. Downers Grove, IL: InterVarsity Press, 1979.

Thielman, Frank. *Ephesians*. Baker Exegetical Commentary on the New Testament. Grand Rapids: Baker, 2010.

Witherington, Ben, III. *The Letters to Philemon, the Colossians, and the Ephesians: A Socio-Rhetorical Commentary on the Captivity Epistles*. Grand Rapids: Eerdmans, 2007.

Philippians

Bockmuehl, Markus. *The Epistle to the Philippians*. Black's New Testament Commentaries. Peabody, MA: Hendrickson, 1998.

Cohick, Lynn. *Philippians*. Story of God Bible Commentary. Grand Rapids: Zondervan, 2013.

*Fee, Gordon D. *Philippians*. New International Commentary on the New Testament. Grand Rapids: Eerdmans, 1995.

*Hansen, G. Walter. *The Letter to the Philippians*. Pillar New Testament Commentaries. Grand Rapids: Eerdmans, 2009.

Hawthorne, Gerald. *Philippians*. Word Biblical Commentary. Revised and expanded by Ralph P. Martin. Nashville: Nelson, 2004.

Keown, Mark J. *Philippians*. 2 vols. Evangelical Exegetical Commentary. Bellingham, WA: Lexham, 2017.

Melick, Richard R., Jr. *Philippians, Colossians, Philemon*. New American Commentary. Nashville: Broadman, 1991.

*Silva, Moisés. *Philippians*. Baker Exegetical Commentary on the New Testament. 2nd ed. Grand Rapids: Baker, 2005.

*Thielman, Frank. *Philippians*. NIV Application Commentary. Grand Rapids: Zondervan, 1995.

Thompson, James W., and Bruce W. Longenecker. *Philippians and Philemon*. Paideia. Grand Rapids: Baker, 2016.

Witherington, Ben, III. *Paul's Letter to the Philippians: A Socio-Rhetorical Commentary*. Grand Rapids: Eerdmans, 2011.

Colossians and Philemon

Barth, Markus, and Helmut Blanke. *The Letter to Philemon*. Eerdmans Critical Commentary. Grand Rapids: Eerdmans, 2000.

Beale, G. K. *Colossians and Philemon*. Baker Exegetical Commentary on the New Testament. Grand Rapids: Baker, 2019.

*Bruce, F. F. *The Epistles to the Colossians, to Philemon, and to the Ephesians*. New International Commentary on the New Testament. Grand Rapids: Eerdmans, 1984.

Dunn, James D. G. *Epistles to the Colossians and to Philemon: A Commentary on the Greek Text*. New International Greek Testament Commentary. Grand Rapids: Eerdmans, 1996.

*Garland, David E. *Colossians and Philemon*. NIV Application Commentary. Grand Rapids: Zondervan, 1998.

*Harris, Murray J. *Colossians and Philemon*. Exegetical Guide to the Greek New Testament. Nashville: B&H, 2010.

Martin, Ralph P. *Colossians and Philemon*. New Century Bible. Grand Rapids: Eerdmans, 1973.

McKnight, Scot. *The Letter to the Colossians*. New International Commentary on the New Testament. Rev. ed. Grand Rapids: Eerdmans, 2018.

———. *The Letter to Philemon*. New International Commentary on the New Testament. Grand Rapids: Eerdmans, 2017.

*Moo, Douglas J. *The Letters to the Colossians and to Philemon*. Pillar New Testament Commentary. Grand Rapids: Eerdmans, 2008.

Pao, David W. *Colossians and Philemon*. Zondervan Exegetical Commentary on the New Testament. Grand Rapids: Zondervan, 2012.

Thompson, Marianne Meye. *Colossians and Philemon*. Two Horizons New Testament Commentary. Grand Rapids: Eerdmans, 2005.

Witherington, Ben, III. *The Letters to Philemon, the Colossians, and the Ephesians: A Socio-Rhetorical Commentary on the Captivity Epistles*. Grand Rapids: Eerdmans, 2007.

Wright, N. T. *Colossians and Philemon*. Tyndale New Testament Commentaries. Downers Grove, IL: IVP Academic, 2008.

First and Second Thessalonians

Beale, G. K. *1–2 Thessalonians*. IVP New Testament Commentary. Downers Grove, IL: InterVarsity Press, 2004.

Bruce, F. F. *I and II Thessalonians*. Word Biblical Commentary. Waco, TX: Word, 1982.

*Fee, Gordon D. *The First and Second Letters to the Thessalonians*. New International Commentary on the New Testament. Rev. ed. Grand Rapids: Eerdmans, 2009.

*Green, Gene. *The Letters to the Thessalonians*. Pillar New Testament Commentary. Grand Rapids: Eerdmans, 2002.

Gupta, Nijay. *1–2 Thessalonians*. New Covenant Commentary Series. Eugene, OR: Cascade, 2016.

*Holmes, Michael W. *1 and 2 Thessalonians*. NIV Application Commentary. Grand Rapids: Zondervan, 1998.

Malherbe, Abraham. *The Letters to the Thessalonians*. Anchor Bible. New York: Doubleday, 2000.

Marshall, I. Howard. *I and II Thessalonians*. New Century Bible. Grand Rapids: Eerdmans, 1983.

Martin, Michael D. *1, 2 Thessalonians*. New American Commentary. Nashville: B&H, 1995.

Morris, Leon. *The First and Second Epistles to the Thessalonians*. Rev. ed. New International Commentary on the New Testament. Grand Rapids: Eerdmans, 1991.

Shogren, Gary. *1 and 2 Thessalonians*. Zondervan Exegetical Commentary on the New Testament. Grand Rapids: Zondervan, 2012.

*Stott, John R. W. *The Gospel and Time: The Message of 1 and 2 Thessalonians*. Downers Grove, IL: InterVarsity Press, 1991.

Wanamaker, Charles A. *The Epistles to the Thessalonians*. New International Greek Testament Commentary. Grand Rapids: Eerdmans, 1990.

*Weima, Jeffrey A. D. *1–2 Thessalonians*. Baker Exegetical Commentary on the New Testament. Grand Rapids: Baker Academic, 2014.

Witherington, Ben, III. *1 and 2 Thessalonians: A Socio-Rhetorical Commentary*. Grand Rapids: Eerdmans, 2006.

First and Second Timothy and Titus (Pastoral Epistles)

*Fee, Gordon D. *1 and 2 Timothy, Titus*. New International Biblical Commentary. Peabody, MA: Hendrickson, 1988.

Guthrie, Donald. *The Pastoral Epistles*. Tyndale New Testament Commentaries. Downers Grove, IL: IVP Academic, 2009.

Johnson, Luke T. *The First and Second Letters to Timothy: A New Translation with Introduction and Commentary*. Anchor Bible. New York: Doubleday, 2001.

———. *Letters to Paul's Delegates*. New Testament in Context. Valley Forge, PA: Trinity International, 1996.

Kelly, J. N. D. *A Commentary on the Pastoral Epistles*. Harper's New Testament Commentaries. New York: Harper & Row, 1963.

Knight, George W., III. *The Pastoral Epistles*. New International Greek Testament Commentary. Grand Rapids: Eerdmans, 1992.

Lea, Thomas D., and Hayne P. Griffin Jr. *1, 2 Timothy, Titus*. New American Commentary. Nashville: Broadman, 1992.

Liefeld, Walter L. *1 and 2 Timothy, Titus*. NIV Application Commentary. Grand Rapids: Zondervan, 1999.

Marshall, I. Howard, and Philip H. Towner. *A Critical and Exegetical Commentary on the Pastoral Epistles*. International Critical Commentary. Rev. ed. Edinburgh: T&T Clark, 1999.

*Mounce, William D. *Pastoral Epistles*. Word Biblical Commentary. Nashville: Nelson, 2000.

Quinn, Jerome D., and William C. Wacker. *The First and Second Letters to Timothy*. Eerdmans Critical Commentary. Grand Rapids: Eerdmans, 2000.

Towner, Philip. *1–2 Timothy and Titus*. IVP New Testament Commentary. Downers Grove, IL: InterVarsity Press, 2010.

*———. *The Letters to Timothy and Titus*. New International Commentary on the New Testament. Grand Rapids: Eerdmans, 2006.

Wall, Robert W., and Richard B. Steele, *1 and 2 Timothy and Titus*. Two Horizons New Testament Commentary. Grand Rapids: Eerdmans, 2012.

Witherington, Ben, III. *Letters and Homilies for Hellenized Christians: A Socio-Rhetorical Commentary on Titus, 1–2 Timothy and 1–3 John*. Downers Grove, IL: InterVarsity Press, 2006.

*Yarbrough, Robert W. *The Letters to Timothy and Titus*. Pillar New Testament Commentary. Grand Rapids: Eerdmans, 2018.

Hebrews

Attridge, Harold. *The Epistle to the Hebrews*. Hermeneia. Philadelphia: Fortress, 1989.

Bruce, F. F. *The Epistle to the Hebrews*. New International Commentary on the New Testament. 2nd ed. Grand Rapids: Eerdmans, 1990.

Cockerill, Gareth L. *The Epistle to the Hebrews*. New International Commentary on the New Testament. Grand Rapids: Eerdmans, 2012.

deSilva, David A. *Perseverance in Gratitude: A Socio-Rhetorical Commentary on the Epistle to the Hebrews*. Grand Rapids: Eerdmans, 2000.

Ellingworth, Paul. *The Epistle to the Hebrews*. New International Greek Testament Commentary. Grand Rapids: Eerdmans, 1993.

France, R. T. "Hebrews." In *Expositor's Bible Commentary*, 13:19–208. Rev. ed. Grand Rapids: Zondervan, 2006.

Guthrie, Donald. *Hebrews*. Tyndale New Testament Commentaries. Downers Grove, IL: IVP Academic, 2009.

*Guthrie, George H. *Hebrews*. NIV Application Commentary. Grand Rapids: Zondervan, 1998.

Hagner, Donald A. *Hebrews*. New International Biblical Commentary. Peabody, MA: Hendrickson, 1990.

Koester, Craig A. *Hebrews*. Anchor Bible. Rev. ed. New York: Doubleday, 2001.

*Lane, William L. *Hebrews*. Word Biblical Commentary. 2 vols. Dallas: Word, 1991.

———. *Hebrews: A Call to Commitment*. Peabody, MA: Hendrickson, 1985.

Schreiner, Thomas R. *Commentary on Hebrews*. Nashville: B&H Academic, 2015.

Witherington, Ben, III. *Letters and Homilies for Jewish Christians: A Socio-Rhetorical Commentary on Hebrews, James, and Jude*. Downers Grove, IL: InterVarsity Press, 2007.

James

Allison, Dale C., Jr. *James: A Critical and Exegetical Commentary*. International Critical Commentary. Rev. ed. London: Bloomsbury T&T Clark, 2013.

*Blomberg, Craig L., and Mariam J. Kamell. *James*. Zondervan Exegetical Commentary on the New Testament. Grand Rapids: Zondervan, 2008.

Davids, Peter H. *Commentary on James*. New International Greek Testament Commentary. Grand Rapids: Eerdmans, 1982.

Johnson, Luke Timothy. *The Letter of James*. Anchor Bible. New York: Doubleday, 1995.

Laws, Sophie. *The Epistle of James*. Black's New Testament Commentaries. Peabody, MA: Hendrickson, 1980.

Martin, Ralph P. *James*. Word Biblical Commentary. Waco, TX: Word, 1988.

McCartney, Dan G. *James*. Baker Exegetical Commentary on the New Testament. Grand Rapids: Baker, 2009.

*McKnight, Scot. *The Letter of James*. New International Commentary on the New Testament. Rev. ed. Grand Rapids: Eerdmans, 2011.

*Moo, Douglas J. *The Letter of James*. Pillar New Testament Commentary. Grand Rapids: Eerdmans, 2000.

*———. *James*. Tyndale New Testament Commentary. 2nd ed. Downers Grove, IL: IVP Academic, 2015.

Motyer, J. A. *The Message of James: The Test of Faith*. Bible Speaks Today. Downers Grove, IL: InterVarsity Press, 1985.

*Nystrom, David P. *James*. NIV Application Commentary. Grand Rapids: Zondervan, 1997.

Richardson, Kurt. *James*. New American Commentary. Nashville: B&H, 1997.

First and Second Peter and Jude

Achtemeier, Paul D. *1 Peter*. Hermeneia. Minneapolis: Fortress, 1996.

Bauckham, Richard J. *Jude, 2 Peter*. Word Biblical Commentary. Waco, TX: Word, 1983.

Clowney, Edmund P. *The Message of 1 Peter*. Bible Speaks Today. Downers Grove, IL: InterVarsity Press, 1989.

Davids, Peter H. *The First Epistle of Peter*. New International Commentary on the New Testament. Grand Rapids: Eerdmans, 1990.

———. *The Letters of 2 Peter and Jude*. Pillar New Testament Commentary. Grand Rapids: Eerdmans, 2006.

Edwards, Dennis R. *1 Peter*. Story of God Bible Commentary. Grand Rapids: Zondervan, 2017.

Elliott, John H. *First Peter: A New Translation with Introduction and Commentary*. Anchor Bible. New York: Doubleday, 2001.

Goppelt, Leonhard. *A Commentary on 1 Peter*. Grand Rapids: Eerdmans, 1993.

*Green, Gene L. *Jude and 2 Peter*. Baker Exegetical Commentary on the New Testament. Grand Rapids: Baker Academic, 2008.

*Green, Michael. *2 Peter and Jude*. Tyndale New Testament Commentaries. Downers Grove, IL: IVP Academic, 2009.

Grudem, Wayne A. *1 Peter*. Tyndale New Testament Commentaries. Downers Grove, IL: IVP Academic, 2009.

*Jobes, Karen H. *1 Peter*. Baker Exegetical Commentary on the New Testament. Grand Rapids: Baker, 2005.

Kelly, J. N. D. *Commentary on the Epistles of Peter and Jude*. Harper's New Testament Commentaries. Peabody, MA: Hendrickson, 1969.

Marshall, I. Howard. *1 Peter*. IVP New Testament Commentary. Downers Grove, IL: InterVarsity Press, 1990.

*McKnight, Scot. *1 Peter*. NIV Application Commentary. Grand Rapids: Zondervan, 1996.

*Michaels, J. Ramsey. *1 Peter*. Word Biblical Commentary. Waco, TX: Word, 1988.

*Moo, Douglas J. *2 Peter and Jude*. NIV Application Commentary. Grand Rapids: Zondervan, 1996.

Neyrey, Jerome H. *2 Peter, Jude*. Anchor Bible. New York: Doubleday, 1993.

*Schreiner, Thomas. *1, 2 Peter, Jude*. New American Commentary. Nashville: B&H, 2003.

Tamfu, Dieudonné. *2 Peter and Jude*. Africa Bible Commentary Series. Grand Rapids: Zondervan, 2018.

Witherington, Ben, III. *Letters and Homilies for Jewish Christians: A Socio-Rhetorical Commentary on 1–2 Peter*. Downers Grove, IL: InterVarsity Press, 2007.

First, Second, and Third John

Akin, Daniel L. *1, 2, 3 John*. New American Commentary. Nashville: B&H, 2001.

Brown, Raymond E. *The Epistles of John*. Anchor Bible. Garden City, NY: Doubleday, 1982.

*Burge, Gary M. *Letters of John*. NIV Application Commentary. Grand Rapids: Zondervan, 1996.

Campbell, Constantine R. *1, 2, and 3 John*. Story of God Bible Commentary. Grand Rapids: Zondervan, 2017.

Derickson, Gary W. *1, 2, and 3 John*. Evangelical Exegetical Commentary. Bellingham, WA: Lexham, 2014.

*Jobes, Karen H. *1, 2, and 3 John*. Zondervan Exegetical Commentary on the New Testament. Grand Rapids: Zondervan, 2014.

*Kruse, Colin G. *The Letters of John*. Pillar New Testament Commentary. Grand Rapids: Eerdmans, 2000.

*Marshall, I. Howard. *The Epistles of John*. New International Commentary on the New Testament. Grand Rapids: Eerdmans, 1978.

Smalley, Stephen S. *1, 2, 3 John*. Word Biblical Commentary. Grand Rapids: Zondervan, 2015.

Stott, John R. W. *The Letters of John*. Tyndale New Testament Commentaries. Downers Grove, IL: IVP Academic, 2009.

Thompson, Marianne Meye. *1–3 John*. IVP New Testament Commentary. Downers Grove, IL: InterVarsity Press, 1992.

*Yarbrough, Robert W. *1–3 John*. Baker Exegetical Commentary on the New Testament. Grand Rapids: Baker, 2008.

Revelation

Aune, David E. *Revelation*. Word Biblical Commentary. 3 vols. Grand Rapids: Zondervan, 2017.
Beale, G. K. *The Book of Revelation*. New International Greek Testament Commentary. Grand Rapids: Eerdmans, 1999.
Beasley-Murray, George R. *The Book of Revelation*. New Century Bible. Rev. ed. Grand Rapids: Eerdmans, 1981.
*Duvall, J. Scott, *Revelation*. Teach the Text Commentary. Grand Rapids: Baker, 2014.
Fee, Gordon D. *Revelation*. New Covenant Commentary Series. Eugene, OR: Cascade, 2011.
*Keener, Craig S. *Revelation*. NIV Application Commentary. Grand Rapids: Zondervan, 2000.
Koester, Craig. *Revelation*. Anchor Bible. Rev. ed. New Haven, CT: Yale University Press, 2014.
———. *Revelation and the End of All Things*. Grand Rapids: Eerdmans, 2001.
Ladd, George E. *A Commentary on the Revelation of John*. Grand Rapids: Eerdmans, 1972.
Leithart, Peter. *Revelation*. International Theological Commentary. 2 vols. London: Bloomsbury T&T Clark, 2018.
Mangina, Joseph L. *Revelation*. Brazos Theological Commentary on the Bible. Grand Rapids: Brazos, 2010.
Michaels, J. Ramsey. *Revelation*. IVP New Testament Commentary. Downers Grove, IL: InterVarsity Press, 1997.
Morris, Leon. *The Book of Revelation*. Tyndale New Testament Commentaries. Downers Grove, IL: IVP Academic, 2009.
*Mounce, Robert H. *The Book of Revelation*. New International Commentary on the New Testament. Rev. ed. Grand Rapids: Eerdmans, 1997.
*Osborne, Grant. *Revelation*. Baker Exegetical Commentary. Grand Rapids: Baker, 2001.
Paul, Ian. *Revelation*. Tyndale New Testament Commentary. Downers Grove, IL: IVP Academic, 2018.
Reddish, Mitchell. *Revelation*. Smyth & Helwys Bible Commentary. Macon, GA: Smyth & Helwys, 2001.
Resseguie, James L. *The Revelation of John: A Narrative Commentary*. Grand Rapids: Baker Academic, 2009.
*Smalley, Stephen S. *The Revelation to John*. Downers Grove, IL: InterVarsity Press, 2005.
Thomas, John Christopher, and Frank D. Macchia. *Revelation*. Two Horizons New Testament Commentary. Grand Rapids: Eerdmans, 2016.
Thomas, Robert L. *Revelation: An Exegetical Commentary*. 2 vols. Chicago: Moody Press, 1992, 1995.
Wall, Robert W. *Revelation*. New International Biblical Commentary. Peabody, MA: Hendrickson, 1991.
Walvoord, John F. *The Revelation of Jesus Christ*. Chicago: Moody Press, 1966.
Witherington, Ben, III. *Revelation*. New York: Cambridge University Press, 2003.

Computer Software and the Internet

Some of the resources mentioned above are available in electronic format. We encourage you to take full advantage of computer software packages that include the best resources. Often the convenience and price are hard to beat. But remember that you are after the best tools, not simply the least expensive deal. You can use the recommended list above to evaluate the various software packages.

Be cautious when using internet resources. This is a rapidly changing environment, and it has not traditionally represented the best in biblical scholarship. While the internet is certainly convenient, you do not always know whether you are getting reliable information. We recommend that you stick with works by respected authors.

SCRIPTURE INDEX

MARK

LUKE

ROMANS

1 CORINTHIANS

2 CORINTHIANS

GALATIANS

SUBJECT INDEX

AUTHOR INDEX

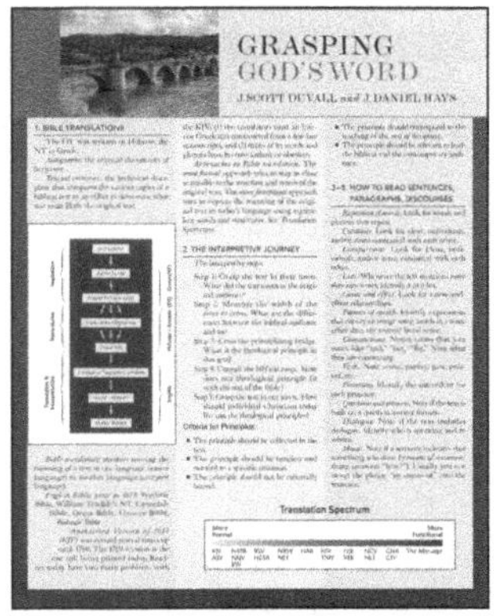

GRASPING
GOD'S WORD
J. SCOTT DUVALL and J. DANIEL HAYS
Translation Spectrum

Journey into God's Word, Second Edition

A Guide to Learn the Skills You Need to Understand and Apply God's Word. Now Revised and Updated!

Life is a journey, and like any journey it requires an accurate, reliable roadmap to get us where we need to go. God has provided such a guide in his Word. But just as a navigator needs to learn how to interpret all the contours and symbols of a map, so also we need to be able to understand how the Bible communicates its directions to us.

In *Journey into God's Word, Second Edition* readers will:

- Be introduced to the Interpretive Journey, a five-step framework for understanding how to read any Bible passage
- Learn vital reading skills that aid in their comprehension of not just the Bible, but of any piece of literature
- Discover the importance of understanding historical-cultural and literary contexts
- Receive guidance on choosing a Bible translation for their study
- Be given practical tips for reading specific genres in the Bible like, Gospels, letters, Law, prophecy, poetry, and more

Journey into God's Word, Second Edition helps Bible readers acquire these skills and become better at reading, interpreting, and applying the Bible to life. Based on the bestselling college/seminary textbook *Grasping God's Word*, it takes the proven principles from that book and makes them accessible to people in the church. It starts with general principles of interpretation, then moves on to apply those principles to specific genres and contexts. Hands-on exercises guide readers through the interpretation process, with an emphasis on real-life application. This second edition has been revised and updated to match the fourth edition of *Grasping God's Word* with a five-step Interpretive Journey.

Available in stores and online!

ZONDERVAN®
.com